D1084076

HISTORICAL DICTIONARY

The historical dictionaries present essential information on a broad range of subjects, including American and world history, art, business, cities, countries, cultures, customs, film, global conflicts, international relations, literature, music, philosophy, religion, sports, and theater. Written by experts, all contain highly informative introductory essays of the topic and detailed chronologies that, in some cases, cover vast historical time periods but still manage to heavily feature more recent events.

Brief A–Z entries describe the main people, events, politics, social issues, institutions, and policies that make the topic unique, and entries are cross-referenced for ease of browsing. Extensive bibliographies are divided into several general subject areas, providing excellent access points for students, researchers, and anyone wanting to know more. Additionally, maps, photographs, and appendixes of supplemental information aid high school and college students doing term papers or introductory research projects. In short, the historical dictionaries are the perfect starting point for anyone looking to research in these fields.

HISTORICAL DICTIONARIES OF RELIGIONS, PHILOSOPHIES, AND MOVEMENTS

Jon Woronoff, Series Editor

Orthodox Church, by Michael Prokurat, Alexander Golitzin, and Michael D. Peterson, 1996

Civil Rights Movement, by Ralph E. Luker, 1997

North American Environmentalism, by Edward R. Wells and Alan M. Schwartz, 1997

Taoism, by Julian F. Pas in cooperation with Man Kam Leung, 1998

Gay Liberation Movement, by Ronald J. Hunt, 1999

Islamic Fundamentalist Movements in the Arab World, Iran, and Turkey, by Ahmad S. Moussalli, 1999

Cooperative Movement, by Jack Shaffer, 1999

Kierkegaard's Philosophy, by Julia Watkin, 2001

Slavery and Abolition, by Martin A. Klein, 2002

Prophets in Islam and Judaism, by Scott B. Noegel and Brannon M. Wheeler, 2002

Lesbian Liberation Movement: Still the Rage, by JoAnne Myers, 2003

Descartes and Cartesian Philosophy, by Roger Ariew, Dennis Des Chene, Douglas M. Jesseph, Tad M. Schmaltz, and Theo Verbeek, 2003

Witchcraft, by Michael D. Bailey, 2003

Unitarian Universalism, by Mark W. Harris, 2004

New Age Movements, by Michael York, 2004

Utopianism, by James M. Morris and Andrea L. Kross, 2004

Feminism, Second Edition, by Janet K. Boles and Diane Long Hoeveler, 2004

Jainism, by Kristi L. Wiley, 2004

Wittgenstein's Philosophy, by Duncan Richter, 2004

Schopenhauer's Philosophy, by David E. Cartwright, 2005

Seventh-day Adventists, by Gary Land, 2005

Methodism, Second Edition, by Charles Yrigoyen Jr. and Susan E. Warrick, 2005

Sufism, by John Renard, 2005

Sikhism, Second Edition, by W. H. McLeod, 2005

Kant and Kantianism, by Helmut Holzhey and Vilem Mudroch, 2005

Olympic Movement, Third Edition, by Bill Mallon with Ian Buchanan, 2006

Anglicanism, by Colin Buchanan, 2006

Welfare State, Second Edition, by Bent Greve, 2006

Feminist Philosophy, by Catherine Villanueva Gardner, 2006

Logic, by Harry J. Gensler, 2006

Jesus, by Daniel J. Harrington, S.J., 2010

Metaphysics, by Gary Rosenkrantz and Joshua Hoffman, 2011

Shinto, Second Edition, by Stuart D. B. Picken, 2011

The Friends (Quakers), Second Edition, by Margery Post Abbott, Mary Ellen Chijioke, Pink Dandelion, and John William Oliver Jr., 2011

Lutheranism, Second Edition, by Günther Gassmann with Duane H. Larson, and Mark W. Oldenburg, 2011

Hinduism, New Edition, by Jeffery D. Long, 2011

Calvinism, by Stuart D. B. Picken, 2012

Hobbes's Philosophy, by Juhana Lemetti, 2012

Historical Dictionary of the Chinese Communist Party, by Lawrence R. Sullivan, 2012

New Religious Movements, Second Edition, by George D. Chryssides, 2012

Catholicism, Second Edition, by William J. Collinge, 2012

Radical Christianity, William H. Brackney, 2012

Organized Labor, Third Edition, by James C. Docherty and Sjaak van der Velden, 2012

Islamic Fundamentalism, by Mathieu Guidère, 2012

Historical Dictionary of Islamic Fundamentalism

Mathieu Guidère

The Scarecrow Press, Inc.
Lanham • Toronto • Plymouth, UK
2012

Published by Scarecrow Press, Inc.
A wholly owned subsidiary of The Rowman & Littlefield Publishing Group, Inc.
4501 Forbes Boulevard, Suite 200, Lanham, Maryland 20706
www.rowman.com

10 Thornbury Road, Plymouth PL6 7PP, United Kingdom

British Library Cataloguing in Publication Information Available

Library of Congress Cataloging-in-Publication Data

Guidère, Mathieu.
  Historical dictionary of Islamic fundamentalism / Mathieu Guidère.
      p. cm. — (Historical dictionaries of religions, philosophies, and movements)
  Includes bibliographical references.
  ISBN 978-0-8108-7821-1 (cloth : alk. paper) — ISBN 978-0-8108-7965-2 (ebook)
  1. Islamic fundamentalism—History—Dictionaries. I. Title.
  BP166.14.F85G85 2012
  297.803—dc23   2012008210

∞™ The paper used in this publication meets the minimum requirements of
American National Standard for Information Sciences—Permanence of Paper
for Printed Library Materials, ANSI/NISO Z39.48-1992.

Printed in the United States of America

Contents

Editor's Foreword

Islamic fundamentalism is fraught with confusion and misunderstanding, not surprisingly given the divisions within Islam itself and the multitude of fundamentalist groups. Indeed, for virtually any statement that can be made about the movement in general, there are exceptions and caveats. Almost all the groups hark back to earlier times and want to return to the fundamentals of the religion. But there are disagreements on exactly which time that was, let alone what the fundamentals were. And while some want to purify the religion and shed all recent accretions, others argue that there is a pressing need for modernization and adaptation.

While many are willing to teach by example or preach to the unknowing, others want to impose their views through force and violence, and obviously the more violent groups are the more visible ones, although the majority of Muslims do not approve of violence. And who should be taught: Muslims who have strayed, infidels who never believed to begin with, or Arabs and others in the Middle East or even farther afield?

It is clear that much of the West does not understand Islam and especially fundamentalist Islam. Even Muslims do not often know what to make of Islamic fundamentalism since it is usually directed against the coterie of kings, sheiks, presidents, and dictators who still rule in most Muslim countries. Nor is the civilian population spared from fundamentalist Islamic fervor.

This incredible confusion and misunderstanding makes the *Historical Dictionary of Islamic Fundamentalism* one of the most important in this series. It is truly historical in that it starts at the beginnings and traces the religion's very long and complicated trajectory up to the present day in the chronology. The introduction provides insight into the theory and motivations of Islamic fundamentalists. The dictionary section includes entries on people, not only those whose names are both infamous and widely known, such as the late Osama bin Laden, but some earlier figures who are quite familiar to Muslims. It also profiles dozens of more shadowy leaders, scarcely known except to members of their own groups. Then there are the movements, not just al-Qaeda and the Taliban army but many more, as well as the often complicated situation in many of the Muslim countries and events like the attack on the World Trade Center and other bloody attacks and more ordinary events that have influenced the movements. Finally, there are entries on crucial concepts. The glossary is a handy guide, and the extensive bibliography provides sources for further research.

This book was written by one of the finest experts and scholars on the subject. Mathieu Guidère spent his childhood and youth in the Middle East, studying at local and French schools before receiving his doctorate at the Sorbonne, with further diplomas from the University of Lyon 2, one of them in Arabic. He was an associate professor at the University of Lyon 2 until 1998, at which time he became a resident professor at the French Military Academy of Saint-Cyr. After being senior fellow at the Center for Advanced Defense Studies in Washington, D.C., he taught at the University of Geneva, Switzerland, until becoming a full professor at the University of Toulouse, France, in 2011. And during his academic career, Dr. Guidère has written articles and papers and served as a television commentator on the subject of Islamic fundamentalism and related topics, meanwhile producing a growing list of books in French, the most recent being *Le Printemps islamiste* (2012), *Le Choc des révolutions arabes* (2011), *Les Nouveaux terroristes* (2010), *Irak in Translation* (2008), and *Al-Qaida à la conquête du Maghreb* (2007). In this, his first work in English, he was aided by Amanda Gawlowicz, who, at the time of this publication, was a candidate for a master's degree in global communications at the American University of Paris. She began her work on Islam while serving as a research assistant for the Descartes Institute, a think tank based in Paris. The result of their efforts is impressive, as readers will quickly realize.

Jon Woronoff
Series Editor

Preface

The task that presented itself with this publication is, how does one write a historical dictionary on Islamic fundamentalism following the events of the Arab Spring and why? First, what is essential is that many of these groups that were treated and analyzed as terrorists or Islamic extremists are now in partnership and affiliated with many of the revolutionaries in these countries. This is particularly true for Egypt and Libya. With this evolution in mind, one must move from the perception of the "terrorism decade" to the "new democracy" era that is present. To make this transition possible, these groups need to be evaluated through an ideological and sociopolitical lens while taking into account the major changes that occurred during 2011 in the Arab world.

Therefore, one cannot discuss Islamic fundamentalism today without taking into account the Arab Spring. Likewise, it must be remembered that the exact results and effects of these revolutions have yet to be seen. What was of great benefit to the formation of this dictionary is that it was being formed and written while these events were unfolding. The transitory nature of 2011 was remarkable in that it allowed for this text to be ever evolving and contemporary. This historical era has influenced the context and information of this dictionary so much so that it can facilitate the reader in looking through this lens of Islamic fundamentalism.

What the whole world saw in 2011 was a breathtaking rise of the Islamic parties and forces in almost all the revolutionized countries. In Tunisia, the *Ennhada* (Renaissance) Party won the first free elections in the country. In Morocco, the Justice and Development Party won the majority of the parliamentary seats. Then, in Egypt (which also had its first free elections), the historic Muslim Brotherhood won a majority of the votes and was followed by the Salafist party *al-Nour* (The Light). Not only did *al-Nour* come in second at the voting booths, but it won almost 25 percent of the votes. This formidable number shows that about a quarter of the Egyptian population wants to enact the sociopolitical views of Salafism throughout the country. This is especially interesting since the platform of the Salafists rests on the application of Islamic law (*sharia*).

The Libyan case is an amazing one as well, especially since during the revolution, groups that are ideologically jihadist and Salafist fought on the side of the Libyan rebels, assisting in the liberation. What is unique about this alliance is that it was the first time in Arabic and Islamic history that an Islamic group (here, the Libyan Combatant Group) was part of a country's revolution. This assistance in ending the long dictatorship of Muammar Qadhafi, which lasted from 1969 to 2011, will no doubt result in an amicable relationship between the Islamists and the new state of Libya.

As illustrated by just these few examples, the political events and social consequences occurring after the Arab Spring have effectively changed the nature of studying Islamic fundamentalism.

While living in different countries in the Arab world during the 1970s and 1980s, I had the impression that I was living in a world that was still very much set in an ancient time. But life and perception there changed indefinitely after the collapse of the Soviet Union and then later after the September 11, 2001, attacks. Now, the West has created new enemies, called terrorism and Islamic fundamentalism, that have effectively replaced the former enemy: communism. This transition was made possible since many Eastern people and experts maintained their reflections, visions, and perceptions that were formed because of the Soviet Union. So as the Western world replaced the Eastern bloc, these perceptions were not so much changed as redirected.

During the 1990s, the al-Qaeda organization was still in its formative period and was, arguably, almost invisible. So during this decade, the major players in Islamic fundamentalism and terrorism were the armed Islamic Algerian groups. These groups were also the first to attempt to destroy a cultural landmark through air traffic. This plan was in 1994, and the target was the Eiffel Tower. Thankfully, the French government succeeded in countering this terrorist attack by forcing the plane to land in Marseille. But nevertheless, this action (and many others) inspired leaders such as Osama bin Laden. Although similar and related in many regards, these two groups did not share in the same enemy. For the Algerian groups, the enemy was the Arab Muslim regimes and governments, but to bin Laden, it was the Western governments and countries. In both of these cases, international relations, occupation of the Islamic countries, and the "theft" of the Muslim resources was at the center. Living in France by this time, I saw the rise of this phenomenon and a shift from France being the main target of the Algerian groups to the United States as the major enemy of the Saudi groups.

So, for a person who was well aware of this occurring dynamic, September 11, 2001, was a predictable event. There were many indicators of this rising hostility, including the 1993 bombing in the basement of the World Trade Center, the 1998 attacks on the American embassies in Nairobi and Dar es Salaam, and the 2000 bombing of the USS *Cole*.

During this time of great insurgencies between the Muslim neofundamentalists and the American neoconservatives, the Islamic fundamentalist groups were watching so as to understand how they should function in this climate. In the 1990s and 2000s, the Islamic fundamentalists learned two essential things: first, that the Muslim people as a whole reject violence as a way to impose the Islamist political agenda and, second, that the enemy was not outside but within the Arab countries.

So with this knowledge at hand and in witnessing the outcomes of the Arab Spring, it is evident that the major victory of the Islamic fundamentalist groups, movements, and leaders was to accept the give-and-take of democracy. Realizing that joining with rather than against the Arab and Muslim people was the way to influence the populace, these groups entered into this democratic platform. Before the popular uprisings, these groups were totally against and refusing to cooperate with any form of democracy (deeming it "the religion of the West"), but seeing the ways in which to enter into the Arab-Muslim sociopolitical realm, these ideals were adopted so as to have a position in the future of the revolutionized countries.

These Islamic fundamentalists groups have only converted to the program of democracy and have adopted this double language very strategically to gain the popular votes and favor of the Arab society. Although these groups have adopted only the vocabulary and platform of democracy, not its true spirit, to further fundamentalist goals, at least the logic of democracy was too adopted. This evolution needs to be kept in mind while reviewing and studying all the historic and contemporary groups, movements, leaders, and goals of Islamic fundamentalism.

I would like to thank the series editor, Jon Woronoff, for his great insights and professionalism while this dictionary was being developed. A work of such length can be successful only with guidance and experience such as his. Finally, I would like to give my utmost thanks to Amanda Gawlowicz. I brought her into this project not only for the logical reason of her native fluency in English but also because of her remarkable and objective understanding of the evolution of these groups and movements. Her ease in researching and writing about this subject should make reading about this complex and nuanced subject easier for the user of this dictionary.

Reader's Notes

The main focus of this dictionary is to provide the reader with the essential information on the basic ideas, concepts, ideologies, leaders, intellectuals, dogmas, groups, events, and movements that have shaped the contemporary world of Islamic fundamentalism and Islamism. Although there is a relative focus on the more recent figures, movements, and actions, the historic influences have been included as well so that the reader can understand the foundation of the Islamic fundamentalist movement. Ideological concepts such as *shura* (consultation), *sharia* (Islamic law), *umma* (nation), *hakimiyya* (governance), and *tawhid* (oneness of Allah) have been explained at length in their individual entries and are cross-referenced throughout others. This has been done so as not to distract the reader from the entry in which they are mentioned. Therefore, this dictionary is heavily cross-referenced to help explain the ideological discourses of various groups and figures.

Distinctions have also been made between radical and moderate movements and groups so that the basis of their behaviors can be better understood. These ideas are also explained through the fundamentalist lens so that the reader can ascertain the perspective of these groups, which is truly the most advantageous way to approach this diverse field. Thus, when philosophy, the West, theology, or jihad is explained, it is from the fundamentalist perspective. Also, some care should be taken regarding the groups and parties listed in this dictionary as fundamentalist that have been very active since and during the 2011 Arab Spring, such as the Libyan Combatant Group. Even though some of them seem to now have adapted the rules of democracy, it is their historical background that has been thoroughly explained in the corresponding entries. These groups also include the Salafi parties in Egypt like *al-Nour* and in Tunisia like the Supporters of *Sharia*. The focus of this dictionary is then to explain the reasons and purposes as well as the developments of these fundamentalist reinterpretations. This dictionary seeks to cover all the ideas and rhetoric that distinguish Islamic fundamentalism from the other forms of Islam.

Moreover, great attention has been given to leaders and groups that have been most formidable to Islamic fundamentalism, such as the al-Qaeda organization, *Hizbullah*, the Muslim Brotherhood, Ayatollah Ruhollah al-Musawi

Khomeini, and Osama bin Laden. On the opposite end, the minor players and movements have also been included but have not been explained in such great detail. Nevertheless, this dictionary includes all the major and minor features of Islamic Fundamentalism and everything in between.

Being a dictionary, these entries have been listed alphabetically, and all have been transliterated. However, doctrinal and political concepts such as *hudud, dar al-harb, fitna*, and *fitra* will be found under their transliterated forms. But the glossary should also be of great assistance for the reader who would like to easily access the English forms of these and other terms. The chronology also has included a good deal of historic events from the 13th to 18th centuries that are not investigated within the dictionary but have been included to provide a greater historical context to the Arab world.

A note on the transliterations of the Arabian, Indonesian, and Persian words: the most phonetically accurate transliterations have been used, although this may not fall into any one of the conventions of transliteration. The efforts of linguists to create universally accepted transliterations of such words are formidable and impressive, but we have taken into account the popular transliterations that readers are used to as well. So, for example, we have used the more accurate "Quran" rather than the popular "Koran" but the popular "Osama bin Laden" rather than the more accurate "Usama bin Laden." Taking this nuance into consideration, we have included many cross-references throughout the dictionary to better assist the reader in finding terms or names with many alternative spellings. All cross-references, if within an entry, are in boldface type, and the other form used is "See also," which is for items related to the entry but not made explicit in the entry. There are also individual references that are separate from the entries throughout the dictionary.

Also, names of groups are listed according to their more popular or well-known uses, not necessarily their English transliterations. For example, *Hizbullah* is listed rather than "Party of God." However, groups that are more commonly known by their French names, such as the Algerian group *Front Islamique du Salut*, will be found under "Islamic Salvation Front." Cross-references have been added in numerous parts of this dictionary to better assist the reader in this matter. In addition to the cross-references, the reader is encouraged to use the list of acronyms and abbreviations where the national and English name of the group is provided. These acronyms should also be very familiar to readers, as they are commonly used in the popular press. The reader is also encouraged to make use of the figures, which depict the Islamic splinter groups in various countries. Although these charts are not exhaustive, they do include the major relationships and alliances that are discussed within the text. Therefore, if the reader is interested in analyzing a specific dynamic or the movements within a specific country, the reader should consult these charts as a quick guide to getting started with research.

Some aspects of this dictionary to keep in mind is that when looking up the Arabic and Persian transliterations, it is essential to remember that the articles *al-* and *el-* were not taken into account while alphabetizing, and readers should go to the main noun that follows to find the entry. For example, "al-Qaeda" will be found under "Q," not "A." As for "Muslim Brotherhood," the term always refers to the Egyptian Muslim Brotherhood unless otherwise noted. The convention for calendar dates is day-month-year, but for date-significant terms, such as the September 11 attacks, the month-day-year has been used sometimes since the reader is more familiar with this standard. However, the entry will be found under "World Trade Center and Pentagon Attacks of September 11, 2001." But all such possibly confusing entries have been thoroughly cross-referenced in order to facilitate the rapid and efficient location of information and to make this book as useful a reference tool as possible.

Acronyms and Abbreviations

AIAI	Al-Itihad Al-Islami/Islamic Union
AIG	Armed Islamic Group/Groupe Islamique Armé (GIA)
AIS	Armée Islamique du Salut/Islamic Salvation Army
AJD/MR	Alliance for Justice and Democracy/Movement for Renewal
AL-AQSA	Al-Aqsa Martyrs' Brigade (al-Fatah Group)
ALF	Arab Liberation Front/Jabhat al-Tahrir al-'Arabiyah
ABIM	Angkatan Belia Islam Malaysia/Movement of the Malaysian Youth
AML	Association of Muslim Lawyers
APHC	All-Parties Hurriyat Conference
AQAP	Al-Qaeda in the Arabian Peninsula
AQI	Al-Qaeda in Iraq
AQIM	Al-Qaeda in the Islamic Maghreb
ASG	Abu Sayyaf Group
ASWJ	Ahl As-Sunnah Wal-Jammah/Adherents of the Sunna and the Community
AUM	Al-Umar Mujahideen/The Mujahideen of Umar
BIF	Benevolence International Foundation
BKPMI	Badan Komunikasi Pemuda Masjid Indonesia/Association for Communication between the Youth of Indonesian Mosques
BRN	Barisan Revolusi Nasional/Front of the National Revolution
BSO	Black September Organization
CIA	Central Intelligence Agency
CSAMEPP	Committee for Solidarity with Arab and Middle Eastern Political Prisoners/Comité de soutien aux prisonniers politiques arabes et du Moyen-Orient
CSSW	Charitable Society for Social Welfare
DDII	Dewan Dakwah Islamiyah Indonesia/Council of Predication for Indonesian Islam
DEM	Dukhtaraan-e-Millat/Daughters of the Nation
DFLP	Democratic Front for the Liberation of Palestine
ETIM	East Turkestan Islamic Movement
FBI	Federal Bureau of Investigation

FIS	Front Islamique du Salut/Islamic Salvation Front
FIT	Front Islamique Tunisien/Tunisian Islamic Front
FKASWJ	Forum Komunikasi Ahlu Sunnah wal-Jama'ah/Forum of the Communication of the Faithful of the Sunna and the Prophet
FLN	Front de Libération Nationale/National Liberation Front (Algerian Nationalist political party)
FPI	Front Pembelam Islam/Front of the Defenders of Islam
FRC	Fatah Revolutionary Council
GAM	Gerakan Aceh Merdeka/Movement for the Independence of Aceh
GAMPAR	Gabungan Melayu Patani Raya/Association for a Large Malaysian Pattani
GIA	Groupe Islamique Armé/Armed Islamic Group
GICM	Groupe Islamique Combattant Morocain/Moroccan Islamic Combatant Group (also referred to as Moroccan Islamic Fighting Group)
GMIP	Gerakan Mujahidin Islam Pattani/Movement of Holy Warriors of Islam Pattani
GPII	Gerakan Pemuda Islam Indonesia/Movement of the Young Indonesian Muslims
HIG	Hizb-e-Islami Gulbuddin
HM	Hizb-ul-Mujahideen/Party of the Mujahideen
HSM	Harakat Al-Shabaab Al-Mujahideen/Mujahideen Youth Movement (also referred to simply as al-Shabaab)
HuA	Harakat-ul-Ansar/Movement of Supporters
HuJI	Harakat-ul-Jihad Al-Islami/Islamic Struggle Movement
HuJI-B	Harakat-ul-Jihad Al-Islami Bangladesh/Islamic Struggle Movement in Bangladesh
HuM	Harakat-ul-Mujahideen/Mujahideen Movement
HuMA	Harakat-ul-Mujahideen Al-Alami/The Global Mujahideen Movement
IAF	Islamic Action Front
ICC	International Criminal Court
ICU	Islamic Courts Union
IDF	Israeli Defense Forces
IED	Improvised Explosive Devices
IJU	Islamic Jihad Union
ILO	Islamic Liberation Organization
IMT	Islamic Movement of Turkistan
IMU	Islamic Movement of Uzbekistan
IPP	Islamic Political Parties

IRP	Islamic Renaissance Party of Tajikistan
ISAF	International Security Assistance Force
ISCI	Islamic Supreme Council of Iraq
ISE	Islamic Society of Engineers
ISI	Inter-Services Intelligence (Pakistan)
IUPA	Islamic Unity Party of Afghanistan/Hizb-e-Wahdat e-Islamic Afghanistan
JC	Justice and Charity Movement/Jamaat al-'adl wa al-Ihsan
JeM	Jaish-e-Muhammad/Army of Muhammad
JI	Jamaat-e-Islami/Islamic Party
JKIF	Jammu and Kashmir Islamic Front
JKJI	Jammu and Kashmir Jamaat-e-Islami/Jammu and Kashmir Islamic Party
JMB	Jamaat-ul-Mujahideen in Bangladesh/Assembly of the Mujahideen in Bangladesh
JRTN	Jaysh Rijal al-Tariqah al-Naqshabandia/Army of the Naqshabandi Sufists
JTJ	Jamaat Al-Tawhid wa Al-Jihad/Group of Monotheism and Jihad
JuI	Jamaat-ul-Ulema-e-Islam/Assembly of the Islamic Clergy
JuM	Jamaat-ul-Mujahideen/Assembly of the Mujahideen
KISDI	Komite Indonesia untuk Solidaritas dengan Dunia Islam/Indonesia Committee for Solidarity with the Muslim World
KOMPAK	Komite Aksi Penanggulungan Akribat Krisis/Action Committee for a Crisis Solution
KRN	Kampulan Revolusi Nasional/National Revolutionary Movement
LDK	Lembaga Dakwah Kampus/Dakwah Campus Centers
LeJ	Lashkar-e-Jabbar/Army of the Mighty
LeT	Lashkar-e-Tayyiba/Army of the Pure
LH	Lashkar Hizbullah/Group of the Party of God
LIFG	Libyan Islamic Fighting Group (also referred to as Libyan Islamic Combatant Group)
LJ	Lashkar-e-Jhangvi/Army of Jhangvi
MAB	Muslim Association of Britain
MB	Muslim Brotherhood
MBG	Misuari Breakaway Group
MEK	Mujahideen-e-Khalq/People's Mujahideen Organization of Iran
MILF	Moro Islamic Liberation Front
MLF	Moro Liberation Front

MMA	Muttahida Majlis-e-Amal/United Council of Action
MMI	Majlis Mujahidin Indonesia/Council of Indonesian Mujahideen
MSC	Mujahideen Shura Council
MSP	Movement for the Society of Peace
NATO	North Atlantic Treaty Organization
NIF	National Islamic Front
NII	Negara Islam Indonesia/Islamic State of Indonesia
NTC	National Transitional Council (Libya)
OIC	Organization of the Islamic Conference
OPEC	Organization of Petroleum Exporting Countries
PAS	Pan-Malaysian Islamic Party/Parti Islam Se-Malaysia
PDPA	People's Democratic Party of Afghanistan
PFLP	Popular Front for the Liberation of Palestine
PIJ	Palestinian Islamic Jihad
PJD	Parti de la Justice et du Développement/Justice and Development Party (in Arabic: Hizb Al-Adala wa Al-Tanmia)
PLO	Palestinian Liberation Organization
PRMI	People's Resistance Movement of Iran/Jund Allah in Iran
PSI	Pan-Sahel Initiative
PULO	Patani United Liberation Organization/United Organization for the Pattani Liberation
RAI	Rabitat al-Alam al-Islami/Muslim World League
RSM	Rajah Suleiman Movement
RSO	Rohingya Solidarity Organization
SGPC	Salafi Group for Preaching and Combat
SIMI	Students Islamic Movement of India
SSP	Sipah-e-Sahaba Pakistan/Army of the Friends of Sahaba
TCG	Tunisian Combatant Group
TII	Tentara Islam Indonesia/Indonesian Islamic Army
TJP	Tehrik-e-Jafaria Pakistan/Movement of the Pakistani Shiites
TSCTI	Trans-Saharan Counter-Terrorism Initiative
TuM	Tehrik-ul-Mujahideen/Mujahideen Movement
UDP	United Development Party
UJC	United Jihad Council
UMNO	United Malays National Organization
UN	United Nations
UNESCO	United Nations Educational Scientific and Cultural Organization
UTO	United Tajik Opposition

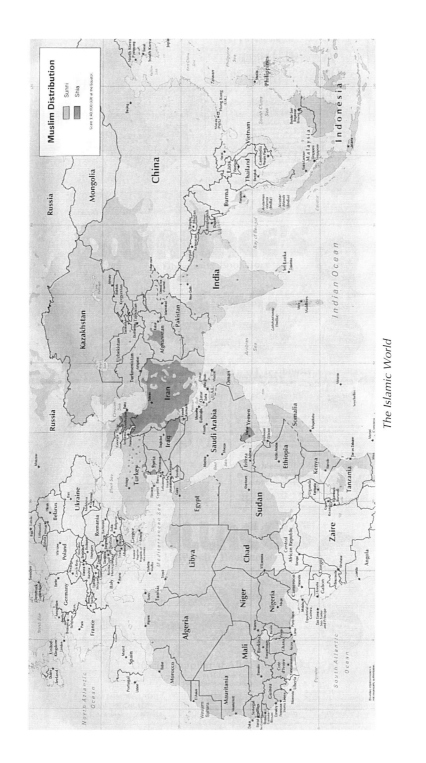

The Islamic World

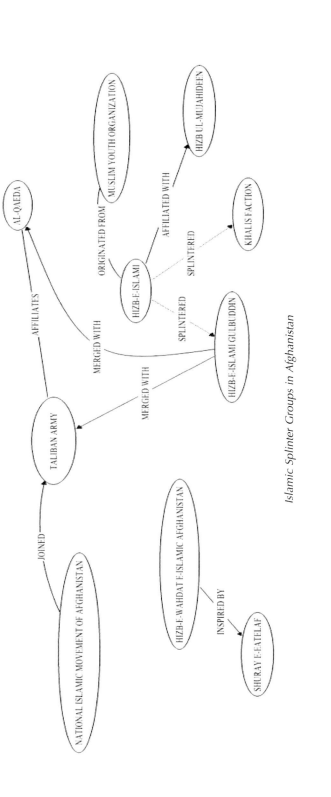

Islamic Splinter Groups in Afghanistan

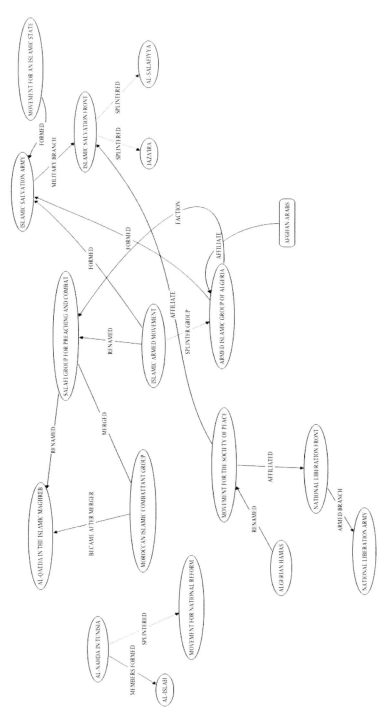

Islamic Splinter Groups in Algeria

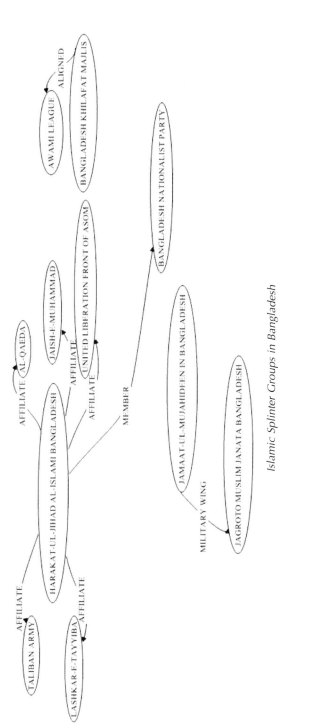

Islamic Splinter Groups in Bangladesh

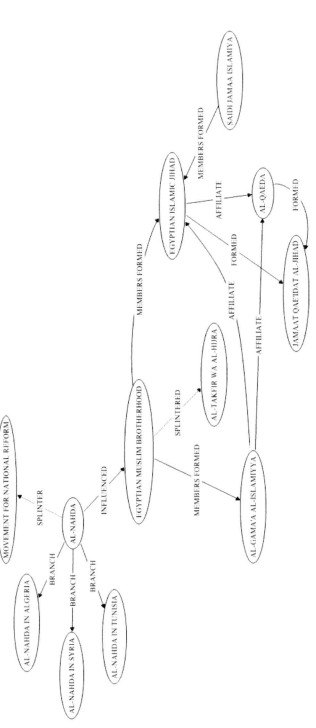

Islamic Splinter Groups in Egypt

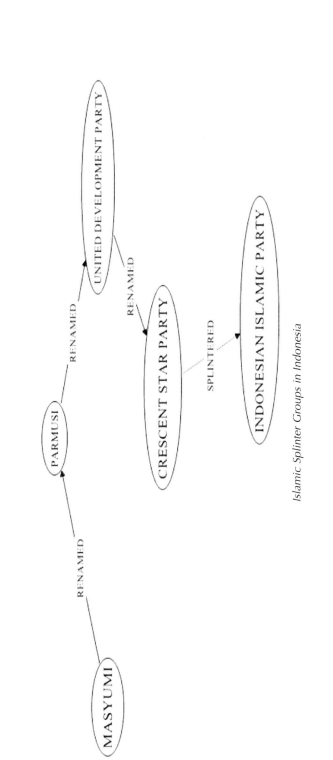

Islamic Splinter Groups in Indonesia

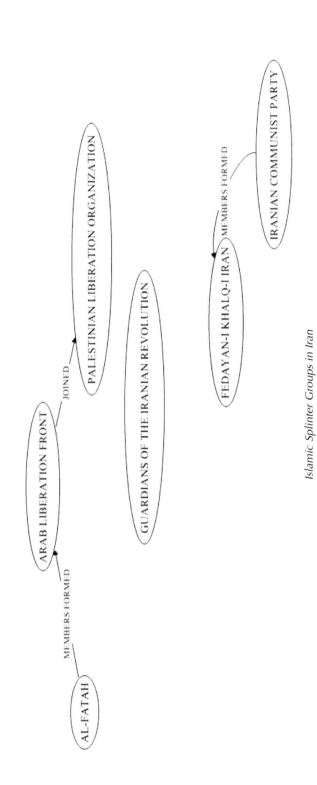

Islamic Splinter Groups in Iran

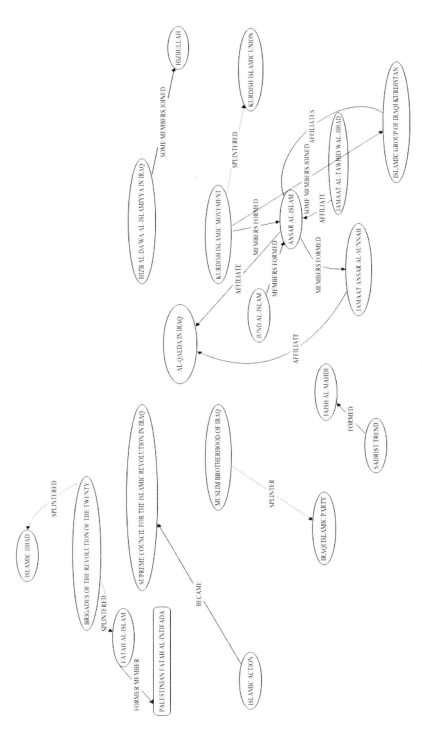

Islamic Splinter Groups in Iraq

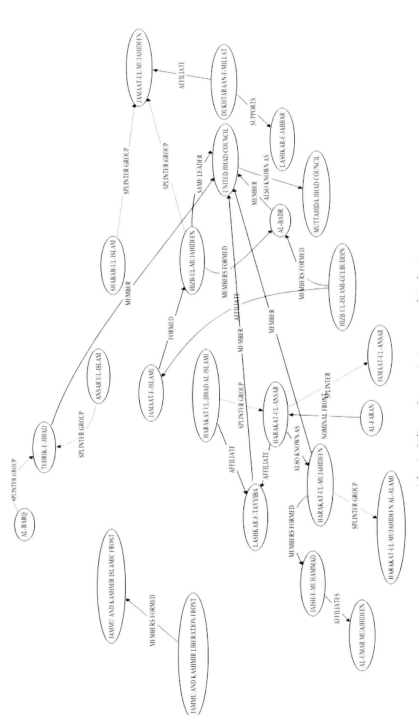

Islamic Splinter Groups in Jammu and Kashmir

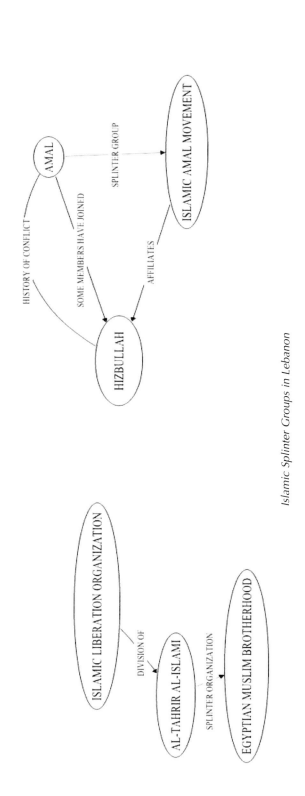

Islamic Splinter Groups in Lebanon

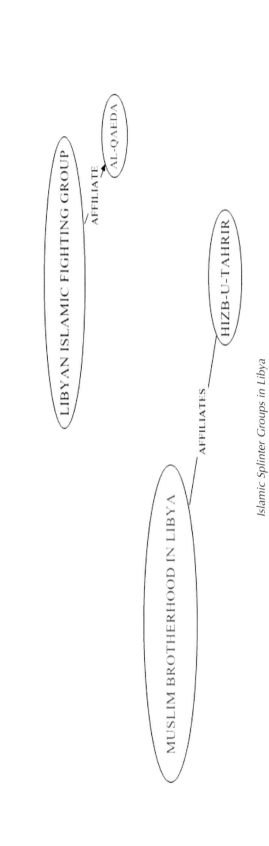

Islamic Splinter Groups in Libya

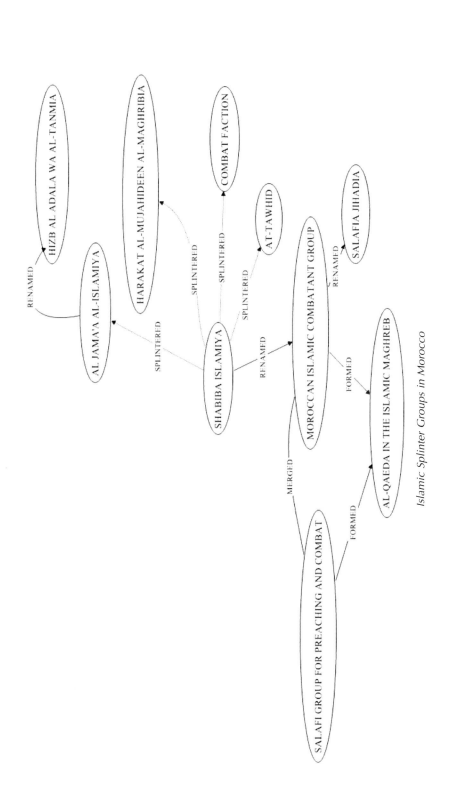

Islamic Splinter Groups in Morocco

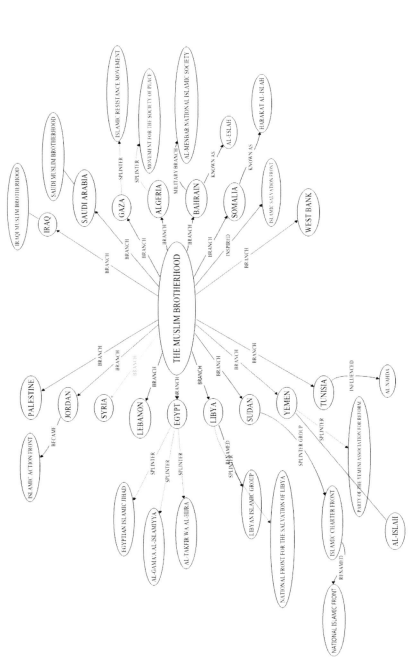

Islamic Splinter Groups of the Muslim Brotherhood

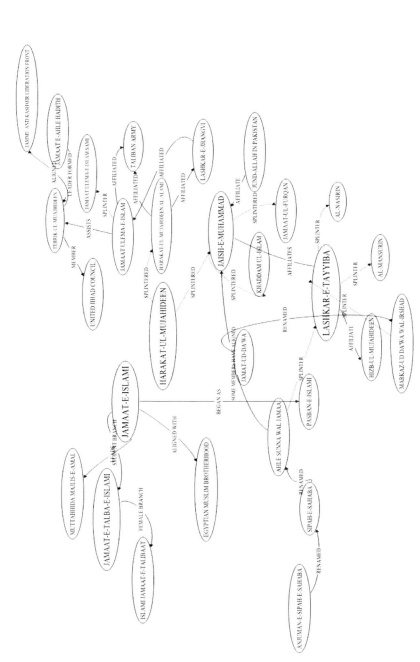

Islamic Splinter Groups in Pakistan

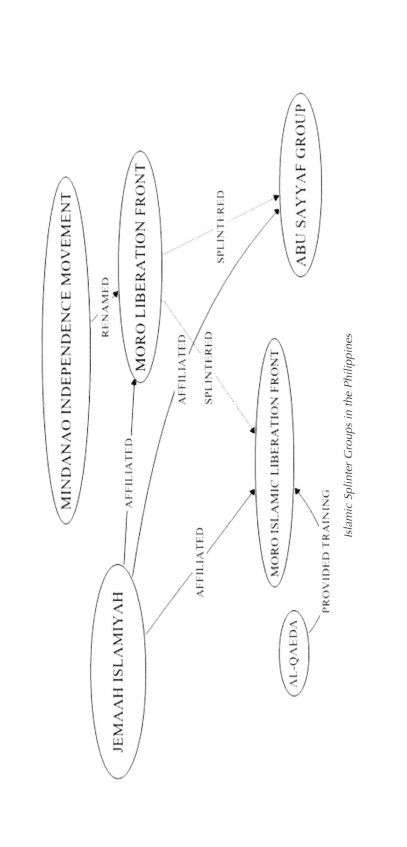

Islamic Splinter Groups in the Philippines

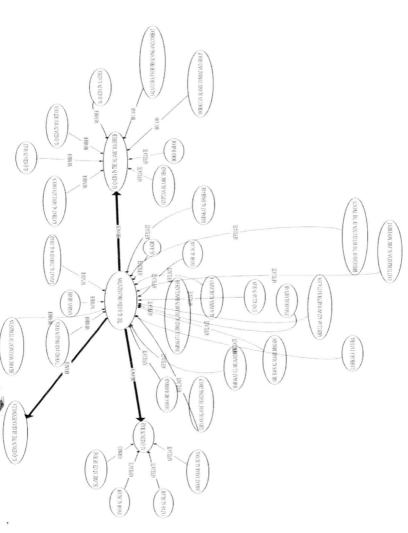

Al-Qaeda Splinter Groups and Affiliates

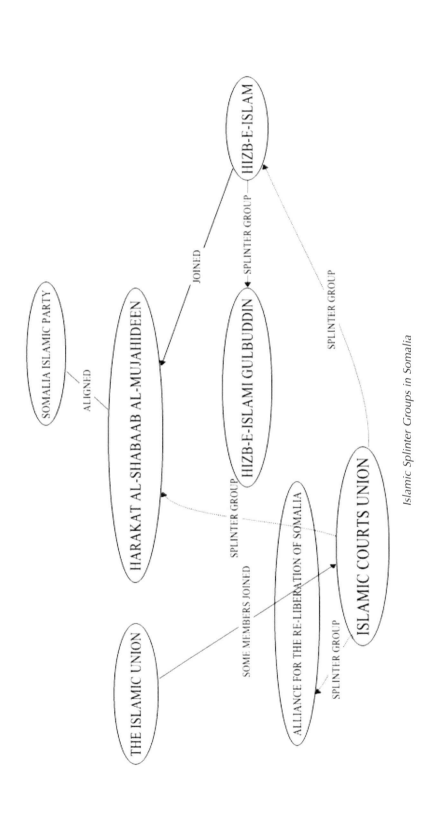

Islamic Splinter Groups in Somalia

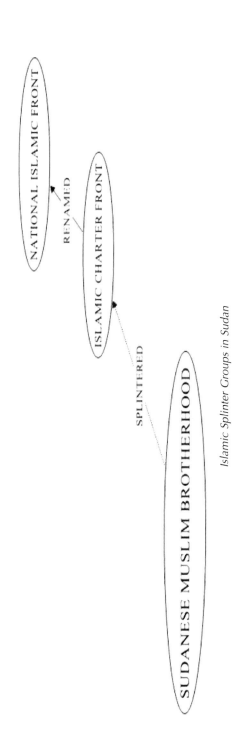

Islamic Splinter Groups in Sudan

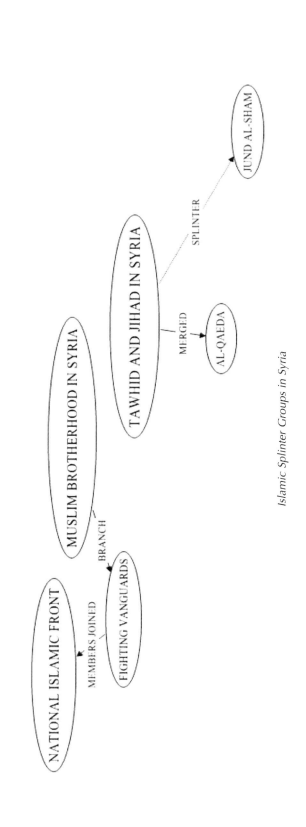

Islamic Splinter Groups in Syria

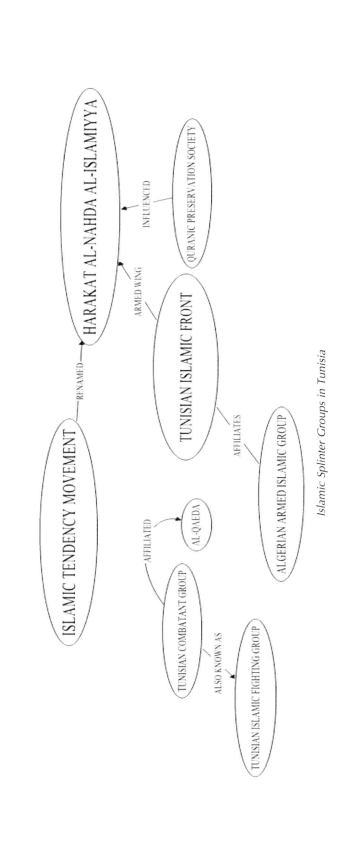

Islamic Splinter Groups in Tunisia

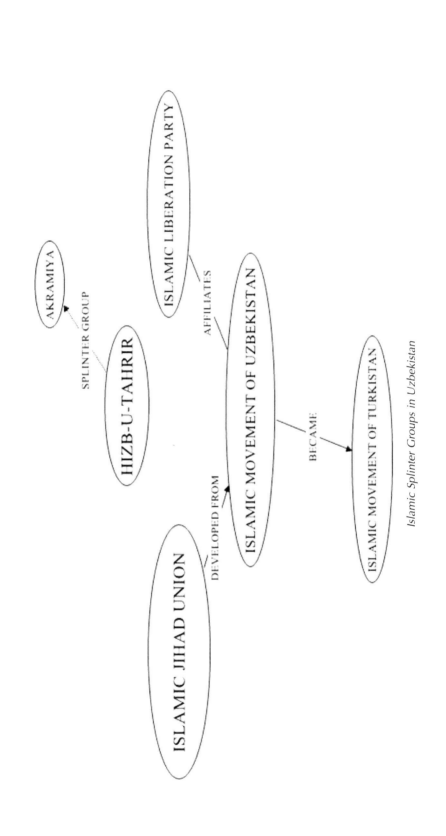

Islamic Splinter Groups in Uzbekistan

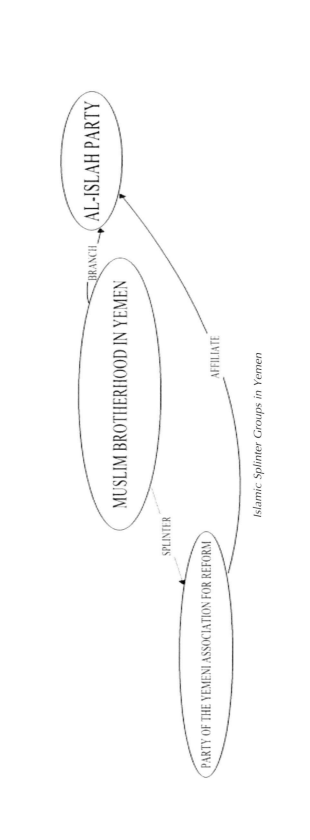

Islamic Splinter Groups in Yemen

Chronology

1258 January: The Mongols under the rule of Hulagu Khan (grandson of Genghis Khan) sack Baghdad, marking the end of the Abbasid caliphate rule. **February:** The Mongols establish their dynasty in what was to become present-day Iran and Iraq.

1263 January: Birth of Ahmad ibn Taymiyya, who lived until 1328 and who is often considered as the real founder of Islamic fundamentalism. Many Islamic thinkers, such as Ibn Abd al-Wahhab and Abu Alaa al-Maududi, borrowed extensively from Taymiyya's writings, which continue to influence various facets of rigorist Islam to this day.

1266 Death of Berek Khan, who was the first ruler of the Golden Horde to convert to Islam.

1270 The Eighth Crusade, which failed within the year after the crusaders under King Louis IX invaded Tunisia.

1281 Beginning of the reign of Osman I, founder of the Ottoman Empire who died in 1324.

1299 The Mongols invade Syria, and the Marinids besiege the Ziyyanid capital of Tlemcen in present-day Algeria.

1393 Ottoman invasion of Bulgaria, resulting in the conquest of Bulgaria up to the Balkans by the Turks.

1448 October: Second battle of Kosovo, which was victorious for the Turks and resulted in Serbia being annexed to Turkey and Bosnia becoming its territorial vassal.

1453 6 April: Mehmed II conquers Constantinople and rules it until 1481. The two halves of the Ottoman Empire are thereby united, and the end of the Byzantine Empire occurs.

1492 The united lands of Aragon and Castile capture Granada, resulting in the expulsion of all Muslims, Jews, and other non-Catholics from Spain.

1501 Isma'il I (1487–1524), the founder of the Safavi Empire, proclaims himself shah (king) of Iran. Twelver Shi'ism is then announced as the official religion of Persia.

1516 The Ottoman Empire conquers Egypt and Syria.

1517 The Ottoman Empire gains control over Mecca and Medina, the two holiest places in Islam.

1520 Start of the reign of Suleiman the Magnificent. This is considered the time when the Ottoman Empire reached its peak. Hungary and the Mediterranean coastlands of Algeria and Tunisia also come under Ottoman control during this period.

1556 Akbar the Great (1542–1605) establishes the Mughal dynasty in northern India.

1625 Java comes under the rule of the Islamic Mataram Sultanate.

1703 Birth of Ibn Abd al-Wahhab, who initiated an all-inclusive reform of Islam that would later be referred to as Wahhabism. The teaching of al-Wahhab, founded on that of Ibn Taymiyya (1263–1328) and on an austere rendition of traditional Islam, is based on the literal interpretation of the Quran and is one of the most dominant schools of Islam today. His influence has been felt mostly in the Gulf States.

1740 Muhammad ibn Saud, head of the al-Saud dynastic family, and theologian Ibn Abd al-Wahhab swear an oath to each other promising to work together to establish a true Islamic state within the kingdom of Saudi Arabia. Wahhabism remains Saudi Arabia's principal religion.

1794 The Afghans are driven from modern-day Iran by the Qajar dynasty, which then rules Persia from 1795 to 1925.

1798 Napoleon's famous campaign in Egypt.

1804 The Mughal Empire officially ends when Shah Alam II accepts the protection of the British East India Company.

1805 Egypt gains independence from the Ottoman Empire, then takes control of western Arabia and extends its boundaries to the Sudan.

1813 Mecca and Taif are captured by the Egyptian army, resulting in all Saudis being expelled from the Hijaz.

1818 **September:** End of the Ottoman-Saudi War with the surrender of Saudi military leaders.

1828 Beginning of the Russo-Turkish War.

1829 **14 September:** Treaty of Adrianople ends the Russo-Turkish War.

1830 French forces enter Algiers and end Ottoman rule in Algeria.

1832 Prince Abd al-Qadir is recognized by the French as the *amir* of Algeria. **21 December:** The Turkish army is defeated at the Battle of Konya by the Egyptian forces.

1839 The start of the *Tanzimat* ("reorganizational") period throughout the Ottoman Empire. A widespread program of modernization in various areas of political administration, judicial practices, and medical science takes place throughout the Ottoman lands.

1840 A powerful European alliance obliges Egypt to withdraw its forces from Syria.

1847 **21 December:** Abd al-Qadir of Algeria surrenders to the French army after being denied entry into Morocco.

1849 Reformist Egyptian ruler Muhammad Ali Pasha dies.

1850 In Istanbul, non-Muslim citizens are declared legally equal to practicing Muslims throughout the Ottoman Empire.

1857 **10 May:** The Indian Rebellion results in the last Mughal ruler in India, Bahadur Shah Zafar, being ousted from power. India then comes under British sovereignty.

1871 Jamal al-Din al-Afghani settles in Egypt after being exiled from Afghanistan for his aggressive Islamic views.

1876 **31 August:** Beginning of the reign of Abd al-Hamid II, which is regarded as one of the most religiously conservative periods within the Ottoman Empire.

1878 **13 June–13 July:** Congress of Berlin recognizes the independence of the Balkan states, which were previously under Islamic control. This also results in Turkey losing the bulk of its territory within the European continent.

1879 Jamal al-Din al-Afghani is expelled from Egypt again for his sociopolitical views.

1881 **12 May:** Treaty of Bardo allows the French armed forces to occupy Tunisia. This occupation will last until 1956. **29 June:** Muhammad Ahmad declares himself to be the mahdi of Sudan.

1882 **April:** Egypt is occupied by the British.

1884 Muhammad 'Abdu joins Jamal al-Din al-Afghani in Paris, and together they publish the influential journal *al-Urwa al-Wuthqa*.

1885 Muhammad Ahmad declares that the government of Sudan will enforce the *sharia* laws of Islam.

1886 Abdullah Suhrawardy establishes the Anjuman-e-Islam in London, later named the Pan-Islamic Society of London.

1899 Sudan is officially administered by Great Britain, and Muhammad 'Abdu becomes the mufti of Egypt.

1902 Ibn Saud captures Riyadh, the future capital of Saudi Arabia.

1906 **7 April:** Morocco becomes a French and Spanish protectorate as a result of the Conference of Algeciras. **5 August:** The Persian constitution is reworked and publicized as a result of the Persian Constitutional Revolution.

1912 The start of the Muhammadiyya reform movement in Indonesia; founding of the Islamic Union, a movement in Southeast Asia that sought to modernize Islam in the region.

1914 **2 November:** The Ottoman Empire enters World War I, siding with the Central Powers.

1916 **16 May:** The Sykes-Picot Agreement divides the Middle East between the British and the French governments. **June:** The Arab revolt against the Ottoman rule begins.

1917 **2 November:** The British government issues the Balfour Declaration, the document that proposed Palestine as the homeland for Jews.

1918 **30 October:** The Ottoman Empire loses a majority of its territories after the signing of the Armistice of Mudros. **11 November:** World War I ends.

1920 **25 April:** The British Mandate for Palestine and the French Mandate for Syria and Lebanon are signed.

1921 **1 April:** Abdullah I becomes the king of Jordan. **23 August:** Faisal I becomes the king of Iraq. Both leaders are sons of the former sharif of Mecca.

1924 **3 March:** Turkey officially abolishes the Islamic caliphate by dismissing 'Abdul Majid II.

1925 **15 December:** Reza Shah Pahlavi overthrows the Qajar dynasty in Persia and establishes the Pahlavi dynasty.

1926 The *Tablighi Jamaat* Islamic reform movement is founded in northern India. **10 January:** King Abdul-Aziz of Saudi Arabia declares himself king of Mecca and the Hijaz.

1928 The Muslim Brotherhood is established in Egypt by Hassan al-Banna with the desire to resurrect the Muslim Empire. To further illustrate their motives, the group took on the motto, "Allah is our purpose, the Prophet our leader, the Quran our constitution, jihad our way and dying for Allah our supreme objective."

1932 **3 October:** Iraq is granted independence by Great Britain and enters the League of Nations.

1935 Persia is renamed Iran by Reza Shah Pahlavi. The Muslim Brotherhood is established in Palestine by Abd al-Rahman al-Banna, brother of the movement's founder, Hasan al-Banna.

1939 World War II begins.

1941 **26 August:** *Jamaat e-Islami* is founded in Lahore, India.

1942 A Muslim Brotherhood faction is established in Jordan.

1943 **22 November:** Lebanon gains its independence from France.

1945 End of World War II. A Muslim Brotherhood faction is established in Syria. **17 August:** Indonesia is proclaimed an independent republic.

1946 **17 April:** Syria is granted independence from France. **25 May:** Jordan gains independence from Great Britain.

1947 **14 August:** Pakistan breaks away from India and becomes an independent Islamic nation.

1948 **Spring:** Hostilities escalate between the Arab armies and the Jewish state. **14 May:** The creation of Israel. **November:** The United Nations partitions Palestine.

1949 **12 February:** Hasan al-Banna is assassinated in Egypt.

1951 **24 December:** Libya gains independence from Italy.

1952 **23 July:** King Faruq of Egypt is forced to abdicate his throne after a military coup led by Gamal Abd al-Nasser. This day is referred to as the Egyptian Revolution of 1952.

1953 *Hizb at-Tahrir al-Islami* is established in Jerusalem by Taqiy al-Din al-Nabhani. **19 August:** Iranian Prime Minister Muhammad Mosaddegh is removed from power following a coup d'état. **9 November:** King Abd al-Aziz of Saudi Arabia dies.

1954 **26 October:** An attempt to assassinate Egyptian President Nasser results in the incarceration of hundreds of Muslim Brotherhood members in Egypt. The group was then subsequently banned in Egypt.

1956 *Jam'iyyat al-'Ulama' al-Muslimin* is disbanded in Algeria. **20 March:** Tunisia becomes independent from France. **7 April:** Morocco gains independence from France.

1957 A pan-Islamic congress is held in Lahore. **31 August:** Malaysia gains independence from Great Britain and declares Islam to be the national religion.

1958 **14 July:** Iraq is declared a republic after Brigadier General Abd al-Karim Qasim carries out a coup d'état against King Faisal II.

1960 The independence of Mali, Niger, and other former French colonies in Africa. **26 April:** The Iraqi Islamic Party is formed out of the Iraqi Muslim Brotherhood but is banned for one year by Iraqi Prime Minister Abd al-Karim Qasim.

1962 **19 March:** Algeria becomes an independent state after the Algerian War for Independence with France, which began on 1 November 1954.

1964 *Al-Jama'a al-Islamiyya* in Lebanon is established by Fathi Yakan. The Islamic theologian Hasan al-Turabi becomes the secretary-general of the Islamic Charter Front in Sudan. The Muslim Women's Association in Egypt is dissolved.

1965 *Mujahideen-e-Khalq* is founded in Iran.

1966 **29 August:** The influential Egyptian Muslim Brotherhood extremist and theologian Sayyid Qutb is executed for allegedly plotting to overthrow the government.

1967 **10 June:** Israel gains control of East Jerusalem, the Gaza Strip, the Golan Heights, the Sinai Peninsula, and the West Bank after defeating the Arabic armies during the Six-Day War.

1968 The International Islamic Union for Student Organizations is established during a pilgrimage to Mecca. The extremist group *al-Takfir wa al-Hijra* is created in Egypt by Shukri Mustapha.

1969 **1 September:** King Idris of Libya is removed from power after a successful coup d'état led by Colonel Muammar Qadhafi.

1970 The *Mujahideen* movement in Morocco is established by 'Abd al-'Aziz al-Na'mani. **26 October:** *Milli Nizam Partisi* is founded in Turkey by Necmettin Erbakan.

1971 The influential female Islamist Zaynab al-Ghazali is released from prison by Egyptian President Anwar al-Sadat.

1972 October: The *Milli Nizam Partisi* is dissolved in Turkey and is reorganized into *Milli Selamat Partisi*.

1973 17 July: Afghani King Zahir Shah is overthrown. **6 October:** The Yom Kippur War breaks out between the Arab states and Israel and ends with an Israeli victory on 25 October of that year.

1975 The *Amal* movement is formed in Lebanon. **25 February:** The leader of the group The Nation of Islam, Elijah Muhammad, is killed by civilians in North America.

1976 November: Salih Sirriyya, leader of *Tanzim al-Fanniyya al-'Askariyya* (Organization of the Military Techniques), is executed in Egypt.

1977 20 December: *Hizb al-Tahrir al-Islami* founder, Taqiy ad-Din al-Nabhani, dies in Beirut.

1978 A Muslim Brotherhood branch is founded in Somalia and takes the name *Harakat Al-Islah*. **August:** Leader of the Shiite Twelvers in Lebanon, Musa al-Sadr, disappears during a trip to Libya. **17 September:** The Camp David Accords are signed between Israel and Egypt.

1979 The National Islamic Front begins to influence the Sudanese government. **11 February:** The Pahlavi dynasty falls in Iran as a result of the Iranian Islamic Revolution led by Ayatollah Ruhollah al-Musawi Khomeini. **26 March:** Peace accords are signed between Egypt and Israel. **20 November:** Islamic fundamentalists barricade themselves in the al-Masjid al-Haram of Mecca against the Saudi security forces for two weeks, resulting in the deaths of more than 200.

1980 9 April: Muhammad Baqir al-Sadr, the *Hizb al-Da'wa al-Islamiyya* spiritual guide, and his sister, Amina Sadr bint al-Huda, are executed in Iraq. **22 September:** Start of the Iran-Iraq War, which lasts until 20 August 1988. **End of September:** *Tanzim al-Jihad* is formed from a merging of Muhammad Abd al-Salam Faraj's and Karam Zuhdi's Egyptian groups.

1981 6 June: *Harakat al-Ittijah al-Islami* (future *Harakat al-Nahda al-Islamiyya*) is formed. **6 October:** Khalid Islambouli leads a group of militant extremists who assassinate Egyptian President Anwar al-Sadat during a military parade in Cairo.

1982 *Hizbullah* in Lebanon is formed. **February:** Known as the Hama massacre, Syrian forces suppress an Islamist rebellion, resulting in thousands of deaths. **6 June:** Israel invades southern Lebanon, beginning the First Lebanon War. **16–18 September:** A massacre occurs at the Sabra and Shatila Palestinian refugee camps in Beirut.

1983 The Second Sudanese Civil War begins. **23 October:** The Beirut barracks bombing results in the withdrawal of the American and French troops from Lebanon.

1985 **14 June:** Shiite extremists hijack a Trans-World Airlines flight going from Athens to Rome and then force it to reroute to Beirut. Eight crew members and 145 passengers were held for 17 days, and one American hostage, a U.S. Navy sailor, was killed. The incident finally concluded after Israel released 435 Lebanese and Palestinian prisoners.

1987 **7 November:** General Zine al-Abidine Ben Ali overthrows Tunisian President Habib Bourguiba.

1988 **20 August:** The Iran-Iraq War comes to a conclusion.

1989 **14 February:** Ayatollah Khomeini issues a *fatwa* calling for the death of *The Satanic Verses* author Salman Rushdie. **18 February:** The Islamic Salvation Front is established in Algiers by Abbassi Madani. **June:** A group of militants led by General Omar al-Bashir and Hassan al-Turabi's National Islamic Front seize control of Sudan in a bloodless coup d'état.

1990 **August:** Kuwait is annexed by Iraqi Baathist leader Saddam Hussein.

1991 **28 February:** The Gulf War ends, and the Iraqi troops are expelled from Kuwait. **25–28 April:** The first and only International Islamic Congress is organized in Khartoum, Sudan, by Hasan al-Turabi. **December:** Beginning of the Algerian Civil War, which results in the deaths of 100,000 to 150,000 people.

1992 *Hizb Jabhat al-'Amal al-Islami* (Islamic Action Front) is formed in Jordan. **16 February:** Sheikh 'Abbas al-Musawi, *Hizbullah* in Lebanon leader, is killed by Israeli forces. **28 August:** Rashed al-Ghannoushi, *Ennahda* leader, is sentenced to death in Tunisia but flees to London.

1993 **26 February:** Bombing in the basement of the World Trade Center's North Tower in New York City marks a new phase of international terrorism that targets solely civilians. **18 March:** Professor Hamid Nasr Abu Zayd is charged with apostasy in Egypt.

1994 **September:** The Taliban army is formed. **26 October:** Peace accords are signed between Israel and Jordan, leading to many Islamic insurgencies against the Jordanian King Hussein I. Hamas still continues to carry out terrorist attacks against Israel.

1995 **Summer:** The Algerian Armed Islamic Group conducts a series of attacks against the French public transportation system. **June:** Islamists attempt to assassinate Egyptian President Hosni Mubarak in Ethiopia. **26 October:** Fathi Shaqaqi, cofounder of the Palestinian Islamic Jihad, is killed in Malta. **4 November:** Israeli Prime Minister Yitzhak Rabin is assassinated in Tel Aviv.

1996   5 January: Explosives expert Yahya Abd-al-Latif 'Ayyash is killed in Gaza by Israeli forces, spawning the creation of the Yahya 'Ayyash Brigades in Palestine. **25 June:** The Khobar Towers are bombed in Riyadh, Saudi Arabia. **28 June:** Necmettin Erbakan is elected prime minister of Turkey.

1997   Former Syrian Muslim Brotherhood leader 'Abd al-Fattah Abu Ghudda dies in exile. **25 September:** Ahmad Yassin, leader of Hamas, is released from an Israeli jail. **17 November:** The Luxor massacre occurs at the hands of the Egyptian Islamic Group.

1998   23 February: Osama bin Laden issues his "call for a global jihad against all Westerners and Jews." **7 August:** The United States embassies are bombed in Nairobi, Kenya, and Dar es-Salaam, Tanzania, killing 263 people and injuring more than 5,000.

2000   12 October: The USS *Cole* is bombed, killing 17 sailors and wounding 39 others.

2001   2 March: The Taliban army dynamites the sixth-century Bamiyan Buddha statues in Afghanistan. **11 September:** Four American commercial airliners are hijacked and crashed into the Pentagon in Washington, D.C.; a field in Pennsylvania; and New York City's World Trade Center, which is completely destroyed. Leaving 2,973 dead, this provokes the U.S. military Operation Enduring Freedom in Afghanistan and the "War on Terror."

2002   1 March: The United States first invades Afghanistan with Operation Anaconda in the hope of ousting the Taliban army.

2003   February: The Darfur conflict begins to develop in Sudan. **19 March:** The United States invades Iraq and overthrows Saddam Hussein and his Baathist regime, resulting in Hussein's eventual capture and execution six months later. This resulted in a growth of jihadist organizations throughout the country. **16 May:** The *Salafia Jihadia* group conducts the Casablanca suicide bombings, killing more than 30 people and injuring more than 100. **14 April:** The Association of Muslim Scholars is formed in Iraq.

2004   11 March: Madrid is devastatingly bombed by Islamic militants, leaving 191 dead and 1,824 injured. **October:** Al-Qaeda is established in Iraq and proclaims Abu Musab al-Zarqawi to be its leader.

2005   **7 July:** The London Transportation System is bombed by Islamic militants. **3 August:** Mahmoud Ahmadinejad rises to power in the Islamic Republic of Iran and becomes president of the country.

2006   **22 February:** The destruction of the Golden Mosque in Iraq further disturbs the tense Shiite-Sunni relations. **Summer:** The *Al-Shabaab* movement begins in the hope of taking over the Somali government. **7 June:** Al-Qaeda in Iraq leader Abu Musab al-Zarqawi is killed during a U.S. airstrike in Baqouba. **12 July:** *Hizbullah* ignites the Israeli-Lebanese conflict. **11 December:** The International Conference to Review the Global Vision of the Holocaust takes place in Tehran. Headed by Iranian President Mahmoud Ahmadinejad, it was condemned as a symposium to deny the legitimacy of the Holocaust.

2007   **January:** Al-Qaeda in the Islamic Maghreb is established in North Africa, and the Algerian Abu Mussab 'Abd al-Wadud (a.k.a. Abdelmalek Droukdal) is named its leader. **11 April:** A series of suicide bombings takes place in Algiers, Algeria, and Casablanca, Morocco. **June:** Hamas removes the *al-Fatah* leaders from the Gaza Strip. **11 December:** Al-Qaeda in the Islamic Maghreb conducts bombings against the office of the UN High Commissioner for Refugees in Algiers, killing more than 40 people.

2008   **February:** Al-Qaeda in the Islamic Maghreb kidnaps two Austrian tourists in Tunisia and brings them to Mali. Rise of Abdelhamid Abu Zeid, leader of the Tariq bin Ziyad Brigade.

2009   **January:** Al-Qaeda's Saudi and Yemeni branches merge to create al-Qaeda in the Arabian Peninsula. **4 June:** Newly elected American President Barack Obama makes a historical speech to the Muslim nation in Cairo. **5 November:** The Fort Hood shooting takes place at the hands of Nidal Malik Hasan, killing 12 soldiers and one civilian while also wounding 38. **8 December:** Al-Qaeda in the Islamic Maghreb claims responsibility for the kidnapping of a French citizen and three Spanish humanitarian workers in Mauritania. **25 December:** Al-Qaeda in the Arabian Peninsula claims responsibility for the attempted hijacking of an Amsterdam flight en route to Detroit.

2010   **24 July:** Al-Qaeda in the Islamic Maghreb leader Abdelmalek Droukdal announces the execution of a kidnapped French citizen. **16 September:** Five French citizens are kidnapped in Arlit, Niger. **2 October:** The Nigerian Islamic militant group *Boko Haram* pledges its allegiance to al-Qaeda in the Islamic Maghreb. **18 December:** Civil riots and demonstrations erupt in Tunisia, resulting in the Arab Spring revolutions, which continue into 2011.

2011   The Arabic Spring civil protests continue to erupt throughout the Arabic world, resulting in the overthrow of the Tunisian, Egyptian, and Libyan leaders. Bahrain, Iraq, Jordan, Kuwait, Lebanon, Libya, Morocco, Oman, and Syria are also affected by the revolutionary climate. **January:** The Muslim Brotherhood in Egypt announces that it will run its candidate Abdel Moneim Abul Fotouh during the fall legislative elections; other Islamic organizations' leaders and influential figures run for the presidency as well. **2 May:** Osama bin Laden is killed by U.S. Navy SEALs in Abbottabad, Pakistan. **12 June:** The Turkish Islamic Party triumphs in national elections, revolutionizing the country's foreign policy. **30 September:** The American-born al-Qaeda recruiter Anwar al-Awlaki is killed in Yemen. **18 October:** Israel exchanges 1,024 Hamas prisoners for one abducted Israeli soldier, Gilad Shalit. **23 October:** *Ennahda* wins the first free elections in Tunisia. **26 November:** The Morocco Islamist party, Justice and Development, wins in the new elections. **30 November:** The Egyptian Muslim Brotherhood Party wins the elections in Egypt. The country's Salafi party *al-Nour* comes in second with 25 percent of the votes. It should be noted that many members of *al-Nour* were supporters of the jihad and were even imprisoned for their activities.

2012   21 January: *Boko Haram* kills almost 200 civilians in the Nigerian town of Kano. The group presents itself to be more and more well trained and armed, leaving experts to believe that this is a direct result of its relationship with al-Qaeda in the Islamic Maghreb. **30 January:** It is announced that peace talks will take place between the Taliban army and the United States in Qatar.

Introduction

Fundamentalism, or the practicing of the basics of a creed's doctrines, is not unique to Islam or to the ideological world. In fact, every religion has experienced some form of fundamentalism at one point in history. These forms of fundamentalist mentalities, from the moderate to the radical, have been in reaction to their own contemporary sociopolitical climates. With regard to Islamic fundamentalism, those who desire this return to the "fundamentals" do so because they feel that today's changing modern world is blemishing the "sanctity" or "purity" of Islam and therefore that a return to the religion's basics will preserve the faith and provide for a morally just life for its believers. This life, to the Islamic fundamentalists, should be based on the ancient Islamic societies of the seventh century in which the Prophet Muhammad, his companions, and the four subsequent rulers (caliphs) after them lived.

Today, Islamic fundamentalism has also been instrumental for various groups to promote its sociopolitical agendas in their respective countries. But, although related, this breed of fundamentalism should not be confused with Islam itself. A complex religion rich in history and culture, Islam has been marred by the many extreme acts of violence that have aligned actions with faith. It has then been speculated as to whether these acts are a result of the poor economic, political, and social conditions that exist in many of the Muslim countries or whether they are due to a grave misinterpretation of the religion by these radicals.

This growing trend has had a tremendous impact the world over and has dictated a great deal of foreign policy in both Western and Middle Eastern diplomacy. This dictionary aims at exploring and illustrating the historical premise that these fundamentalist movements have grown from and the contemporary situation in which they reside. The goal here is to break down the cultural barriers that may prevent many Western minds from understanding Islam's past—a past that has led to this movement and needs to be viewed from an objective point of historical consideration while keeping in mind the Islamic perspectives. Perhaps topics that are notorious from a Western perspective (such as martyrdom operations, austere religious devotion, dress codes, and control of daily activities) can be regarded in a new light devoid

1

of judgment or misconception. This unbiased and factual account is an attempt to dissipate the atmosphere of the "clash of civilizations" that has been particularly prevalent in the past two decades.

Misinterpretation and false apprehensions have steered the course of the general opinion of the Islamic fundamentalist movement and, to a point, the Islamic culture in general. Here, the views of the Islamic fundamentalists, the history from which they come, and the psychology fueling their beliefs will be carefully represented while retaining the notion that (like many other similar movements of the past) extremist factions and therefore violence can occur and is a very serious reality.

This dictionary can also be used as a simple guide for the most basic dogmas and customs in Islam. Although the text focuses on contemporary fundamentalist activities, the essential qualities that define Islam as a religion and culture are explored. Therefore, this work has an array of uses that can lead to a variety of considerations and research topics.

A BRIEF HISTORY OF THE RISE OF ISLAMIC FUNDAMENTALISM

Since the European colonial period in the Middle East and Northern Africa in the late 18th century, the Islamic fundamentalist movement has been on the rise. Reactionary to the Western presence, many believe that the deterioration of Islam has been a complete consequence of European influence. The "founding fathers" of Islamic fundamentalism, such as Muhammad 'Abdu and Jamal al-Din al-Afghani, began by preaching against the impact that the Western technologies and cultural influences did have and would continue to have on the state of Islam. The European dominance over these regions remained until the end of World War II, leaving a long-standing mark on the Islamic world. The formidable Egyptian Muslim Brotherhood emerged in 1928 as a result of these strong anticolonist sentiments that were pervading much of the Arabic world. Today, the group continues to impact various trends and groups while remaining innovative and ever present, especially in Egyptian society.

After the independence of the African and Middle Eastern countries around the middle of the 20th century, secularism began to prevail, and colonial masters were soon replaced by authoritarian regimes in many of these countries, straying even more society from the traditional and basic principles of the religion. By the end of the century, a majority of the Arab world had been "westernized" in the eyes of the fundamentalists. Even the various coups d'état that have resulted in nationalistic governments have further suppressed socioeconomic growth in a majority of the Muslim countries. From this poverty and social instability, a desire to revolutionize the political structure has arisen. This accounts for the majority of desirable recruits being of the male middle-to-lower-class demographic (those who feel the straining effects of the socioeconomic current the most). However, contrary to popular belief, a large share of the Islamic leaders and participants are rather highly educated. Their time spent in academia has helped them to understand how social rebellion can change the course of a civilization, and their knowledge of the Islam of the past, which is seen as "a true Islamic society," has become that much more appealing. In short, these participants are far from the "Third World, uneducated" perception that exists in many Western minds.

Contemporarily, the European and American militant presence in Saudi Arabia (the country of the holiest lands in Islam: Mecca and Medina), Iraq (the historical capital of the Islamic Caliphate), and Afghanistan (the country of the *mujahideen*) has further promoted anti-American/anti-European animosity. This resentment of the military presence has also then led to a general resentment of Western culture as a whole by many. This can be understood in simple terms by the post-9/11 sentiments many Americans felt about Muslims: an aggressive action took place by members of a culture that led to the attacked culture having bias and judgment against that culture from which those belligerents came. Therefore, it is more about a "clash of perceptions" than about a "clash of civilizations."

From this perspective, a rise in fundamentalism and anti-Western sentiments can be reasonably explained. The small percentage of extremists who have taken this view to violent levels not only want American and European citizens (military and civilian alike) to be absolutely expelled from their land but desire to wage war on Western soil as well. However, a majority of the Arabic world remains moderate and accepting of democratic and secularist ideals. Many want to "Islamize" Western ideals: combining both cultures in order to create one unified compromising society. This widely held notion represents a celebration of identity, diversity, and tolerance.

Historically, the Islamic fundamentalist movement is a conscious perspective that is derived from historical experiences. The central structure and method of the fundamentalists is based primarily on a particular point of view. This dictionary hopes to facilitate in understanding the cultural and doctrinal opinions from which these participants are coming. A difficult task, yes, but understanding from an objective perspective can lead to great advances in personal and, perhaps in turn, cultural psychology.

It must also be remembered that this fundamentalist mentality is not restricted only to the Arabic world but has also spread to the wider Muslim world in parts of India, southern Asia, Russia, North America, and Europe.

AN APPROACH TO ISLAMIC FUNDAMENTALISM: INTERNAL, COMPARATIVE, CULTURAL, AND HISTORICAL

The perspective of this introduction has been through cultural intelligence, meaning that the way in which Islamic fundamentalism is researched and information is gathered is through strategic monitoring by cultural awareness. This allows for an internal point of view to be reached while the evolution of the groups and movements is therefore constantly updated. Through strategic monitoring, trends, common points, and differences are focused on. Since this type of approach has been applied to this dictionary, it is diverse, absolutely contemporary, and researched using a unique and modern method of observation.

The historical dimension of this dictionary lies in the references of the contemporary groups and organizations to the ancient Islamic doctrines, trends, and movements on which they rely. It must be stressed that this is not a history of Islam or Islamic movements (this type of general information would be best found in a general encyclopedia of Islam) but rather refers to the main milestones in Islamic fundamentalist history and the most basic of the creed's doctrines that help shape it. Therefore, this dictionary is Islamic in the sense that Islam is simply emphasized. The following pages deal rather with ideological Islamism—that is, the use of the Islamic religion within and for the sociopolitical agenda of these groups. Quite simply, "Islam is a religion, Islamism is an ideology." This difference must be wholly understood for the concepts behind the content to be perceived correctly.

THE DEFINITION OF ISLAMIC FUNDAMENTALISM

Space

Islamic, here, refers to all the countries where some groups are defined as or refer to themselves as Islamic. Therefore, not only the Arab world is covered but all of the continents. For many of these places, even when the majority of the population is not Muslim, there are some groups that claim to be Islamic or are related to Islamic fundamentalism even though their national heritage dictates otherwise. However, there is an obvious focus on the countries that are part of the Organization of the Islamic Cooperation (comprising 57 member states and known as the Organization of the Islamic Conference until 28 June 2011).

Time

This dictionary deals primarily with the contemporary Islamic fundamentalist groups, movements, and entities that were created after World War

I (1914) and up until 2012. However, this does not mean that groups and movements that existed prior to this time frame are not included. Rather, all historical groups and movements that have influenced or are referred to by the contemporaries in focus are discussed so that the reader may better ascertain their historical background, inspirations, and aspirations.

Ideology

As previously discussed, the main idea of Islamic fundamentalism is just that—the fundamentals. This ideology designates all groups and movements that want to return to the foundations of Islam. The term "foundation" is specifically historical and refers to the era of the Prophet Muhammad and the subsequent generations of his companions that followed him, especially what is referred to as "the four well-guided caliphs" (*al-khulafa' al-rashidun*). All the groups that aim at making the Islamic societies live in the same manner as these previous generations define themselves and are labeled as fundamentalists. They are called fundamentalists simply because they want the absolute application of the fundamentals of Islam. The foundations are therefore time relevant, thus making time and ideology intertwined.

Agenda

The agenda is also intertwined with the ideology. Islamic fundamentalists' agenda is to apply those doctrines and laws that existed during the foundation period of Islam in the seventh century. They seek to establish a caliphate (Islamic government) and strictly apply *sharia* (Islamic law) in public affairs and daily life. However, the defining agendas and the degree of strictness in the application of these fundamentals depend entirely on the individual group. To the Islamic fundamentalists, this agenda is seen as an entirely achievable utopia since it did exist before.

ISLAMIC FUNDAMENTALISM IN THE INDIVIDUAL'S LIFE: MEN, WOMEN, FAMILY, THE BODY, AND THE SENSES

From the view of the Islamic fundamentalists, men and women are completely distinct from one another. For men, they are to adhere to the regulations of the personal and familial life according to a rigorous, religious model. This is founded on the basis that man is the applicant of Allah's prescriptions and guidelines to the family cell. Man is therefore responsible for his own salvation as well as that of all the members of his family. Also, it should be noted that the family is defined as an extended one, not composed only of the immediate members. This tribal system is very much active within the Islamic society and has been for centuries, making the blood link between people very extensive. These regulations also include personal stipulations regarding the daily life of the man. The Islamic fundamentalists give precise recommendations on how the man should dress, eat, pray, groom, and procreate.

Islamic fundamentalists also give strict and compulsory prescriptions about how women should live, act, and behave. Schematically, there are two categories of feminine being that are defined: being a mother and being a wife. Being a mother is the optimal status that any women can achieve according to the Islamic fundamentalists. It also requires that a respectful attitude be always given toward the mother. The opposition of roles between mother and wife deal directly with the relationship that a woman has with a man, be it son, husband, father, brother, and so on. In Islamic fundamentalism, the woman is always submitted to the man's will and directions as long as they correspond to Islamic law.

An episteme that exists on a major level in Islamic fundamentalism and that directly concerns the female body is that of the veil. There are three types of veils in the Islamic fundamentalist perception: the *burka*, the *khimar*, and the *hijab*. What is interesting about the veil is that the degree of fundamentalism that each group exhibits will dictate which type of veil is worn and which body parts are hidden or shown. For the most radical of the groups, showing the entire face and body (including the hands) of a woman is considered a sin that is able to distract man from adoring Allah. So, they impose the use of the *burka*, which covers the whole body and the entire face. For some less extremist groups, the entire body and face of the woman are considered sinful except for the eyes only if the woman never looks directly at the man whom she is communicating with. Therefore, these groups recommend that the woman wear a *khimar*, which allows for the eyes to be seen. Finally, for the more moderate Islamic fundamentalist groups, the entire body is still considered just as sinful except for the face only if the woman never applies makeup to it. This group therefore prescribes the *hijab*, which reveals the woman's face only, covering her neck, ears, and hair.

Based on these views, it is then possible to distinguish between the three major degrees of Islamic fundamentalism by observing the extent to which they desire to control the believers' body and five senses. For example, some groups even have the will to control their senses—smell, taste, sound, touch, and sight. However, most do not possess the will to control smell and taste, but the majority does have strict recommendations for the regulation of sight, touch, and sound.

ISLAMIC FUNDAMENTALISM IN PUBLIC LIFE

With regard to public affairs, the Islamic fundamentalist movements and groups can be recognized by the political projects that they defend. These projects revolve around their desire to organize power in order to manage the area and its public affairs based on the historic model of the Prophetic Era (the time of the Prophet Muhammad, his immediate followers, and the first four caliphs). This means that they desire a political system that is guided by religious preoccupations and dominated by religious people in a theocratic manner. Most of these Islamic fundamentalist movements and groups have been greatly influenced on the political level by the 1979 Iranian Islamic Revolution, which resulted in Iran's current theocracy. Along with the revolution itself, its leader, Ayatollah Ruhollah al-Musawi Khomeini, emerged as the model of Islamic leadership in contemporary history.

Besides that, what distinguishes or characterizes these groups on the political level is the fact that they oppose Western culture and its hegemony (specifically, democracy and military interventions). For the more moderate groups, however, Western concepts of governance are reworded and rethought into Islamic concepts such as *shura* (consultation) for elections and *al-'adala* (justice) for equality.

There are also some other key civil concepts that should be noted. First, the *umma* (nation), in Islamic fundamentalist political ideology, is considered to be a universal community of believers as opposed to a civil society with a national identity. The *umma* is an extranational, extraterritorial, and extraracial concept. *Hukuma*, or government, is also completely based on the guidance of Allah, or *hukumiyya*. The one who would then carnally govern the people (*hakim*) is therefore perceived and considered to be the successor of the Prophet and the first four caliphs. In fact, "caliph" translates as "successor"—further emphasizing the historicism behind Islamic fundamentalism. The *hakim* is also expected to rule in the same manner as the Prophet Muhammad and the first caliphs. The governed (*mahkum*) are then expected to submit to the *hukumiyya* of Allah, and the country should be ruled on the basis of religious opinion, *fatwa* (Islamic legal decree), and *sharia* (Islamic law). So, since the governed are to submit themselves to Allah and his governance and the governor should be ruling in the likeness of Allah, the people are to trust that all decisions that he makes are reflective of Allah's will.

ISLAMIC FUNDAMENTALISM AND DIPLOMACY

Historically, there have been two types of areas that have been designated since the ancient times in Islam. The Islamic fundamentalists still refer to them today, and they are *dar al-Islam* (land of Islam) and *dar-al-harb* (land of war). The former is designated as any place regardless of man-made boundaries or territorial divisions in which an Islamic state is installed. These places are considered sacred and pure and therefore must be preserved and not disrupted in any way. *Dar al-harb* is quite the opposite. This refers to any land in which Islamic law does not exist and therefore is worthy of warfare or aggression since it does not adhere to the governance of Allah.

The Islamic fundamentalists also do not honor any peace with a non-Islamic body but accept only a temporary truce or armistice (*hudna*; cease-fire). According to many medieval Islamic scholars, *hudnas* with a non-Muslim enemy should be limited to only a period not exceeding 10 years. Since the non-Islamic state does not abide by Islamic law, any treaty or policy introduced by it is not deemed valid to the Islamic fundamentalists. Even more so, it is considered forbidden to align with non-Islamic states, especially against other Islamic states. It is also acceptable to annul all agreements made with any non-Islamic state since that state is not based on Islamic principles or because it may target other Muslims.

To the Islamic fundamentalists, the *dhimmi*, or non-Muslims who live in an Islamic country, are allowed to continue to live within the Islamic state but have fewer rights. Although they are permitted to stay within the Islamic state, they cannot partake in any Muslim activity but are obliged to publicly adhere to the laws of the state. For example, under Islamic law, a *dhimmi* may consume pork but must do so in private. Restrictions and persecutions against the non-Muslims depends on the degree of fundamentalism spread within an Islamic state, and so are the levies (*jizya*) that the *dhimmi* must pay to the Islamic state for allowing them to live there. A *dhimmi* also can never hold judicial or political power over a Muslim in an Islamic state.

THE EVOLUTION OF ISLAMIC FUNDAMENTALISM

Prior to the collapse of the Soviet Union in 1991, the enemy for the Islamic fundamentalists was the communists and all atheists. Many of the current adherents to Islamic fundamentalism were also Arab soldiers (*mujahideen*) who fought against the Soviets in the Soviet-Afghan War (1979–1989). After the 1991 Gulf War and even more so since the 11 September 2001 attacks, the enemy for the Islamic fundamentalists has been designated as Western culture and American imperialism. The similarity here is that both the past (the communists) and current (all westerners) enemies of the Islamic fundamentalists had or have a strong military presence in the Arab world and sought to adjust and change the Islamic culture to be more in the guise of their own. The difference between the two, however slight, is perceived and understood, but the differences in ideology are emphasized. For example, the communists were ideological atheists (devoid of any religious prescriptions), whereas Western civilization is viewed as crusaders—invaders of the Islamic lands in the name of Christ, or pagans focused purely on materialism and consumerism. To the Islamic fundamentalists, the enemy may be different, but the overarching perspective is not.

Another evolution that has been recently taking place in Islamic fundamentalism is the extensive use of technology and media by the groups and its members. Referred to as "Islamic neofundamentalism," this new trend has made it possible for many groups to reach a wider audience. This advantage that technology has brought to the Islamic fundamentalists has affected not only their media outlets but their tactical warfare as well. This Islamic neofundamentalism has made it possible for groups and members to better broadcast their agendas, communicate with each other, and attract a larger range of people. In short, Islamic neofundamentalism has spread and gone global thanks to media and communication technologies, especially with the rise of the Internet.

ISLAMIC FUNDAMENTALISM AND TERRORISM: CONNECTIONS AND DIFFERENCES

A common misconception in Western thought is that all Islamic fundamentalists are terrorists or that Islamic fundamentalism is a "politically correct" label for terrorism. Although some groups and individuals who have committed extreme acts of violence do subscribe to Islamic fundamentalism, this is by no means an umbrella term. Islamic fundamentalism, like any other social movement, spawns violent radicals just as easily as it does peaceful members. Before looking into the connections and differences between Islamic fundamentalists and terrorists, a clarification must be made: as of this writing, there is no common consensus as to what defines a terrorist. The word exists purely colloquially and is used sparingly in this dictionary for that very reason. However, when it is used, "terrorism" here refers to violent acts that are targeted at civilians just as frequently as security forces. The term "terrorists" is then used to describe militant extremists who participate in those acts.

As previously mentioned, the largest connection between terrorism and Islamic fundamentalism is that some groups and figures fall into both categories. Furthermore, many terrorists believe in the same ideologies that Islamic fundamentalists do: the application of *sharia*, the installation of a caliphate, and an austere interpretation of the Quran and the Hadiths that dictates their lives. In fact, many acts of terrorism are done with the hope of destroying a society's infrastructure and economy so that the Islamic state can flourish in its place (which is the case with most domestic terrorism within the Muslim countries). Also, many extremist groups have grown out of the moderate ones. As is the case with many terrorist outfits, those who break away from their father groups often do so because they feel that a more aggressive approach should be taken and because they are unhappy with the moderate methods.

Both Islamic fundamentalists and terrorists feel that the society that surrounds them (a majority of the Arabic world and the entire Western world) is corrupt and in dire need of change. The key differences, here, lie in approach. Islamic fundamentalists are actually often more focused on the smaller, regional changes that they want to enact in their own tribes or communities. Few even possess the resources to conduct violent acts on a large scale, let alone the international level. Many Islamic fundamentalist groups and members also only use Islamic law and doctrine to improve their own daily lives and do not wish to incorporate "outsiders" into their groups, wishing to keep their communities as tightly knit as possible. On the contrary, other terrorist outfits seek membership from a wide range of communities and demographics in the hope of gaining even more recruits. Although many terrorists desire a society based on the fundamentals of Islam, all people who wish for this way of life are by no means terrorists. These extremists are merely a marginal (but resilient) faction of the movement.

ISLAMIC FUNDAMENTALISM TYPOLOGY

The various Islamic fundamentalist groups can best be classified and most easily understood by focusing on the basic concerns of each type of group. These concerns can be categorized most accurately by rites and symbols, government and governance, and diplomacy and foreigners. The groups should then be segmented into popular Islamic fundamentalism, political Islamic fundamentalism, and jihadi Islamic fundamentalism so that all factions of the movement are represented.

Popular Islamic Fundamentalism

Popular Islamic fundamentalists or, rather, the brand of Islamic fundamentalism that is adhered to by the majority of the people is most directly affected by the rites and symbols of Islam. For example, when sacred figures (such as the Prophet Muhammad) or a pilgrimage (*hajj*) are disturbed, the popular Islamic fundamentalists are far more likely to rebel against those who desecrate these symbols than if someone hinders their legislation or government. Popular Islamic fundamentalists are even far more unlikely to concern themselves over issues involving foreigners or diplomacy.

Political Islamic Fundamentalism

As the label suggests, political Islamic fundamentalists are much more focused on the current status of the government and those who are governing the Muslim countries. These adherents apply their efforts directly to revolutionizing or altering the contemporary legislature. They also then use symbols of Islam to further gain influence among the Islamic fundamentalist community and networks. However, they too are less likely to focus on the diplomatic relations of the government, although such issues may be occasionally discussed and utilized in delegitimizing a government.

Jihadi Islamic Fundamentalism

The jihadi Islamic fundamentalists muster all their resources and completely direct their focus on the foreigners who are present within and outside their state as well as their state's diplomacy with other nations. A foreign presence will serve only to increase their activities, just as unfavorable (from the point of view of the jihadi Islamic fundamentalists) diplomatic relations will. Therefore, there is a greater focus on international affairs than on domestic ones for the jihadi Islamic fundamentalists. Its adherents stress that through proper foreign relations (or lack thereof), domestic tranquillity can be achieved and the symbols of Islam better preserved.

A SOMETIMES DIVISIVE FORCE

A symbol of unity and of the ancient prosperity of Islam, the caliphate is therefore one of the central components of Islamic fundamentalism because of what it represents. After the dismissal of 'Abdul Majid II of Turkey in 1924, the caliphate has ceased to exist. However, when the various caliphs were in power, the Islamic world grew to encompass northern Africa, the Arabian Peninsula, eastern and southern Asia, and Indonesia—an impressive feat. This vast territory that the Islamic nation encompassed translated into a sense of superiority and grandeur of the caliphate. Since its dissolution, many Muslims (not just the Islamic fundamentalists) wish to see a return to the "glory days" of Islam. The caliphate represented for many an idyllic dream of utopia where many Muslims lived together under a single unifying system that was based solely on the holy texts of Islam. This way of the past was seen for a long time as unlikely to resurface again, which is why the 1979 Iranian Islamic Revolution had such a powerful impact. With the success of the Iranian people, it now seems possible to others that such changes can continue to take place throughout the Arabic world.

Further encouraging this notion is the Arab Spring of 2011. After decades of authoritative rule, one by one the people of Tunisia, Egypt, Libya, Syria, Yemen, Algeria, Bahrain, and other Arab countries began to demonstrate against their regimes, which have exerted a constant state of repression for decades. Revolutionary to say the least, these acts, which had an inspiring domino effect on each other, have been embraced by all sectors of the population the world over. Although these rebellions are more about socioeconomic reforms rather than doctrinal fundamentalism, they nevertheless represent how the Islamic nation can still rally together in a unifying force as it once did hundreds of years ago.

However, Islamic fundamentalism has a great opportunity to surpass itself with the onset of the Arab Spring. These countries, now given the chance to rebuild and empowered with their successes, may be susceptible to the fundamentalist doctrine and desire the return of the caliphate as well. These nations may be wary of such Western ideas as democracy but are definitely against a dictatorship or an all-powerful regime that leaves room for fundamentalism. In its moderate form, the nation is ruled on the basis of unifying principles that all are familiar with (i.e., Quranic doctrine) and is led by a figure (the caliph) who is merely a figure-head to enforce the Islamic laws. If a caliphate could be formed throughout these newly liberated states, the opportunity to install an austere Islamic state would definitely be there. However, many feel wary about the extremism that has grown out of Islamic fundamentalism in the past few decades and therefore are apprehensive about this hypothesis as well. Interestingly enough, during the spring of 2011, many Islamic fundamentalist groups and figures were rather silent during the protests, leading to the belief that perhaps these groups were waiting for the dust to settle before trying to impose their ideas of reform. This is why one should be vigilant to see how the newly elected Islamic parties in Tunisia and Egypt will act as time progresses. However, in Libya, the Islamic fundamentalists took an active part in the liberation of their country from the 42-year Qadhafi regime. This is the first time that militants of Islamic fundamentalism partook as liberators, not as political opponents. This is also a unique opportunity for them to demonstrate whether they are able to build a new system based on peace and respect for human rights. To be sure, the upcoming years in the Arab world will be those of interest and intrigue.

'ABDU, MUHAMMAD (1849–1905). A major reformist of Islamic **theology** and considered to be one of the founders of Islamic **Modernism**, Muhammad 'Abdu maintained a close relationship with **Jamal al-Din al-Afghani** but was expelled from **Egypt** in 1881 for supporting the 'Urabi Revolution (although years later, in 1899, he would return and become the mufti of Egypt). After his expulsion, 'Abdu re-joined al-Afghani in Paris in 1887 and together they published *Al-'Uraw Al-Wuthqa* (The Tightest Bond). Unlike al-Afghani, 'Abdu wished to concentrate more on educational and scholastic reforms throughout the Islamic world rather than political ones. However, his **interpretation** of **Islam** under the lens of modernity created some critics, especially as he also claimed that there is no divide between **Islam** and the modern world. Despite this non**fundamentalist** approach to the religion, 'Abdu also advocated for the application of the *shura* (consultation) council in political activities and the purification of Islamic practices in daily life. Most significant in his theories on Islam is 'Abdu's support for the application of **reason** when interpreting the **Quran**. He died on 11 July 1905.

ABDUL-JALIL, MUSTAFA (1952–). Mustafa Abdul-Jalil has been the chair of the National Transitional Council (NTC) of **Libya** since its inception following the 2011 Libyan Revolution, which overthrew **Muammar Qadhafi**'s 42-year rule of the country. Prior to leading the NTC, Abdul-Jalil actually served in the Qadhafi government as minister of justice. Educated at the University of Libya and also appointed as a judge, and despite his position within the former regime, he constantly spoke out against the injustices that were taking place within the country. His outspokenness and advocacy for the freeing of political prisoners enhanced his reputation while at his post as minister of justice.

Abdul-Jalil resigned on 21 February 2011 in protest against the Qadhafi regime in light of the protests that raged in Libya during the **Arab Spring**. He publicly encouraged the resistance fighters to continue their struggle against Qadhafi in the hopes that the ruler would soon step down. Abdul-Jalil was also one of the major promoters of Libya's need for an interim government because of its civil unrest. When that body, the NTC, was finally set up in

Benghazi, it named Abdul-Jalil its leader and chairman on 5 March 2011. Although he has decided not to take part in the 2011 elections, he is still an active member in the NTC.

ABDUL RAHMAN, SHEIKH OMAR (1938–). Leader of the **Islamic Group** in **Egypt**, Abdul Rahman was accused of participating in the assassination of Egyptian President Anwar al-Sadat in 1981. This accusation was based on the fact that he issued a *fatwa* against Sadat prior to his murder. However, Abdul Rahman was acquitted of the charges. Afterward, he orchestrated the establishment of an Islamic **fundamentalist** organization that sought to oust President Hosni Mubarak and replace the government with an **Islamic state**. He was also implicated in the 1993 World Trade Center bombing and intended to conduct other attacks in New York City that targeted the United Nations building and the heavily used Holland and Lincoln Tunnels. Finally, on 1 October 1995, Abdul Rahman was convicted of conspiring to assassinate Mubarak and attack the New York City locales as well as a **United States** military outpost in Egypt. Sentenced three months later to life imprisonment, the extremist is currently serving his sentence in the U.S. federal penitentiary system. Many terrorist attacks have been conducted in the hope of releasing him, such as the **Luxor massacre** in 1997. The **al-Qaeda** leader **al-Zawahiri** has also called for him to be freed many times. *See also* SUPPORTERS OF THE *SHARIA*.

ABDULLAH AZZAM MARTYR BATTALION/KATIBAT AL-SHA-HID. The Abdullah Azzam Martyr Battalion is an **al-Qaeda** affiliate that supports opposition to **Western**-aligned **governments** and other non-Muslim forces. The name comes from the mentor of **Osama bin Laden**, Abdullah Azzam, who has been noted as the "godfather of the modern **jihad** movement." The Abdullah Azzam Martyr's Battalion was specifically dedicated to the opposition of former president Hosni Mubarak of **Egypt**. Like most Islamist groups, the Abdullah Azzam Martyr's Battalion attacks tourists in the Egyptian region, hindering one of the country's greatest sources of earnings and thereby helping to perpetuate the cycle of poverty and oppression through which the group finds supporters. Notably in October 2004, the battalion attacked Sinai resorts in Taba, Ra's Al-Sultan, and Nuwayba, killing 34 people, mostly Egyptian and **Israeli** nationals. In July 2005, the organization again attacked a tourist site, this time in Sharm Al-Sheikh, Egypt. Using car bombs, the group killed 88 and wounded 200. While the battalion has splinter cells and related organizations, the Abdullah Azzam Martyr's Battalion is still highly active even in the post-Mubarak era. The group is characterized by its use of explosives and the targeting of civilians. More recently, on 4

August 2010, a suicide bomber attacked a Japanese oil tanker in the Strait of Hormuz, and in May 2011, the group bombed multiple NATO fuel vehicles in **Pakistan**. *See also* BOMBING; VIOLENCE.

ABU GHUDDA, 'ABD AL-FATTAH (?–1997). A founding member of the Muslim World League (*Rabitat al-'Alam al-Islami*) and former spiritual leader of the **Muslim Brotherhood in Syria**, 'Abd al-Fattah Abu Ghudda also taught at various mosques and educational institutions (*madrasas*) throughout **Syria**. In 1962, he became a member of Syria's parliament and, therefore, the only **fundamentalist** representative there. However, a year later he was briefly imprisoned for antiestablishment statements he made. Considered to represent a wide range of Islamic ideologies, Abu Ghudda increasingly gained popularity before his death in 1997 while in exile.

ABU HAFS AL-MASRI BRIGADE. This group took its name from **al-Qaeda** leader Mohammad Atef (a.k.a. Abu Hafs al-Masri), who was killed during an air raid in **Afghanistan** in November 2001. The Brigade conducted subway **bombings** in Madrid and London in 2004 and 2005, respectively. Interestingly enough, the group claimed to have been instrumental in the 2003 blackouts in North America, although this was later denied by analysts who attribute the incident to electrical problems. This false claim has led experts to believe that perhaps the group is not a true organization and is merely a group of militants who conducted a few attacks. *See also* LONDON BOMBINGS OF 7 JULY 2005; MADRID BOMBINGS OF 11 MARCH 2004.

ABU NIDAL ORGANIZATION. An umbrella name given to the **Arab Revolutionary Brigades**, **Black June**, the **Fatah Revolutionary Council**, and the Revolutionary Organization of Socialist Muslims by **Western** intelligence agencies, the Abu Nidal Organization and its affiliates were all led by Sabri Kahlil al-Banna, whose nom de guerre was **Abu Nidal**.

ABU QURAH, 'ABD AL-LATIF (1908–1967). 'Abd al-Latif Abu Qurah founded such organizations as the Jordanian Red Cross and the **Palestinian** Islamic Conference as well as establishing the Jordanian branch of the **Muslim Brotherhood** in 1942. Abu Qurah led the **Muslim Brotherhood in Jordan** until 1953, during which time he served as the Brotherhood's commander in the 1948 Arab-Israeli War.

ABU SAYYAF GROUP (ASG). A splinter organization from the **Moro Liberation Front**, the ASG formed in 1991 after disagreeing with the former's negotiations with the Philippines. ASG hoped to establish an **Islamic** republic in the Philippine islands of Mindanao and Sulu based on the republic that was formed in **Iran**. Originally led by **Abubakar Janjalani** (d. 18 December 1998), **Khaddafi Janjalani** led the group for some time until his death on 4 September 2006, when his brother, Omar Janjalani, took over. The group has conducted countless **bombings** and kidnappings and has even been linked to the 1993 World Trade Center bombing attackers. The most notable of the group's attacks is probably the 7 April 1995 assault on the Roman Catholic town of Ipil on Mindanao Island. ASG militants stormed the town and opened fire on its citizens, killing dozens and kidnapping several. Moreover, on 20 March 2000, the group kidnapped 50 from the island of Basilan. Although the group has continued to conduct kidnappings and other such attacks, it was reported that by 2002, its membership had decreased significantly.

ABU ZAYD, HAMID NASR (1943–2010). Raised in a town near Cairo, Hamid Nasr Abu Zayd dedicated his scholastic training to Islamic studies and wrote many works that focused on various hermeneutic **interpretations** of the **Quran**. In a life full of legal confrontations and ideological persecutions, Abu Nasr was imprisoned at the early age of 12 for having **Muslim Brotherhood** sympathies. While teaching at Cairo University (1982–1993), he had charges of apostasy (*ridda*), **blasphemy**, and **heresy** brought against him by his colleague 'Abd Al-Sabur Shahin, allegedly because of his controversial academic publications. The allegations happened after Abu Nasr applied for a promotion within the university and Shahin, a member of the Standing Committee of Academic Tenure and Promotion, stated his accusations. Declared an apostate (*murtadd*) after the *hisbah* trial, his marriage to fellow Cairo University professor Ibtihal Younis was annulled because of the regulations of *sharia* (Islamic law). Both appealed the conviction but then fled **Egypt** (after the **Egyptian Islamic Jihad** called for his death) and took up residency in Holland and taught at Leiden University. However, despite the hearing within the courts, in 1995 Cairo University granted Abu Nasr his promotion based on his works *Imam Shafi'I and the Founding of Medieval Ideology* and *The Critique of Religious Discourse*.

Although Abu Nasr still lives in Holland, he frequently returns to Egypt for academic discussions and lectures. Abu Nasr's situation caused great interest and intrigue as **human rights** organizations were incredibly vocal in their criticism of the professor's mistreatment. In legislative terms, the Egyptian Penal Code does not recognize apostasy unless another religious institution declares the defendant's conversion to that faith or the said defendant publicly announces his conversion—hence the controversy of Abu Nasr's trial. In addition, during this time, Abu Nasr was not the only Muslim coming under fire for liberal thoughts on **Islam**. This simply illustrates what was a period of intellectual repression and assault on the part of the Egyptian government, which also repressed various professors, writers, and intellectuals, such as Youssef Chahine, Atif Al-Iraqi, and Naguib Mahfouz.

ACTIVISM. *See HARAKIYYA.*

ACTIVIST. *See HARAKIYYA.*

ADEN-ABYAN ISLAMIC ARMY. An **Islamic group** in southern **Yemen**, the Aden-Abyan Islamic army is known for its December 1998 kidnapping of 16 tourists in Abyan, Yemen, and was allegedly involved in the 2000 **bombing** of the USS *Cole* off the coast of Aden, Yemen. The 1998 hostage situation left four of the kidnapped dead, while the destruction of the *Cole* killed 17 American sailors. This group is presumed to have links with **al-Qaeda in the Arabian Peninsula**.

ADHAALATH **PARTY/JUSTICE PARTY.** Created in August 2005, the *Adhaalath* Party is one of the **Islamic political parties** in the Maldives. Sheikh Hussein Rashed Ahmed was named the party's first president, and the group heads the Ministry of Islamic Affairs (which is led by prominent *Adhaalath* member Abdul Majeed Abdul Bari). However, the group has not been electorally successful because of its antisecular aims. Since the general opinion in the Maldives is one for pluralism and **democracy**, **Sunni Islam** (the *Adhaalath* ideological platform) and the establishment of an **Islamic state** are not highly sought after in the country. Critically, the group has come under attack by many stating that it is exploiting **religion** to gain a political foothold within the country, not having an economic or diplomatic platform or any declared constitution or manifesto. The group also endorsed the statement released by the Ministry of Islamic Affairs, which supported the implementation of a **theocratic** legislative ruling—the first time such clerical liberties were discussed in the Maldives.

AL-ADL WAL IHSANE. Founded by **Sheikh Abdesslam Yassine**, *Al-Adl Wal Ihsane* is a Moroccan **Islamic group** associated with the **Salafi** school of **Islam**. Ideologically, the group seeks the establishment of an **Islamic state** and the application of *sharia* (Islamic law) throughout **Morocco**. *Al-Adl Wal Ihsane* has a large following in the university system and has labeled itself a social welfare organization since it has not achieved legal status as a **political party** because of its religious affiliations—although the group claims that it does not wish to enter into the legislative realm. Leader Yassine has also developed a sort of cult following in Morocco, and his daughter, Nadia

Yassine, heads the feminine branch of the group. *Al-Adl Wal Ihsane* has strongly voiced its opposition to the Moroccan monarchy and advocates for its replacement by an Islamic **caliphate**. *See also* WOMEN.

AL-AFGHAN AL-'ARAB/**AFGHAN ARABS.** During the Soviet-Afghan War (1979–1989), the term *Al-Afghan al-'Arab* was applied to the many Arab volunteer soldiers who fought in the insurrection. Anti-Soviet sentiments throughout many parts of the world led to the support of the Afghan Arabs regardless of their ideological convictions that they were fighting a **jihad**. Since the end of the war, many members have joined and formed different organizations that now form the contemporary militant Islamic **fundamentalist** groups (however, this does not apply to all former Afghan Arabs). In particular, the groups that have a significant number of Afghan Arabs in their membership are the Algerian Armed Islamic Group (*Al-Jama'a al-Islamiyya al-Mussallaha*), *Jamaat al-Muslimin* (The Group of Muslims), *Al-'Ama'im al-Sawda'* (Black Turbans), **al-Qaeda**, and the **Taliban army**, among others. *See also* AL-TAKFIR WA AL-HIJRA.

AFGHAN ARABS. *See AL-AFGHAN AL-'ARAB.*

AL-AFGHANI, JAMAL AL-DIN (1838–1897). Credited with being one of the most revolutionary and active **Sunni** scholars, Jamal al-Din al-Afghani is also known by the nickname of *Hakim al-Sharq* (Sage of the East). After being expelled from Istanbul in 1871, he relocated to Cairo, where his ideological influence began to take hold. Followers, including fellow Islamic reformist **Muhammad 'Abdu**, were attracted to his anti-British sentiments, although this led to his expulsion from **Egypt** in 1879. During his later years, al-Afghani became involved with the pan-Islamic movement and wrote *Al-Urwa al-Wurthqa* (The Tightest Bond) with 'Abdu. His views on **Islam** were reformist in the sense that they placed an emphasis on the mixture of **science** with intellectual development in Islamic life. According to Al-Afghani, all three should be conjoined to create a more prosperous and renewed **Islamic society**, especially since scientific advancements are not abhorrent to the doctrines of the faith. It is in these ideas of "**modernizing**" Islam that the role of **pan-Islamism** should take place, according to al-Afghani.

AFGHANISTAN. To Western minds, Afghanistan is synonymous with militant Islamic **extremism** and the home of various radical **Islamic groups**. The predominantly **Sunni** Muslim country has been increasingly visible in the contemporary media ever since the **World Trade Center and Pentagon attacks of September 11, 2001**, which then resulted in the October 2001 deployment of U.S. troops within the country under the initiative Operation

Enduring Freedom. The main objectives of the Western involvement there were to eliminate and suppress the **Taliban army** and **Osama bin Laden**'s **al-Qaeda** contingents that were operating within the vast tribal regions of the country. The ongoing presence of the Taliban army within the country was also becoming an international concern (although the force had lost much of its power by November 2001). Afghanistan has also attracted many foreign **jihadists** to the country over the past decade. In turn, they have then aligned themselves with the al-Qaeda organization. Ideologically, the country has many Sufi adherents in addition to the dominating Sunni community. **Sufism**, or the mystical side of **Islam**, has also manifested itself in the form of *al-Naqshabandiyya* and *al-Qadiriyya* within Afghanistan. The **Deoband Islamic Movement** has also been incredibly influential, especially to the Pashtun tribes.

Politically, the country has a contemporary history of not establishing a strong central **government**. The past governments have also been characterized by being both secular and sectarian but not consistently maintaining an influential moderate government. This led to the influence of the Communist Party within Afghanistan in the 1950s, as it was believed that it could revive the Afghani socioeconomic situation. The Soviet Union has been accused of encouraging the coup that ousted King Zahir Shah on 17 July 1973 and led to the Saur Revolution (27 April 1978)—all precursors to the Soviet-Afghan War (1979–1989). Even after successfully defeating the Soviet regime in 1989, the state was unable to secure itself internally, and in 1992 civil war broke out, finally ending in 1996.

Following this, the Taliban army came to power (although created in September 1994), and the country became even more segmented tribally. In fact, this resulted in the country becoming strongly divided between the Tajik and Uzbek north and the Pashtun south. The end of the Soviet-Afghan War also left the *mujahideen* without their aggressive schedules, and many of these veterans began to be lured by militant groups throughout the Arabic world. When the Taliban was in power, *sharia* (Islamic law) was installed and strictly enforced, especially in the south. However, the group lacked any substantial foreign support and domestically was limited to the Pashtuns in membership. So it was in response to this concern that the group began attracting foreign Islamic militant groups and eventually Osama bin Laden's organizations. By 2001, the army controlled an estimated 95 percent of Afghanistan. The strict enforcement of Islamic law also resulted in the Taliban's March 2001 destruction of one of the most notable sites in the country's landscape: the **Bamiyan Buddhas**.

Its use of Islam has helped the Taliban army become a formidable force in Afghani life throughout the 1990s. Since Islam plays such an integral role within the community, its platform of being the "protectors" of the religion allowed for a greater acceptance throughout the population. Even with the International Security Assistance Force (ISAF) invasion in 2001, the population was still in favor of the Taliban regime since it associated the NATO forces with the previous enemies—the Soviets. This was due simply to the fact that, in the Afghani popular perception, both groups (the **West** and the former Eastern bloc) were foreign powers seeking to change the legislative and cultural Islamic climate of Afghanistan. The Afghani popular mind-set has then been pro-jihadi because of this. Since many members of the Taliban were also *mujahideen*, there is an association that this group can again successfully thwart the enemy as the **Afghan Arabs** did during the Soviet-Afghan War. But after losing power in 2001, the Taliban began to create civil chaos in order to remind the masses that a much more tranquil climate existed when it was in power prior to the Western invasion.

An interesting aspect of Afghanistan that should be noted is its opium trade. For centuries, opium cultivation dominated the country and was used as a viable resource to gain economic growth through trade with India and Asia. However, while this cultivation was drastically limited throughout the 20th century, in the past decade it has been used again as a source of income. The ideal area for the growth of the poppy plant (from which opium is derived) is in southern Afghanistan, which, because of proximity, the militant Islamic groups active in the south have recently begun recultivating and trading throughout the Muslim world to gain finances. Some experts have even reported that an estimated $4 billion annually is earned by the opium trade for these radical organizations.

Afghanistan's weak political structure makes it dependent on foreign aid and the country's wealthy tribal leaders. The northern Uzbeks and Tajik tribes also play an extraordinary role in the **government** of the country. The country has also declared Islam as the official religion, leading to a greater resistance to the quasi democracy that is currently led by Hamid Karzai, the first president of Afghanistan, who was elected in 2004. In fact, the southern regions reported almost zero voter turnout for the 2010 elections. However, in the north, it is quite the opposite both ideologically (a greater adherence to Sufism exists there) and politically. Currently, it seems as if the Karzai government is trying to attain a stronger sense of Islamic **legitimacy** while trying to suppress Islamic extremism (which seeks a return to Islamic law and the installation of an **Islamic state**) and establishing a positive Islamic voice within the government.

The presence of influential extremist leaders within Afghanistan also helped the militant Islamic groups gain a stronger presence within the country itself and in neighboring **Pakistan**. Moreover, most Western tactical attention started to shift to **Iraq** during this time, and the Afghani extremists began to adopt the Iraqi militant methods of domestic **terrorism** and the use of improvised explosive devices (IEDs). The targeting of foreigners, especially aid workers and diplomats, was the most common form of Afghani militancy along with the use of IEDs at this time. By 2008, the tide seemed to have shifted within the country, and the government of Karzai began to deteriorate. Infiltrations in the legislature and the domestic security forces, as well as a shortage of ISAF troops, led to the Taliban regaining much of its previously lost territories and then some.

The 2005–2008 period saw a heavy upswing of **suicide bombings** and other attacks within the country as the Taliban reorganized and became increasingly more aggressive. Recently, Afghanistan is marked by internal strife and disarray, with the countryside being controlled by the militant groups and the capitals and larger cities being controlled by NATO's ISAF. However, a scheduled withdrawal of Western troops from the country is supposed to take place beginning in 2012. Yet it is still not certain what will happen to the country once this takes place.

*AL-AHBASH/JAM'IYYAT AL-MASHARI' AL-KHAIRIYYA AL-IS-LAMIYYA/***ASSOCIATION OF ISLAMIC PHILANTHROPIC PROJECTS.** A **Sunni** Islamic **fundamentalist** group, *Al-Ahbash* retains its headquarters in Beirut and is headed by Sheikh 'Abd Allah al-Habashi. The group is reportedly financed by **Syria** and has provided many civil services through its intricate system of educational and extracurricular programs. Among its ideologies, *Al-Ahbash* believes that the modern **Islamists** neglect the teachings of the **Prophet Muhammad** and therefore are guilty of nonbelief (*kufr*).

AHL AS-SUNNA WAL-JAMMAH **(ASWJ)/ADHERENTS OF THE SUNNA AND THE COMMUNITY.** Based in Great Britain, this **Islamic group** was established in November 2005 by Sulayman Keeler. Its membership is approximately 1,000, and the group operates primarily through its Internet forum titled *Muntada Ahl as-Sunna wal-Jammah*. The content on the website (which was launched in 2006) varies from anti-**Western** propaganda to voice recordings of many Islamic extremists, such as **Osama bin Laden** and **Ayman al-Zawahiri**. ASWJ functions primarily to organize demonstrations throughout London, especially outside particular foreign embassy offices. The group advocates for the **jihad** and supports the **Islamic Courts Union**.

AHL-E-HADITH. See BANGLADESH.

AHMADIYYA MUSLIM COMMUNITY/*JAMAAT AHMADIYYA*. The Indian Ahmadiyya movement, which began in 1889, spawned two groups: the Ahmadiyya Muslim Community and the smaller Lahore Ahmadiyya Movement (*Ahmadiyya Anjuman Ishaat-e-Islam*). The split occurred in 1914 over ideological differences. The leader of the Ahmadiyya community is known as a Khalifatul Masih (Successor of the Messiah) and is currently Mirza Masroor Ahmad (the fifth Khalifatul Masih). The community was originally led by Mirza Ghulam Ahmad, who claimed that he was the fulfiller of all eschatological and messianic prophecies. Essentially, the Ahmadiyya movement combines **Christianity**, **Islam**, and **Judaism** in the hopes of creating a **universal**, all-encompassing faith. The community is based on six specific precepts: **Monotheism**, the existence of angels (the belief in spiritually manifested beings that were created by **Allah** to implement His will), **divine texts** (the Gospels, the Kitab, the Psalms of David, the **Quran**, the Scrolls of Abraham, and the Torah), prophets (law bearing and non–law bearing), Judgment Day, and divine decree.

Similar to traditional Islam, denying *tawhid* is probably the severest sin one can commit in the **religion**, and, with regard to the angels, the Ahmadiyyas believe that there are four main ones (Azrael, Gabriel, Michael, and Raphael). The divine decree is essentially the belief that Allah controls all actions and outcomes of the world. However, in the Ahmadiyya faith, it is also understood that **science** and religion should never be in conflict. Essentially, this movement stresses that all the divine texts, prophets, and other figures of various religions have contributed to the development of Islam. Ahmadiyya Muslim Community adherents believe that the existence of other faiths is primarily to help promote the Muslim doctrine, and therefore the Ahmadiyya founder, Ghulam Ahmad, is a "prophet" similar to the **Prophet Muhammad** but subordinate to him. It is thought that Ahmad is the "continuation" of the Prophet Muhammad and is essential to the reformation and **liberation** of Islam.

Demographically, the country with the largest population of Ahmadiyya Muslim Community members is **Pakistan** with an estimated 4 million believers. **Bangladesh**, India, and Indonesia also have a large number of adherents. Ahmadiyyan scholars also claimed to have translated the Quran into over 100 languages. However, in 1970, the *Jamaat-e-Islami* began to ostracize and condemn the Muslim Ahmadiyya Community within Pakistan, leading the country to officially declare its members as "non-Muslims" in 1974. As a result, any Ahmadiyya who openly declares that he is a Muslim can be punished by law. Because of these repressions, the headquarters of the movement was moved to London. A majority of Muslims still condemn the Ahmadiyya Muslim Community, especially because of their doctrinal rejection of the finality of "prophethood." *See also* HERESY; *PASBAN KHATM E-NABUWWAT*; *TEHRIK-E-KHATME NABUWWAT*.

AKRAMIYA. Founded by Akrom Yo'ldoshev, *Akramiya* is a splinter **Islamic group** from the *Hizb-u-Tahrir* organization. Established in 1996 in the Fergana Valley, Uzbekistan, the group's main ideological platform is the establishment of an Islamic **caliphate** at the local, not international, level. *Akramiya* also publishes a periodical, *Yimonga Yul* (Way to Faith), that states the reasons why a national, global caliphate is unrealistic and impractical.

ALGERIA. In Algeria, **Islam** is not only the dominant **religion** but also the main institution of culture and identity throughout the country. Societal and cultural practices are directly related to the ideologies of Islam, and Algeria's **history** is completely intertwined not only with the religion but with the actions of the Islamists as well. French colonial rule from 1830 to 1962 and the modern economic failures have totally influenced the rise of Islam throughout society and have made it easier for Islamists to make headway in Algeria as opposed to other countries that did not undergo the religious oppression that Algeria did. The 132 years of colonial rule led to such grave religious and social despondency that the ideologies of Islam have provided a comforting sense of identity for much of the population. This history in Algeria has therefore paved the way for the radical Islamists to gain support in a country where there was already a deep-seated anti-**Western** mentality. Current Islamists believe that their modern-day cause is a direct relative of the past war against the Western culture and often utilize the motto "Islam is our religion; Arabic is our language; Algeria is our motherland," which was made famous by **'Abd Al-Hamid Ibn Badis**.

Since the Algerian War of Independence from France (1954–1962), no other group has caused as much warfare and strife in Algeria as the Islamists. Between 1988 and 1999, Islamist militants exercised so much brutality that the decadelong turbulence took over 150,000 lives, most of which were civilian. The Algerian **government** enacted policies of amnesty in September 1999 (**Algerian Civil Concord**) and September 2005 (**Charter for Peace and National Reconciliation**) in the hope of limiting the armed Islamists, but the policies have served only to legitimize and empower political Islamism. Islamism has continuously grown in the Algerian political sector since **Islamic political parties** and their affiliates have won seats in the country's parliament in national elections. These actions have undoubtedly led to the widespread growth of Islamism in Algeria. However, the brutal tactics used by the **extremists** have led to a decline in overall popular support and have marginalized them in many circles. This is indicated by the April 2009 election, where the Islamist *Ennahda* candidate, Djahid Younsi, received only 1.3 percent of the votes—this, of course, all changed after the 2011 **Arab Spring**.

Therefore, it is hard to ascertain exactly how much general support Islamists receive throughout the country since there are many conflicting factors. Although the population has voted against the political factions and has expressed disapproval of their barbaric tactics, the religious ideologies are supported and used as a means of camaraderie. Still, **Islamic groups** have surprisingly gained an incredible amount of organization and resources through the **jihadist** groups, to the amazement of Algerian security forces. Unabashed destruction and insurrection were carried out by various groups throughout Algeria, and many foreign agencies refused to assist the ailing country. It was not until the **World Trade Center and Pentagon attacks of September 11, 2001** that Algeria finally received assistance to combat the Islamists. But a lack of internal security in the private and public sectors of Algeria has made it difficult for countermeasures to have any real effect against the extremists, and the country had to resort to using military and civilian task forces. Known as *gardes communaux*, or communal guards, Algeria armed thousands of youths from the lower classes to help combat the Islamist insurrections.

Historically in the Algerian political realm, Islamic parties have gained legal status because of a subsequent political liberalization in 1989, when the Algerian government authorized the legitimacy of religious-based political parties even though such parties were deemed unconstitutional. A domineering and eclectic Islamist movement was the basis for this legalization, and from it grew the **Islamic Salvation Front** (ISF). The most abrasive and formidable Islamic political party, the ISF was composed of various militants, including **jihad** supporters from **Afghanistan**. During the June 1990 municipal and December 1991 legislative elections in Algeria, when it was perceived that the ISF was going to overwhelmingly succeed, a coup d'état erupted, and the party was swiftly disbanded by a civilian-military regime under President Abdelaziz Bouteflika (in power since 1999), who feared the group's irrational ideologies. Despite these events, the ISF still remains influential throughout the Islamist population in Algeria.

As of 2011, three Islamist political parties remain in Algeria: the **Movement for Society and Peace**, the Movement for Islamic Renaissance (*Ennahda*), and the **Movement for National Reform**, which is an offshoot of *Ennahda*. All three of these parties seek to instill *sharia* (Islamic law) throughout Algeria and the Muslim world. In 2009, during the presidential elections, all three parties endorsed President Bouteflika for a third term in order to retain their legitimacy. However, there was a consequent decline in Islamist political party support throughout Algeria at this time due to restlessness within the groups. Nevertheless, Islamist ideologies throughout the country remained. This division within the country has led to countless confrontations between the state and its citizens, including the civil uprisings of the Arab Spring.

Beginning in January 2011, the civil protests reached such a pitch that Bouteflika promised civil reforms and a constitutional revision and that a new election would take place on May 2012. It is expected that he will not be reinstated and that one of the Islamic parties will be voted into office instead. Algeria did not see such a violent climate in the 2011 Arab Spring revolts, perhaps because of the population's trauma and therefore hesitation after the Algerian Civil War (1992–2002), which took over 150,000 lives.

ALGERIAN CIVIL CONCORD/CIVIL HARMONY ACT. Put up for vote on 16 September 1999 in **Algeria**, this referendum granted **Islamist** fighters not guilty of rape or murder amnesty if they surrendered to the Algeria **government** and thereby ceased their participation in the Algerian Civil War (1992–2002). The vote had an impressively high voter turnout (85 percent) and was supported by an overwhelming 98 percent of voters. The main objective of this legislation was to end the ongoing Algerian Civil War (1992–2002) between the Algerian government and the country's various **Islamic groups** that took from 150,000 to 200,000 lives. According to the referendum's general provisions, "The Act of Civil Concord is part of the grand design of restoring **peace** and harmony to society." The result of this vote led to the pardoning of numerous insurgents and was met with mixed opinion throughout the civil and militant populations. This law was pushed through the Algerian Parliament by the then newly elected President Abdelaziz Bouteflika. The act was instrumental in the dissolution of the **Armed Islamic Group**, as it resulted in many of its militants deserting the organization. However, in turn, this led to the subsequent rise of the **Salafist Group for Preaching and Combat** as the most active Islamist group within the country, a group that would soon form **al-Qaeda in the Islamic Maghreb**. *See also* CHARTER FOR PEACE AND NATIONAL RECONCILIATION.

ALL PARTIES HURRIYAT CONFERENCE (APHC). Formed on 10 March 1993, the APHC is a conglomerate of 27 Kashmiri **Islamic** and sociopolitical groups. These groups all share the same separatist cause to see Kashmir liberated from Indian control and are the political face of the Jammu and Kashmir Liberation Front. Originally, the APHC had six members: the **Organization of Islamic Students**, *Ittihadul Muslimeen*, the Jammu and Kashmir Liberation Front, the Jammu and Kashmir People's League, the

Muslim Conference, and the People's Democratic Front. Etymologically, "*hurriyat*" is the transliteration of the Kashmiri word for "liberty."

The conference refuses to recognize India's claim on the Jammu and Kashmir region and has accused Indian security forces of **human rights** violations even though many groups within the APHC have had the same charges made against them. They use the UN decree of the right to self-determination to gain diplomatic recognition for Kashmir. The group is divided into two separate factions although still working as a basic whole, one (led by Sayed Ali Shah Geelani) named *Tehreek-e-Hurriyat*, which refuses to enter into agreements with India, and the other (led by Mirwaiz Omar Farooq), which has been engaged in talks with India since 2004. Each organization that is part of the APHC is represented by its respective leader. All the leaders sit in the conference together, acting as one unified body to bolster their own individual goals.

Currently, the main groups that are part of the APHC are the Awami Action Committee, All Jammu and Kashmir Employees' Confederation, *Anjamani Auqafi Jama Masjid*, *Anjaman-e-Tabligh-ul Islam*, *Auquaf Jama Masjid*, Employees and Workers Confederation, Employees and Workers Confederation Arsawi Group, Imam Ahmad Raza Islamic Mission, Organization of Islamic Students, *Ittihad-ul-Muslimeen*, *Jamaat-e-Ahle Hadith*, *Jamaat-e-Hamdania*, **Jamaat-e-Islami**, **Jamaat Ulama-e-Islam**, Jammu and Kashmir Human Rights Committee, Jammu and Kashmir Liberation Front, Jammu and Kashmir People's Basic Rights/Protection Committee, Jammu and Kashmir People's Conference, Jammu and Kashmir People's Freedom League, Kashmir Bar Association, Kashmir *Bazme Tawheed*, Liberation Council, Muslim Conference, People's League, Political Conference, *Saut-ul-Aliya*, *Tehreek-e-Huriati Kashmiri*, and *Ummat Islami*. The Executive Council of the APHC also has members within the representative body of the conference. Those currently are Moulvi Abbas Ansari (*Ittihad-ul-Muslimeen*), Sheikh Abdul Aziz (People's League), Abdul Ghani Bhat (Muslim Conference), Mirwaiz Omar Farooq (Awami Action Committee), Syed Ali Shah Geelani (*Jamaat-e-Islami*), and Yasin Malik (Jammu and Kashmir Liberation Front). In January 2010, Tabish Bhat was named the organization's leader. *See also* KASHMIRI SEPARATISM.

ALLAH/GOD. Formed by the Arabic article *al* meaning "the" and *Lâh* for "God," Allah is unique and the only deity in **Islam** having "neither father nor son," as stated in the *Surat al-Samad* passages of the **Quran**.

In Arabic, there are 99 different names for Allah. To the faithful, He is the most powerful, omnipresent figure within the religion. Allah is all that encompasses the faith, and it is also believed that the Arabic language is the direct word of God. Belief in Allah, His divine governance (*hakimiyya*), and Oneness (*tawhid*) is just one of the many cornerstones of the Islamic faith. All the Islamic concepts and notions, both moderate and extreme, are centered on the belief in Allah and adherence to his word.

ALLEGIANCE. A system of leadership that exists within Islamic **fundamentalist** extremist groups and has been utilized most notably by the **al-Qaeda** organization. Allegiance could better be referred to as a pledge (*bay'a*). This allegiance system is based on the traditional and historic tribal allegiance system, which many of these operatives work within and are familiar with. Many times when new leaders become affiliated and merge their organizations with al-Qaeda (e.g., **Abdelmalek Droukdel**'s **Salafist Group for Preaching and Combat** on 24 January 2007), they announce a change in name (here, **al-Qaeda in the Islamic Maghreb**), and those affiliates claim all their actions in the name of the group in which they are joining the leader (in this case, **Osama bin Laden**). Thus, when an attack takes place, there are a number of different figures who claim responsibility for the same attack. Many have viewed this as dissension within the group or competition. When different leaders or members all make commentaries on attacks, those commentaries should not be viewed as a shift in responsibility or leadership or even as promoting one figure over another. Rather, it is a demonstration of hierarchical links, internal oaths of allegiance, and an expression of each member's duties.

Furthermore, a pledge is not just an initial or initiating statement but can also be used to demonstrate a renewal or confirm obedience. In addition, a pledge can be made in the name and on behalf of another individual within the organization without that person being a direct participant. Because of the hierarchical top-down structure of many extremist organizations, this system of allegiance is understood to apply to all members of the group, while the main figurehead resides at the top but does not have to give direct commands.

The history of this tribal allegiance system is geographically and dogmatically founded. Geographically, since the groups operate in such a vast territory, shifting leadership is the best way to maintain a stable command system. Since these leaders have taken the same oath to each other and the group as a whole, each leader is entrusted to give similar commands and direct each of his regions in the same way. These rules of the allegiance system date back to ancient Arabic tribal practices and therefore maintain a cultural and historical foundation. Dogmatically, an oath of *hudaybiyya* was known to be taken by Muslims before the **Prophet Muhammad**. As stated in the **Quran**, this oath renewed both trust and loyalty in Muhammad and, by proxy, to **Allah**.

These oaths can vary from one organization or group to another, but they always represent the same system of allegiance and always include the high-ranking figure to which these oaths are directed. These oaths can also be made to a leader of one group from an outside source that is not completely incorporated into the former's group. For example, one leader may claim allegiance to another, but that leader's group still maintains its own identity and is not merged with the other. An example of this is **Boko Haram**'s allegiance to al-Qaeda in the Islamic Maghreb. These types of oaths still retain their symbolic effects but are even more practical. The system is manifold, as it provides a driving force for expansion, satisfies historical and symbolic desires, allows the commander in chief to manage a vast area effectively, and placates a desire for acknowledgment from the bottom up.

ALLIANCE FOR JUSTICE AND DEMOCRACY/MOVEMENT FOR RENEWAL (AJD/MR). The AJD/MR is a Mauritanian **political party** that was formed in August 2007 by activist Ibrahima Moctar Sarr. Demographically, the party is based in the Senegal River valley in the southern part of **Mauritania**. The party was formed out of the merger between Sarr's former Movement for National Reconciliation party and the preexisting Alliance for Justice and Democracy Party. During the August 2008 coup d'état that took place in the country, the AJD/MR (along with the Rally of Democratic Forces and the Movement for Direct Democracy parties, among others) announced its dissension with the political regime of Sidi Ould Cheikh Abdallahi and expressed its desire to run candidates in the upcoming elections (originally scheduled for 6 June 2009). Sarr ran as an AJD/MR candidate during the 18 July 2009 presidential elections but was defeated by **Muhammad Ould Abdel Aziz**, leader of the coup and president of the High Council of State, which assumed power after orchestrating the 2008 political overthrow.

AMAL. A political Islamic **fundamentalist** organization comprised of **Shia** Muslims from **Lebanon**, *Amal*'s name comes from the Arabic word for "hope" and is also the acronym of *Afwaj al Muqawama al Lubnaniya* (Lebanese Resistance Detachments). The group was established in 1975 as a military organization by Iranian-born cleric Musa Sadr, who also formed the Movement of the Deprived in 1974. Financially, *Amal* was supported for a period of time by **Iran**, especially in the aftermath of the **Iranian Islamic Revolution of 1979**, but after *Hizbullah* **in Lebanon** emerged in 1982, *Amal*'s support from that country waned (and slowly completely disappeared), and then it turned to **Syria** for sponsorship. Ideologically, *Amal* hoped to see the Shiite community gain control over its own people in Lebanon but did not seek a total **Islamic state** in the country, especially one modeled after the new Iranian state. However, this lack of desire for the Iranian model of an

Islamic state and the lack of militant force used by *Amal* led to many of its members leaving to form the **Islamic *Amal* Movement** (many also joined *Hizbullah* in Lebanon). Nevertheless, the Lebanese Shiite community was generally supportive of *Amal* since it wanted to protect and secure its livelihood. In August 1978, Sadr disappeared while visiting **Libya**, leading many *Amal* members to suspect **Muammar Qadhafi** as being responsible, also further harming *Amal*'s relationship with Iran, as Iran and Libya had a viable diplomatic connection.

Hizbullah and *Amal* have been at odds with each other almost since the former's establishment in the early 1980s. Much of *Amal*'s membership strength was absorbed by *Hizbullah*, and there was often a mistaken link between the two, resulting in *Amal* being accused of many attacks that were in fact *Hizbullah* orchestrated. Furthermore, after the 1985 TWA Flight 847 incident, *Hizbullah* and *Amal* were openly at war with each other, resulting in *Amal* seeking financial support from Syria. However, in the aftermath of the Lebanese Civil War in 1990, the two groups reconciled and joined forces with the southern Lebanese to combat the **Israeli** army. Nabih Berri (Sadr's successor) was then instrumental in mending the relationship between *Amal* and Iran. *Amal* still supports Syria and continues to have a political presence in Lebanon, winning 14 of the 128 seats in the Lebanese parliamentary elections in 2005. The relationship between *Amal* and *Hizbullah* is still one of delicate alliance even though *Amal* members fought alongside *Hizbullah* in the 2006 Israeli-*Hizbullah* war.

'*AMAL* ORGANIZATION. *See* ISLAMIC ACTION.

AMIR. Literally meaning "prince," *amir* is a term that is most commonly applied to the commanders of the militant **fundamentalist Islamic groups**.

AMMARI, SAIFI (1968–). Born in Kef Rih, **Algeria**, on 1 January 1968, Saifi Ammari has adopted the moniker "*El Para*" or Abderrazak al-Para. The name "*El Para*" is a derivative from "paratrooper," as Ammari was trained and highly skilled in that branch of the Algerian forces before joining the Islamist forces in 1992. In November 2002, Ammari formed his own division within the **Salafi Group for Preaching and Combat**, whose primary goal was the abduction and ransoming of foreign tourists. Known as the "Al-Para Group," the group utilized and preferred to operate in the Sahara region of southern Algeria. Between 23 February and 30 March 2003, the group kidnapped 32 hostages (mostly German nationals) and was pursued into **Mali**, Chad, and eventually Niger by counter-Algerian and -Malian forces. In March 2004, Ammari was captured by the rebel group the Movement for

Democracy and Justice in Chad. Although the group tried to have him sent to Germany to stand trial, he was turned over to Algerian security forces in October 2004 and has remained in Algeria ever since. In June 2005, Algeria announced that *"El Para"* will remain imprisoned indefinitely because of his heinous criminal record.

AL-ANDALUS. The official name of the media division of **al-Qaeda in the Islamic Maghreb** (AQIM), *Al-Andalus* was announced by AQIM in October 2009. A Web-based platform for the group to spread its ideologies, the name comes from the southern land in the Iberian Peninsula that was controlled by the Islamic Umayyad **caliphate** from 711 to 1492, when it was seized by the Catholic Empire of Spain, thereby marking the end of the Muslim presence in the Iberian Peninsula. This platform aims to report on the activities of AQIM as well as the **al-Qaeda** organization as a whole and seeks to unite the communication policies of all the al-Qaeda groups. Its website encourages the Islamic insurgency in North Africa and is vocal in criticizing the **Western** influences in the Maghreb.

ANGKATAN BELIA ISLAM MALAYSIA (ABIM)/MOVEMENT OF THE MALAYSIAN YOUTH. A **fundamentalist** Malaysia movement, the ABIM is ideologically inspired by the **Muslim Brotherhood**. Founded in 1972, the group is considered the most formidable force in Malaysian Islamic revivalism. The group's objectives include establishing an **Islamic state** and implementing *sharia* (Islamic law) within the country. Highly critical of the Malaysian government, ABIM hopes to mobilize the youth within the country to expose the corruption and "westernization" taking place in Malaysia. In doing this, the group feels that the country would be more prone to opt for an Islamic **government**. Relatively successful, members of the group have entered the political, social, and educational fields. Perhaps the most prominent member of the group is Anwar Ibrahim, who was the former deputy prime minister of Malaysia.

ANSAR AL-ISLAM/SUPPORTERS OF ISLAM. *Ansar al-Islam* is a Kurdish **Sunni** Muslim **Islamic group** that applies a radical view of **Islam** and *sharia* (Islamic law) to its practices. Geographically, the group began in the northeastern mountainous region of Halabja, **Iraq**, near **Iran** and has established military training camps within this area—specifically in the villages of Biyara and Tawela. The group is the result of the September 2001 merger between *Jund al-Islam* (Soldiers of Islam) and a fraction of the **Kurdish Islamic Movement**. Mullah Krekar, former leader of the Kurdish Islamic Movement, emerged as *Ansar al-Islam*'s leader. Reputedly pugnacious in their practices, most members are veterans of the Soviet war in **Afghanistan** (*mujahideen*) and have repeatedly announced their dissension from the Patriotic Union of Kurdistan. There have been a number of attacks conducted by *Ansar al-Islam*, which implements mostly **suicide bombings** (*istishhad*) and **assassinations**. However, *Ansar al-Islam* has also repeatedly kidnapped hostages and killed many of them as well.

The group also maintains an alliance with *Jamaat Ansar al-Sunna* (Group of the Followers of the *Sunna*) and the **Kurdistan Islamic Group**. Although the group has worked with **al-Qaeda** and has received assistance from the organization, it has insisted that *Ansar al-Islam* is not a branch of the group, merely an affiliate. In the later part of 2003, it was announced that Abu Abdallah al-Shafi'i had replaced Krekar as the group's leader since the latter was sentenced to house arrest in Norway. Reportedly, the group has approximately several hundred to 1,000 members.

ANSAR AL-SUNNA. See ANSAR AL-ISLAM.

APOSTASY/*RIDDA*. According to Islamic **fundamentalists**, apostasy occurs whenever a Muslim refuses to adhere to the **Quranic** teachings and *sharia* (Islamic law). Historically, *ridda* was applied to anyone who denied his or her faith in **Islam** or ridiculed any of its doctrines. Contemporarily, apostasy has taken on a connotation of disbelief (*kufr*), which applies not only to a person's religious activities but to his or her daily and political ones as well.

The Islamic fundamentalists believe that since Islam **governs** all aspects of daily life, apostasy can occur when one differs from the **religion** in even the minutest respect. The role of apostasy in the political sphere has become an increasingly large topic for concern according to the fundamentalists. These strict abiders in Islam feel that if a ruler does not apply *sharia* to the land he is governing, then he is guilty of apostasy. Furthermore, if he applies foreign, **pagan**, or **Western** laws to the land ruled, he is also guilty of apostasy. Doctrinally, apostasy is considered such a serious matter because it reflects the Muslim's activities in the earthly realm, which is seen as of the utmost significance because it is where one bridges toward the sacred world.

AL-AQSA MARTYRS' BRIGADE. Also known simply as Al-Aqsa or Kata'ib Shuhada' al-Aqsa, the brigade is a **Palestinian** nationalist group that derived its name from Al-Aqsa Mosque on the Temple Mount in Jerusalem. The brigade is allegedly associated with **Al-Fatah**, **Hamas**, and the **Islamic Jihad of Palestine**. It has carried out a number of **assassinations**, **suicide bombings**, and other types of attacks on Israeli nationals (military and civilian alike). On 11 November 2004, the group announced its new name: the Brigades of the Martyr Yasir Arafat.

ARAB LIBERATION FRONT (ALF)/*JABHAT AL-TAHRIR AL-'ARABIYAH.* Established by Zeid Heidar in April 1969, the ALF is composed mostly of former *Al-Fatah* members from **Iran**. Although the group's strength is reportedly small, during Saddam Hussein's **Baathist** regime in **Iraq**, the front became the leading **Palestinian political party** within the country and quickly joined the **Palestinian Liberation Organization** (PLO) just months after its formation. Currently, the ALF is led by Rakad Salem (a.k.a. Abu Mahmoud), who is incarcerated in **Israel**. Politically, the group follows the Baathist Pan-Arab platform and believes that the PLO needs to increase its aggressions and has become too moderate. In addition, when the Oslo Accords were signed in 1993, a split within the ALF occurred as not all members agreed with the PLO's participation in the truce. The members who did side with the PLO eventually relocated to the Palestinian territories and formed the Palestinian Arab Front.

Although for years the ALF was the leading group within Iraq's rather small Palestinian population, with the **United States** occupation of Iraq in 2003, many of the Iraqi-Palestinian nationals were forced to leave the country. With the dissolution of the Baathist party, many ALF members fled the country for security reasons and became refugees mostly in **Lebanon** and the West Bank. Recently, the group has been militarily silent and has not claimed responsibility for an attack since the early 1990s.

ARAB REVOLUTIONARY BRIGADES. *See* FATAH REVOLUTIONARY COUNCIL.

ARAB SOCIALIST BAATH PARTY. *See* BAATH PARTY.

ARAB SPRING. Commencing in the early part of 2011, the Arab Spring (also called the Arab Awakening or Arab Uprisings) refers to the major revolutionary groundswell of social protests and civil demonstrations that resulted in the complete overturning of the dictatorships in **Egypt**, **Libya**, and **Tunisia**. Large protests and uprisings also took place in **Algeria**, **Bahrain**, **Iraq**, **Jordan**, **Morocco**, Oman, **Syria**, and **Yemen**—but not to as great an extent as in Egypt, Libya, and Tunisia. Kuwait, **Lebanon**, Mauritania, **Saudi Arabia**, and **Sudan** also saw some minor civil unrest. Although each country experienced the Arab Spring in different ways, marches, strikes, protests, and rallies were always present. The use of social media networks as a way to unite and mobilize a good percentage of the population was another defining feature.

It could be argued that the wave of protests actually began with the 18 December 2010 protest in Tunisia that was sparked by Muhammad Bouazizi's public self-immolation, which was done to protest against the corruption prevalent within the country. This resulted in mass public demonstrations that had a ripple effect on Algeria, Jordan, Egypt, and finally Yemen until spreading even farther across the Muslim world. A majority of the most violent and decisive rallies often occurred on Fridays after the noon prayers at the local mosques. The most generally agreed on causes of the Arab Spring have been the ongoing corruption of the totalitarian regimes and absolute monarchies that existed and continue to exist in many of the countries, and the terrible socioeconomic conditions that have gone on unresolved for decades, such as drastic poverty and widespread unemployment. In addition, many members of the population who are highly educated and conscious of this need to provoke social reform refused to accept the existing state of affairs and were well aware that a change needed to take place.

Factors such as rising food prices, the increased cost of living, a decrease in the human development index, and a serious lack of legislative reforms have been occurring over decades in these countries. So, although one particular incident may have sparked these uprisings, this was a cause that has been simmering for years and was bound to explode. There have also been plenty of social activists and reformist organizations present in many of these countries (particularly Algeria, Egypt, and Tunisia) for decades.

When the civil protests and demonstrations began, many of those in power were unwilling or perhaps unable to satisfy the demands of the protestors, and this served only to intensify the conflicts. On 14 January 2011, Tunisia's President Zine El Abidine Ben Ali fled to Saudi Arabia; on 11 February 2011, Egyptian President Hosni Mubarak resigned; and on 23 August 2011, **Muammar Qadhafi** was overthrown by the rebels after months of violence and resistance. While fellow leaders of the Muslim states witnessed these events, many announced their intentions to not seek reelection, such as Sudanese President **Omar al-Bashir** and Iraqi Prime Minister Nouri al-Maliki. Others, such as Yemeni President Ali Abdullah Saleh, have tried to negotiate deals with the protestors, but this, especially in Saleh's case, only encouraged the civil unrest. On 4 June 2011, he sustained injuries when his compound was attacked by the rebel forces, but he returned again on 23 September 2011. More than 1,500 have been reported killed as a result of the Yemeni uprisings.

The fighting began to subside in many of the countries by the summer of 2011 and thereafter, and while great sociopolitical strides were made in many of these oppressed countries, many died as a result of the fighting as well. For example, the resistance began to subside in Tunisia in March 2011 with an estimated 223 dead. Then, on 23 October 2011, the Tunisians went to their first-ever free elections, electing a Constituent Assembly. In Algeria, the protests decreased in April 2011 with the lifting of the 19-year-old state of emergency. Sudan also began to resolve its conflicts in April. The Mauritanian and Omani protests began to subside in May 2011. June saw the end of the Saudi rallies, and municipal elections were held on 22 September 2011. In addition, **women** will participate in the *shura* (consultation) council and in elections in Saudi Arabia during the 2015 elections. Moroccan protests decreased in July, and the Iraqi uprisings ended in August 2011.

Moreover, Egypt's situation resulted in the suspension of its constitution and parliament, and the former ruler Mubarak and his associates are subject to prosecution. In Bahrain, an estimated 36 were killed, and many political prisoners have been released. Libya has been arguably the most volatile country throughout the Arab Spring. Over 25,000 have been reported killed as a full-scale civil revolution raged. The rebel forces known as the National Transitional Council (NTC) seized control of not only Bab al-Azizia, the headquarters of the Qadhafi regime, but other major cities as well, such as Tripoli and Benghazi. The NTC took control of the country after a UN-mandated military intervention was enacted, complemented by NATO forces. Qadhafi was killed by rebels on 20 October 2011. In Syria, over 3,500 have been reported dead during countless demonstrations, and members of the parliament and provincial governors have resigned. The National Council of Syria has been formed subsequently.

Aside from the overarching historical impact of the Arab Spring, many smaller incidents will undoubtedly become landmark events, such as the attack and death of Libya's Qadhafi on 20 October 2011 and the Tahrir Square demonstrations in Egypt on 25 January 2011. In fact, Tawakkul Karman, a journalist and leading member of the Yemen protests, was awarded the 2011 Nobel Peace Prize, while other notable members of the Arab Spring were nominated for the prize as well—further illustrating just how incredibly significant these events have become. Moreover, these protests also aligned different groups that rallied under the same flag of dissatisfaction even though in the past they were often at odds. Although the peoples participating in the Arab Spring were widely spread geographically, ideologically they were all united. Each cause may have had its minor differences, but these momentous events brought all types of Tunisians, Egyptians, Omanis, Jordanians, and others together under the cause of reform. A notable lack of nationalist banners and slogans further emphasized this desire for basic **human rights** and freedoms.

Of particular significance, it should also be noted that even though this period is referred to as the Arab Spring, it was not only Arabic people who participated in these protests—many non-Arabs, especially of the minority populations, were incredibly active in each country involved. This included Copts in Egypt, other Christians in various countries, and Kurds in Syria and Iraq. In addition, the world over, many countries of varying nationalities were supportive of the revolutionary actions of these people. Whether from Asia, Europe, North America, or Russia, the participants in the Arab Spring were encouraged by the international community.

ARMED ISLAMIC GROUP (AIG)/*GROUPE ISLAMIQUE ARMÉ* (GIA)/ARMED ISLAMIC GROUP OF ALGERIA/*AL-JAMA'A AL-ISLAMIYYA AL-MUSALLAH.* The GIA adopted brutal tactics in hopes of overthrowing the **government** of **Algeria** and replacing it with a completely **Islamic state** after Algerian forces preempted the obvious win of the **Islamic Salvation Front** in the December 1991 legislative elections. The GIA is a splinter group of the **Islamic Armed Movement** and was originally headed by Mansour Meliani, who was executed in May 1993 for his participation in the August 1992 airport attack in Algiers. The main difference between the Islamic Armed Movement and the GIA is that the former insisted that members have proper **Islamist** ideological training (and are mostly former fighters from the Soviet-Afghan War [1979–1989]), whereas the latter did not impose such requirements. Although the GIA took on radical Islamist Omar el-Eulmi as its spiritual mentor, the lack of religious rigor resulted in many militant infiltrations and transfers of leadership. Throughout the 1990s, the GIA committed numerous acts of barbarism and civil massacres, notably the 29 August 1997 Rais massacre and the 22–23 September 1997 Bentalha massacre. Completely hostile and malevolent, the GIA waged war on all civil service members, government officials, political pluralists, Algerian authoritative supporters, artists, foreigners, and practically any individual who deviates from their strict Islamist ideologies, making the GIA the most high-profile Islamist organization.

This Islamic **fundamentalist** group also took an active part in the 1992–2000 Algerian Civil War in hopes of creating an Islamic state within the country, seeing the warfare as an opportunity to do so. Ideologically, the group believes that only through **jihad** can an **Islamic society** take hold throughout Algeria, and since many members are former *mujahideen* of the Soviet-Afghan War, combat has come easily to the GIA. The group also targeted France as an a priori enemy and conducted attacks on the French territories, notably the 24 December 1994 Air France Flight 8969 hijacking and the Saint-Michel metro station bombing on 25 July 1995, killing eight people and injuring 150. This tactic of attacking **Western** countries that were invested in the resources of Algeria (like France) was another way, besides internal conflict, that the GIA hoped to topple the Algerian government.

Throughout the 1990s, the group was very successful with this plan of attacking westerners and, by the close of 1995, had killed approximately 100 foreigners. The GIA's indiscriminate **violence** and draconian practices caused dissension and schism within the organization and warfare between other **Islamic groups**, such as the Islamic Salvation Front and the **Islamic Salvation Army**. However, with the end of the Algerian Civil War in 2000, over 2,100 GIA members surrendered or took up the conditions of amnesty.

The last known leader, or *amir* (Arabic for "general" or "commander"), was Nourredine Boudiafi, whose arrest was announced in January 2005 by the Algerian government. Since 1998, however, the **Salafi Group for Preaching and Combat** (now **al-Qaeda in the Islamic Maghreb**), a GIA faction, seems to have overshadowed its father organization in its ability to be an equally effective militant Islamist group. *See also* AFGHANISTAN; *TAKFIR.*

ARMY OF THE SUPPORTERS OF ALLAH. *See JUND ANSAR ALLAH.*

ART. The Islamic **fundamentalist** perception of art is that it should be permitted and tolerated only if it leads to the worship of **Allah**. However, it is deemed forbidden to figuratively represent or depict Allah, the **Prophet Muhammad**, or his companions. This point of view is especially enforced in the **Sunni** tradition of **Islam**, which accounts for 85 percent of the entire Muslim population worldwide (approximately 1.3 billion).

In contemporary history, the *Jyllands-Posten* **Muhammad cartoons controversy**, the outrage that **Salman Rushdie** provoked with his publication *The Satanic Verses*, and the **Taliban**'s destruction of the **Buddhas of Bamiyan** on 8 September 2008 are just three examples of the control and sensitivity that can occur with regard to images in Islam. In popular culture, for the Islamic fundamentalists, all cinematic scenes of nudity are also strictly forbidden. Moreover, while the Taliban was in power in **Afghanistan** (1996–2001), songs and music albums were banned because of their seemingly indecent artistic creativity.

What is then preferred are traditional calligraphic images of **Quranic** versus and recitations from the **Hadiths**. Ornamental in their nature, these designed writings can take the form of architectural adornment, manuscript illuminations, and simple panel motifs, among others.

AL-ASALAH ISLAMIC SOCIETY. The dominant **Salafi Islamic political party** in **Bahrain**, al-Asalah is also a branch of the Islamic Education Society and has been led by Ghanim al-Buaneen since 2005. Conservative in its ideological platforms, the main support of the group comes from the Muharraq and Riffa areas (two of the three largest cities in Bahrain). Members reject any application of **modernism** within the country and are completely austere in their **interpretations** and practices of **Islam**. Spokespeople for the group have been active in declaring their disagreement over **women**'s rights, veneration, icon worship, and divination—all of which have become increasingly popular subjects in Bahraini society. Although they are also in opposition to the **Shiite** ideology, most al-Asalah followers agree with their Islamic counterparts' desire for a return to religious conservatism despite the difference between the schools.

ASBAT AL-ANSAR/**THE LEAGUE OF FOLLOWERS.** This **Salafi** Islamic **fundamentalist** group is also known as the Partisans' League and seeks to establish an **Islamic state** within **Lebanon** since they view the country as being dominated by **Western** secularist influence. Also believed to be allegedly associated with **al-Qaeda**, the group has conducted a series of **assassinations** and **bombings** on civilian social structures throughout the 2000s. Ahmad Abdulkarim as-Sa'idi (a.k.a. Abu Mahjin), who leads the group, has been sentenced to death in absentia and was a supposed affiliate of **Abu Musab al-Zarqawi** until 2006.

AL-ASHA'RIYYA/**THE TRADITIONALISTS.** An early school of Islamic theology, *al-Asha'riyya* is named after its founder, Abu al-Hasan al-Ash'ari (d. 936). Its adherents were incredibly influential in changing certain ideas in **Islam**. Ideologically, they firmly believed that human **reason** is not capable of fully understand **Allah** and that all that man creates belongs to Allah since he is the absolute creator. In addition, they stipulate that all forms of moral truth should be left to religious scholars. Although these thoughts could be considered traditionalistic, or based on *taqlid*, *al-Asha'riyya* did support rationality as a means to understanding that Allah controls all reason and has given humanity free will. The most influential pieces of literature for this school were *The Incoherence of the Philosophers* and *The Revival of the Religious Sciences in Islam*, which were written in the 10th century by a Persian scholar, al-Ghazali. Some contemporary Muslim thinkers believe that *al-Asha'riyya* was responsible for the decline of applying rational thought to Islamic doctrine, although the subsequent 12th through 14th centuries saw an increase in **innovation** in Islam. In addition, many pioneers of the scientific improvements of this time were adherents of this school of Islam.

ASSASSIN/*HASHASHIN*/ASSASSINATION. Historically, the etymological provenance of the term "assassin" can be traced to the name given to the *Isma'ili Fedayin* group, which was called *hashashin* (which refers to those who take the drug hashish). Over time, the word had been altered in English as "assassin." During the **Sunni** Abbasid dynasty (750–1517), the *Isma'ili Fedayin* assaulted high-ranking officials of the dynasty specifically through attacks in which the attacker was understood to be killed as well (what is now known as suicide attacks). These acts started to awe the populace, as they were seen as both honorable and bold. The members of the dynasty, not wanting the *Isma'ili Fedayin* to achieve a positive reputation for their acts, claimed that they were merely under the influence of hashish, or *hashshishi*. The term is usually applicable only when prominent figures are killed, but many assassins have proven to be driven by psychological deviance rather than sociopolitical motives.

Assassinations are known as probably the oldest, most effective, and most common tool used by radical Islamic **fundamentalists**. Usually opportunistic in nature, assassins most often believe that through their acts, they can help destabilize existing regimes and win public support for their causes. *See also ISTISHHAD*; SUICIDE BOMBING; VIOLENCE.

ASSASSINATION. *See* ASSASSIN.

ASSOCIATION OF MUSLIM LAWYERS (AML). Although officially established in 1995, the AML has been active in Great Britain since 1993. Steadily growing in both influence and membership, AML has organized numerous conferences and symposiums to increase the application of *sharia* (Islamic law) throughout the Muslim community. Its logo, meaning "Act with hope," demonstrates the group's desire to apply its barrister training in the hope of gaining a positive relationship between British and Islamic law. Members also, through their symposiums, encourage scholarship and research in both fields to better facilitate an understanding between the two. Through this interrelationship, it is claimed that a fair and just society can be established throughout the country.

AML members are active lobbyists, educators, developers, and organizers who work with both Muslims and non-Muslim lawyers and do not try to achieve equality in the judicial and social facets of the culture. Along with the Muslim Council of Britain and the Union of Muslim Organizations, AML has also worked with the House of Commons and the House of Lords. This working relationship with British legislative bodies is extremely important in achieving one of the group's primary goals: equal rights of Muslims under the British domestic code. The organization achieved some success in this area with the 2003 decree of Employment Equality Regulations, which protected minority groups from religious discrimination in the workplace. However, the equality ends there. Because of the efforts of the AML, the House of Parliament is debating a law that would protect Muslims more fully from racial discrimination. The organization has also worked with other lobbying groups in Belgium, Germany, and France to achieve similar goals of Muslim equality in those countries.

Legislatively, AML hopes to have matters such as Muslim marriage and property ownership get treated in accordance with Islamic law and that this application be accepted by the British legal system. This would mean that British common law would recognize the legality of *sharia* in specific Muslim matters. AML members have claimed that this decree could serve as an alternative dispute resolution that would also be beneficial to the traffic in the civil courts. However, the onslaught of **violence** conducted by certain Muslims over the past decade has made the legislature in Great Britain (and many other countries for that matter) very hesitant to pass laws that would provide legal security for them. This stance, viewed as hypocritical, has prompted the AML to form the Working Party on **Human Rights** and Civil Liberties to ensure that unjust oppression (toward Muslims and non-Muslims alike) does not take place within the courts.

ASSOCIATION OF MUSLIM SCHOLARS/*JAM'IYYAT AL-'ULAMA' AL-MUSLIMIN.* Although dissolved in 1956, this reformist movement set out to revolutionize Algerian cultural and religious affairs. Formed in the 1920s, most of its members and leaders (including **'Abd al-Hamid Ibn Badis** and Bashir al-Ibrahimi) were educated middle-class Muslims. In fact, it was established by students from the universities of Al-Azhar, **Egypt**, and Al-Zaytuna, **Tunisia**, who wanted to fight against the **Sufi** Muslim orders. Inspired by **Muhammad 'Abdu, Jamal al-Din al-Afghani**, and **Muhammad Iqbal**, the Association of Muslim Scholars encouraged the use of nationalism and Arabic identity to create unity that could be strong enough to fight against the French presence in **Algeria**.

AT-TAWHID. Translated to literarily mean "monotheism," this group was created in 1996 by former members of the militant Islamist movement, *ash-Shabiba al-Islamiya.* At-Tawhid was formed as a way for its fragmented members to gain political influence and legitimacy in **Morocco**. However, former King Hassan II refused to recognize the party, and therefore *At-Tawhid* assimilated into the Constitutional and Democratic Popular Movement, which since 1998 has been known as the **Justice and Development Party**. *See also* ISLAMIC GROUPS; ISLAMIC POLITICAL PARTIES; MOROCCAN ISLAMIC COMBATANT GROUP; *TAWHID.*

AUTHENTICITY/*ASALA.* ** *Asala*, according to the Islamic **fundamentalists, is the way in which **Islam** can return to a "purer" form devoid of any and all **Western** influence. *Asala* refers to acting within the constraints of a very literal **interpretation** of and adherence to Islam, not necessarily the rejection of **scientific** advancements (although opinions differ between the Islamic modernists and the fundamentalists) but always the rejection of Western stimuli. The **Islamization** of political or social matters can also authenticate **legitimacy**. This idea of authenticity and thereby "purity" not only distinguishes the Islamic faith from all others but also places it in a perceived superior position according to the fundamentalists. *See also* GOVERNMENT; ISLAMIC GOVERNMENT.

AWAMI LEAGUE/BANGLADESH PEOPLE'S LEAGUE. Currently the leading political party in Bangladesh, the Awami League is a leftist anti-Islamic **fundamentalist** group founded in 1949 at the capital of the former Pakistani province of East Bengal. Developed by Maulana Abdul Hamid Khan Bhashani, Shamsul Huq, and Huseyn Shaheed Suhrawardy, the league was created to oppose the dominant Muslim League in Pakistan and quickly attracted immense popular support in East Bengal (currently East Pakistan). Politically, the group runs on a platform of nationalism, secularism, **democracy**, and socialism. A majority of the original members of the league came from the University of Dhaka, and it was reportedly 1,000 members strong.

The league was also an incredibly influential force during the 1952 Bengali Language Movement, which involved students protesting that Bengali be recognized as an official language by **Pakistan**. Resulting in the deaths of many students at the hands of Pakistani security forces, this movement is seen as the turning point in Bengali nationalism and the catalyst for the Bangladesh Liberation War (26 March–16 December 1971). During the conflict, members of the Awami League were exceptionally instrumental both tactically and politically, and the group was able to mobilize the population primarily because of its pronationalist stance. Therefore, when Bangladesh won its independence on 16 December 1971, the group won the country's first general elections in 1973.

However, with the 1975 **assassination** of Bangladesh's "father" Sheikh Mujibur Rahman, the group was overthrown, and its members retreated into the rural areas of the country as many of its leaders were executed and jailed. Years later, in 1990, when democracy was restored in Bangladesh, the Awami League returned and regained its position as a formidable organization within Bangladeshi politics. The group continued to be successful, as five members have become the president of Bangladesh, four became prime minister, and one even became the prime minister of Pakistan. Rahman's daughter, Hasina (one of the two surviving members of her family), has been leading the party since 1981 and has been the prime minister of Bangladesh since January 2009. At present, the Awami League has developed into different sociopolitical wings, including the Bangladesh Awami Jubo League and the Bangladesh Students League.

'AWDA, 'ABD AL-'AZIZ (1950–). Born on 20 December 1950, 'Abd al-'Aziz 'Awda was one of the founders of *Al-Jihad al-Islami* **in the West Bank and Gaza Strip** who also called for the eradication of the traditional **Muslim Brotherhood** ideologies. While studying **Islam** in Cairo, 'Awda became involved with such organizations as the **Islamic Jihad Group** and *Tanzim al-Kuliyya al-Fanniyya al-'Askariyyy*, leading to his future activism (*harakiyya*) as an Islamic **fundamentalist**. Currently, 'Awda also serves as the spiritual potentate of the **Palestinian Islamic Jihad**. (Located in Damascus, **Syria**, it is a branch of the **Egyptian Islamic Jihad**.) 'Awda's anti-Egyptian sentiments could be a result of his youth, as he was born in Jabaliyah, Gaza Strip, during the beginning of **Egypt**'s occupation there (1949–1967) following the 1949 armistice agreement made between Egypt and **Israel**.

AL-AWLAKI, ANWAR (1971–2011). Born in Las Cruces, New Mexico, on 22 April 1971 to a prominent family from **Yemen**, Anwar al-Awlaki was an Islamic lecturer who previously trained with the *mujahideen* fighters from **Afghanistan** and was a former *imam* who had served as spiritual guide for many Islamists. Gifted in the art of recruitment and motivation, al-Awlaki inspired numerous attacks within and outside the **United States** and counseled **jihadists** from all branches of **al-Qaeda**. He had also been suspected of conniving with the 24 December 2009 "Christmas Day Bomber" Umar Farouk Abdulmutallab and the 5 November 2009 Fort Hood shooter, **Nidal Malik Hasan**, among others. According to reports, in 2007 he was promoted to regional commander within al-Qaeda—a distinct rank of honor within the group. He was known for his use of the Internet in gaining support and spreading his ideologies, especially with the online magazine *Inspire* and the forum *Sada Al-Malahim*. Considered one of the most notorious and conspicuous figures in Islamic **fundamentalism** next to **Osama bin Laden**, al-Awlaki was killed on 30 September 2011 in Yemen.

A committed supporter of any and all harm inflicted on the United States and other **Western** countries, al-Awlaki provided ideological justification for these acts through his sermons and lectures. It is, however, interesting to note al-Awlaki's popularity among the Islamists, considering his American origin, the fact that he dictates primarily in English, and his lack of formal Islamic scholastic training. He used the writings and works of **jihadi** ideologist **Sayyid Qutb** and Abdullah Azzam to perpetuate his *takfirist* and jihadist teachings to reach numerous young followers. From 1998 to 2000, al-Awlaki was under investigation for his involvement in many organizations that were set up as fronts to supply finances to groups like al-Qaeda and **Hamas**.

In 2004, he took up residence in Yemen and began teaching at the Iman University in Sanaa, the curriculum of which has a reputation for promoting radical Islamic **theologies** and **extremism**. On 31 August 2006, he was arrested with four others for the kidnapping and ransoming of a **Shiite** teenager and for allegedly plotting to kidnap a U.S. military attaché but was released on 12 December 2007. While in Yemen, the jihadists provided safety and protection for other Islamists under his tribe, fittingly known as the Awlakis. By December 2009, it was believed that al-Awlaki was hiding in the Shabwa and Ma'rib regions of central Yemen, two areas known for its al-Qaeda refugees who are safeguarded by local tribes that are opposed to the central government of Yemen in Sanaa. As a senior recruiter and spiritual leader, al-Awlaki had been one of the most dominant and influential figures in American and British domestic Islamic fundamentalist movements and attacks in the first decade of the 21st century. The ideologue was at the top of countless watch lists in Great Britain, the United States, the United Nations, and others yet remained for some time under the protective shroud of **al-Qaeda in the Arabian Peninsula** (AQAP) and his tribe. He was also one of the first American-born citizens to be placed on the U.S. National Security Council's targeted killings list.

On 30 September 2011, al-Awlaki, Samir Khan (top explosive maker for AQAP), Ibrahim al-Asiri (another AQAP operative), and three others were killed just outside the town of al-Khasaf, Yemen as a result of a U.S. Joint Special Operations Command air strike that targeted their convoy. Although there was some critical backlash from civil liberty groups over the U.S. strike since al-Awlaki and Khan were American-born citizens, their involvement in hostilities and conspiracies against other Americans could not be denied, and therefore the acts were justified according to the U.S. Department of Defense. According to reports, the attack was a success because of the Yemeni intelligence and operational support that was given. *See also* MUSLIM ASSOCIATION OF BRITAIN.

AL-'AWWA, MUHAMMAD SALIM (1942–). An **Egyptian** Islamic **fundamentalist** and practicing attorney, Muhammad Salim al-'Awwa is known for his discourses on the necessity of **pluralism** within **Islamic society**. A once high-ranking member of the **Muslim Brotherhood**, the litigator also serves as head of the defense council for various Islamic fundamentalists who are on trial in Egypt. According to al-'Awwa, in order for a society to become civil, it must embrace different societal measures, but this does not make it a society influenced by **Western** ideas. To him, individuality comes through diversity, and **pluralism** is the tolerance of this diversity that is encouraged by the **Quran**. Al-'Awwa states that the **divine text** does not identify a particular political order (*nizam*), does encourage the election of rulers through *shura* (consultation), and allows for religious freedoms as long as they do not contradict with the fundamentals of **Islam**. Al-'Awwa also serves as the secretary general of the International Union for Muslim Scholars and wrote *Pluralism in Islamic Political Thought* (1993).

'AYYASH, YAHYA ABD-AL-LATIF (1966–1996). A member of **Hamas** and the leader of the West Bank legion of the **Izz ad-Din Al-Qassam Brigades**, 'Ayyash became known under the nickname "the engineer" for his extended implementation of improvised explosive devices. Responsible for countless attacks, 'Ayyash was eventually killed by an explosive planted in the headset of a telephone by the **Israeli** secret service on 5 January 1996. 'Ayyash coordinated many attacks that resulted in the deaths of numerous Israelis and thus is seen as a **martyr** by many. These attacks include the 6 April 1994 Afula Bus massacre, the 13 April 1994 Hadera Central Station **suicide bombing**, and the 19 October 1994 Tel Aviv Bus 5 massacre. In the aftermath of 'Ayyash's death, a group of Izz ad-Din Al-Qassam brigadiers and members of Hamas formed the Yahya 'Ayyash Units (or Disciples of 'Ayyash) and conducted a series of suicide bombings in his honor in February and March 1996, killing over 60 Israelis.

AZHAR, MASOOD (1968–). Leader and founder of *Jaish-e-Muhammad*, Masood Azhar was born on 10 July 1968 in Bahawalpur, **Pakistan**. During his studies at *Jamia Uloom ul Islamia* (a *madrasa* in Karachi, Pakistan), Azhar joined *Harakat-ul-Ansar* and became a *mujahideen* fighter during the Soviet-Afghan War (1979–1989). Throughout the years, he rose to top positions in *Harakat-ul-Ansar*, including that of general secretary, which allowed him to more effectively spread the group's ideology of **pan-Islamism** in the South Asian countries. He has also been associated with leaders of *Al-Itihad al-Islami*. Azhar has repeatedly stated his desire to rid the Muslim community of **Western** and Indian influences. When Azhar left *Harkat-ul-Ansar* (which is now known as *Harakat-ul-Mujahideen*) to form *Jaish-e-Muhammad*, he intensified his **extremist** convictions. His new militant organization carried out countless attacks on Indian targets, notably on India's parliament in December 2001. He was also accused of helping to orchestrate the **Mumbai attacks of November 2008**, which killed and injured hundreds. The militant wrote a number of books as well in the Hindustani language of Urdu, including *Fazail e Jihad* (The Benefits of Jihad) and *Zaad e Mujahid* (The Ammunition of the *Mujahid*), all pertaining to the **jihad**.

AZIZ, GENERAL MUHAMMAD OULD ABDEL (1956–). Assuming the presidential office of **Mauritania** on 5 August 2009, General Muhammad Ould Abdel Aziz was a leading figure in the August 2005 coup d'état that deposed then President **Maouya Ould Sid Ahmed Taya**. A career solider born on 20 December 1956 in Akjoujt, of then French Mauritania, Aziz was also extremely influential in the August 2008 coup d'état of Sidi Ould Cheikh Abdallahi's presidential regime. Ironically, while Aziz was a colonel in the Presidential Security Battalion, he was awarded Mauritania's highest military award for suppressing insurrections in June 2003 and August 2004. Under Cheikh Abdallahi's administration, General Aziz was named his presidential chief of staff. The 6 August 2008 coup d'état began when Aziz and other senior officers were ordered to be removed by Abdallahi. Hours later, troops seized the president and prime minister of Mauritania and announced the termination of their power. After the 2008 political upheaval, Aziz became president of the High Council of State during Mauritania's political transition. In order to run in the July 2009 presidential election, he stepped down from that post in April 2009. The **United States** and African Union have declared President Aziz's government and the 2008 coup d'état illegal and unconstitutional, whereas **Morocco**, **Libya**, and Senegal have expressed their support.

B

BAATH PARTY/ARAB SOCIALIST BAATH PARTY. An **Islamic political party** comprised of both Arab nationalists and socialists, the Arab Socialists Baath Party seeks to remove all traces of **Western** imperialism from the Arabic world. The party has also adopted the motto "Unity, Liberty, Socialism," which illustrates its desire to join national unity with **social justice**. As Baath is translated from Arabic to mean "resurrection," its ideologies are clearly defined as a return to a pure Arab state that operates completely separate from non-Arab forces and influence.

Founded in 1947 in Damascus, **Syria**, by Michel Aflaq and Salah al-Bitar, the group has tried to establish branches in other Arabic countries, but its main foothold is in **Iraq** and **Syria**. In Iraq, the group attained sole political power following a coup d'état in February 1963 that expelled procommunist President Abd Al-Karim Qasim, but it was quickly ousted a few months later. The Baath Party returned to power in Iraq in July 1968 (after a coup d'état led by Generals Ahmad Hasan al-Bakr and Saddam Hussein) and remained as the dominant political authority until 2003. In 1974, the party in Iraq reformed itself under the National Progressive Front in hopes of gaining wider support. Saddam Hussein experienced growing support and emerged as the party's leader and used this increased power to move al-Bakr out of the political spotlight. Saddam Hussein remained as the party's leader until the June 2003 invasion led by the **United States**, which left it banned by the Coalition Provisional Authority.

After the fall of Hussein's government, many Baathist branches (such as in **Jordan**, **Lebanon**, **Mauritania**, **Sudan**, and **Yemen**) dissolved so as to distance themselves from the Iraqi problem. However, in Syria, the party has been the commanding political force there since 8 March 1963. In Iraq the party is known as the *Qawmi* (Nationalists) and in Syria the *Qotri* (Regionalists), which function as two separate entities. Interestingly enough, although the group emphasizes a non-Western Arabic nation, its political and social theories are based on European ones of nationalism and socialism. Both Aflaq and al-Bitar even studied at the Sorbonne in France, where they came into contact with French positivists and the German *Kulturnation* concepts that helped shape their doctrines. Aflaq's ideas are synthesized in his five-volume work, *On the Way of Resurrection*.

Structurally, the group organized multiple cells with a hierarchical command arrangement in which communication was passed solely from the upper levels down to the cells. Although this construction was somewhat cumbersome, it did prove to be resilient against dissension and infiltration. The Baath Party was also designed to operate under a unifying Regional Command that would be at the top of the organization and would enforce the pan-Arab nationalism of the group. Not only did the Baath Party seek political dominance, but it also sought social support and hoped to gain military recruits. *See also* MUSLIM BROTHERHOOD IN SYRIA.

BADAN KOMUNIKASI PEMUDA MASJID INDONESIA (BKPMI)/ASSOCIATION FOR COMMUNICATION BETWEEN THE YOUTH OF INDONESIAN MOSQUES. This group is a radical Indonesian organization founded in 1976. The BKPMI currently has a branch in each district in Indonesia. Its foundation was based on Toto Tasmara's idea that one organization should be created so that various Muslim youths from various areas could assemble together. The first assembly in 1976 took place in the Istiqamah Mosque during Ramadan and had Muslims from mosques in Surabaya, Yogyakarta, Jakarta, and Bandung in attendance. After witnessing this success, the Indonesian Council of Religious Clergy allowed for BKPMI to be established. Tasmara was then named its leader.

The goal of this group is to use the mosques not only to develop the spiritual lives of the society but also to encourage a social camaraderie and therefore build a greater Islamic nation (***umma***). BKPMI's slogan is "back to the mosque," which illustrates its ideal that it is in the mosque that communication and ***shura*** (consultation) can grow. BKPMI also inspired many other youth-orientated Muslim groups and continued to create transregional activities to unify the Indonesian Muslim community. Once every three years, BKPMI holds a national conference to discuss new activities that should take place and to elect new members to its board. The first meeting was held in 1992, and the group continues to spread throughout the whole country.

AL-BADR. Active in the Jammu and Kashmir regions, this militant **Islamic group** was formed in June 1998 and is commanded by Jasniel Rihal. Created out of members from **Hizb ul-Mujahedeen** and **Hizb-ul-Islami Gulbuddin**, a majority of the members are veteran fighters from the Soviet-Afghan War (1979–1989) (***mujahideen***). The group participates in the **jihad** against the U.S. occupation in **Afghanistan** and supports the acquisition of Jammu and Kashmir by **Pakistan**. *Al-Badr* is also associated with the **United Jihad**

Council, *Jamaat-e-Islami*, and **al-Qaeda**. Membership is estimated to be relatively low at only 200 to 300, and it is one of the few Kashmiri separatist groups that implements **suicide bombings** in their insurgencies. The group also makes considerable use of foreign mercenaries, a unique characteristic for such organizations. Based in Mansehra, Pakistan, *Al-Badr* also has a significant presence in Muzaffarabad in the Pakistan-occupied region of Kashmir. The militants have targeted mainly Indian government officials and military installations throughout the Jammu and Kashmir region. Virulently denouncing the effectiveness of any proposed negotiations between India and Pakistan, the group insists that only through jihadi efforts can Pakistan gain control of the desired territories. *See also* KASHMIRI SEPARATISM.

BAHRAIN. What is most interesting about Bahrain's Islamic demographic is that although the al-Khalifa ruling family adheres to the **Sunni** school of **Islam**, a majority of the population is **Shiite**. Economically, the country was one of the first in the Persian Gulf to become a major oil-exporting state, but a rapid depletion in its resources has resulted in the state's having to find alternative sources for its economic future. With regard to society and culture, Bahrain is quite lenient and open in comparison to its neighboring states. However, **Islamic political parties** are banned in the country, but those who desire a voice in the legislative realm have revamped themselves into political social organizations, although they are mostly Islamic in nature. The ruling family (which has been in power since the country gained independence on 15 August 1971 from Great Britain) has played off the various religious cultures and diverse ideologies against one another in order to gain a stronger degree of stability. This tactic proved to be quite successful until the onset of the **Arab Spring** in 2011.

Another economic aspect that should be noted is that the Shiite community as a whole is considerably poorer than the Sunni minority. The Shiite people have also claimed that there has been a great deal of discrimination against them in the job sector and with regard to civil programs. This could be due to the ruling family's subscription to Sunni Islam. This inequality has been the basis for many of the Shiite population's grievances and a basic platform in their "political social organizations." In addition, the more traditional Islamists wish to impose *sharia* (Islamic law), have a louder voice in legislative matters, amend the Bahraini constitution so that these changes could take place, downgrade the intense internal security forces, limit Sunni immigration (an aspect that has been viewed as the government's attempt to stifle the Shiite demographic), and restrict "immoral" activities as proscribed by Islamic law. They also desire a **government** that is guided by Shiite clerics but not a direct **theocracy**.

Although the Shiites have claimed to be loyal to Bahrain and its ruling family, preferring rather to make changes to the government peacefully and internally, the Sunni population has been skeptical of their ideological and cultural closeness to **Iran**. In fact, many commentators on the Arab Spring unrest have blamed Iranian influence for the social demonstrations, although participants in the demonstrations claim that the unrest is purely a result of internal strife.

In comparison to the Shiite political parties, not all the Sunni parties have Islamic platforms. Some are purely secular, whereas others are independent. Therefore, there is much more competition between Sunni groups than there is between the Shiites because of the range in diversity. Another interesting factor is that since the Sunni population makes up the elite minority within the country, there is little to no platforms that are based on political reforms. Rather, these groups ask for the general improvement in Bahraini life for all. This often includes calling for economic stability but never involves equality for the Shiite populations or the removal of the **Western** presence within the country. Both of these would directly affect the lifestyle of the Sunni elite if any changes were to be made. Although the Shiite and Sunni groups in Bahrain disagree on a variety of issues, some clerics from both of these schools of **Islam** have joined forces in the past. The issues that they aligned themselves on have been the banning of the sale and consumption of alcohol, the eradication of prostitution, and the stifling of other forms of illicit cultural activities.

With regard to Islamic aggressions within the state, the government has been rather successful in limiting and controlling militant **extremism** within its borders. Domestic policies such as four-year election periods and parliamentary approval of King al-Khalifa's appointments have been enacted with the hope of pacifying any antilegislative animosities. However, Bahrain's lower chamber of parliament (which is elected by the people) still has limited powers in comparison to the upper chamber (which is appointed by the monarchy). Although this limited form of **democracy** that pervades the Bahraini system is not entirely favored by the majority, its population is still allowed many rights in comparison to other Gulf emirates. Still, Prime Minister Prince Khalifa ibn Sulman al-Khalifa has held his post since the 1971 independence and is the world's longest-reigning prime minister.

Diplomatically, the only notable problems that Bahrain has seen are with regard to *al-Islah*'s support for **Hamas** in the Gaza Strip. This has also spawned a number of anti-Zionist sentiments throughout the country. Bahrain, though, has not been known to be much of a scene of militant extremism with regard to providing military or financial aid. This may be due to the country's generally flourishing economic situation or its lack of having radical brands of Islamic **fundamentalism** within its borders. The monarchy has also established severe punishments in its penal code for those who are accused of participating in or providing assistance to jihadists.

However, Bahrain's main problems lie internally with the agitated Shiite population rather than with the international **jihad** movement. February 2011 saw the first wave of social demonstrations to hit the country after civil revolutions in **Egypt** and **Tunisia** began to influence the majority population. The country's first counteraction to suppress the riots was heavy-handed, but after that resulted in casualties and therefore even more civil unrest, the monarchy decided that a lighter stance should be taken. Despite the government's desire to cooperate with the Shiite public, grave damage has been done to their relationship after its initially aggressive tactics destroyed much of the morale that the Shiite community had. Countries such as **Saudi Arabia** that possess the same socioeconomic and demographic characteristics as Bahrain have even vowed to help dispel the unrest. Although it would take a great deal to overthrow the powerful al-Khalifa family, the turbulence and discontent within the country remains to be settled. *See also* BAHRAIN FREEDOM MOVEMENT; HAQ MOVEMENT FOR LIBERTY AND DEMOCRACY.

BAHRAIN FREEDOM MOVEMENT. Established in a northern London mosque, the Bahrain Freedom Movement became popular after its leading involvement with the 1994–1999 uprisings in **Bahrain**, which resulted in King Hamad ibn Isa al-Khalifa becoming *amir* in 1999. Its leader, Sayyed Shehabi, was formerly a member of the **Shiite al-Wefaq Islamic National Society**. After King Hamad instituted his reforms, which allowed for the return of former political exiles, many Bahrain Freedom Movement members returned from Great Britain to Bahrain. This resulted in the movement losing many of its key members, but still a large number remained in asylum in London. Those who returned received amnesty and participated in the renewed legislative and electoral processes in Bahrain. However, with the onset of the revolutions brought on by the **Arab Spring** civil protests, many activists were again prosecuted by the kingdom in the hope of dispelling further unrest.

BALANCE/*TAWAZUN*. In Islamic **fundamentalist theology**, balance occurs between the known and the unknown workings of **Allah**. For example, the student of **Islam** must accept the actions of Allah as axioms since the work of Allah is beyond human **reason**. In addition, the student should actively search and study those concepts that are within the boundaries of the human mind. In fundamentalist ideology, the attainment of such a balance should be **intuitive** and achieved with caution so as not to blur the boundaries of the two realms. *See also* PEACE.

BALIK **ISLAM/RETURN TO ISLAM.** Founded in 1990, *Balik* Islam is a predication movement in the Philippines. It was set up by Christians who converted to **Islam** after traveling as missionaries in the Middle East. The group is active primarily in the Manilla region and is influenced by the *Wahabbi* ideology.

BANGLADESH. With Bangladesh's wide variety of Islamic and secularist groups and adherents, it has developed into a more moderate **Islamic state** that uses its Muslim culture as a source of nationalist identity. Almost all the country adheres to the **Sunni** school of **Islam**, and it possesses over 100,000 mosques. These religious centers operate as community centers that provide education as well as spiritual guidance. This has then led to the majority of the population following a traditional, orthodox version of Islam. There are also many *madrasas* that operate within Bangladesh, further promoting this brand of Islam.

Legislatively, this devotion to Islam has been acknowledged successfully by all the leading rulers of Bangladesh since its independence in 1971—even by the more secular ones. This relationship could be described as a sort of embrace between the governmental and the ideological, although Islam's presence in the political sector has been rather limited (with the exception of the 1975 coup d'état that resulted in the removal of the secularist regime and its replacement with a sectarian one that lasted until 1990). In recent politics, secularist policies have been enacted purely to combat the militant **extremist** factions within the country. So far, this has been seen as a progressive policy but with many contradictions and risks of corruption.

The Islamic movement in Bangladesh has manifested itself into three groups: **traditionalists**, **Islamic political parties**, and radical extremists. The traditionalists, also known as revivalists, are represented by two different groups: *Ahl-e-Hadith* and *Tablighi Jamaat*. *Ahl-e-Hadith* has origins reaching as far back as 1830s British India, where it then spread to Bengal and then to the newly independent **Pakistan**. Ideologically, the group does not recognize any individual branch of Islam but rather relies simply on an austere interpretation of the **divine texts**. The group claims to have approximately 25 million adherents worldwide. The group does not involve itself with Bangladeshi politics and prefers to purely spread its interpretations of the **Quran** and the **Hadiths** throughout the state. *Tablighi Jamaat* could be considered a kind of missionary group in the sense that it focuses its efforts on spreading the doctrines and rites of Islam primarily to non-Muslims within the country. Its headquarters are in Dhaka, and members orchestrate an annual assembly that is attended by millions. Although the group refrains from being involved in state politics, it is state sponsored by Bangladesh.

With regard to political Islam in Bangladesh, *Jamaat-e-Islami* has been the most influential group in comparison to its radical counterpart *Harakat-ul-Jihad al-Islami* in Bangladesh (HuJI-B). *Jamaat-e-Islami*, originally from India, spread to Bangladesh in 1979 and was headed by Abbas Ali Khan. Currently, it is led by Maulana Motiur Rahman Nijami. Although the group wishes to install an Islamic state based on *sharia* in the country, it desires to do so through democratic and nationalistic means. Through its **Islamization** of **democracy**, it has achieved a good amount of public support in a range of demographics. However, the party has been only mildly successful when it comes to the polls. It is also allegedly funded by many internal groups and international organizations.

HuJI-B emerged in 1992 in Bangladesh particularly because Islamic extremists were drawn to the country's weak internal security force and unstable economy. Ideologically, this group wishes to establish Islamic law by means of an aggressive policy inspired by that of the **Taliban army**. Many of its members are former Afghan *mujahideen*, and it has allegedly some links with the **al-Qaeda** organization. Although the group was officially banned by the Bangladesh government in October 2008, HuJI-B still has a number of units throughout the country despite the actions the state has taken to prevent their insurgencies. *Jamaat-ul-Mujahideen* in Bangladesh is another radical Islamic party operating within the country and has been ever since 1998. Ideologically similar to HuJI-B in wanting to aggressively establish *sharia*, it possesses an alternative military wing: *Jagroto Muslim Janata* Bangladesh. *See also* AWAMI LEAGUE; BANGLADESH *KHILAFAT MAJLIS*.

BANGLADESH *KHILAFAT MAJLIS*. An **Islamic political party** in **Bangladesh** that seeks to establish an **Islamic state** based on *sharia* (Islamic law) and headed by a **caliph** within the country, the *Khilafat Majlis* was formed in 1989. Islamic scholars Maulana Abdul Gaffar and Ahmad Abdul Quader founded the group to represent the traditionalists within Bangladesh. Many members of the group have come from intellectual communities, such as the universities and the *madrasas*. The group also has a central executive committee that oversees the basic undertakings of *Khilafat Majlis*.

Members were active in protests against the 2006 Lebanon War and participated in the 2011 **Arab Spring** protests, resulting in the arrest and imprisonment of many of its affiliates. Also in 2006, the group formed an electoral alliance with the **Awami League** with the hope of further consolidating the Muslim vote. However, this pact was broadly criticized since the Awami League is known for its secularist agenda—one that is largely contrary to that of the *Khilafat Majlis*. However, in the 29 December 2008 elections, the group ran independently yet won only 8 of the 345 seats within the Bangladeshi Parliament. *See also* TRADITIONALISM.

AL-BANNA, HASSAN (1906–1949). Born on 14 October 1906, this influential Muslim revivalist and one of the most prominent **modern** Islamic thinkers founded the **Muslim Brotherhood** in March 1928. At an early age, the charismatic al-Banna studied **Sufism** (the mystical side of **Islam**) and actively participated in the Egyptian Revolution of 1919 against British colonial rule. These activities formed the basis of his Muslim Brotherhood organization, which quickly spread to numerous areas throughout **Egypt**. The Brotherhood's popularity was due mainly to al-Banna's charismatic direction and his scrutiny of the gravely unbalanced distribution of wealth. Soon, the impoverished, the working class, and professionals alike were joined through this network, which increased loyalty and support for the organization and for al-Banna himself.

Al-Banna also used mosques, hospitals, cafés, and various other locations when giving his lectures to further demonstrate the breadth that his movement could have. In addition to his religious reforms, Al-Banna wanted to enter the political sector in order to revolutionize **Islamic society** from within, having run twice as a candidate with other Brotherhood members, but was forced to withdraw in 1942 and then lost in 1945. In December 1948, growing tensions mounted in Egypt between the monarchy and the Brotherhood, which spoke out against the regime, resulting in the group's being declared illegal. Many members of the group were imprisoned, and weeks later Egyptian Prime Minister Mahmoud an-Nukrashi Pasha was assassinated by a Brotherhood member, Abdul Majid Ahmad Hasan. Although al-Banna released a statement anathematizing the attack (although he had previously declared support of the **jihad**), he was later killed the following February while leaving the *Jamiyyat al-Shubban al-Muslimeen* headquarters in Cairo on 12 February 1949. *See also* HASAN AL-BANNA IDEOLOGY.

AL-BANNA, SABRI KHALIL. *See* ABU NIDAL ORGANIZATION.

***BARISAN REVOLUSI NASIONAL* (BRN)/FRONT OF THE NATIONAL REVOLUTION.** Based in the south of Thailand, BRN is an Islamic separatist movement. Founded in 1960 by religious teachers, BRN hopes to create an **Islamic state** based on *sharia* (Islamic law). At the end of the 1970s, there was a split within the group when some members did not wish to be part of the Malaysian state (like the BRN wanted) but rather totally independent. This group is known as the BRN Coordinate. By the end of the 1980s, BRN changed its nature and founded an informal network of associates and moved toward religious predication. But since January 2004, BRN Coordinate has been conducting insurgencies in southern Thailand.

AL-BASHIR, 'UMAR (1944–). Head of the **National Congress Party** and president of **Sudan**, al-Bashir also served as a general in the Sudanese army. During his participation in the Sudanese armed forces, he led the military coup d'état that removed then Prime Minister Sadiq al-Mahdi on 30 June 1989. The coup was supported by the **National Islamic Front** and came to be known as *Thawrat al-Inqadh al-Watani* (National Salvation Revolution). After the coup, the Revolutionary Command Council for National Salvation took control over Sudan and tried to establish a *Majlis-al-Shura* (consultation council). However, al-Bashir dissolved the council after it failed to succeed and appointed himself president on 16 October 1993. Al-Bashir still maintains his associations with the National Islamic Front and has been involved with the Second Sudanese Civil War (1983–2005) and the Darfur conflict (2003–2010). The numerous civilian atrocities that have taken place in Sudan have been a result of the *Janjaweed* (militant Arabic tribesmen) conducting raids against the non-Arabs within the country.

Al-Bashir's association with Islamic **fundamentalist** groups has made him a figure of controversy, even though his relationship with National Islamic Front founder **Hassan al-Turabi** dissolved at the end of the 1990s after the latter tried twice to overthrow him. Accused of genocide and war crimes for the incidents in Darfur, on 12 July 2010 the International Criminal Court (ICC) issued a warrant to the Sudanese government for al-Bashir, making him the first sitting head of state to be indicted by the court. However, despite this indictment, he has continued to rule as head of the Sudanese government and has not been turned over to the ICC tribunal when visiting other states. This is due mostly to his decision to travel only to nations with which he has a close relationship and alliance.

BASRA, RIAZ (1967–2002). Founder of *Lashkar-e-Jhangvi* in 1996, Riaz Basra was born in Sargodha, **Pakistan**. In 1985, he joined *Sipha-e-Sahaba* and fought in the Soviet-Afghan War (1979–1989) alongside his fellow *mujahideen*. Basra formed *Lashkar-e-Jhangvi* along with other former members of *Sipha-e-Sahaba* because they felt that their father group should be more aggressive in its implementation of *sharia*. This **Sunni** Muslim group targeted members of the **Shiite** school of **Islam** and was banned in August 2001. Basra was killed during a botched attack in Punjab, Pakistan, at a Shia village on 14 May 2002.

BAY'A. *See* ALLEGIANCE.

BELHADJ, ABDUL HAKIM (1966–). Former leader of the **Libyan Islamic Combatant Group**, Abdul Hakim Belhadj emerged as the leader of the Tripoli Military Council of the Libyan rebellion after playing a formidable role during the 17 February 2011 battle at Bab Azizia. Bab Azizia was the headquarters of **Muammar Qadhafi**. He is arguably one of the most prominent members of what is referred to as "The Dawn of the Mermaid," or the period of the liberalization of Tripoli.

His military life began in 1988 when he went to **Afghanistan** to join the **jihadists** there. After relocating to various countries, he joined the Libyan Islamic Combatant Group during its inception. He returned to **Libya** in 1994 and began to fully promote the downfall of the Qadhafi regime but then returned to Afghanistan because of security threats and continued to travel extensively. He was arrested in Malaysia in February 2004 and was transferred to Bangkok to be interrogated by the Central Intelligence Agency (CIA). Afterwards, the CIA deported him to Libya, and he was released along with 214 other incarcerated militants from the Abu Slim jail in March 2010 by Qadhafi's son, Saif al-Islam, in the hope of bringing about reconciliation and **peace**. But not a year later, he joined the Libyan insurgency against Qadhafi in February 2011 and has been influencing and inspiring the rebels ever since. *See also* AL-HASADI, ABDUL HAKIM.

BELHADJ, 'ALI (1955–). Born in **Tunisia**, Belhadj is the vice president of the **Islamic Salvation Front** in **Algeria** and represents its **Salafi** branch. Ideologically inspired by Islamic thinkers such as **Hasan al-Banna** and **Sayyid Qutb**, Belhadj is a spiritual leader for many of his followers. At an early age, he was involved with the **Armed Islamic Group** and was jailed from 1982 to 1983 for his participation in the Algerian Islamic movement. Strict in his **interpretation** of **Islam** and politically extreme, he developed a relationship with the Algerian **Abbasi Madani** and formed the Islamic Salvation Front with him in 1989. Although both were arrested for their antiestablishment actions and demonstrations in Algiers in 1991, Belhadj was released in 1997. As part of his release conditions (he was originally sentenced to 12 years), Belhadj was ordered to abstain from any and all political activity. Again, in July 2005, he was held in custody until March 2006 for advocating for the insurgents in **Iraq** while on Al-Jazeera television; he was released under the **Charter for Peace and National Reconciliation**. Belhadj was also active in the 5 January 2011 Bab El Oued, Algeria, protests and was arrested the same day for "inciting an armed rebellion."

BELMOKHTAR, MOKHTAR (1972–). Born in Ghardaïa, **Algeria**, on 1 June 1972, this prominent **Islamist** is the head of one of the major brigades of **al-Qaeda in the Islamic Maghreb**'s (AQIM) *Katibat el Moulanthamoun* (literally translates to "those who hide their face"). Active in northern **Mali** and a former Algerian soldier, Mokhtar Belmokhtar is the longest-serving active group leader. In 1991, at the age of 19, he trained in **Afghanistan**'s *Khalden* and *Jihad Wal* camps as well as **al-Qaeda**'s *Jalalabad* camp. He has been incredibly successful in establishing familial connections with the Muslim and Tuareg tribes in northern Mali, southern Algeria, Chad, Niger, and **Mauritania**, allowing for easier transport of goods and hostages by AQIM. In 2003, Belmokhtar also worked with the Algerian extremist Saifi Ammari to master and utilize the Saharan environment for the **Salafist Group for Preaching and Combat** (SGPC), now AQIM.

Belmokhtar officially joined the Islamist organization in 1998. In 2003, when **Abdelmalek Droukdel** was named **Hassan Hattab**'s successor of the SGPC, Belmokhtar broke his ties with the group since Belmokhtar believed that he should have been chosen as the new leader. Since then, he is supposedly pursuing his own form of the **jihad** in the Sahara, but he is still in connection with AQIM leaders. A subject of international arrest warrants for his participation in countless Islamist activities, Belmokhtar has been sentenced to life imprisonment (in absentia) in June 2004, March 2007, and March 2008 in Algeria.

Among many crimes, he was instrumental in the December 2008 kidnapping of two Canadian UN diplomats and the January 2011 abduction of two French nationals in Niger. Belmokhtar has mastered navigating the Sahara, maneuvers small yet extremely mobile battalions of troops, and is constantly moving across the borders to avoid detection. For years, the experienced militant has been the key facilitator between Algerian jihadi groups and al-Qaeda as well as the main weapons and materials supplier in the North African desert. Belmokhtar's reliability in the supplying of troops and goods into the Sahara and Sahel regions has made him one of the most important figures in the Islamist movement.

BENEVOLENCE INTERNATIONAL FOUNDATION (BIF). Once regarded as a nonprofit charity group in **Saudi Arabia**, the BIF (originally named the Benevolence International Committee) was realized to be merely a financial front for **al-Qaeda** before being banned by the UN Security Council. Established in 1988 by Adel bin Abdul-Jalil Batterjee (brother-in-law of **Osama bin Laden**), BIF reached numerous countries and established offices in many of them, extracting funds from each one. The group explained to its donors that the funds were going toward "those afflicted by war" and that the donations were being used for providing food for the poor, improving education, giving medical treatment, and providing housing for refugees.

By 1993, BIF assumed its official name and took an office in Chicago, Illinois, that was headed by Enaam Arnaout. Indeed, on 15 June 1994, an American ambassador visited the Chicago office and declared it to be a humanitarian organization—unaware of its true objectives. Finally, in December of that same year, the U.S. Federal Bureau of Investigation received intelligence of two men (also members of BIF) who were funding a **terrorist** plot that was meant to take place the following month. After a formal investigation, the objectives and activities of BIF were found out. It was revealed that the organization not only provided funding but directly purchased ammunition for al-Qaeda as well as other **extremist** groups in **Afghanistan**, Chechnya, and **Pakistan**. However, during the 2003 trial, Arnaout was convicted only of racketeering as part of a plea bargain. *See also* CHECHEN TERRORISM.

BENKIRANE, ABDELILAH (1954–). A **Sunni** politician from **Morocco**, Abdelilah Benkirane is also the leader of the **Justice and Development Party**. He entered this position in July 2008 and is moderate in his Islamist sociopolitical stance. After his **Islamic political party** won a majority of the parliamentary seats during the November 2011 elections, he was appointed prime minister of Morocco on 29 November 2011.

BERSATU/**UNITY.** A Unitarian separatist movement, *Bersatu* has been active in the south of Thailand since 1991. When the Thai government wanted to begin formal negotiations in June 2005 with the Islamic separatist groups, the government chose this group to initiate the discussions with. The negotiations took place in the hope of stopping the Islamic insurgencies in Thailand. *Bersatu* was chosen because of its good relationship with Malaysia since the Thai government wanted to strengthen its ties with the Malayan government to counter the Islamic threats.

BESLAN SCHOOL SIEGE. Conducted by an Islamic **fundamentalist** Chechen separatist group known as the **Riyad as-Saliheen Martyrs' Brigade**, the school siege was launched on 1 September 2004 at approximately 9:30 a.m. at School Number One in the city of Beslan in North Ossetian, Russia. There, roughly 30 male and female members of the brigade stormed the school donning explosive belts while the school (roughly 1,200 people—800 schoolchildren approximately ages 5 to 14 along with their teachers and parents) was in assembly celebrating the beginning of the new school year. Immediately, the attackers confined everyone to the gymnasium, 82 feet long by 33 feet wide, and executed 20 of the seemingly strongest men. It was here in the gymnasium that the captives and their captors stayed for days without water or food in approximately 90-degree heat. The Riyad as-Saliheen Martyrs'

Brigade placed explosive detonators around the gym, threatening to explode the building with everyone inside if any rescue attempt was made. It had also previously placed guns and weapons underneath the floorboards prior to the operation and made its captives retrieve them during the takeover. Early on in the incident, one child was released with a list of demands that focused mostly on the release of imprisoned comrades. Among their other demands was also to be in contact with the presidents of the regional governments and with Dr. Leonid Roshal, a pediatrician who was instrumental in helping the hostages of the October 2002 Moscow theater siege. The president of the nearby Ingushtian region spoke to the insurgents, and afterward they released 26 women who then carried out a child each. During the entire event, approximately 65 children and one adult were able to escape on their own.

The next day of the takeover saw conflict and frustration as the attackers spoke to Dr. Roshal but were unable to be convinced to release children hostages and were uncompromising on the release of their fellow imprisoned Brigade members. Later in the afternoon, they finally acted with extreme aggression and fired two rocket-propelled grenades at the security vehicles surrounding the school. On the third day, gunfire and explosions began to come from within the building, although there are conflicting reports on why the **violence** began. Nevertheless, the attackers opened fire on their victims and security forces outside. Immediately, the Russian task team responded by blowing up specific parts of the walls so that the hostages could escape, but the incident still resulted in the death of over 300 people and an injury count of over 700—only one of the Brigade members was taken alive.

In the aftermath, Chechen separatist leader Shamil Basayev took full responsibility for the organization of the attack. It was also later reported that the captives were not merely held in confinement but tortured as well. Furthermore, it appears that the attackers took stimulants in order to stay awake during the event and also to counteract any possible use of fentanyl-based gases that the Russian security forces could have used (as they did in the Moscow theater incident). *See also* CHECHEN TERRORISM.

BIN LADEN, OSAMA (1957–2011). Founder of the **al-Qaeda** organization and probably the most universally recognized figure of the contemporary Islamic **fundamentalist** movement, Osama bin Laden was born to a wealthy family in Riyadh, **Saudi Arabia**, on 10 March 1957 and raised under the **Wahhabi** school of **Islam**.

After achieving his education in engineering at King 'Abd al-'Aziz University in Jeddah, Saudi Arabia, Osama bin Laden joined the Afghani war against the Soviet Union (1979–1989) and quickly became one of the leaders of the Afghan Arabs (*Al-Afghan al-'Arab*). It was during this time that he developed his skills of recruitment and influence among fellow Islamic militants. He began to employ hundreds of fellow Afghan Arabs and established training camps to further promote radical fundamentalist actions. His followers were estimated in the thousands as he financially supported many **Islamic groups** and movements that in turn led to more movements forming alliances with him. To further enhance his abilities to finance and arm Islamic militant groups, bin Laden created *Maktab al-Khadamat*, a precursor to al-Qaeda that made the funneling of goods easier and more efficient.

In August 1988, the al-Qaeda organization was officially established after his split from Abdullah Azzam's organization. Wanting to create a stronger military force that would expand after the Soviet withdrawal from **Afghanistan**, he was also ideologically inspired by **Sayyid Qutb**. Through al-Qaeda, bin Laden sought to restore *sharia* (Islamic law) throughout the Muslim world, supported the necessity of the **jihad**, and opposed **Western** forms of civil and political policy. The elimination of the state of **Israel** and the eradication of U.S. forces within the Muslim world was also of the utmost importance to bin Laden. According to bin Laden, the Afghani **Taliban** regime created the only "true" **Islamic state**, and therefore he provided militant assistance to their forces. In return, Afghanistan's Taliban army refused to extradite bin Laden despite the numerous calls for it.

After the end of the conflict in 1989, bin Laden returned to Saudi Arabia as a hero of the jihad. After the Iraqi invasion of Kuwait on 2 August 1990, bin Laden offered his *mujahideen* support to Saudi Arabia but was refused, and U.S. forces entered the skirmish instead. This event heightened his anti-American feelings and strained his relations with Saudi Arabia even further. He was exiled to **Sudan** in 1991 as a result of his radical antigovernment speeches and was stripped of his Saudi Arabian citizenship.

Bin Laden viewed the presence of westerners in the Gulf as an insult to Islam and considered them to be infidels occupying the holy lands of Mecca and Medina. After declaring a *fatwa* against any American occupying force, he was expelled from Sudan and went to Afghanistan in 1996. During this time, he developed a relationship with Islamic militant **Ayman Al-Zawahiri** (now in command of al-Qaeda), and in February 1998 the two declared a *fatwa* under the World Islamic Front for Jihad against Jews and Crusaders, targeting America and all its allies and declaring their wish to regain Mecca and Jerusalem solely for the Muslim people. He continued to stay under the protection of the Taliban army until 2001, when he then went to Waziristan for two years. In 2003, bin Laden finally moved to **Pakistan**, where he remained hidden until his death in 2011.

Bin Laden had been implicated in the financing of various jihadist groups in **Algeria**, Afghanistan, and **Egypt**. He also had ties with extremists in

Bosnia and Sarajevo and was involved with or implicated in numerous mass-casualty attacks against both civilian and military targets. These include the 1993 bombing of the World Trade Center in New York City; the 1996 **Khobar Towers bombing** in Dhahran, Saudi Arabia; and the 7 August 1998 **East African United States embassy attacks**. When he officially claimed responsibility for the **World Trade Center and Pentagon attacks of September 11, 2001**, he became the most wanted terrorist in the world and was declared the major target of the "War on Terror" by the George W. Bush administration of the United States. However, it was the embassy bombings in East Africa that initially placed him on the Federal Bureau of Investigation's Ten Most Wanted List in 1999.

In the wake of these incidents, many countries heightened their security efforts, and the U.S. Special Activities Division was assigned to find and eliminate bin Laden. Countless attempts were made by various Special Forces divisions of not only the United States but also Great Britain, Israel, and France to capture and/or kill bin Laden and Al-Zawahiri at all costs. Finally, on 2 May 2011 (after almost 10 years of tracking) in Abbottabad, Pakistan, a U.S. Navy SEALs operation approved by American President Barack Obama succeeded in killing him. However, many still debate the exact circumstances of his death since the U.S. government stated that his body had been buried at sea. *See also* EXTREMISM; ISLAMIC *SHURA* ARMY.

BIN OMAR, ABDULLAH (1958–). Founder of the **Tunisian Islamic Front** and an extremist Islamic **fundamentalist**, Abdullah bin Omar was imprisoned in 2002 in Guantanamo Bay for his actions in **Afghanistan** and **Pakistan** but was released in 2011 after the **Arab Spring** rebellion in **Tunisia** as part of a compromise to free political prisoners.

For a short period (1990–1992), bin Omar lived in Lahore, Pakistan, as his son-in-law became one of the higher operatives in the **al-Qaeda** organization. According to reports, he was active in the militant Islamist movement as early as the 1980s and stayed for some time in Afghanistan while being completely incorporated with the al-Qaeda militants and their associates as well as receiving financial assistance from the group. During this time, he also held the position of training operatives in various al-Qaeda camps and specialized in antiaircraft missiles. When bin Omar was arrested in spring 2002, he was found staying in the Pakistani home of a *Lashkar-e-Tayyiba* member.

BLACK HAND ORGANIZATION/*AL-KAFF AL-ASWAD*. Founded in 1930 by Izz ad-Din al-Qassam in the then British Mandate of **Palestine**, the Black Hand was an anti-Zionist organization that al-Qassam led until his death in 1935. The origins of the group go back to a revolt that al-Qassam led in 1921 in **Syria**. After its failure, he went into exile in Haifa, **Israel**, and there began to recruit and train Arabs to fight against the Jews in Palestine—it was from this that the Black Hand Organization began. From 1930 to 1935, the group claimed responsibility for the deaths of nearly 10 Jews and was comprised of approximately 200 to 800 militants.

After al-Qassam's death on 20 November 1935, the group largely disbanded, but much of it remained intact and continued to promote the group's anti-British/anti-Zionist platform. Some even participated in the Arab revolt that took place from 1936 to 1939 in Palestine and called themselves *Qassamiyun* (Followers of al-Qassam). *See also* IZZ AD-DIN AL-QASSAM BRIGADES.

BLACK SEPTEMBER ORGANIZATION (BSO). Established in December 1971 in order to gain retribution for the ousting of the **Palestinian Liberation Organization** (PLO) from **Jordan** during the "Black September" of 1970, the BSO was established by the PLO majority group, **Al-Fatah**. The actions of "Black September" involved the hijacking of four commercial airliners all from different companies (British Overseas Air Company, Pan American World Airways, SwissAir, and Trans World Atlantic) that were destined for New York City, except the British Overseas Air Company flight, which was headed to London. Occurring on 6 September 1970, the Pan American World Airways flight was redirected to Cairo and the others to Jordan. Orchestrated by the Popular Front for the Liberation of Palestine (PFLP), finally, on 12 September, approximately 400 passengers were released from custody, and the aircraft were bombed. In the wake of this event, Jordanian King Hussein declared martial law on 16 September and ordered an attack on and expulsion of all Palestinian forces within the country, resulting in a large number of Palestinian deaths and the elimination of the PLO in Jordan. It was in reaction to this suppression of Palestinians within Jordan that the BSO was established.

However, even though the organization was originally set up to defend Palestinian interests in Jordan, the BSO began to spread its **violence** to other countries, such as Israel, and targeted all **Western** forces as well. The group was led the whole time by Salah Khalaf (a.k.a. Abu Iyad) and had made numerous **assassination** attempts on King Hussein of Jordan. The group's most infamous act is the murder of the Israeli Olympic team during the 1972 Summer Olympics in Munich, Germany. During the incident, all 11 members of the Israeli team were killed along with a German civilian and five of the eight BSO aggressors. Consistently violent, the organization carried out at least 35 attacks, including assassinations, **bombings**, and kidnappings. As the years passed, it seems as though the BSO focused almost all of its efforts on targeting Israeli citizens, military, and politicians. With the increased security threat to the country and its citizens, Israel used the Israeli Wrath of God and Israeli Defense Forces to target and to eliminate BSO operatives. Finally, *Al-Fatah* announced its decision to dissolve the organization in December 1974. Many members of the group then joined the PFLP or the **Fatah Revolutionary Council**.

BLASPHEMY/*TAJDEEF*/*SUBB*. Punishable by death in **Islam**, in accordance with *sharia* (Islamic law), blasphemy is defined as slandering or maligning the faith or any aspect of it. Such affronts include defiling a mosque, making ill-intentioned statements about **Allah** or the **Prophet Muhammad**, or not partaking properly in daily prayers or rituals, to name a few. When a state adheres to the jurisdictions on blasphemy, such as in **Pakistan**, other consequences include imprisonment or fines. Usually, a *fatwa* is also declared against that person. As such, blasphemy is one of the gravest crimes in Islam.

For radical Islamists, there is a range of acts that are considered to be blasphemous, such as merely expressing different opinions besides the common ones about Islam or Islamic history (e.g., the ancient times, the **Prophet Muhammad**'s Companions, the gathering of the **Quran**, the origin of the **Hadiths**, and the life of the Prophet, to name a few). When Islamic **fundamentalists** carry out their punishment on blasphemers, torture and mutilation can also occur besides death. In addition, many times, not only the blasphemer but also his or her family and friends can be threatened because they are considered to be responsible for not stopping his or her blasphemy. Islamic **extremists** also consider those who speak out against condemning one of blasphemy as blasphemers themselves. This is found in the Islamic principle of "Ordering the Good and Blaming the Bad" (*al-amr bil maaruf wal nahy 'an al-munkar*). A contemporary example of this occurred on 4 January 2011, when Salmaan Taseer, the governor of Punjab, was killed by his own bodyguard (an adherent of Islamic fundamentalism) for supporting amendments to the Pakistani blasphemy laws.

However, the seriousness of blasphemy does not exist just within Islam. **Christianity** also takes the matter quite seriously. But the difference is in its contemporary reactions. For example, although an act may offend many Christians or is deemed to be blasphemous, no modern "Christian state" would punish such a crime, as is the case in the **Islamic states**. In fact, the last blasphemy-related corporal punishment in the Christian world took place in 1697 in Great Britain. This is due to the fact that most Christian-dominated nations are also **democracies**, which separate the powers of church and state. This is not the case in Islam, where the dogma is to unwaveringly guide both the political and the religious lives of the people. In addition, most Muslims believe that a blasphemer is beyond salvation, whereas in Christianity, reparations can be made in the name of the sinner.

Some of the most notable public cases of blasphemy are **Salman Rushdie**'s 1988 publication of *The Satanic Verses*, which defamed the history of Islam to its adherents by telling imaginary stories about the Prophet Muhammad; the 2005 ***Jyllands-Posten* Muhammad cartoon controversy**, which insulted the image of the Prophet to Muslims; and the condemnation of Asia Bibi in 2010. Asia Bibi's case is interesting not only because it took place in Pakistan but also because her arrest was called for by the Islamists within the country. Bibi, a Pakistani Christian, was sentenced to death in November 2010 for verbally praising her faith to her Muslim coworkers. It was considered as a missionary action that aimed to make these people leave Islam and convert to Christianity. She has been imprisoned since, and her family went into hiding. Even when Pakistani President Asif Ali Zardari (in office from 2008 to the present) called for a pardon of Bibi, Pakistani protestors took to the streets. It should be noted that almost the entire population in Pakistan supports the death penalty for a blasphemy conviction, but the accusation is taken very seriously throughout the Muslim world as well.

Individuals have been accused of blasphemy or of insulting Islam in various countries for speaking ill of Allah, finding fault with Islam or with Muhammad (**Afghanistan**), slighting the Prophet or a member of his family or writing Muhammad's name on the walls of a toilet, damaging a Quran, spitting at the wall of a mosque (Pakistan), figuratively depicting Allah or Muhammad (**Egypt**), invoking Allah while committing a forbidden act (**Sudan**), expressing an atheist or a secular point of view, publishing or distributing such a point of view (**Nigeria**), flouting the rules prescribed for Ramadan, whistling during prayers (Indonesia), insulting religious scholarship, or claiming that forbidden acts are not forbidden (**Iran**). *See also* APOSTASY; HERESY; *JAHILI* SOCIETIES.

BOKO HARAM. An **Islamic group** based in Nigeria, *Boko Haram* seeks the application of *sharia* (Islamic law) and the establishment of an **Islamic state**, particularly in northern Nigeria, and was established in 2002 in Maiduguri, Nigeria. Officially, the group is named *Jama'at Ahl as-Sunna Li-adda'awa wa al-Jihad* (Association of Sunnis for the Propagation of Islam and for Holy War), but it is more commonly referred to as *Boko Haram*, which is a phrase that loosely translates to "Non-Islamic education is forbidden." The use of *Boko Haram* reflects the group's opposition to all **Western** influences.

Since its inception, the group was led by **Muhammad Yusuf**, who forcefully advocated for a social and educational reform throughout the country that would eliminate all Western influences and purely promote Islamic-based **methods**. Thoroughly ideologically austere, members of the group are forbidden to partake in any activity that is Western or Western based. This resistance can be traced back to the 1903 fall of the Sokoto **caliphate** to the British forces. Since the British control, many have resisted Western influences of all kinds.

Yusuf and his followers have created an Islamic school (*madrasa*) and mosque that have attracted non-Nigerians as well. However, the *madrasa* came under criticism for just being a recruiting center for future **jihadists**. The group also received a lot of international attention following a great deal of violence that took place in Nigeria in 2009. In July of that year, the Nigerian police began an official investigation of the group after allegations that *Boko Haram* was aggressively arming itself. In response, several of the group's leaders were imprisoned in Bauchi, and an ensuing fight with the Nigerian security forces began, resulting in the deaths of hundreds. During these attacks, Yusuf was killed on 30 July and was succeeded by **Abubakar Shekau**, Yusuf's deputy.

More recently, the group was responsible for the 7 September 2010 release of over 700 inmates from a Bauchi prison. On 2 October 2010, *Boko Harum* pledged **allegiance** to **al-Qaeda in the Islamic Maghreb** (AQIM) during an announcement through AQIM's media division *al-Andalus* calling on Nigerians to wage jihad. It was actually a *Boko Haram* leader, Muhammad Abu Bakr bin Muhammad al-Shakwa, who pledged allegiance to AQIM leader **Abdelmalek Droukdel** in response to an offer of assistance that Droukdel had made several months prior. This offer was not only symbolic but also practical since it allowed for the exchange of expertise, training of Nigerian fighters, and greater finances.

In the days leading up to the 26 April 2011 Nigerian presidential election, *Boko Haram* conducted multiple operations: on 28 January, a candidate was assassinated; on 1 April, a Bauchi police station was attacked; 9 April saw the bombing of a polling facility; the office of the Independent National Electoral Commission was bombed on 15 April; and 14 prisoners at an Adamawa state prison were freed on 22 April. The group announced that it would stop the attacks if its conditions (the removal of Senator Ali Modu Sheriff from office and the return of its mosque in Maiduguri) were met, but the amnesty was rejected on 9 May. On 29 May, the group conducted a series of bombings in northern Nigeria that killed approximately 15 people. A suicide bomber from the group then attacked the UN headquarters in Abuja, the federal capital of Nigeria, on 26 August 2011, killing more than 20 people. On 25 December 2011, the group conducted a suicide attack in Madalla, located near Abuja, against Christians in Nigeria, killing dozens. This same type of attack occurred a year earlier in 2010. On 21 January 2012, the group killed approximately 185 people in the Nigerian town of Kano. As of this writing, the group continues with its policies of violence and aggression against all those who do not succumb to its radical ideologies. Yet, increasingly, *Boko Haram* has been focusing its efforts to liberate northern Nigeria (which is mainly Muslim) from southern Nigeria (which is where the Christian community resides). The events of the **Arab Spring** and the independence of southern **Sudan** have given more hope that the group is succeeding in its endeavors.

BOMBING. A typical modus operandi of Islamic **fundamentalist** groups, bombings of governmental and administrative buildings of heavily populated public zones have become popular since the 23 October 1983 Beirut airport bombing. The incident was part of a series of anti-**Western** attacks that also included the 18 April 1983 bombing of the U.S. embassy in West Beirut, a 4 November 1983 bombing of **Israeli** security forces in Tyre, and an attack that occurred the same day as the Beirut airport bombing that was directed at a French military headquarters in Beirut. The airport bombing was carried out by a **suicide bomber** who drove a truck into a building at a location that was currently being used as a temporary barracks for U.S. military personnel. It resulted in the death of more than 241 U.S. soldiers and wounded over 60. All the previously mentioned attacks in the series had definite similarities: "**martyrs**" driving trucks into their targets with incredible precision, causing huge amounts of damage and great loss of life. For the Beirut airport bombing, the bomb on the truck was equipped with the equivalent of 12,000 pounds of TNT that was combined with hexogen (a highly complex and potent explosive) that was wrapped around cylinders of gas and driven into a structural pillar in order to create the most damage.

The great amount of expense and technical knowledge that was needed not only to make the explosive itself but also to reconnoiter the places attacked led many experts to believe that the attacks were government sponsored. In addition, for two years, no group or organization took responsibility for the attacks. Both of these features are common characteristics of explosive operations conducted by Islamic **extremists**.

However, an undisclosed report stated that Abu Mushlih ('Imad Mughniyah), leader of the **Islamic Revolutionary Guards** in Baalbak, **Lebanon**, was the commander of the operation. Finally, on 16 February 1985, the **Iranian** *Hizbullah* claimed responsibility under the name **Islamic Jihad**. In the aftermath of these attacks, the harsh and brutal tactics of the Lebanese became too dangerous for American military interests, and in February 1984, the **United States** military withdrew its forces from Lebanon. Effects are still being felt from the Beirut airport bombing, as family members of some of the servicemen killed filed lawsuits in 2001 against the **Iranian** government under the Antiterrorism and Effective Death Penalty Act of 1996. The Beirut incident is unique not only because it was one of the first major contemporary Islamist attacks but also because it could be seen as a type of standard that occurs in both execution and effect. Other examples include the **East African United States embassy attacks**, the **London bombings of 7 July 2005**, the **Madrid bombings of 11 March 2004**, and the bombing of the USS *Cole*. *See also* BROOKLYN BOMBING PLOT; VIOLENCE.

BRIGADES OF THE MARTYR YASIR ARAFAT. *See* AL-AQSA MARTYRS' BRIGADE.

BRIGADES OF THE REVOLUTION OF THE TWENTY. Comprised mostly of former militants from the disbanded Iraqi army, the 1920 Revolution Brigades is an aggressive **Sunni** Muslim group active in **Iraq**. Members of the group have announced their intention to create an **Islamic state** throughout the country through brutal tactics, opting for **martyrdom** over surrender or the abandonment of their cause. Primarily active in and around Baghdad, the group's name references the Iraqi revolution against English colonial rule in 1920. In adopting this moniker, the group makes analogous the goals of the nationalists during the colonial revolution and the current cause of the Islamists. Using guerilla tactics to perpetuate its **jihad** against the coalition forces' occupation, the group has also been accused of numerous **bombings** and kidnappings. On 18 March 2007, the group announced its division into two units: **Conquest of Islam** and **Islamic Jihad**.

Shortly before this separation, the 1920 Revolution Brigades rejected an offer by the Islamic state in Iraq to form an alliance. In retaliation for their refusal, the Islamic state in Iraq took up arms against the group. During a 27 March 2007 attack, the leader of the 1920 Revolution Brigades, Harith Dhahir Khamis al-Dari, was killed. Ever since, there have been periodic skirmishes between the two groups. The **United States** has also claimed that the group was working with the **Western** powers to combat **al-Qaeda** cells. However, 1920 Revolution Brigade spokespeople have consistently denied this claim.

BROOKLYN BOMBING PLOT. On 29 July 1997, the U.S. State Department received a threatening letter stating that unless **Sheikh Omar Abul Rahman**, **Sheikh Ahmad Yasin**, and **Ahmad Ramzi Yusuf** were released from prison, a series of **bombings** would soon take place throughout New York City. Days later, on 31 July, the New York City police force raided a Brooklyn apartment in which the suspected plotters were staying (this information was based on an anonymous tip that was called in). The suspects, Lafi

Khalil and Gazi Ibrahim Abu Mezer from **Palestine**, were detained by the police force as they were about to set off a series of explosions during the raid. Inside the apartment, bomb-making materials and a copy of the letter that was sent to the State Department were found. Detailed plans were also found inside the apartment that indicated a plot to bomb a public transportation bus and a subway station on Atlantic Avenue in New York City. However, neither one of the suspects seemed to have any connection with a militant or political **Islamic group**. A year after the incident, on 23 July 1998, Khalil was acquitted of the charges and was convicted of possessing a false alien registration document, whereas Mezer was convicted of attempting to use a weapon of mass destruction. *See also* UNITED STATES OF AMERICA.

BUDDHAS OF BAMIYAN. Carved from 544 to 644 into a sandstone cliff in the Hindu Kush mountain region in the Bamyan Valley of **Afghanistan**, the Buddhas of Bamiyan were two standing figures of Vairocana and Sakyamuni that were 180 and 121 feet tall (55 and 37 meters, respectively). Until the ninth-century Islamic invasion, the area was controlled by the Buddhist kingdom of Gandhara and was the place of many Kushan monasteries. It was the monks who lived in these monasteries who carved the statues and, at the time, decorated the site with frescoes, jewels, and other adornments. They were the largest standing sculpted Buddhas in the world until their destruction.

On 2 March 2001, the **Taliban** army, using dynamite, blew up the statues over a period of several days, as the Buddhas were declared idolatrous. The international condemnation of their destruction (and, in turn, the Buddhist heritage in Afghanistan) was immediate, and it proved just how serious the Taliban army's **fundamentalist** ideologies are. The site was designated by the UN Educational Scientific and Cultural Organization as an endangered World Heritage site in 2003. The destruction of the Bamyan Buddhas has come to represent the religious oppression of Islamic fundamentalism in Afghanistan. In fact, the Taliban had announced its desire to destroy the statues in 1997, but since, at that time, it did not control the area, the plans were not put into effect until some years later. Once the Taliban took control of the area (and most of the country), it stated that these statues were anti-**Islam** and must be destroyed. This is just one of the major examples of the censorship and strict outlawing of all things deemed "un-Islamic" to the Taliban regime in 1996–2001. Their destruction was officially ordered by Abdul Wali, the minister for the propagation of virtue and the prevention of vice in Afghanistan under the Taliban, as he declared it justified by *sharia* (Islamic law). *See also* ART.

C

CALIPH. *See* CALIPHATE.

CALIPHATE. Historically, the caliphate has been an ideal representative of unity in **Islam** for the past 14 centuries. In medieval Islamic history, a caliphate is the supreme political power that **governs** all aspects of life in all of the Islamic territories. During the medieval period, three major caliphates existed: the Umayyad caliphate (661–750), the Abbasid caliphate (750–1258), and the Ottoman caliphate (1517–1924). The establishment of the caliphate has been the focal point for many Islamic **fundamentalists**, and its implementation is desired among almost all the fundamentalist organizations. The caliphate combines **theology** and **jurisprudence**, which should vary with the changes in **society** over time but still should never separate from its Islamic basis. For many fundamentalists, the caliphate is a unifying force that brings with this unity a sense of purity and superiority to Islam.

According to contemporary Islamic fundamentalists such as **Hassan al-Banna**, the new caliphate in Islam cannot exist without social, economic, and educational reformation throughout. Therefore, the caliphate will operate best if it is governing a society that is already on a path of religious and intellectual advancement. Structurally, the caliphate must be supported by different councils and leagues that would be responsible for the electing of the caliphs (those who head the caliphate). The caliph, in return, applies the commands of *sharia* (Islamic law), which is outlined in the **divine texts**. Since this mode of **government** is complicated and not easily attained, it has been argued that a caliphate was not enacted in many Muslim countries because the need for a structurally practical organization was of greater concern. The establishment of a caliphate is completely related and interwoven with the concept of a pure and united **Islamic state**. The Islamic system (*nizam*) of the caliphate is also supported by *Hizb ut-Tahrir al-Islami*, *Jamaat al-Jihad al-Islami*, and the **Muslim Brotherhood**, among many others.

CALL. *See* DA'WA.

CARLOS THE JACKAL (1949–). Born Ilich Ramírez Sánchez, this Venezuelan militant was incredibly active throughout the 1970s while he was head of the Popular Front for the Liberation of Palestine. His most infamous operation is probably a siege at the Organization of Petroleum Exporting Countries (OPEC) Secretariat headquarters in Vienna, Austria, on 21 December 1975. During this attack, "Carlos the Jackal" held 11 OPEC heads hostage and collected a ransom totaling over $50 million from **Iran** and **Saudi Arabia**. However, after this incident, he was rarely heard from or seen again, and many experts believed that he was either killed or covertly working at a training camp in **Libya** or **Syria**. Finally, in 1993, the French government was made aware that he was living in Syria, and his extradition was repeatedly called for. Feeling pressure from other governments as well, Syria eventually expelled Sánchez, and he relocated to **Sudan**. On 14 August 1994, the Sudanese police force arrested him, and he was given to the French officials. While in captivity, he openly admitted that he had murdered 83 people in the 1970s and 1980s and was also suspected of being involved with over 30 other aggressive attacks besides the OPEC incident. He received a trial (which lasted only 10 days) and was sentenced to life imprisonment on 24 December 1997. Sánchez is currently serving his sentence in Clairvaux prison and claims that he has converted to **Islam** while in detention.

CEASE-FIRE. *See HUDNA.*

CENTRAL ASIAN ISLAMIC ACTIVITY. The spread of Islamic activity to Central Asia is a direct result of the Soviet War in **Afghanistan**, which lasted from 1979 until 1989. Prior to this occupation, the Soviet Union was completely cut off from its neighboring Muslim world to the south, and Islamic tendencies within the Union of Soviet Socialist Republics were totally suppressed. After the Soviet War in Afghanistan, many soldiers returned to their native land, inspired by the very same Afghan *mujahideen* that they had been fighting. Feelings of distinction and abhorrence toward the Soviet rulers that some of these soldiers now felt were coupled with the new fascination for the Muslim world that they were so severed from. This dynamic was the basis for the Islamic movement within Soviet Central Asia, and many groups, such as the **Islamic Movement of Uzbekistan**, were created in Kazakhstan, Kyrgyzstan, Tajikistan, and Uzbekistan. *See also* EAST TURKESTAN ISLAMIC MOVEMENT; ISLAMIC RENAISSANCE PARTY OF TAJIKISTAN.

CENTRAL INTELLIGENCE AGENCY HEADQUARTERS ATTACK. Occurring on 25 January 1993, a gunman entered the Central Intelligence Agency (CIA) headquarters in Langley, Virginia, and opened fire using an

AK-47 machine gun, resulting in the deaths of two CIA employees (analyst Lansing Bennett and communications worker Frank Darling) and injuring two other CIA employees as well as a repair man. After a special operation conducted by the Federal Bureau of Investigation, the assailant was captured on 17 June 1997 in **Pakistan** and was extradited to the **United States** for trial. The gunman was identified as Pakistani immigrant Mir Aimal Kansi, who seemed to use the U.S. involvement in the Middle East and the influence in **Pakistan** as his motives for the attack. After his trial, he was sentenced to life imprisonment for the murder of Bennett and received the death penalty for the murder of Darling (since it was deemed that with Darling, he used excessive brutality). Kansi was executed by lethal injection on 14 November 2002 in a Virginia state penitentiary.

CIVIL HARMONY ACT. *See* ALGERIAN CIVIL CONCORD.

CHARITABLE SOCIETY FOR SOCIAL WELFARE (CSSW). Formed by **Sheikh 'Abd al-Majid Zandani**, the CSSW was set up as a funding organization that allegedly financed **al-Qaeda**. Another infamous Islamic **extremist, Anwar al-Awlaki**, served as CSSW's vice president from 1998 to 1999. Through his dynamic presentations and lectures, al-Awlaki was able to attract a vast amount of monetary support for the group, as he was a notable member of **al-Qaeda in the Arabian Peninsula**.

CHARTER FOR PEACE AND NATIONAL RECONCILIATION. Promoted by Algerian President Abdelaziz Bouteflika, this charter was another way to bring **peace** and stability to **Algeria** in the wake of the Algerian Civil War (1992–2002). It followed the 1999 **Civil Harmony Act** by offering subsequent amnesty to those guilty of most of the violence committed during the war, including those accused of mass murder, **bombings**, and rape. It even granted exoneration to those sentenced in absentia but still outlawed the **Islamic Salvation Front**. Aside from absolution, the charter granted financial compensation to civilians who lost family members during the hostilities and reinstated employees who lost their positions on political grounds. The vote took place on 29 September 2005 and passed with 97.36 percent before finally being approved as law on 28 February 2006. However, the Charter for Peace and National Reconciliation was harshly criticized by **human rights** groups and families of the victims for its lack of judgment and **justice**, which, they argued, comes before reconciliation.

The figures released by the state in October 2010 reported that since this clemency act was established, roughly 7,500 insurgents had given up their arms and surrendered to the state. This legislation also led to the March 2006 release of **'Ali Belhaj** and Abdelhak Layada, two of the most radical Islamists and leader of the Islamic Salvation Front and founder of the **Armed Islamic Group**, respectively. Despite the advancement of peace that this charter was aimed at bringing, the last armed group in Algeria, the **Salafist Group for Preaching and Combat**, rejected the terms of the charter and announced a continuation of its warfare against the Algerian **government**.

CHECHEN TERRORISM. In the aftermath of the fall of the Soviet Union in 1991, a major nationalist and Islamic **fundamentalist** movement began to take hold in the Chechnya region of Russia. The **extremists** hoped to detach Chechnya from Russia, making it its own republic. Ethnographically speaking, the area is comprised mainly of non-Russian Muslims and borders Georgia in the Caucasus Mountain region. If the area successfully gained independence from Russia, then this would have serious implications for the rest of the country. Chechen extremists allegedly received a majority of their tactical support from Georgia, which allowed the rebels to use its Pankisi Gorge and Tbilisi territories for attacks and training. The Chechen militants were mostly former *mujahideen* from the Soviet-Afghan War (1979–1989) and have formed an estimated 15,000-person force.

The events to try to have the region secede from Russia began on 6 September 1991, when a former Soviet militant, Dzhukar Dudayev, led a coup d'état and declared Chechnya an independent state. Problems continued to escalate between the Russian government and the Chechen nationalists when Russia redrafted its constitution on 12 December 1993 and did not recognize the independence of Chechnya. Furthermore, from December 1994 until May 1996, Russian forces tried to regain the territory and suppress the rebellion, but to little avail. The feeble Russian military force resulted only in large Russian casualties and national embarrassment, as the Chechen guerillas conducted numerous **bombings**, kidnappings, and **suicide attacks** on foreigners, Russians, and fellow Chechens alike.

One of the rebels' largest attacks was on a hospital in Kizlyar, Daghestan, on 9 January 1996 in which they captured over 3,000 hostages. Even after a minor **peace** agreement was made between Chechnya and Russia on 27 May 1996, attacks still continued to take place in the Chechnya region. However, these attacks now seemed to result more from friction between the moderate and extremist Chechens. The moderates hoped for a peaceful solution and open **dialogue** with the mother country, whereas the extremist groups desired to no longer have any diplomatic relation with Russia and wanted Chechnya to become an **Islamic state**. Throughout the 1990s, Chechen extremists continued to use aggressive tactics to further push their Islamic agenda, even attempting to **assassinate** Chechen President Aslan Maskhadov on numerous occasions. In fact, many of their methods of **Islamization** proved to be effective, and this convinced Russia to commence another campaign against the extremists in Chechnya on 1 October 1999—usually referred to as the Second Chechen War. Soon after, in December 1999, the Russian security forces occupied most of the region.

More recently, many extremists and their leaders have been allegedly linked to **al-Qaeda**, an accusation that was supported by the 27 December 2002 arrest by French forces that detained a few Arab rebels who claimed that they had ties with al-Qaeda and the Chechen rebels and plotted to attack the Russian embassy in Paris. The increasing acts of **violence** against Chechen civilians increased the population's dislike of the formation of an independent Islamic state of Chechnya. A vote held in the country on 23 March 2003 confirmed that a majority of the population wanted to remain a part of Russia. This resulted in a large number of attacks throughout Chechnya during the beginning of 2003, interestingly enough by **suicide bombers** (*shahidki*) who were **women** and then gained the name "black widows" through the media. The violence continued to increase in 2004, notably with one attack (9 May 2004 at the Dynamo Stadium in Grozny) that resulted in the assassination of Chechen President Akhmed Kadyrov. The al-Qaeda Islambouli Brigades also used a *shahidka* (singular female martyr) in the bombing of a Moscow subway station that killed nine and injured over 50. However, the most recent and most infamous attack by Chechen rebels is the September 2004 **Beslan school siege**. Extremists also tried to hijack a commercial airliner in the Kabardino-Balkaria region capital of Nalchik on 13 October 2005 in hopes of creating an attack similar to that of **11 September 2001**, but it was thwarted by security forces.

The Russian security forces seemed to have attained better counterintelligence information as compared to the beginning of the rebellion in the early 1990s. This may be due to the weakening of the Chechen extremists and the waning popular support throughout the region especially in light of the Beslan school siege, numerous attacks on civilians, use of female suicide bombers, the opposition to the radical Islamic agenda that was being pushed, and the increasing amount of nonnationals in the Chechen army. On 10 July 2006, the Russian security forces killed extremist leader Shamil Basayev, marking the beginning of the decline of the rebel movement. Since his death, only minor attacks have occurred within the region. The decrease in extremist activity has also been secured by the elimination of other leaders within the movement.

CHRISTIANITY. According to the Islamic **fundamentalists**, Christianity (along with **Judaism**) is recognized as an important **religion** for society, but it has been tainted and corrupted throughout **history**. Because of this corruption, Christianity has lost its spiritual relevance and is now simply a product of **Western** materialism. This is because Christianity has also been associated with nondivine elements and has attributed divine characteristics to a man (in Jesus Christ); this has further distanced the religion from its Oneness with God (*tawhid*). Since Christianity is associated with Western society and it was the West that brought imperialism and colonization to the Muslim world, Christianity is regarded with disdain by many Muslims, especially the Islamic fundamentalists. The other problem with Christianity lies with the conflict in **Palestine**. By aiding the Jews in **Israel** to acquire Palestine and the holy lands of **Islam** that lie in that area, Christians are further resented, and some Islamic fundamentalists have even talked about a "Jewish-Christian coalition."

However, the fundamentalist position on Christianity is not just with regard to its relationship with the West but also concerns the more delicate issue of how to deal with Christians living in Arab and Muslim countries. Some counterarguments have also been made that the Christian population even existed within these territories prior to the emergence of Islam. Notably, there is presently a very large Christian community in **Lebanon** and a sizable one among the Palestinians, and over 10 percent of the population in **Egypt** is Coptic. In addition, there are large, if dwindling, numbers of Russian Orthodox Christians in the Central Asian republics that were once part of the Soviet Empire. Within the Russian Federation, there are even more acute problems within Chechnya.

Therefore, these communities have been caught up in the contest between Islam and Christianity not just theoretically but through actual acts of **terrorism** against them. For example, in Egypt the **Muslim Brotherhood** has been very moderate on its views and relations toward the Coptic Christians there and has never been hostile toward them. In addition, any group inspired by the Muslim Brotherhood, *al-Islah*, or *Ennahda* will be moderate in its relationship with Christians. However, the **Egyptian Salafi** movement has constantly been hostile against its Christian population. Two notable acts recently occurred in January 2010, when Egyptian Salafi militants allegedly killed six Coptics in a church in Upper Egypt, and in late 2011 several Coptic churches were burned in Egypt. Other groups that are hostile toward Christians include **al-Qaeda**, *Tehrik-e-Jihad*, *Jamaat-e-Islami*, *al-Takfir wa al-Hijra*, and *al-Muhajiroun*.

COMMITTEE FOR SOLIDARITY WITH ARAB AND MIDDLE EASTERN POLITICAL PRISONERS (CSAMEPP). A **Lebanese** organization that directed much of its aggressive efforts against the French government in the hopes of releasing Georges Ibrahim Abdallah (leader of the Lebanese Armed Revolution Factions), the group is also known as *Comité de soutien aux prisonniers politiques arabes et du Moyen-Orient*. Abdallah was arrested in 1984 in France because of his continued aggressions against **Israeli** and U.S. diplomats within the country. In order to pressure the French government to release him, the CSAMEPP carried out a total of 14 attacks that injured over 170 people and killed 6. Wanting to end the aggressions against civilians, French Prime Minister Jacques Chirac eventually agreed to release Abdallah or impose a light sentence when his case came to court. However, after his trial, Abdallah still received a life sentence of imprisonment. It was in the wake of this trial that it became evident that CSAMEPP was supported by **Iran**. Later, the leader of CSAMEPP, Fouad Ben Ali Saleh, was arrested and sentenced to life imprisonment in 1992, further marking the end of the organization.

CONQUEST OF ISLAM. *See FATAH AL-ISLAM.*

CONSENSUS. *See IJMA'.*

CONSTITUTION/CONSTITUTIONAL RULE. Since **legislation** is viewed by many **fundamentalists** as a divine institution, the **Quran** and the **Hadiths** are used as the ultimate text in forming *sharia* (Islamic law). However, a variation has been formed in contemporary history. Some Islamic fundamentalists (like **Rashed al-Ghannushi**) believe that a **modern** constitution can exist but must be based on the Quran. This has come to be a more moderate view of constitutional rule. However, this method of legislation failed in **Egypt** and came under considerable criticisms. Some **extremists** (such as **Sayyid Qutb**), on the other hand, believe that no human law can ever properly exist and that legislation must look only to the **divine texts** of **Islam** for political guidance. Therefore, *sharia* is often used as the basis for an Islamic constitution since it relies purely on these texts. More recently, events in **Tunisia**, **Egypt**, and other countries involved in the **Arab Spring** have reignited interest in a constitution. *See also* GOVERNMENT.

COUSINAGE. Described as a local mode of verbal sparring between different ethnic groups, *cousinage* creates a **dialogue** of banter in place of conflict. This conflict resolution tactic originated in **Mali** and supports the country's relative cultural stability through the celebration of diversity. While other mechanisms exist to create **peace** and promote tolerance, *cousinage* has been seen as the most successful.

CRESCENT STAR PARTY/CRESCENT STAR FAMILY/*KELUARGA BULAN BINTANG.* The Crescent Star Party is an **Islamic political party** in Indonesia formed in 1960 after the banning of the Masyumi Party by the first president of Indonesia, Kusno Sukarno. When Sukarno was replaced by the New Order in 1965, the Masyumi Party could not be legally revived, so members created the *Parmusi*, the Muslim Party of Indonesia (*Partai Muslimin Indonesia*), in 1971. By 1973, Parmusi merged with other, similar parties and became part of the **United Development Party**. However, on 21 May 1998, when President Suharto resigned, the Masyumi members again sought to revive their group and in doing so renamed themselves the Crescent Star Party. Yusril Ihza Mahendra emerged as the new party's leader and was interestingly enough a former speechwriter to Suharto.

The group desires the implementation of ***sharia*** (Islamic law) within Indonesia and advocates for the total application of a traditional Islamic educational system. During the 1999 elections (the first for the newly organized group), the Crescent Star Party received only 13 of the 560 seats in the People's Representative Council of Indonesia, but Mahendra was appointed minister of justice and law. The spring of 2000 saw a divide within the group and therefore the establishment of the splinter organization, the Indonesian Islamic Party (*Partai Islam Indonesia*). In the 2004 and 2009 elections, the Crescent Star Party increasingly lost votes, and Mahendra was replaced by Malem Sambat Kaban. As of 2011, the party no longer holds any seats in the People's Representative Council but still garnishes some marginal support from over 20 of the 33 Indonesian provinces. *See also MAJLIS SYURO MUSLIMIN INDONESIA.*

D

DAR AL-ISLAM/**ABODE OF ISLAM.** *See DAR AL-HARB.*

DAR AL-HARB/**ABODE OF WAR.** Designated as the land where **Islam** does not rule, *Dar al-Harb* is a territory where, according to Islamic **fundamentalists**, fighting can occur. Therefore, *Dar al-Harb* is not a Muslim area because *sharia* (Islamic law) is not enacted there (not because the population is not Muslim). According to fundamentalist ideologies, the Abode of War is anywhere where *sharia* is not applied regardless of territorial boundaries or demographics. However, if the ruler of the considered land asks for a ceasefire (*hudna*), then the territory ceases momentarily to be considered as an Abode of War. When applying this doctrine to Islamic lands, some contemporary Muslim societies are, however, perceived as not Islamic, and therefore Islam must be augmented. Conversely, the Abode of Islam (*Dar al-Islam*) is the territory where Islam is enacted, and therefore no warfare can take place within it. *See also DAR AL-SULH.*

DAR AL-SULH/**LAND OF TRUCE.** *Dar al-Sulh* is the territory where Muslims accept the presence of infidels on the condition that they recognize the supremacy of **Islam** by paying tribute to the **Islamic state** and honoring the prohibitions set up by that state. Interestingly, this truce can be declared for a set period of time. For example, it can be instated for 10 years, and then the terms will have to be renegotiated or annulled. *See also DAR AL-HARB.*

DARUL ISLAM/**LAND OF ISLAM PARTY.** This is an Indonesian combatant group founded by a radical Muslim politician, Sekarmadjj Maridjan Kartosurwiryo, in West Java on 7 August 1949. This group led a rebellion in Aceh, South Sulawesi, and Kalimantan, Indonesia. In these regions, *Darul Islam* was able to attract even more fighters to its ranks. The group desires to establish an **Islamic state** based on *sharia* (Islamic law) in Indonesia and was comprised mostly of former servicemen at its establishment. Over the years, *Darul Islam* has split into both moderate and extremist (*Jemaah Islamiyah*) factions.

The instability of the Indonesian government during the 1950s allowed the group to grow and eventually control a large part of Java. In addition, the group often referred to itself as "Tentara Islam Indonesia," the Indonesian Islamic Army. However, the strict control of Indonesia that was implemented by President Sukarno (in office, 1945–1967) in 1957 led to the group losing much of its territory and leaders. In June 1962, Kartosurwiryo was captured and executed by the state. His successor, Kahar Muzakkar, was then killed by the state military during an ambush in February 1965. After these events, the group lost much of its vigor and halted its insurgencies in Indonesia. However, although the group was officially deemed as dismantled, some underground groups began to form in the 1970s and 1980s. Known as *Komando Jihad*, most of its members were *Darul Islam* veterans. *See also DAULAH ISLAMIYAH*; *NEGARA ISLAM INDONESIA*.

DAULAH ISLAMIYAH*/ISLAMIC TERRITORY.** This is the name of the project presented by **Jemaah Islamiyah** for the foundation of an **Islamic state** in the entire Southeast Asia. Its specificity lies in its difference from the ***Negara Islam of Sekarmadjj Maridjan Kartosurwiryo (founder of ***Darul Islam***), which accepts the frontiers of the Indonesian state as a transregional Islamic state. Yet both of these platforms aim to unify the same political entities in all the historical regions where **Islam** was spread. These are Indonesia, Malaysia, Singapore, Brunei, South Philippines, and South Thailand.

***DA'WA*/CALL.** Etymologically, *da'wa* translates from Arabic to mean "making an invitation" or "to summon" and signifies the preaching of **Islam** since it is understood as the action of calling people to the truth of Islam. This truth also means that Islam must fight against the distrust in society, which the Islamic **fundamentalists** view as coming from the **West**. It is said that *da'wa* must first be used at the personal level and gradually rise to the international stage, where the true power of Islam will be realized. Through *da'wa*, the *jahili* **society** can no longer exist since its corruption will be removed by the *da'i* (caller or preacher), according to the fundamentalists. Muslims who focus on *da'wa* may be considered a type of missionary in the sense that they encourage people to participate in Islamic prayer, veneration, and piety. Contemporarily, *da'wa* is emphasized as the complete effort of applying Islam to all aspects of life. Using this definition, Islamic fundamentalists have placed *da'wa* at the center of their dogmatic thought. *See also DA'WA IN KUWAIT AND SAUDI ARABIA*; *HIZB-U-TAHRIR*; ISLAMIC CALL IN IRAQ; *JAMAAT-E-ISLAMI*.

***DA'WA* IN KUWAIT AND SAUDI ARABIA.** Active in Kuwait and eastern **Saudi Arabia** during the 1970s and 1980s, *Da'wa* in Kuwait and Saudi

Arabia was a **Shiite**-based **Islamic political party**. The aims of the group centered on replacing the current regimes in those countries with one based on the **Islamic Republic of Iran**. Activities of this group were suppressed by their respective **governments**, but they still managed to gather support and membership. Evidence of Iranian support can be seen as far back as 1992 in Saudi Arabia.

DEMOCRACY/*AL-DIMUCRATIYYA*. To the Islamic **fundamentalists**, the ultimate sovereignty comes only from **Allah**, and man's sovereignty can only be within the boundaries of Islamic law (*sharia*) and consultation (*shura*). Therefore, a democracy practiced within **Islam** must adhere to the aforementioned guidelines. Through the contemporary **history** of Islam, despotic or authoritarian **governments** have ruled in many of the Arabic countries. Some feel that as long the Muslim **interpretation** of democracy remains faithful to the guidelines previously mentioned, it will also be a successful bridge between the East and **West**. Many popular Islamic fundamentalists, such as **Hasan al-Banna**, **Rashed al-Ghannushi**, and **Hasan al-Turabi**, have discussed the democratic possibilities in Islam. However, the more radical fundamentalists have denied any desire to open any such **dialogue** and want an Islam based purely on the **Quran** and completely separate of any Western influence—an association that democracy has. The main stumbling block in democratizing Islam is the difference between **divine governance** (*hakimiyya*), which is emphasized in Islam, and human governance, which is emphasized in a democracy.

In practice, this broad range in perspective can especially be seen when one investigates different **Islamic groups** and their relationship toward and perception of democracy. There are **Islamic political parties** that derive their ideologies from democracy (considered the more moderate groups) or are influenced by the concept. The **Alliance for Justice and Democracy** is an example of one such group. Many have even announced promises of installing and adhering to democratic practices if elected. However, there are some which still wish to have *sharia* be the dominant form of **legislation**—this is where "**Islamization**" comes in. *Hizb-u-Tahrir* and the **Islamic Iran Participation Front** are examples of this type of party. More radical movements, on the other hand, have very little concern for democracy in their programs and discourse, although they repeatedly claim to represent the people or be acting for the good of the people. These statements are usually made to mobilize an opposition against despots, be they dictators or aristocrats. Yet, within their own movements, there is precious little internal democracy, and the ways in which leaders or policies are chosen is very obscure. Indeed, in many cases, the leader of a particular group is deemed *amir* and has superior authority.

In 2011, the **Muslim Brotherhood** created the political party Liberty and Justice (*al-Hurriya wal Adala*) to run in the Egyptian legislative elections. The **Egyptian Salafists** did the same and founded, months before the election, the Light Party (*Al-Nour*). The same trend occurred with the **Muslim Brotherhood in Libya** and the **Tunisian** Islamists. Many new Islamist parties were created in order to take part in these elections. Notably, in Egypt, *al-Wasat* (Middle), *al-Asalah* (Authenticity), and *al-Fadyla* (Virtue) were founded.

Finally, whatever the views on democracy in the political sense, these groups are not offering democratic ideals to half the population, namely, **women**. This gender is to follow the dictates of men in political and social life as concerns their limited rights and substantial obligations, their behavior, and even their dress. However, Tunisian politics following the **Arab Spring** rebellion had mandated that within the 1,500 lists for the October 2011 election, at least half the names be female. In addition, in 2005, Iraqi legislation declared that 25 percent of their electoral seats be reserved for women politicians. *See also* EQUALITY; INNOVATION; ISLAMIC STATE.

DEMOCRATIC FRONT FOR THE LIBERATION OF PALESTINE (DFLP). A member of the **Palestinian Liberation Organization**, the DFLP seeks to create an independent Palestinian state in the Gaza Strip and West Bank. Formerly known as the Popular Democratic Front for the Liberation of Palestine, the group changed its name to the DFLP in August 1974. It has emphasized the need for a rebellion within the working classes in order to remove imperialist and capitalist influences and thereby create a free Islamic **economy**. This socialist economic ideology has also made the group reject **pan-Islamism** and therefore rename itself. The group now desires only internal financial support, although it used to receive sponsorship from **Syria**, **Libya**, and South **Yemen**. The DFLP also supports the use of militant tactics but stipulates that they should be used only within **Israel** and other occupied areas.

During the 1970s, DFLP's **violence** manifested itself in the form of **bombings** and kidnappings of Israeli nationals. The group's most infamous operation was on 15 May 1974, when three DFLP members stormed a school in Ma'alot, **Israel**, taking 90 schoolchildren hostage. In exchange for the children, the attackers requested the release of 23 Arab prisoners. When negotiations proved to be unsuccessful, the Israeli security forces tried to take over the school, but the DFLP members killed 21 children and 7 adults and injured over 70 more hostages.

The group's membership during its most active years in the 1970s and early 1980s was estimated at about 1,000 to 2,000. Currently, the group might have at most 500. It was also removed from many countries' watch lists because of the sudden lack of activity and sharp decrease in membership. However, the group's activities are still monitored, and its financial assets are subject to sequestration. Politically, the DFLP has also suffered, as in the 2005 **Palestinian Authority** presidential elections, when its candidate won only 3.5 percent of the votes. The year 2006 did see an upswing in the group's activity (it conducted several attacks from June to August 2006), but it has been theorized that this could have been due to the group wanting to still be visible on the Palestinian platform as groups like *Al-Fatah* and **Hamas** became more dominant.

DEMOCRATIC ISLAMIC ARAB MOVEMENT/*AL-HARAKAT AL-ISLAMIYYA AL-'ARABIYYA AL-DIMUCRATIYYA*. Founded in **Jordan** by Yusuf Abu Bakir in 1990, the Democratic Islamic Arab Movement sought total adherence to the **Quran** and the **Hadiths**. Members believed that the **divine texts** and living in the likeness of the **Prophet Muhammad** was the pathway to socioeconomic stability and cultural advancement. However, the group has criticized other Islamic **fundamentalists** for being too rigid and focusing on "frivolous" issues of **Islam**. The group also believes that *sharia* (Islamic law) should not be immediately enacted in a society until proper requirements have been met. Ideologically, the movement believes that the Quran should be implemented in accordance with contemporary society and calls for an open **dialogue** with the **West**.

DEOBAND ISLAMIC MOVEMENT. Founded in the Darul Uloom Deoband *madrasa* in Deoband, India, the movement's adherents (known as Deobandis or the singular Deobandi) claim 1867 as the program's official year of inception. The Deoband movement was founded by scholars Sayyid Muhammad Abid, Zulfigar Ali, Shah Rafi al-Din, Rashed Ahmad Gangohi, Muhammad Yaqub Nanautawi, Muhammad Qasim Nanotvi, and Fadhl al-Rahman 'Usmani, who were committed to austere **interpretations** of the **divine texts** and completely against the British occupants within India. Ideologically influenced by the **Sunni** school of **Islam**, the group also adheres to the Hanafi Islamic school of **jurisprudence**. Politically, the Deoband foundation is not one of legislative affairs, and members had no desire to enter into politics—this apolitical platform has inspired many other groups, such as *Jamaat Ulema-e-Hind*, *Jamaat Ulema-e-Islam*, and *Tablighi Jamaat*. With regard to **Western** civilization, the Deobandis believe (along with many Islamic **fundamentalists**) that Islam has fallen behind socially and culturally because of the West's materialistic and unscrupulous influence on the culture. This "westernization" is the reason, according to the Deobandis, why many Muslims have turned their backs on the teachings of the **Quran** and the **Prophet Muhammad**.

During the early 1900s, the group gained significant influence and saw the establishment of similar movements throughout India and other countries, most notably **Pakistan**. The spreading of the Deoband movement and its ideologies is particularly due to the **activism** of its founding members and original students. Eventually, over 100 **madrasas** associated with the Deoband movement arose within the movement's first years. The Deoband *madrasas* have been consistent in their hopes of "purifying" Islam by looking solely to the Quran and the teachings of Muhammad (the **Hadiths**) for guidance. Adherents state that a Muslim's first obligation is to Islam, then his **nation**—justifying the necessity of the **jihad** as a means of protection. The group has also expressed its desire for a return to the past political structure that used to exist in Islam (specifically during the time of Muhammad), which called for a commander (*amir*) who would ensure an egalitarian system (*nizam*).

However, the movement has not gone without criticism from both religious and secular institutions. These critiques include its lack of progress in the **modernization** of Islam, its conservative stance on the Islamic dress code (especially with regard to **women**), its oppression of the **Shiite** communities, and its constant issuing of *fatwas*, especially on mundane matters. Contemporarily, the Deoband movement continues to influence various fundamentalist groups and movements, specifically the **Taliban** army in **Afghanistan** (many of its leaders attended Deobandi *madrasas* in **Pakistan**).

DEWAN DAKWAH ISLAMIYAH INDONESIA (DDII)/COUNCIL OF PREDICATION FOR INDONESIAN ISLAM. Founded in 1967, DDII was comprised of members from Masyumi (an abbreviation of *Majlis Syuro Muslimin* **Indonesia**, "Assembly of Indonesian Muslims"). DDII was influenced by the **Salafi** ideology and is considered a radical **Islamic group**. The group publishes a newspaper, *Media Dakwah*, in which it expresses the superiority of **Islam** compared to the worldly anti-Islam threats that surround it. The group was led by Muhamaad Natsir until his death in 1993. Since then, DDII has been relatively inactive.

DIALOGUE/*AL-HIWAR***.** For the moderate Islamists, an open dialogue between the East and the **West** is of importance for the progress of civil **society**. They believe that through an open dialogue, both cultures can achieve intellectual and diplomatic advancement. This possible result is seen as more beneficial than the current relationship and therefore should be promoted, according to the moderates. It is also believed that a dialogue between the East and the West could transcend stereotypes, demolish false representations, and bring understanding between the two cultures.

DIVINE GOVERNANCE/*HAKIMIYYA*. The doctrine of divine governance, or *hakimiyya*, is basically the absolute sovereignty of **Allah** in the universality of **Islam**. The **fundamentalists** believe that there is no other authority than He, and therefore man must apply His *sharia* (Islamic law) legislation to **society**. *Hakimiyya* therefore works in conjunction with *tawhid* (oneness of Allah). Islamic scholars like **Abu al-A'la al-Mawdudi** have supported this **theology** of Allah's ultimate governance and furthermore state that any man who claims governance over Allah's is an **apostate**. The radical fundamentalists use *hakimiyya* as a justification for a **jihad** against any group or **government** that does not make *tawhid* its basis. It reasons that humans follow Allah's pathway (**method**) and are therefore followers of Allah, or members of *Hizb Allah* (also referred to as ***Hizbullah***, or Party of God). However, *hakimiyya* is conducted by humans because no person can claim absolute finality of his **interpretation**. *See also* UNIVERSALISM.

DIVINE TEXTS. The divine texts in **Islam** are the **Quran** and the *Sunna* (tradition) of the Prophet, which are also known as the Hadiths. These texts are quintessential to the religion, as they are the only recognized and **legitimate** sources for **interpretation** and guidance in Islam. Moderate **fundamentalists** believe that interpretation of the holy texts, especially the Quran, should be constantly evolving and subject to review since society is continuously changing. This adaptation of the text and its application to every facet of daily activities (from the personal to the administrative) is seen as a must for any solid development of **Islamic society**. Since the Quran is the foundation of Islam, any deviation from that text will negate any advancement that the society wishes to procure. Most fundamentalists (moderate and radical alike) agree that separating the texts from daily life has historically proven to transform the individual's mind-set into one that focuses more on the earthly than the divine. This separation can lead to the development of **paganism**, an impious life, and unbelief (***kufr***).

AL-DJIHAD AL-ISLAMI. *See* ISLAMIC JIHAD UNION.

DJOUADI, YAHIA (1967–). Yahia Djouadi, or Yahia Abu Amar, is known as the leader of **al-Qaeda in the Islamic Maghreb** (AQIM) in the Sahel-Sahara region, which is based in northern **Mali**. Since AQIM's commencement on 11 September 2006, the **Islamic groups** in the Sahel-Sahara region have been trying to concentrate their power in the northern region of the Sahel. Djouadi has been instrumental in financing, preparing, and executing AQIM attacks through this desert area. In order to help **al-Qaeda** achieve its objectives in northern Africa, Djouadi and other AQIM leaders have carried out actions such as the kidnapping and ransoming of hostages and trafficking of weapons and arms. He carried out 11 attacks against the armed forces in **Mauritania** between 2005 and 2011. The most significant of these were one against the Lemgheity military base in June 2005, a **suicide bombing** against the French embassy in the capital of Nouakchott in August 2009, another against the Mauritanian army's Nema camp in August 2010, and the 1 February 2011 suicide attack that targeted Mauritanian President **Mohamed Ould Adbel Aziz**.

DROUKDEL, ABDELMALEK (1971–). Born in Meftah, **Algeria**, Abdelmalek Droukdel (a.k.a. Abu Musab Abdel Wadoud) is the commander of **al-Qaeda in the Islamic Maghreb**. Droukdel joined the **Islamic** cause in 1994 and was trained as an explosives expert while with the **Armed Islamic Group**. After the July 2004 death of Nabil Sahraoui, Droukdel assumed power and became the commander of the **Salafist Group for Preaching and Combat** (SGPC). Under Droukdel's influence, the group formed an official alliance with **al-Qaeda** on 11 September 2006 and then on 11 January 2007 publicly announced that the SGPC would be known as al-Qaeda in the Islamic Maghreb. This alliance is proof of Droukdel's desire to expand the Islamist insurgency to a more global, international stage. A series of attacks, mostly car and **suicide bombings**, targeting everything from government buildings to civilians, has been launched under the control of Droukdel throughout Algeria and the rest of the Islamic Maghreb and Sahel countries. Droukdel and his soldiers also implement the tactic of kidnapping and ransoming hostages to fund their activities. Because of his actions, Droukdel was sentenced to life imprisonment in absentia in Algeria on 27 March 2007. *See also* ABU ZEID, ABDELHAMID.

DUKHTARAAN-E-MILLAT (DeM)/DAUGHTERS OF THE NATION. What is unique to DeM is that it is an all-**women** Islamic organization. Mildly aggressive but nonetheless **fundamentalist** in its ideologies, the group has tried to resort to political means to achieve its goals. Formed in 1987 and based in Kashmir, the organization advocates the merging of Kashmir with **Pakistan**, particularly through the **jihad**. Its membership strength is approximately 350, and it is led by Ayesha Andrabi. DeM has gained media attention mostly because of the contentious remarks Andrabi has made over the past decade. She has regularly and publicly supported *Lashkar-e-Jabbar*, which is actually known for its oppression of women. DeM claims that its advocacy of the traditional role of Muslim women is one of the ways in which social reform can take hold and pure Islamism can reign. The group has also supported other militant **Islamic groups**, such as *Lashkar-e-Tayyiba*, and has opposed **peace** initiatives to help perpetuate the jihad. This radical orthodox outfit has especially been critical of Muslim women who do not adhere to the traditional dress code of Islam. Although DeM has yet to use violent tactics (despite the allegation that a member was responsible for a **bombing** in Srinagar in 1995), experts believe that it acts as envoys for other fundamentalist groups. The group has also been suspected of participating in the *hawala* system, an allegation that has been supported by Andrabi's marriage to the financial chief of ***Jamaat-ul-Mujahideen***, Qasim Faktu. *See also* KASHMIRI SEPARATISM.

E

EAST AFRICAN UNITED STATES EMBASSY ATTACKS. This entry refers to the two simultaneous **bombings** that occurred at two different U.S. embassies in Nairobi, Kenya, and Dar es Salaam, Tanzania, that were allegedly conducted by **al-Qaeda**. The attacks occurred on 7 August 1998. In Nairobi, at approximately 10:30 a.m., a truck riddled with explosives was set off outside the embassy, killing 291 people and injuring more than 5,000. Only 18 of the dead and injured were American nationals, while all the remaining were Kenyans. In Dar es Salaam, a gasoline carrier was allowed entrance into the compound and was then ignited, killing 10 and injuring 77. It was this event that resulted in **Osama bin Laden** and his al-Qaeda organization being placed on the U.S. Foreign Terrorist Organization list. The same day the U.S. administration placed the group on the list (20 August 1998), it launched a rocket attack on three suspected al-Qaeda bases in **Afghanistan** and **Sudan**. Although several suspects were arrested in connection with the 7 August attacks, the detonators were identified as Muhammad Saddiq Odeh and Muhammad Rashed al-Owhali. Odeh was captured by **Pakistani** officials and was extradited to Kenya before being placed in U.S. custody. Al-Owhali, who was originally designated a **martyr** during this attack but instead fled, was captured while receiving medical help at a nearby hospital. Both were sentenced to life imprisonment in 2001. The hunt for the suspects and the investigation of the attacks was the largest conducted by the Federal Bureau of Investigation at that time and also brought to light the lack of security within foreign compounds. This resulted in the tightening of security measures in all U.S. foreign structures worldwide. The investigation also saw the merger and cooperation of the Central Intelligence Agency with the Kenyan, Pakistani, and Tanzanian authorities.

EAST TURKESTAN ISLAMIC MOVEMENT (ETIM). Allegedly affiliated with **al-Qaeda** and other international **jihadist** groups, this Uighur **Islamic** fundamentalist group hopes to create an independent state in East Turkestan (China's western Xinjian-Uighur autonomous region). The group primarily uses car **bombings** as its means of aggression and was especially active during the 1990s. ETIM is linked with the pan-Turkish Islamic movement that exists throughout Central Asia and also includes the **Islamic Movement of Turkistan**. *See also* CENTRAL ASIAN ISLAMIC ACTIVITY.

ECONOMIC THEORY. In Islamic **fundamentalist** ideology, economic theory is transcendental (originating in **Allah**) and should be morally compliant (based on religious rules and not economic theories). Therefore, the right to private ownership is essential in **Islam**, but it exists under the stipulations that it is Allah who grants this right. Therefore, according to *sharia* (Islamic law), to privately own a business or any entity is not a natural right but rather Allah given. Allah then is the owner of all, and man is but His vicegerent who is given ownership based on physical and spiritual requirements. If a man lacks the positive Islamic qualities that allow ownership, then that ownership is deemed illegal because Allah would not naturally grant it to him. So, in accordance with *sharia*, ownership is deemed legal only if the owner complies within the framework of Islamic **morality**. In addition, if the owned enterprise receives monetary gain through morally harmful actions like gambling or cheating, the enterprise is deemed illegal.

In Islamic doctrines, the economy is submitted to moral and religious principles. This means that the Muslim investor invests depending on rules that are determined morally and ethically by *sharia* committees. From the Islamic perspective, the objective is not to produce the maximum wealth for the individual but to make the majority of the people feel like the system is fair and that there is solidarity and brotherhood (***ukhuwwa***) with the implementation of Islamic doctrines to the economy. For example, in Islamic finance, usury is frowned on, and the lender cannot charge any interest to the borrower since the banker and the depositor agree on the fact that if a person deposits money in the bank, he or she is giving that money to the bank, harking back to the concept of charity in Islam.

There is an ideology that you invest in real, tangible things—that it is labor that makes money. The fluctuation of the monetary rates is how the bank turns a profit, but it is a risk because these rates can go up or down. However, it is a system that works in this society because charity is a pillar of Islam and because the Muslim thinks that work is what makes money, not that money can make more money.

The principles of Islamic finance are the following. First, the prohibition of taking or receiving is called *riba*, but this does not preclude a rate of return on investment. Second, risk in any transaction must be shared between at least two parties so that the provider of capital and the entrepreneur share the business risks in return for a share in the profit. Third is the prohibition of speculation. Therefore, gambling and extreme risks are prohibited and are considered contractual obligations. This restricts all derivatives of financial products. In all cases, investment should not violate the rules of *sharia* as set out by the *sharia* committees. These *sharia* boards define what nonethical investments are and even forbid investment in businesses related to alcohol, pork, conventional finances, gambling, casinos, hotels, cinemas, pornography, and the music industry. Some of the *sharia* boards even recommend against investing in tobacco, weapons, and defense.

An example of such restrictions can be found in the Dow Jones Islamic Market Index. These principles are applicable in more than 500 financial institutions and in more than 75 countries. The Islamic financial industry sector had a growth of 15 percent annually over the last 10 years. But because of the financial crisis that began in 2009, this growth is forecast to continue in the coming years, especially because more Muslims around the world are starting to use *sharia*-compliance products that were once marginalized before by the old regimes in, for example, **Libya** and **Egypt**. *See also* SOCIAL JUSTICE.

EGYPT. Egypt has been an important and influential country with regard to the role of political **Islamism** throughout the Islamic Maghreb. Particularly noteworthy is the establishment in 1928 of the **Muslim Brotherhood**, which is still an active group that has spread its ideological values in many countries. The Brotherhood has been decisive in the proliferation of Islamic **theology** within Egyptian **society** but also detrimental in that many religious-oriented groups (whether or not they are militant in nature) have been continuously and vigorously suppressed by the country's security forces since the 1970s. Although an overwhelming majority of the population is **Sunni** Muslim, the relationship between current **government** policies and desired Islamic laws remains delicate.

Today, the government is in a period of reform and change after the resignation of President Hosni Mubarak on 11 February 2011 (his rule as the fourth president of Egypt began on 14 October 1981). **Fundamental** Islamists see this as an opportunity to instill *sharia* (Islamic law) throughout the country, but there still remains heavy opposition, as the people are hesitant to replace one dictator with another form of totalitarian rule. Egypt's adaptation of Islamic doctrine within the government (or lack thereof) will most likely dictate how other countries will respond to the 2011 **Arab Spring** revolutions (e.g., in **Libya** and **Tunisia**).

Fundamental **Islamic groups** have been emerging and reemerging in Egypt over the past few decades. In particular, three groups have dominated the Egyptian Islamic movement: *Al-Gama'a Al-Islamiyya*, *Al-Islami*, and the **Egyptian Islamic Jihad**. **Extremist** attacks in places such as Cairo and the Red Sea areas have greatly hindered the country's most viable industry— tourism. With an economic decline taking place because of this, the country's poverty line continues to rise and thereby perpetuates a cycle of disaffected civilians who are targeted as members by the **extremist** groups. These insurgencies, which peaked between 2003 and 2006, demonstrate how a moderate take on Islamism is in the decline and is being replaced by more radical oppositions. More brutal but lesser-known groups are the **Abdullah Azzam Martyr Battalion** and the Holy Warriors of Egypt. The general population of Egypt has even repeatedly spoken out against the use of **violence** by these groups.

There has been an overall consensus that although the groups maintain a radical **interpretation** of **Islam**, they must not use radical means to spread their ideologies. This "deradicalization" has been one of the most significant factors in Egyptian Islamism popular support. Of the main Islamist groups, the Muslim Brotherhood has proven to be the only one that has successfully adopted this policy, announcing its disapproval of **jihad** and instead favoring moderate political reforms. This, of course, has led to strife between the moderate and extremist Islamic groups—each condemning the other. Unique to Egypt, a great amount of this deradicalization has taken place within the prison system, especially after the government offered amnesties that would release captives if they renounced their brutal ways. However, there has also been a backlash to these conciliatory acts, and constitutional restrictions still make it almost impossible for a moderate faction to make headway, leaving radical ideologies room to grow. Although minor in presence compared to the groups mentioned above, **Hamas** and *Hizbullah* have also gained support throughout the lower-class population in Egypt over the years. *See also* EGYPTIAN SALAFI; *ENNAHDA*.

EGYPTIAN ISLAMIC GROUP. *See AL-GAMA'A AL-ISLAMIYYA.*

EGYPTIAN ISLAMIC JIHAD/*AL-ISLAMI***.** Established in the 1970s, the Egyptian Islamic Jihad was announced as an official group by its founding leaders Karam Zuhdi (leader of the *Saidi Jamaa Islamiya*), **'Abd al-Salam Faraj** (ideological leader of an Islamic cell in Cairo), and **Ayman al-Zawahiri** (now leader of **al-Qaeda**). Most of the membership consists of former **Muslim Brotherhood** affiliates who left the group complaining that the Brotherhood was not aggressive enough and had turned its back on the **jihad**. Some members were also *mujahideen* from the Soviet-Afghan War (1979–1989). The goals of the group were not only to establish an Islamic **caliphate** throughout **Egypt** but also to attack **Israeli** and **Western** forces. On 6 April 1981, a member of the group assassinated Egyptian President Anwar al-Sadat, giving it global recognition. After this incident, many members and leaders, including Faraj and Zuhdi, were imprisoned (Zuhdi until 2003) and some executed (Faraj on 15 April 1982). Leadership of the Egyptian Islamic Jihad was assumed by the imprisoned Abud al-Zumur and Sayyed Imam al-Sharif (a.k.a. Dr. Fadl). Al-Zawahiri still maintained his position as an influential member and in 1991 became the sole leader of the group.

During this time, the group became increasingly volatile and executed a number of persons it claimed to be **apostates** and infidels. *Al-Jihad* also started to adopt the technique of **suicide bombings**, which it claims was inspired by *Hizbullah* **in Lebanon**. June 2001 saw the merger of *Al-Jihad* with al-Qaeda, creating *Jamaat Qae'idat al-Jihad*, led by al-Zawahiri (who had become the second in command to **Osama bin Laden**). Despite substantial security enforcements on the part of the Egyptian **government**, this consolidation with al-Qaeda has proven a large role in the longevity of the Egyptian Islamic Jihad movement—without this relationship, it is doubtful that the latter would have survived. The group continued its insurgencies particularly targeting foreign embassy buildings and has spread to other countries, such as **Sudan**, but in incredibly small numbers. *Jamaat Qae'idat Al-Jihad* has now been considered almost synonymous with al-Qaeda, and a majority of the members on its *shura* (consultation) council are originally from the Egyptian Islamic Jihad. *See also* ISLAMIC JIHAD UNION; *JAMAAT AL-JIHAD AL-ISLAMI*.

EGYPTIAN SALAFI. Salafism has increasingly spread among **Egypt**'s younger people, most likely because of the radical Islamist support of the aforementioned ideology. As is the case in most of the Islamic Maghreb, the poor socioeconomic conditions, coupled with the restrictive political system, have made the Salafi dogmas attractive to many. Since Salafi teaches that only through complete adherence to the **Quran** and the **Hadiths** can Muslims attain a life of purity, this straightforward **theology** serves as a pathway to a higher quality of life for numerous Egyptians. An increasing trend within the **extreme** Salafi movement in Egypt is aggressive attacks on Coptic **Christians** within the country (in January 2010, Salafi militants apparently killed six Coptics leaving a church in Naga Hammadi, Upper Egypt), as they are viewed as **apostates** by the Salafs. However, security forces, **Sufi** Muslims (adherents to the mystical side of **Islam**), and **Western** tourists have been targeted as well. The **government**'s task forces have repeatedly announced their plans to arrest and jail anyone suspected of membership, spreading their ideologies, participating in antiregime actions, and making claims of **apostasy** in hopes to suppress the extremist Salafis.

EMIR. *See AMIR.*

ENNAHDA/HIZB AL-NAHDA/HARAKAT AL-NAHDA AL-ISLAMI-YYA. From the Arabic for "awakening" or "renaissance," this **Islamic** cultural movement began in **Egypt** before moving to **Lebanon**, **Syria**, **Tunisia**, and other Muslim countries. Seen as a period of intellectual **modernization** and reformation, *Hizb al-Nahda* sought to institutionalize Islamic politics and create a new political class among the educated Muslim elite. Geographically, the movement was based in Cairo but soon spread to other Arab capitals, such as Beirut and Damascus. The Arab language was primarily utilized as the unifying force between the Muslim countries to gain support through universality. The founding force of *Ennahda* was Egyptian scholar Rifa'a Al-Tahtawi (1801–1873), who studied **Western** military methods and **science** in Paris, France. He became a supporter of the parliamentary system of **government** and returned to Egypt in the hope of implementing reforms based on the social **philosophies** he learned there. He published these views in his book *Takhlis Al-Ibriz fi Talkhis Bariz* (The Quintessence of Paris), which offered the view that the Muslim world, specifically Egypt, could adopt Western ideologies but reform them in ways that would be applicable to Islamic culture—known as **Islamization**. This credo of receptive modernism is the basis of *Ennahda*. Tahtawi's theories on the reorganization of the **Islamic state** have remained influential on Islamist **political parties**, most notably the **Muslim Brotherhood** and other Arab political parties like *Ennahda* **in Tunisia** and **Algeria**, which adopted the movement's name. *See also* AL-GHANNUSHI, RASHED; MOVEMENT FOR NATIONAL REFORM; MUSLIM BROTHERHOOD IN TUNISIA; TUNISIAN ISLAMIC FRONT.

ENNAHDA **IN TUNISIA.** Arabic for "The Renaissance Party," this group is an Islamic movement from **Tunisia** that was founded by **Rashed al-Ghannushi**. Originally named Islamic Action, it was then renamed to the Movement of the Islamic Tendency and then, in February 1989, *Hizb al-Nahda* (or *Ennahda*) as a way to superficially distance itself from **Islam** and therefore become active on the Tunisian political front. The group derives its political ideologies from the **Muslim Brotherhood** founder **Hassan al-Banna**, from the **Pakistani** philosopher and Muslim revivalist leader **Abul Alaa al-Maududi**, and from the theologian **Sayyid Qutb**. One of the main reasons for the strictly secular Tunisian **government**'s opposition to the group is its religious nature.

Throughout the 1980s and 1990s, *Ennahda* was accused of a violent plot to overthrow the secular regime of Tunisian President Ben Ali. Despite these accusations, the Renaissance Party insists that it is nonviolent and a victim of government repression. During the 1989 elections, the party was banned, yet the members ran as Independents and obtained 17 percent of the votes in the legislative elections. This same year, Ghannushi left for political exile in **Algeria** and then went to London. Presented as a danger to the stability of the country of Tunisia, officers of the group were tortured and imprisoned, and the party was officially banned in 1991. In the early 1990s, hundreds of *Ennahda* supporters were put on trial or fled into exile. Then, in 1999, one of *Ennahda*'s leaders, Abdallah Djaballah, left the party and created the **Movement for National Reform**.

In the wake of the 2011 Tunisian Revolution, Rashed al-Ghannushi reentered the country on 30 January to take part in the elections after President Ben Ali fled the country under popular pressure. Finally legalized in March 2011, the party reclaimed its original name Islamic Action and claimed to be like the Turkish Islamic Party, aiming to take part in the political future of Tunisia. In the October 2011 elections, it won approximately 40 percent of the votes. *See also* ARAB SPRING; *ENNAHDA*; JEBALI, HAMADI.

EQUALITY/*AL-MUSAWAT.* The **Quran** stipulates that men are equal to each other and that no one can claim superiority over another. It is **Allah** who is above all else, and all of humanity is then equally below. Therefore, all men have equal say in political and religious matters since all fall below Allah. This explanation of equality has been used more often in theory than in practice since some Muslims have engaged in the slave trade in the medieval period and beyond, and others feel that Muslims (and, individually, certain sects) are of a higher status than non-Muslims. However, many Islamic **fundamentalists** have been using the Quranic definition of equal rights to gain support since a majority of the Islamic population has been economically suppressed by many of the existing regimes that have claimed socioeconomic dominance. *See also* DEMOCRACY; HUMAN RIGHTS; WOMEN.

ERBAKAN, NECMETTIN (1926–2011). The most significant figure in Turkish Islamic contemporary history, Necmettin Erbakan was born on 29 October 1926 and received his doctorate in mechanics in 1953 at the Aachen Technische Hochschule in Germany. His political career began with the publication of his manifesto *Millî Görüs* (National View) in 1969. His views inspired and attracted many followers, and soon he became a solid figure in Turkish religious-based politics. Erbakan also led the *Al-Refah Partisi* (Welfare Party), *Milli Selamet Partisi* (National Salvation Party), and *Milli Nizam Partisi* (National Order Party). Through his political activities, Erbakan hoped to positively develop diplomatic relations between Turkey and the Arab states and to improve the economic situation in Turkey.

He became the first Muslim **fundamentalist** prime minister of Turkey in 1996 after running under his *Al-Refah Partisi* but was forced to resign a year later after military and secular pressure mounted following comments Erbakan made about the Susurluk scandal (an incident that involved drug trafficking and organized crime, all thought to be allowed by the Turkish government). After he resigned, he was banned from reentering politics by the Turkish constitutional court, and the *Al-Refah Partisi* was expelled from politics as well. Despite these events, he continued to influence and mentor individuals who still believed in his policies. After his period of political exclusion ceased, he founded the Felicity Party (***Saadet Partisi***) in 2001. On 27 February 2011, Erbakan died in Ankara, Turkey, from heart failure.

EXTREMISM/*TATARRUF*. **Islamic** extremism has manifested itself in a number of **Islamic groups** and movements, including the ***al-Tahwid***, ***al-Tahrir***, and ***al-Jamaat*** and ***al-Jihad*** movements. This brand of extremism is a result of radical ideologies that permit, in the view of the believer, **violence** or combat. Most important, and what has been a trend in the Arab states, is that moderate religious-political groups have been suppressed. This suppression is what paved the way for the more radical, extremist groups to form. This extremism has also bred a platform for **activism** (*harakiyya*) in politics.

F

FADLALLAH, MUHAMMAD HUSAYN (1935–2010). A prominent **Shiite** Twelver *marja* (*marja* literally means "source to follow/imitate") in **Lebanon**, Muhammad Husayn Fadlallah is more commonly known as being the spiritual leader of *Hizbullah* **in Lebanon** (although he has denied this claim). Also the founder of the *Mabarrat* Association and the Islamic *Sharia* Institute, he participated in intensive scholarship, wrote many literary works, and gave countless lectures on **Islam**. Born on 16 November 1935 in Najaf, **Iraq**, it is understood that Fadlallah inherited his academic success from his father, who was a Muslim scholar. Fadlallah has also been the target of many **assassination** attempts, as he was allegedly a leader of *Hizbullah* (most notably an attack on 8 March 1985 in Beirut that resulted in the deaths of 80 people). The 2006 *Hizbullah* war in **Israel** (12 July–14 August) only heightened these attempts on Fadlallah's life. Despite his extensive Muslim scholastic training, he has been criticized by many grand ayatollahs for his anti-Semitism. He supported the **Iranian Islamic Revolution** (January 1978–February 1979) and was an avid advocate of a progressive academic system throughout the Muslim world. On 4 July 2010, Fadlallah died, and the day of his memorial (6 July 2010) was marked as a national day of mourning in Lebanon as thousands attended. Fadlallah was a person of influence throughout the Islamic scholastic community, and his legacy continues to be celebrated.

FARAJ, 'ABD AL-SALAM (?–1982). After gaining an engineering degree at the Cairo University, Faraj joined *Al-Jamaat Al-Islamiya* (Islamic Groups). He was ideologically inspired by the writings of **Abu al-A'la al-Mawdudi**, **Sayyid Qutb**, and **Muhammad Ibn 'Abd al-Wahhab**, leading him to work at a private mosque where he regularly gave sermons. His speeches there usually revolved around the problems with the Muslim community due to the un-Islamic political rule that was pervading **Egypt**. He was the mastermind behind many of the actions of *Jamaat Al-Jihad Al-Islami* (Islamic Jihad Group) as well as *Tanzim Al-Jihad* (Al-Jihad Organization). He believed that the people of Egypt were true Muslims but that the **government** of the country had tainted itself and fallen to **paganism**. Faraj expressed these views in his small book *Al-Farida Al-Gha'iba* (The Absent Duty; the absent duty being **jihad**).

AL-FATAH. The most dominant group within the **Palestinian Liberation Organization** (PLO), *Al-Fatah* was established in 1957, making it the oldest of the Palestinian militant groups. Etymologically, *fatah* is Arabic for "conquest" and is also the reverse acronym for the transliterated Palestinian Liberation Movement: *Harakat Al-Tahrir Al-Filastiniyya.* Yasir Arafat (1929–2004), an influential Palestinian politician, was the group's leader for most of its existence. *Al-Fatah* was created in the hopes of establishing an independent and secular state of Palestine, to promote and protect the PLO along with the **Palestinian Authority** (PA), and to politically represent the legislative desires of the Palestinian people.

Despite its goal of creating a pan-Arab unifying force, *Al-Fatah* also supports the personal freedoms and self-determination of Palestinians. *Al-Fatah* believes that the Palestinian population should take up its own arms and **struggle** against occupation without the interference of foreign armed services. Even though the group has pledged that it will not become associated with another state's armed forces, it did receive various forms of support from a majority of other Arab states. However, during the Gulf War (1990–1991), when *Al-Fatah* sided with **Iraq**, it led Kuwait, the Persian Gulf emirates, and **Saudi Arabia** to withdraw their sponsorship. This alliance with the Iraqi invasion of Kuwait undercut the group's political influence that it had with many states as well as with the United Nations.

Al-Fatah first received notoriety and support from the Palestinian community when **Israel** attacked an *Al-Fatah* training camp in March 1968 in **Jordan** only to receive strong resistance from the Palestinian group. *Al-Fatah*'s military perseverance against the Israeli forces also resulted in an increase in new recruits and stature. By July of that year, *Al-Fatah* was allowed into the PLO and, in February 1969, took control of the organization. However, during the 1972 Olympic Games in Munich, Germany, an *Al-Fatah* splinter group, the **Black September Organization**, kidnapped and killed 11 members of the Israeli Olympic team. This incident resulted in a tarnishing of the reputation that *Al-Fatah* had and gave the group international notoriety as an organization that is a breeding ground for **extremism**. In attempts to repair its name, *Al-Fatah* revised its stated goals in 1974 and declared that although a jihad is necessary, it must also coincide with political developments and have legislative achievements that are commensurate with the loss of life.

The group continued to have a tumultuous relationship with Israel throughout the 1970s and 1980s, resulting in numerous attacks and **assassinations** on both sides, notably, on 16 April 1988, when founding *Al-Fatwa* member (second only to Yasir Arafat) and leader of the *Al-Fatah*'s **Force 17** Khalil al-Wazir (a.k.a. Abu Jihad) was killed by Israeli forces. However, *Al-Fatah* has seen a significant increase in diplomatic success, and on 13 September 1993 Arafat (then PLO chairman) and Israel's Prime Minister Yitzhak Rabin signed a peace accord that allowed the Palestinians to create their own state in the areas of Gaza and the West Bank. Yet the group incurred some difficulties with the creation of **Hamas** and the **Islamic Jihad of Palestine**, which drew support and attention away from *Al-Fatah*. Nevertheless, it still remains the dominant party in the PLO and also controls a majority of the security forces within the PA. With the establishment of Hamas and Islamic Jihad of Palestine, the country also saw an increase of **suicide bombings**. To counteract the popularity that the groups were receiving from this tactic, *Al-Fatah* fathered the **Al-Aqsa Martyrs' Brigade**.

However, on 11 November 2004, Arafat died, and Farouk Kaddoumi was announced as his successor. *Al-Fatah* continues to vie for electoral success against Hamas despite its commanding position in the PLO. For example, during the 2004 elections in the West Bank, *Al-Fatah* received a majority in 12 councils, whereas Hamas won a majority in seven councils. The next year, during the Palestinian legislative elections, Hamas won 74 seats to *Al-Fatah*'s 45. This divergence between the Palestinian Legislative Council (led by Hamas) and the Executive Council (led by *Al-Fatah*) has further promoted conflicts between the two groups. This clash has resulted in both organizations losing aid from the European Union and the **United States**.

Although the two sides have tried to reconcile and form a coalition **government**, attempts have proven unsuccessful, and fighting has continued. This conflict escalated and reached a pinnacle on 15 June 2007, when Hamas took control over the Gaza Strip from *Al-Fatah*. Now, with Hamas and *Al-Fatah* sharing rule over Gaza and the West Bank, peace accords with Israel have fallen aside, and Hamas emerged as an even greater threat to Israel than *Al-Fatah*. Despite the history of constant fighting between the groups, members from both parties have tried to make amends and find a common ground so as to heal the division within Palestine. *See also HAWARI.*

FATAH AL-ISLAM/CONQUEST OF ISLAM. Established in November 2006, *Fatah al-Islam* is one of the youngest militant **Sunni** Islamist groups. This **jihadist** organization is led by Shaker al-Abssi. However, it must be noted that Conquest of Islam is not affiliated with **Al-Fatah** or the **Fatah Revolutionary Council**. In 2003, al-Abssi went to **Iraq** to take up arms against the U.S. occupying forces and there became associated with the **al-Qaeda** organization—a relationship that has continued throughout the decade, although it has been officially denied by Al-Abssi. On its establishment, the group made its headquarters in the northern **Lebanon** camp of Nahr al-Bared by seizing it from *Fatah al-Intifada*. The group is thought to possess training camps in **Jordan** and **Syria**. Although membership is reportedly marginal (the group's strength is approximately in the low hundreds), it is comprised of mostly Lebanese, **Palestinian**, and Syrian Sunni **extremists**. Former veterans who fought against the U.S. occupation in **Iraq** are also within the ranks of *Fatah al-Islam*. Among its goals, *Fatah al-Islam* wants to dissolve **Israel**, remove all **Western** occupation, and institute *sharia* (Islamic law) throughout Lebanon, Syria, and Palestine.

Constantly in conflict with the Lebanese army, the group has conducted a series of **bombings** on civilian and political targets. On 2 September 2007, the Lebanese army overran the *Fatah al-Islam* camp at Nahr al-Bared after three months of fighting, resulting in the deaths of approximately 222 militants (along with a number of civilians). The actions undertaken by the group have also instigated conflicts and turmoil between other parochial groups and have led to further discord within Lebanon and the Palestine territories. Financially, the organization was allegedly supported by Syria, but after Al-Abssi lost his leadership position to Abd al-Rahman Awad, the group turned primarily to **Saudi Arabia** for sponsorship. Al-Abssi's fall as leader of *Fatah al-Islam* was a direct result of the September 2007 raid, which concluded with the organization being forced out of their Nahr al-Bared camp. In August 2010, Awad was killed in Lebanon during a skirmish with Lebanese security forces. This, in effect, marked the end of *Fatah al-Islam*. Its low level of activity allowed for the group to even be removed from several federal watch lists by the fall of 2010.

FATAH REVOLUTIONARY COUNCIL (FRC). Established in 1974 by **Abu Nidal** (Sabri Khalil al-Banna), the FRC is a militant group from **Palestine** that was one of the most brutal organizations of the late 20th century. Responsible for over 100 attacks from its establishment until 1991, it has targeted various ethnic groups and was comprised of several hundred at its peak. Nidal's establishment of the FRC was a direct result of his split with *Al-Fatah* and, in effect, the **Palestinian Liberation Organization**. Supported by various countries, the group hoped to see a social revolution take place that would destroy **Israel**, expel "undesirables" from the Palestinian territories, and spread throughout the Arab world. Among the countries that supported the FRC were **Iraq** (1974–1983), **Libya** (1987–1999), **Syria** (1974–1987), and **Egypt** (1997–1998).

Listed as a group under the umbrella term the **Abu Nidal Organization**, the FRC is also known as the Arab Revolutionary Brigades, the Arab Revolutionary Council, Black June, the **Black September Organization**, and the Revolutionary Organization of Socialist Muslims. The group was also responsible for a number of **assassinations**: six under the Arab Revolutionary Brigades, two under Black June, six as the Black September Organization, and another two under the Revolutionary Organization of Socialist Muslims.

During the group's later years, it seemed to grow from being an **extremist** group with revolutionary foundations to a militant organization that would lend its services to various states regardless of their political discourses. Some experts even believe that two-thirds of its financial support came from extortion and from businesses that hired its abilities. In 1988, it had also been speculated that Abu Nidal carried out a massive internal expulsion of untrusted members within his group, resulting in the deaths of over 150 affiliates. However, in the wake of Nidal's death in August 2002, the group seemed to not be able to recover from this "cleansing" and failed to retain its founding ferocity.

FATWA/**LEGAL OPINION.** Basically a decision on a matter in agreement with *sharia* (Islamic law), a *fatwa* can be issued only by a person who is scholastically familiar with and knowledgeable on Islamic law. The individual issuing the *fatwa* must also be communally acknowledged as a strict adherent of **Islam**, **moral**, and not acting in any self-regard or forced motivation. What types of matters constitute a *fatwa* has a very broad range. It could be something simple (as in the correct way for a Muslim to pray) or something more grave (such as murder or warfare). There are various types of *fatwas* as well, the most significant being *takfir*. *Takfirs* have been most commonly used in recent years by radical Islamic **fundamentalists** who use this specific type of *fatwa* to justify their attacks against those deemed as **apostates**. Another *fatwa* can be used to declare a general state of **jihad** that allowed for all individuals of that state to participate in the struggle since it was deemed to be their Islamic duty. A *fatwa* of this magnitude may be issued only by a member of a high-ranking religious authority. If an individual issues this type of *fatwa* and lacks the authority to do so, the issuance is not deemed **legitimate**.

Some well-known *fatwas* include **Ayatollah Khomeini**'s call for **Salman Rushdie**'s death after his publication of *The Satanic Verses* and **Osama bin Laden**'s declaration of a jihad against the **West** in 1998. In the case of Khomeini's *fatwa*, in accordance with **Shiite** law, which stipulates that a *fatwa* will end on the death of the issuer, the *fatwa* ended when Khomeini died in 1989. However, some Shiite scholars have stated that Khomeini's declaration was not a *fatwa* but a *hukm* (distinct jurisdictional order), so the call for Rushdie's death should remain in effect since a *hukm* does not end with the death of its issuer.

FEDAYEEN/FIDA'IYIN. Plural for the Arabic *fida'i*, meaning "one who offers himself," as in self-sacrifice, the term has been adopted by multiple **jihadist** groups to illustrate the groups' desires to die in the holy struggle for **Islam**. These groups include *Isma'ili Fedayeen* (**Shiite** militants active in the 11th and 12th centuries in Asia who attacked the **Sunni** Abbasid dynasty using mainly the tactic of suicide missions), *Fedayan-i Islam* (an **Iranian** organization founded in 1944 by Navab Safavi, who targeted Iranian scholars and public officials whom it felt led to the decline of Islam throughout Iran), the Palestinian *Fedayeen* (which used the term "*fedayeen*" especially for those militants conducting attacks within Israel but not specifically affiliated with any particular group in **Palestine**), *Fedayan-i Khalq-i Iran* (also known as The People's *Fedayan* of Iran, a splinter group from the Iranian Communist Party that was comprised mostly of students who trained in the **Palestinian Liberation Organization**'s camps during the 1960s and that tried to create a militant revolution against the state), and *Fedayeen* of Saddam (established by Saddam Hussein in 1995 with the hopes of protecting his **Baathist** organization by attacking those deemed to be disloyal to the state). *See also* ASSASSIN; *ISTISHHAD*.

FELICITY PARTY. *See SAADET PARTISI.*

FIGHTING VANGUARDS/*AL-TALAI' AL-MUQATILA*. A small contingent of militant members of the **Muslim Brotherhood in Syria**, the Fighting Vanguards were led by Marwan Hadid during the late 1960s and were inspired by **Sayyid Qutb**. What particularly inspired the group was Qutb's argument that the **Muslim Brotherhood** would eventually dissolve if it did not defend itself from the state through a **jihad**. Comprised of only a dozen or so members, the group participated in a number of anti-**Baath** strikes and even gained the attention of Said Hawwa. The insurrections against Baathists continued throughout the 1970s, and Hadid was captured during a strike in 1976 and died shortly thereafter in prison. The group carried on despite the loss of its leader, and the fighting finally peaked in a brief but brutal civil war in 1980 in the north-central cities of **Syria**. After this, Syrian security forces destroyed most of the Fighting Vanguards contingents (then being led by Adnan 'Uqla), and the remaining joined the **National Islamic Front**. While still being pursued by the authorities, the rest of the Fighting Vanguards surrendered under a general amnesty.

FITNA/DIVISION. The Arabic term *fitna* refers to a division within a Muslim nation (**umma**) that includes a test of faith that can even lead to rebellions, chaos, or sedition. Historically, it is derived from the first Islamic civil war that occurred following the assassination of **Caliph** Uthman in 656. This war, which lasted from 656 to 661, was called the *fitna*. The term has since been used to describe a period when a Muslim community becomes unbalanced and then fragmented. Moreover, it can mean that a person or group intentionally causes upheaval between people to create a situation to test the peoples' faith. *Fitna* is also often used to illustrate a group that has undergone extreme moral and emotional grievances that then may compromise their faith and lead to a greater focus on material or worldly gains rather than spiritual ones.

For example, the **Arab Spring** has been qualified in **Saudi Arabia** as a *fitna* because it can weaken the community from within. The duality that occurs when being affected by a rebellion or a revolution is what can tempt Muslims to shy away from or even deny the authority of the Muslim leaders who are ruling in the name of **Allah**. Also, the temptations brought on by **Western** societies are another example of how division can occur. The fear of *fitna* by the **fundamentalists** is a major reason why secular or pluralist **governments** are forbidden by *sharia* (Islamic law). The elements of such forms of government are seen to give too much temptation and lead to an inevitable division among the *umma*. For Islamic fundamentalists, there is only one true party: the Party of Allah (*Hizbullah*). This is so important because the **Islamic state** is based on the rhetoric of solidarity and unification.

FITRA. See INTUITION.

FIZAZI, MUHAMMAD (1945–). Muhammad Fizazi is the spiritual leader of the *Salafia Jihadia* movement and the *imam* at the al Quds mosque (also known as the Taiba mosque) in Hamburg, Germany. Allegedly linked to several **bombings** and other aggressive **Islamic** activities, Fizazi has also preached at mosques in his hometown of Tangiers, **Morocco**. His introduction to the **fundamentalists** most likely came from his move to the impoverished suburb of Casablanca, Sidi Moumen, which had a high degree of Islamic militancy because of its poor socioeconomic conditions. Fizazi obtained his religious indoctrination in **Saudi Arabia,** and on his return to Morocco, he began preaching **extreme** forms of **Salafi** doctrinal philosophy and formed the group *Salafia Jihadia*. He has direct ties with the May 2003 Casablanca attacks, and it has been speculated that many of the **suicide bombers** were from the *Salafia Jihadia*. In the wake of the attack in August 2003, Fizazi was arrested along with 86 other people (a majority were *Salafia Jihadia* members) suspected of involvement. Fizazi was sentenced to 30 years in prison for his radical statements and links to the Casablanca violence.

FORCE 17. The security organization and extended branch of *Al-Fatah*, Force 17 was organized in the 1970s with the intention of providing added protection to the **Palestinian Liberation Organization** (PLO) and leaders of *Al-Fatah*. The group acted primarily as a guerilla police force, imprisoning and punishing people who seemed to be counteractive to the program that the PLO was trying to maintain throughout **Palestine**. Commanded by Khalil al-Wazir, from its inception until his death at the hands of **Israeli** security forces on 16 April 1988, the group also served to direct the actions of the Palestinian militant groups in **Lebanon**. Even in the aftermath of the Palestinian-Israeli peace accord on 13 September 1993, Force 17 allegedly conducted numerous attacks and arrests against Israelis and rebellious Palestinians alike. However, with the creation of the Palestinian Authority (PA) in 1994, Force 17 was renamed the Palestinian Authority Presidential Security Unit and is still dominated by *Al-Fatah* proponents. The newly renamed group still acted in the same fashion as it had under its former name, but now it also provided the security during legislative and ceremonial events. The group continues to serve as a security organization for the PA, PLO, and *Al-Fatah* even after the death of *Al-Fatah* leader Yasir Arafat in November 2004.

FORT HOOD SHOOTING. *See* HASAN, NIDAL MALIK.

***FORUM KOMUNIKASI AHLU SUNNAH WAL-JAMAAH* (FKASWJ)/ FORUM OF COMMUNICATION OF THE FAITHFUL OF THE SUNNAH AND THE PROPHET.** This Indonesian **Islamic group** was formed by Jaffar Umar Thalib in Yogyakarta, Indonesia. The group also possessed an armed wing, *Lashkar Jihad*, and was active mainly from 1998 to 2002.

FREEDOM/*AL-HURRIYYA*. An essential component of **Islam**, almost all **Islamic groups** have called for the existence of freedom. Islamic scholars have stated that *al-hurriyya* is a basic and understandable right to all people of Islam. In politics, it is considered a rupture of *sharia* (Islamic law) if freedom is denied to any people by the **government**. This idea was discussed by many doctrinal schools, such as *Al-Asha 'riyya*, *Al-Mu'tazila*, and *Al-Qadariyya*.

FRONT DE LIBÉRATION NATIONALE. *See* NATIONAL LIBERATION FRONT.

***FRONT PEMBELAN ISLAM* (FPI)/FRONT OF THE DEFENDERS OF ISLAM.** Founded in 1998, FPI is a militia that was created by Habib Rizieq to restore order in the Muslim districts of Jakarta and other major cities in

Indonesia. Its members are largely desocialized individuals who find identity in criminal activities.

FUNDAMENTALISM/*USULIYA*. Referring to the fundamentals, founding principles, practices, foundations, and the founders of **Islam** who should be imitated, the term has been used recently as an all-encompassing term for an assortment of **activism** that ranges from moderate pluralism to radical **extremism**. For example, the moderate fundamentalists are considered to be **Hasan al-Banna**, **Rashed al-Ghannushi**, and **Hasan al-Turabi**, whereas **Ayatollah Khomeini**, **Abu al-A 'la al-Mawdudi**, and **Sayyid Qutb** are proscribed as extremists.

Purely, Islamic fundamentalism means a desire to return to the basic (or fundamental) doctrines of Islam. Yet Islamic fundamentalism has, in recent history, developed connotations of negativity because of the actions of some extremist groups. Nevertheless, it must be stressed that Islamic fundamentalists wish to return their **society** to an **Islamic state** where the absolute adherence to the **divine texts** of Islam (the **Quran** and the **Hadiths**) govern everyday life. Fundamentalism is viewed as an idealistic return to the past way of life, which was ethical and glorious. For the fundamentalists, this return would reestablish the glory of Islamic civilization and identity while absorbing **modernity** and change. However, this is expanded on by being also a critique of **philosophy**, politics, and **science** within the context of modernity. Fundamentalist ideology is based on the institution of *sharia* (Islamic law), adhering to **divine governance** (*hakimiyya*), refuting **paganism**, and creating a society that is overall regulated by Islamic doctrine. Fundamentalists also state that nobody can understand the ultimate truth and therefore that all our **knowledge** is relative. This acceptance of the insufficiency of human **reason** is supported doctrinally, according to the fundamentalists, since man is composed only of *fitra* (intuition), which would lead him to the revelation (*wahy*) of **Allah** since it is He who created all the formal laws of the universe. Therefore, man is subservient to Allah since all the laws and orders of the universe were created by Allah in order for man to serve Him.

Although both moderates and extremists agree on the preeminence of Allah's rule (divine governance), there are significant differences between the two spectrums of fundamentalist ideology. The extremists, for example, desire no compromise or gradual change in **Islamic society**; rather, they desire the immediate overthrow of the secular governments and their replacement with *sharia*. Their discourses are rigid and adamant. In comparison, the moderate discourse is one of readiness to compromise and is practically and theoretically more open. Moderates often transfer cardinal authority to the community but stipulate that if the society does not implement an **Islamic state**, then there is no infraction done to the quintessence of Islam itself.

FUNDAMENTALIST. *See* FUNDAMENTALISM.

FURQAN/**PROOF.** Founded in 1978 and short lived, *Furqan* was a political group based in **Iran**. It came to national attention when it took responsibility for the **assassination** of Ayatollah Murtaza Mutahhari, one of Iran's most prominent scholars. It defended its insurgencies by stating that the **Iranian Revolution of 1979** was tainted by the rich and stained by the Marxists.

G

GABUNGAN MELAYU PATANI RAYA (GAMPAR)/ASSOCIATION FOR A LARGE MALAYSIAN PATTANI. This was the first Muslim separatist movement in southern Thailand. Formed in the early 1950s, GAMPAR was a vehicle for the pan-Malaysian ideology.

AL-GAMA'A AL-ISLAMIYYA/AL-JAMAAT AL-ISLAMIYA/THE ISLAMIC GROUP. *Al-Gama'a al-Islamiyya* began as a dissident group of former members of the **Muslim Brotherhood**. Originally an assemblage of local Islamic **fundamentalist** groups, by the late 1980s the group formed an official structure. Chief among its concerns were replacing **Egypt**'s **government** with an **Islamic state**, the dissolution of the Hosni Mubarak regime, and the rejection of Egypt's treaty with **Israel**. The group began recruiting and influencing young male students but then turned to the prisons and impoverished urban areas to boost membership, especially in the southern region of the country. Ideologically led by **Omar Abdel-Rahman**, the group has developed a fearsome reputation because of its countless campaigns of **violence** against civilians and armed forces alike that took place throughout the 1990s. *Al-Gama'a al-Islamiya* also targeted foreigners and prominent dignitaries, greatly hindering the country's tourist industry. After a June 1995 **assassination** attempt on Mubarak by members of The Islamic Group, the Egyptian ruler sought to repress and dissolve any opposition group, whether radical, moderate, political, religious, social, or intellectual.

Financially and militarily supported by sympathizers from **Afghanistan** and **Sudan**, an estimated 1,200 deaths occurred at the hands of *Al-Gama'a al-Islamiyya* between 1992 and 1997. The group's former leader, Karam Zuhdi, also stated that the group acted with the **Egyptian Islamic Jihad** in the assassination of Egyptian President Anwar Al-Sadat in 1981. After many more insurrections and assassination attempts, the Egyptian security forces strongly suppressed the group, along with other similar organizations, almost incapacitating it by 1997. In fact, Abdel-Rahman was sentenced to life in prison on 17 January 1996. By the summer of 1997, over 20,000 Islamists had been arrested and were kept in custody. In retaliation, exiled leaders Mustafa Hamza and Rifai Ahmed Taha along with **al-Qaeda** deputy **Ayman al-**

Zawahiri conducted the 17 November 1997 **Luxor massacre** at the Temple of Hatshepsut in Egypt. Resulting in the deaths of 71 people (foreigners and nationals alike), the incident crippled the Egyptian tourism market for a period of time and reduced popular support for the Islamic movements. Among its many attacks, some notable ones include the 13 November 1995 assassination of an Egyptian diplomat visiting Geneva, Switzerland; the **bombing** of the Egyptian embassy in Islamabad, Pakistan, on 19 November 1995; the 18 September 1997 shooting on a tour bus; and the 22 March 1998 attack on police forces in Meni Mazar.

In 2003, while most of its leaders were imprisoned in Egypt, the group rejected its violent ways, and many members were released from custody under the government's Non-violence Initiative in September of that year. In April 2006, a reported 1,200 *Al-Gama'a al-Islamiyya* associates were released from custody, including founding member Najeh Ibrahim. Despite many members of the group renouncing their **jihadist** ways, on 5 August 2006, al-Zawahiri stated that a contingent of the organization had aligned itself with al-Qaeda. The announcement, a recorded video, also included then *Al-Gama'a al-Islamiyya* leader Muhammad Al-Hukaymah confirming this merger.

GERAKAN ACEH MERDEKA (GAM)/MOVEMENT FOR THE INDEPENDENCE OF ACEH. Founded on 4 December 1976, GAM was a separatist organization created by Hassan di Tiro. It hoped to reestablish the ancient sultanate of Aceh, known as the "veranda of Mecca." GAM also had a military wing, *Agakan Gerakan Aceh Merdeka* (Army of the Movement for the Independence of Aceh). After over 30 years of fighting, GAM agreed in 2006 to abandon the armed struggle in exchange for the liberation of the province of Aceh. The guerilla war between GAM and the Indonesian military finally ended with over 30,000 dead.

GERAKAN MUJAHIDIN ISLAM PATTANI (GMIP)/MOVEMENT OF THE HOLY WARRIORS OF ISLAM PATTANI. Founded in 1994 in southern Thailand by veteran *mujahideen* and **Afghan Arab** Nasori Saeseng, the group is similar in ideology to *Jemaah Islamiyah* and other **jihadist** groups.

GERAKAN PEMUDA ISLAM INDONESIA (GPII)/MOVEMENT OF YOUNG INDONESIAN MUSLIMS. The former youth organization of the *Masyumi* (*Majlis Syuro Muslimin Indonesia*), GPII Indonesia also served as the youth branch of *Dewan Dakwah Islamiyah Indonesia*.

AL-GHAFFOUR, EMAD ABDEL. An Egyptian **Sunni** Islamist, Emad Abdel al-Ghaffour is currently the president of the *al-Nour* **Islamic political party** in **Egypt**.

AL-GHANNUSHI, RASHED (1941–). Born in Hamma in southern **Tunisia** in 1941, Rashed al-Ghannushi is the historical head of the **Islamic political party *Ennahda* in Tunisia** and a thorough advocate of a Tunisian form of **pan-Islamism**. His political beliefs include the destruction of **Israel** and advocating for anti-U.S. **violence**, and he was a supporter of **Iraq**'s invasion of Kuwait. Forced into exile in London in 1989, the leader returned to Tunisia since the autocrat Zine el Abidine Ben Ali left the presidential office of Tunisia on 14 January 2011 and fled to **Saudi Arabia**. During Habib Bourguiba's regime in Tunisia (1957–1987), Ghannushi was imprisoned several times because of his political activities. While in exile, he remained adamantly separate and marginal with regard to Tunisian affairs. In the wake of the January 2011 **Arab Spring** protests and demonstrations in Tunisia, Ghannushi stated in an interview that *Ennahda* "signed a shared statement of principles with the other Tunisian opposition groups." Soon after, on 22 January 2011, the television station Al-Jazeera also confirmed that he is against an Islamic **caliphate** and wants to "work to build a new state law." When Ghannushi declared his sentiments, members of *Ennahda* were split between the two opposing political ideologies. However, the leader has insisted on his desire to form a **government** of "national union."

His party *Ennahda* won more than 40 percent of the votes in the elections for the Tunisian Constitutional Assembly on 23 September 2011. Even if he did not take any official position in the new government or assembly, he remains the president of *Ennahda* and the main leader of the Islamists in Tunisia. *See also* MUSLIM BROTHERHOOD IN TUNISIA; TUNISIAN ISLAMIC FRONT.

AL-GHAZALI, MUHAMMAD (1917–1996). A leading member of the **Muslim Brotherhood** during the 1940s, Muhammad al-Ghazali joined the group in 1938 and was imprisoned along with many other members in 1949 after the death of **Hasan al-Banna**. Known for his writings, which influenced many, he is seen as one of the most prolific moderate **Islamic** thinkers of contemporary history. His written works deal with many of the recent issues in the Muslim world and gained him many followers. Ideologically, he advocated enacting *sharia* (Islamic law) and the *shura* (consultation) council throughout **Islamic society**.

AL-GHAZALI, ZAYNAB. The leader and founder of the Muslim Women's Association, which was created in 1936, Zaynab al-Ghazali later became the leader of the Muslim Sisters, which was the female branch of the **Muslim Brotherhood**. She was incredibly successful in fund-raising and taking care of the families whose members were jailed because of their association with the Muslim Brotherhood. A frequent visitor to the prison, she was indispensable in smuggling out **Sayyid Qutb**'s writings while he was in custody. Although she was imprisoned in 1965, she was released by Anwar al-Sadat in 1971. Afterward, she became an active member in *Al-Da'wa* and *Al-Liwa' Al-Islami*. *See also* WOMEN.

AL-GHURABAA/THE STRANGERS. A British **Islamic group** that allegedly grew out of the *Al-Muhajiroun* organization when it was disbanded in 2005, *al-Ghurabaa* took its name from a passage in the **Hadiths** that states, "*Paradise is for al-Ghurabaa.*" Its leader, Anjem Choudary, has also been the leader of Islam4UK since its 2010 inception. The group has organized protests in reaction to the *Jyllands-Posten* newspaper, which published a controversial cartoon of the **Prophet Muhammad** and has demonstrated in front of the Danish embassy in London. In November 2005, some members (including Choudary) of *al-Ghurabaa* splintered off and established *Ahl as-Sunna wal-Jamaah*. Choudary now maintains the Internet forum for *Ahl as-Sunna wal-Jamaah*. *Al-Ghurabaa* was officially banned in 2006.

AL-GHURABAA PAKISTAN/THE STRANGERS IN PAKISTAN. The group members refer to themselves as "the strangers" because they consider themselves to be strangers even in Muslim **Pakistan** since the adherents think that it is not a true **Islamic state**. Therefore, its members feel the same as if they were in an infidel country.

This group is an offshoot of *Jemaat Islamiyaah*, which was founded in 1999 in Pakistan. It was led by Riduan Isamuddin Hambali in order to form a new generation of leaders of the **jihad** and to tighten relations with **al-Qaeda** at that time. The organization was officially dismantled in September 2003 following Hambali's capture on 11 August 2003. *See also AL-GHURABAA*.

GOD. *See* ALLAH.

GOVERNMENT/*HUKUMA*/*HUKM*. Most **fundamentalists** deny any and all forms of **democratic** government, but they do favor a **theocratic** form of government since its basic foundation lies in *sharia* (Islamic law). Some of them advocate for the *shura* (consultation), which has **historically** required Islamic scholars to advise the **caliph** (supreme ruler). The function of the government is then to enforce *fitra* (law of nature) and *sharia* as explained in the **divine texts** (**Quran** and **Hadiths**). The moderates also agree on the point that a government exists to represent the needs of its people but always within the constraints of *sharia*. However, there is a lack of desire for state authority, as it is understood that more power should be given to the individual practice of **religion**. *See also* ISLAMIC GOVERNMENT.

GUARDIANS OF THE ISLAMIC REVOLUTION. A **Shiite** militant group from **Iran**, the Guardians of the Islamic Revolution has been accused of being formed by and an extension of the Iranian government. Some experts believe that the group is given Iranian-gained intelligence details and state-affiliated military personnel to conduct attacks outside the country. However, some observers disagree and speculate that the group is an independent organization that simply is sponsored by the Iranian government. Highly protective of its name, the group has released communiqués only to certain media outlets in order to legitimize its identity and prevent other **jihadist** groups from claiming responsibility under its name.

H

HADITHS. A collection of the sayings and acts of the **Prophet Muhammad**, the Hadiths (literally meaning "recitations") were collected between the eighth and ninth centuries and are also referred to as the "traditions of the Prophet." The texts are regarded by **Islam** as being one of the **fundamentals** of the **religion** and are used primarily to validate **Quranic interpretations** and in matters of *sharia* (Islamic law). The Hadiths also have included information about Muhammad's companions and early successors (known as *athar*). A subcategory of the Hadiths also exists, the Hadith *Qudsi*, or Sacred Hadith. These are specifically the words of **Allah** as conveyed by Muhammad and therefore are regarded by many Muslims as the actual words of Allah.

Historically, the Hadiths were originally heard by the Prophet's companions who preserved them after his death in 632 CE. The following generation then received the words and continued to spread them essentially through oral tradition until they were finally officially collected and written down. By the time the Abbasid dynasty scholars were collecting the Hadiths in the ninth century, it became obvious that there was a huge body of "traditions," and deciding which ones were legitimate became known as the "science of the Hadiths" (*'Ilm Al-Hadith*).

The basic guidelines for determining and evaluating the Hadiths are analyzing the actual text, the scale of the transmission, the routes through which the traditions were passed down, and the individuals involved in transmitting these words. These criteria in the science of the Hadiths have resulted in numerous scholastic studies and classifications. A backlash has occurred among some Muslims who do not agree with the various interpretations of the Hadiths and its oral nature. These people (known as Quranists) disregard the Hadiths and rely only on the Quran. In addition, starting in the beginning of the 20th century, **Western** scholars began to analyze the Hadiths in a similar manner that was done to the **Christian** Bible. This scholarship was largely criticized and considered to seriously question the historicity and validity of the Hadiths.

This field is also debated on by contemporary Muslim scholars. It is interesting to note that both the **Shiite** and the **Sunni** schools of Islam have their own individual interpretations of the Hadiths. These differences are based primarily on the fact that the two schools are in conflict over the science of the Hadiths. The Shiite community prefers the interpretation as laid out by the family of Muhammad, whereas the Sunni community prefers the collection of Aisha bint Abu Bakr (Muhammad's second and favorite wife). This difference is one of the quintessential dissimilarities between the two schools and is a main reason behind their individual stances on worship and **jurisprudence** in Islam.

HAIDALLAH, COLONEL MUHAMMAD KHOUNA OULD (1940–). Colonel Muhammad Khouna Ould Haidallah assumed power in **Mauritania** from 4 January 1980 until 12 December 1984. His reign was marked by increased political turbulence and faced multiple coup attempts, troop clashes, military tensions, and conspiracies. From 1980 to 1983, he implemented *sharia* (Islamic law) with the desire to entrench **Islam** in the country. In November 1981, he made an official decree that outlawed slavery in the country, but the practice is still present to this day. Haidallah's political opponents were also treated severely through imprisonments and executions. A coup d'état took place in 1984 while Haidallah was in Burundi. On his return to Mauritania, he was arrested at the airport of Nouakchott and was eventually released in December 1988. It appears that Haidallah's recognition of the Sahrawi Arab Democratic Republic as a sovereign nation was a large cause for the political takeover. He was succeeded by **Colonel Maouya Ould Sid Ahmed Taya**. In 2003, he returned to the political structure in Mauritania by running against President Taya and came in second with 19 percent of the votes but was immediately arrested after the elections under suspicions of plotting a countercoup. Again, on 3 November 2004, he was arrested under conspiracy allegations but was acquitted on 3 February 2005. During the 2007 elections, Haidallah ran again but placed only tenth and received a mere 1.73 percent of the votes.

HAMAS. *See HARAKAT AL-MUQAWAMA AL-ISLAMIYYAH.*

HAMAS IN ALGERIA. *See* ISLAMIC SOCIETY MOVEMENT.

HAQ MOVEMENT FOR LIBERTY AND DEMOCRACY. Founded in 2005, the Haq Movement for Liberty and Democracy is an **Islamic political party** in **Bahrain**. Many members came from the **Al-Wefaq National Islamic Society** and the National Democratic Action Society. Hasan Mushaima has served as its secretary-general since its inception, and Sheikh Jalil al-Singace, a prominent **Sunni** cleric, has been influential in the movement as well.

Haq was especially in opposition to the 2002 Bahraini **constitution**, which it viewed as illegal and an abusive exercise of King Hamad ibn Isa al-Khalifa's powers. In protest, the movement withdrew from the 2002 elections and urged others to do so as well. More recently, on 15 November 2006, the group made an official plea to the United Nations claiming that secretive government committees were set up specifically in order to rig both municipal and parliamentary elections in Bahrain. In their claim, the movement requested the formation of a group to further investigate the situation. This report of accusation is known as the "Bandar Gate," named after its author Salah al-Bandar. It also stated that the granting of citizenship has become a highly selective process in order to alter the demographics of the nation.

HARAKAT-UL-ANSAR (HuA)/MOVEMENT OF SUPPORTERS. Founded by Abdelkader Mokhtari in 1993 as a splinter organization from the *Harakat-ul-Jihad al-Islami*, HuA operates primarily in Jammu and Kashmir. But, since 1998, the group has been known as *Harakat-ul-Mujahedeen*. Soon after its inception, the Indian Security Forces arrested many of its prominent members because of their violent tactics. This **jihadist** group is currently led by Maulana Saadatullah Khan and hopes to have the Jammu and Kashmir regions secede from India and become part of **Pakistan**. Its militants are mostly of **Afghani** and Pakistani origin, and membership is believed to be about 1,000. The group is based in Muzaffarabad, Pakistan, and has carried out numerous attacks throughout southern Asia on both military and civilian targets. HuA is reportedly affiliated with *Lashkar-e-Tayyiba* and Pakistan's Inter-Services Intelligence. The organization *Al-Faran* is allegedly a nominal front of HuA. However, after numerous arrests and losses of the group's main leaders, it seems that the group is hardly active, although the Islamic organization *Jamaat-ul-Ansar* seems to be a continuation of HuA. *See also* AZHAR, MASOOD; KASHMIRI SEPARATISM; VIOLENCE.

HARAKAT AL-ISLAH. See MUSLIM BROTHERHOOD IN SOMALIA.

HARAKAT-UL-JIHAD-AL-ISLAMI (HuJI)/ISLAMIC STRUGGLE MOVEMENT. This Islamic **fundamentalist** militant group was formed in 1984 during the Soviet-Afghan War (1979–1989). As of its inception, HuJI was the first Islamic Pakistani **jihadist** group. Currently operating primarily in **Bangladesh** (banned there in October 2005), India, and **Pakistan**, its leader is Ilyas Kashmiri, although the group was formed by **Fazal ur-Rehman** and Qari Saifullah Akhtar. Ur-Rehman, however, left the group to form the more brutal *Harakat-ul-Ansar* (now known as *Harakat-ul-Mujahedeen*). After the Soviet-Afghan War, HuJI was allegedly recruited by the Inter-Services

Intelligence of Pakistan to continue its **jihad** in the Jammu and Kashmir regions. This also helped foster a working relationship with the Pakistani army. In 1992, the group established a unit in Bangladesh, where it received military assistance from **Taliban** leader Mullah Umar.

Similar in ideology to groups like *Lashkar-e-Tayyiba* and *Jaish-e-Muhammad*, HuJI has used aggressive tactics to free Kashmir from Indian governance and make it Pakistani territory. It also hopes to bring about an Islamic **revolution** that would replace the current secular leadership with a **caliphate** throughout southern Asia. Membership is comprised mostly of young males who, on recruitment, receive military training in HuJI-administered camps in **Afghanistan** and Pakistan. Many of these new recruits (especially in Bangladesh) came from the Islamic *madrasas*, or learning institutions. Among its many operations, HuJI was suspected in the attempted **assassination** of Bangladeshi Prime Minister Sheikh Hasina in 2000. Throughout the decade, HuJI has carried out numerous **bombings** on civilian, governmental, and religious entities. *See also HARAKAT-UL-JIHAD-AL-ISLAMI* BANGLADESH; *JAMAAT-UL-MUJAHIDEEN* IN BANGLADESH; KASHMIRI SEPARATISM.

***HARAKAT-UL-JIHAD-AL-ISLAMI* BANGLADESH (HuJI-B).** Created in 1992, HuJI-B was established in the hope of installing an **Islamic state** throughout **Bangladesh**. **Violent** in their tactics and inspired by the **Taliban** army's rise to power in **Afghanistan**, members of the outfit prescribe to the **jihadist** form of radical Islamism. Many of the original members of HuJI-B were also *mujahideen* from the Soviet-Afghan War (1979–1989) who fled to Bangladesh after the conflict and launched the Islamic movement there. Active primarily on the coastal region of southern Bangladesh and the eastern corridor of India, HuJI-B receives a majority of its funds through arms smuggling and has created training camps in the Chittagong region. Experts have also speculated that membership is approximately around 15,000 and is comprised of both Bangladeshi nationals and foreigners alike, such as Myanmar refugees. A main source of recruitment for HuJI-B has been various *madrasas* throughout Afghanistan, Chechnya, and Jammu and Kashmir.

The organization maintains an affiliation with the Asif Reza Commando Force, *Jaish-e-Muhammad*, *Lashkar-e-Tayyiba*, the Taliban army, the United Liberation Front of Asom, and **al-Qaeda**. Members of HuJI-B were also implicated in the July 2000 attempted **assassination** of Bangladeshi Prime Minister Sheikh Hasina. Reports following the incident stated that there may be a possible relationship between the Pakistani Inter-Services Intelligence and HuJI-B, especially with regard to the assassination plot. Currently, the group is led by Shawkat Osman (a.k.a. Sheikh Farid) and is a member of the Bangladesh Nationalist Party. *See also HARAKAT-UL-JIHAD AL-ISLAMI.*

HARAKAT-UL-MUJAHIDEEN (HuM)/MUJAHIDEEN MOVEMENT. Operating primarily in Kashmir, HuM is a militant **Islamic group** from **Pakistan** that was established in 1989. In 1993, the group merged with *Harakat-ul-Jihad-al-Islami* and was known as *Harakat-ul-Ansar* until its name change in 1997 in response to being listed as an **extremist** organization. HuM sought to enter Kashmiri politics through the use of military influence and conducted a series of kidnappings throughout the mid-1990s. Some members, most notably **Masood Azhar**, left the group to form *Jaish-e-Muhammad*, as it was felt that HuM was not as aggressive as it could be. In February 2000, the group's leader, **Fazal ur-Rehman**, passed his high position on to Farooq Kashmiri, and Rehman in turn became HuM secretary-general. Although some membership was lost to *Jaish-e-Muhammad*, it is estimated that support ranges in the thousands and is primarily in the Pakistani and Indo-Kashmir regions with a large base in Muzaffarabad, Pakistan. *See also HARAKAT-UL-MUJAHIDEEN-AL-ALAMI*; *JAMAAT-UL-MUJAHIDEEN IN BANGLADESH*; *JAMAAT-ULEMA-E-ISLAM*; KASHMIRI SEPARATISM; *MUJAHIDEEN*; AL-QAEDA.

HARAKAT-UL-MUJAHIDEEN-AL-ALAMI (HuMA)/GLOBAL MUJAHIDEEN MOVEMENT. This is a splinter organization from *Harakat-ul-Mujahedeen*. Formed in 2002 after conflicts with its father group over internal organizational structures, the group is based in Karachi, **Pakistan**. Reportedly well armed, the group has targeted **Western** sympathizers and has made several attempts to **assassinate** Pakistani President Pervez Musharraf as well as many other high-ranking officials. Muhammad Imran served as the group's commander until his arrest on 7 July 2002 for his involvement in an assassination attempt (he was sentenced to death on 14 April 2003). Since many of its leaders and members are imprisoned by the Pakistani government, the group is relatively small in size. The remaining cadres have been operating independently of each other and are controlled by a consultative committee. HuMA has received arms and ammunition from some tribes in the North-West Frontier province and the Sindh province. The group has also worked with *Lashkar-e-Jhangvi* and the **Taliban** army on a few occasions.

HARAKAT-AL-MUQAWAMA-AL-ISLAMIYYAH/HAMAS IN PALESTINE/ISLAMIC RESISTANCE MOVEMENT. Widely known as Hamas, this is an Islamic **fundamentalist** group that emerged in **Palestine** in 1987 and is currently led by Khaled Meshaal. Etymologically symbolic to the group, Hamas is also an Arabic word that refers to a devoted path toward **Allah** and is interpreted to more loosely refer to "strength and bravery." Structurally, Hamas has a military branch known as the **Izz ad-Din Al-Qassam Brigades** as well as political and social branches. Each branch oversees its relevant field, but they remain an interwoven network to ensure efficiency and unity within the group. Hamas's consultative council, the *Majlis-al-Shura*, is comprised of various local and foreign leaders (especially the exiled Political Bureau, which is now based in Damascus, **Syria**, and controls most of the decision making in Hamas). Although the different segments of Hamas work together, the direct orders come from the *Majlis-al-Shura*. In the social welfare sector, Hamas has provided financial assistance, Islamic education, and hospitality to many afflicted Muslims, especially in Palestinian territories. Despite many criticisms, Hamas has increasingly risen in popularity among the Palestinian population. It is financially supported allegedly by **Iran** and through private donations.

In 1988, the group's founders developed a charter outlining their principles, and chief among them was the liberation of Palestine from **Israel**. Hamas also hopes to develop a pure **Islamic state** in the territories of Gaza Strip and the West Bank as well as reclaim Jerusalem in the name of **Islam**, in accordance with the 1967 boundary marker, which made Jerusalem Palestinian territory. In the declaration of its covenant, Hamas also identified itself as the **Muslim Brotherhood in Palestine**. **Ahmad Yasin**, leader of the **Muslim Brotherhood in Gaza**, was also an influential spiritual mentor and founding member of Hamas but was killed by Ismeli Shabak on 22 March 2004. The overarching concerns of Hamas are directly related to a **jihad** in and dissolution of Israel—as the group makes use of the **divine texts** of Islam to justify its insurgencies. Ideologically, the group is very similar to the **Egyptian Islamic Jihad**, espoused the views of radical fundamentalist **Sayyid Qutb**, and took inspiration from **Ayatollah Khomeini**'s influence over the Iranian people during the **Iranian Islamic Revolution of 1979**.

The event that preceded the formation of Hamas was the Palestinian uprising in 1987 against the Israeli forces occupying Gaza and the West Bank. After the event, which is known as the First **Intifada**, Gaza Muslim Brotherhood members decided to create Hamas in order to further support the Palestinian expulsion of Israeli influence from the country's territories, although Hamas has explicitly stated that it is not a member of the **Palestinian Liberation Organization** (PLO). The Muslim Brotherhood in Gaza announced Hamas's formation by publishing the "Covenant of the Islamic Resistance Movement" on 18 August 1988. The next year saw the first Hamas offensive, in which members of the group abducted and killed two soldiers in Israel. Shortly after the incident, 415 leading members and activists of the group were deported to **Lebanon**, and Hamas subsequently developed a relationship with *Hizbullah* **in Lebanon**. The relationship between Hamas and *Hizbullah* continued to grow, and in 1992, *Hizbullah* even provided military assistance to Hamas when many were expelled into southern Lebanon that year. Following this, Hamas began to accept financial and strategic aid from **Iran**. Throughout the 1990s, Hamas continued to come into conflict with the PLO's *Al-Fatah*, mainly because of the Arab-Israeli peace accords that the PLO was active in.

Hamas continued to employ its tactics of **suicide bombings** and kidnappings to further suppress Israel. Numerous cases of aggressions took place at the hands of Hamas—at least five per year throughout the 1990s. Palestine imposed countless sanctions and made multiple arrests of Hamas members and leaders in hopes of dispelling their **violence**. Because of their brutality, on 31 August 1999, Hamas was officially banned in **Jordan**, and a year later, in September 2000, the Second Intifada occurred, lasting until August 2005. Much more ferocious than the first, an estimated 5,500 Palestinians, 1,100 Israelis, and 64 foreigners were killed, civilian and military alike. The Intifada grew because of a lack of peaceful resolution to the Palestinian issue. During the Intifada, Israel assassinated longtime Hamas leader Yasin on 22 March 2004 and then a month later his successor Abelaziz Rantissi on 17 April. During this period, the Izz ad-Din Al-Qassam Brigades lost many leaders and were constantly under heavy bombardment from the Israeli forces. It is believed that Israel thought that in killing the main leaders within Hamas, the group would be dramatically weakened, but in reality it served only to increase membership, especially in Palestine. Although there have been a few cease-fire (*hudna*) agreements between Hamas and Israel (most recently on 19 June 2008 and 18 January 2009), the fighting sporadically continues between these two opponents.

During the January 2006 legislative elections in Palestine, Hamas became a direct beneficiary of the social uprising. The party attained the majority of votes (76 of 132 parliamentary seats), whereas the opposing and long-standing PLO party *Al-Fatah* only won 43 seats. On 20 March 2006, the Hamas cabinet was installed in Palestine's parliament, and tensions between the two groups continued to mount, especially in the Gaza Strip. Despite a February 2007 reconciliation agreement signed in Mecca by Palestinian President Mahmoud Abbas of *Al-Fatah* and Hamas leader **Khalid Mashaal** to create a national unifying government, conflicts resumed between the two groups four months later. Known as the June 2007 Battle of Gaza, Hamas gained control over the Gaza Strip by taking advantage of the lack of *Al-Fatah* forces there, resulting in the deaths of over 700. As a result of these events, many countries, such as **Egypt** and the **United States** as well as the European Union, stopped providing economic assistance to Palestine and the Gaza Strip. The group has also been subsequently banned and put on many watch lists in numerous countries because of its continuing brutality and lack of desire to adhere to **peace** accords. *See also* AL-AWLAKI, ANWAR; 'AYYASH, YAHYA ABD-AL-LATIF; ISLAMIC SOCIETY MOVEMENT; *JAYSH-AL-ISLAM*; *JUND ANSAR ALLAH*; MOVEMENT FOR THE SOCIETY OF PEACE; MUSLIM BROTHERHOOD IN JORDAN; POPULAR ARAB AND ISLAMIC CONFERENCE.

HARAKAT AL-NAHDA AL-ISLAMIYYA. *See ENNAHDA*.

HARAKAT-AL-SHABAAB-AL-MUJAHIDEEN (HSM)/AL-SHABAAB/ MUJAHIDEEN YOUTH MOVEMENT. Based in **Somalia**, HSM is a militant **Islamic group** that controls a majority of southern and central Somalia. It is also known as *Ash-Shabaab*, *Hizbul Shabaab* (Arabic for "The Party of the Youth"), and the Popular Resistance Movement in the Land of the Two Migrations. With the aim of overthrowing the current **government** (the Transitional Federal Government) and waging **jihad** against all **Western** forces in the country, *al-Shabaab* also has a large support system in the capital city of Mogadishu. Its members have been known to be increasingly brutal and **violent** in their applications of *sharia* (Islamic law). As of December 2008, the membership was estimated at 3,000 to 7,000. This group is one of the splinter organizations that originated in the **Islamic Courts Union**. The group's first major attack took place on 11 July 2010 during the World Cup final in Kampala, Uganda. A twin **bombing**, the attack killed over 70 people. Their latest large-scale attack was on 4 October 2011, when an *istishhad* of the group detonated a truck just outside a Somali ministry building, killing over 50 people. In response, the Kenyan government, on 16 October 2011, sent support to Somalia to help combat *al-Shabaab*.

Originally, the group was led by Aden Hashi Farah Ayro from 2002 until 2008 and has since seen three other **amirs**, including the current Ibrahim al-Afghani, who has been in power since 2010. Fazul Abdullah Muhammad, East Africa **al-Qaeda** leader since late 2009, is the group's military leader, and it has named Muktar Abdelrahman Abu Zubeyr as its spiritual leader. On 26 January 2009, *al-Shabaab* successfully stormed the base of the Transitional Federal Parliament in Baidoa, furthering its moves to destroy the Transitional Federal Government, which, since 31 January 2009, is headed by President Sharif Ahmed, a former Islamic Courts Union leader and one-time ally of *al-Shabaab*. The group regularly attacks international aid workers and relief organizations, putting them under even harsher pressure, as an estimated 3.5 million people in Somalia are dependent on the supplies and food that these organizations bring. The organization has also attacked the

Sufi Muslim population in the country, opposed the influence of the African Union, implemented the use of **suicide bombings**, and displaced tens of thousands of Somalis because of the attacks.

The increasing savagery and barbarism that has come to characterize the group has led many fighters and leaders to renounce their membership. One such high-profile departure was Mohamed Abdullahi (also known as Sheikh Pakistani), a commander of the group's Maymana Brigade, in 2009. *Al-Shabaab* also lost its deputy commander in chief, Ali Hassan Gheddi, in December 2009. On 1 February 2010, *al-Shabaab* officially announced its ties and allegiance to al-Qaeda and on 23–24 August 2010 carried out a series of assaults on Mogadishu, resulting in the killing of over 300 persons. *Al-Shabaab* experienced an increase in support on 20 December 2010, when *Hizb-e-Islam* and the Somalia Islamic Party joined the *Al-Shabaab* movement. *See also BOKO HARAM.*

HARAKIYYA/**ACTIVISM.** According to Islamic **fundamentalist** ideologies, actions are the result of conceptualizing based on a true formulation of **knowledge**. Therefore, correct and pious ideas are based on activism and the understanding of the **divine texts** based on those actions. Simply put, to be active and thereby take part in activism, one must have an intellect that has applied the doctrines of **Islam**. More so, a fundamentalist believes that activism in the political realm is of the utmost importance since the true values of **society** will be found within the sacred texts. Contemporarily, Islamic **extremists** have often used political activism as an outlet for their agenda.

AL-HASADI, ABDUL HAKIM. An Islamic militant from the **Libyan Islamic Combatant Group**, Abdul Hakim al-Hasadi fought with the **al-Qaeda** affiliates in **Afghanistan** and is the military governor of Derna, a port city in **Libya** that came under rebel control on 18 February 2011. He has been an active member of the Libyan uprising since it began in early 2011. Controversy surrounding his leadership in the Libyan Islamic Combatant Group (which was the al-Qaeda syndicate in Libya) and his dominant role in the Libyan rebellion has made many wonder if an **Islamic state** would be imposed on the country with figures such as al-Hasadi in strong positions. Also known as Abu Abdallah al-Sadek, in 2003 he was arrested and interrogated by the Central Intelligence Agency in Bangkok and then handed over to **Muammar Qadhafi**'s regime, which imprisoned him. He was released along with 214 other incarcerated militants in Libya in March 2010 by Qadhafi's son, Saif al-Islam, in the hope of bringing about reconciliation and **peace**. But not even a year later, al-Hasadi and many of his comrades who were released (including **Abdul Hakim Belhadj**) joined the anti-Qadhafi rebellion.

HASAN, NIDAL MALIK (1970–). Known for the 5 November 2009 shooting in Fort Hood, Texas, Nidal Malik Hasan has come to exemplify the breaking down of trust and infiltration of **extremists** within the military ranks of the **United States**. Since Hasan's actions were not unique to the Western military force (101st Airborne Operations Center insurgent Hasan Karim Akbar attacked his fellow soldiers while stationed in Kuwait, and Oklahoma City bomber Timothy McVeigh joined the U.S. Army in 1988 and even served in the Gulf War), it called for a reexamination of the American military's internal structure and members.

Born in Arlington, Virginia, to Palestinian-born parents, Hasan joined the U.S. Army in 1988, eventually gaining a degree as a psychiatrist and attaining the rank of major. After his attack (which occurred just a month before he was supposed to be deployed to **Afghanistan**), the military's ability to properly recruit and train its own soldiers to act against extremism was severely questioned. However, following an investigation of the attack, it seemed that Hasan had acted alone and was not aligned with any extremist group or movement, but there was sufficient evidence that he was in correspondence with American-born **al-Qaeda** spokesperson **Anwar al-Awlaki**.

Killing 13 of his fellow servicemen and wounding 30 others, Hasan's November 2009 actions prompted an in-depth look into his radicalization and led experts to analyze how such a "lone wolf" could emerge, especially within the system of armed services. Particular to Hasan's case were a number of factors that supposedly drove him toward his extremism. The death of his mother in May 2001 left him searching for a more pious life—one that he found in **Islam**. His views then became drastically conservative, and he soon began to adhere to the austere school of Islamic **fundamentalism**. During this period, he also started to attend the Dar al-Hijrah mosque in Virginia, which is known for being attended by two of the **World Trade Center and Pentagon attacks of September 11, 2001** hijackers as well. This exposure to the extremist trend of Islam did not combine well with his latest work as a military psychiatrist. His daily work was another factor that led to his radicalization. Ironically, he worked in the behavioral health field, and a majority of his work included counseling those returning from service in the Middle East. Speaking to his fellow soldiers about their time on deployment even more greatly affected his mental health during this vulnerable time in Hasan's life.

By 2003, his fellow colleagues at the Walter Reed Medical Center, where he was a resident, began noticing a change in his behavior, especially since he did not keep his extremist ideologies all that secret. In fact, he led a discussion at the military hospital that focused on questioning the American involvement in the Arab world and even called for the release of extremist Muslim militant prisoners. Some of his co-officers even made reports about his condition and the effect that his new religious convictions were having on his impending duties overseas. However, the military was most likely reluctant to lose a service member whom they had invested in like Hasan, and the reports filed for his removal from service were ignored.

Throughout the years, Hasan also donated thousands of dollars annually to various Islamic charity groups, constantly was in correspondence with al-Awlaki, and was continuously referring to online forums seeking justifications for **jihadist** actions. Despite all this communicative activity, especially from a service member, the information monitoring system that the George W. Bush administration prided itself on failed to detect Hasan's activities. However, despite the tragedy of the Fort Hood shootings, researchers of behavioral analysis have used this incident to develop a systemized method for identifying these types of perpetrators in the hope of eliminating such national security threats in the future.

In the wake of the attack, many pointed the finger of blame at Islam, but one specific ideology is not always the cause. Many different beliefs (both secular and sectarian) have resulted in domestic terrorism throughout the years. Comparative research has now become the way in which the military can identify and rehabilitate these "lone wolves." Also as a result, more and more anti-American, proviolence online resources have also been thoroughly monitored by the National Security Agency and the Federal Bureau of Investigation, and officers have been trained about these modern techniques of identifying and resolving such troubled individuals within the service ranks.

HASAN AL-BANNA IDEOLOGY. Hasan al-Banna believed that **religion** should touch every aspect of Islamic life and therefore involved different segments of **society** with his **Muslim Brotherhood**. Despite the wide array of platforms he used for discussion, all actions where based on **Islam**, the weakness of the Islamic world on the international stage, and the increasingly hostile situation in the **Palestinian Authority**. Al-Banna created a structured organization that implemented various communication, societal, and religious tools that were orchestrated by both **traditional** and **modern** means. These basic ideas helped effectively spread the Muslim Brotherhood movement all across the Islamic world and led it to become one of the most important Islamic **fundamentalist** movements. Al-Banna also declared the necessity to remove **Western** influences in education and the importance of the *shura* (consultation) council, whose members should (according to al-Banna) have thoroughly studied religious discipline. Despite his death, the ideologies of the Muslim Brotherhood continued on and blossomed into a new form of Islamic fundamentalism that focused on political reformation. Al-Banna's organization still continues to influence and inspire many

Islamic groups (militant and political alike). Today, the Muslim Brotherhood remains the largest Islamic organization in the world.

HASHASHIN. See ASSASSIN.

HATTAB, HASSAN (1967–). Founder of the Algerian **Islamic group** the **Salafi Group for Preaching and Combat** (SGPC), Hassan Hattab was born on 14 January 1967 in Rouiba, **Algeria**, and enlisted in the Algerian National Service, where he trained as a paratrooper along with **Saifi Ammari**. Like many members of the **Armed Islamic Group** (AIG), he joined after the 1992 canceled elections in Algeria and rose to the level of *amir*, or leader, of the Kabylia region. His dissension with the AIG occurred on 14 September 1998 because of his disapproval of the group's attacks on civilian lives, and he then formed the SGPC. The SGPC began operating primarily in the northeastern part of Algeria, but it then soon surpassed the AIG in its power and dominance. However, on 23 October 2003, Hattab lost his leadership position to Nabil Sahraoui, and the latter became the official head of the SGPC. During an announcement made by the SGPC on 9 February 2005, the group claimed that Hattab was completely excluded from the Islamist group and was deemed a "stranger to **jihad**."

HAWALA/HUNDI. A monetary transfer system based on informal arrangements and agreements, *hawala* is used by a large network of groups throughout North Africa, the Middle East, and South Asia. *Hawala* actually originated from eighth-century *sharia* (Islamic law) practices and is, in practice, a way of distributing funds or even settling debts through a type of honor system. In many countries, it remains the most reliable and well-functioning institution. This was the common financial practice throughout Africa and the Middle East until the modern banking system was introduced in the 19th century by the Europeans.

In *hawala*, the individuals who are responsible for the moving of funds are called *hawaladars* (in India, *angadia*) and usually receive a small stipend for the services provided. However, *hawala* is not limited to just monetary sums; goods and services may be exchanged as well. Quick, easy, and free of any **government** regulations or controls, *hawala* is often used by the majority of **extremist** groups and Islamists whose assets have been frozen by government sanctions. The system's verbal arrangements and lack of written records also make it attractive to illegal groups and militants who need to transfer finances between each other. Because of this, the practice has come under scrutiny by many governments and is criticized as nothing more than a money-laundering system. However, attempts to suppress or control the network have proven to be unsuccessful. *See also DUKHTARAAN-E-MILLAT*; ECONOMIC THEORY.

HAWARI. Hawari was the special forces and operations unit used by *Al-Fatah* and the **Palestinian Liberation Organization**. It also served as an intelligence organization especially under Yasir Arafat's leadership of *Al-Fatah*. Etymologically, the group derived its name from one Colonel Hawari (a.k.a. Abdullah Abdulhamid Labib) and has been active since 1985. Many members of *Hawari* were also former militants of the **May 15 Organization**. The group is most widely known for its April 1985 attack on the **Syrian** state airline company's office in Rome; the June 1985 bombing of the Geneva, Switzerland, train station; and the April 1986 bombing of TWA Flight 840 from Cairo to Athens. *Hawari* has also conducted attacks under the names of the Martyrs of Amn Araissi and the Martyrs of Tal Al-Za'atar.

HAWWA, SA'ID (1935–1989). Leader of the **Muslim Brotherhood in Syria**, Hawwa's ideology was based on the argument of **equality** for the people and their need for protection against regimes that might try to pervert their faith. According to Hawwa, power must have its basis in the *shura* (consultation), and there must be the choice to establish any **political party** or civil organization since the one-party system had proven to be unmanageable in the Islamic world. He also advocated for freedom of expression, equal rights, and accessibility to the courts. Hawwa added that members from minority groups should also be allowed to occupy parliamentary posts, thereby making representation equal and proportionate. *See also* DEMOCRACY.

HERESY/*BID'A*. Considered to be the most heinous crime in **Islam**, heresy is defined as deviating from the doctrines of the faith. This type of dissent, to Islamic **fundamentalists**, can occur when Muslims pray to any other person besides **Allah**, when **interpretations** of the **divine texts** are considered to be more liberal than austere, or when *sharia* (Islamic law) is not applied in an **Islamic state**.

Interestingly enough, many of the historical schools and sects of Islam are considered to be heretical as well. For example, **Sunni** Muslims in **Pakistan** feel that the **Ahmadiyya Muslims community**, the **Shia** Muslims, and the followers of **Sufism** are all heretics. The reverse happens as well with Shiites claiming that Sunnis are not true adherents to Islam and so forth. The points of contention between these groups are usually based on specific although serious differences. This makes heresy, in Islam, a matter of perception, depending on which school one adheres to. It has also resulted in many fellow Muslims being accused of **apostasy** and **blasphemy**.

This perception of heresy differs from that in **Christianity** and in the West more generally since, over time, slight variations of faith have become more acceptable. Most have also come to tolerate different forms of religion as long as there is some adherence to a broader creed. It has rather become more important in the West that a person or group believe in some form of doctrine rather than being completely atheistic, whereas most Muslims believe in a strict adherence devoid of any deviation. In addition, Islamic fundamentalists believe that Christians are heretics just as much as Christian fundamentalists believe that adherents of Islam are heretics too. *See also* INNOVATION.

HISTORY/*AL-TARIKH*. History is the way that **Allah** has envisioned the world's events, and since the Islamic **fundamentalists** believe that man is to model his actions in accordance with the **divine texts** of **Islam**, they should dismiss **modern** history because that history has separated man from the teachings of the texts. They feel that history has proven to be an obscuring force in man that has prevented him from understanding the true teachings of Allah. However, the fundamentalists participate indirectly in historicism by relating all matters in terms of political, quantifiable, and social circumstances. Yet it should be noted that historicism is relative to the fundamentalist's belief that natural laws that are beyond human control determine past events. *See also* PAST.

HIZB-AL-ADALA WA AL-TANMIA/*PARTI DE LA JUSTICE ET DU DÉVELOPPEMENT* (PJD)/JUSTICE AND DEVELOPMENT PARTY. Originally named the Constitutional and Democratic Popular Movement (which began in 1969), the PJD, in 1998, was formed out of a synthesis of smaller, promonarchial, moderate Islamist organizations in **Morocco** and since took on its new name. It is still often referred to in the media by the initials "PJD" for its French name.

As an **Islamic political party**, the PJD has participated in every Moroccan parliamentary election since 1997 and has obtained decent electoral results. The main reason for Morocco's tolerance of the PJD is because of the group's acceptance of the Moroccan **constitutional** system and its moderation in the promotion of the religious platform of the group. PJD prefers to use **Islam** as a way to safeguard Muslim identity and maintain traditions rather than resort to advocating an **Islamic state**, which could compromise the character of the **religion** in Morocco. The PJD is the pacifying, moderate Islamic group in the country that seeks to preserve Muslim cultural integrity through positive means. The group is currently led by Saad Eddine Othmani. *See also* AT-TAWHID; *SHABIBA ISLAMIYA* (ISLAMIC YOUTH)/MOROCCAN ISLAMIC YOUTH MOVEMENT.

HIZB-AL-NAHDA. *See ENNAHDA.*

HIZB-E-ISLAMI/ISLAMIC PARTY. Organized at Kabul University in 1975, *Hizb-e-Islami* was founded by Abduraheem Naizai. The group was inspired and originated from the Muslim Youth Organization, which was founded in 1969 at the same university to fight the growing communist forces in **Afghanistan** at the time. Ideologically similar to the **Muslim Brotherhood** and *Jamaat-e-Islami*, *Hizb-e-Islami* sought to replace the Afghan **government** and the numerous tribal factions with a unified **fundamental** Islamic **caliphate**.

In 1979, *Hizb-e-Islami* split into two groups, one led by Gulbuddin Hekmatyar (*Hizb-e-Islami Gulbuddin*) and the other by Mulavi Younas Khalis (the Khalis faction). However, on the political level, the nonviolent faction of the *Hizb-e-Islami* is a registered **Islamic political party** in Afghanistan. Led by Abdul Hadi Arghandiwal, in 2010 it was reported that the faction held 19 of the 246 parliamentary seats. *See also HIZB-UL-MUJAHIDEEN.*

HIZB-E-ISLAMI GULBUDDIN (HIG). Formed by Gulbuddin Hekmatyar in 1977, HIG splintered from *Hizb-e-Islami* when dissension within the group led to Mulavi Younas Khalis forming his own *Hizb-e-Islami* in 1979, known as the Khalis faction. Therefore, the group still led by Hekmatyar is referred to as HIG. An **Islamic political party** in **Afghanistan**, HIG was funded by the anti-Soviet forces during the Soviet-Afghan War (1979–1989) and retained a considerable dominance until the emergence of the **Taliban army** in the mid-1990s. Despite its decline in the early 2000s, HIG soon resurfaced and continued its program of brutal military insurgencies. The group's origins in the Soviet-Afghan War also led to financial ties with **Pakistan** and **Saudi Arabia**. Most of its members are veteran *mujahideen* from the war who also share the same goal of expelling the current political regime in Afghanistan and forcibly imposing an **Islamic state** based on *sharia* (Islamic law) and **fundamentalism** throughout the country.

The group has been noted for its intense training of militant Islamic **extremists** and its radical anti-**Western** posture. Notably, HIG attacked Kabul repeatedly in 1994, resulting in the deaths of more than 25,000 civilians. The group also tried to dissolve the individual tribal communities in hopes of an easier transition to an Islamic state, but this led to greater conflicts with the emerging Taliban army. Aggressions that did occur with the Taliban were a result of this goal to dissolve the tribal communities. The Taliban replaced the organization in September 1996, and many of the HIG militants took up arms with the new Afghan army, and many of its Pakistani training camps were taken over by the Taliban as well. Thus, HIG was predominantly and unofficially merged with **al-Qaeda** and the Taliban for ideological and logistical reasons. *See also AL-BADR.*

HIZB-E-WAHDAT-E-ISLAMI   AFGHANISTAN/ISLAMIC   UNITY PARTY OF AFGHANISTAN (IUPA). Established in 1989, the IUPA has been a viable militant and **Islamic political party** formed in order to bring together doctrinally similar, aggressive **Shiite** Islamic *mujahideen* groups under one body. The group acted as a major player in the Kabul skirmishes of 1992–1994 and the ensuing Afghan Civil War.

Inspired by the *Shuray-e-Eatelaf* alliance from 1985, the IUPA strove to stabilize the fighting as well as the politics in **Afghanistan**. This participation helped make its political platform more influential. In addition, the country's depredations from the war left a desire for an all-encompassing group that could properly represent the people's desires and ideological like-mindedness. A majority of its support also comes from the Hazara (Persian-language people mainly relocated in central Afghanistan) community, which has a long history in the political activities of the country, further increasing its vitality. However, throughout the 1990s and early 2000s, the organization became so broken up that it fragmented by 2009 into various groups that all took the name *Hizb-e-Wahdat* in some form.

HIZBULLAH/PARTY OF GOD. Basically, the term *Hizbullah* is a political one that is used to differentiate between those who adhere to *tawhid* (oneness of **Allah**), *sharia* (Islamic law), and the divine governance of Allah (*hakimiyya*) and those who do not (*Hizb-al-Shaytan*, Party of Satan). Those who fall under the *Hizb-al-Shaytan* label prefer an ideology that is consistent with *kufr* (unbelief), the laws of human governance, and **paganism**. Most **fundamentalists** argue that many Muslims are part of *Hizb-al-Shaytan* because they prefer a society based on the laws of man and do not adhere to *sharia*. Since members of *Hizb-al-Shaytan* do not implement a "true" Islamic way of life, they are therefore living in *dar al-harb* (abode of war), and a **jihad** against them is thus legitimized. *See also* BLASPHEMY; HERESY.

HIZBULLAH IN THE HIJAZ. *See* ISLAMIC JIHAD IN THE HIJAZ.

HIZBULLAH IN LEBANON. In **Lebanon**, *Hizbullah* is the name of the leading Islamic **fundamentalist** group in the country. When clashes erupted within the **Shiite** population after the **Israeli** invasion of Lebanon in 1982, the party was formed. Organized by a group of militant Shiites, the group considers **Muhammad Husayn Fadlallah** as its spiritual leader. Formed under the supposed sponsorship of the **Iranian Revolutionary Guards**, the group is based in the Biqa' Valley but also has contingents in Beirut and southern Lebanon. *Hizbullah* is considered a resistance group by most Lebanese people and a **terrorist** group by many countries. The organization officially announced its presence when it released a signed statement in 1994 memorializing the 18 September 1982 massacre at the Sabra and Shatila refugee camps in Beirut. It has been speculated that the group was formed by **Iranian** militants in order to gain popular support within the Shiite community. The U.S. Marines and Israeli army occupation in Lebanon in the early 1980s also provided opportunities for the Iranian forces to gain popularity within the country.

Ideologically, *Hizbullah* possesses a strong adherence to the **Quran** and uses Quranic terminology and justification in almost all its political writings. However, Quranic **interpretations** are limited to a small group of Islamic scholars (*ulama*) who are deemed to be the most learned men on **Islam**. This is in accordance with Shiite tradition, which believes that Quranic interpretation does not belong to the average Muslim. Members of *Hizbullah* also believe that the framework of the *ulama* can bring unification to Islam.

Structurally, an *'alim-qa'id* (scholastic leader) leads the *ulama*, who then directs the people, but the way in which any act is performed is up to the discretion of the people. At the top of the organization is the ***Majlis-al-Shura*** (Consultative Council), chaired by the charismatic leader of *Hizbullah*, Hasan Nasrallah. There are also several committees that exist within the organization: ideology, information, finance, judicial affairs, military affairs, political affairs, and social affairs. The group also believes that through *al-jihad al-akbar* (the greater struggle), it participates in a more encompassing service to Islam. Ideologically based on orthodox Shiite traditions, *Hizbullah* members also feel that **peace** and unity will come through the return of the Twelfth Imam, the *Mahdi*. This would lead to a revolution of the Islamic order and is a title that **Ayatollah Khomeini** first held.

Although the party began quietly, after the 1984 occupations in Lebanon, it started to create more of a stir within the media. A year later, in 1985, it declared its manifesto that sought a state based on ***sharia*** (Islamic law), expressed its disdain for the current **government** in Lebanon, and underlined its doctrinal uniqueness. The year 1988 saw the beginning of a war between *Hizbullah* and the ***Amal*** Party that lasted until 1990. The former was reasonably successful in both the military and political arenas as it continued to stress its goal of overthrowing the Lebanese government and installing *sharia*.

The group has also taken its membership conditions very seriously and has developed a very sophisticated propaganda and recruitment system. It holds lectures, seminars, and sermons; publishes a variety of literature; and reaches a wide audience that stretches from children to **women** to militants. Part of its success also comes from the social aid that the group has provided for many of the impoverished Shiites in the country. Financially, the group has supposedly received aid from Iran, but this information has been disputed. Currently, the group has focused more on political reforms than on engaging in armed attacks, but members stress that they have not given up on their *al-jihad al-akbar*. In many elections, *Hizbullah* won seats in the Lebanese Parliament, making it the largest group in the syndicate. In addition, in 2006, the Party of God proved its military efficiency when it took up arms against the Israeli army.

HIZBULLAH SHIITE MILITIA. *Hizbullah* in **Lebanon** began to train Iraqi **Shiite** militants in the southern parts of **Iraq** in 2003, presumably to avoid using the Farsi language of the Shiite in **Iran** and therefore to avoid a great amount of counter**terrorist** monitoring. In addition, the unstable conditions in Iraq in 2003 allowed various **extremist** groups to infiltrate the country and attract followers. However, the militia eventually did relocate to Iran by 2006 when the U.S. forces (still in Iraq) began to attack its contingents, especially those in Basra. This illustrates the resources that *Hizbullah* in Lebanon has to create an international training and operative presence that thereby can attract more support or influence. The Shiite populations in Iraq, which were given new freedom with the overthrow of Saddam Hussein in 2003, along with the dominant Shiite population in Iran, can serve to promote the interests of Iran and *Hizbullah* only through a brotherhood of faith. Its placement within Iraq was also instrumental in its anti-**Western** campaign, as a majority of Iraqis still held strong anti-American sentiments because of the 2003 invasion, which still has a military presence. It is also believed that the *Hizbullah* Shiite Militia gained support from the Iranian al-Quds Force and *Jaish-al-Mahdi*.

HIZB-UL-MOMINEEN. A **Shiite** sectarian group in Kashmir, *Hizb-ul-Momineen* has taken up arms to free Kashmir from Indian control. Although the **Pakistani** forces have tried to dissuade Shiite militant groups from entering into the Kashmir conflict, *Hizb-ul-Momineen* was the only group that was encouraged by **Pakistan**'s Inter-Services Intelligence (ISI). Comprised purely of Shia Muslims, the group took root in the early 1990s. Its first leader, Shuja Abbas, continued to clash with the ISI and was forced to resign from his post. The group is currently under the command of Sayed Ijaz. *Hizb-ul-Momineen* has not engaged in many aggressive actions; instead, it insists on focusing its efforts on avoiding any Shia-**Sunni** discord that may take place in Kashmir. In fact, this was instigated when Pakistan's ISI asked the organization to take responsibility for the murder of Shiite Indian sympathizers that was conducted by Sunni **extremists**. The reason for this claim was ironically to prevent India from orchestrating Shia-Sunni tensions after the killings. *See also* KASHMIRI SEPARATISM.

HIZB-UL-MUJAHIDEEN **(HuM)/MUJAHIDEEN MOVEMENT.** Established in the Kashmir Valley in 1989 by Ahsan Dar, *Hizb-ul-Mujahedeen* is a Kashmir liberation group that is based in Muzaffarabad, **Pakistan**. The group was formed by *Jamaat-e-Islami* at the reported behest of Pakistan's Inter-Services Intelligence to become another aggressive force against the Jammu and Kashmir Liberation Front (a group that desires total independence in the area). The goals of the HuM are not only to make Jammu and Kashmir part of Pakistan but to implement *sharia* (Islamic law) throughout the area as well. Sayeed Salahudeen (a.k.a. Muhammad Yusuf Shah) is the group's current leader, and it has become the largest and most widely supported **Islamic group** in Jammu and Kashmir. HuM has proven itself to be effective despite its limited personnel strength, which is estimated at only 1,500. The group has divided itself into five cells operating in six different locations throughout Jammu and Kashmir: the Central, Chenab, Gool, Northern, Southern, and Pir Panjal Divisions.

In 2000, when Dar initiated cease-fire (*hudna*) accords with the Pakistani government, dissension ran high throughout the HuM, resulting in Salahudeen breaking away and creating the **United Jihad Council**. Although the accords never came to fruition, members of HuM were still torn between which of their two leaders to follow. In January 2002, Dar was replaced by Saiful Islam as HuM's commander in Kashmir, although he was killed in an attack shortly after on 2 April. Ghazi Nasiruddin is now the operations commander in the Kashmir Valley region. Dar's followers were quickly marginalized by Salahudeen's faction, which was becoming increasingly more pernicious. HuM has worked closely with both the *Hizb-e-Islami* and different *mujahedeen* groups by providing training and arms for one another. The group's actions are limited to the Jammu and Kashmir areas, and, although some civilian deaths have occurred because of its attacks, the group insists that it is targeting solely Indian security forces. *See also* AL-BADR; KASHMIRI SEPARATISM; *LASHKAR-E-TAYYIBA*.

HIZB-U-TAHRIR/**PARTY OF LIBERATION.** *Hizb-u-Tahrir* is an **Islamic political party** that seeks an integral **Islamic state** based on *sharia* (Islamic law) and ruled under a unifying elected **caliphate** for the entire Muslim world. Established in 1953 by **Palestinian** Islamic scholar **Taqiuddin al-Nabhani** in Jerusalem, the movement has spread to numerous

Arabic countries, although it is deemed illegal in many of them. According to *Hizb-u-Tahrir*, the establishment of a caliphate would bring unity and security through the doctrines of *sharia* and ***da'wa***. Like most political **Islamic groups**, it believes that the influence of **Western** civilization has been the primary source of corruption within the Islamic nation (***umma***) and therefore must be completely eradicated if a "pure" state of **Islam** is to exist. This translates into the overthrow of many **governmental** regimes since they have a loosely **democratic** construction and are part of the Western world. *Hizb-u-Tahrir* also has a strong anti-Zionist position and calls for the dissolution of **Israel**. Al-Nabhani has further stated in his writings that this unified, transnational Islamic state is not only a religious duty but also an obligation to **Allah** that is punishable if not pursued.

Although the group uses the word *hizb*, it is not a true political party. Structurally, the group is incredibly centralized with its core leadership being based in the Palestinian Territories. Throughout the regions where *Hizb-u-Tahrir* has a presence, there are underlying networks of local leaders and committee members with a head, called a *mushrif* (supervisor), who is the only one in contact with the other factions of *Hizb-u-Tahrir*. When al-Nabhani died in 1977, he was succeeded by Abd al-Qadim Zallum, who was then replaced in 2003 by Ata Khalil Abu-Rashta. The group has also produced a draft **constitution**; among its clauses is the formation of an *Amir al-Jihad* (Commander of the Jihad) that would regulate the defense of the state, under the direction of the caliph, and calls for any male over 15 years to take military training. The proposed document also calls for the formation of a ***shura*** (consultation) council and the banning of non-Muslims from secular occupations and forbids participation in any organization that is not Islamic (such as the World Bank and the International Monetary Fund).

Reportedly, *Hizb-u-Tahrir* has active branches in 40 countries with a total membership reaching the tens of thousands. It is listed as a legitimate organization in the United Arab Emirates, **Lebanon**, and **Yemen**, while arrests and suppression frequently take place in countries such as **Egypt**, **Jordan**, **Morocco**, **Syria**, and **Tunisia**. The group has also been noticeably active in **Libya**, working alongside the **Muslim Brotherhood in Libya**. In Central Asian Islamic countries such as Azerbaijan, Kazakhstan, Tajikistan, and Uzbekistan, the group has attracted numerous followers who have carried out attacks in the name of *Hizb-u-Tahrir*, leading to the suppression and detainment of many alleged members. **Bangladesh**, Indonesia, and Malaysia have also experienced a *Hizb-u-Tahrir* presence. A notable satellite group is active in Great Britain and is the leading British Islamist organization followed by the **Muslim Association of Britain**. *See also* CENTRAL ASIAN ISLAMIC ACTIVITY.

HIZB UT-TAHRIR AL-ISLAMI. See ISLAMIC LIBERATION PARTY.

HOLY TEXTS. *See* DIVINE TEXTS.

HOLY WAR. *See* JIHAD.

AL-HOUTHI, SAYYID YAHIA BADREDDIN (1965–). Shiite leader of the *Shabaab al-Munimin* **Islamic political party** in **Yemen**, Sayyid Yahia Badreddin al-Houthi's brothers were political activists as well: Abdul Malik al-Houthi also leads the group and Hussein Badreddin al-Houthi and Abdul Karim al-Houthi once did as well. This has made *Shabaab al-Munimin* also become known as the al-Houthis. As he and the group were key players in the Houthi Rebellion, he was sentenced to imprisonment on 5 February 2010 by the Yemeni government, but he still remains at large. Opposed to the Yemenite people, who are predominantly **Sunni**, the al-Houthis are allegedly funded by the **Islamic Republic of Iran**.

AL-HUDAYBI, HASAN (?–1972). In the wake of **Hasan al-Banna**'s death, Hasan al-Husaybi became the leader of the **Muslim Brotherhood** in 1949. Although not very well known within the group, he represented the middle ground between the radical and moderate branches of the Brotherhood. This compromise helped him eventually gain popularity within the organization. During his time as leader of the Brotherhood, he appointed **Sayyid Qutb** editor of the group's periodical, *Al-Ikwan al-Muslimun* (Muslim Brethren), and made him a member of the *Maktab al-Irshad* (Guidance Bureau), the highest body within the Brotherhood's structure. Although the two men were influential within the organization, al-Hudaybi disagreed with Qutb's **radicalism** and in turn published his own book, *Du'at La Qudat* (Callers, Not Judges). Al-Hudaybi was arrested and sentenced to death along with Qutb, but the former's term was commuted to a life sentence.

HUDNA/**CEASE-FIRE.** A truce or agreement among fighting opponents, the *sharia* (Islamic law) on *hudna* stipulates that a cease-fire between Muslim and non-Muslim parties can last no longer than 10 years. In contemporary history, the term is most commonly used to refer to the cease-fires between **Israel, Palestine, Jordan, Hamas**, and the **Islamic Jihad of Palestine**.

HUDUD/**DETERRENTS.** In **Islam**, legal restrictions (or deterrents) have been set up within the realm of social crimes. This was done to ensure social **justice** within the community. *Hudud* are therefore seen as not only legal doctrines but also social and political boundaries that will help create **peace**.

Examples of *hudud* include the death penalty for adultery, **apostasy**, **blasphemy**, **heresy**, and so on.

HUMAN RIGHTS/*HUQUQ AL-INSAN***.** Most Islamic **fundamentalists** do not acknowledge human rights with the exception of those outlined by the **Quran** and proposed by *sharia* (Islamic law). Any ideas about human rights as outlined by a philosophical or secular system are not credible to the fundamentalists. Some radicals, such as **Abu al-A'la al-Mawdudi** and **Sayyid Qutb**, believe that the issue of human rights is simply a political platform being used by **Western** forces to gain influence in the Islamic world. With regard to the moderate Islamists, they believe that the **divine texts** (**Quran** and **Hadiths**) are the source of human rights and that **Islam** was the first **system** (*nizam*) to provide such a luxury to its people. The moderates (e.g., **Muhammad Salim al-'Awwa** and **Rashed al-Ghannushi**) also feel that the **modern** ideas of *huquq al-insan* should be viewed under the lens of the Islamic perspective and therefore would be acceptable to be incorporated into Muslim society.

However, these human rights are not precisely the same or as numerous as the human rights proclaimed by Western countries and, indeed, adopted by universal organizations, such as the United Nations, in numerous conventions, declarations, and resolutions. If not completely adopted, they are at least appreciated and respected by at least the moderate Islamists. This was illustrated in their repeated demands for human rights in the struggles against countless dictatorships and, most remarkably, by the Arab Spring. However, this view does not seem to prevail among the radical Islamists. These groups rather resort to actions that disregard even such elementary rights as the right to life and liberty, which is violated by **assassinations**, **bombings** (including **suicide bombings**), and kidnappings. This is also seen in undermining the rights of **democracy** and equality for **women**, to say nothing of inhibiting freedom of speech and freedom of **religion**. Such acts contributed to the hatred of **extremism** abroad but also a growing distaste for these ideological hard-liners even in the Islamic countries. *See also* AL-TURABI, HASSAN 'ABD ALLAH.

HUNDI. *See HAWALA.*

I

IBN BADIS, 'ABD AL-HAMID (1889–1940). Born in Constantine, **Algeria**, **'Abd al-Hamid Ibn Badis** was one of the most influential and renowned Islamic reformers of the early 20th century. Supposedly influenced by **Muhammad 'Abdu** and **Jamal al-Din al-Afghani**, Ibn Badis formed *Jam'iyyat al-'Ulama' al-Muslimin* (Association of Muslim Scholars) in 1931. With the goal to reform **Islam**, his movement began as a way to emphasize the Islamic identity against the French colonial power in Algeria. Ideologically, he advocated for the "rebirth" of Islam and religious tolerance (although he regularly condemned the **Sufists** for their rituals), asked for Arabic to be recognized as the official language of Algeria, and stressed the importance of nationalism. Ibn Badis believed that through educational reforms and the glorification of free will, Islam could be improved.

IBN TAYMIYYA, TAQIY AL-DIN AHMAD (1263–1328). The most influential thinker of the **Sunni** Islam medieval period, Ibn Taymiyya still remains an important figure to the contemporary radical **fundamentalists**, such as **'Abd al-Salam Faraj** and **Sayyid Qutb**. A Hanafli scholar and often referred to as "Sheikh al-Islam" (a title of the utmost superiority in Islamic scholarship), Ibn Taymiyya lived during the time of the Mongol invasions of the Islamic world (1257 and 1258), which deeply influenced and prompted his doctrinal writings. Ideologically, he believed in the absolute supremacy and literalism of the **Quran**, the *Sunna* of the Prophet, and the *Salaf al-Salih* (the pious ancestors). To him, any deviation from these three facets of **Islam** constituted *bid'a* (**innovation**) and should be forbidden. He also felt that **theology** weakened society, and his views on the *kufr* (unbelief) of the Mongol rulers of his time are likened to the radicals' views on the modern rulers in the Islamic world.

In fact, he famously declared a *fatwa* against the Mongol invaders while he was in **Syria**, stating that a **jihad** against them was an obligation of every Muslim. This was based on the Mongols' adherence to their Yassa legal code, which was not founded on *sharia* (Islamic law) and therefore made them akin to *jahiliyya* (paganists). His devotion to the Holy Struggle was so great that he is credited with stating that the jihad is the greatest act of voluntary service any man could do for **Allah**.

He was also avidly against **traditionalism** (*taqlid*), which has influenced groups such as the **Muslim Brotherhood**, among others. Considered the thinker who brought **Salafism** to the Islamic world, Ibn Taymiyya believed that the first three generations of Islam (Salafists)—the **Prophet Muhammad**, his companions, and the followers of the companions—were the ultimate models of how to live a pure Islamic life. His most notable text is *Kitab iqtida al-sirat al-mustaqim* (On the Necessity of the Straight Path), in which he strongly expressed his abhorrence to borrowing any type of traditions or doctrines from non-Muslim religions, such as **Christianity**, including celebrating the Prophet's birthday or constructing mosques around the burial grounds of prominent figures of Islam. Ibn Taymiyyah's work influenced a number of Islamic thinkers, such as **Abul Alaa al-Maududi** and **Muhammad Ibn Abd al-Wahhab** (founder of **Wahhabism**).

IJMA'/**CONSENSUS.** Consensus has been seen as the source of political authority in **Islam** since it is the foundation of the *shura* (consultation) council, as the council depends on consent from all its members. Muslim scholars have also attributed the term *'aqd al-bay'a* (the contract of **allegiance**) to the idea of the consensus. In other words, it is the social contract between the ruler and the ruled in order to reduce the threat of despotism and increase the rights of the individual. Islamic **fundamentalists** have also argued that this concept is rooted in Islam and that **Western** culture has taken from it. However, most scholars tend to underscore the importance of *ijma'* in Islamic textual **interpretations**. *Ijma'* has been seen as the way to reduce the ideological and political problems that exist within the current **Islamic society**. The moderates agree that **democracy** should be reevaluated in terms of consensus and Islamic law *sharia* (Islamic law) in order to remove the corruption that currently exists.

Although *ijma'* is sometimes seen as theoretical, its application can lead to a much-needed reformation. Radical fundamentalists believe that consensus will free and liberate Islam from the tyranny of the political traditions that have existed within contemporary Muslim society. Both moderates and radicals have agreed on the idea of consensus since they believe in the communal interpretation of the holy texts to evaluate actions and elect leaders. If there is no popular approval (consensus), then *sharia* is not properly being enacted.

AL-IKHWAN/**BRETHREN.** Composed of **Wahhabists**, this group was used by 'Abd al-'Aziz Ibn Saud (who established the current kingdom of **Saudi Arabia** in the early 20th century) to provide inspiration for the followers of the strict cultural practices within his kingdom. *Al-Ikhwan* is then also the label that is sometimes affixed to Wahhabi activists. When the new state of Saudi Arabia came to power in the 1930s, the group was suppressed, but it has persevered and is still in existence today. Currently, the group prefers the name *Al-Muwahhidin*—the monotheists. *See also* AL-SAUD; AL-WAH-HAB, MUHAMMAD IBN ABD.

ILYAS, MUHAMMAD (1885–1944). Born in the then United Province of British India in 1885, Ilyas is known for his theory of what he describes as "the mission of the Prophets." Essentially, it calls for the creation of *jamaats*, Arabic for "assemblies," which would then go to various tribal regions and **call** for those Muslims to return with the *jamaat* to different mosques. Each *jamaat* would be comprised of at least 10 men and would preach Ilyas's constructed "Six Principles." These principles (similar to the Five Pillars of **Islam**) are *kalimah* (the profession that the only figures in Islam are **Allah** and the **Prophet Muhammad**), *salah* (five daily prayers), *ilm* and *dhikr* (reciting passages from the **Quran** and **Hadiths** while in congregation and listening to the words of an *amir*), *ikram-i-Muslim* (the respectful and civil treatment of fellow Muslims), *tashih-i-niyyat* (living one's life in the image and likeness of Allah), and *tafrigh-i-waqt* (following the message of the Prophet and revealing it to others). *See also* TABLIGHI JAMAAT.

INNOVATION/*BID'A*. For Islamic **fundamentalists**, *bid'a* describes the un-Islamic doctrines of contemporary society in opposition to the rules of the earlier period of **Islam**. It is the fact of bringing new or "alien" elements within the **Islamic societies** as opposed to the way of the Salafia (pious ancestors). Innovation, to them, is a negative term that has tainted Muslim society. However, the moderate fundamentalists may see innovations, such as **democracy**, as positive cultural borrowings or social advancements. *See also* HERESY; HISTORY; MODERNISM.

INSPIRE. The first English-language online periodical published by **al-Qaeda in the Arabic Peninsula**, *Inspire*'s premiere issue was released in July 2010. In creating a publication in English, **al-Qaeda** hopes to attract American and British insurgents to join the Islamic cause and encourage dissension within the two countries. The magazine possesses a range of information from translated messages from **Osama bin Laden** to propagandistic articles that encourage violent acts of **extremism** and slander of the **Western** governments. It has been reported that Samir Khan, an American-born **Yemenite** and al-Qaeda affiliate, is the main author of *Inspire* and that al-Qaeda in the Arabic Peninsula leading member **Anwar al-Awlaki**, also born in the

United States, is its creator. Thought to be a variant of the Arabic online magazine *Sada al-Malahim* (Echo of the Battlefield), *Inspire* has thus far released new editions every three months. According to *Inspire*, its name comes from a transliterated verse in the **Quran** that states, "Inspire the believers to fight." Clearly targeting **Islamic** sympathizers in the United States and Great Britain, readers are also able to submit their own articles for publication and are allowed to comment on already published ones. The 2011 issues mostly focused on the "new techniques of **jihad**."

INTERPRETATION/*TAFSIR*. The term "interpretation" in **Islam** is relegated to the attempts of humans to decipher and read the **holy texts** of Islam, specifically the **Quran**. It can also refer to the effects that a current cultural climate might have on the reading of the text (although this view is more often used by the radical **fundamentalists**). Many Islamic fundamentalists believe that Islam's fall from global dominance is a result of a failed *tafsir* of the holy texts. They feel that if *tafsir* were conducted properly, Islam would be the contemporary source of influence and a social powerhouse of the world. Many fundamentalists then agree that Islam should reinterpret the Quran so as to shed the culture of the previously staining **interpretations**, which left **Islamic society** open to injustices.

INTIFADA. Arabic for "an uprising or revolt," the term refers specifically to two popular rebellions that took place in the Gaza Strip and the West Bank. Both events revolved around **Palestinians** revolting against the **Israeli** occupying forces within those territories.

The First Intifada started on 9 December 1987 in the Gaza Strip as a direct result of an automobile accident in which the Israeli driver killed some Palestinian pedestrians. It began mildly with a group of university students taunting and throwing debris at Israeli troops but then quickly escalated to a point where almost the entire Palestinian population in the Gaza Strip began to form demonstrations and boycotts and to partake in various forms of civil disobedience. Although the outbreak and political violence of this uprising seemed to occur spontaneously, it was revealed that, in fact, the **Islamic Jihad of Palestine**, **Hamas**, and the **Palestinian Liberation Organization** orchestrated many of the leading insurgencies of the First Intifada. However, a global concern over the unbridled **violence** taking place at the hands of the Israeli security forces on the Palestinian activists began to take hold. By 1989, the Israel Defense Forces was charged by the U.S. government with **human rights** violations and for causing many unwarranted deaths of Palestinian protestors. By 1990, the intifada began to lose its energy, and its conclusion can be officially marked by the signing of the Oslo Accords in 1993. In the end, it was reported that 1,162 Palestinians and 160 Israelis died during the revolt.

The Second Intifada began on 28 September 2000 and was based around the attacks and **suicide bombings** of various Islamic militants, such as the **Al-Aqsa Martyrs' Brigade**, *Al-Fatah*, **Hamas**, and **jihadist** groups, throughout the Gaza Strip and the West Bank. However, the rebellion began as a protest against the arrival of the Israeli Ariel Sharon (then head of the Likud Party) at the Temple Mount (*Haram al-Sharif*) in Jerusalem, which is considered the third-holiest shrine in **Islam**. The violence and force that took place during the Second Intifada was much higher than that of the first. Israel resorted to aerial strikes and launched rockets, and the **peace** agreements made in 1993 between Israel and Palestine were completely abolished. This was also more than likely attributed to Sharon's election as Israel's prime minister on 6 February 2001.

This intifada lasted for approximately eight years, during which the Israeli and Palestinian forces attacked each other's military and civilian posts with countless **bombings**, raids, and **suicide bombings** on the Palestinian side, resulting in a strict travel ban in Israel. Both governments also went through a great amount of political upheaval and legislative changes. In hopes of subduing the violence, Sharon called for all Israeli nationals residing in the occupied territories of Gaza and the West Bank to return to Israel. Meanwhile, the Palestinian attacks actually increased. Finally, on 8 February 2005, newly elected Palestinian Authority President Mahmoud Abbas entered into negotiations with Sharon at the Sharm al-Sheikh Summit to end the fighting. Despite the diplomats' efforts to negotiate a **cease-fire** and peace, Israel and Hamas continued to target each other's leaders and military cadres. With the fighting reaching an absolute peak, a peace agreement was finalized between Abbas and Sharon on 18 June 2008. During these eight years of the Second Intifada, an estimated 5,322 Palestinians and 1,057 Israelis died. *See also* HARAKIYYA.

INTUITION/*FITRA*. Intuition is the contrary of reflection. It is viewed as the law of nature to the **fundamentalists**. According to them, it is the natural force that drives all men to seek out the good as well as **Allah**. *Fitra* comes as naturally to men as a physical law does and is also used as a replacement for **philosophy** (*falsafa*) in the fundamentalist debates.

IQBAL, MUHAMMAD (1877–1938). A Pakistani reformist, philosopher, and poet, Muhammad Iqbal left an intellectual legacy that is still felt widely today. Influenced by the works of Sayyid Ahmad Khan, he was involved in the political scene of India and was instrumental in the creation of **Pakistan**.

This was due largely to the All-India Muslim League, of which he was a member. Iqbal was also elected to India's Parliament from 1930 to 1936.

IRAN, ISLAMIC REPUBLIC OF. The success of the **Iranian Islamic Revolution of 1979** has resulted in the country becoming the primary exporter of influence with regard to how the successful installations of an **Islamic state** can occur. Because of this, the country has also been accused of providing not only ideological support but also financial and military aid to various **Islamic groups**, both moderate and radical, sometimes correctly, sometimes not. The specific accusations of the state-sponsored **extremist** activities can be traced back to **Ayatollah Khomeini**'s insistence that an aggressive approach be used in order to properly oust any current authority and replace it with an Islamic one. When Khomeini and his adherents finally removed the Pahlavi monarchy on 11 February 1979, all the radical militant groups were amalgamated into the **Iranian Revolutionary Guards**, which has had an influence both domestically and internationally over the past few decades.

As the Islamic Republic of Iran continued to grow in power, its militancy also increased, culminating in the Iraq-Iran War (1980–1988), which was launched by Saddam Hussein of **Iraq**. This bloody battle served only to further encourage the Iranian belief that tactical, bellicose approaches were the most desirable, leading them to spread this doctrine even farther throughout the rest of the Muslim world. When Khomeini died in 1989, the next 10 years witnessed only an even more dramatic increase in Iranian hostilities both internally and externally. The republic and its **Iranian Revolutionary Guards** were held responsible for a number of political **assassinations** and **bombings** and for assisting **jihadist** groups in a number of countries. The country has even strengthened its ties with *Hizbullah* **in Lebanon** and the **al-Qaeda** organization over the recent years.

Although the Republic of Iran was founded on **Shiite** doctrines of **Islam**, the country has not based its international assistance on other countries' ideological commitments. While the different organizations and individuals that Iran has sponsored have not necessarily always been Shiite adherents, their commonality has always been to serve the interest of Iran as a whole. This sponsorship has allegedly reached *Hizbullah* in Lebanon and its insurgencies against **Israel** (specifically in providing arms), the post-**Baathist** Iraq (in the form of political support for the Shiite political groups and anti-**Western** militants), **Afghanistan**'s **Taliban army** (in providing ammunition and training for its militants), and **Palestine** (giving financial support to such groups as **Hamas** and the **Islamic Jihad of Palestine**).

The 2003 removal of Saddam Hussein from power in Iraq had a significant impact on Iranian diplomacy within that country. Viewed as Iran's greatest enemy, the removal of the Baathist Party was an opportunity for Shiites to gain religious influence within Iraq—since the Shiite population was notably suppressed during Hussein's reign. Iranian Shiite interests have even tried to infiltrate the Shiite communities in **Egypt**, **Morocco**, and **Yemen** as well. The 2011 **Arab Spring** protests have also been an avenue by which Iran has tried to influence foreign populations. Many have even called these social revolutions the start of the "Islamic awakening"—merely a continuation of the Iranian Revolution on the international level. However, when this Iranian support reached **Bahrain** (a kingdom that quickly and forcefully tried to squash the rebellion), **Saudi Arabia** also got involved to try and eliminate Iranian influence there and increase its own.

Yet it must be noted that a nationwide desire for the Iranian exportation of its revolutionary ideas does not really exist, especially since this has translated into radical Islamism in many countries. So the funding of international Islamic groups remains a concern within the state and a small percent of the upper-class elite—this is not a communal exportation. Public support also seemed to wane with Iran's financial assistance during the 2006 Israeli-*Hizbullah* conflict in **Lebanon**; many Iranians objected to the state giving money to international causes rather than providing its own people with financial assistance and civil aid. However, there does seem to be greater popular support for the Palestinian conflicts with Israel—although it still is marginal in comparison to the desire for internal aid, as the country has suffered from a tremendous economic downswing which began in 2008.

There also exists a wide array of religious minorities within the country. Although all are relatively small in size compared to the Shiite majority, they nevertheless exist and are frequently subjected to religious persecution by the state. This religious animosity against the minority has also made these groups dread any presence of Islamic **radicalism** within the country—fearing that it would lead only to greater persecution.

Radical Islam makes itself felt within Iran through a number of outlets. First and foremost, as previously mentioned is the Iranian Revolutionary Guards (domestically referred to as *Pasdaran*). The organization is not only domestic but also international in providing military training, arms supplies, and finances for political and radical operations. The Ministry of Intelligence and Security is another oppressive group but one that is controlled by the ruling clerical body. The organization has also allegedly used Iranian job posts that require an international presence as a front to conduct operations against any group or movement that seeks to undermine the Iranian state, including such bodies as the Ministry of Foreign Affairs and the Cultural Affairs Ministry. A more domestically oriented group focused on control is *Basij*. Originally established as a militant force during the Iran-Iraq War, the group now operates internally to regulate and monitor daily life in Iran. It also partici- pates in the training of militants. The *Ansar-e-Hizbullah* was also created to conduct similar activities as *Basij*, but it is focused more on the universities.

Despite all the provisions the state has made to suppress opposition, two groups have been noteworthy in targeting Iran: the **Mujahideen-e-Khalq** and the Free Life Party of Kurdistan. *Mujahideen-e-Khalq* is an extremist group ideologically based on an Islamic-socialist doctrine. Although present in the country before the 1979 revolution, afterward it relocated to Iraq to avoid being swiftly eliminated by the new republic. With the group now being sup- ported by Iraq, it was seen as an even greater threat to Iran. The group's ac- tivities and gains declined significantly following the 2003 Baathist removal, and it is currently all but defunct. The Free Life Party of Kurdistan, although small, has been successful in conducting attacks against Iran since its incep- tion in 2004. Tactically, the group targeted Iranian military camps and runs on a platform of installing **democracy** by force and defending the Kurdish minority within the state.

Domestically, June 2009 saw an immense amount of civil protests within the country—arguably the greatest since the 1979 Revolution. Brought on by the reelection of Mahmoud Ahmadinejad as the sixth president of Iran, it was widely believed that this member of the **Islamic Society of Engineers** was reelected fraudulently. Since Iran is governed in a **theocratic** manner, a deep questioning of the clerical body that oversees the government was severely repressed. In response to the riots, the state began to crack down on media outlets and opposition party members and even suppressed foreign anti-Iranian sentiments. The country has continued with this control of the opposition, and the media continue to be regulated. Since the uprisings, hundreds of Iranians have been imprisoned and executed for speaking out against the republic. This domestic policy has only intensified with the onset of the Arab Spring in 2011.

IRANIAN ISLAMIC REVOLUTION OF 1979. Arguably the greatest modern example of Islamic **activism** (*harakiyya*), the basis of this revolution (1977–1979) was the opposition to the shah of **Iran** and led to his eventual ousting. It was in the aftermath of the Iranian Revolution that an overwhelm- ing sense of Islamic awakening erupted all over the Islamic world. The revo- lutionaries wished to change the political, economic, and religious climate of Iran as well as spread the **Shiite** doctrines throughout the Islamic world whose majority is **Sunni**. The revolution also led to the appearance of *Harakat Amal al-Islamiyya* (the Islamic *Amal* Movement) and *Hizbullah* **in Lebanon**. The main activists who supported the revolution were religious scholars, militant groups, **political parties** (notably the communist Tudeh Party and *Mujahi- deen-e-Khalq*), and various intellectuals—but it was the religious scholars who proved to be most influential. After the overthrow of Muhammad Reza Shah Pahlavi on 11 February 1979, the Islamic scholars acted as custodians of the new political **system** of the republic and also seemed to incite the most **activism** throughout the population during the rebellion.

Of these scholars, **Ayatollah Ruhollah al-Musawi Khomeini** was the most influential and quickly gravitated to the center of the revolution. His urge for the removal of the Pahlavi dynasty was shown by his persistent activism and preaching. Interestingly enough, he was in exile for 13 years before becoming the leading voice in the revolution, making his prominence that much more unexpected. Through Khomeini's enforcement of **Islam**, the opposing groups united: the middle classes supported the right for private ownership, foreign interference was rejected, social justice was advocated, and the support of agriculture as an economic base was encouraged. *Istishhad* (martyrdom), *Ramadan* (the month of fasting), and *'Ashura* (the day of remembering the martyrdom of Husayn ibn Ali, grandson of the **Prophet Muhammad**) all proved to be viable Islamic symbols that helped mobilize the people even further.

After the monarchy was deposed, an Islamic Revolutionary Council and temporary revolutionary government along with the Islamic Republican Party were formed as the ruling bodies of Iran. The religious scholars assumed the powers of the **government** and established the Assembly of Experts (*Majles-e-Khebregan-e-Rahbar*), which drafted the new **constitution** based on Shiite ideologies and *sharia* (Islamic law). However, shortly after its victory, the new Republic of Iran faced an economic downturn as the **West** placed a boycott on the country in 1980. Shortly after, the country was also dragged into the Iraqi War until 1989, creating more financial instability for the new state. *See also* IRANIAN REVOLUTIONARY GUARDS.

IRANIAN REVOLUTIONARY GUARDS. Established in 1979 as a protective organization, the Revolutionary Guards are now considered one of the most important militant groups in **Iran**. Originally formed to militarily help protect **Ayatollah Ruhollah al-Musawi Khomeini**'s rebel forces, the group became integrated into the security forces of the country after the revolution. It is also a formidable entity that deals with political and social matters of the state as well. The end of the 1988 war in **Iraq** further enhanced the group's influence as it became the majority contingent in the Iranian military organization. To this day, it continues to play the dual role of being a military and civil defense unit. Politically, the group has also had influence with the appointment of many of its members into the Iranian bureaucracy, parliament, and the Guardian Council of the Constitution (*Shora-ye Negahban-e-Qanun-e-Assassi*). Structurally, the Revolutionary Guards (also known as *Pasdaran*) have maintained a complex network of internal security apparatuses that has helped further their longevity. The group also developed into an international front when they provided assistance to **Hizbullah** **in Lebanon**. *See also* IRANIAN ISLAMIC REVOLUTION OF 1979.

IRAQ. This Arabic country has a long and rich history that includes secular, **Islamic**, **Shiite**, and **Sunni** movements and also has a large Kurdish minority population. Iraq has a rich and diverse heritage comprised of many groups, yet about 97 percent of Iraqis are practicing Muslims with a majority being adherents of the Shiite branch of Islam. Demographically, the Sunni Iraqis inhabit most of the northern and central regions of the country. Since 2003, both branches have been allowed the freedom of open expression—a luxury most appreciated by the once-repressed Shiite population. It is a direct result of the removal of Saddam Hussein's **Baathist Party** in 2003 that **Islamic groups** have reentered the Iraqi sociopolitical circuit.

However, this is also true for the militant Islamic groups as well. The waning security forces and the inability for the country to establish a strong **government** has allowed these groups to foster. This is most felt in the northern regions, where the militants have been strictly enforcing their austere prescriptions of *sharia* (Islamic law). However, the overwhelming current in the country is one of incredible dissatisfaction with the sectarian violence, which reached its peak in 2007. It has been estimated that from just 2004 to 2007, an approximate 77,000 Iraqis were killed as a result of these insurgencies, which took place at the hands of the Islamic militants and the U.S. security forces as well.

The fall of Hussein in 2003 marked a serious turning point in the contemporary history of Iraq. When the nationalist party was in power (1968–2003), many of the **Islamic political parties** went into exile or into hiding to escape persecution. Now, both Sunni and Shiite groups have a strong voice on the Iraqi political platform (although there is still a notable secularist presence). After the American occupation in 2003, an interim government was established in Iraq (2004–2005), and, although nascent, it also saw the rise of Islamic militant groups and thereby an increase in aggressions and **extremism** throughout the country. So, in Iraq, there is a very recent yet strong struggle for power between the secular and Islamic groups.

With regard to Islamic activity, Iraq possesses three types: Shiite, Sunni, and Kurdish. The most dominant Shiite groups in Iraq are *Hizb al-Da'wa al-Islamiyya* in Iraq (**Islamic Call in Iraq**), the **Sadrist Trend**, and the **Islamic Supreme Council of Iraq** (ISCI). The similarities between these Shiite parties lie in their objection to the American occupation forces within Iraq and the desire for a sturdy central Iraqi government (although ISCI is more in favor of stronger regional governments). While differences exist between all the Shiite parties, the groups' wish to form a unified Shiite front has been the current climate in all their political platforms.

With regard to the Sunni groups in Iraq, there has been a great change since 2009 because of the increased presence of Islamic political parties within the country. This presence has resulted in a majority of the Sunni community turning in favor of a more secularist, nationalist political agenda. The main Iraqi Sunni political group is the **Iraqi Islamic Party**. Established in the mid-1940s, the group was modeled after the **Muslim Brotherhood** and officially emerged on the Iraqi political circuit in the 1960s after Abd al-Karim Qassem's regime allowed Islamic parties to be recognized by the state. However, when the Baath Party came to power in 1963, the group was sharply repressed, and many leaders went into exile, but the group still continued its work surreptitiously. With the toppling of the Baathist regime, the group returned to the Iraqi political scene, and in the December 2005 elections, it headed the Sunni electoral coalition *Tawafuq* (Iraqi Accord Front), winning 44 of the 275 parliamentary seats and maintaining its position as the dominant player in Iraqi Islamic politics. However, by 2009, the group began to suffer some internal divisions so that by the 2010 elections, the Sunni power has been relocated to a secular coalition—the *Iraqiyah*. The current Sunni political trend is now defined as more nationalist than Islamist because of its difficulty in gaining a wide range of support because of the large Shiite population within the country. But it is still the most successful Sunni political party in Iraq.

As the Sunni Islamist political influence has gone into decline, so too have Sunni Islamist militant groups. In fact, since 2007, very few aggressive Sunni Islamic groups are still substantially active in Iraq. The reason for this could be the opposition groups' renunciation of **violence** in hopes for a better support base in the elections. However, **al-Qaeda in Iraq** (AQI) still continues its aggressive agenda throughout the country. With the goal of establishing an **Islamic state** in Iraq, AQI has also been working with the Kurdish *Ansar al-Islam* in order to increase its strength. AQI has claimed responsibility for some of the deadliest attacks and **bombings** that Iraq has seen in recent years. Although the group lost a great deal of its territory in 2007 because of the *Sahwa* (Surge) movement, it remains quite active in the northern regions of the country.

An interesting Sunni militant group that entered the Iraqi militant stage in December 2006 is *Jaysh Rijal al-Tariqah al-Naqshabandia* (JRTN), or "Army of the Naqshabandia Sufists." Formed as a direct result of the execution of Saddam Hussein (30 December 2006), the group was allegedly organized by former Baathist leaders who are now living in exile in **Syria**. JRTN wishes to reestablish the Baathist regime in Iraq and has conducted attacks against the American security forces, particularly in the northern regions (where AQI has a strong presence as well).

Although there is strong trend among a majority of the Sunni population to see the withdrawal of the American occupying forces (which began in 2011), there is a growing fear throughout Iraq that with their absence, extremist groups may grab even more power and return Iraq to a state of oppression and violence. Currently, Iraq seems to be teetering on the edge of wishing for the removal of the **Western** security teams but anxiety over its possible negative consequences. This could be easily understood since the country has recently gotten rid of one tyrannical and aggressive regime.

The Kurdish Islamic sphere has been comprised of the **Kurdistan Islamic Union** (*Yekgirtu*) and the **Islamic Group of Iraqi Kurdistan**. Both groups are ideologically similar and were based on the Muslim Brotherhood model of political Sunni Islamism. The Kurdistan Islamic Union emerged in 1994 as a sociopolitical reform party that concerns itself with improving the Kurdistan community through Islamic ideals. The group has been consistently nonaggressive and most active in charitable outlets. In 2001, the Islamic Group of Iraqi Kurdistan emerged after members of the Kurdish Islamic Union were dissatisfied with the nonaggressive stance of the party. The group has been blamed for a series of political **assassinations** and attacks, especially against Kurdish leaders. It is also allegedly aligned with *Ansar al-Islam* and has announced its desire to strike a brotherhood with other Islamic militant groups. However, these two groups have had little success in the Kurdish parliamentary elections—combined, they only hold eight of the 111 seats. The state's parliament has been dominated by the Kurdistan Democratic Party and the Patriotic Union of Kurdistan for decades. Therefore, the Kurdish Islamic parties are quite marginal in the Iraqi political sector.

Currently, Iraq remains a parliamentary **democracy**, although Islam has been announced as the official creed of the state. This has led to the ambiguous application of *sharia* in many of the areas. The government has also had various responses to the militant Islamism in the north. The height of the parliament's support to oppose these groups came in 2006–2007 after the American military announced that it would be deploying more of its troops into the country. The Iraqi security forces have since decided to work in cooperation with the Western troops and have improved their own tactical methods. Because of this, extremism has decreased by an estimated 90 percent in just the few short years of 2008–2011, but no one knows what will happen after the Western withdrawal. *See also* ISLAMIC ACTION; KURDISH ISLAMIC MOVEMENT; MUSLIM BROTHERHOOD IN IRAQ.

IRAQI ISLAMIC PARTY. The largest **Sunni** Muslim **Islamic political party** in **Iraq** and the foremost member of the Iraqi Accord Front, the Iraqi Islamic party was banned from 1961 under the socialist **Baath Party** rule until the 2003 U.S. invasion of Iraq. The party has been led by Osama Tawfiq al-Tikriti since 24 May 2009. Originally a splinter group from the **Muslim Brotherhood in Iraq**, the party's Sunni ideologies have made it difficult for it to gain proper support throughout **Shiite** Iraq.

After being banned in 1961, some members finally took up political exile in Great Britain and during the 1970s reactivated their movement there, even publishing a periodical called *Dar as-Salam*. After the 2003 invasion of Iraq, many members served on the interim Iraqi Governing Council. However, in protest against the American assault on the Iraqi provincial town of Fallujah, many members withdrew their participation in the interim **government**. The Iraqi Islamic Party also boycotted and withdrew from the 2005 elections, stating that increased **violence** throughout the country was corrupting the electoral process. Instead, the group urged Iraqis to vote for constitutional amendments. By the close of the year, the party reentered the elections under the Iraqi Accord Front and succeeded in gaining 44 of the 275 seats in the parliament—the largest success of any Sunni political party.

Ideologically, the Iraqi Islamic Party called for the withdrawal of the American-led Multinational Force in Iraq and the complete promotion of Islamic values. Although the group was able to reenter Iraqi politics after the U.S. military invaded the country in 2003, members still call for the removal of the **Western** military presence. This attitude is due in part to the increased hostilities that have been pervading the country over the past few years.

AL-ISLAH/AT-TAJAMMU AL-YEMENI LIL-ISLAH/**YEMENI CONGREGATION FOR REFORM.** The foremost political opposition party in **Yemen**, *al-Islah* is divided into three different segments: the political branch, the tribal confederacy, and the mainstream **Salafists** within the country. The political faction is essentially the **Muslim Brotherhood** in Yemen, which is led by Muhammad Qahtan. The tribal confederacy is led by Sadiq al-Ahmar, and the **Salafists** are under the spiritual guidance of Abdul Majeed al-Zindani. Moderately successful as an **Islamic political party**, in the last legislative elections in the country in 2003, *al-Islah* won 46 of the 301 parliamentary seats. The group has also been instrumental in organizing demonstrations and protests during the 2011 political discord occurring within Yemen as part of the **Arab Spring**. Currently, the group has been most active in challenging a possible constitutional amendment that would allow the Yemeni president to serve a lifelong term.

ISLAM. Islam is the most rapidly growing **religion** in the world and is second in followers only to **Christianity**. Although the Muslim **nation** (*umma*) stretches over the entire globe, the majority of its adherents are concentrated in the Middle East, North Africa, and Asia. Islam has two main fundamental values: **peace** and submission to **Allah** (*tawhid*). Muslims doctrinally believe that the **religion** is the only true faith and that it was revealed to the **Prophet Muhammad** in **Saudi Arabia** during the seventh century. Structurally, the most pious of Muslims adhere to what are known as the Five Pillars of Islam: acknowledging that there is no true god except Allah and that Muhammad is the sole prophet of Allah (*shahada*), praying five times a day facing in the direction of Mecca (*salat*), almsgiving (*zakāt*), fasting during Ramadan (*sawm*), and, for those who are able, making an annual pilgrimage to Mecca (*hajj*).

The religion also requires belief in six articles of faith, which are the belief in Allah, belief in the messengers and Prophet of Allah, belief in the Revelations and the **Quran**, belief in angels, belief in Judgment Day, and belief in the omnificence of Allah and His decree. Even though all Muslims believe in the six articles of faith and adhere to the Five Pillars, they differ in how they interpret the Quran and apply *sharia* (Islamic law). *Tawhid* is often seen as the **fundamental** belief within the religion. The fundamentalists argue that *tawhid* leads to a **unity** with the universe as well as *fitra* (intuition), therefore making this doctrine supreme. Moderate to radical fundamentalists can agree that Islam does not only imply the devotion and literal **interpretation** of the **divine texts** (Quran and **Hadiths**); it is also a way of life that is present in all facets of daily activity aside from worship, such as diet, dress, hygiene, business ethics, responsibility for family members, marriage, divorce, inheritance, civil and criminal law, fighting in defense of Islam (**jihad**), relations with non-Muslims, and much more.

Islam is therefore not merely a religion but also a system (*nizam*) that entails **economic theory** and **Islamic political parties** as well. To the most devout Muslims, happiness will come from obeying Islam in its totality, and, conversely, unhappiness will come from not adhering completely to its doctrines. However, there is flexibility within Islam that allows for changes that would meet the needs of the current societal climate or situation. With this changeability, it is viewed that the religion and therefore the culture can progress. Islam presents all men as equals (or man as man) and also gives due consideration, acknowledgment, and cooperation to the other religions provided that they do not try to undermine or destroy the sanctity of Islam. *See also* APOSTASY; HERESY; SHIA ISLAM; SUNNI ISLAMISM; THEOCRACY; WOMEN.

AL-ISLAMI. See EGYPTIAN ISLAMIC JIHAD.

ISLAMIC ACTION/'*AMAL* **ORGANIZATION.** This group was formed in 1982 during the Iran-Iraq War (1980–1988) in the hopes of ousting the former **Baathist** government in **Iraq**. However, it must be stressed that there is no link between the *Amal* organization in Iraq, the *Amal* group in **Lebanon**, and the **Islamic** *Amal* **Movement**. The group joined the Supreme Assembly for the Islamic Revolution of Iraq and since 2003 has become known as the Supreme Council for the Islamic Revolution in Iraq. It is currently the largest party in the Iraqi United Alliance.

ISLAMIC ACTION FRONT PARTY/*HIZB JABHAT AL-'AMAL AL-ISLAMI.* Founded in 1992 as the political branch of the **Muslim Brotherhood in Jordan**, the Islamic Action Front based its function on those similar to the Muslim Brotherhood but called for the application of *sharia* (Islamic law) and social justice, which would also dictate the country's economic practices. The Islamic Action Front also called for a society that would adhere to the teachings of **Islam**, implement a **theocratic** approach to the political realm, and liberate **Palestine** through the **jihad**. The group also published a small newspaper called *Al-Ribat*, which expressed its ideologies and goals and enabled it to win approximately one-third of the parliamentary seats in the 1993 elections in **Jordan**.

ISLAMIC ACTION SOCIETY/*JAMA'AT AL-'AMAL AL-ISLAMI.* See ISLAMIC FRONT FOR THE LIBERATION OF BAHRAIN.

ISLAMIC *AMAL* **MOVEMENT/***HARAKAT AMAL AL-ISLAMIYYA.* *Amal* is the Arabic acronym for *Al-Muqawama al-Islamiyya* (Islamic resistance). An offshoot of the **Shiite** *Amal* movement in **Lebanon** and led by Husayn al-Musawi, *Harakat Amal al-Islamiyya* split from its father organization in June 1982. The reason was noted as Nabih Berri's (the *Amal* movement's leader) participation in the Salvation Committee. Formed by the Lebanese government, Berri's partaking in the Salvation Committee was viewed as treason, and members wanted to distance themselves from any secular orientation that the *Amal* movement now had. Husayn al-Musawi was a formative leader whose prestigious family claims to be descendants of the Prophet Muhammad. He was expelled from the *Amal* movement in the mid-1970s because of his belief that Lebanon should become an **Islamic state**. The Islamic *Amal* Movement is supported by the **Islamic Republic of Iran** and is based near Baalbak, Lebanon (a location also used by the **Iranian Revolutionary Guards**). The group sought a **pan-Islamic** revolution throughout the Middle East and believed that only through aggression could this take place. Al-Musawi had deep relations with *Hizbullah* **in Lebanon** and later became one of the highest ruling members of the organization. It also believed that the Islamic *Amal* Movement has been completely absorbed by *Hizbullah* and that a distinction has been kept alive only to counteract intelligence agencies.

ISLAMIC ARMY OF ADEN-ABYAN. *See* ISLAMIC JIHAD IN YEMEN.

ISLAMIC CALL IN IRAQ. Established in 1968, Islamic Call in Iraq (*Hizb al-Da'wa al-Islamiyya*) is the oldest of the **Shiite** parties in **Iraq** and was originally a political opposition group formed to thwart the growing communist trend. The group continued with its opposition platform throughout the 1970s and 1980s, inciting the **Baathist** regime to harshly repress its efforts. However, with the removal of the Baathist forces, Islamic Call in Iraq has reemerged as a formidable Iraqi **Islamic political party**. In fact, Prime Minister Nuri al-Maliki (b. 1950) is also a member of the group, serving only to increase its influence.

ISLAMIC CHARTER FRONT. *See* NATIONAL ISLAMIC FRONT.

ISLAMIC COURTS UNION (ICU). Headed by Sheikh Sharif Ahmed, the Islamic Courts Union was a group of Somali Islamists who banded together to rival the current Somali administration, the Transitional Federal Government. The organization has also been referred to as the Joint Islamic Courts and the Supreme Islamic Courts Council. The individual groups that made up the ICU were all *sharia* (Islamic law) courts (the members of the governing system of judges that took control after the 1991 collapse of the Somali **government**), which determined that through unifying around the same cause, they could gain more influence and control more territory in **Somalia**. The goal of the ICU was to create social justice through the application of *sharia* across the country, which it believed would unify Somalia and combat iniquity. Structurally, the ICU was comprised of members who were *sharia* judges in the sense that they control a specified area and are in charge of enforcing *sharia* in that particular district. Various orientations exist, depending on the individual and ranging from incredibly strict adherence to the **divine texts** to a more relaxed level of social liberty.

Successful in their attempts, throughout 2006 the ICU controlled most of southern Somalia, including major cities such as Mogadishu (which occurred in the spring of 2006 as a result of conflict between the ICU and the Alliance for the Restoration of Peace and Counter-Terrorism). On 5 October 2006, the ICU announced the establishment of the Supreme Islamic *Sharia* Court of Banadir, which brought an end to all tribal-related power in the capital in hopes of better unifying the organization. However, throughout the war in

Somalia, which lasted from 2006 until 2009, the ICU was forced to abandon many of its holdings as Somali task forces along with the assistance of Ethiopian battalions suppressed the ICU, stripping it of its territories.

As a result, the ICU disbanded, and many of the extreme Islamists split to form splinter organizations, such as the *Al-Shabaab*, *Hizbul Islam*, and the Alliance for the Re-Liberation of Somalia. On 1 February 2009, Sharif Ahmed was elected president of the Transitional National Government as a result of reconciliation agreements. *See also AL-ITIHAD AL-ISLAMI.*

ISLAMIC *DA'WA* ORGANIZATION OF AFGHANISTAN. Originally part of the **Islamic** Union for the Liberation of **Afghanistan** (*Ittehad e-Islami bara-ye Azadi-ye Afghanistan*), this **Islamic political party** was established in the early 1980s by Abdul Rasul Sayyaf after members split from its father organization. However, it was not known under its current name until 2005, when it registered as a political party with the Afghani Ministry of Justice. The Islamic *Da'wa* Organization of Afghanistan hopes to bring together the various Afghani Islamic opposition forces in order to create a united front and was a member of the **Peshawar Seven**—an alliance of *mujahideen* forces that were supported militarily and financially by countries that wanted to eliminate the People's Democratic Party of Afghanistan (PDPA).

The group's membership is comprised mostly of Arab volunteers, and after successfully ousting the PDPA, the organization tried (along with other similar groups) to take control of Kabul in 1993. Notoriously, the Islamic *Da'wa* Organization of Afghanistan conducted a series of massacres in western Kabul on 11 February 1993 in coordination with the *Jamaat-e-Islami* forces. When the **Taliban army** came to power in 1994, the organization actually became part of the Northern Alliance, which was formed in September 1996. *See also DA'WA.*

ISLAMIC FRONT FOR THE LIBERATION OF BAHRAIN/*AL-JABHA AL-ISLAMIYYA LI TAHRIR AL-BAHRAIN*. A **Shiite** Islamic **fundamentalist** group that sought to bring about a revolution in **Bahrain**, the Islamic Front for the Liberation of Bahrain was established in March 1979 and was allegedly supported by **Iran** (notably by the Foundation for the Oppressed and the Liberation Movements Office) and *Al-Da'wa Al-Islamiyya* (Islamic Call) **in Iraq**. The group has carried out numerous attempts to overthrow the **government** and replace it with an **Islamic state**, and after these insurgencies, many members were arrested by the state's security forces. Exiled Iraqi Hujjatulislam Hadi Al-Mudarrisi, brother of **Islamic *'Amal* Party** founder Muhammad Taqi Al-Mudarrisi, founded the group and returned to Iraq following Saddam Hussein's fall from power in 2003.

Of the many attacks, the most notable of the group's was the 17 January 1996 **bombing** at the Middle East Petroleum and Gas Conference and the 11 February 1996 Diplomat Hotel bombing, both in Manama, Bahrain. Although the group was banned practically since its inception, the 2001 legislative reforms conducted by King Hamad bin Isa Al-Khalifa pardoned the group and legitimately recognized it. As a result, the Islamic Front for the Liberation of Bahrain renamed itself Islamic Action Society (*Jama'at Al-'Amal Al-Islami*) and entered the political realm of Bahrain. Although banned for a brief period in 2005, the group still functions as an opposition party within the country. It is currently led by Sheikh Muhammad Ali Mahfuz, long-time associate of Al-Mudarissi.

ISLAMIC GOVERNMENT/*AL-HUKUMA AL-ISLAMIYYA*. Fundamentally, the Islamic government symbolizes the ***governance*** (*hakimiyya*) of the **Islamic system** (*nizam*) and gains its power through ***shura*** (consultation). The responsibility of the Islamic government is both a religious and a political one that is based on ***ijma'*** (consensus). The stipulation of consensus is of great importance to the Islamic government, for the Islamic culture believes that a harmonious society will exist only if there is agreement between the ruler and the ruled. Therefore, the leader of the society (or the government itself as a whole) must always look to the *shura* for guidance since the *shura* represents the interests of society. However, the aspect of the Islamic government that is of most significance is that despite any form of government that an Islamic society may undertake, it must be rooted in the **fundamentals** of **Islam**.

THE ISLAMIC GROUP. *See AL-GAMA'A AL-ISLAMIYYA/AL-JAMAAT AL-ISLAMIYA.*

ISLAMIC GROUP OF IRAQI KURDISTAN. Established in May 2001 in Iraqi Kurdistan (the autonomous region of Northern **Iraq**), the Islamic Group of Iraqi Kurdistan is comprised of many former members of the **Kurdish Islamic Movement**. An **Islamic political party** with **Sunni** ideologies, the group allegedly has links to *Ansar al-Islam* and is supposedly financed by the Patriotic Union of Kurdistan (a similar political group). Ideologically, the group supports relations with all **Islamic groups**, claiming that the umbrella of **Islam** should be a source of camaraderie. Members also state that doctrinal differences between the varying schools of Islam are gateways to fraternity, not opposition.

Electorally, the group has not been very successful, receiving only 7 percent of the popular vote at the January 2005 elections for the National Assembly of Iraq and 6 seats in the 111-seat Kurdish National Assembly. Following this election, the Islamic Group of Iraqi Kurdistan joined the Democratic Patriotic Alliance of Kurdistan in December 2005. Finally, during the 2009 Iraqi Kurdistan elections, the group joined three other political groups and named the coalition the Service and Reform List, resulting in the allocation of 13 seats. However, on 7 March 2010, the Islamic Group of Iraqi Kurdistan removed itself from the Service and Reform List and received only 1.32 percent (two seats) of the votes. *See also* ISLAMIC POLITICAL PARTIES.

ISLAMIC GROUPS/*AL-JAMAAT AL-ISLAMIYYA*. Many of the Islamic groups have transcended past moderate ideologies and crossed into **radicalism**. Here, *Al-Jamaat Al-Islamiyya* strictly refers to those Islamic groups that are labeled as **fundamental** extremists. Advocating revolution, using violent methods, and showing unwavering adherence to Islamic doctrines are the defining characteristics of many of these Islamic groups. Their use of brutal tactics has led to their illegality, and therefore many of the groups remain underground so as to evade security forces. Because of this, it is hard to determine exactly their range of support, but it is certain that their influence is still formidable. Yet there is a **consensus** that a majority of the support comes from the urban middle-class and university students—which is characteristic of many sociopolitical organizations whether they be extremist or not. However, the strong antiestablishment stance and increasingly violent actions have made these movements controversial among many other Muslims in the general population.

The groups, often influenced by radical scholars or writers (like **Sayyid Qutb**), target those who are deemed infidels and betrayers of **Islam**, therefore justifying the **jihad** against them. The conservative application of *sharia* (Islamic law), the removal of **Western** influences from the Muslim world, and the absolute dissolution of **Israel** are also common goals of the Islamic groups. Different Islamic organizations have also conducted educational and social programs to gain a wider range of support. Since the late 1970s, these types of groups and activities have been especially dominant in the Egyptian universities, where *Al-Jamaat Al-Islamiyya*'s ideology first started to gain momentum and even set up a union during the 1980s. Many other groups throughout the Islamic world have adopted the name *Al-Jamaat Al-Islamiyya* to illustrate the essence of their dogmas and relate their goals to these previously mentioned. However, adherents prefer to refer to themselves as Muslims and rarely use the term "Islamist." *See also* EXTREMISM; VIOLENCE.

ISLAMIC GUERILLAS IN AMERICA. Comprised of Islamic African Americans who were inspired by **Ayatollah Ruhollah al-Musawi Khomeini**, it is believed that the Islamic Guerillas in America were supported by the **Islamic Republic of Iran** in order to repress anti-Iranian sentiments in the **United States**. The group resorted to **assassination** as its means of stifling the Iranian nonconformists and most infamously killed 'Ali Akbar Tabataba'i (a well-known anti-Khomeini **activist**) in Washington, D.C., on 22 July 1980. It is believed that the group was formed by an Iranian immigrant who obtained citizenship and lived within the Washington, D.C., area. Although little is known about the individual's identity, experts believe that most of the organization's members were recruited through the local prison system.

ISLAMIC IRAN PARTICIPATION FRONT/*JEBHEYE MOSHARE-KATE IRAN E-ISLAMI.* Unique to the Islamic Iran Participation Front is that, while it supports **Islam** as the official creed of **Iran**, members also advocate for a democratic state within the country. Established in 1998, the front is led by Mohsen Mirdamadi and has the motto "Iran for all Iranians." Its desire for a merging of **democracy** with Islam and therefore **Islamization** has resulted in its exclusion from the parliamentary elections as ordered by the Council of Guardians, the **theocratic** body of Iran. Despite not being able to run its own candidates, the Islamic Iran Participation Front has supported other contenders. Structurally, the front possesses a Central Council consisting of 30 members that deal with the decision making of the group. *See also* ISLAMIC POLITICAL PARTIES.

ISLAMIC JIHAD IN THE HIJAZ/*HIZBULLAH* IN THE HIJAZ/ PARTY OF GOD IN THE HIJAZ. A **Shiite** Islamic **fundamentalist** group, the Islamic **Jihad** in the Hijaz hopes to overthrow the **Saudi Arabian** kingdom and replace it with an **Islamic state** based on the one implemented in **Iran**. Allegedly sponsored by Iranian interests, the group claims that it is in effect an extension of *Hizbullah* **in Lebanon**, and it is unlikely that many of its members are from Saudi Arabia, especially the Hijaz area. This assumption is based on the fact that a very small contingent of Shiite Muslims live in the Hijaz region, and, in fact, the population of Saudi Arabia counts only 3 million to 4 million Shiites in a country of 27 million people. It is believed, then, that the group is comprised of Iranian, Kuwaiti, and Lebanese Shiites, especially since its father organization, *Hizbullah*, is made up primarily of militants from those countries.

The group allegedly conducted the 1996 **Khobar Towers bombing** and **assassinated** the Saudi diplomat Salah Abdullah Al-Maliki on 7 January 1989. In the wake of the 31 July 1987 Mecca riots, which resulted in the deaths of over 400, the group claimed revenge against the Saudi Arabian regime, which it blamed for the **violence**. Two days after the events in Mecca, the Saudi Arabian embassy in Tehran was attacked, killing one diplomat. The group continued to target both Saudi and American interests, resulting in the former severing all diplomatic ties with Iran and restricting the number of pilgrims admitted into the country for the Hajj.

The area of the Hijaz is of particular importance because within it lies two of the holiest places in Islam—Mecca and Medina. Therefore, control over this region is absolutely vital to Islamic rulers, as the one who controls the area is deemed "Protector of the Two Holy Places," making said ruler preeminent in Muslim society. Since Saudi Arabia controls these areas and consists of predominantly Sunni Muslims, Shiite rulers want to gain control of the Hijaz, especially since the Saudi regime has continuously repressed Shiite sects for decades. *See also* LEBANON.

ISLAMIC JIHAD IN YEMEN/ISLAMIC ARMY OF ADEN-ABYAN. A small, radical **Islamic** group of little renown, the Islamic Jihad in Yemen operates primarily in the areas surrounding Aden, **Yemen**. Active mostly in the late 1990s, the group tried to establish and enforce its own doctrine of *sharia* (Islamic law) throughout the area. Allegedly affiliated with the **al-Qaeda** organization, the group has used the tactic of **suicide bombings** and kidnappings in the hopes of overthrowing the Yemenite **government**. During 1998, the Islamic Jihad in Yemen abducted 20 foreigners, resulting in the death of four of them. After Yemeni security forces bombarded one of the group's camps, five members were arrested; three were sentenced to death, one was sentenced to life imprisonment, and another was acquitted. One of the three executed was Zein Abu Bakr Al-Mihdar (a.k.a. Abu Al-Hassan Al-Mohady), leader of the group. Since then, the Islamic Jihad in Yemen resorts mostly to blowing up explosive-ridden boats while they are near foreign vessels. From 2000 to 2002, the group allegedly attacked the USS *The Sullivans*, the USS *Cole*, and the tanker MV *Limburg* and has been driven away from the Aden-Abyan regions by the Yemen security forces. *See also* BOMBING.

ISLAMIC JIHAD OF PALESTINE/*HARAKAT AL-JIHAD AL-ISLAMI FI FILASTIN*/MOVEMENT OF THE ISLAMIC JIHAD IN PALESTINE. Also commonly known as the Palestinian Islamic Jihad (PIJ), this **Sunni** separatist group is reportedly financially supported by **Iran** and **Syria**. Although membership is rather low (less than 1,000), the group has allegedly trained with Iran's **Islamic Revolutionary Guards**, and many members were once aligned with the **Muslim Brotherhood** in Gaza. The group is headquartered in Damascus, Syria, and was the first Palestinian Islamic group to employ the tactic of **suicide bombings** against **Israel** (believed to have been adopted from the Iranian militants). Founded in the 1970s by Sheikh ʻ**Abd**

al-'Aziz Awda and Fathi Shaqaqi in the Gaza Strip, the group was formed after being inspired by the **Iranian Islamic Revolution**. After seeing the success in Iran, members from the Muslim Brotherhood split to form this more radical group, but the two (the Muslim Brotherhood in Gaza and the Islamic Jihad of Palestine) still retain a working relationship.

Ideologically, the group believes that in order to expel Israeli occupants from the Palestinian territories, a **jihad** is absolutely necessary. The Islamic Jihad of Palestine also targets British nationals, as it feels that they protect the Zionists' interests. These sentiments originated in the 1920s, when the militant group, then simply known as the **Islamic Jihad**, was formed by Sheikh Izz ad-Din Al-Qassam to combat the British and Jewish settlers in the British Mandate for **Palestine**. The group's ideological foundation as such has led to the creation of the **Izz ad-Din Al-Qassam Brigades**, a splinter organization of the Islamic Jihad of Palestine that is, in effect, the militant branch of the group. However, the group has also worked under the name of the Al-Quds Brigade.

Interestingly enough, the group uses numeric labels to identify one another—each member is known by a six-digit code. By the late 1980s, the Islamic Jihad of Palestine also formed an alliance with the **Palestinian Liberation Organization** (PLO) and was remarkably influential during the First **Intifada**. The group also formed a relationship with *Hizbullah* **in Lebanon** after members of the PIJ were exiled to **Lebanon** from Israel. In the wake of the 1991 Gulf War, the Islamic Jihad of Palestine moved even closer to Iran and continued with its jihadist activities. In the latter part of 1994, the PIJ killed at least 4 and injured approximately 12 others in two attacks. This resulted in the PLO arresting many members of the Palestinian Islamic Jihad as well as many other jihadi affiliates; 160 PIJ members were arrested in response to the 1994 actions. In retaliation, the radical organization bombed an Israeli commuter bus on 22 January 1995, killing 19 and injuring 61. When Fathi Shaqaqi was **assassinated** on 26 October 1995 in Malta, the PIJ announced his successor as former University of South Florida professor Dr. Ramadan Abdullah Shallah; however, little action was seen by the group during the remainder of 1995 and throughout 1996. The group resurfaced in 1997 and 1998 with small suicide bombings that resulted in little destruction and no loss of life.

With the outbreak of the Second **Intifada** in 2000, the Islamic Jihad of Palestine reemerged in full force and conducted numerous suicide bombings, a tactic that was soon used by the equally active **Hamas** and **Al-Aqsa Martyrs' Brigades** as well during the **violence**. Throughout the eight-year intifada, the PIJ conducted at least 207 attacks (including suicide bombings, rocket launchings, kidnappings, and various other forms of insurrection), resulting in the death of approximately 154 and injury of a reported 3,734. The Palestinian Authority continues to try and repress the group, but it still remains active and does not acknowledge any prior **cease-fire** agreements that Israel made with other groups, such as Hamas or *Al-Fatah*.

ISLAMIC JIHAD UNION (IJU)/*AL-DJIHAD AL-ISLAMI.* Dzhamaat *Modzhakhedov* in Uzbek, the Islamic Jihad Union is an **extremist** organization that developed from the **Islamic Movement of Uzbekistan** in 2002. The group has been accused of launching numerous insurgencies against the Uzbekistan **government**. In April 2004, the group conducted its first major attack, which took place on multiple police checkpoints during a public event, resulting in the killing of an estimated 47 people through the use of **suicide bombings**. Ideologically, the group advocates for the destruction of **Western** influences in the Islamic countries and seeks to replace the secular regime of Uzbekistan with a **government** based on Islamic *sharia* (Islamic law). The IJU has also claimed an alliance and brotherhood with insurgents from **Afghanistan**, emulating their devotion in the global **jihad**. Although the group has its origins in Uzbekistan, it is understood that members are scattered throughout Central Asia and as far away as Turkey and Germany. *See also* CENTRAL ASIAN ISLAMIC ACTIVITY.

ISLAMIC LABOR PARTY. This **Islamic political party** from **Egypt**, formerly the Socialist Labor Party, has been particularly active in calling for the implementation of *sharia* (Islamic law), especially with regard to the economic system in Egypt. The Socialist Labor Party was formed on 9 September 1978 by Ibrahim Shoukry but then, by 1986, underwent major ideological changes and became the Islamic Labor Party. This was officially announced at the group's fifth conference in 1989 by calling the meeting "Reform from an Islamic Prospective."

The group seeks to protect the country's natural resources and domestic industries as well as achieve equal distribution. With regard to foreign diplomacy, the Islamic Labor Party hopes for a peaceful Egyptian unity with **Sudan** and **Libya**, among other countries. In addition, it has been active in advocating for the liberation of **Palestine**. In 1990, the organization even tried to join hands with the **Muslim Brotherhood** but was rebuffed since the Brotherhood did not want to boycott the elections as the Labor Party did.

However, on 20 May 2000, the Egyptian Political Parties' Affairs Committee banned the Islamic Labor Party and its publication, *al-Shaab*. The committee's reason was that the activities of the group were not in the best interest of the general public and thus worthy of suspension. This was instigated by complaints within the group over a recent division between its leaders, but many contested that the ban was and still is illegal. *See also* ECONOMIC THEORY.

ISLAMIC LAW. *See AL SHARI'A.*

ISLAMIC LIBERATION ORGANIZATION (ILO). A division of *al-Tahrir al-Islami* (a **Muslim Brotherhood** splinter organization) in **Lebanon**, the group is known primarily for the 30 September 1985 kidnapping of four diplomats from the Soviet embassy in Beirut: a commercial attaché, an embassy second secretary, a cultural attaché, and an embassy physician. The group sent photographs of the kidnapped men and demanded that the Soviets convince **Syria** to stop its aggressions against the **Sunni** Muslim **Tawhid** group in Tripoli, or else they were going to **assassinate** the hostages. On 2 October, the cultural attaché, Arkady Katvok, was killed by the ILO, and the remaining three were released on 30 October after the events in Tripoli came to an end. The group has been inactive ever since the 1985 incident.

ISLAMIC LIBERATION PARTY/*HIZB UT-TAHRIR AL-ISLAMI.* The Islamic Liberation Party is an **extremist** movement that has set out to implement pure Islamic doctrine in the law and establish a **caliphate** throughout the Muslim world. Using *da'wa* to create unity, the group seeks to have *sharia* (Islamic law) dominate the Islamic lands. The group defines success as having *sharia* executed in everyday life as well as the political and religious realms. As is common in most of the other **Islamist groups**, the Islamic Liberation Party turns solely to the **divine texts** of Islam for guidance and justice. Members believe that the only way to implement a caliphate is through the **jihad** and hence have used **violence** to attain their ends. It is the perception of the group that the Islamic world has been so demoralized and corrupted by **modernity** that the only way to revert back to a traditional and "true" Muslim life is through these extreme measures. Thought of by its members as a utopian state, the party believes that through the education and subsequent spreading of the *sharia* philosophies throughout civilian and **governmental** circles, a purely Muslim and orthodox society will be achieved.

The group was founded in 1953 in Jerusalem by a former judge, Taqiuddin Al-Nabhani, and has spread throughout many countries, including **Iraq**, **Egypt**, **Jordan**, **Libya**, **Saudi Arabia**, **Syria**, and **Tunisia**. However, it is believed that many of the members are Uzbekistani in origin and have been focusing their efforts on Central Asia since the dissolution of the Soviet Union in 1991. This radical **Sunni** Muslim group has refused to take part in any local or national politics and is clearly not a political movement, even though it hopes to see legislative changes. The subversive acts of the Islamic Liberation Party have led to its repression and the imprisonment of hundreds of its constituents. The Russian Federal Security Service has also claimed that the party is linked with the **Islamic Movement of Uzbekistan**, which has an alliance with the **Taliban**, and therefore is incriminated. According to the Russian security forces, there are numerous *Hizb ut-Tahrir Al-Islami* cells throughout Russia, and the group was led by a Kyrgyzstani national, Alisher Musayev, and Akram Jalolov of Tajikistan, although both men were arrested in Moscow on 6 June 2003. *See also* CENTRAL ASIAN ISLAMIC ACTIVITY; AL-NABHANI, TAQIYUDDIN; THE WEST.

ISLAMIC MOVEMENT OF AFGHANISTAN/*HARAKAT E-ISLAMI-YI AFGHANISTAN.* Once a member of the Northern Alliance in **Afghanistan**, this **Islamic political party** was founded in 1978 and was led by Ayatollah Muhammad Asif Muhsini from its inception until 2005. Ideologically inspired by the Iranian socialist revolutionary Ali Shari'ati, the group fought against the People's Democratic Party of Afghanistan (*Hizb e-Democratik e-Khalq*) as part of the **Tehran Eight**—a coalition of Shiite *mujahideen*. In 2001, with the U.S. occupation of Afghanistan, the Islamic Movement of Afghanistan split, and one faction became the People's Islamic Movement of Afghanistan. Secularist in its political ideologies, the People's Islamic Movement of Afghanistan is led by Sayyed Muhammad Ali Jawid and joined the short-lived National Understanding Front of Afghanistan in April 2005. *See also* SHIA ISLAM.

ISLAMIC MOVEMENT OF TURKISTAN (IMT)/ISLAMIC PARTY OF TURKISTAN. Originally called the **Islamic Movement of Uzbekistan**, this nationalist Islamic **fundamentalist** organization seeks to create an **Islamic state** throughout Kazakhstan, Kyrgyzstan, Tajikistan, Turkmenistan, Uzbekistan, and Xinjiang. This pan-Turkish notion of instilling *sharia* (Islamic law) in these Central Asian states (all of which have significant Muslim populations) is illustrated by the Islamic Movement of Uzbekistan's name change to the Islamic Movement of Turkistan. Once their goal is reached, the members hope to then call this unified state "Turkistan." The IMT allegedly has aligned itself with the Afghani **Taliban** regime, is based in **Afghanistan** (from 1999 to 2001 the group was in the Tavildara Valley of Tajikistan but relocated after Russian pressure forced Tajikistan to expel the group), and has several hundred members. The organization is also comprised of youths from the Fergana Valley region in Uzbekistan as well as former Uighur militants from Xinjiang. Reportedly, the group received a majority of its financing from participating in the illicit Central Asian opium trade.

Of its many violent acts, the most notable is the 16 February 1999 explosion of six car bombs that were placed outside the legislative offices in Tashkent, Uzbekistan, resulting in killing 16 and injuring 128. However, after the U.S. occupation of Afghanistan in 2001, the IMT was largely destroyed, and its remaining militants took up arms with their allied Taliban and **al-Qaeda** forces. Now mainly active in the tribal regions of **Pakistan**, Tohrir Yuldashev continues to lead the group, which still hopes to attain the goal of achieving the desired pan-Turkish state. *See also* BOMBING; CENTRAL ASIAN ISLAMIC ACTIVITY; VIOLENCE.

ISLAMIC MOVEMENT OF UZBEKISTAN (IMU). Formed by Islamic zealot Tahir Yuldashev (b. Tohir Yo'Idosh) and former paratrooper Juma Namangani (b. Jumaboi Khojayev in 1969), the Islamic Movement of Uzbekistan was originally created as a militant organization with the goal of replacing Uzbekistani President Islam Karimov (in office since 24 March 1990) with an **Islamic state** based on *sharia* (Islamic law). Namangani was a fighter, and on his return to his hometown of Namangan (from which he took his name), Uzbekistan, he developed a camaraderie with Yuldashev, and the two men created *Adolat*, Uzbek for "justice," in 1991. The same year that Uzbekistan gained independence from the Soviet Union, the group flourished in Namangan with its radical **Salafi** ideologies and assumed governance in the area, applying *sharia* there. However, the group became increasingly brutal, and Uzbekistani President Islam Karimov, once tolerant of *Adolat*, outlawed the group in 1992 and dismantled the Islamic law there. Afterward, members of *Adolat* fled to Tajikistan and joined forces with the **Islamic Renaissance Party of Tajikistan** during the 1992–1997 Tajikistan Civil War.

During this time, while Namangani fought, Yuldashev toured most of the Muslim world developing contacts with numerous **Islamic groups** and **fundamentalists**, including **Osama bin Laden** and the **Afghan Arabs**. In 1998, after being disenchanted by the concessions the Islamic Renaissance Party made during the Tajikistan peace accords, *Adolat* officially became the Islamic Movement of Uzbekistan (now named the **Islamic Movement of Turkistan**). Suspected of receiving financial support from **Pakistan**'s Inter-Services Intelligence, the organization created bases in the Tavildara Valley of eastern Tajikistan and in northern **Afghanistan**. The IMU focused a great deal of its military operations on the southern region of neighboring Kyrgyzstan and was successful in recruiting a large following of economically "oppressed and religiously" persecuted citizens who also sought the end of Karimov's despotic rule. The IMU has been held responsible for numerous **assassination** attempts on the president's life but official attribution has yet to be placed. In retaliation for the attacks, Karimov reinforced his repression of **Islam** in the country which resulted in an increased opposition to his regime. Yuldeshev continued to harvest the alliances he previously made with other Islamists, and the IMU became intertwined with **Taliban** operations in Afghanistan and Pakistan (Namangani even became the Taliban's deputy defense minister).

In 2001, a majority of the IMU fighters, including Namangani, were killed by a U.S.-led air strike while fighting in Afghanistan. In the aftermath of this event, Yuldeshev and many others from the remaining insurgency dispersed into the Waziristan region of Pakistan in the Federal Administered Tribal Areas in attempts to create training camps in the Waziristan area to help the Pakistani Islamic cause. On 27 August 2009, Yuldashev was killed in South Waziristan, in the same manner as his partner Juma Namangani, by a U.S. Air Force–led operation. Despite the loss of its founding leaders, the IMU remains active and incredibly influential (along with the Islamic Liberation Party) in Central Asia, particularly Kazakhstan, Kyrgyzstan, Tajikistan, and Uzbekistan. On 17 August 2010, the group announced the appointment of Abu Usman Adil, Yuldashev's former deputy, as its new *amir*. On his inauguration, Adil proclaimed that the IMU will continue to focus its jihadist efforts on southern Kyrgyzstan. *See also* CENTRAL ASIAN ISLAMIC ACTIVITY; ISLAMIC JIHAD UNION; ISLAMIC LIBERATION PARTY; YO'IDOSH, TOHIR.

ISLAMIC NATIONAL ACCORD ASSOCIATION. *See* AL-WEFAQ NATIONAL ISLAMIC SOCIETY.

ISLAMIC PARTY OF AZERBAIJAN. Created in 1991 at Nardaran, Azerbaijan, the Islamic Party of Azerbaijan is comprised mainly of conservative **Shiite** Muslims. However, since the political climate of the country is mainly secular and religiously progressive, the group's legitimacy was only experienced from 1992 to 1995 (allegations of the group being financed by **Iran** also helped lead to its illegality). Following its ban, many members were arrested, and the Azerbaijan laws were altered to prohibit any **Islamic political party** from forming or existing.

Ideologically, the party seeks the establishment of an Islamic republic within the country modeled after Iran. Members, although nationalistic, do not agree with the pan-Turkish sentiments and were adamantly against the Armenian occupation of the Nagorno-Karabakh regions of northwestern Azerbaijan (1988–1994). Led by Movsum Samadov, the group repeatedly voiced its support for *Hizbullah* **in Lebanon** and the rejection of **Western** and Zionist mentalities.

ISLAMIC PARTY OF TURKISTAN. *See* ISLAMIC MOVEMENT OF TURKISTAN.

ISLAMIC POLITICAL PARTIES. Working toward the promotion of **Islam** as a viable **legislative** alternative, the difference between these groups and militant **Islamic groups** or socioideological Islamic parties should be stressed. The political parties announce and offer candidates for upcoming governmental elections who pledge to promote Islamic ideals throughout the country if elected. Socioideological Islamic groups simply work toward the promotion of Islam but do not necessarily involve themselves in electoral or legislative processes. Similarly, militant Islamic groups do not always have political interests and focus rather on aggressive combatant strategies. However, it must be noted that socioideological Islamic groups may resort to hostile tactics as well. In addition, some political parties (in the traditional sense) have derived from militant groups and vice versa. Therefore, there are groups that transcend the lines of both political and militant motivations.

There are also some countries that have banned the formation of religious-oriented political parties, such as **Bahrain**, **Jordan**, and **Mali**. In these cases, groups that have Islamic motivations present the party not as a political one but rather as a social group. In Bahrain, these are the **Al-Menbar National Islamic Society** and the **Al-Wefaq National Islamic Society**. Jordan's main sociopolitical group, **Islamic Action Front**, has done the same and has formed under the socioideological group the **Muslim Brotherhood in Jordan**.

With regard to the Muslim Brethren, this extraordinary multinational sociopolitical group has emerged in numerous forms. Almost every faction of the **Muslim Brotherhood** is a political player in some capacity. This pertains specifically to the **Muslim Brotherhood in Algeria**, **Muslim Brotherhood in Bahrain**, **Muslim Brotherhood in Iraq**, **Muslim Brotherhood in Palestine**, **Muslim Brotherhood in Saudi Arabia**, **Muslim Brotherhood in Somalia**, **Muslim Brotherhood in Sudan**, **Muslim Brotherhood in Syria**, and **Muslim Brotherhood in Tunisia**.

Just as there are states that repress the formation of Islamic political parties, there are some that encourage it in order to maintain the status quo and as long as their ideologies are not outwardly religious. However, that is not to say that groups do not come under pressure from the state. This can be seen mainly in **Algeria** with the **Movement for National Reform**, the **Movement for the Society of Peace**, and the **National Liberation Front**—the largest in the country. In addition, within Algeria, there are **extremist** political parties, such as the **Islamic Salvation Front**, which includes a number of **jihadists** within its membership. A similar climate exists in **Morocco** as well. There, the **Justice and Development Party** dominates the socioideological political platform. Turkey, too, has this variant in the *Saadet Partisi*. However, **Sudan**, a declared **Islamic state**, is dominated by the brutal **National Congress Party**.

In Malaysia, the key groups are the **United Malays National Organization** (which is the largest and seeks to implement *sharia* [Islamic law] throughout the country) and the **Pan-Malaysian Islamic Party** (which is militant in its tactics). Other aggressive political groups include the **National Islamic Movement of Afghanistan**, which aligned with the **Taliban army**; *Jamaat Ulema-e-Islam*, which is one of the largest political parties in Pakistan and is also affiliated with the Taliban; the **Islamic** *Amal* **Movement**, which formed out of the Lebanese *Amal*, is affiliated with *Hizbullah*, and implements aggressive tactics to form an Islamic state; the **Arab Liberation Front**; and **Islamic Call in Iraq**.

However, a majority of the Islamic political parties simply seek the establishment of an Islamic state and wish to see this occur through moderate, nonviolent, political means. These include the **Adhaalath Party**, *Amal*, the *Al-Asalah* **Islamic Society**, the **Awami League** (which is more democratically based), *Ennahda*, *Fedayan-I Khalq-I Iran*, *Hizb-e-Islami*, *Hizb-u-Tahrir*, the **Iraqi Islamic Party**, the **Islamic Iran Participation Front**, the **Islamic Supreme Council of Iraq**, *Jamaat-e-Islami*, the **Justice and Charity Movement**, *Tanzeem-e-Islami*, the **United Development Party**, and the **Yemeni Association for Reform**.

There are also coalition groups that exist and are comprised of many like-minded groups, such as the **United Council of Action** and the **Palestinian Liberation Organization**. Interestingly enough, Egypt possessed a Political Parties' Affairs Committee, which monitored the actions of these groups and was influential in banning a number of groups, including the **Islamic Labor Party**. In addition, some important Islamic political figures are **Hasan al-Banna**, **Taqiy al-Din al-Nabhani**, **Hassan 'Abd Allah al-Turabi**, and **Abdul Majeed al-Zindani**. *See also* BAATH PARTY; BANGLADESH *KHILAFAT MAJLIS*; CRESCENT STAR PARTY; DEMOCRACY; GOVERNMENT; *HIZB-E-ISLAMI GULBUDDIN*; *AL-ISLAH*; ISLAMIC *DA'WA* ORGANIZATION OF AFGHANISTAN; ISLAMIC GOVERNMENT; ISLAMIC GROUP OF IRAQI KURDISTAN; ISLAMIC MOVEMENT OF AFGHANISTAN; ISLAMIC MOVEMENT OF TURKISTAN; ISLAMIC MOVEMENT OF UZBEKISTAN; ISLAMIC PARTY OF AZERBAIJAN; ISLAMIC RENAISSANCE PARTY OF TAJIKISTAN; ISLAMIC SOCIETY OF ENGINEERS; *JAMAAT AHL AL-HADITH*; JUSTICE AND PROSPERITY PARTY; KURDISTAN ISLAMIC UNION; *MILLI NIZAM PARTISI*; NATIONAL AWAKENING PARTY; REFORM STAR PARTY; *SIPAH-E-SAHABA PAKISTAN*; *TEHRIK-E-JAFARIA PAKISTAN*.

ISLAMIC RENAISSANCE PARTY OF TAJIKISTAN (IRP)/ISLAMIC REVIVAL PARTY OF TAJIKISTAN. Also known as the Islamic Revival Party of Tajikistan, the IRP was the only legal **Islamic political party** in Central Asia (with a brief period of prohibition from 1993 to 1998 that coincided with the Tajik Civil War). The party was founded in 1990, and when Tajikistan gained its independence from the Soviet Union in September 1991, it was officially established. Despite its legality, the party came into constant conflict with the communist government that still ruled Tajikistan. When IRP members tried to replace the current regime with an **Islamic state**, the group was swiftly banned from 1993 to 1998. During this period, many members and its leader fled to **Afghanistan** and **Iran** and there formed the **United Tajik Opposition** (UTO). Fighting broke out between the UTO and the Tajik forces, leading to the deaths of tens of thousands of persons before peace accords were signed in March of 1997. After the amnesty agreements, IRP and UTO members returned to Tajikistan, and the IRP was registered as an official political party for the 1999 elections. However, it met with mediocre success, and the IRP has won a minimal amount of seats in the country's parliament since running on a platform of Islamic revivalist ideals. Until his death in 2006, Sayid Abdullod Nuri was the leader of the IRP. *See also* CENTRAL ASIAN ISLAMIC ACTIVITY; ISLAMIC MOVEMENT OF UZBEKISTAN.

ISLAMIC RESISTANCE MOVEMENT. *See* HAMAS.

ISLAMIC REVOLUTIONARY GUARDS. *See* IRANIAN REVOLUTIONARY GUARDS.

ISLAMIC REVOLUTIONARY ORGANIZATION. An Islamic **fundamentalist** organization based in **Lebanon** that hopes to overthrow the **government** of **Saudi Arabia** and replace it with a **Shiite** state similar to that in **Iran**, the Islamic Revolutionary Organization is strikingly similar to other groups, such as the **Islamic Jihad in Hijaz** and the Soldiers of Justice. Relatively unknown and not very active, the group is most known for its attacks on the oil-producing eastern province of Saudi Arabia. *See also* ISLAMIC REVOLUTIONARY ORGANIZATION OF THE ARABIAN PENINSULA.

ISLAMIC REVOLUTIONARY ORGANIZATION OF THE ARABIAN PENINSULA/*AL-MUNAZZAMA AL-THAWRIYYA AL-ISLAMIYYA FI SHIBH AL-JAZIRA AL-'ARABIYYA.* Active in eastern **Saudi Arabia**, the Islamic Revolutionary Organization of the Arabian Peninsula was an underground **Shiite** organization. Believed to have been formed as a direct result of the 1979 **Islamic Revolution in Iran,** the group allegedly has ties with other political groups in the Persian Gulf, such as **Islamic Jihad** in Saudi Arabia and possibly *Hizbullah* **in Lebanon**. *See also* ISLAMIC REVOLUTIONARY ORGANIZATION.

ISLAMIC SALVATION ARMY. The military branch of the banned **Islamic political organization** from **Algeria**, the **Islamic Salvation Front** (known as FIS for *Front Islamique du Salut*), the Islamic Salvation Army (AIS: after the French *Armé Islamique du Salut*) was formed in July 1994 after the Armed Islamic Movement, the Movement for an Islamic State (*Harakat Al-Dawla Al-Islamiyya*), and the **Armed Islamic Group** (also known by its French acronym GIA for *Groupe Islamique Armé*) joined together. As a result, the AIS declared its allegiance to the Islamic Salvation Front in the hope of strengthening FIS influence during the Algerian Civil War (1992–2002). The term "Islamic Salvation Army" has a symbolic meaning, as it was often used to refer to guerrilla warriors who supported the FIS.

The AIS and the GIA were the two strongest and most aggressive Islamic militant groups during the war, although the GIA remained more active in comparison. In fact, under control of **Djamal Zitouni,** the GIA even attacked the AIS on occasion, furthering reports that even though both groups were rivals of the ruling Algerian **government**, they were also rivals of each other, especially since the AIS condemned the GIA's increasingly barbaric tactics.

The AIS was first briefly led by the Armed Islamic Movement's Abdelkader Chebouti until November 1994, when the Movement for an Islamic State's Madani Mezrag took over the leadership position. By the end of that year, the AIS controlled nearly half the militants outside Algiers, as the capital city remained the base of the GIA. The military base for the AIS was in the Beni Khettab Mountains on the Mediterranean coast of northern Algeria. As the Algerian Civil War raged on, the AIS wanted to disconnect itself from the GIA's civilian massacres and declared a cease-fire within the group on 21 September 1997. In 1999, the AIS officially disbanded as thousands of its members took advantage of the **Algerian Civil Concord Act,** which was enacted that year under Algerian President Abdelaziz Bouteflika.

ISLAMIC SALVATION FRONT/*AL-JABHA AL-ISLAMIYYA LI AL-INQADH.* Usually referred to by the French acronym for the *Front Islamique du Salut* (FIS), the Islamic Salvation Front is an Islamist sociopolitical movement based in **Algeria**. It is rooted in the Algerian Islamic movement, which played a key role in the Algerian war for independence against the French colonialists (1954–1962). From this Algerian Islamic movement came three groups: the Algerianization Party, the Islamic Society Movement, and the

Islamic Salvation Front. The main objective of the FIS, like most Islamic **fundamentalist** groups, is to implement *sharia* (Islamic law) throughout the Muslim world, establish a society of economic self-sufficiency, and prohibit forms of economic exploitation, such as monopolies and usury. The FIS can be considered more of a social protest movement that dealt with both moral and ideological issues in order to attain a cultural **authenticity**, which it believed to be beneficial to Algerian and Muslim society.

Established on 18 February 1989 in Algiers as a political opposition force, the FIS created socioeconomic platforms that focused on the "Arabization" of the country. That same year, the Islamic Salvation Front won 60 percent of the votes in the municipal elections. The group's formation was a direct result of the 3 November 1988 amendment to the Algerian **constitution** that allowed **Islamic political parties** other than the **National Liberation Front** (*Front de Libération Nationale*) to become active in the Algerian **government**. The FIS's inception was orchestrated by Sheikh **Abbasi al-Madani** and '**Ali Belhadj**. The two leaders' range and variety in political ideology reflects the broad span of convictions throughout the FIS. Madani, a former fighter in the Algerian War for Independence and a professor at the University of Algiers, represented the more moderate Islamic conservatism and often connected the FIS to the ideals of the independence fighters during the former war. Belhadj conversely made use of his appeal to the younger lower-class citizens through his radical speeches, which reflected a more stringent Islamic conservatism, such as the installation of *sharia*. Many of the FIS members also worked at various mosques and universities, frequently speaking out against **westernization** in Algeria. Supporters often represented an array of occupations but were mostly from the educated sector of the population. Allegedly, the group was financed through private contributions and commercial enterprises.

During the 12 June 1990 elections, the FIS produced impressive results in winning 93 percent of the local towns and cities that had populations exceeding 50,000. The Gulf War (2 August 1990–28 February 1991), which immediately followed the elections, further helped the FIS gain momentum and support throughout the country as the group organized anti–Desert Storm rallies and events that were generally supported throughout the population. However, prolonged demonstrations and bloody encounters with Algerian security forces led to a belief within the Algerian government that the FIS was a formidable threat, and therefore, on 30 June 1991, both al-Madani and Belhadj were taken into custody. Despite the arrests of its founders, the party remained active and legal, and soon Abdelkader Hachani attained leadership (Muhammad Said was briefly head of the group for four days prior to Hachani's appointment). The FIS saw another electoral success on 26 December 1991, when the party won 48 percent (188 of the 231 seats) of the overall popular vote; however, this win was quickly smothered.

On 11 January 1992, fearing the coming of FIS rule, the Algerian army forced FIS candidate and president-elect Chadli Bendjedid out of office and replaced him with the formerly exiled militant Muhammad Boudaif. Resulting in a national state of emergency, FIS members (including Hachani) were arrested, and the organization was officially deemed illegal on 4 March 1992. Subsequently, al-Madani and Belhadj were sentenced to 12 years' imprisonment on 12 July of the same year but were later released on 13 September 1994. The remaining FIS activists declared war on the Algerian government in the wake of these events, and the group officially announced its call to arms against the state the following year, leading to discord and civil war. In July 1994, the radical Islamic Salvation Army (*Armé Islamique du Salut*) united with other smaller opposition forces and declared allegiance to the FIS in hopes of increasing the group's ability to defeat the Algerian government.

With the terms set out by the 1999 **Algerian Civil Concord Act**, many members of FIS deserted the group, and the organization's power began to wane, paving the way for the rise of the more brutal **Armed Islamic Group** (*Groupe Islamique Armé*) and the equally hostile **Salafi Group for Preaching and Combat**. However, at its height, FIS had a solid internal structure that consisted of a hierarchical *Majlis-al-Shura* (consultative council) whose members were rarely disclosed, as al-Madani was the only member to make public addresses. This of course changed when al-Madani was imprisoned and 'Abd Al-Qadir Hashshani became the new spokesperson. When Hashshani came to power in the group, the FIS was split in two: *Jaza'ira* (led by Hashshani) and *Al-Salafyya* (comprised of former *Majlis-al-Shura* members). *See also* ECONOMIC THEORY; ISLAMIC SALVATION ARMY; ISLAMIC SOCIETY MOVEMENT; MUSLIM BROTHERHOOD IN ALGERIA; NATIONAL LIBERATION FRONT.

ISLAMIC *SHURA* ARMY. Created by **Osama bin Laden** during his time in **Sudan** from 1992–1996, the Islamic *Shura* Army, or the Islamic Consultative Army, was created in order to coordinate all the new foreign militant bodies that were now aligning themselves with the Islamic **fundamentalists**. More of a derivative organization, members included the leaders or high-ranking representatives of these groups. Because of their broad ancestral range, various countries, such as **Algeria**, **Egypt**, **Iraq**, **Libya**, **Saudi Arabia**, **Somalia**, and **Tunisia**, were represented. The formation of the Islamic *Shura* Council is actually the original framework of the international organization of **al-Qaeda**. Once **Ayman al-Zawahiri** and his **Egyptian Islamic Jihad** aligned with bin Laden, the Islamic *Shura* Army was no longer needed, as al-Qaeda finally blossomed. This entity shows how organized and multifaceted the al-Qaeda organization has been as a military alliance since its founding years.

ISLAMIC SOCIETY/*AL-MUJTAMA' AL-ISLAMI*. An Islamic society is one that is simply based on *sharia* (Islamic law). It is argued that having a basis of *sharia* will lead to a complete and morally upright sociopolitical society that governs over all, from the individual to the **nation**. Because of this universality, *sharia* is desired. Islamic **fundamentalists** also argue that since an Islamic society is based on adherence to Islamic doctrines and thereby the codes of how to live a moral life, an Islamic society is the most honorable and distinguished society. They also agree that the total application of Islamic law will lead to a modern Islamic society imbued with superior and positive values. *See also* DEMOCRACY; ISLAMIC STATE.

ISLAMIC SOCIETY OF ENGINEERS (ISE). A member of the religiously conservative Alliance of Builders of Islamic Iran, the ISE is an **Islamic political party** from **Iran** that was created in August 1988 following the end of the Iran-Iraq War. Ideologically, the ISE seeks to increase the role of **Islam** in the administrative, scientific, and technological fields. Members feel that by applying Islam to these civil fields, an increase in popular knowledge and therefore cultural prominence can occur. Although the ISE supports the freedom of assembly and expression, it does not advocate the influence of foreign cultures—both Eastern and **Western**. Many members of the ISE have gone on to prominent roles in Iranian society. For example, Mahmoud Ahmadinejad became the sixth president of Iran in 2006 (although the ISE did not support his campaign), and Muhammad Reza Bahonar became the first deputy speaker of the Iranian Parliament. *See also* SCIENCE.

ISLAMIC SOCIETY MOVEMENT/*HARAKAT AL-MUJTAMA' AL-ISLAMI*/HAMAS IN ALGERIA. Founded in 1990 by Mahfoudh Nahnah, this moderate **Islamic political party** was one of the leading sociopolitical movements in **Algeria**. As a leader, Nahnah was one of the more exceptional public figures in the country's Islamic **activism**. The group fought for a politically plural society and also desired to have an open dialogue with the non-Islamic parties, making the Islamic Society Movement one of the most moderate groups in the country. Also among its ideologies was the desire for a morally and spiritually sound population because, without this, according to the group, good relations in political affairs cannot be attained. Membership of the group represented a range from the working middle class to the educated upper class. Entrepreneurs and members of the private sector allegedly provided financial support to the group. An outstanding achievement of the Islamic Society Movement came in 1997, when Nahnah was elected to the parliament in Algeria.

ISLAMIC STATE. Historically, during the sixth and seventh centuries in **Islam** when the **caliphate**'s power was waning, the idea of an Islamic state as an independent institution apart from the caliphate (in which the caliph would be a figurehead) was first introduced. This was brought on by a series of foreign invasions that led to a revivalist movement throughout many of the Muslim lands. The *Khawarij* (Seceders) of the seventh century were also the first ones to theorize that dogma and **legislation** can be interwoven. This dogma was based on **divine governance** and the ultimate adherence to the **Quran**. Contemporary scholars have supported the application of a societal state based on *tawhid* and the doctrines of the **Salafi** (or *Al-Salaf Al-Salih*, "righteous ancestors"). Other contemporary movements for an Islamic state are the pietistic movements called *Al-Sunusiyya* and *Al-Mahdiyya* and also the **Muslim Brotherhood**. Whereas the Sufi movements called for a purification of society in order to establish an Islamic state, the Brotherhood focused on the reinterpretation of the basics of Islam to remake the idea of the Islamic state.

Many Islamic **fundamentalists** agree on the urgency of establishing the Islamic state, although some extremists feel that this should be done with absolutely no influence from **Western** ideologies. In other words, the radical fundamentalists believe in restricting the foundations of the Islamic state. They also feel that if any non-Islamic influence is placed on the state, then all **legitimacy** will be gone. However, radical and moderate Islamists alike absolutely agree on the application of *sharia* (Islamic law) within the state. The concept of the Islamic state has also been the driving force behind practically all the Islamic fundamentalist movements throughout the Arab world and has been part of both conservative and radical movements alike.

The state, in Islam, is more than just a **system** that controls the affairs of its people; it is also involved in exerting a moral and religious influence on the population, especially throughout its daily affairs. Although the state's function should be limited, it nevertheless can provide ethical guidance for the society based on the teachings of Islam. The role of the state is continuously a moral one, even on international platforms. It also creates a social contract between the state and the people that, once created, cannot be negated. The fundamentalists believe that the creation of the Islamic state is essential to creating a virtuous society since it acts as a guiding agency based on *sharia*. Although the state can rework the principles of *sharia* to comply with contemporary concerns, it should never diverge from its basic outlines.

An Islamic state is also a unifying force, not a segmented authority that is rooted in the traditions of the Prophet, and therefore is the best example of an **Islamic society**. Since the state is founded on unity and the Quran's teachings are those of unity, the state reflects Quranic dogma, which is the foundation of the legitimacy of the Islamic state. It is believed that the Islamic state is based on divine law, which provides a constitutional framework, and it is through the establishment of a pure Islamic state that the Islamic world can gain economic, political, and social dominance throughout the world. Another essential function of the Islamic state is to ensure that philosophies or foreign ideologies are not influencing the society, for they can lead to denying **Allah**'s divinity or principles and therefore disrupt the unity that the Islamic state is trying to achieve. Supporters of the state also feel that although patriotism and nationalism are ways in which a society can strengthen itself, they are still too narrow and must be used in moderation and with caution. Overall, the Islamic state is not only an institution but a also doctrinal body that helps to bring the Islamic society to a higher standard of living based on moral purity and agenda. *See also* DEMOCRACY; GOVERNMENT; INTERPRETATION.

ISLAMIC STRUGGLE MOVEMENT. *See HARAKAT-UL-JIHAD AL-ISLAMI.*

ISLAMIC SUPREME COUNCIL OF IRAQ (ISCI). One of the most influential **Islamic political parties** in **Iraq**, the ISCI was the largest group in the Iraqi Council of Representatives from 2005 to 2010. Supported by the **Shiite** Muslim community, the group was originally known as the Supreme Council of the Islamic Revolution of Iraq and was established in 1982 during the Iran-Iraq War and in response to the weakening of the *Hizb al-Da'wa al-Islamiyya* **in Iraq**. Based in Tehran and state funded by the Iranian **government**, the group was originally led by Ayatollah Muhammad Baqir al-Hakim. The main objective of the group during its time as the Supreme Council of the Islamic Revolution of Iraq was to eliminate the **Baathist** regime of Saddam Hussein and establish an Islamic republic like that in **Iran**. Ideologically, the group desired a **theocratic government** based on the post-**1979 Iranian Islamic Revolution** model installed by **Ayatollah Ruhollah al-Musawi Khomeini**. Many members from *Hizb al-Da'wa al-Islamiyya* in Iraq also joined the Supreme Council of the Islamic Revolution, something that was controversial considering the volatile character of the former.

Following the U.S. invasion of Iraq in 2003 and the subsequent fall of the Hussein regime, the group quickly rose in popularity. This rise was due to the council's many social services that it provided, making it similar to the **Muslim Brotherhood** and **Hamas**. Reported membership is in the thousands, and most of the support comes from the southern regions of the country. On 29 August 2003, its leader, al-Hakim, was killed in Najaf by a car **bombing** that also killed approximately 85 others. Still, the group persevered, joined the United Iraqi Alliance, and during the January 2005 elections won six of the eight Shiite seats in the government. The group also won the majority in Baghdad and then gained favorable positions within the Interior Ministry. On 11 May 2009, the group officially changed its name to the Islamic Supreme Council of Iraq, claiming that the use of the word "revolution" was no longer applicable.

ISCI support grew so large in the south that it has been named its de facto government and has made statements about creating an autonomous Shiite state there. Recently, the ISCI has also been criticized for its **theocratic** approach to government and its alleged oppression of **Sunni** Muslims in the southern areas. During the 2009 elections, the group ran under the name *al-Mehrab* Martyr List and came in second at the polls. Since 2009, the group has been led by Ammar al-Hakim.

ISLAMIC TENDENCY MOVEMENT/*HARAKAT AL-ITTIJAH AL-ISLAMI***.** Essentially founded in 1970 by Tunisian Islamist leader **Rashed Al-Ghannushi**, *Harakat Al-Ittijah Al-Islami* was the predecessor of *Harakat Al-Nahda Al-Islamiyya*. The most significant Islamic organization in **Tunisia**, the Islamic Tendency Movement was formed along with 'Abd al-Fattah Moro as an educational movement that was then called *Jam'iyyat Al-Hifaadh 'ala Al-Qur'an* (**Quranic Preservation Society**). After making progress with its cultural and missionary objectives, the group developed into a political movement and was renamed *Harakat Al-Ittijah Al-Islami* in June 1981. Ideologically, the group hoped to spread its political-Islamic beliefs on both the national and the local level. However, many members were arrested and jailed because of their association with the **Islamic political party**. The group was nevertheless successful in recruiting young members, especially from the mosques and universities.

By 1985, the Islamic Tendency Movement had become the largest student association and workers' union in Tunisia. Financially, the group raised funds through commercial enterprises (the selling of periodicals and such) and membership dues (each member paid 5 percent of his income to the movement). Structurally, the party was led by an *amir* who was assisted by a consultative council (*majlis-al-shura*). The movement possessed this structure in 14 different regions in Tunisia. When, in 1989, parties that were racially or doctrinally affiliated were banned, the party was renamed *Harakat Al-Nahda Al-Islamiyya* (Islamic Renaissance Movement).

ISLAMIC UNITY OF AFGHANISTAN *MUJAHIDEEN*. *See* PESHAWAR SEVEN.

ISLAMIZATION/*ASLAMA*. Basically, "Islamization" is a word used to describe the process used by the Islamic **fundamentalists** to adopt other discourses and concepts into Islamic thought. The term can be applied to a wide variety of topics, such as **philosophy**, order, **science**, and technology. For example, when dealing with ideas like **human rights** and **democracy**, they were looked at through the lens of **Islam** (Islamization) and get legitimate rights (*Al-Huquq Al-Shar'iyya*) and Islamic *shura* (consultation). As a process, Islamization depends on deconstructing old or new concepts and reconstructing them into concepts that are presumed to be Islamic compliant. Therefore, to partake in Islamization, one participates in the unique historicist process of human thought and **interpretation**. This process has been used both directly and indirectly by many Islamic fundamentalists. An institution, the International Institute for Islamic Thought, has undertaken serious studies of Islamization and has published numerous works on the subject. From a sociocultural perspective, "Islamization" is also a word used to describe a form of Islamic **activism** aiming to making the society live in a more Islamic manner. This is done through *da'wa* (missionary actions), conducted by educational and social programs to gain more adherence to Islamic principles. *See also* HISTORY; ISLAMIC SOCIETY; LEGITIMACY.

ISMA'ILI FEDAYIN. See ASSASSIN.

ISRAEL. The state of Israel was established in 1948 after the end of the British Mandate, and although the nation was largely able to contain Islamic supporters for some time, a strong anti-Zionist movement began to take hold during the 1970s. Many experts have stated that this was due mostly to the success of the **Iranian Islamic Revolution of 1979**, the pro-**Islam** politics of which spread throughout the Arab world and was felt mainly in the **Palestinian Territories**. The issue with Israel is one of contrasting views of nationalism and sensitive tensions of the reappropriation of the land itself by the Israelis. To Palestinians, the land of Israel is conquered, taken land as well as a place where the Palestinian Arabs have been chastised and repressed. To Israelis, their people deserve a place of settlement and claim that the land is historically theirs. The Nazi genocide of Jews during World War II was, in fact, the main reason that a Jewish sovereign land was created and supported by the **West**. Therefore, there have been a constant duality and nationalistic problems surrounding this territory. Fighting is a constant between the Jews within Israel and the Arabs (even the secularists) living within and outside its borders.

Even though it is not recognized by the international community, according to Israeli law on Jerusalem, Israel's capital is Jerusalem—a city that holds significant meaning not only to the Jewish people but to Muslims and **Christians** as well. This threefold "right to possession" and constant security threats have been staples of the state of Israel and its relationship especially with Palestine. Since the Zionist movement is viewed as a threat to Islam, **jihadists** have also seen good reason to attack the nation and ostracize its inhabitants. In 1964, the **Palestinian Liberation Organization** was established with the intent of combining the efforts of multiple groups that fly the same banner of pan-Arabism and anti-Zionism. This movement and its affiliates have posed the largest threat to Israel within the past half century.

When Israel gained its independence, large populations of Arabs (mostly Palestinians) fled the country or were pushed into exile. This displacement of thousands and Israel's continued criticism of Islam is at the heart of the strife. In addition, many of the Arabs who continue to be within Israel's borders live under constant surveillance and military rule. Israel's policy of its people serving a minimum of four years of military or state service after the age of 18 allows it to have a constant security force within and surrounding its borders.

Noticing these tensions early on in the formation of the state, the government tried to unify the Jewish and Arabic communities within Israel by allowing the formation of Arab political groups. The only stipulation was that these parties be based on an Israeli-Arab and therefore Jewish-Arab identity. This attempt at unity was successful for some groups but as a whole failed. Ideas of nationality and freedom of identity are constantly in flux within the country and the surrounding territories. This resulted in a more hard-line, austere prescription of Islam to be promoted within the surrounding Arab nations and among Arabs living within Israel. The outcome was religious **extremism**, segregation, and **radicalism**. However, all these aggressions did not entirely manifest themselves until the 1980s.

Israel has seen the creation of **Islamic groups**, most notably *Usrat al-Jihad* (The Family of Jihad) in 1979. Formed by Farid Ibrahim Abu Mukh (student of the founder of the Islamic Movement in Israel), the group was staunchly militaristic even though it subscribed to the ideologies of the **Muslim Brotherhood**. The goal of *Usrat al-Jihad* was to forcibly retake the land in the name of Islam and establish an **Islamic state** in its place. However, the Israeli security forces rendered the group inactive by 1981, although the Islamic Movement in Israel still operates. More of a sociopolitical group, the Islamic Movement in Israel is focused more on bringing Muslims back to Israel and improving the public services that the Israeli government did not provide for its Arab population.

One of the biggest events that affected Israel even to this day is the formation of **Hamas**. In the 1970s, the Israeli government allowed the creation of an **Islamic group**, *Mujama al-Islamiya*, to be formed in the nearby Gaza

Strip. This was due mainly to the Israeli perception, at this time, that the main threat to Israel was not Islamic Palestine but rather secular Palestine. Although *Mujama al-Islamiya* functioned as a social organization for some years after the 1987 **Intifada**, many of its members formed Hamas. Hamas then emerged as a militant organization whose main goal was to eliminate the state of Israel. These military aggressions continued to rise especially after the 1993 Oslo Accords, which redrew the boundaries of Israel and the Palestinian Territories, displacing even more people, although the goal was to encourage peaceful relations.

Because of the constant security threats, the Israeli Security Agency (*Shin Bet*) continuously patrols its borders and has a large amount of jurisdiction and leeway to search and seize under any pretense. This heavy-handed military presence has made it incredibly difficult for any Islamic organization or group to gain a significant presence within Israel. Many of the Islamic contingents that do exist within are under the guise of public and social reformists to simply provide basic needs for the Arab and Muslim populations.

As Israeli Arabs continue to be repressed and segregated by the state, discontent continues to grow, and it is estimated that by 2020, this community will make up approximately 20 to 30 percent of the Israeli population. Even today, not even half (an estimated 41 percent) of the Israeli Arabs agree with Israel's right to exist as a nation. Patriotism has been even more stressed with the Israeli war with **Lebanon** in 2006 and has allowed for the population to become influenced further by foreign Islamic groups. This is most evident with the relationship that radical Islamists operating in the Gaza Strip have with the Israeli Arabs. Even **al-Qaeda** operatives have reached some Muslims within Israel, but they never succeeded in creating a branch or constituting a threat to the Hebrew state.

Since 1996, there have been a substantial number of arrests by *Shin Bet* of those accused of conspiring against Israel and/or working with **terrorist** operatives. Israeli Arabs have also supposedly had relations with extremists in **Iran**, **Iraq**, and particularly **Lebanon**. *Hizbullah* **in Lebanon** specifically is attracted to an alliance with Israeli Arabs for obvious tactical reasons. In addition, since these Arabs already operate within the state of Israel, they can maneuver within the country easily and can have access to intelligence information. This relationship between Israeli Arabs and *Hizbullah* can also foster an affiliation with the **al-Aqsa Martyrs' Brigade**. In fact, some experts claim that the internal threat caused by this influence from outside forces is even more dangerous than the outside threats themselves.

Perhaps the state's largest failure is in not achieving a sense of unity between the Israeli Jews and Arabs. The differences between the two communities seem to have been only highlighted rather than used as a way to encourage nationalism or even camaraderie. Although Israel is slow to provide its Arabs a socioeconomic system that is equal to that of Jews, the state has made the educational system equal. However, this has led only to further division, as Islamic studies are not present and the Arab students must, on the contrary, learn about the Jewish heritage and adhere to their teaching practices. Another point of discontent is that, for security reasons, Israeli Arabs are exempt from participating in the mandatory civil service. This is perceived as another form of segregation since some Israeli Arabs volunteer to do so and feel rejected by the system and therefore do not desire to be integrated in the nation. This act then pits citizen against citizen and weakens even further any acceptance of the state of Israel by Israeli Arabs. *See also* UNITED STATES OF AMERICA.

***ISTISHHAD*/MARTYRDOM.** *Istishhad* is translated from Arabic to mean the act of martyrdom or the seeking thereof. It is derived from the Arabic word *shahada*, which means to testify in the eyes of **Allah** for some action. The word is used synonymously with the recently developed **suicide bombing** operations, but it has a heroic emphasis rather than a victimizing one in Islamic **fundamentalism**. Islamists prefer the term "martyrdom" over "suicide bombings/attacks" because suicide is forbidden under *sharia* (Islamic law), and martyrdom is a magnanimous act that could lead to the preservation of **Islam** and is therefore advocated. These who perform the act of *istishhad* (plural, *istishhady*) are seen as the noblest of Muslims, receiving a glorious and sublime death. Many believe that martyrdom is the ultimate act of piety, and it is most commonly found in the radical **Islamic groups**. The radicals view *istishhad* as the illustration of their activism (*harakiyya*).

Historically in Islam, martyrdom was not something attained by fighting among Muslims, but that has changed to mean fighting any person or group, Muslim or not, who sullies the sanctity of the religion. *Istishhad* has contemporary militant origins in the Iran-Iraq War (1980–1988) and the term `amaliyat istishhadiya* (martyrdom operations) was first used by members of **Hamas** in the spring of 1994.

However, there are various types of martyrdom, including suicide bombing and other attacks (gun and knife) in which it is clear that the attacker will not escape. The defining characteristic of martyrdom (in Islamic fundamentalism) is that in killing others, the individual sacrificed him- or herself as well. It also included mainly men throwing themselves at a superior enemy in the knowledge that they would probably die as well.

Many Islamic militant groups engage in *istishhad* or use it as their primary means of insurgency. These include the **Egyptian Islamic Jihad**, **al-Qaeda**, and *al-Shabaab*.

Attacks that have been conducted at the hands of *istishhadyun* include the 14 August 2003 UN embassy bombing in Baghdad conducted by Abu Osama al-Maghrebi and the attack against the Algerian government in 11 April 2007 by Abu Jandal. From 2004 to 2006, in Iraq, over 900 attacks were conducted by *istishhadyun*—this accounts for almost all the attacks in the country during that period. Although the number of suicide bombings has decreased in the past few years, they are still prevalent. Some of these attacks were conducted at the same time by different *istishhadyun* simultaneously. The idea, of course, was to create the largest amount of destruction and, from their point of view, to arrive in paradise together. Recently, there has been a trend in martyrdom operations in that they employ **women** as well as men. *See also* ASSASSIN; BOMBING; EXTREMISM; JIHAD; VIOLENCE.

ISTISHHADYUN. Meaning "martyrdom seekers," **al-Qaeda** has adopted the tactic of recruiting young (generally 15 to 25 years of age) members to become part of this new aspect of its **jihad**. Evidence has shown that these *istishhadyun*, or *istishhadyin*, join the organization's branches in **Iraq** and North Africa to kill themselves in **suicide bombing** attacks against U.S. or other foreign government structures.

These "martyrdom operations" were first implemented by **Iran** during the Iraq-Iran War (1979–1989) as a military strategy in detonating buried land mines to clear paths for the advancing fighters. Using the glorification of martyrdom, **al-Qaeda** has successfully recruited many youths to participate in suicide bombings that result in a wake of devastation. Over the years, these actions have developed into an inspirational path for people who seek a noble death and have become the archetype in extreme Islamist warfare. **Al-Qaeda in the Islamic Maghreb**, **Hamas**, and other **Islamic groups** use the dogmatic doctrine of the *istishhad* (being a martyr) to entice their recruits. Although suicide is antithetical to **Islam**, supporters have made fine distinctions between what constitutes suicide and martyrdom. In these distinctions, it is concluded by the Islamists that the two are not the same, and therefore martyrdom is not abhorrent to *sharia* (Islamic law) but rather the opposite, although this is far from generally accepted.

However, there is reason to believe that not all the martyrdom seekers are volunteers and that considerable social pressure is brought to bear on the young (especially girls), particularly if relatives of that person died in the jihad. It is then seen as a duty to take retribution on the enemy in this way. There are also financial inducements in the sense that the family that the *istishhadyun* leaves behind will be taken care of.

AL-ITIHAD AL-ISLAMI (AIAI)/THE ISLAMIC UNION. Formed in 1994, AIAI was the largest militant **Islamic group** in **Somalia**. Allegedly funded by **Osama bin Laden**, it has been reported that after the fall of President Siad Barre's regime in Somalia on 26 January 1991, bin Laden decided to send military and financial support to the group in hopes of gaining a foothold in the country. Reputed to be a violent organization that sought to impose *sharia* (Islamic law) throughout the country, the AIAI also was instrumental in founding the *sharia* courts in Somalia. Extremely aggressive, the group claimed responsibility for numerous **assassination** attempts, governmental and civilian **bombings**, kidnappings, and raids on clan areas that opposed its presence (although many members were harbored by some clans that supported its cause). Prominent leaders of the AIAI include Hassan Dahir Aweys, Hassan Abdullah Hersi al-Turki, and Muhammad Haji Yusuf. The organization was also believed to have allies in nearby Eritrea, Ethiopia, Kenya, and **Yemen**, allowing the AIAI to establish training camps and operational bases there. However, the AIAI started to suffer significant losses at the hands of Ethiopian security forces in 2002 and never quite recovered. When the AIAI began to demobilize, Aweys became a prominent figure in the **Islamic Court Union**, and al-Turki headed its *Hizb Al-Shabaab* faction as many militants fled to Yemen. *See also* AZHAR, MASOOD.

IZZ AD-DIN AL-QASSAM BRIGADES. Targeting civilians, Egyptians, Israelis, and rival Palestinian groups in the Palestinian territories, the Izz ad-Din Al-Qassam Brigades (often referred to simply as the Al-Qassam Brigades) are the military wing of **Hamas**. They have made use of **suicide bombings** in addition to other tactics to inflict their ideological agenda on the people they deem a threat or insubordinate to their Islamist cause. Formed in December 1987, their name was chosen in honor of the Palestinian militant nationalist Izz ad-Din Al-Qassam (19 November 1882–20 November 1935), who, in 1930, founded the **Black Hand Organization** anti-Zionist movement. Although exact membership of the Brigade is open to speculation, it is believed that their number reaches several hundred with a supportive security force of an estimated 10,000 operatives who are designated to reinforce the Brigade if need be. Most of the militants were trained in **Iran** and **Syria** and work as a collective entity with the political faction of Hamas. The Gaza Strip is their primary base of operations. The Al-Qassan Brigades have also proven themselves entirely capable of performing large-scale and complex lethal assaults, reinforcing the speculation as to their size and support.

Throughout the 1990s, the Izz ad-Din Al-Qassan Brigades were known for their suicide bombings, which were especially directed at civilians, helping the group attain international notoriety for its atrocities. In 1996, the leader of the Brigades' West Bank battalion and senior explosives coordinator, Yahya Ayyash, was killed by the Israeli secret services (*Shabah*). In remembrance, some members of Hamas's military branch call themselves "Disciples of Ayyash" or "Yahya Ayyash Units."

The uniform of the Al-Qassan Brigade members consists of a black hood with a green sash tied around the forehead, as seen on the group's insignia. On 3 September 2005, the Brigades posted via their website the names and ranks of the top seven operatives. This mentioned Mohammed Deif as head and general commander, Marwan Isa and Ahmed Jaabari as his assistants, Raid Said as the Gaza City commander, Ahmad Al-Ghandur as the northern Gaza Strip commander, Muhammad Abu Shamala as the southern Gaza Strip commander, and Muhammad Al-Sanwar as the Khan Younis commander. On 6 September 2006, an Egyptian media source reported that Egyptian authorities had captured Deif. Throughout 2009 and 2010, the Israeli secret service had seen progress in successfully carrying out air strikes aimed at Hamas and Al-Qassam Brigades leaders, resulting in the deaths of many of the organization's chief commanders. *See also* 'AYYASH, YAHYA ABD-AL-LATIF; ISRAEL; PALESTINE.

J

JAHILI SOCIETIES. A *jahili* society, or pagan society, is one that is based on human governance rather than **divine governance**, or *hakimiyya*. *Jahiliyya*, or **paganism**, happens when man follows a human system of belief or philosophy rather than one based on the divine. According to many **fundamentalists**, **Western** society is an example of a *jahili* society because the populations have separated the doctrinal from the political—a quality that would never be found in a true **Islamic state**.

JAISH AL-MAHDI/MAHDI ARMY. Established in June 2003 by Muqtada Al-Sadr, *Jaish Al-Mahdi* is a **Shiite** Islamic **fundamentalist** group in **Iraq** that began in the northeastern part of Baghdad called Saddam City (now Sadr City). The group's formation is a direct result of the April 2003 fall of Saddam Hussein's regime at the hands of the U.S. military forces. *Jaish Al-Mahdi* hoped to be a security force within the chaotic area as well as an opposition group against not only the American occupying forces but the installed Iyad Allawi legislature as well. The *Mahdi* Army also hoped to protect and represent Shiite sociopolitical interests within the new **government**. After the **United States** banned one of Al-Sadr's newspapers on 2 April 2004, the group became hostile and began to attack numerous civil structures and police barracks throughout the surrounding areas of Baghdad. However, the American security forces were able to contain much of the activity, and the counterinsurgencies resulted in the deaths of hundreds of *Jaish Al-Mahdi* members. Faced with the loss of many of his followers, the conflict ended on 6 June 2004 when Al-Sadr signed a **peace** agreement with the **Western** forces.

Jaish Al-Mahdi continued to have a turbulent relationship with the occupying American forces in Iraq, especially within Baghdad. Just two months after the June truce, hostilities began again between the two military opponents, resulting in a standoff due to Al-Sadr barricading himself within the Shiite Imam 'Ali Shrine in Najaf. Although the *Mahdi* Army was outnumbered by at least 1,000, the American and Iraqi security teams were not able to enter the shrine so as to not upset the already unstable public. Again, a truce was agreed on with the mediation of Grand Ayatollah Sayyid 'Ali Hussaini al-Sistani.

Experts have reported that since 2006, the group has grown exponentially, and membership is between 20,000 and 60,000 participants. Some also believe that the organization is split into different cadres with various leaders for each although all are still working under the same umbrella *Mahdi* Army group. The group has also been more vicious in its actions against **Sunni** Muslims within the Iraqi capital area, especially in places where the Shiite population is dominant. Investigators furthermore have concluded that the *Mahdi* Army may have possibly received military training and tactical support from the **Iranian Revolutionary Guards**. Al-Sadr still continues to inspire and publicly speak to his followers from time to time despite the U.S. efforts to detain him. The group has maintained its platform of rebelling against the American occupants but has been rather inactive for the past few years because of its leader, Al-Sadr, being in **Iran**. As soon as he reentered the country in 2011, he threatened to reactivate the *Mahdi* Army if the occupying American forces did not withdraw from Iraq by the end of the year as planned. *See also* ISLAMIC GROUPS; VIOLENCE.

JAISH-E-MUHAMMAD **(JeM).** Translated as "The Army of Muhammad," JeM is a Pakistani *mujahideen* organization that has stated its primary goal as separating the area of Kashmir from Indian control and incorporating it into **Pakistan**. In the hope of doing so, JeM has carried out numerous strikes against the Indian region of Kashmir and has been officially banned in Pakistan since January 2002. Considered one of the most violent militant **Islamic groups**, it was formed in March 2000 by **Masood Azhar** after his split with *Harakat-ul-Mujahideen* and his release from an Indian prison in 1999. Many members from *Harakat-ul-Mujahideen* followed Azhar to JeM, and after its banning in 2002, the group splintered into *Khaddam-ul-Islam* and *Jamaat-ul-Furqan* (both were banned by Pakistan in November 2003). The group is aligned with *Lashkar-e-Tayyiba* and has jointly conducted attacks on **government** agents and facilities. JeM has also claimed responsibility for kidnapping and killing journalists and American and European nationals and suicide attacks on legislative buildings.

Its membership is reportedly in the several hundreds and includes Afghans, Kashmiris, Pakistanis, and veterans of the Soviet-Afghan War (1979–1989). The force briefly maintained training camps in **Afghanistan** until the later part of 2001 and received armed support from *Harakat ul-Jihad Al-Islami* and the **Taliban army**. Although its main contingents lay in Peshawar and Muzaffarabad in Pakistan, the group is notably present in a large portion of Kashmir. *See also JAMAAT ULEMA-E-ISLAM*; KASHMIRI SEPARATISM; *SIPAH-E-SAHABA PAKISTAN; AL-UMAR MUJAHIDEEN.*

JAMAAT AHL AL-HADITH/**ASSEMBLY OF THE FOLLOWERS OF THE SAYINGS OF THE PROPHET.** An **Islamic political party** from **Pakistan**, *Jamaat Ahl al-Hadith* is part of the *Ahl al-Hadith* reformist movement, which is similar to the **Salafi** movement and strictly emphasizes the austere devotion to the **Hadiths**. The group is also part of the **Islamic Council of Action**. In 2002, *Jamaat Ahl al-Hadith* won 53 of the 272 legislative seats in Pakistan. Led by Dr. Sajid Mir, the group has also spoken out against the involvement of the **government** in affairs dealing with *sharia* (Islamic law). It was formed shortly after the separation of Pakistan from India in 1947 and took up headquarters in Karachi. Membership began to grow substantially by the late 1980s and reached over 300 by 2000. The group constantly affiliates itself with the other *Ahl al-Hadith* factions and has been slandered for its alleged associations with various **jihadist** groups.

JAMAAT ANSAR AL-SUNNA/**GROUP OF THE FOLLOWERS OF THE SUNNA.** Founded in September 2003, *Jamaat Ansar Al-Sunna* is a militant **Islamic group** that is based in northern and central **Iraq**. Members are of both Kurdish and Arab **Sunni** descent, and many have formerly been part of the *Ansar Al-Islam* group. This **salafi** group has taken up arms in the hope of expelling the U.S. occupation in Iraq and the **government** of Nouri Al-Maliki (prime minister of Iraq since 20 May 2006). The group is allegedly known to have close connections with *Jamaat Al-Tawhid wal-Jihad* (which later become **al-Qaeda in Iraq**), among other militant Islamic groups. *Jamaat Ansar Al-Sunna* has carried out numerous attacks on secular and civilian entities since its inception, turning mostly to improvised explosive devices and **suicide bombings** to achieve its goals. The group has also claimed responsibility for numerous kidnappings and subsequent executions of its hostages, a majority of whom were Iraqi nationals. The group distributes propaganda in the forms of pamphlets, audio recordings, and Internet messages to attract support, spread its ideologies, and proclaim its continuing presence.

JAMAAT-UL-FURQAN. Led by Umar Farooq, *Jamaat-ul-Furqan* was established after some members of *Jaish-e-Muhammad* left in 2000. Active in **Afghanistan** and **Pakistan**, the group has been known for the ferocity of its attacks on **westerners**. Among its notable attacks was the 17 March 2002 incident when five people were killed and 45 injured during a hand grenade **bombing** at a Protestant church in Pakistan's capital of Islamabad. Little is known about the group, and it was officially banned in November 2003.

JAMAAT-E-ISLAMI (**JI**)/**ISLAMIC PARTY.** The oldest Islamic **fundamentalist political party** in **Pakistan**, JI was established in Lahore, Pakistan, on 26 August 1941 by theologian **Maulana Sayyid Abul Alaa Maududi**. The group has an Indian faction (*Jamaat-e-Islami Hind*) and a Bangladeshi faction (*Jamaat-e-Islami* in **Bangladesh**). JI also is head of the **United Council of Action** (*Muttahida Majlis-e-Amal*), a Pakistani coalition of Islamic political groups, and is closely aligned with the **Muslim Brotherhood**. The group is divided between *mutaffiq*, or "affiliates" (the elite tier); the *handard*, or "sympathizers" (the middle tier); and the *arkan*, or "members" (the rest of the group). Ideologically, JI seeks an integral **Islamic state** totally devoid of **Western** influence and based on *sharia* (Islamic law) throughout the Muslim world, particularly in Bangladesh, India, and Pakistan. The group relies solely on the sacred texts of **Islam** and the most fundamental dogmatic practices.

JI was established because of the population's desire to adopt an Islamic **constitution** after the withdrawal of the British colonial forces in Pakistan. Successful in its goals, the *Qaraardad-e-Maqasid* (the country's constitutional preamble) states that all laws will be made in conformity with the **Quran**. The group was deemed by the Pakistani Supreme Court a legal political party and ran in elections from 1950 to 1977. Although originally in support of Pervez Musharraf's political rule as Pakistan's president, JI began to discount Musharraf after he started to make anti-Islamic reforms to the nation's constitution.

Although the group does not have a formal armed presence in the Indo-Pakistani War for Kashmir, it has nevertheless supported the Kashmiri Muslims and their **jihad**. Currently, the group is led by Ghulam Muhammad Butt and has continually gained support and membership through the use of *da'wa*. Its conviction of the Islamic jihad has made the group exceedingly popular with various *mujahideen* organizations, especially *Hizb-e-Islami*. JI has come under scrutiny, as critics have claimed that it is simply an **extremist** group, using the advocacy of education of Muslims as a front for propagating a militant Islamic dictatorship. In fact, JI does possess a training camp in Kashmir, and it has been reported that the *Hizb-ul-Mujahideen* is the group's military outfit. The group has also gained support and membership through university students and Islamic student groups, notably the *Jamaat-i-Tulaba-i-Islam*. *See also* AL-BADR; ALL PARTIES HURRIYAT CONFERENCE; JAMMU AND KASHMIR *JAMAAT-E-ISLAMI*; KASHMIRI SEPARATISM; *PASBAN-E-ISLAMI*.

AL-JAMAAT AL-ISLAMIYA. *See AL-GAMA'A AL-ISLAMIYYA*; ISLAMIC GROUPS.

JAMAAT AL-JIHAD AL-ISLAMI/ISLAMIC JIHAD GROUP. The Islamic Jihad Group was founded in **Egypt** in 1979 by **Muhammad 'abd Al-**

Salam Faraj, although it did not establish its *Majlis-al-Shura* (consultative council) until 1981. Ideologically, the group sought to establish an **Islamic state** and **caliphate**. The group also encouraged all Muslims to participate in the **jihad**, as it is seen as their duty. Based on Faraj's writings, the group believes that the Muslim world has turned into a *jahili* society and is now at the mercy of imperialism and Zionism. This belief that the **government** should be returned to a pure **Islamic society** was the driving force behind the group's **assassination** of Egyptian President Anwar Al-Sadat in 1981. This plot was further triggered by Sadat's peace accord with **Israel**. **'Abbud Al-Zumar** also became a leading figure in *Jamaat Al-Jihad Al-Islami* and encouraged the overthrow of the states (especially Egypt) that were deemed un-Islamic and *jahili*. Taking contemporary inspiration from **Ayatollah Ruhollah al-Musawi Khomeini**, the armed revolution of the people was seen as the only way to return **Islam** to its true values. **'Abd al-Rahman** also emerged as an influential figure in the Islamic Jihad Group. He helped maintain the group in its later years and further encouraged the application of *sharia* (Islamic law) in order to achieve justice within the **Islamic societies**.

JAMAAT-UL-MUJAHIDEEN **(JuM)/ASSEMBLY OF THE** *MUJAHI-DEEN.* The first splinter group to form out of *Hizb-ul-Mujahideen*, JuM was established in 1990 and is comprised mostly of Kashmiri **Deoband** adherents and former members of *Shabaab-ul-Islam*. A political *amir* leads the group as chief, and the organization as a whole has a military structure with a commander in chief and vice commander in chief who each control underlying divisional, district, and area commanders. Although the group is brutal in its tactics, it has yet to grow into a substantial size; membership is estimated in only the low hundreds. One reason for JuM's lack of strength is the huge number of arrests and deaths of key members since 1997. In fact, during the spring of 2001, it seemed as though the whole group was about to crumble because of the rampant incarcerations. However, the group has become a significant organization in the Jammu and Kashmiri separatist movement. It also claims that participants in JuM are purely Kashmiri, whereas many similar groups have a lot of **Pakistani** nationals within their ranks as well.

Aside from seeking the independence of Kashmir, the group has also been vocally opposed to the **All Parties Hurriyat Conference** and any attempts at **peace** agreements between India and Pakistan. Radical in its ideologies, JuM feels that only through aggression, not diplomatic negotiations, can the territories be liberated. The group has claimed responsibility for the March 1993 Badami Bagh explosion, which left 29 dead, and the attack on the Beerwah army barracks on 12 September 2000. The group also stated that it conducted the 25 December 2000 bombing at the Batwara, Srinigar, army headquarters, which killed nine. However, some experts believe that the perpetrators of the attack were actually members of **Jaish-e-Muhammad** and **Al-Umar Mujahideen**. *See also JAMAAT-UL-MUJAHIDEEN* IN BANGLADESH; KASHMIRI SEPARATISM.

***JAMAAT-UL-MUJAHIDEEN* IN BANGLADESH (JMB)/ASSEMBLY OF THE *MUJAHIDEEN* IN BANGLADESH.** Founded in 1998 by Abdur Rahman, JMB is an Islamic militant organization that was first established in Dhaka, Bangladesh. Using mostly improvised explosive devices (IEDs), the group has carried out numerous aggressions throughout the country and was officially banned by the **government** of Bangladesh on 23 February 2005. In particular, on 17 August 2005, members of the group reportedly detonated over 500 IEDs in 300 different locations across 50 cities in Bangladesh. On 30 March 2007, Rahman and five other heads of JMB were executed for the August 2005 **bombings** and the murder of two judiciary figures. Afterward, Maulana Saidur Rahman assumed the leadership of JMB.

Reportedly 100,000 strong, JMB has created affiliations and a working relationship with a number of Islamic organizations. It also used a number of **madrasas** to recruit and train young members in the ideologies and militant structure of the group. The internal structure of the group works on a hierarchical scale, as different segments of JMB are dispersed throughout Bangladesh to ensure cohesion and effectiveness. Ideologically, the group hopes to replace the current government of Bangladesh with an **Islamic state** based on **sharia** (Islamic law) and the **holy texts** of **Islam** through aggressive tactics. Although JMB is doctrinally similar to other **Salafi** Islamic fundamentalist organizations, the group has also announced that it was heavily influenced by the **Taliban** in **Afghanistan**.

Closely adhering to the strictest forms of **Islam**, JMB opposes all non-Muslim forms of government and civic life. The group is also considered, along with various organizations like *Hizb-ut-Tawhid* and **Harakat-ul-Jihad Al-Islami**, to be part of the **Harakat-ul-Mujahedeen** organization. Financially, the group is supported by private donations from **Bahrain**, Kuwait, **Libya**, **Pakistan**, **Saudi Arabia**, and the United Arab Emirates. Although most of the founding leaders, high commanders, and members of the group have been arrested or executed, the group nevertheless is still presently active, albeit on a small scale. *See also JAMAAT-UL-MUJAHIDEEN.*

JAMAAT AL-MUSLIMIN. *See AL-TAKFIR WA AL-HIJRA.*

***JAMAAT-E-TALBA-E-ISLAMI*/ISLAMIC ORGANIZATION OF ISLAMIC STUDENTS.** An Islamic organization influenced by the works of **Abul Alaa Al-Maududi**, the group hoped to spread the **fundamentalist** program of **Islam** throughout different universities throughout **Pakistan**. It is considered to be the student branch of the party *Jamaat-e-Islami* in Pakistan and is the largest student organization in the country. It is headquartered in Lahore, Pakistan, and was founded on 23 December 1947. It also has a female counterpart, which is called *Islami Jamaat-e-Talibaat*. During the 1971 Indo-Pakistani War, the group took up arms and was truly instrumental in the fight against India, as an alleged 10,000 members died protecting East Pakistan from falling under Indian control.

Ideologically, the group promotes the doctrine of *tawhid* (oneness of **Allah**) and the *khatm* (finality) of the **Prophet Muhammad**. The group was also a formidable influence in declaring the **Ahmadiyya Muslim Community** non-Muslims within Pakistan. Members also believe, like many other **funda-mentalists**, that an **Islamic society** cannot exist without completely adhering to *sharia* (Islamic law). The group has also been exceptionally influential in the sociopolitical activities of Pakistan, transcending the various rulers the country has had. Despite the bans that the **government** has placed on student organizations being involved in the country's politics, the group continues its work of spreading its fundamentalist ideologies throughout the university system. Currently, *Jamaat-e-Talba-e-Islami* is led by Sayyid Abdul Rashed. Allegedly, the group received financial assistance from **Saudi Arabia** and has been accused of being affiliated with the extremist *Hizb-ul-Mujahideen*.

JAMAAT AL-TAWHID WAL-JIHAD (JTJ)/*TAWHID AL-JIHAD*/ GROUP OF MONOTHEISM AND JIHAD. Established in 2003 and led by Jordanian **Abu Musab Al-Zarqawi**, the JTJ was a militant Islamic **fun-damentalist** group that formed an alliance with the **al-Qaeda** organization in September 2004. After the merger of these two groups, the organization became known as *Tanzim Qaidat Al-Jihad fi Bilad Al-Rafidayn* (Organization of the Jihad in the Land of the Two Rivers, the two rivers being the Euphrates and Tigris in Mesopotamia [**Iraq**]), or **al-Qaeda in Iraq**. Many of the members of the JTJ were non-Iraqi, mostly Kurdish **jihadists** and *mujahideen* from the Soviet-Afghan War (1979–1989). The original goal of the group was to overthrow the monarchy in **Jordan**, and Zarqawi even established a training camp in Heart, **Afghanistan**. After the 2001 U.S. occupation in Af-ghanistan, the JTJ relocated to Iraq and there developed a relationship with the Kurdish *Ansar Al-Islam*. For the next two years, the Saddam Hussein regime (which was already monitoring the actions of *Ansar Al-Islam*) would try, unsuccessfully, to capture al-Zarqawi and dissolve the JTJ.

After the 2003 U.S. invasion of Iraq, the JTJ grew stronger and larger af-ter absorbing remnant militants from organizations that were dissolved and foreign fighters who took up arms against the **Western** forces and needed al-Zarqawi's military connections to advance tactically. During this time, the group focused its efforts on removing the U.S. forces within Iraq, ousting the interim **government** that was formed after the fall of Saddam Hussein's regime, replacing that government with an **Islamic state**, and marginalizing the **Shiite** community within Iraq. The JTJ kept away from the use of predictable tactics of warfare (guerilla fighting, conventional weaponry, and so on) and instead turned to **suicide bombings**, improvised explosive devices, and kidnappings that targeted military forces, diplomats, and civilians alike. The group also became known for taping its executions and publishing them online—a propagandistic tactic of terror that has been adopted by many other groups. Spiritually led by Abu Anas Al-Shami, the cleric cited verses from the **Quran** to justify the group's brutal tactics and legitimize its jihad.

Of its many attacks, the most notable are the August 2003 **bombing** of the Jordanian embassy in Baghdad, which killed 17; an attack on the Imam Ali mosque in Najaf, which left 86 dead; the Day of Ashura bombing in 2004, which killed 178; the May 2004 **assassination** of Iraqi interim government President Ezzedine Salim in Baghdad; a car bomb that killed 47 in September 2004; and the October 2004 massacre of 49 Iraqi National Guardsmen. After having dominated the Islamic insurgency for the two-year period of 2004–2006, JTJ leader al-Zarqawi was killed in a U.S. air strike on 6 June 2006. The group still remains part of the al-Qaeda network.

***JAMAAT ULEMA-E-HIND*/ORGANIZATION OF INDIAN SCHOLARS.** Established by four prominent Indian scholars (Qazi Hussein Ahmed, Ahmed Sayyid Dehlvi, Abdul Bari Firangi Mehli, and Abdul Mohasim Sajjad) in 1919, *Jamaat Ulema-e-Hind* is an Indian Islamic organization. Opposed to an independent **Islamic state** of **Pakistan**, the group is also affiliated with the Indian National Congress. The group's sociopolitical belief is that Indian Muslims and non-Muslims should live together under a secular **government** within the country. This theory is known in Urdu as *mu'ahadah* (treaty agreement) and is, in fact, the basis of the Indian **constitution**.

***JAMAAT-UL-ULEMA-E-ISLAM* (JUI)/ASSEMBLY OF THE ISLAMIC CLERGY.** JUI is part of the **Deoband Islamic movement** and is also a Pakistani **political party**. First led by Allamah Shabbir Ahmad Usmanni, JUI was formed by ex-members of *Jamaat-ul-Ulema-e-Hind* in 1945. Originally a religiously motivated group, JUI's presence on the Pakistani political arena began with the modernized, **Western**-influenced policies enacted by then President Ayub Khan from 27 October 1958 to 25 March 1969. Opposed to these new **government** measures, the party ran in the country's first general election on 7 December 1970 in the hope of gaining influence and applying its strict **interpretations** of *sharia* (Islamic law) to the government.

Allegedly affiliated with **Afghanistan**'s **Taliban**, the group has also created more *madrasas* in **Pakistan** than any other similar organization. JUI is also part of the **United Council of Action** alliance of religious parties that also includes *Jamaat-e-Islami*. Chief among the group's goals is to establish a purely independent Islamic Pakistan. The activities conducted by JUI, especially through its domination of the political and ideological realms, have helped make way for groups such as *Harakat-ul-Mujahedeen* and *Jaish-e-Muhammad*, among others. Currently, the party has split into two factions known as *Jamaat-ul-Ulema-e-Islam Fazal*, led by **Fazal ur-Rehman**, and *Jamaat-ul-Ulema-e-Islam Sami*, led by Sami ul Haq. *See also* ALL PARTIES HURRIYAT CONFERENCE.

JAMMU AND KASHMIR ISLAMIC FRONT (JKIF). Initiated and supported allegedly by the Pakistani Inter-Services Intelligence in 1994, the JKIF is a group that was formed primarily from the Jammu and Kashmir Liberation Front. However, its leaders, Bilal Ahmad Baig, Hilal Ahmad Baig, Sajjad Ahmad Keno, and Javed Ahmad Krava, all originated from the Student's Liberation Front (which broke away from the Jammu and Kashmir Liberation Front a few years prior). At the time of its inception, the JKIF was unique in that it had no political associations. However, the organization seeks the acquisition of Jammu and Kashmir by **Pakistan** through increasingly **violent** means. The group was ideologically led by Maulana Abdul Rahman Makki. The JKIF has carried out numerous large-scale explosions in highly populated urban areas throughout India. In 2001, the Indian **government** passed the Prevention of Terrorism Ordinance, allowing far-ranging arrests of anyone even merely suspected of membership in **extremist** organizations. Consequently, numerous JKIF members were jailed, and the outfit nearly became extinct by 2002. Although the group has been in dire straits, its revanchist, militant ideologies have inspired many other organizations to take root. *See also* KASHMIRI SEPARATISM; TERRORISM.

JAMMU AND KASHMIR *JAMAAT-E-ISLAMI* (JKJI)/JAMMU AND KASHMIR ISLAMIC PARTY. Using its foothold in Jammu and Kashmir to gain a distinct advantage in the liberation from India, the JKJI is a segmented group from **Abul Alaa Maududi**'s *Jamaat-e-Islami*. It was established by the theologian Saaduddin Tarabali, whose primary goal was to eradicate the tribal folk practices that were believed to be corrupting the sanctity of **Islam** in Jammu and Kashmir. Prominent in the political realm of Jammu and Kashmir since its formation in the late 1940s, the group began its affiliation with the Pakistani Inter-Services Intelligence when the Indo-Kashmir aggressions started in the 1980s. However, in July 2000, JKJI agreed with the *Hizb-ul-Mujahideen*'s moves for peace in the hope that the acquisition of the territories could be faster if solved diplomatically rather than by **violence**. However, by 2005, the group was subject to internal splintering, and leadership was frequently rotated. The group has been led by Mohammad Hassan Tarigami since 10 August 2006. *See also* KASHMIRI SEPARATISM.

JANJALANI, ABUBAKAR (1959–1998). A Filipino veteran *mujahideen* of the Soviet-Afghan War (1979–1989), Abubakar Janjalani also studied in various Islamic countries, such as **Saudi Arabia**. While serving in the war, Janjalani became close with **Osama bin Laden**, who provided him with the capital to create the **Abu Sayyaf** (the nom de guerre of Janjalani) group in the Philippines. Janjalani recruited members out of the **Moro National Liberation Front** (MNLF), making Abu Sayyaf, in effect, a splinter group of the MNLF. The group was fully active by the early 1990s and conducted numerous **bombings**. His younger brother, **Qadhafi Janjalani**, eventually joined the group as well. However, on 18 December 1998, Abubakar Janjalani was killed on Basilan Island during a fight with the Filipino National Police. Following his death, Qadhafi Janjalani took over the group.

JANJALANI, QADHAFI (1975–2006). Leader of **Abu Sayyaf**, Qadhafi Janjalani was a Filipino militant who was accused of partaking in numerous kidnappings and various acts of **terrorism**. Born in Isabela City, he joined in the early 1990s his brother's **Abubakar Janjalani** group but was imprisoned in Manila in 1995. However, he eventually escaped from the Camp Crame jail. Later, in December 1998, after the death of his brother, he took control of Abu Sayyaf. After this, the group was inactive for a period of time as it consolidated its power and reformulated its methods to be more financially oriented as it began to take hostages. For years, Abu Sayyaf under Qadhafi's control continued to kidnap and terrorize many throughout the Filipino area. By the mid-2000s, Janjalani and other members of Abu Sayyaf were among the most wanted men in the world. However, on 26 December 2006, a body that was confirmed to be that of Qadhafi Janjalani was found buried in the Philippines. The exact circumstances of his death remain unknown.

JAYSH AL-ISLAM/**ARMY OF ISLAM.** Located in the Gaza Strip, the Army of Islam is an Islamic militant group comprised of the Durmush Palestinian clan from the Gaza Strip. The group came into the public sphere after its kidnapping of BBC journalist Alan Johnston on 17 March 2007, an act that attracted a huge amount of media attention. The group has been linked to **al-**

Qaeda and **Hamas**, although the latter has denied such claims of an alliance. In fact, Johnston was released to Hamas officials 114 days after his capture. Key leaders of the group were killed in November 2010 by **Israeli** Air Force strikes: Muhammad Namnam along with two others on 3 November as well as Islam and Mohammed Yassif on 17 November. The attacks apparently took place after Israeli security forces were informed of the army's plot to strike in the Sinai. The Army of Islam is also the suspected perpetrator of the 2011 New Year's Day **bombing** of a Coptic Christian church in Alexandria, **Egypt**, resulting in 23 deaths. The group denied any role in the attack yet supported the rumors before **al-Qaeda in Iraq** claimed responsibility.

JEBALI, HAMADI (1949–). Cofounder of *Ennahda* in Tunisia, Hamadi Jebali was elected as Tunisia's prime minister on 14 December 2011. Prior to his involvement with the *Ennahda* Party, he was an accomplished engineer and even created his own engineering company. He joined *Ennahda* in 1981 and was the editor of the group's newspaper *Al-Fajr* (The Dawn). After publishing an essay with **Rashed al-Ghannushi** speaking out against the corrupt military courts in Tunisia, he was imprisoned by the state for one year in 1990. Then again, in 1992, he was accused of plotting to overthrow the Tunisian **government** and replace it with an **Islamic state**. On this charge, he was sentenced to 15 years' imprisonment. However, in February 2006, he was released. But since the events of the 2011 **Arab Spring**, the *Ennahda* Party has become legalized and became the most powerful **Islamic political party** in the country. Jebali, despite his incarceration, has always remained a viable figure in the movement.

   In fact, Jebali's election has reinforced the dominance of the *Ennahda* Party within the country, as it is expected that the new government of the country will be dominated by the ideologies and sociopolitical views of this party. Jebali assumed office on 24 December 2011.

JEMAAH ISLAMIYAH. Established in 1993, this Islamic **fundamentalist** group sought to install an **Islamic state** throughout Brunei, Indonesia, Malaysia, the southern Philippines, and Singapore. *Jemaah Islamiyah* is allegedly affiliated with the **Abu Sayyaf Group**, the **Moro Islamic Liberation Front, al-Qaeda**, and the **Taliban army**. Founded by Indonesians Abu Bakar Bashir and Abdullah Sungkar (formerly members of *Darul Islam*), the group boasts an estimated 1,000 members. A formidable leader of the group, Riduan Isamuddin (a.k.a. Hanbali), has also become a leader of operations and a strong affiliate of al-Qaeda. Brutal in its tactics, the group has allegedly conducted numerous attacks that have resulted in the deaths of 260 people and injured a reported 700. *Jemaah Islamiyah* was originally formed to specifically attack the secular regime of Suharto in Indonesia and replace it with an **Islamic state**. However, on 21 May 1998, the Suharto regime fell, and the group returned to Indonesia and continued to use **violence** throughout the area.

Of its many attacks, the most notable are the 12 September 2000 Jakarta Stock Exchange car **bombing**, which killed 15 and injured 20; the 12 October 2002 Bali bombings; and the 1 October 2005 Bali bombings, which resulted in the total combined deaths of 222 and injured 338. Despite these insurgencies, the group has been severely damaged because of its loss of key leaders and members. For example, Sungkar died in 1998, Bashiri was arrested on 15 October 2004 (but was released on 14 June 2006), and Hanbali was arrested on 11 August 2003. The group continued to be weakened after the October 2002 Bali bombing when members broke off into three separate groups: one led by Bashiri, another led by Noordin Muhammad Top, and the third led by Abu Dujana, active in the island of Sulawesi. By 2008, it seemed as if *Jemaah Islamiyah* was slowly deteriorating, but research showed that the organization still had roughly 1,000 members and was, in fact, actively building more refined and dangerous weapons. On the basis of these observations, the group has recently been less focused on short-term, immediate operations and rather has been concentrating its resources on building up arms and finding recruits. *See also JIHAD FI SABILILIYAH.*

JEMAAH MUJAHIDEEN ANSHUROLLAH/FIGHTERS ACTING IN THE WAY OF GOD. *Jemaah Mujahideen Anshurollah* was an informal network of Indonesian **activists** that was founded in the early 1970s by Abdullah Sungkhar in central Java. It was formed to perpetuate the ideology of **Darul Islam** and fight against the injustices taking place in the Indonesian state.

JIHAD/HOLY WAR/STRUGGLE. In the most basic of terms, jihad is simply an armed struggle against any institution or force that opposes or restricts **Islam**. There is, however, a difference between how the moderate and radical **fundamentalists** view jihad. For example, a moderate view on jihad is that it is not a means of aggression and expansion but rather a protection of *da'wa*, a way to gain **peace**, a right of every Muslim, and the fulfillment of **Allah**'s mission of justice against powers that seek to destroy Islam. There is also no definitive time frame for jihad—it could last for any length of time and be composed of multiple phases. There is an agreement among the fundamentalists that it should have strong, solid organization as well as continuity.

Radical fundamentalists, however, see jihad as not only a defensive action but also a way to establish Islam in the lands where it does not exist. In other words, jihad should not just protect Islam, but it should also destroy *jahili* **societies** and transform them into Islamic ones. Some radical fundamentalists have even gone so far as to condemn every society as *jahili*. It is claimed that with the combination of these two actions (defense and transformation), the **divine governance** of Allah will prevail. Jihad is then viewed as a way to liberate society from oppressive **governments** or institutions.

An agenda for jihad was theorized both in **Shiite** and in **Sunni** Islam by leaders like **Ayatollah Khomeini** and **Sayyid Qutb**: substantial defense of the nation, the removal of any obstacle preventing *da'wa*, and then the establishment of Allah's governance. Many Islamic fundamentalists have found passages in the **Quran** that advocate and support the importance of the jihad, thereby further instilling the Islamic foundations of the struggle. According to their Quranic **interpretations**, Allah proclaims that it is the responsibility of every Muslim to have a morally prosperous society free of tyranny and oppression. If the Muslim finds himself in a repressive society, it is his duty and obligation to struggle against the current regime and replace it with an **Islamic society**.

Some of the major groups that adhere to the jihadist platform are *Boko Haram*, **East Turkestan Islamic Movement**, **Egyptian Islamic Jihad**, **Egyptian Salafi**, the **Islamic Salvation Front**, *Harakat-ul-Ansar*, *Harakat-ul-Jihad al-Islami*, *Harakat-ul-Jihad al-Islami* **Bangladesh**, **Islamic Jihad in the Hijaz**, **Islamic Jihad of Palestine**, *Jund Ansar Allah*, **Islamic Jihad of Palestine**, **Islamic Jihad in Yemen**, *Jamaat al-Jihad al-Islami*, *Jamaat al-Tawhid wa al-Jihad*, *al-Jihad al-Islami* **in the West Bank and Gaza Strip**, **Libyan Islamic Fighting Group**, and the **al-Qaeda** organization and its affiliates and branches, including **al-Qaeda in Iraq**, **al-Qaeda in the Islamic Maghreb**, **al-Qaeda in the Arabian Peninsula**, *Shabiba Islamiya*, *Salafia Jihadia*, **Salafi Group for Preaching and Combat**, *Shabiba Islamiya*, the **Taliban army**, *Tawhid and Jihad* **in Syria**, and *Tehrik-e-Jihad*, among others.

All these groups are composed of those who are referred to as *fedayeen*, or those who are willing to die in the struggle. The inclusion of these individuals is one of the defining characteristics which label these groups as jihadi. In addition, the **Islamic Jihad Union** is a conglomerate of various jihadi groups of which many of the above are members. Some influential and pertinent figures in the holy struggle are **Anwar al-Awlaki**, **Osama bin Laden**, **Abdel Latif Moussa**, **Hasan 'abd Allah al-Turabi**, and **Abu Musab al-Zarqawi**, to name a few. It should also be noted that almost every nation discussed in this dictionary has been susceptible to jihadi activity in some way. Most notable are **Afghanistan**, **Egypt**, **Iraq**, **Libya**, **Palestine**, **Sudan**, **Syria**, and **Yemen**. *See also* EXTREMISM; *INSPIRE*; ISLAMIC POLITICAL PARTIES; MASTER NARRATIVES; *SADA AL-MALAHIM*; TERRORISM.

JIHAD FI SABILILIYAH/**JIHAD ON THE PATH OF GOD.** This was the term used by ***Jemaah Islamiyah*** to justify the permanence of the **jihad** to the implementation of *sharia* (Islamic law) and the establishment of a **caliphate** in Southeast Asia.

***AL-JIHAD AL-ISLAMI* IN THE WEST BANK AND GAZA STRIP.** The *Al-Jihad Al-Islami* organization does not have one central base; rather, it is an umbrella term used by many **Islamic groups** from different countries that share in the same ideologies. However, the largest concentration of *Al-Jihad Al-Islami* affiliates is in the West Bank and Gaza Strip of **Palestine**. Members of *Al-Jihad* are mostly middle-age, middle-class militants who are eager to conduct the **jihad** in the name of **Islam**. In addition, many members joined the group after being influenced by many other members or leaders of the group while staying in prison together—many in **Israel**. Ideologically, the group is influenced by **Sayyid Qutb** (whose discourses on the armed revolution were of great influence) and Sheikh 'Izz Al-Din Al-Qassam.

Al-Qassam is considered the leading symbol of the movement since he was the trailblazer of the Palestinian armed revolution. Many members of *Al-Jihad* see similarities between al-Qassam's actions in Palestine against the British and Zionists and their own struggle against the Israelis. *Al-Jihad Al-Islami* also adopted al-Qassam's strict organizational methods and recruitment of the politically oppressed lower class. The group has also been influenced by the **Egyptian Islamic Jihad**. Tactically, the group relies on **suicide bombings** (*istishhad*) since they are viewed as most effective. The group hopes to establish an **Islamic state** in Palestine and eradicate the state of Israel. This elimination of Israel is one of the defining characteristics of *Al-Jihad Al-Islami*, which has separated it from many of the other Islamic groups and has led to conflicts with the **Palestinian Liberation Organization**. *See also* IZZ AD-DIN AL-QASSAM BRIGADES.

JORDAN. The constitutional monarchy of the Hashemite Kingdom of Jordan has had a reputation of successfully suppressing any foreign or domestic militant Islamic insurgencies since its inception in 1921, when Great Britain created the Amirate of Transjordan. The kingdom, which is comprised mostly of **Sunni** Muslims, has encouraged both moderate and **traditional** practices of **Islam** in the hopes of discouraging any **extremist** activity. In addition, the Hashemite family's claim of being descendants from the Prophet's tribe has helped create **legitimacy** and encourage a traditionalistic brand of Islam. This was further reinforced in 1952, when Islam was proclaimed as the official religion of Jordan and *sharia* (Islamic law) was introduced into its **constitution**. However, it is not the exclusive source of **legislation**.

Although extremist movements have historically been repressed, two factions of radical Islamic **fundamentalism** do exist within the country: the Jordanian Islamists, which originated in the **Muslim Brotherhood of Jordan** (which spawned the **Islamic Action Front**), and the *Salaf* Jihadism movement, which was encouraged by **al-Qaeda**. These groups often have overlapping membership and ideologies, but the Jordanian Islamists receive more popular support because of their Muslim Brotherhood roots. Reasons for the rise of radical Islamists within Jordan are the ongoing conflicts within **Afghanistan**, Gaza, **Iraq**, and **Palestine** as well as the **government**'s inherently weak religious structure, which has been recently unsuccessful in immobilizing the opposition groups. Many of the groups' problems with the Jordanian regime are related to its **peace** treaty with **Israel** and its strict control over the religious system within the country.

Currently, the leaders of the Jordanian Muslim Brotherhood faction feel that the country should serve as the ultimate military and tactical base to "liberate" Israel because of its geographical proximity. However, the monarchy (and a majority of the public) has not been willing to enter into the Israeli conflict since it is viewed as a Palestinian matter. Jordan's reluctance to join in the fight against Israel has helped provoke these radical groups, especially since a large number of Jordanians have a Palestinian heritage (actually more than half are refugees from the Palestinian territories), and this demographic makes up a majority of the membership within **Islamic groups**.

As is the case with most **jihadist** groups, the main means of recruitment has been through propagandistic publications produced by the organizations. Yet, since the monarchy has been swift in banning such materials, the groups have begun to use the Internet and other means of technological communication to reach potential members—mostly young men. Although a small percentage of the population supports the extremists, these tactics of recruitment have proven to be invaluable and very effective, especially since the ideal recruits are more prone to using the modern modes of technology.

The Salafi Jihadists have gained popular support by being viewed as the protectors of Islam. The Jordanian community has been a particular witness to the insurgencies taking place in Israel and Iraq because of its geographical proximity and feels that specifically the **al-Qaeda in Iraq** (AQI) presence within its borders will help establish an **Islamic state** throughout the country. However, the repression of the group by the Jordanian government, the death of AQI leader **Abu Musab al-Zarqawi** in 2006, and the popular desire to eliminate violence from the country have led to a decrease in overall support. In the hope of regaining support, the Salafi Jihadist supporter **Abu Muhammad al-Maqdisi** began to promote another view of **extremism** that was ideologically similar to AQI but emphasized that no attacks should occur within Jordanian boundaries. However, in the past few years, the Jordanian security forces have been increasingly successful in capturing Salafi Jihadist members and thwarting their plans. Jailing groups of members for a time and public trials have been used to help decrease their influence on the public.

Currently, the Jordanian Islamists or, rather, the Islamic Action Front (IAF) has claimed to want to establish a more cooperative relationship between the group and the Jordanian government. This was announced by the new secretary-general of the IAF, Ishak al-Farhan, after the 30 May 2009 resignation of Zaki Irsheid from that position. However, throughout the population, it seems as if there has been a recent trend that is in favor of the Islamic penal code (*hudud*)—an aspect supported by the Islamic fundamentalist organizations. It must be recognized that the increasing support for the fundamentalists is due to the community's wish to apply conservative Islam to daily life and legislation, not to their desire for an extremist regime within the country.

In addition, Jordanians who are members of the Muslim Brotherhood are more likely to join the Palestinian **Hamas**, and the two organizations have been increasingly intertwined. However, this relationship came under pressure in 2009, when the more moderate members of the Brotherhood did not approve of being associated with the increasingly violent Hamas. The Palestinian question remains an integral part of Jordanian life, and this relationship with Hamas continues to infuse a great deal of Islamic expression throughout the community.

Politically, November 2009 saw far-reaching internal reforms within the Jordanian Parliament as enacted by King Abdallah II. This reshaping gave hope to many within the Jordanian Muslim Brotherhood (especially after its huge defeat in the 2007 elections) and other reformist groups, yet skepticism remains with regard to the sincerity of the king's political agenda. Some also feared that the onset of the **Arab Spring** in 2011 would affect Jordan as well. However, this shock wave has yet to be seriously felt within the country (in comparison to other Muslim countries), although opposition groups have taken this opportunity to orchestrate some demonstrations. In March 2011, some Jordanians were killed in a protest regarding the Israeli peace treaty. Still, many regard this climate in Jordan as a Palestinian tactic to undermine the kingdom.

JUDAISM. Although the **Quran** acknowledges the divine message of Judaism, it also takes note of the Jews's disobedience to **God**, specifically, their deviation from the divine laws in order to prosper financially and politically. Along with **Christianity**, Muslims do acknowledge that once Judaism was a decent, **monotheistic religion** but that it has now lost its divine message in favor of personal interests. The occupation of **Palestine** and formation of Israel is the ultimate contemporary example, in the eyes of Islamic **fundamen-**

talists, of the dependence on physical power that Jews possess. It is viewed that the land in question is sacred to both Christians and Muslims and should not be occupied by any one people. *See also* ISLAM.

JUND ALLAH **IN IRAN/PEOPLE'S RESISTANCE MOVEMENT OF IRAN (PRMI).** Also known as the PRMI, *Jund Allah* (also *Jund-Allah* or *Jundallah*) is translated as "soldiers of God." A **Sunni** Muslim organization founded by Abdulmalek Rigi, the group has significant positions in the Sistan and Baluchistan provinces of **Iran**. There is also another *Jundallah* group operating in Balochistan, **Pakistan**. Reportedly linked to **al-Qaeda**, *Jund Allah* has claimed responsibility for many kidnappings, smugglings, and attacks throughout Iran on civilian and military targets. Supported militarily by **Afghanistan** and Pakistan, the PRMI was most likely established in 2003 as an offshoot of the Baluchi Autonomist Movement, which was created to support the regime of Saddam Hussein. Ideologically, the group insists that it is fighting for the rights of all Sunni Muslims in **Shia**-dominated Iran, although it has been accused of having a proxy agenda of trying to dissolve the republic.

Great Britain and the **United States** have been regularly accused of providing financial and military support to the PRMI in the hope of disrupting the Iranian government, although none of these reports have been confirmed and are left merely to speculation. On 23 February 2010, the group's founder was captured in Iran and subsequently executed on 20 June 2010. *Jund Allah* announced Muhammad Dhahir Baluch as the new leader of the organization. More recently, the group coordinated a **suicide bombing** on 14 December 2010 near a mosque in Chah Bahar, Iran, killing approximately 39 Shia worshippers. *See also JUND-ALLAH* IN PAKISTAN.

JUND-ALLAH **IN PAKISTAN.** Although it shares its name with the *Jund Allah* organization in **Iran**, *Jund-Allah* in **Pakistan** works independently of that group and has a reputation for being much more vicious in its tactics. Affiliated with **al-Qaeda**, *Jaish-e-Muhammad*, and the **Taliban army**, this militant **Islamic group** has taken responsibility for numerous insurgencies against civilian, governmental, and military groups. Qasim Toori, a well-known **extremist fundamentalist**, is also a member of *Jund-Allah* in Pakistan. What distinguishes this group from other militant organizations is that its membership has come predominantly from Pakistani security and military forces, although it is reported that the group's membership is shrinking. *See also JUND ALLAH* IN IRAN.

JUND ANSAR ALLAH/**ARMY OF THE SUPPORTERS OF ALLAH.** Led by Sheikh **Abdel Latif Moussa**, *Jund Ansar Allah* is an armed Islamist organization that operates primarily in the Gaza Strip. In November 2008, the group announced its inception and dedication to the global **jihad**. The first known operation that took place under *Jund Ansar Allah*'s direction was the 8 June 2009 military attack in which the Islamist members assaulted Israel Defense Forces stationed near the Nahal Oz border in the northern Gaza Strip. Using improvised explosive devices, the IDF successfully thwarted the attack, and five *Jund Ansar Allah* members subsequently died. Ideologically inspired by **al-Qaeda**, the organization attracted its members through Moussa's sermons at his Ibn-Taymiyah mosque in Rafah, Gaza Strip. In his sermons, which took place on Fridays, Moussa regularly verbally attacked the Palestinian ruling power and Islamist rival group **Hamas** for its lack of implementing *sharia* (Islamic law) throughout the country.

The group continued to clash with Hamas, and on 22 July 2009, three *Jund Ansar Allah* militants participated in a standoff with Hamas police in the southern Gaza Strip location of Khan Younis until eventually surrendering. Finally, on 14 August 2009, after announcing the installation of an Islamic amirate in the Palestinian territories, including the Gaza Strip, and again criticizing Hamas, the Rafah mosque was destroyed by Hamas police forces the next day, and 24 people died, including the group's leader, Moussa. After the August 2009 attack, Hamas was condemned by numerous al-Qaeda groups as being a secular movement that was dedicated to the massacre of Islamists. On 29 August 2009, *Jund Ansar Al-Jihad wal Sunna* (a *Jund Ansar Allah* splinter group) took responsibility for an attack on a Hamas security compound in Gaza City in retaliation for the 14 August attack and released a declaration calling for other jihadists to join forces against the "apostate[s]" Hamas.

JURISPRUDENCE/*AL-FIQH*. *Fiqh* is the theological corpus used by Islamic scholars to deal with legal issues. Many moderate **fundamentalists** believe that jurisprudence is one way that **Islam** can operate within a modern society. They feel that *sharia* (Islamic law) must be adjusted in ways that will accommodate **modernity**, or else it will fail. They argue that jurisprudence should be based on the freedom of researching different legal systems so that the Muslim community can have many options and tools to create its revived society. Conservatively, the **Islamic state** should base its jurisprudence on consultation (*shura*) and consensus (*ijma'*) so that multiple needs are met. The fundamentalists agree that the development of an Islamic jurisprudence should be left to Islamic scholars and that no particular view of **government** should ever be imposed on a society. *See also* ISLAMIC SOCIETY; THEOCRACY.

JUSTICE/*AL-'ADALA*. For many Islamic **fundamentalists**, justice can take place only after the establishment of an **Islamic state**, or else that state has not fulfilled its obligation to society. Justice can take international, legal, and social forms to ensure that it provides security to all of humanity. To the fundamentalists, moderate and radical alike, **Islam** is the basis of **world order**, and therefore its arms of justice must be wide. The moral idealism of Islam is the way to defend different societies from injustice and spread justice all the same—it is one of the most distinct marks of the **religion**. Some Islamic fundamentalists like **Hasan al-Banna** have even stipulated that proper worship of **Allah** or any future success of Islam cannot exist without justice. **Sayyid Qutb** goes even further to state that a lack of justice means an increase in self-interest, which can erode a community's solidarity. Justice is therefore the reason why the state must interfere in some cases not only to uphold justice but also to perpetuate the morality of the society. It can be argued, then, that justice is at the center of an **Islamic state** and therefore a good society. *See also* ISLAMIC SOCIETY; PEACE.

JUSTICE AND CHARITY MOVEMENT (JC)/*JAMAAT AL-'ADL WA AL-IHSAN.* One of the largest and most powerful **Islamic political parties** in **Morocco**, JC was formed in 1988. A major platform of the group has been its abhorrence of the autocratic monarchy, and therefore it has been deemed illegal and is unrecognized as a political party. An indigenous movement, the group regularly advocates the overthrow of the monarchy and the implementation of *sharia* (Islamic law). Furthermore, it believes that only through **justice** and educational reforms within the community (not radical actions) can a free **Islamic society** exist in Morocco. Founded by **'Abd Al-Salam Yasin**, a former regional inspector of the Ministry of National Education in Morocco, the group is better known by his spokeswoman-daughter Nadia Yasin. Because of its criticisms of the monarchy, the group has repeatedly been in conflict with the Moroccan government since its inception.

In 1996, JC created the Muslim Participation and Spirituality Association as a way for the group to generate further support outside the country in order to achieve success within it. The association has developed chapters in some of Europe's major cities, and those are led by JC activists who expatriated from Morocco. Funding for JC comes solely from membership contributions, as each member of the group is required to donate 2.5 percent of his or her salary to the movement. The group has also had incredible success in university circles, from which most of its members come.

JUSTICE AND DEVELOPMENT PARTY. *See HIZB AL-ADALA WA AL-TANMIA.*

JUSTICE AND PROSPERITY PARTY/*PARTAI KEADILAN SEJAHTERA.* Seeking the dominance of **Islam** in Indonesian public life, the

Justice and Prosperity Party is an **Islamic political party** in Indonesia. First called the Justice Party at its inception on 20 July 1998, the group adopted its current name in April 2002. First led by Nurmahmudi Ismail, Justice and Prosperity is now headed by the radical Luthfi Hasan Ishaaq. By 2004, the group became the seventh-largest **political party** in the Indonesian Parliament (the People's Representative Council), gaining 45 of the 560 seats in the elections. A prominent member, Hidayat nur Wahid, was also elected speaker of the People's Consultative Assembly. The basis of the party's support comes from the urban areas of Jakarta, constituting a major voting demographic that led to the 2009 electoral gain of 12 more seats in the parliament.

The group has been very active in speaking out against the political corruption that has tainted the Indonesian government, a position that has helped gain it popular support. Although Justice and Prosperity advocates for the role of Islam in Indonesian life, it strongly asserts that it does not support a complete **Islamic state** based on *sharia* (Islamic law). This is due mostly to its members' belief in the freedom of **religion** since *sharia* requires all constituents to adhere to Islam. Still, its ideological platform is largely conservative, has ties with the **Muslim Brotherhood**, supports the liberation of **Palestine**, and is against the rising American/**Western** influence in Indonesia.

***JYLLANDS-POSTEN* MUHAMMAD CARTOONS CONTROVERSY.** On 30 September 2005, the Danish newspaper *Jyllands-Posten* published 12 editorial cartoons of the **Prophet Muhammad** titled "The Face of Muhammad." Created by 12 different political cartoonists who regularly published for the periodical, the series was written as a commentary on a debate between self-imposed censorship and a social critique of **Islam**. The Muslim population within the country strongly protested the publication by holding demonstrations in response. The controversy heightened as various newspapers throughout the world reprinted the images in their own pages. As the cartoons circulated, protests began within the Islamic world as well.

Danish (and in some cases European) embassies in **Iran**, **Lebanon**, **Pakistan**, and **Syria** were attacked by some outraged members of the population. Deemed racist and blasphemous, many Muslims took great offense to the images, and the Danish government was attacked as being anti-Muslim. However, the illustrators and representatives from *Jyllands-Posten* defended the cartoons as being simply an act of free speech, intended not to criticize the nation of Islam as a whole but rather to exemplify a pressing issue of **extremist** Islamic ideology.

Despite the publication's defense of the cartoons and its explanation of their meaning, protests and demonstrations continued. This served only to encourage already palpable anti-**Western** sentiments throughout the Muslim world. In fact, on 27 October 2005, Muslim organizations filed a lawsuit against *Jyllands-Posten* under Danish criminal code, which prohibits any public ridiculing of religious faiths. However, this case never made it to the courtroom, as the publication was deemed not guilty of any criminal offense at the prosecution level. Still, outrage persisted and demonstrations continued. In the escalating protests, an approximate 139 people were killed as a result of local security forces trying to subdue the crowds.

Fatwas were issued by some **extremists**, calling for the deaths of the cartoonists and resulting in many of them going into hiding or coming under police protection. In addition, it was reported that toward the end of 2006, the Muslim boycott of Danish products accounted for an estimated 15 percent decrease in total Danish exports since the time of the publication. Even in 2010, animosity over these images continued as one of the artists was bombed in his home on 1 January by a Somali extremist who intended to kill him. However, his attempt was thwarted by local police forces. This incredible backlash against the satirical cartoons is due primarily to the severe punishment that insulting Muhammad warrants in Muslim culture. Considered one of the gravest infractions, these images were seen not as a critical social commentary but rather as a direct insult to a way of life and dogmatic tradition to those outraged within the Muslim community. The provenance of the periodical (i.e., Western) served only to underline the tensions. *See also* ART; BLASPHEMY.

K

KAMPULAN MAHADI/MAHADI MOVEMENT. Formed in 1970, the Mahadi Movement was a Malaysian **Islamic group** established by Imam Mahdi to demand the introduction of *sharia* (Islamic law). Short lived, the group disbanded in 1972.

KAMPULAN REVOLUSI NASIONAL (KRN)/NATIONAL REVOLUTIONARY MOVEMENT. The National Revolutionary Movement was a Malaysian Islamic group formed in 1980 by the Libyan Ibrahim Mahmoud. It was disbanded in 1995.

KASHMIRI SEPARATISM. The areas of Jammu and Kashmir have been under Indian control since the Indian-Pakistani War in 1947, making the areas technically under Indian jurisdiction. Given the Hindu majority in India, many Islamic **fundamentalists** sought to reclaim the territories and reintegrate them into **Pakistan** or see Jammu and Kashmir become their own separate **Islamic states**. Groups involved in this movement are *Al-Faran*, *Al-Hadid*, *Harakat ul-Muminim*, *Harakat- ul-Mujahideen* (formerly *Harakat- ul-Ansar*), *Jaish e-Muhammad*, the **Kashmir Liberation Front**, and *Lashkar e-Tayyaba*. This separatist movement has easily occurred since the territories are the only ones within India that have a Muslim majority. Allegedly financially and militarily supported by Pakistan, many members of these groups are also veteran *mujahideen* of the Soviet-Afghan War (1979–1989).

The contemporary Jammu and Kashmir violence for the liberation against Indian control started in 1989, when separatists began attacking Hindu civilians within the territories, Indian security forces, and foreign tourists. The insurgencies reached a peak during the 1990s, when over 12,000 died, resulting in India declaring a state of martial law from 1994 to 1995 within the areas. Despite the militant rule, approximately 8,000 more people were killed from 1995 to 1997. The brutality continued to mount, especially in 1998, when militant separatists began attacking Hindu villages, leading to a great exodus of people fleeing the Vale of Kashmir into the more secure city of Jammu.

Pakistan's interest in the Kashmiri separatist movement has come under question, especially since many experts believe that the state has supported this violent rebellion since the end of the Indian-Pakistan War. Recently, many have also suspected that the Afghani **Taliban** regime has played a major role in the insurgency as well. However, after the **World Trade Center and Pentagon attacks of September 11, 2001**, it seems as if the Pakistani government has distanced itself from the militant Kashmiri bodies, but many experts feel that Pakistan is clandestinely operating within the territories through its Inter-Services Intelligence. *See also HIZB-UL-MOMINEEN*; *HIZB-UL-MUJAHIDEEN*; *KHADDAM-UL-ISLAM*.

KATIBAT AL-ABU GHUDDA. *See* ABDULLAH AZZAM MARTYR BATTALION.

KATIBAT AL-MOULATHAMOUN/BRIGADE OF THE TURBANED PEOPLE. *Katibat Al-Moulathamoun* is one of the most famous Malian extremist groups that are part of **al-Qaeda in the Islamic Maghreb** and is led by **Mokhtar Belmokhtar**. Also known informally as the *Moulathamoun* group, this organization operates in the vast Sahel Desert region in central **Mali** and utilizes familial connections with the Tuareg tribes in the north to imprison hostages and establish training bases in the area.

KHADDAM-UL-ISLAM. A splinter group from *Jaish-e-Muhammad*, *Khaddam-ul-Islam* was established in 2002 following the former being banned by the Pakistani **government**. Allegedly aligned with *Jamaat Ulema-e-Islam*, the group is led by Abdul Rauf and *Jaish-e-Muhammad*, founder **Masood Azhar**'s brother. Some believe that *Khaddam-ul-Islam* is just a continuation of Azhar's organization. The group receives tactical support from various radical Islamic **Sunni** groups and continues the *Jaish-e-Muhammad*'s efforts to oust India from Kashmir. Financially, *Khaddam-ul-Islam* has been known to use racketeering to generate funds in addition to receiving donations from allies. In addition to conducting insurgencies against Indian-occupied Kashmir, the group has declared its willingness to take up arms against **Western** forces in any Islamic country. It is speculated that the group's strength is low and possibly only in the hundreds. *See also* KASHMIRI SEPARATISM.

KHALIFA, MUHAMMAD 'ABD AL-RAHMAN (1919–). The general guide of the **Muslim Brotherhood in Jordan**, Khalifa also held the position of prosecutor and judge. Before becoming the Brotherhood's general guide, he was the deputy general guide and a member of **Jordan**'s Lower House of Parliament from 1959 to 1961. Having received a law degree at the law university in Jerusalem, he also works as an independent litigator.

KHAMENEI, 'ALI (1939–). After the death of **Ayatollah Ruhollah al-Musawi Khomeini** in 1989, Khamenei became the supreme spiritual guide (*waliy al-faqih*) of the **Islamic Republic of Iran**. Previously, in 1981, he also served as the third president of the Islamic Republic. Active in the **Iranian Islamic Revolution of 1979**, he also sat on the Council of Defense in the wake of the rebellion. While serving as secretary-general of the Islamic Republican Party, he was a key player in the ousting of President **Abul Hasan Bani Sadr** and Muhammad Shari'atmadari.

KHOBAR TOWERS BOMBING. Occurring at 9:50 p.m. on 25 June 1996, a truck laden with explosives was detonated outside the Khobar Towers apartment complex in Dhahran, **Saudi Arabia**. At the time, the complex was being used to house U.S. Air Force personnel from the 4404th Air Wing. Although the explosion took place 35 yards away from the entrance of the complex, the force was so powerful that it left a crater 30 feet deep by 80 feet wide, damaged six buildings within the complex, and destroyed an entire facade of an eight-story building that housed approximately 2,500 troops. According to the observations made by on-duty security forces, the truck was driven to be parked just outside the safety perimeter, and then the driver sped away in another vehicle.

Because of this incident, the **United States** relocated over 4,200 of its military recruits in Saudi Arabia to a remote desert region that was largely desolate. Following an investigation, many believed that the **bombing** was conducted by Iranian-affiliated militants or even the work of the **al-Qaeda** organization. Yet the Saudi interior minister stated that the attack was carried out solely by Saudi nationals after their research, which concluded on 22 May 1998. However, in early 2000, information surfaced that the domestic extremist group *Hizbullah* **in the Hijaz** was responsible for the attack. *See also* SUICIDE BOMBING.

KHOMEINI, AYATOLLAH RUHOLLAH AL-MUSAWI (1902–1989). Best known as being the leading figure in the **Iranian Islamic Revolution of 1979**, Khomeini also received a notable education in **jurisprudence**. When the socioeconomic conditions in **Iran** were not being improved by the shah in the 1940s, Khomeini began his protests. He openly stated how the large lower class should rebel against the oppressive regime in order to create a better **Shiite** society. The foreign influence on Iran (allegedly the CIA aided the Shah's SAVAK security force) was also another problem that Khomeini openly objected to. Ideologically, Khomeini believed in the **jihad** as an effective method for Iran to return to **divine governance**, **unity**, and **reason**. Continuously incarcerated, Khomeini was once released under popular demand in 1963 but was then rearrested in 1964 and exiled to Turkey after inciting a boycott of that year's elections. Following his stay in Turkey, he moved to **Iraq** and then to France.

Despite being abroad, Khomeini continued to influence the masses through his writings, recordings, and the strong network of religious clerics that he established. A charismatic figure, Khomeini easily appealed and related to the lower classes—a characteristic that helped him gain influence and later become the supposed spiritual leader of *Hizbullah* **in Lebanon**. Even after the revolution in Iran, he continued to be active in the country's politics and has left a legacy of being one of the most successful leaders of any contemporary revolution. *See also* KHOMEINISM.

KHOMEINISM/*KHOMEINIYYA*. After the success of the **Iranian Islamic Revolution of 1979**, **Ayatollah Ruhollah al-Musawi Khomeini** and his ideologies were hailed as being the foundation of the **Islamic Republic of Iran**'s new political agenda. Now the principal authority on legal, religious, and social matters, Ayatollah Khomeini's guidance became known as Khomeinism. The basis of Khomeinism is the combination of **religion** and nationalism, thus creating an **Islamic society** rooted in the **fundamentals** of **Islam**. His policies were applicable to both foreign and domestic matters of the state as well. After many countries in the Islamic world witnessed the success of Iran's revolution, they sought to adapt Khomeini's policies in order to be successful in their own rebellions. It was here that Khomeinism began to take hold and was seen as catalytic to any global Islamic revolution.

Soon, movements in **Bahrain**, **Egypt**, **Iraq**, Kuwait, **Pakistan**, and **Saudi Arabia** all began to use Khomeinism in their own rebellions. However, this led to a number of riots, repeated coup d'état attempts, **bombings**, hijackings, and demonstrations throughout all of these countries (although Bahrain was influenced the most because of its **Shiite** majority). **Lebanon** was also greatly influenced by Khomeinism because of its large Shiite population and the **Israeli** invasion in 1981, which springboarded the rebellion. The militant **Islamic political group *Hizbullah* in Lebanon** also claimed that Khomeini was its spiritual leader (even though he repeatedly denied any relationship with the group). The Iranian Revolution and, in effect, Khomeinism had a great influence on many of the Islamic countries during the 1980s and 1990s as the Muslim world began to experience upheaval and revolt against many of its regimes. Although Khomeini himself denied supporting any acts of **violence** or affiliation with such groups, his revolutionary ideas nevertheless inspired many of them.

KNOWLEDGE/*MA'RIFA*. Knowledge, in the eyes of the Islamic **funda-mentalists**, is the most motivating force for action as it leads to the revival of **Islam** because it is the result of **consciousness**. Since consciousness allows the individual to see what is good or bad, just or unjust, man can then real-ize when a society is corrupt and not an **Islamic society**. A good, developed knowledge will then lead to an Islamic way of life. However, this is also deemed a more moderate view since many **extremists** believe that knowledge should be suppressed since only **Allah** possesses pure knowledge. Knowl-edge, from their point of view, should be restricted to what can be gained from the **interpretation** of the **Quran**. Any attempts to gain knowledge through **philosophy** or **science** should also be relegated to textual interpreta-tions and therefore be purely practical, not abstract.

***KOMITE AKSI PENANGGULUNGAN AKRIBAT KRISIS* (KOMPAK)/ ACTION COMMITTEE FOR A CRISIS SOLUTION.** A **Salafist** Indo-nesian nongovernmental organization founded on 1 August 1998, KOMPAK was established by businessman Tamsil Linrung from Makassar. Linrung and KOMPAK played an active role in the **jihadi** movement of the Moluccas and Celebes. Although the group was disbanded, a number of supporters are still involved in the armed violence movement in Indonesia, often in conjunction with members of *Jemaah Islamiyah*.

***KOMITE INDONESIA UNTUK SOLIDARITAS DENGAN DUNIA ISLAM* (KISDI)/INDONESIAN COMMITTEE FOR SOLIDARITY WITH THE MUSLIM WORLD.** Founded in 1987, KISDI was established by militants belonging to the most conservative wing of *Dewan Dakwah Is-lamiyah Indonesia*. This group hoped to denounce the political anti-Muslim conspiracy that it felt was pervading the country.

***KUFR*/UNBELIEF.** According to **fundamental** Islamic doctrine, any non-adherence to *tawhid* (oneness of **Allah**) from political to theological devi-ance is considered *kufr*. There is, however, a difference in what justifies *kufr* from the moderate to the radical point of view. Moderate fundamentalists typically are lax in condemning a person of unbelief since they acknowledge the natural weakness of man and allow for more ideological and administra-tive freedoms. Radical fundamentalists are markedly more rigid on what is deemed *kufr*. They believe that any submission to any entity or institution that is not firmly based on Allah's teachings constitutes unbelief and therefore legitimizes the killing of the assumed nonbelievers. *See also* BLASPHEMY; HERESY; *JAHILI* SOCIETIES.

KURDISH ISLAMIC MOVEMENT/*AL-HARAKAT AL-ISLAMIYYA AL-KURDIYYA*. The foundation of this group was a direct result of the destruction of Halbaja, Kurdistan, in 1988 at the hands of Saddam Hussein's regime in **Iraq**. During the regime's attacks on Kurdistan from 1988 to 1991, religious sentiments increased within the country, and the group's support grew. The brothers Mulla 'Uthman 'Abd Al-'Aziz and Mulla 'Ali Al-'Aziz led the Kurdish Islamic movement that fought against the Iraqi militants' occupation in the country. Some experts have attributed the group's increase in power to the return of the **Afghan Arabs** (*Al-Afghan Al-'Arab*) and to Iranian support, but members of *Al-Haraka Al-Islamiyya Al-Kurdiyya* have denied any associations with the **Islamic Republic of Iran**.

KURDISTAN ISLAMIC GROUP. *See* IRAQ.

KURDISTAN ISLAMIC UNION. An **Islamic political party** in Kurdistan (a part of **Iraq** heavily populated by Kurds), the Kurdistan Islamic Union was formed in 1994 and named Salaheddine Bahaaeddine its secretary-general. Structurally, the group has a governing council comprised of approximately 40 members that determines the most important actions of the organization. The Kurdistan Islamic Union obtains a majority of its support through the university system.

A scandal occurred in November 2005, when the party withdrew from the Democratic Patriotic Alliance of Kurdistan just before the Iraqi legislative elections in December of that year. This move resulted in the gathering of thousands of protestors outside the group's offices that got so hostile that four of the Kurdistan Islamic Union's members were killed. In the ensuing elections, the party only won 5 of the 275 seats available in the Iraqi Council of Representatives. A member of the Islamic Kurdish League, the group is also represented on the Iraqi Governing Council.

Ideologically, the party advocates the establishment of a federal Kurdistan region, securing stability within Iraq, creating a dialogue of equality between the various Kurdish religious groups, eradicating economic and political corruption, improving the housing situation (which has been in impoverished conditions), increasing the potential for education among all the classes, and developing a private sector of entrepreneurship and industry within the economy.

L

LASHKAR HIZBULLAH (LH)/GROUP OF THE PARTY OF GOD. An Indonesian organization founded in Banten, West Java, in July 1998, LH was first led by Cecep Bustomi. He took the name of the Islamist militia that was allowed under Japanese occupation. It has been strongly linked to the Vanguard of the Defenders of **Islam** and calls for the introduction of *sharia* (Islamic law) in Indonesia. Several hundred members participated in the **jihad** of Celebes, where they played an active role in the attack on Christian villages in the Poso area. The organization claimed to have sent militants to **Afghanistan** in late 2001 to fight alongside the **Taliban** against the U.S. invasion, but this information was never confirmed. *See also HIZBULLAH.*

LASHKAR-E-JABBAR (LeJ)/ARMY OF THE MIGHTY. The group first became publicly recognized after two attacks on 7–8 August 2001 by two men who later identified themselves as being part of LeJ. The armed incidents took place at a girls' school in Srinigar, India, where the two men attacked a teacher and threatened **violence** unless the **women** adhered to the Islamic dress code. Attracting a fair amount of media coverage in Jammu and Kashmir, the group stressed its seriousness on the need to wear the *burka* in public. However, the LeJ was operational before the August 2001 event and allegedly conducted similar attacks—most of which centered on violations of a strict Islamic dress code in public for women. The all-female *Dukhtaraan-e-Millat* soon pledged its support for the group in light of the condemnation that LeJ was receiving. However, the group is not entirely supported by other Islamic **Kashmiri separatist** organizations (notably the **All Party Hurriyat Conference**, *Hizb-ul-Mujahideen*, and *Lashkar-e-Tayyiba*). Ideologically, the group's main focus is on strictly implementing conservative Islamic practices regarding women, including proper dress, segregation in public spaces, and accompaniment outside domestic spaces. Little is known about LeJ's establishment and membership, but it has been speculated that the Pakistani Darul Uloom Haqqania *madrasa* has financially aided the organization in the past.

LASHKAR-E-JHANGVI **(LJ)/ARMY OF JHANGVI.** Formed in 1996 by former *Sipah-e-Sahaba* member **Riaz Basra**, *Lashkar-e-Jhangvi* means "army of Jhangvi." Haq Nawaz Jhangvi, after whom the group is named, was a founder of ***Sipah-e-Sahaba*** and was killed by a **Shiite** group in 1990. LJ is an extremist **Sunni** Islamic militant organization that has directed the bulk of its force to fighting Pakistani Shia Muslims in order to establish a Sunni Muslim *caliphate* throughout the country as part of the **Deoband** movement. In 2002, Basra was killed during a failed attack on a Shia outfit in Punjab, **Pakistan**. Akram Lahori (a.k.a Muhammad Ajmal), also a former *Sipah-e-Sahaba* member, is currently the leading commander of LJ.

The group is best known as being responsible for the kidnapping of the American journalist Daniel Pearl in January 2002 and his subsequent beheading. LJ has also been suspect in the **assassination** of Benazir Bhutto on 27 December 2007. The group has carried out a number of attacks and has formed alliances with the **Islamic Movement of Uzbekistan**, *Jamaat Ulema-e-Islam*, and the **Taliban**, among others. Members of each of these groups have trained and fought alongside each other on a number of occasions, especially against the United Islamic Front for the Salvation of Afghanistan. *See also HARAKAT-UL-MUJAHIDEEN AL-ALAMI.*

*LASHKAR JIHAD/***ARMY OF THE HOLY STRUGGLE.** Led by Umar Thalib, *Lashkar Jihad* was a militant Indonesian **Islamic group**. It was particularly active in the **jihad** in Moluccas and Celebes. After being put under extreme pressure from the Indonesian authorities, the group disbanded in October 2002.

*LASHKAR KHOS/***MILITIA OF ACTION.** This was a special operation group of *Jemaah Islamiyah*. *Lashkar Khos* was made up of experienced military men and was placed under the direct authority of the **amir** of Mantiq. A portion of the *Lashkar Khos* militants was killed in various insurgencies, while the rest attacked the Marriott Hotel in 2003 in Jakarta.

LASHKAR-E-TAYYIBA **(LeT)/ARMY OF THE PURE.** *Lashkar-e-Tayyba* is one of the most active militant **Islamic groups** in **Pakistan**. The group has conducted a series of attacks on Indian Kashmir in the hopes of liberating the area from Indian rule and imposing an **Islamic state** over all of South Asia. LeT has training camps in the Pakistani area of Kashmir and was established in 1990 in **Afghanistan** by Hafiz Muhammad Saeed and Zafar Iqbal. Although it is currently based in Muridke, Pakistan, the group was banned by the Pakistani government on 12 January 2002. LeT, like most other Islamic **fundamentalist** groups, seeks to unify the Muslim **nation** through the establishment of an **Islamic state** and has called for a **jihad** against all foreign influences that may corrupt this ideal. The group sees the recovery of Kashmir as a piece of the larger Islamic struggle to return **Islam** to its purest form, specifically in the regions surrounding Pakistan.

Beginning as a splinter organization from *Jamaat-ud-Da'wa* (now known as *Markaz-ud Da'wa wAl-Irshad*), the original reason for the group's formation was to provide further military aid in the form of veterans from the Soviet–Afghan War (1979–1989) (*mujahideen*) to the Pakistani army fighting in Kashmir. The group has additionally claimed that it receives military aid from the Pakistan army, specifically from Azad Kashmir's 12th Infantry Division, although this has been denied by the country's government. Pakistan's powerful main intelligence agency, the Inter-Services Intelligence, has also provided tactical aid to LeT and its Kashmir jihad, although the extent of this is unknown.

The group has been accused of and claimed responsibility for a number of civilian offenses and assaults on legislative buildings and public and military facilities. Most notably, the group is suspected of carrying out the **Mumbai attacks of November 2008**, which lasted three days and killed about 164 people while injuring another 308. The organization's operations have proven to be a considerable weight on the Indo-Pakistani relationship, which is already under stress. LeT has developed ties with the **al-Qaeda** network, *Jaish-e-Muhammad*, *Hizb-ul-Mujahideen*, and the **Taliban** regime. Financially, LeT receives funds purely through private donations from Pakistanis, Kashmiris, Saudi Arabians, and other Muslim communities. Although the actual strength of its membership is unknown, it has been speculated to be around several thousand. Currently, the group has experienced some discord and division in the form of the *Al-Mansurin* and *Al-Nasirin* factions. *See also DUKHTARAAN-E-MILLAT*; *HARAKAT UL-ANSAR*; *HARAKAT-UL-JIHAD AL-ISLAMI*; KASHMIRI SEPARATISM; *AL-UMAR MUJAHIDEEN*.

LATIF MOUSSA, ABDEL (1959–2009). Born in the Gaza Strip, Abdel Latif Moussa was the former leader of the **Salafi Jihadist** group *Jund Ansar Allah*, which was based in Rafah, Gaza Strip. Although he attended the University of Alexandria's Faculty of Medicine and excelled in the field of science, he spent 15 years working for the *Ahl Al Sunna* mosque in Khan Yunis, Gaza Strip. From 2006 until the time of his death in 2009, Moussa was the *imam* of the Sheikh Al Islam Bin Taymiyah mosque in Rafah, Gaza Strip. He also authored a number of books regarding the issue of faith. His final book, *As'illa Wa Ajwiba Shariya Hawl Al Qadiyah Al Filistiniyah* (Juristic Questions and Answers regarding the Palestinian Cause), resulted in consolidating his reputation as an international *mufti*, or a scholar of **Sunni Islam**

who specializes in expounding *sharia* (Islamic law). On 14 August 2009, he publicly proclaimed the establishment of an Islamic amirate in the Palestinian territories and criticized the **Hamas** movement for not properly implementing *sharia* within the region. The next day, on 15 August 2009, forces from Hamas stormed Moussa's Rafah mosque, and bitter fighting ensued. Moussa died in an explosion, and 23 other people were killed and over 130 were injured during the battle.

LEAGUE OF ARAB STATES. Geographically, the League of Arab States consists of 22 countries located in Southwest Asia, North Africa, and northeastern Africa. As of 2012, more than 350,000,000 people lived in the boundaries of the League of Arab States. Founded on 22 March 1945 in Cairo, the original members were **Egypt**, **Iraq**, **Jordan**, **Yemen**, **Lebanon**, **Saudi Arabia**, and **Syria**. According to the Pact of the League of Arab States, their main objective is to "draw closer the relations between member States and co-ordinate collaboration between them, to safeguard their independence and sovereignty, and to consider in a general way the affairs and interests of the Arab countries." Over the decades, the organziation has served to promote political, socioeconomic, and cultural interests as well as serve as an arena to sort out policies, disputes, and conflicts. However, the League of Arab States does not rely on geography to constitute membership; rather, it is based on support and promotion of a unified Arab nationalism. For decades, it has been a major ideological bulwark against Islamist **fundamentalism**. Its main figure for a long time was the Egyptian president Gamal Abdel Nasser (1918–1970).

LEBANON. When Lebanon was established as an independent state in 1943, it was created to be a **democracy** that could serve the needs and interests of all the religious groups within the country. Diversity was encouraged in the political and religious realms, but over time this platform seemed only to encourage groups that would be hostile toward ideological opponents. At the same time, groups within Lebanon began advocating for **Islam** to be the solution to any problems within the state. This notion of the saving quality of Islam reached its peak especially after the Arab-Israeli War in 1967, the **Iranian Revolution of 1979**, and the 1982 Israeli occupation of Lebanon. The events of 1982 were particularly significant in that they led to the creation of *Hizbullah* **in Lebanon**. Acting as a military and sociopolitical force, *Hizbullah* managed to regain control of Beirut in 2008, but this resulted in an increase of sectarian friction and insurgencies. The group and its large amount of supporters have continued to spread the notions of **Islamization** throughout Lebanon.

The large Christian populations within Lebanon and the executive inequalities that have been perpetuated over the decades have also encouraged the Islamic movements. Yet the anti-Zionist movements and **Shiite** groups have been the main forces in mobilizing the Lebanese. The most active **Islamic groups** within Lebanon, besides the radical *Hizbullah*, are *Amal*, **Islamic Liberation Organization**, and *al-Tahrir al-Islami*. A faction of *Hizb-u-Tahrir* also exists but remains largely underground because of its violent activities. *Amal* in particular is influenced by the **Muslim Brotherhood** and the works of **Hassan al-Banna** and **Sayyid Qutb** but has been at odds with *Hizbullah* for quite some time. This tension is politically based, as *Amal* has supported the executives within the Lebanese **government** and *Hizbullah* has tried to promote its own figures instead. However, there has been some division within *Amal* in the form of the creation of the splinter group the **Islamic Amal Movement**. This group wishes to see Lebanon become an **Islamic state** and is more aggressive in its actions than its father organization.

Salafi Jihadists have also had a presence within the country, but this has been minor mostly because of the Lebanese security forces repressing their actions. In fact, many of the Islamic militants who operate within the country are from **Palestine**. This demographic makes sense considering the strife that Lebanon has continuously had with Israel. Perhaps the most present and aggressive group within Lebanon is *Fatah al-Islam*, which is comprised mostly of Palestinians but is based in northern Lebanon. This group has been linked to the 2002 **assassination** of Lawrence Foley, an American diplomat, and the 13 February 2007 bus **bombing**, which killed three. The Lebanese security forces tried repeatedly to suppress this group, and eventually, from 20 May 2007 to 2 September 2007, the state security and *Fatah al-Islam* erupted into open battle. The **al-Qaeda** organization claimed to have encouraged this action, resulting in the deaths of approximately 160 Lebanese troops, and was giving provisions to *Fatah al-Islam*.

Interestingly enough, the leadership within Lebanon consists largely of **Sunni** (Muslim) and Maronite (Christian) adherents, but after the emergence of *Hizbullah* as a formidable political force, the Shiite community has been more and more prevalent within the administration. The party's success is due mostly to its use of the holy struggle against **Israel** to obtain support among the masses. Even if the majority of Lebanese people do not encourage a full **jihad**, they still are against occupation, and therefore *Hizbullah* is deemed patriotic and pro-Lebanon.

The political system within Lebanon has been increasingly problematic and has struggled with internal strife for quite some time. During the 1970s and 1980s, it was even suggested that Lebanon should amalgamate into **Syria** because the internal strife was so horrible. A civil war that lasted from 1975 to 1990 was due mainly to the Islamic and pan-Arabic groups joining arms against the Maronite administrative powers. This period also saw the First **Intifada** of 1987, which was spearheaded by *Hizbullah* and resulted in Lebanon adopting more and more **legislation** to make it an Islamic state. It could be compared to the Islamic **system** in **Iran** but was short lived. The country has been marked by countless insurgencies, civil wars, and aggressive diplomatic disputes. The 2006 war between *Hizbullah* and Israel increased the tensions within the population as a whole. Communities began to be pockmarked with internal fighting at an alarming rate. This was especially evident in West Beirut.

Hizbullah continues to be a key player in the Lebanese political system ever since it entered the system officially in 1990 after the civil war by running its own candidates. Its strong, absolute desire to create an **Islamic state** within the country has served only to increase the **violence** against not only non-Muslims but Sunnis as well. The group's successful operations in liberating Beirut and then ousting the Israeli forces are the main reason why public support remains strong. The group often reminds the population of the military successes when opposition comes to light. Hence, the Lebanese population is caught in a balancing act between nationalism, **theocracy**, and security.

LEGISLATION/*TASHRI'*. Since many of the Islamic **fundamentalists** have included practical political discourses in addition to their societal and religious ones, legislation must be taken into account when discussing their views on the role of the state as an authority. Many of these theories on the role of legislation within the **Islamic state** are based on the doctrine of **divine governance** (*hakimiyya*). When applying *hakimiyya* to legislation, the state has a limited role since **Allah** is the only source of the law, and a true **Islamic society** will then adhere to his legislation only. Furthermore, since legislation is subject to **interpretations** of the **Quran**, the state cannot impose any regulations that would differ from those set out in the **divine texts**. An Islamic state then becomes a moral society since it upholds only the values of Allah. For the fundamentalists, the application of *sharia* (Islamic law) is not a social phenomenon but rather naturally occurring in any Islamic society. Man's role in legislation then becomes one of interpretation and adherence, not creativity or innovation. *See also* LEGITIMACY.

LEGITIMACY/*AL-SHAR'IYYA*. Legitimacy, to the **fundamentalists**, comes from **divine governance** (*hakimiyya*) and can result only from social and political adherence to **Islam**. Fundamentalists believe that since many **Islamic societies** lack any real human **liberation**, **freedom**, or **consciousness**, their **governments** are not legitimate. They further believe that a government based on the laws of man can never be legitimate unless it is liberated and made into an **Islamic society**, whose laws would then be based on those of **Allah** and, thereby, legitimate. *See also* LEGISLATION.

***LEMBAGA DAKWAH KAMPUS/DAKWAH* CAMPUS CENTERS.** *Lembaga Dakwah Kampus* was a network of Indonesian students who participated in the 1980s revival of political **Islam**.

LIBERATION/*AL-TAHRIR*. Theoretically, freedom will come only from the individual's liberation from mortal pleasures and subsequent devotion to *tawhid* (oneness of **Allah**). Central to Islamic **fundamentalist** thought, liberation is viewed as the way to bring about the necessary changes needed to reform the Muslim world without weakening Islamic doctrine. Liberation is applicable to economic, political, and social freedoms as well as religious ones. Liberation is thought to happen when man devotes himself to *tawhid* and thereby submits himself to **Islam** and is free of the constraints of humanity. *Tawhid* is therefore central to a fundamentalist **interpretation** of liberation because it separates man from the artificial laws of humanity and connects him with Allah. Liberation also connects man to the **divine governance** and reinforces the legitimacy of a **jihad** against *jahili* **societies**.

LIBYA. During the 1980s, the poor economic conditions and the dictatorial regime of Libyan ruler Colonel **Muammar Qadhafi** (in power 1969–2011) have favored the emergence of **extremist** groups within Libya. The unsatisfactory conditions in the country have allowed **Islamic groups**, like the **Libyan Islamic Fighting Group** and the **Muslim Brotherhood in Libya**, to gain significant popular support. Libya has been under the domination of an Arab nationalist regime that adhered at least verbally to socialism since 1 September 1969, when Qadhafi staged a military coup d'état against the hereditary monarch King Idris (who was in power since Libya gained independence from Italy on 24 December 1951). Qadhafi was the sole leader of the country thereafter, and this had an enormous influence on the increase of rebel movements and political insurgencies that came to a peak during the **Arab Spring**. The large cadre of radical Islamists and revolutionaries, tired of the autocrat, finally exploded on 14 February 2011, a day that saw the first protests of the Libyan uprising. This contempt for Qadhafi's regime had been the soil in which Islamist movements had grown.

This resistance gained its first foothold in the late 1970s, when Qadhafi issued his *Green Book* and imposed it as the only source of governance for the country until his regime's fall in October 2011. Since the 1990s, Libya has been prey to chronic socioeconomic problems that have also helped foster the growth of political Islamism. Political opposition groups continued to be spawned and receive support from the country's population since there was no governmental alternative to Qadhafi's rule. The Islamic Gathering Movement (*Harakat Al-Tajamu' Al-Islami*) is one such group and has obtained great support in the eastern region of the country, its doctrines being similar to those of the Muslim Brotherhood in Libya. The *Tabligh* group also attracted popular support (although mainly in the west) and is small. Despite Qadhafi's policies of banning and eliminating all Islamic oppositional organizations, their presence was still evident and ideologically influenced a great deal of the population who wanted an end to Qadhafi's rule and therefore political reform. When the civil war in Libya, which sprung from the public demonstrations of the Arab Spring, began in April 2011, the Islamists took an active part in the fight against the pro-Qadhafi forces. The current governing body within the country, the National Transitional Council, is comprised of some former **al-Qaeda** affiliates who wish to implement an **Islamic state** within the newly liberated country. The Libyan people, freed from Qadhafi's leadership and encouraged by their great actions, seem eager to accept this new society, which would provide a traditional Islamic life, not like the one implemented by the Qadhafi regime.

Although Qadhafi's Libya lacked a traditional **constitution**, it did set up a ban on extremist Islamic groups with the adoption of the Great Green Charter on Human Rights in 1988. According to the charter, militant Islamists were banned because of security threats, not their doctrinal positions. The **government** under Qadhafi also prohibited any and all religious practices that conflicted with the regime's interpretation of *sharia* (Islamic law). This strict administrative control on **Islam** within Libya was further imposed by the constant monitoring of Islamic practices by the government. Any form of political Islam and religious extremism was deemed a threat to the Qadhafi regime and was therefore constantly watched. The regulation was even extended to censoring religious literature, restricting public access to Islamic organization's websites, and monitoring the activities within mosques.

Libyan Islamism used to be one that was completely controlled by the state and dictated by the government's interpretation of it. The former government also set up the World Islamic Call Society, which was a state-regulated university that trained students in the government-mandated form of Islamic history, thought, and practices. Contrary to its goals, this strong control of Islam actually generated more opposition than adherence within the country, something that is clearly evident in the uprising that took place in early 2011. Arguably one of the most successful rebellions of the Arab Spring, the Qadhafi government was officially ousted on 21 August 2011, when the rebels stormed the capital city of Tripoli and removed the pro-Qadhafi forces. While in hiding in his hometown of Syrte with what was left of his supporters, a small group of rebels captured and killed Qadhafi on 20 October 2011.

It should also be noted that in 2006, Qadhafi declared that 12,000 tons of chemicals weapons were stored in the south of Libya and accepted to destroy two-thirds of them under international supervision. Currently, the remaining one-third of these chemical weapons are under the control of the National Transitory Council (NTC) and have been put under the supervision of the UN agency for the control of weapons of mass destruction after the 2011 fall of Qadhafi.

The Qadhafi regime was interested in developing some nuclear facilities but finally agreed after more than 10 years of embargo to give up developing these weapons and asked for the development of a civil nuclear industry to produce electricity. Since the new Libyan government seems to have chosen to develop more of the oil industry and to rely on its gas and petroleum reserves, the major problem is the proliferation of conventional weapons, such as AK47s and other assault weapons, that were stored in the military ammunitions barracks. Both Europe and the **United States** are working together with the United Nations to convince the NTC to get these weapons back under the control of the military. Otherwise, it is feared that some of these weapons can be stolen or can be bought by terrorist organizations, such as **al-Qaeda in the Islamic Maghreb**, and then taken to its sanctuaries in the Sahara, especially in northern **Mali**. Some of these weapons, such as SAM-7 missiles, are incredibly dangerous for civil airplanes, but they need a lot of expertise and maintenance to operate properly. This leads most experts to believe that the **terrorist** groups have no pressing urge to acquire these weapons since they do not possess the know-how to maintain these weapons.

LIBYAN ISLAMIC FIGHTING GROUP (LIFG)/LIBYAN ISLAMIC COMBATANT GROUP. The LIFG was the dominant Islamic political resistance group in **Libya**. Members officially announced its establishment in 1995, but the group has technically been in existence since the late 1980s, when it was a secretive **jihadist** organization formed by Awatha al-Zuwawi. Many of the LIFG's members also gained military training fighting the Soviets in the Soviet-Afghan War (1979–1989). While in Afghanistan, the organization also developed close ties with **al-Qaeda** and other jihadist groups that shared the same beliefs and implemented the same harsh tactics in order to bring about a political upheaval. In 1989, the Libyan authorities found out about the group's formation and arrested or exiled many members, including al-Zuwawi. The group believed that only through violent and militant strategies could the regime of **Muammar Qadhafi** be overthrown. This ideology made it a formidable player in the 2011 **Arab Spring** civil uprising in Libya that toppled the Qadhafi regime in August of that year. Its activities during the Afghan-Soviet War had also provided internal strength within the group, and it developed strong alliances with other Islamists, such as the **Algerian Armed Islamic Group**, the **Egyptian** *Al-Gama`a Al-Islamiyya*, and the **Moroccan Islamic Combatant Group**.

Throughout the 1990s, the LIFG carried out a series of **assassination** attempts on Qadhafi and was involved in many conflicts with the Libyan security forces. Repression by the government's military branch led to many members fleeing the country and continuing their operations in exile. A majority of these militant LIFG members were operating in Afghanistan and some also in Great Britain to establish support (notably Abu Anas Al-Libi, who is also in affiliation with al-Qaeda and has commanded training camps in Kabul, Afghanistan). Thus, after the Libyan rebellion in early 2011, many members of the group returned home and joined the rebels in the fight against the Qadhafi regime. The group's support and involvement in the Libyan revolution only underscored its own legitimacy and abilities.

The group is rumored to be led by Abu Abdullah al-Sadek and shares financial resources and ideologies with al-Qaeda. Many prominent members of the LIFG have also become significant al-Qaeda figures in Afghanistan, such as Abu Laith Al-Libi. The alliance between the LIFG and **al-Qaeda in the Islamic Maghreb** was made official via an Internet statement released in 2007.

LONDON BOMBINGS OF 7 JULY 2005. Also known as the 7/7 Bombings, these four nearly simultaneous attacks were the most heinous acts of domestic **bombing** in British history as well as the first incident using **suicide bombers**. The attackers were four persons of whom three were British Muslim nationalists (two of Pakistani origin, the other born in Jamaica) who struck two London Underground trains and one double-decker public transportation bus. The first bomb exploded at approximately 8:50 a.m. on London Underground train 204 and was triggered by Shehzad Tanweer, killing 8 and injuring 171. Not a minute later, another bomb was detonated by Muhammad Siddiq Khan, killlling 7 and injuring 163 on London Underground train 216. At the same time, Jermaine Lindsay set off a bomb on train 311, killing 27 and injuring 340. Finally, at 9:47 a.m., Hasib Hussein blew up a public bus at Tavistock Square, killing 13 and injuring 110. Following the incident, the London transit authority completely shut down the public transportation network and evacuated all stations and platforms. London security agencies and the Metropolitan Police Service continued to deal with the repercussions of the bombings until 15 July.

During the investigation, the technical accuracy, the range of devastation, and the Muslim prescriptions of the killers led many experts to believe that it was the work of the **al-Qaeda** organization. It was also concluded that the bombs, although nearly doing so, were intended to explode at exactly the same time and were placed in such a way that the explosions would form a cross traversing central London. Interestingly enough, all four assailants were from decent socioeconomic surroundings and all well educated. In addition, the only one with a criminal record was Lindsay, who was born in Jamaica but raised in the United Kingdom and converted to **Islam** at age 15. Khan was the oldest at only 31, while Hussein was 18, Lindsay 19, and Tanweer 22. After forensic analysis was conducted, it was also concluded that all the explosives were highly technically complex and sophisticated. Furthermore, it perplexed investigators how easily the four men were able to attain the materials to create such bombs and go undetected during both acquisition and assembly. It was also revealed that the men supposedly carried out this attack to express their resentment of the British support of the U.S. invasion of **Iraq** in 2003.

LUXOR MASSACRE. Taking place on 17 November 1997, the Luxor massacre became infamous not only for the number of victims (59 foreigners all from Bulgaria, Colombia, France, Germany, Great Britain, Japan, and Switzerland) but also for the brutality with which the attack occurred. Six members of the **Egyptian Islamic Group** and *Munazzamat Al-Jihad* (Jihad Organization) stormed the archaeological site and tourist attraction of the Temple of Hatshepsut in **Egypt**, trapped the victims in the temple's middle courtyard, and began the massacre. The survivors' accounts, which detailed the viciousness of the attack, led to the worldwide coverage and infamy of the event. As a result, Egyptian President Hosni Mubarak (in office 1981–2011) began to repress many of the **Islamic groups** within the country, especially the **Muslim Brotherhood** and its affiliates. Many groups that were not affiliated with either the Egyptian Islamic Group or *Munazzamat Al-Jihad* felt the repercussions from this massacre, especially as many states began to withhold support from Islamic groups so as to avoid being associated with these atrocious acts against foreigners. The public disdain for the act also forced the leaders of the two groups to reassess their campaign strategies and strive for more peaceful ways to topple the Egyptian regime (their sociopolitical goal). In 1998, the Egyptian Islamic Group officially announced that it would cease all **violent** methods and agreed to an end of hostilities with the Egyptian **government** the following year.

M

AL-MADANI, ABBASI (1931–). President of the **Islamic Salvation Front** in **Algeria**, Madani began his career as a political Islamic **fundamentalist** in 1954, when he joined the **National Liberation Front**. On 1 November 1954 (the first day of the Algerian War for Independence), he placed a bomb in an Algerian radio studio and was arrested for his actions and jailed until the conclusion of the war in 1962. Shortly thereafter, he was imprisoned for eight years because of attacks he conducted against the French while with the group. After serving his time, he joined the short-lived (1963–1966) Value Society. Throughout the 1970s, Madani gained more education and eventually received his doctorate from London University and became a professor at the University of Algiers.

However, after signing a letter that criticized the Algerian secular **government**, he was jailed again from 1982 to 1984. The Islamic Salvation Front was later established in 1988 because of an amendment to the country's **constitution** that allowed for a multiparty parliament. Since Madani was one of the charismatic and influential founders of the group, he was elected its leader and became inspirational to many of the youths in the Algerian population. Successful, the Islamic Salvation Front became nationally recognized and was made **legitimate** by the Algerian government—even winning large majorities in municipal elections in 1991. Madani published many intellectual and Islamic works that illustrate his views on Islamic fundamentalism and political pluralism. His moderate views are largely contrasted to his colleague **Ali Belhadj**, as Madani supports the **Islamization** of government and educational practices. Since the January 2011 protests in Algeria, he has relocated to Doha, Qatar.

MADI, ABU AL-'ULA (1958–). Madi first became active in the political arena of **Egypt** during his years as a university student. While gaining his engineering degree in 1976, he joined *Al-Jamaat Al-Islamiyya* and a year later was elected president of a student union that the group controlled. Protesting against President Anwar Al-Sadat's foreign and domestic policies (especially in the wake of Egypt's defeat in the 1973 war with **Israel**), Madi's influence even won him election to the vice presidency of Egypt's national student union. However, his political **activism** earned him jail time, and it was during his incarceration that he joined the **Muslim Brotherhood**. After some years, he increasingly began to oppose the violent trend that was taking hold in the **Islamic groups** and called for compromise between the moderate and extremist organizations. His resistance against many of the Brotherhood's actions got him expelled from the Brethren in 1996. He then tried to establish *Al-Wasat* (The Moderates) but with little success. This party was finally legalized after the Egyptian Revolution on 11 February 2011.

MADRASA. Although *madrasa* simply refers to any type of learning institution, its use in this dictionary is to refer specially to an Islamic educational institution (*madrasa Islamiyya*). However, it must be noted that there are nonreligious, secular, and private *madrasas* as well. A *madrasa Islamiyya* has a structure that is divided into two parts: a course that focuses on the memorization of the **Quran** and a course that helps individual students become scholars of **Islam**. There are also other courses offered, such as Arabic literature, calligraphic sciences, the **Hadiths**, Islamic **history**, **Islamic law**, and Quranic **interpretation**, **science**, and **theology**. Yet each individual *madrasa* varies in the different courses it offers, and some have even more advanced seminars. A wide range of ages can attend these institutions, and many of the attendees eventually become *imams*. In many areas, the *madrasa* plays a sociocultural role throughout the community as well and are usually attached to an endowed mosque. The mission of most of these structures is to admit the poorer classes as well as **women** so as to educate a wider population and enhance the academic system of Islam. The *madrasa* system was founded during the Middle Ages by Nizam Al-Mulk (1018–1092).

However, while the primary function of this entity is education, many of these have become recruiting grounds for extremist movements, and, indeed, some of them were specifically set up by such organization to find recruits. As many of these *madrasas* are located in poorer, underdeveloped neighborhoods, they are often endowed and financed by wealthy Arabs who are located in other states, such as **Saudi Arabia** or elsewhere on the Persian Gulf coast. However, since such allegations have come forth, there has been a decline in donations from the wealthy and private benefactors.

However, because of the Islamic system of charity between Muslims that obliges every believer to give approximately 10 percent of his yearly income to the poor, a huge amount of money was driven from the Gulf states, especially to the poor countries of Asia. These transactions were often handled by organizations that have some linkage to **jihadi** or **terrorist** groups. This was the case for organizations such as *Tehrik-e-Taliban* **Pakistan**, which was directing and managing a number of religious schools using the charity money from the Gulf countries and educating young men on a radical ideology that made them easy recruits for organizations such as **al-Qaeda**.

Thus, the criticism was more about the content of the educational system (what these *madrasas* were teaching) rather than the fact of helping the educational system itself. In short, what the students were learning was critiqued more than the fact that the schools were built. After the **World Trade Center and Pentagon attacks of September 11, 2001**, this "Islamic charity system" was considered and dealt with as a money-laundering system and has been under strict surveillance by most countries ever since. Monitoring both simple money transactions and the SWIFT system (Society for Worldwide Interbank Financial Telecommunications) dried the financial situation and made it very difficult to finance such institutions or schools. However, this did not stop the recruitment of radical people since these people are engaged in the fight because of resentment toward their country's sociopolitical climate more so than their education in the *madrasa*.

MADRID BOMBINGS OF 11 MARCH 2004. This event involved the **bombing** of four public transportation trains using 10 explosive devices that resulted in the deaths of 191 and injured an estimated 2,050. More commonly known in Spain as "3/11" or "M-11," the devices used were backpacks filled with explosive materials that were then detonated off-site using cellular phones. Three other bombs were found that were unsuccessfully discharged but were neutralized by the Madrid bomb disposal units. The incident occurred between 7:37 and 7:40 a.m., all on the same train line, located in a highly populated area in northeastern Madrid. Investigation of the unexploded bombs led authorities to Moroccan Jamal Zougam, a leader of an **extremist** cell of **Islamic** militants.

Similar to the **London bombings of 7 July 2005**, the simultaneous nature and high mortality rates led many experts to believe that **al-Qaeda** conducted this attack, although that day the **Abu Hafs Al-Masri Brigade** claimed responsibility for it. In addition, like the London bombings, it seems as if the motive behind the attacks was retaliation for Spain's support of the 2003 U.S. invasion of **Iraq**. The deadliest and most catastrophic bombing in Spanish history, the incident may also have led to the victory of the Spanish Socialist Workers' Party in the 14 March 2004 elections; the group repeatedly supported the withdrawal of Spanish troops from the Iraqi occupation. Furthermore, on 19 April 2004, Spain did indeed withdraw its troops from Iraq, although its military presence still remained in **Afghanistan**.

Responsibility for the 11 March attacks was first thought to be the work of the Basque Fatherland and Liberty organization, which conducted bombings in the past in the area in the late 1980s. Investigators also believed that the bombers were Algerian, Moroccan, and Syrian members of the **Moroccan**

Islamic Combatant Group. However, others maintain that the insurgents were not affiliated with any particular group but instead acted independently and were merely inspired by the actions of other militant organizations.

MAHDI **ARMY.** *See JAISH AL-MAHDI.*

AL-MAHDIYYA. Founded in June 1881 by Muhammad Ahmad Ibn'Abd Allah Al-Mahdi Al-Sudani (1843–1885), *Al-Mahdiyya* called for the **liberation** of **Islam** by returning to its **fundamentals**, the *Sunna* (tradition) of the Prophet, and rejecting traditional **interpretations** of the **Quran**. Named *Al-Mahdi Al-Muntazar* (The Awaited Guide) by his followers, Al-Mahdi Al-Sudani created strong tribal relationships through marriage that he used to try to encourage those tribes to begin a **jihad**. The Sudanese capital of Khartoum fell under his control in January 1885, when his followers seized the city in response to a number of campaigns by the Turkiyah government to capture Al-Mahdi Al-Sudani. With the city under his control, he spread his ideologies throughout the area and gained even more support. However, he died shortly after in June 1885 and was replaced by Abdallahi Ibn Muhammad as leader of *Al-Mahdiyya. See also* SUDAN; TRADITIONALISM.

MAJLIS MUJAHIDEEN INDONESIA **(MMI)/COUNCIL OF INDONESIAN** *MUJAHIDEEN.* An Indonesian radical organization founded in August 2000, MMI was established to achieve, by political means, the application of *sharia* (Islamic law) in Indonesia. It was considered as the political showcase of *Jemaah Islamiyah* even though some of its members belong to a wider circle and do not support the **jihad**.

MAJLIS AL-SHURA/MAJLIS ASH-SHURA. Arabic for "consultative council," during the medieval period, the *Majlis ash-Shura* was responsible for the most important decisions of the *caliphate*, including electing the *caliph* or even removing him. Although no strict guidelines appear as to who may be on the council, it is understood that members must be well educated in *sharia* (Islamic law) and possess a complete understanding of the role of the *caliph*. The *Majlis ash-Shura* deals only with the issues of the *caliph* and is more or less the advisory council that oversees issues related to him. As they aim to reestablish the *caliphate*, all **al-Qaeda** branches and affiliate organizations, such as **al-Qaeda in the Arabian Peninsula** and **al-Qaeda in the Islamic Maghreb**, today have a *Majlis ash-Shura*. Almost all Islamic **fundamentalist** groups call for the establishment of the *Majlis al-Shura* in place of the current parliaments that exist in many of the Islamic countries. The advisory council on **Islamic law**, the *Majlis al-Shura*, is the term used for the group of individuals who possess legislative and consultative powers in the Muslim and Arabic countries.

Depending on the governmental situation, the power and influence of the *Majlis al-Shura* varies, although al-Qaeda, **Bahrain**, **Egypt**, **Iran**, Oman, **Pakistan**, Qatar, and **Saudi Arabia** all possess this type of structure. Members share in the wish to enact *sharia* throughout the Muslim world, and all adhere to the strictest of Islamic guidelines as the group acts as a united whole to discuss and determine a number of policies that affect religious and secular activities. The *Majlis al-Shura* always turns to the **Quran** and the *Hadiths* for spiritual guidance and reaffirms that it is the Quran that declares that a spiritual-oriented governing body should exist for the people of Islam. In effect, the *Majlis al-Shura* merges contemporary political practices with Islamic law. *See also SHURA.*

***MAJLIS SYURO MUSLIMIN INDONESIA*/MASYUMI/COUNCIL OF INDONESIAN MUSLIMS.** Established in 1943, Masyumi became the party of the modernist Muslims until it was banned by President Sukarno in 1960. A few of its officers who participated mostly in covert operations eventually went on to form different movements of radical **Islam** in Indonesia that were based on **Salafism**.

MALI. Roughly 90 percent of the Malian population adheres to **Sunni Islam**, but there is a large difference in religious practices in Mali compared to other Islamic countries. In Mali, animism is almost entirely fused into the practice of **Islam** as well as many other mystical components. There is also a deep regard for the veneration of ancestors and the promotion and invocation of past Muslim rulers, clerics, and prophets into their religious practices. For centuries, Islam and animism have accompanied each other in Mali, making it difficult for the radical Islamists to appeal to a majority of the citizenry.

This landlocked country in North Africa has seen increased Islamist **violence**, and its northern regions are currently occupied by **al-Qaeda in the Islamic Maghreb** (AQIM). Although the country is somewhat successfully democratic, the AQIM activity has posed countless security threats to Mali. Mali also possesses a state **constitution** that bans religious-based **political parties**, putting some limitations on the influence of Islamists in the country even though the majority of the population is Muslim. There has also been a cultural attempt within Mali to create a syncretic belief structure that preaches religious forbearance and encourages animist traditions in the hope of dispelling the growing Islamist ideologies. This fusion of Islam with animism and tolerance contrasts greatly with the doctrinal teachings of the Islamic **fundamentalists** and has therefore made it difficult for any **extremist** group to gain significant popular support in the country.

Thus, the violence that has occurred in Mali has been directly associated with the AQIM. Mali's desolate northern regions, which account for two-thirds of the country's territory, have been desirable for the radical **Islamic groups**, especially since the country's government and population have little oversight there. AQIM is benefiting from Mali's economic difficulties, the interfering Tuareg tribe in the north, and widespread **Salafi** ideology. The first example of the ease with which Islamist organizations can operate in northern Mali happened in May 2010, when the AQIM forced 15 hostages to walk from southern **Algeria**, where they were captured, across the desert area of northern Mali. One hostage died of heat stroke during the captivity, and the remaining were released in August 2010 for a reported 5 million euros. For such reasons, Mali has given French, Mauritanian, and Algerian troops permission to conduct attacks on Islamist forces within the Malian borders, proving the country's desire to rid itself of this problem. *See also* COUSIN-AGE; MALI HIGH ISLAMIC COUNCIL; MAURITANIA.

MALI HIGH ISLAMIC COUNCIL. Formed by the **government** of **Mali** in 2002, the High Islamic Council oversees the increasing number of **Islamic groups** and associations within the country. Since the 1990s, there has been a dramatic rise in the amount of these groups even though the country's **constitution** from 1992 declares Mali to be a secular state and bans religious **political parties**. Although a vast majority of the Malian population is Muslim, this is considered to be of a personal and private nature. The High Islamic Council serves as the official intermediary between the political authorities and religious practitioners in Mali. It is also considered to be the most senior body of **Islam** in the country and correlates religious affairs, such as the standardization of preaching. However, this council is sometimes seen as the **government**'s attempt to interfere with Islamic practices and is contradictory to the Malian secular constitution.

AL-MAQDISI, ABU MUHAMMAD (1959–). Also known as 'Isam Muhammad Tahir, Al-Maqdisi is best known as being the spiritual guide to **Abu Musab Al-Zarqawi** and the founder of the group *Bay'at Al-Imam* (Oath of Allegiance to the Imam). Palestinian by birth but raised in Kuwait, Al-Maqdisi wrote *Millat Ibrahim* (Abraham's Sect), which outlines his ideologies. He called for a violent and radical **Salafi** program and renounced many of the Islamic **fundamentalist** groups (especially the **Jordanian Muslim Brotherhood**) as being too moderate and guilty of *takfir* (unbelief). He was also once a member of the Salafi group *Jam'iyyat Ihya 'Al-Turath Al-Islami*. Al-Maqdisi also supports the **divine governance** of **Allah** and has been implicated as being involved with (or influencing) many acts of violence in **Afghanistan**, **Iraq**, **Jordan**, and **Saudi Arabia**.

MARJI' AL-TAQLID/**AUTHORITY FOR IMITATION.** This group is comprised of the highest-ranking clerics of the Twelvers's **Shiite** organization. In order to be placed on the council, one must be influential within the religious community and have attained a significant amount of followers. The *maraji'* do not always need to share in the same beliefs or social discourses, but all of them must have scholastic knowledge and be able to properly exercise **reason**. Characteristically, it is understood that all members are persuasive, modest, respectable, and virtuous. *Marji' Al-Taqlid* is not an officially established organization, and there is no council that elects the individual *maraji'*. Rather, the position is granted by the other *maraji'*. The group exists because within the Shiite community there is a belief that the thoughts and ideologies of the living scholars, not the dead ones, should be imitated. There is a limit to the number of *maraji'* who can exist in the group at one time, and the most famous member of the *Marji' Al-Taqlid* was probably **Ayatollah Ruhollah al-Musawi Khomeini**, the leader of the **Iranian Islamic Revolution**.

MARTYRDOM. *See ISTISHHAD.*

MASHAAL, KHALID (1956–). The head of **Hamas** since 2004, Mashaal joined the group in 1987, when it was first established, and led its Kuwaiti branch. While a student at Kuwait University, he began his political **activism** and joined the Islamic *Haqq* Bloc (Islamic Truth Bloc), the General Union of Palestinian Students, and the **Muslim Brotherhood**. He even orchestrated the establishment of *Al-Rabita Al-Islamiyya Li Talabat Filastin* (Islamic League for Palestinian Students) in 1980. Mashaal was introduced to the up-and-coming Hamas organization when he moved to **Jordan** from Kuwait and devoted himself to the Islamic political cause. He continued to work with Hamas and became the leader of many different factions within the political bureau. On 25 September 1997, he was the target of an **assassination** attempt conducted by Israeli Mossad (national intelligence agency) members. This incident led to a series of prisoner exchanges between **Jordan** and **Israel**, notably the release of **Ahmad Yasin** (founder and spiritual guide of Hamas). When the Jordanian **government** banned Hamas in 1999, Mashaal (along with many others) was arrested and expelled from Jordan. He then moved to Qatar but in 2001 relocated to Damascus, **Syria**.

MASHHUR, MUSTAPHA (1924–2002). Formerly a deputy to the supreme guide of the **Muslim Brotherhood**, Muhammad Hamid Abu al-Nasr, Mashhur himself became the fifth supreme guide of the group in 1996 until his death in 2002.

AL-MASRI, ABU AYYUB (1968–2010). Born in **Egypt** and formerly a member of the **Muslim Brotherhood**, he joined the **Egyptian Islamic Jihad** in 1982 and began to work closely with leading **jihadist Ayman al-Zawahiri**. He also trained in the Afghani al-Farouk camp by 1999 and became an expert in constructing explosives. After the American invasion of **Afghanistan** in 2001, he relocated to **Iraq** in 2002 and became a dominant figure in **al-Qaeda in Iraq** (AQI), operating mostly in the central and southern regions of the country. By early 2003, he successfully helped to establish the AQI presence in Baghdad and became second in command of AQI next to **Abu Mussab al-Zarqawi**. When al-Zarqawi was killed by U.S. forces on 7 June 2006, al-Masri replaced him as the group's main figure. His ascension to power was officially announced by AQI on 12 June 2006. It should also be noted that al-Masri went by quite a few aliases, such as Abu Hamza al-Muhajir, Abdul-Monim al-Badawi, Yusif al-Dardiri, and Sharif Hazaa.

Al-Masri was killed on 18 April 2010 as a result of a joint U.S.-Iraqi operation that took place in Tikrit, Iraq. Three other men were killed after the fire-fight, which took place when al-Masri's and the military force's men clashed with each other at the home where the former was staying. Considered to be a huge success against the jihadists, information on **Osama bin Laden** and Ayman al-Zawahiri was confiscated from within the housing compound after the fighting subsided. AQI announced that al-Nasser Lideen Illah Abu Suleiman was al-Masri's replacement on 14 May 2010. *See also* SALAFI JIHADISM.

MASTER NARRATIVES. Commonly used genres in the Islamic **fundamentalist** narratives are referred to as "master narratives." These are the typical and most frequently used kinds of stories that the groups use to convey their message. They have been labeled combat narratives (*Qital*), oneness narratives (***Tawhid***), prediction narratives (*Maktoob*), election narratives (*Ikhtiyar*), achievement narratives (*Tamkin*), self-organizing narratives (*Walâ'*), and the legitimizing narratives (*Tabrir*).

The combat narrative focuses on conflict and aggression throughout the story even if, in reality, the conflict itself is particularly minute. For example, this type of story will focus on the specific aggression that arises between various groups. The oneness narrative is based on a completely biased view of the issues in the story. Another conflicting or even similar perspective will be suppressed in order to highlight the ideas of the group that produces this specific narrative in order to appear as the "one" or the "unique" able to bring about the solution. In the prediction narrative, the assignment of roles and characteristics of events, individuals, or groups are focused on. One example might be the illustration that the ***mujahideen*** will continue to fight against the

Western forces as they have in the past (i.e., the Soviet-Afghan War [1979–1989]), and this defense of **Islam** makes them pious, adherent Muslims. The election narrative emphasizes that jihadists are chosen, or "elected," by **Allah** to protect Islam and therefore should not have to pay dues to any other force besides Him. Similar to the combat narrative, larger and more meaningful issues are underscored by thin or superficial events. A self-organizing narrative stresses the Muslim concept of **unity** and allegiance. This type of story particularly focuses on the fact that decent Muslims should not fraternize with non-Muslims. The term comes from the Arabic for "loyalty and disavowal," which is the name given to the Muslim allegiance system *Al-Wala' wa Al-Bara'*. The legitimizing narrative does just what the name suggests; it gives legitimacy to certain actions by explaining events within a totalizing framework. For example, this particular story would illustrate to the audience that kidnappings are valid forms of **jihad** since it is the infidel who is besieged. *See also* NARRATIVES.

AL-MAUDUDI, ABUL ALAA (1903–1979). Born in present-day Maharashtra, India, on 25 September 1903 to a prominent family with a deep lineage in the **Sufi** dogmatic tradition, many of his ancestors were leading luminaries of the faith. Allegedly, his paternal ancestry can be traced back to the **Prophet Muhammad**. Maududi has published a number of works on the treatises of **Islam**, notably *Al-Jihad fi Al-Islam* (Dealing with Jihad in Islam). His publications have been praised for their comprehensive and direct explanations of the ideology and their application to **government**. He also regularly criticized the **Western** influence on Islam and the newfangled **religion** that it produced. According to Maududi, Islam is not merely a religion but an all-encompassing way of life. Islam, from his perspective, must be applied to all facets of life and all areas of the world. It is in these arguments that he justified *sharia* (Islamic law) and the need for the **jihad**.

From 1941 to 1972, Maududi was the commander of *Jamaat-e-Islami*, the oldest Islamic party in **Pakistan**, using this position to spread his new philosophies. In August 1947, he relocated to Pakistan in the hope of establishing an **Islamic state** within the newly partitioned country. Other factions of *Jamaat-e-Islami* spread to **Bangladesh**, India, Kashmir, and Sri Lanka. He wrote continuously in criticism of the Pakistani government's failure to create a **caliphate** and impose *sharia*. His actions led him to be jailed numerous times, and he was even sentenced to corporal punishment in 1953 by the Pakistani government, but the public outrage was so great that he was eventually pardoned and released. The *amir* left the organization in April 1979 to better tend to his ailing health. While being treated by his doctor-son in Buffalo, New York, he died of kidney and heart problems on 22 September 1979.

MAURITANIA. Mauritania faces a host of political, economic, and social challenges, and this has led to an increase of Islamist activity. In 1982, *sharia* (Islamic law) was implemented in the country. However, Mauritania's problems are due primarily to its geography. Situated between the sub-Saharan portion of Africa and the Arab Maghreb, Mauritania is shared by the diverse African and Arab populations. Nearly the entirety of the Malian population is **Sunni** Muslim. The country has gone through about a dozen military and political coups since its independence from France in 1960 and has seen the emergence of a **jihadi**-oriented movement in the form of **al-Qaeda of the Islamic Maghreb**. Mauritanian Islamist activity is particularly evident in the political arena, where the country's unstable political situation, sensitive slavery issues, and socioeconomic problems have developed new opportunities for radical Islamist **violence**. **Islamic groups** use urban poverty, the rejection of **Western** culture, and criticisms of the political class as strategies for attracting support of their organizations and ideologies.

In addition, Mauritania has seen groups that were influenced by the Sudanese **Hassan al-Turabi**, **Salafism**, and the **Muslim Brotherhood**. Violent Islamism has been seen as the primary source of disorderly instability and is a foreign ideology that is detrimental to the Mauritanian traditional views of society. On 28 October 1999, Mauritanian Foreign Minister Ahmed Sid'Ahmed signed an agreement in Washington, D.C., that established full diplomatic relations and thereafter joined **Egypt**, **Palestine**, and **Jordan** as the only members of the **League of Arab States** to officially recognize **Israel**. However, this was criticized as being an attempt to gain aid projects and achieve geopolitical aims. In March 2010, Mauritania's Foreign Minister Naha Mint Hamdi Ould Mouknass announced that the country had completely cut ties with Israel.

AL-MAWDUDI, ABU AL-A 'LA (1903–1979). An extremely influential Islamic **fundamentalist** whose impacts are still felt throughout the Islamic world, Al-Mawdudi is one of the most significant figures of 20th-century **Islam**. His ideologies of **divine governance** and the abolishment of all forms of **paganism** had a notable impact on writers like **Sayyid Qutb**. Al-Mawdudi's most lasting impact is probably his establishment in 1941 of the Pakistani and Indian *Jamaat-i Islami*, which still serves as the model for many Islamic fundamentalist groups. His most influential book, *Al-Jihad fil Islam* (Struggle in Islam), has been translated into several languages.

MAY 15TH ORGANIZATION. A rather small branch of the Popular Front for the Liberation of Palestine—Special Operations Group (a member of the Popular Front for the Liberation of Palestine), the May 15th organization took its name from the date on which the first declaration of war against **Israel** by the Arab states was announced. Based in Baghdad, **Iraq**, the group was originally led by Abu Ibrahim and carried out several attacks between 1978 and 1985. Often referred to simply as May 15th, the group's attacks often used highly technical bombs planted on aircraft that were barometrically detonated. In total, the organization's attacks led to the death of seven and injured 43. The bombings included a Tokyo-to-Honolulu Pan American World Airways flight; the Israeli embassy in Athens, Greece; the Mount Royal Hotel in London; and a Rome-to-Athens TWA flight. Despite the number of attacks, the group was reported to contain only an estimated 50 to 60 members. Deemed inactive since 1986, it is believed that many members took up arms with *Hawari*.

AL-MENBAR NATIONAL ISLAMIC SOCIETY. A **Sunni** Muslim **Islamic political party**, al-Menbar is associated with the **Muslim Brotherhood in Bahrain**. Conservative in its legislative demands, the group adheres to the belief that cooperation with the kingdom can lead to a quicker Islamic progress. Accused by many hardline Islamists as being too liberal, the group has been active in supporting the freedom of assembly, **religion** within the kingdom, and **women**'s rights within the electoral process. Despite its differences with the **al-Asalah** Party, al-Menbar has worked with the group on a number of occasions to keep a unified Sunni force within the country.

METHOD/*MANHAJ*. Many Islamic **fundamentalists** believe that **Islam** is the most perfect method of gaining **knowledge**. They state that Islam is the perfect method because it unites **justice** with the intellectual and with the spiritual—in other words, it is based on *tawhid* (oneness with God). The fundamentalists then believe that any person or group that diverges from the method of Islam is considered *jahili* and subject to the **jihad**. Methods of the West are then considered to be undesirable since they are based on domination, human knowledge, and **philosophy**. Especially with regard to **reason** (*'aql*), the central debate is method as opposed to **imitation** (*taqlid*).

AL-MIDKHALI, RABI (1931–). A **Salafist** scholar and professor from Saamitah, **Saudi Arabia**, Rabi al-Midkhali studied *sharia* (Islamic law) in Riyadh and Medina. After finishing his studies, he became the chair of the *Sunnah* Department and a member of the Faculty of **Hadith** at the Islamic University of Medina. He is best known for founding the Midkhaliya Movement in Saudi Arabia and has published multiple books, including *A Study of the Prophetic Hadith* and *Clarity in Defending the Sunnah*.

***MILLI NIZAM PARTISI*/PARTY FOR NATIONAL ORDER.** Established by **Necmettin Erbakan** in January 1970, *Milli Nizam Partisi* was the first legitimate **Islamic political party** in Turkey. However, it was dissolved a year later when the group was prosecuted in the Turkish Constitutional Court for exploiting **Islam** to gain political advantages. After this accusation, many members created *Milli Selamet Partisi* (National Salvation Party), and some even tried to revive the group in 1976, but the attempt was unsuccessful. Ideologically, *Milli Nizam Partisi* opposed secularism and false doctrinal interpretations and supported the moral basis of social **justice** in order to create a peaceful society in Turkey. Although the group could not publicly impose its Islamic ideologies, it did call for the application of religious programs in the education system.

MISUARI BREAKAWAY GROUP (MBG). A Filipino fighting group formed in Jolo by the last supporters of Nur Misuari, former head of **Moro National Liberation Front** (MNLF). The MBG was established so that Misuari could prevent his removal from the post of governor of the Autonomous Region of Muslim Mindanao after the elections in November 2001. The group was aligned with **Abu Sayyaf**, another associate of the MNLF.

MODERNISM. The current modernist trend in Islamic **fundamentalism** is the belief that **reason** can be applied to the **interpretations** of **Islam** in order to give the **religion** universality. Reason is the cornerstone of the modern fundamentalist schools of thought, for they argue that it is reason that connects man to his *fitra* (intuition) and thereby his **morality**. They also agree that if it were not for reason, **science** and technology could not grow. Modernists often try to reinterpret Islam as a **philosophy** and apply the **Western** political and metaphysical models to it. Their justification is that those modes will give the religion scientific and rational support. When applying Western ideas, they employ **Islamization** and turn theories such as constitutional rule into *ijma'* (consensus), for example.

Although the modernists have come under attack by many other fundamentalists (especially the radicals) for their Western inspirations, the group defends its notions by looking back to the **history** of Islam. Members claim that throughout the **past** in the Muslim world, the culture came into contact with different societies and cultures and dealt with their interpretations accordingly to increase the Islamic corpus of knowledge. The use of Islamization and progressiveness in the modernist trend is hoping to revive the intellect within Islam and instill a belief that the East and West can exist in harmony. In recent decades, modernism was criticized by Islamic fundamentalists as synonymous with the "westernization" of Islamic thought. *See also* MODERNITY.

MODERNITY/*HADATHA*. With regard to modernity, although some **fundamentalists** believe that the Islamic world should "update" itself, there is a hesitation by many to embrace **modernism** because of its associations with **Western** culture. To many Muslims, modernity is synonymous with the West, which is often characterized by being power hungry and materialistic—making the West an undesirable model for modern **Islam**. Those who support the idea of a new Islam claim that perhaps modernity will free them from the economic, political, and social strains that exist in the current **Islamic society**. Conversely, those opposed to the application of modernity to Islamic life state that the modern West has its own sociopolitical problems, too.

However, there is an overall consensus that Islam needs to change its current priorities, and **liberation** through modernism could be the way by which to reform the society. Supporters of this belief argue that a religious liberation will lead to a political liberation and then economic and social freedom. With regard to **science** and technology, it is felt that they should be an intricate part of the new, modern Islam only as long as they are disconnected from any philosophical theories. **Islamization** is also an intrinsic part of the modern Islamic thought. Basically, what is "modernizing" Islamic thought, in comparison to the more rigid fundamentalist view, is the application of **reason** to the Islamic doctrines. *See also* PHILOSOPHY.

MOMBASA ATTACK OF 2002. On 28 November 2002 (the day before the 55th anniversary of the UN Partition Plan for Palestine), an Israeli-owned and -operated hotel called the Paradise Hotel and an Israeli-owned Arkia Airlines charter plane were targeted in Mombasa, Kenya. At the Paradise Hotel, a bomb-laden vehicle crashed into the lobby of the structure and exploded, and two Strela II surface-to-air missiles were fired at the aircraft during its takeoff from the Mombasa International Airport but failed to impact the plane.

The hotel was the only Israeli-operated hotel in the region and was frequented by many Israeli tourists, a reason for its being targeted. Thirteen people were killed and 80 were injured as a result. The Israeli government sent military planes into the site to evacuate guests and assist in the damage control. The missile attack on the Arkia aircraft happened almost simultaneously with the Paradise Hotel explosion. The plane was en route to Tel Aviv, and it is suspected that an antimissile defense system embedded in the aircraft led to the missiles' failure. The aircraft was then followed by Israeli fighter jets until it made a safe landing in Tel Aviv at Ben Gurion Airport.

Interestingly enough, for several days leading up to the attacks, there were multiple warnings issued by Australian, British, and German intelligence agencies of possible attacks that would take place in Nairobi and Mombasa.

Following the attacks, the **Lebanon**-based group known as the Army of Palestine claimed responsibility. *See also* BOMBING; ISRAEL; PALESTINE.

MONOTHEISM. Monotheism is the belief in one God, as exists for Muslims, Christians, and Jews. However, for Muslims specifically, monotheism is the belief in *tawhid* (oneness of **Allah**). A devotion to *tawhid* also means that the individual will follow Allah's guidelines in all respects of life from the religious to the political and from the ritualistic to the everyday. Other monotheistic religions, such as **Christianity** and **Judaism**, are perceived as corrupted by many **fundamentalists** although once pure since they are not based on *tawhid*. Some moderate fundamentalists have even been in support of working out a relationship between the **religions** as long as the **freedoms** and sanctity of **Islam** are not harmed.

MORALITY. Morality, according to the **fundamentalists**, is the most important aspect of the **religion** and is therefore the factor that distinguishes **Islam** from other faiths or **philosophies**. For many Muslims, morality is the manifestation of one's commitment to **Allah** and *tawhid*. Morality is the key to avoiding corruption and exploitation; without morals, **justice** can never prevail in an **Islamic society**. Furthermore, without a good grasp of morality, humans will move toward an existence of **paganism** and spiritual impoverishment.

MORO ISLAMIC LIBERATION FRONT (MILF). When the **Moro Liberation Front** agreed to a cease-fire (*hudna*) with the Filipino **government** in 1987, many members believed that the leadership of the group was steering the movement in a direction where independence of the Muslim-populated regions could not be attained. These members then established the MILF in return. The MILF soon became an **extremist** Islamic **fundamentalist** group that hoped to see an **Islamic state** develop throughout the Moro region of the Philippines. More aggressive in their ideologies and methods than the Moro Liberation Front and the **Abu Sayyaf Group**, members of the MILF also allegedly received training in the *Jemaah Islamiyah* and **al-Qaeda** camps. Throughout the group's existence, there have been multiple cease-fires with the Filipino government (in 1997, 2000, 2003, and 2006) between bouts of fighting that resulted in numerous casualties for both the MILF and the Filipino forces.

MORO LIBERATION FRONT (MLF)/MORO NATIONAL LIBERATION FRONT. A group comprised of separatist Islamic **fundamentalists**, the MLF sought to detach the islands of Mindanao and the Sulu archipelago in the southern Philippines from **government** control and establish an **Islamic state** there instead. Allegedly supported by **Iran**, **Libya**, and Sabah in Malaysia, the group also received assistance from the Organization of the Islamic Conference (OIC), which helped to mediate disputes between the MLF and the Filipino government. Not originally an Islamic fundamentalist group, the MLF began as a leftist political organization (named the Mindanao Independence Movement, established in 1972 by Nur Misuari) but by 1973 began to recruit an estimated 15,000 militants and occupied most of the Cotabato province and Jolo Town a year later. It has been speculated that the assaults on these territories were specifically designed to coincide with the Islamic Foreign Ministers' Conferences that were taking place in Benghazi and Lahore in order to gain support from the members of the conference.

Even though the MLF was successful in gaining support throughout the Islamic states, the Filipino populations were not as sympathetic. Even the domestic Muslim communities within the Philippines showed a lack of support for the MLF's goals. This is most likely due to its **violence** and an overwhelming belief that the MLF would limit civil liberties in power. Furthermore, the government's security forces were effective in repelling the rebel forces. Realizing that public support was waning and that militant suppression was rising, Misuari agreed to a peace accord in 1976, but insurgencies from the group still sporadically occurred throughout the next year. Internally, the group also began to split into three different segments: one group sought refuge with the government, another became the radical **Moro Islamic Liberation Front**, and a small contingent formed the **Abu Sayyaf Group**.

The MLF did achieve a remarkable political success on 19 August 1996, when it was welcomed into negotiations by the Filipino government in order to discuss the creation of the Southern Philippine Council for Peace and Development, which would grant the Muslim Philippine territories some autonomy. Weeks later, on 2 September 1996, Misuari and President Fidel Ramos signed a peace agreement that ended the conflicts between the two groups and formed the Autonomous Region of Muslim Mindanao. This settlement sparked outrage among many of the more extremist members of the MLF and especially heightened anti-Misuari sentiments in the Moro Islamic Liberation Front since the arrangement was viewed as a concession to the Filipino government. The splinter groups of the MLF have become more active than its father organization, and little has been heard from the MLF in the past decade. In fact, the last major action carried out by the group was in 2001 on a Filipino military base that killed over 100. The act was apparently due to Misuari's growing distaste for the Filipino government's adjustments to the 1996 accords and in hopes of gaining back support he had lost from within his own organization.

MOROCCAN ISLAMIC COMBATANT GROUP/MOROCCAN IS-LAMIC FIGHTING GROUP/*GROUPE ISLAMIQUE COMBATTANT MAROCAIN* (GICM). This North African **Sunni** Muslim **Islamic group** emerged in the 1990s and is banned in numerous countries as being an affiliate of **al-Qaeda** and, more specifically, of **al-Qaeda in the Islamic Maghreb** (AQIM). Allegedly, the group has members in various countries such as Belgium, Denmark, **Egypt**, France, Great Britain, and Turkey. Like most Islamic **fundamentalist** organizations, GICM wants to transform the national **government** into an **Islamic state**, or **caliphate**, and supports al-Qaeda's hostilities with the **West**. The group has orchestrated and participated in multiple civilian assaults, notably the 16 May 2003 Casablanca attack, which made use of 12 *istishhadyun* and resulted in the deaths of 45 Moroccans; the **Madrid bombings of 11 March 2004**, which killed 200 and injured 1,500; and the Casablanca **suicide bombings** on 10–14 April 2007. The group's splinter organization, *Salafia Jihadia*, has also claimed responsibility for many GICM-related offenses.

Although little is known about the group's formal structure, it is speculated that GICM was founded and is comprised of former *mujahideen* veterans from the Soviet-Afghan War in (1979–1989). Even though GICM is **Morocco**'s predominant Islamic militant group, there is no final conclusion as to who leads the organization, although reports have pointed to Muhammad Guerbouzi and Taeb Bentizi. The organization is derived from the Islamic group *Shabiba Islamiya*, which, in 1993, split in two: the Moroccan Islamic Combatant Group and *At-Tawhid*. The group obtains its monetary resources from arms dealing and trafficking in false documents. In September 2006, GICM joined the Algerian **Salafi Group for Preaching and Combat** to form AQIM.

MOROCCAN SALAFI JIHADISM. What makes **Morocco** so unique in the Islamic Maghreb is that it hosts numerous (some reports have indicated up to 100) yet small **Salafi**-jihadi **extremist** groups. Since September 2006, **al-Qaeda**'s North African branch, **al-Qaeda in the Islamic Maghreb** (AQIM), has been trying to unite these groups under one single front. Many young Moroccans have also taken up arms and joined militant groups in **Afghanistan** and **Iraq** to fight against the U.S. forces. Moroccan nationalists are also among those suspected to be enrolled in AQIM training camps in **Algeria** and **Mali**. Impoverishment in many of Morocco's cities, especially in the north, have been breeding grounds for extremists who see the ideologies of the Salafis as a way to create a better standard of living based on a hard-edged orthodoxy of **Islam**.

Most of the salafist jihadists in the country are disciples of the **Wahhabism** school of Islam and rely solely on the **divine texts** and thereby do not acknowledge the monarchy's lineage, which is deemed to be that of the **Prophet Muhammad**. The jihadists use their extremism in an attempt to create a wholly Islamic **government** in keeping with the strictest laws of the faith. The Salafis' main criticism of Morocco's Islamic **government** is that the monarchy is trying to modernize *sharia* (Islamic law) to be more flexible with regard to contemporary society, which is deemed abominable by the **fundamentalists**.

MOROCCO. The monarchy of Morocco has interestingly enough been one of the few countries in the Islamic Maghreb to encourage the development of **Islamic political parties**. Despite these efforts to involve the **Islamic groups** within the governmental fabric of Morocco, the country has nevertheless been subjected to **jihadist** and Islamist extremist attacks. Although the Moroccan **government** tolerates moderate Islamists, most of these insurgencies prefer to create a **caliphate** throughout the Islamic world, and therefore these groups are prohibited by the monarchy. One of the most brutal and extreme Islamic groups is the **Moroccan Islamic Combatant Group**, which has claimed responsibility for numerous attacks throughout the country.

With regard to the former King Hassan II (who reigned from 26 February 1961 to 23 July 1999), he allowed Islamic-orientated political groups to function only if they used the **religion**'s values as an inspiration for civility, not malcontent. To combat these conflicting elements, the current ruler, King Mohammed VI (who ascended to the throne in July 1999), has implemented a strategy that involves encouraging nonviolent monarchy-supporting Islamists to participate in the country's politics while also suppressing the Islamic **Salafists**, who resort to violence. Chief among these groups is the **Justice and Development Party**. Many different Islamic organizations and movements exist in Morocco and are both domestic and foreign in origin. Their success can be traced in part to the deplorable conditions in the northern urban neighborhoods of Morocco, a result of the monarchy's lack of funding and corruption in the civil service. The citizens have therefore turned to the Islamists, who have provided charity in return for allegiance. *See also* MOROCCAN SALAFI JIHADISM.

MOVEMENT FOR NATIONAL REFORM. A relatively moderate **Islamist political party** in **Algeria**, the Movement for National Reform (*Mouvement pour la Réforme Nationale*) was created as a result of a break within the *Ennahda* political movement. The separation was due to *Ennahda*'s declaration of support of the Algerian secular **government**. Originally led by Abdallah Djaballah, the Movement for National Reform had only slight success in its first election campaign in 2002, receiving 9.5 percent of the vote and a subsequent 43 parliamentary seats. Djaballah eventually left the group and went on to form the more radical *Al-Islah* group. Devastatingly, during the 2007 Algerian elections, the Movement for National Reform won only three seats in the parliament, and its presence has been on the wane ever since.

MOVEMENT FOR THE SOCIETY OF PEACE (MSP). Formerly Algerian **Hamas** (from the Arabic for *Harakat Al-Muqawamat Al-Islamiyyah*, meaning "Islamic Resistance Movement"), this **Islamic political party** operates mainly in **Algeria** and in the 1990s was led by Mahfound Nahnah. After Nahnah's death in 2003, Bouguerra Soltani took control of the group. The organization has been affiliated with the **National Liberation Front** (*Front de Libération Nationale*) and the National Rally for Democracy. The formation of the MSP began when the multiparty system was adopted in Algeria during the early 1990s. As a result, the **Muslim Brotherhood in Algeria**, which had a presence in the country since the end of the French colonial period, created the group in order to gain a political presence. Members of the then-named Hamas represented a wide mixture of nationalists, Islamists, and technocrats.

When religiously affiliated political parties were banned in Algeria, the group changed its name to the Movement for the Society of Peace (*Mouvement pour la Société de la Paix*), although "Hamas" is often used to refer to the organization; therefore, MSP is the Muslim Brotherhood's Algerian presence. The group obtained 5.3 percent of the popular vote during Algeria's first multiparty elections in 1991. When the **Islamic Salvation Front** (*Front Islamique du Salut*) was banned after the second round of elections was canceled in January 1992, MSP sympathized with the banned party, but the group never officially aligned itself with the Islamist insurgency that followed so that it could remain legal in the Algerian political **system**.

When the Algerian Civil War (1992–2002) culminated from these events, the MSP called for a peaceful resolution and a return to political pluralism while criticizing both sides of the conflict. Although MSP was against the political coup d'état that sparked the conflict, the group also did not agree with the Islamist tactics of brutality, especially against Algerian civilians. Throughout the war, MSP continued to run candidates in elections and win seats in the country's parliament. In 1999, Abdelaziz Bouteflika became president of Algeria, and MSP supported the presidency as well as his referenda to grant amnesty to the Islamist militants in the hopes of ending the insurrection. In 2009, the MSP split into two factions because of the loss of the popularity of its president, Aboudjera Soltani. Many members of the party did not agree with Soltani's unconditional support of President Abdelaziz Bouteflika and in June 2009 orchestrated a revolt inside the MSP. Since the 2011 political reforms (and removal of Bouteflika) that came to Algeria, the group has been supporting multiple political parties such as the **Muslim Brotherhood in Algeria** and the National Liberation Front in hope that Algeria will soon see an Islamic society. *See also* ARAB SPRING.

AL-MUHAJIROUN/**THE EMIGRANTS.** An **Islamic group** from Great Britain, *al-Muhajiroun* was brought to the country on 14 January 1986 and was banned by the **government** by August 2005. However, the group was originally founded on 3 March 1983 in Mecca (the 59th anniversary of the fall of the Ottoman **caliphate**) by Omar Bakri Muhammad in the hope of uniting it with *Hizb-u-Tahrir*. *Al-Muhajiroun* in **Saudi Arabia** was banned by the government in January 1986, leading to Omar Bakri reestablishing himself and his group in Great Britain. By 1996, the group had a notable presence on the British-Islamic scene. The organization also fostered the *al-Ghurabaa* group and The Savior Sect. Since its inception, Bakri, along with Anjem Choudary, have led the group until it was banned in reaction to the **London bombings of 7 July 2005**. Yet many experts believed that The Savior Sect was basically operating as *al-Muhajiroun* since October 2004. In June 2009, the organization reemerged in Great Britain but was short lived after another legislative act banned the group in January 2010.

Ideologically, the group seeks to spread **Islam** throughout the kingdom of Great Britain, convince the populace of the advantages of **Islamic law**, introduce Islam into legislative procedures, create a **pan-Islamic** climate throughout the country, and establish a caliphate there. *Al-Muhajiroun* gained infamy for its "Magnificent 19" conference, which was held in praise of the **World Trade Center and Pentagon attacks of September 11, 2001**. This, along with allegations that the group was sending members to Chechnya to fight with the Islamic rebellion there, prompted the Great Britain National Union of Students to originally ban the group in March 2002. *Al-Muhajiroun* also supposedly helped fund the establishment of the Islamic Council of Britain, which also participated in the "Magnificent 19" conference.

Many people who have been associated with *Al-Muhajiroun* have set off explosions throughout the years. This includes Jawad Akbar, Saladhuddin Amin, Anthony Garcia, Omar Khyam, and Waheed Mahmood (all connected with the group), who were convicted in 2007 of planning to bomb multiple places in Kent and London. *See also* BOMBING; CHECHEN TERRORISM.

MUHAMMADIYAH/**FOLLOWERS OF MUHAMMAD.** Founded in 1912 in West Java, *Muhammadiyah* is a reformist group that seeks to purify **Islam** and **Sufism** in the line of **Wahhabism**. Considered to be an Islamic movement of a second "modernism," the group also established schools that taught secular subjects in the hope of better integrating Muslims into the strict national education system. Currently, it is the largest Muslim organization in Indonesia.

AL-MUHANAH*/FRATERNITY OF THE INTERIOR POWER.** This clandestine Malaysian group was founded in 1992 by Muhammad Amin Razali, who is a former member of ***Darul Islam and took part in the Soviet-Afghan War (1979–1989). The group was dissolved by the government in 2000 after having committed different subversive actions in Malaysia.

MUJAHIDEEN. The term is literally translated from Arabic, meaning "strugglers" or "people acting in **jihad**," since *mujahideen* has an etymological basis to the term *jihad* (meaning "struggle"). These warriors of the holy war first came into the public spotlight as loosely aligned Afghan opposition forces during the Soviet-Afghan War (1979–1989). During the war, the *mujahideen* were allegedly financed and armed by the U.S. Central Intelligence Agency under both the Jimmy Carter and the Ronald Reagan administrations because of the *mujahideen* anti-Soviet sentiments. However, the **Pakistani** Inter-Services Intelligence was used as an intermediary to conceal the **Western** origins of the support. Throughout the years following the end of the Soviet-Afghan conflict in 1989, the *mujahideen* parties formed a political organization called the Islamic Unity of Afghanistan *Mujahideen*, and many areas in Afghanistan fell to the *mujahideen* forces. Supported by many other Muslim **extremist** factions, the *mujahideen* began to implement the violent tactic of suicidal warfare, and many veteran *mujahideen* were approached by the extremist group the **Taliban** during its formative years in the mid-1990s.

Contemporarily, the term *mujahideen* has been used to describe not only these veterans of the Soviet-Afghan War but also any militant member of an Islamic insurgent group, especially **al-Qaeda** and the Taliban. *Mujahideen* have also formed **Islamic groups** in **Iran** (***Mujahideen-e-Khalq*** and *Mujahideen* of the Islamic Revolution Organization), **Iraq** (*Mujahideen Shura* Council), and Pakistan (the Pakistan Army National Guard is also known as the "*Mujahideen* Force"). *See also HARAKAT-UL-MUJAHIDEEN*; *HARAKAT-UL-MUJAHIDEEN AL-ALAMI*; *HARAKAT AL-SHABAAB AL-MUJAHIDEEN*; *HIZB-UL-MUJAHIDEEN*; *JAMAAT-UL-MUJAHIDEEN* IN BANGLADESH; SUICIDE BOMBING; VIOLENCE.

***MUJAHIDEEN-E-KHALQ* (MEK)/PEOPLE'S *MUJAHIDEEN* ORGANIZATION OF IRAN.** The dominant militant force in opposition against the **Islamic Republic of Iran** was MEK. Led by a husband-and-wife team, Massoud and Maryam Rajavi, the group was also known under the name of the People's Mujahideen Organization of Iran. The group was established in the 1960s by a group of well-educated Iranians who opposed the rule of then monarch Shah Muhammad Reza Pahlavi, particularly because of his pro-**Western** stance. Although active in the 1979 Revolution, which ousted Pahlavi and replaced him with a **Shiite** Islamic regime, the group's ideologies still conflicted with the country's **government**. Because of this conflict, the group was forcibly relocated to Paris from 1981 until 1986, when it moved to **Iraq** (although it still maintained its Paris office).

It was this move that established MEK's relationship with the Saddam Hussein regime of Iraq. The group's activities included targeting Iranian governmental facilities and officials, especially Muhammad Khatami (Iranian president from 1997 to 2005) and his chiefs of staff. Civilians and military personnel have been targeted as well. Receiving most of its financial and operational support from the regime of Saddam Hussein, MEK suffered greatly from the leader's fall in April 2003. Aligned with the Iraqi administration, the primary activities of MEK were suppressing opposition and providing additional internal protection within **Iran**. The group had a number of training and administrative facilities, but the headquarters was in Camp Ashraf near Baghdad. On 10 May 2003, shortly after the fall of Baghdad on 9 April, MEK agreed to a consolidation of its weapons and arms as a result of a **cease-fire** agreement. Over 4,000 members of the group, most of whom were in Camp Ashraf, were also disarmed and subsequently interned. In June, the Parisian compound of MEK was also investigated, and 160 activists were arrested along with Maryam Rajavi.

MUJAHIDEEN YOUTH MOVEMENT. *See HARAKAT AL-SHABAAB AL-MUJAHIDEEN.*

MUMBAI ATTACKS OF NOVEMBER 2008. These attacks, which lasted from 9:20 a.m. on 26 November 2008 until 8:00 a.m. on 29 November 2008, involved 10 militant extremists who bombed 10 different targets in Mumbai, India. Using grenades and machine guns, the assailants struck the luxury hotels the Taj Mahal Palace and Oberoi Trident, the Chhatrapati Shivaji train station, a Jewish community center named the Chabad House, and the Leopold Café. By the time Indian security forces finally suppressed the fighting, about 173 people had been killed and 308 injured. All the victims, many of them tourists, were of multiple nationalities, including American, Australian, Canadian, Israeli, and German. Only one of the attackers survived, Pakistani Ajmal Amir Kasab, and on interrogation he admitted that he and his comrades conducted the attacks in the name of *Lashkar-e-Tayyiba*.

This event severely hindered the already delicate Indian-Pakistani relationship by being seen as a deliberate attack on India by **Pakistan** and an attempt to make the Indian **government** seem weak and susceptible to foreign aggressions. The Pakistani public was also offended by accusations that the attack was state supported, and this was worsened by the Inter-Services Intelligence (ISI) of Pakistan's disagreement with the state's prime minister, Manmohan Singh, who requested that the head of the ISI go to India to try to pacify the situation by admitting to having had some involvement with the incident. *See also* BOMBING; EXTREMISM.

MUSLIM ASSOCIATION OF BRITAIN (MAB). Established in 1997 by senior member Kemal al-Helbawy, the MAB is an Islamic organization that has directed much of its efforts to opposing the **Western** occupation in **Iraq** and in generating Islamic political ideologies throughout Great Britain. Interestingly enough, members believe that collaboration with non-Muslim groups is permissible as long as they are petitioning against the same anti-Western cause. However, this mutualism is not extended to the Zionists or the Israelis. The MAB worked with the Stop the War Coalition for a period of time but soon severed its ties on the ground that the former was diverging from its cultural and social reformation platform and rather started to focus more on a forced political upheaval. The MAB has supported candidates in various British elections and has been noted as trying to sway voters' opinions to elect Muslim candidates. Currently, the Muslim population in Great Britain constitutes more than 10 percent and adheres to 40 political formations. In the country, individual Islamic schools are recognized and supported, making England fertile soil for the promotion of Muslim *da'wa*. There have also been allegations made that the MAB has close ties with **Anwar al-Awlaqi**, an extreme Islamist **al-Qaeda** affiliate and promoter of Islamic **fundamentalism**. The MAB is the Federation of Islamic Organizations in Europe's official English representative as well. *See also* ISLAM; ISLAMIC POLITICAL PARTIES.

MUSLIM BROTHERHOOD (MB)/AL-IKHWAN AL-MUSLIMUM. Throughout many of the Arabic states, the MB is the largest political opposition organization. This transnational movement is the oldest and most influential **Islamic group**. It uses "Islam is the solution" among its many slogans, clearly illustrating its objective. The MB has also been cited as the main influence on numerous Islamic illegal political groups even in countries where there is not an official MB branch.

Founded in March 1928 in Ismailia, **Egypt**, by **Hassan al-Banna**, the MB seeks to implement the teachings of the **Quran** and the **Hadiths** to develop a structure of purely Islamic life and nation (*umma*) throughout the Arab world. Al-Banna also desired an organization that would awaken society to the necessity of independence and instill *sharia* (Islamic law) to provide the freedom of the people's rule over the **government**. According to MB belief, these practices should shape every aspect of daily life and are seen as a pure way to live an Islamic existence. This extremely orthodox Islamism stemmed from the view that the Islamic world had been tainted by **Western** influences. Al-Banna viewed Western **philosophies** in practical terms and felt that the **modernity** of Islam must take into account all **interpretations**, political ideologies, and **theologies**. Politically, the group believes in the power of the community and stresses the importance of democratization, political pluralism, *tawhid*, and social unity. In his discourses, al-Banna underlines how there should be equality in civic, economic, political, religious, and social matters as well as the avoidance of turning political confrontations into ideological wars.

Originally a social organization, the MB quickly rose in influence and power. It also was allowed to grow largely in part to the secretiveness implemented in its earlier phases, keeping the MB away from the Egyptian government's radar. In addition, when Al-Banna was hired as a teacher in Cairo, he took the opportunity of being in the capital city as a way to further promote his organization. Its **pan-Islamic** ideas helped to spread the doctrine of the MB throughout the Arab world, and soon **Lebanon** (in 1936), **Syria** (in 1937), and Transjordan (in 1946) also established their own MB groups. World War II also saw the doubling of the movement's efforts, an increase of student participation, and greater mobilization of the Egyptian public. By 1936, the organization had 800 members and increased exponentially in two years to 200,000. It has been noted that the group's pan-Islamic ideas are the reason for the great support among the Arab nations, and Cairo became the organization's headquarters for representatives throughout the Muslim world. However, in December 1948, after the November seizure of plans and documents that detailed a military branch of the Egyptian MB, then Egyptian Prime Minister Mahmud Fahmi Nokrashi called for the group's dissolution. In retaliation, member Abdel Meguid Ahmed Hassan assassinated Nokrashi on 28 December 1948.

The group also saw a rise in public support as the MB built mosques and schools—notably in 1946, the Egyptian Ministry of Education donated funds for its administrative expenses (by 1948, there were over 500 MB branches for social service). The construction of schools was especially popular, as the majority of the group's membership was middle-class educated professionals.

Even though the group gained a reputation as a peaceful organization, by the end of the Arab-Israeli War in 1948, the Egyptian government banned and repressed the group after criticisms of the regime were made. In addition, MB members fought alongside Arab forces and gained tactical military training—a quality that the Egyptian government also feared. However, it must be noted that the MB began as a nonviolent, peaceful organization whose members only eventually turned to violence when it became necessary. Other governments in the countries where the MB took hold followed suit in suppressing its affiliates as well. However, there was a resurgence of the MB's movement in 1951, when the group participated in the rebellion against British forces by declaring its political views but not violating any laws. Throughout Gamel Abdel Nasser's presidency, which lasted from 1952 until 1970, members of the group were tortured and imprisoned merely because of their allegiance to the MB. This led to their radicalization, and one of their ideologists, **Sayyid Qutb**, called for the use of **violence** against the government to obtain an Islamist regime in Egypt. He was sentenced to death on 29 August 1966. Some militants related to the organization also participated in the killing of Egyptian President Anwar Al-Sadat in 1981. Under Sadat's successor, President Hosni Mubarak, MB members were persecuted and imprisoned (although by 1982, membership was reported at half a million). Another MB radical, **Ayman Al-Zawahiri**, eventually left the group to join **al-Qaeda** and became the second in command in the **Osama bin Laden** organization.

Cairo has always remained the headquarters for all factions of the MB despite the breadth of its dissemination. Financed by membership and private contributions, certain MB members entered the political arena running on independent platforms with the motive of establishing a **caliphate** in those territories, such as the **Islamic Action Front** in **Jordan** and **Hamas** in Gaza. The MB faction in Jordan has also been an active political party, placing many members in the country's parliament. Inspirational to a number of Islamic **fundamentalist** groups, such as the *Ennahda* **in Tunisia** and the **Islamic Salvation Front**, the MB continues to inspire Islamic movements throughout the Muslim world.

Structurally, the different branches of the MB follow a hierarchy composed of the General Organization Conference (the highest body with members who oversee the actions of the lower bodies), the *Shura* Council (plans and creates programs and/or resolutions), and the Executive/Guidance Office (headed by a general guide, it follows the procedures laid down by the higher-ranking branches, distributes orders, and reports to the *Shura* Council). The general guide (*al-Murshid al-Aman*) of the Egyptian MB is currently Muhammad Badie. The group has seen the following general guides in Egypt since al-Banna (1928–1949): **Hassan al-Hudaybi** (1949–1972), Umar al-Tilmisani (1972–1986), Muhammad Hamid Abu al-Nasr (1986–1996), **Mustafa Mashhur** (1996–2002), Ma'mun al-Hudaybi (2002–2004), Muhammad Mahdi Akef (2004–2010), and Muhammad Badie, who has currently held the position since 16 January 2010. In each country, the MB is organized in this structure in order to effectively and efficiently attain the goals of the organization as a whole.

Although the MB has gone through many phases of success and repression, it continues to have a tremendous effect on Egyptian society to this day. During the 2005 parliamentary elections, MB candidates ran as independents because of their illegality and won 20 percent (88 seats), continuing their status as the largest opposition force in the government. This win demonstrated the organization's ability to become not only an ideological force but a political influence throughout the country as well. With regard to **Israel**, spokespersons for the MB have called for the dissolution of Egypt's 32-year peace treaty with the country. Throughout the Egyptian revolution of February 2011, the group seemed to be reluctant to take part in the events and managed not to appear as an instrumental force in the movement for fear of retaliation by the Egyptian army. However, after Egypt ousted the Hosni Mubarak regime, the party ran under the name "Freedom and Justice Party" and won the majority of the Egyptian votes during the country's first free elections (November 2011–January 2012). *See also* ARAB SPRING; HARAKAT AL-MUQAWAMA AL-ISLAMIYYAH; HASAN AL-BANNA IDEOLOGY; ISLAMIC POLITICAL PARTIES; MUSLIM BROTHERHOOD IN ALGERIA; MUSLIM BROTHERHOOD IN BAHRAIN; MUSLIM BROTHERHOOD IN IRAQ; MUSLIM BROTHERHOOD IN PALESTINE; MUSLIM BROTHERHOOD IN SAUDI ARABIA; MUSLIM BROTHERHOOD IN SOMALIA; MUSLIM BROTHERHOOD IN SUDAN; MUSLIM BROTHERHOOD IN SYRIA; MUSLIM BROTHERHOOD IN TUNISIA; *UKHUWWA.*

MUSLIM BROTHERHOOD IN ALGERIA. During the Algerian revolution against the colonial French forces in the early 1950s, the doctrines of the **Muslim Brotherhood** reached **Algeria** and were extremely influential in the uprising. Between 1953 and 1954, Sheikh Ahmad Sahnoun spearheaded the Brotherhood's Algerian branch, and the group was notably instrumental in the revolution against France (1954–1962), using the Brotherhood doctrine of an Islamic national identity to create a united front against the **Western** force. Despite the Brotherhood's successful influence during the revolution, the **National Liberation Front** (which assumed power over the country after the war and imposed single party rule) marginalized the Brotherhood. Despite this repression, the Algerian Muslim Brotherhood still remains active in religious and educational establishments and continues to argue for a greater role of **Islam** in the politics of Algeria. The group also gained particular momentum when it recruited Arabic teachers from **Egypt**, the Muslim Brotherhood's primary sect, to reinforce its reformist-Islamist ideologies.

Then, after the 1991 political reform, which allowed for the presence of multiple political parties, the Muslim Brotherhood changed its name to the

Movement for the Islamic Society. Soon after, a ban was placed on religiously oriented political parties, and it was then renamed the **Movement for the Society of Peace**. The group was led by Mahfoud Nahnah until his death in 2003; the group has since been led by Boudjerra Soltani. After the outbreak of the Algerian Civil War (1992–2002), the group did not officially join forces with the increasingly brutal **Islamic Salvation Front** or with the **Armed Islamic Group**, thus remaining a legitimate political organization.

MUSLIM BROTHERHOOD IN BAHRAIN. In the Persian Gulf coast monarchy of **Bahrain**, the **Muslim Brotherhood** is installed under the name of *Al-Islah* Society (led by Sheikh Isa bin Muhammad al-Khalifa) with the *Al-Menbar* **National Islamic Society** operating as its political front. *Al-Menbar* has met with moderate success in the political arena of the country, although its electoral victories have been decreasing over the years. The group aligned with its former opposition, the **Salafi** *Al-Salah*, during the 2006 elections in order to keep the **Sunni** Islamic vote united. In particular, the group sharply opposed Bahrain's adoption of the International Covenant on Civil and Political Rights because it would allow Muslims to oppose **Islam** if they so choose. This was completely abhorrent to the strict Islamic doctrine to which the Bahraini Muslim Brotherhood subscribed. In the spring of 2011, the Bahraini Muslim Brotherhood was challenged by **Shiite** groups supported by **Iran** that were attempting to overthrow the Bahraini king.

MUSLIM BROTHERHOOD IN GAZA. *See HARAKAT AL-MUQAWAMA AL-ISLAMIYYAH.*

MUSLIM BROTHERHOOD IN IRAQ. In 1960, the Iraqi Muslim Brotherhood was established under the **Iraqi Islamic Party** but was swiftly banned under the rule of Iraqi nationalist leader Abd al-Karim Qasim. This suppression lasted throughout the remainder of the 20th century, and finally, after the fall of Saddam Hussein in 2003, the Iraqi Islamic Party resurfaced. An advocate for **Sunni Islam** and its social and political applications within the country, the party has also been sharply critical of the U.S. occupation in **Iraq**. The Iraqi Islamic Party, however, has used political means rather than militant ones to gain a presence in the country. Its current leader, Tariq al-Hashimi, is also the country's second vice president. The **Muslim Brotherhood** has also influenced a number of Islamic movements throughout the country, especially in northern Kurdistan.

MUSLIM BROTHERHOOD IN JORDAN. Established in 1942 by 'Abd Al-Latif Abu Qura, the Jordanian Muslim Brotherhood heavily influences the political arena in the country, although it is registered as a charity organization. Ideologically, the group uses **Islam** as the model for attaining socioeconomic and political equality in **Jordan**. This faction of the **Muslim Brotherhood** has also presented itself as a nonviolent organization (as is the basis of the movement) that hopes to instill *sharia* (Islamic law). This group was, in fact, involved in the foundation of the Jordanian monarchy, as King Abdullah I relied partly on the group while establishing his kingdom in 1946. During the 1950s and 1960s, the group saw great electoral successes that continued to last until 1989, when its wins began to upset the equilibrium between the **government** and the group.

Although most **political parties** were banned in the country, the Muslim Brotherhood escaped suppression by the Jordanian monarchy and thereby formed the **Islamic Action Front** (*Jabhat Al-'Amal Al-Islami*) in 1992. Currently, the Islamic Action Front is the dominant party in the country's parliament, holding the majority of seats—the group siding with **Iraq** during the 1991 Gulf War also helped it gain popularity in Jordan. A large factor for its success is that the group has continually appealed to the people, having addressed their problems with social disorder and injustice, and supporting their abhorrence to martial law. In addition, they reject **Western** influences, such as capitalism, and back the Palestinian cause. The head of the Jordanian Muslim Brotherhood is Hammam Saeed, and he has formed an alliance with the **Hamas** leader in Damascus, **Syria**, Khaled Meshaal.

MUSLIM BROTHERHOOD IN LIBYA. One of the first countries to adopt the concepts of the **Muslim Brotherhood**, **Libya**'s relations with the group began by offering refuge. During the late 1940s, when Egyptian Muslim Brotherhood members were being oppressed, King Idris I, Libya's constitutional monarch from 24 December 1951 until 1 September 1969, offered the members political asylum and allowed them a decent amount of freedom to spread their Islamic ideologies. The Brotherhood declared Ezzeddine Ibrahim Mustafa, an Egyptian cleric, to be the leader of the Libyan branch, and the group quickly gained popularity among the people. The establishment of the University of Libya in the city of Benghazi in 1955, geographically close to the Libya-Egypt border, also helped bolster the Brotherhood's influence in the country, as many Egyptian Muslim Brotherhood members became professors there and hence reached many students who were crucial since young university students have repeatedly been the Brotherhood's targeted and most active participants. These roots of intellectual promotion in order to gain social, political, and cultural advancements have remained a constant with the Libyan Muslim Brotherhood.

However, fearing any form of political opposition, **Muammar Qadhafi**, who was Libya's leader since 1 September 1969, expelled many Egyptian Muslim Brotherhood members from the country. In 1973, the Brotherhood was officially banned, and many Libyan Muslim Brotherhood members were arrested, resulting in the practical disbanding of the Brotherhood in Libya for the remainder of the decade. However, in the beginning of the 1980s, the Brotherhood resurfaced in the form of the Libyan Islamic Group (*Al-Jama'a Al-Islamiya Al-Libyia*) as a way to legitimately reenter society. Again, members received a good deal of support from the Libyan population, especially university students and the area of Benghazi, where strong opposition to Qadhafi's rule existed. The Libyan Muslim Brotherhood shares the same unifying ideologies and core operations as the other branches of the Muslim Brotherhood: the replacement of the current political regime with one based on *sharia* (Islamic law). From the Brotherhood faction in Libya, three groups have formed: a Nasirite one, a completely unpolitical group, and another that continues in the likeness of the Brotherhood's ideologies. Despite Qadhafi's attempts to destroy the Brotherhood, the movement sparked a number of other Islamic extremist groups to form, such as the National Front for the Salvation of Libya (*Al-Jabha Al-Wataniyya li Inqadh Libya*), which became one of the most significant political opposition groups in the country.

MUSLIM BROTHERHOOD IN PALESTINE. In 1935, under a strong Egyptian initiative, the brother of **Egypt**'s **Muslim Brotherhood** founder **Hassan al-Banna**, 'Abd Al-Rahman al-Banna, installed a Muslim Brotherhood in the British Mandate for **Palestine** (although it was not made legitimate until October 1946). Jamal Al-Husseini, vice president of the High Islamic Council, also had a significant role in the group's establishment. By 1947, 25 branches of the Muslim Brotherhood existed throughout the region, and membership totaled between 12,000 and 20,000. The group also even asked the Jordanian **government** permission to set up factions in Bethlehem, Jericho, and Jerusalem. The Brotherhood was instrumental in the militant skirmishes of the 1948 Arab-Israeli War, although the group's activities were focused mainly on social and ideological reforms rather than political ones— yet the group still had a critical voice when it came to Palestine's foreign policies and relationship with the West, especially Great Britain.

The Palestinian Muslim Brotherhood's influence was strengthened by a number of factors, primarily the merger of different factions into one unified Muslim Brotherhood (branches in Gaza, **Jordan**, and the West Bank united under the Muslim Brotherhood Society in Jordan and Palestine). The Brotherhood's lack of militant activity also helped to ensure its livelihood because it was not forcibly dismantled like most **Islamic groups** were after the Palestinian wars. The Palestinian Muslim Brotherhood also established hundreds of mosques throughout the Gaza Strip and the West Bank between 1967 and 1987 in order to promote its anti-imperialistic ideologies, recruit members, and gain political influence.

It also gained support by providing aid to lower-class Muslims by creating medical and social aid that were funded by Brotherhood members. Considering its foundations, the group is also exceptionally loyal to the Egyptian movement, further securing its longevity. In 1988, a new wing of the Brotherhood was founded in Gaza, the **Islamic Resistance Movement** (known as **Hamas** for the Arabic *Harakat Al-Muqawama Al-Islamiyya*), and became one of the most powerful and influential Palestinian military rebel groups. This creation helped bolster the Brotherhood's position that it was slowly losing at the time. In 2007, Hamas successfully took over the Gaza Strip and thereby allowed the Muslim Brotherhood to control this very significant territory. There has also been a trend within the movement toward a heavier prescription of violent tactics that are directed toward Israel.

MUSLIM BROTHERHOOD IN SAUDI ARABIA. Even though the kingdom of **Saudi Arabia** p practices mainly the **Salafi Wahhabiyya** school of **Islam**, the **Sunni**-based **Muslim Brotherhood** has been tolerated throughout the country. Although the **government** has yet to suppress the group, not all members of the population and legislation are supportive of its presence in Saudi Arabia.

MUSLIM BROTHERHOOD IN SOMALIA. In the 1960s, the **Muslim Brotherhood** ideology found its way to Somalia and officially developed under the name of *Harakat Al-Islah* (Reform Movement) in 1978. Commonly referred to as *Al-Islah*, the organization's goals are very similar to many other Muslim Brotherhood–inspired groups and Islamic movements. Its members seek a revival of orthodox **Islam** throughout society and the creation of an **Islamic state**. *Al-Islah*'s operational base is in the capital city of Mogadishu on the coast of the Indian Ocean. Its founding leaders were Abdullah Ahmed Abdullah, Muhammad Yusuf Abdi, Ali Ahmed, Ahmed Rashid Hanafi, and Muhammad Ahmed Nur. Fearing political repression from the regime of Siad Barre, who was in office as the third president of Somalia from 21 October 1969 until 26 January 1991, the group remained in secrecy and loosely constructed its organization until Barre's fall.

Unique to *Harakat al-Islah* in comparison to other Brotherhood-based groups is that every five years the organization holds elections for its *Shura* Council chairman. For the past 30 years, these elections have taken place, and currently Dr. Ali Bashi Omar Roraye will lead the organization until 2013.

Al-Islah has taken up humanitarian and educational goals as opposed to militant ones like some Brotherhood-affiliated organizations. The major legacy of the group is the establishment of Mogadishu University. Through educational networking and funding provided by kindred organizations, *Al-Islah* has successfully educated more than 120,000 students in Somalia's capital. These social achievements have led to a reputation of intellectual peacekeeping among its members, who are comprised mostly of the highly educated urban elite. Although this form of the Muslim Brotherhood has been criticized by the extreme Islamists as being too moderate and abhorrently open to **Western** philosophies, *al-Islah* members contest that their platform of social equality and educational superiority derive from the **fundamentals** of Islam. Since civil war broke out in Somalia on 31 January 2009, the group is no longer active as its own entity but has aligned itself with the transitional **government** of Islamic tribunals.

MUSLIM BROTHERHOOD IN SUDAN. Since its inception in 1949, the **Muslim Brotherhood** has had a significant political presence in **Sudan**. Closely following the political dogmas of the Egyptian Muslim Brotherhood, the Sudanese Muslim Brotherhood has been able to gain influence and power throughout the country, making this Brotherhood branch one of the most successful within the organization. As in **Egypt**, the main source of support has been the younger educated population. The Islamic Charter Front (now the National Islamic Front), a splinter organization from the Sudanese Muslim Brotherhood, has worked with Brotherhood members to create a unified Islamic culture throughout Sudan. One of the main priorities of both groups is to institutionalize *sharia* (Islamic law) and implement it in all facets of Sudanese society. Politically successful, the Brotherhood has members in public and private Sudanese institutions, national and regional politics, and the military forces. However, the group has been sharply criticized for its human rights violations, especially in the Darfur conflict and the Southern Sudan Civil War (2003–2005). *See also* NATIONAL ISLAMIC FRONT; AL-TURABI, HASSAN 'ABD ALLAH.

MUSLIM BROTHERHOOD IN SYRIA. Founded in 1945, the Syrian branch of the **Muslim Brotherhood** was part of the legal opposition, especially in the country's war for independence from France. The ideas of the Muslim Brotherhood first came to **Syria** by way of Syrian students who studied at Cairo's university and participated in Egyptian Muslim Brotherhood events. When the students returned to Syria, they established *Shabaab Muhammad* (Muhammad's Youths) based on the ideologies of the Egyptian

Muslim Brotherhood. *Shabaab Muhammad* would eventually come to be known as the Syrian Muslim Brotherhood. Running in the 1961 elections and winning 10 seats in the Syrian Parliament, the group was soon banned in 1963 with the rise of the **Baath** (Baathist) Party, which occurred because of the 8 March military coup d'état that marginalized the **Sunni** Muslims in the country. After the Brotherhood's suppression, the group was instrumental in the Sunni-based resistance movement, which opposed the secularist Baath Party.

During the Lebanese Civil War in 1975, the Syrian government of Hafez al-Assad intervened to technically support Israel, sparking severe agitations within the country. As a result, many prominent members of the Syrian political regime were killed throughout the following years. Responsibility for the murders was claimed by the Syrian Muslim Brotherhood. On 7 July 1980, according to Syrian Emergency Law 49, membership in the Muslim Brotherhood was deemed a capital offense and has remained so ever since. Following this law, thousands of Brotherhood members turned themselves in hoping to avoid capital punishment. This revealed the demographics of the membership: professors, engineers, and mostly young students from Damascus. Nonetheless, this opposition continued to smolder until February 1982, when the Muslim Brotherhood took control of the central Syrian city of Hama. In reprisal, the military forces of the government of Hafez al-Assad heavily bombed the city, killing 10,000 to 30,000 people. Known as the Hama massacre, this incident marked the end of the Brotherhood as an effective Islamic force in Syria.

The Syrian Muslim Brotherhood's political activity in the country has since significantly relaxed, but it has gone on to establish headquarters in London and Cyprus. The group is currently led by Ali Sadreddine Bayanouni, who has taken refuge in London. The Syrian Muslim Brotherhood called for reform of Bashar al-Assad's regime in early 2011 and took part in the popular demonstrations that occurred in the country later that spring.

MUSLIM BROTHERHOOD IN TUNISIA. The **Muslim Brotherhood**'s influence in **Tunisia** has been adopted under the ***Ennahda*** organization. Arabic for "revival" or "renaissance," *ennahda* is Tunisia's most influential and powerful Islamic group. **Rashid Ghannouchi** began the organization in 1969 after returning to Tunisia from his studies in Damascus and Cairo. In Damascus, where the Muslim Brotherhood has a huge presence in the university, he discovered the ideologies of the Brotherhood. He then imitated its program and political agenda when returning to Tunisia, namely, Islamization of the society by the means of **Quranic** revival associations, popular preaching in mosques, and social aid to the poor. *See also ENNAHDA* IN TUNISIA.

AL-MU'TAZILA/**THE RATIONALISTS.** A school of Islamic thought from the 8th to the 10th centuries that has been particularly influential in modern-day **Iraq**, it was originally formed by Wasil ibn Ata (d. 748), and adherents originally referred to themselves as *Ahl al-Tawhid wa al-Adl* (People of Divine Unity and Justice). *Al-Mu'tazila* is most known for its assertion that since **Allah** is eternal and man is unable to completely understand Him, the **Quran** was solely created by man in context and verse. In addition, adherents believed that it is not permissible to reject **reason** based solely on Allah's omnificence, but it is reason that allows the believer to entrust in Allah's will. Although the group adopted **Western** forms of **philosophy**, it nevertheless had its basis in **Islam**. Believers often debated issues such as predestination, the presence of evil, and an allegorical versus literal interpretation of the **Quran**. Yet it was this reliance on Western thought that caused *Al-Mu'tazila* to come under criticism by many of its contemporaries. Thus, since not many Muslims were accepting its ideas, the school did not really flourish until the latter part of the 20th century, when a resurgence of the movement surfaced after the discovery of some *Al-Mu'tazila* texts in **Yemen**.

AL-NABHANI, TAQIYUDDIN (1909–1977). Founder of the Islamic Liberation Party (*Hizb ut-Tahrir Al-Islami*) in **Jordan** and **Palestine**, al-Nabahani once worked at the *sharia* (Islamic law) court and sat as a judge on the Appeals Court in Jerusalem until 1950. While in Palestine, he joined the **Muslim Brotherhood** and wrote extensively on political pluralism, **philosophy**, concepts of human thinking, and the modes of psychology that drive it. Specifically, his earlier publications explored how the internal processes of thoughts and convictions established emotions and sentiments. His work is considered to be a direct result of his education on **Sufism** (the inner, mystical dimension of **Islam**) by his maternal grandfather, Yusuf al-Nabhani. Through his studies of psychology and philosophy, al-Nabhani concluded that the only way to revolutionize Islam is by changing the thoughts and perceptions of Muslims, which, in his opinion, was (in addition to the import of foreign philosophies) what originally led to the decline of the **caliphate**.

Al-Nabhani supported discussion and education as the ways in which to revive traditional Islamic law. Through his publications, he tried to apply rationalist thinking and deductions to axioms in explaining that the **divine texts** of Islam are beyond question because **Allah** is beyond human conception. His school of thought was materialized in the founding of the Islamic Liberation Party. Among his many influential works are *Inqadh Filistin* (Salvation of Palestine) and *Al-Takattul Al-Hizbi* (Party Formation). Ideologically, he believed that the lack of awareness of the importance of the individual in politics was the reason for society's unwillingness to create a communal renaissance and revolutionize the Islamic political system (*nizam*).

Al-Nabahani outlined a three-step, gradual political program: first, communal awareness of the party's political platform and ideologies; second, community outreach, which would heighten support and social **consciousness**; and third, the gaining of power over the existing regime and subsequent rule of the people. He was very careful to note that the political party should never lose itself and became just another mechanism of the state; rather, its independence from the administration would secure its **legitimacy**. To him, the party was an ideological entity that safeguards the population from the

government by becoming a social structure that supervises the state's actions. In doing this, al-Nabahani highlighted the importance of elections and dismantled the power of the executive. *See also* DEMOCRACY.

AL-NADAWI, ABU AL-HASAN (1914–1999). Born to a respectable family in India, Al-Nadawi became one of the most distinguished **Islamic** thinkers of the 20th century. He was also a member of a number of Islamic organizations, especially *Nadwat Al-'Ulama'*. His book from 1944, *Madha Khasia Al-'Alam bi Inhitat Al-Muslimin* (What the World Lost by Muslims' Deterioration), remains influential to many Muslims. While touring **Egypt** in 1951, he became acquainted with many members of the **Muslim Brotherhood**, including **Muhammad Al-Ghazali** and **Sayyid Qutb**. He even received the esteemed International King Faysal Award. It could be argued that Al-Nadawi's impact is rivaled only by that of **Abu Al-A 'la Al-Mawdudi**, as both men contributed greatly to the intellectual basis of many Islamic **fundamentalist** movements. Ideologically, he stressed the importance of Islam for procuring any real **peace** or social order. He often compared and contrasted the **West** with Islam to illustrate the stability that the latter possesses.

NAHDLATUL ULAMA/**SCHOLARS OF THE RENAISSANCE.** An association of scholars formed in 1926 in Java, *Nahdlatul Ulama* was established to defend the practices of traditional **Islam** in Indonesia as new reformist Muslim movements were trying to "purify" Islam. These groups condemned **Sufi** practices and customs of anti-Islamic origin. Today, it is the second-largest Muslim organization in Indonesia.

AL-NAQSHABANDIYYA. Founded by Muhammad Baha' al-Din al-Naqshabandi in Turkey, Al-Naqshabandiyya began as a **Sufi** movement that supported and is similar to many other Islamic parties in the country. Such parties include the *Refah Partisi* and *Al-Watan Al-Umm*. It has been argued that the movement has its origins in the Ottoman Empire when the religious scholar Sheikh Ahmad Hindi promoted the movement throughout Turkey. Currently, the group is led by Muhammad As'ad Kushan.

NARRATIVES. Deeply entrenched within Islamic culture, narratives are stories that are created in order to further emphasize and illustrate the actions, ideologies, and goals of the specific Islamic **fundamentalist** group that created them. Propagandistic in nature, they are also viable tools for attracting new members and are more frequently used by the radical **Islamic groups**. Each narrative often uses the life of a certain **martyr** to convey the story and can be created in various media, such as songs, speeches, videos, or writings.

Although each narrative varies slightly, all adhere to common conventions that are easily recognized by the audience and implement the **Quranic** Arabic language to further engage and captivate the viewers. These narratives have even been translated in such a way that the rhetoric can be understood by non-Muslims, garnishing an even broader support base. However, despite all the attempts that these narratives make at promoting the fundamentalist-**jihadi** agenda, a majority of Muslims refute these since often fellow Muslims are injured as a result, and revolution has taken place without a holy war, most recently in places like **Egypt**, **Libya**, and **Tunisia**. Nevertheless, the fundamentalist narrative still plays an important role in understanding their ideologies, similarities, and recruitment tactics.

These narratives are categorized into three different types based on the goals of each: the local, the regional, and the global. The local narrative is one that, as the name suggests, focuses on local atrocities that have resulted in the deaths, displacement, and injuries of fellow Muslims. Ideally, the viewers are meant to react to these images and conjure up a sense of desire to aid the "Islamic cause" to stop such **violence**. The regional narrative focuses on a broader problem facing the Muslim world according to the fundamentalists—the American military occupation in the Arab states. In these narratives, the **jihad** is romanticized, and its target audience consists of those of better socioeconomic standing who do not see the mayhem personally. In short, the regional narrative brings the plight of the global jihad to the potential recruit. This form of narrative is most often used by **al-Qaeda**. The global narrative is even broader than the regional style and focuses on the corruption, exploitation, and hostilities that the entire **West** has brought and will continue to bring to Islam. Despite the slight differences between the styles, many groups (including al-Qaeda) interweave all three together in their narratives.

Through all these varying styles, the particular group that creates the narrative will always use certain central themes. These usually coincide with their ideological beliefs. These include the problem of the creation of **Israel**, the Palestinian **martyrdom** that followed, and the injustices of the **United States** that ensued; the restoration of the **caliphate**; the exploitation of the resources within the Arabic states by the Western nations and subsequent injustices; and the corruption embedded throughout the Muslim **governments** as they serve Western interests and abuse their own people. *See also* MASTER NARRATIVES.

NASRALLAH, SAYYID HASAN (1960–). The general secretary of *Hizbullah* **in Lebanon** since 1992, Nasrallah has become one of the most dominant and prominent figures in the Lebanese political circuit and is considered to be an Islamic nationalist with tight links to **Iran**, as he is financially and militarily supported by that country.

From an early age, Nasrallah became involved with the Islamic **fundamentalist** movement and became associated with many leading figures, such as **Muhammad Baqir al-Sadr** and 'Abbas al-Musawi. When he was 15 years old, he joined the *Amal* movement and became a chief member. However, Nasrallah took a break from his political **activism** and returned to his studies in 1976. After his separation from the *Amal* movement, Husayn al-Musawi and Nasrallah formed the militant group **Islamic *Amal* Movement** (*Harakat Amal Al-Islamiyya*) in hopes of raising a significant front against **Israel**.

Nasrallah also helped with the formation of *Hizbullah* and in 1987 became the leading member of its executive committee. His promotion to general secretary of *Hizbullah* came after the assassination of 'Abbas al-Musawi. Under Nasrallah's leadership, he claims that the group is concerned with the welfare of the Lebanese people and desires to continue the struggle against Israel. However, during the 2006 Israel-Lebanon conflict, he came under great criticism as the 34-day insurgency between *Hizbullah* and the Israeli army resulted in the deaths of approximately 1,200 people. He also hopes that cooperation can exist among the many different sociopolitical groups operating in the country. Significantly, *Hizbullah* has won seats in the Lebanese Parliament while under his guidance.

With regard to establishing an **Islamic state**, Nasrallah argues that since there would be no **consensus** (because there is a significant number of Muslims and non-Muslims throughout the population who are not in favor of the Islamic state), the state should not try to force its creation. If a state of Islam were established under these forced conditions, Nasrallah claims, social **justice** and **freedom** would be undermined. However, he claimed to be in support of the popular demonstrations that took place during the 2011 **Arab Spring**, especially the activities taking place in **Bahrain**.

NATION/*UMMA*. To the Islamic **fundamentalists**, the *umma* should be a unified, self-sacrificing, and virtuous entity that is based on the foundations of **Islam** and can successfully create an Islamic **government**. This government should also exist purely to serve the needs of the people and adhere to **Islamic law**. For this nation to properly be, it must encourage the community to become closer to **Allah**, properly worship, promote unity, diminish ideological or political tensions, and use the **holy texts** as guidelines for all matters. The *umma* designates the entire Muslim community throughout the world without any distinction to nationality or citizenship; it is transnational.

Most of the time, *umma* is translated in English as "nation," whereas the exact translation of the term under Islamic concepts refers to a universal community of believers in Islam. Here, the community is transnational and trans-territorial and not directly related to a defined boundary as it is in English.

NATIONAL AWAKENING PARTY/*PARTAI KEBANGKITAN BANGSA***.** Founded in 1999, this **Islamic political party** in Indonesia maintains its headquarters in Jakarta and is headed by Muhaimin Iskandar. After the fall of President Suharto on 21 May 1998, a group of various **Sunni** Islamic constituents gathered together and, with the support of the leading Sunni group in Indonesia, *Nahdlatul Ulama*, created the National Awakening Party. By 3 June 1998, 13 politically influential Indonesians were selected, and the creation of the party was marked by the drafting of its constitution.

The group is based on the desire to combine sociopolitical reforms, strategic governance, and a beneficial relationship with *Nahdlatul Ulama* in order to create a progressively **Islamic state** within Indonesia. Strongly influential, a founding member (Abdurrahman Wahid) went on to become president of Indonesia from October 1999 to July 2001. A majority of the group's support comes from the areas of Java and demographically from the conservative Muslim populations. However, although the Awakening Party supports the role of **Islam** within the **legislation**, it by no means advocates for a complete and austere Islamic **nation**. Moderately electorally successful, the party won 27 out the 560 seats in the People's Representative Council in the 2009 polls.

NATIONAL CONGRESS PARTY. The ruling **Islamic political party** in **Sudan**, it has been led by General **'Umar Hasan Ahmed al-Bashir** since he formed the party on 16 October 1993 and declared himself president of Sudan. Since the beginning of his presidency, al-Bashir began to implement *sharia* (Islamic law) throughout the country using a platform of conservative nationalism. However, the National Congress Party and al-Bashir have come under criticism for using the ideology of **pan-Islamism** to increase his power and dictatorship. Ideologically similar to al-Bashir's former party, the **National Islamic Front**, the Congress completely dominates the Sudanese Parliament (in the 2000 elections, the party won 86.5 percent of the votes and 355 of the 360 parliamentary seats). In 2000, an opposition group headed by former al-Bashir associate **Hassan 'Abd Allah al-Turabi** was quickly disbanded by the al-Bashir regime, and its leaders were imprisoned. Since then, little political opposition has gained traction in Sudan.

The National Congress Party did broker a deal with the Sudan People's Liberation Movement, bringing an end to the Second Sudanese Civil War (1983–2003) by allowing the southern region of Sudan autonomy for six years followed by independence as a separate state. However, the onset of the Darfur conflict (2003–2010) between the al-Bashir regime and opposing rebel groups left millions displaced and over 200,000 dead. The National Congress has been accused of supporting the Arabic armies of the Janjaweed in their campaign of murder and violence. Because of these accusations and the violence of the warfare, al-Bashir received 10 criminal charges and a warrant for his arrest from the International Criminal Court. Despite the judgments against him, the National Congress Party leader remains in power and won the majority (68.24 percent) during the April 2010 elections—also the first Sudanese multiparty elections in 10 years.

NATIONAL ISLAMIC FRONT (NIF). Founded by **Hassan al-Turabi**, the NIF is an Islamist group that operates in **Sudan**. The group was originally named the Islamic Charter Front and from 1964 to 1969 was an Islamist student group whose inception took place after the expulsion of then president Ibrahim Abboud. After the 1969 coup d'état, General Gaafar al-Nimeiry took control of Sudan and persecuted members affiliated with the Islamic Charter Front. Because of this, the group reorganized itself into the **Muslim Brotherhood in Sudan** until 1989, when the organization was again rechartered as the NIF after it organized the overthrow of then Sudanese prime minister Sadiq Al-Mahdi. The group strives to implement a purely Islamic state based on *sharia* (Islamic law) and rejects political and civil secularism. Since **Islamic political parties** are banned in the country, the group formed the National Congress to be able to penetrate the government legitimately.

Ruthlessly violent and brutal, the NIF has participated in bloody insurgencies such as the Second Sudanese Civil War (1983–2003) and the Darfur conflict (2003–2010). The NIF has gained military and civilian support even though the group has orchestrated numerous insurgencies and inflicted many **human rights** violations, especially against the southern Sudanese, minority factions, **women**, and marginal religious groups. Around 1999, the NIF's support started to erode primarily because of the decadelong civil war that was ravaging the country, and in 2004 al-Turabi was imprisoned. Although the group saw a steep decline during the early part of the new millennium, the Sudanese government is still dominated by NIF high-ranking officials. *See also* AL-BASHIR, 'UMAR.

NATIONAL ISLAMIC MOVEMENT OF AFGHANISTAN/*JUNBISH-E-MILLI ISLAMI AFGHANISTAN*. An Afghani **Islamic political party** led by General Abdul Rashed Dostum, the National Islamic Movement of **Afghanistan** is comprised mostly of former communists. The group possesses a military wing, Division 53, which was once instrumental in defending the northern Afghan oil fields. In 1988, *Junbish-e-Milli Islami Afghanistan* took control of Kandahar and a year later allegedly had thousands of members within its ranks. After the Soviet Union started withdrawing its troops in 1989, the organization began to take over even more territories in Afghanistan, including Mazar-e-Sharif in March of that year. Dostum's forces also entered in the battle for Kabul after the Afghani government of Muhammad Najibullah collapsed on 16 April 1992. Although *Junbish-e-Milli Islami Afghanistan*'s activity in the fighting began to wane by January 1994, the combat over control for the city lasted until the summer of 1994, resulting in over 25,000 deaths.

Following these events, Dostum moved his militants to northern Afghanistan. However, defections occurred in 1996 when General Abdul Malik Pahlawan accused Dostum of ordering the assassination of his brother. Pahlawan gathered a contingent of followers from within the *Junbish-e-Milli* ranks and eventually joined the **Taliban army**. Dostum and the remainder of his troops eventually joined the Northern Alliance and became notably instrumental in the fall of the Taliban army in 2001.

NATIONAL LIBERATION FRONT. Known more commonly as *Front de Libération Nationale* (FLN), this is an Algerian nationalist political party that was founded on 1 November 1954 by the merging of many smaller groups in the hope of aligning under a stronger force in order to gain Algerian independence from France. The Revolutionary Committee of Unity and Action was the auxiliary military force in **Algeria** that consisted of networks striving to impose the Algerian nationalist movement. It was this organization that helped form the FLN by promoting unity to throw off French rule during the Algerian War for Independence (1954–1962). Within two years of the group's inception, nearly all the nationalist factions had united under the FLN, and it took on the characteristics of a shadow government. The FLN also developed its military branch called the *Armé de Libération Nationale* (ALN), which, along with the rural guerilla forces, put up powerful opposition to the French army occupying Algeria. The FLN finally achieved Algerian independence in May 1962 with the Evian Accords, and the FLN assumed control of the country.

To combat any political opposition, the FLN adopted a single-party **constitution** but immediately experienced severe internal conflicts. Throughout this dissension, the ALN remained the prevailing military force in Algeria. The FLN remained influential in the decades that followed, but in 1988 the Algerian constitution was amended to allow a multiparty system, and therefore the FLN's power decreased while the ALN remained the ultimate authority in Algeria until the end of the Algerian Civil War (1991–2002). Still, despite the actions that took place during the civil war, the FLN will always remain a cornerstone in Algerian history because of its role in achieving independence.

Ideologically, the FLN sought pan-Arab nationalism throughout Algeria, using **Islam** to attain national consciousness and solidarity. The founding anti-imperialist doctrines of the FLN continued to remain at the core even after Algeria's independence and have affected the country's foreign policies. Although the group repeatedly used Islam to rally support throughout the years of its rule, it harshly criticized radical Islamists and especially their opposition group, the **Islamic Salvation Front**. Presently, the FLN remains the largest political party in Algeria but shares the stage with the National Rally for Democracy (known by the French name *Rassemblement National pour la Démocratie*).

NEGARA ISLAM INDONESIA (NII)/ISLAMIC STATE OF INDONE-SIA. The NII was declared by Anak Kartosurwiryo in 1949. This group was comprised mainly of former members of ***Darul Islam***. Over the decades, the NII began to spread throughout the country and is now known as N11, referring to the 11 military regions of the organization.

NIDAL, ABU (1935–2002). Born Sabri Khalil al-Banna, Abu Nidal joined *Al-Fatah* after the 1967 Arab-Israeli War, adopting his nom de guerre "Father of the Struggle." After the insurrection, he joined the **Palestinian Liberation Organization** (PLO) and quickly rose to be a high-ranking member, eventually becoming the PLO's chief representative in Iraq. However, in 1973, he left the group because of disagreements over Yasir Arafat's leadership and formed the **Fatah Revolutionary Council** a year later. Abu Nidal repeatedly attempted to **assassinate** Arafat, resulting in the PLO issuing a death sentence for him. He also had a hand in the founding and organization of many other groups, such as the **Arab Revolutionary Brigades**, **Black June**, and the Revolutionary Organization of Socialist Muslims—although experts tend to refer to these groups under the umbrella name **Abu Nidal Organization,** as it is unclear whether all of them are individualized. His increasingly violent activities resulted in losing a majority of his financial sponsorship, notably from Iraq, which had a longtime relationship with him. In 1983, the Iraqi government ordered Abu Nidal and his affiliates to leave the country.

At one time, the Islamist had a few hundred followers throughout Iraq, **Libya**, **Lebanon** (the majority), and **Syria**. His influence and power eventually eroded, and on 3 July 1998, a small group of his followers confronted Nidal and tried to oust him from his own organization. In response, the Egyptian **government** placed him under protective custody, although the country denied this claim. On 16 August 2002, while living in Baghdad, **Iraq**, he died as a result of gunshot wounds. The Iraqi regime claimed that he committed suicide, whereas Palestinians insist that his murder was ordered by Saddam Hussein.

1920 REVOLUTION BRIGADES. *See* BRIGADES OF THE REVOLUTION OF THE TWENTY.

NIZAM. See SYSTEM.

AL-NOUR/**THE LIGHT.** One of the **Islamic political parties** that grew out of the 2011 **Arab Spring** rebellion in **Egypt**, *al-Nour* is considered to be the most influential of all the **Salafi** parties there. Running on a platform of Islamic **fundamentalism**, the party advocates for a strict application of *sharia* (Islamic law). During the new parliamentary elections that took place from 28 November 2011 to 11 January 2012, *al-Nour* came in second only to the **Muslim Brotherhood**.

The history of the party can be traced back to the 1970s, when the Egyptian Salafi *Da'wa* group was formed by people who did not want to join the Muslim Brotherhood but still wanted to be part of an institutionalized Islamic movement. For years, the group refused to enter the political scene in Egypt, but, because it was not based on **Islam**, an affiliation (even if to reformulate it) was deemed forbidden. Even during the 2011 uprisings, the group maintained a relative silence because President Muhammad Hosni Mubarak (in office 1981–2011) was Muslim, and the group felt it sinful to rebel against him despite the unjustices. However, after Mubarak was ousted in February 2011, the group entered the political scene since it was deemed pure and new and also to protect and unite the Islamic interests within Egypt.

The group gained its legality in June 2011 and since then has been led by **Emad Abdel Ghaffour**. Its campaign policies are based on the application of *sharia*, free education, free health care, agricultural sustainability, an improvement of housing conditions, and various other socioeconomic aids, to name only a few.

NURI, SAYID ABDULLOD (1947–2006). Leader of the **Islamic Renaissance Party of Tajikistan**, Sayid Abdullod Nuri also led the United Tajik Opposition during the Tajik Civil War (1992–1997). Nuri first gained notice when he was instrumental in the Tajik National Peace Accord, which brought an end to the hostilities. Born in Sangvor, Tajikistan, on 15 March 1947, Nuri was briefly imprisoned from 1986 to 1988 by Soviet security for dispensing religiously affiliated propaganda. Among his doctrinal and militant desires, Nuri advocated for an **Islamic state** and supported the **Islamic Movement**

of Uzbekistan, which has been operationally inactive since 2001 because of increasing repression by the country's security forces. An influential figure in the political and military realms, he has also been allegedly affiliated with **al-Qaeda** and other Islamic **fundamentalists**. When Nuri died of cancer on 9 August 2006, his funeral service was attended by thousands, and he has been remembered by his followers as an "irreplaceable personality" who tried to return Tajikistan to a position of Islamic ideals and morality. *See also* CENTRAL ASAIN ISLAMIC ACTIVITY; UNITED TAJIK OPPOSITION.

P

PAGANISM/*JAHILIYYA*. Paganism, the devotion to the materialistic and/or undermining of **monotheism**, has become (according to the Islamic **fundamentalists**) the distinguishing characteristic of the **West**. To many Muslims, Western civilization has turned its back on **morality** and virtue because of its desires and loss of ideological **consciousness**. Paganism results in physical, religious, and social confusion coupled with moral disintegration and spiritual liquidation. Accordingly, this is also the source of many economic and political problems for the United States, Europe, and generally the West. Specifically, the fundamentalists agree that paganism can be defined by an obsession with and/or competition for material wealth or gain, and it is this desire for the physical rather than the spiritual that has generated political and social conflicts within these *jahili* **societies**. Many radical fundamentalists feel that all contemporary societies fall under these prescripts. They use *tawhid*, or the lack thereof, as a way to determine whether a society is pagan. This paganism is the reason that they warn against and disagree with **Islam**'s attempt to assimilate Western ideologies to their culture—for fear that Islam may become corrupted by the material as the West has. In addition, a *jahili* society is one that does not apply *sharia* (Islamic law) and that violates the teachings of the **Quran** and **divine governance**. To the fundamentalists, moderate and radical alike, the essence of Islam is one that focuses on the destruction of paganism.

PAKISTAN. Pakistan was officially created on 14 August 1947 following Great Britain's end of its colonial rule in India. Originally destined to be the land of Asia's Muslim population, the country currently adheres primarily to **Sufi** Islam (mystical Islam). Politically, there are many varied **Islamic political groups** operating within its borders, and its military policies have allowed for an array of relationships with different **Islamic groups** both domestic and foreign. Its border with **Afghanistan** has also made it particularly susceptible to the influences of **al-Qaeda** and the **Taliban army**. Although the country is declared **democratic**, the Islamic political agenda heavily influences policies and practices. Pakistan also has a positive relationship with the **United States**, an alliance that many radical Islamists wish to eliminate.

On the northwestern border of Afghanistan lies the Federal Administered Tribal Areas, which have become home to some of the most radical Islamic militant groups today. Aside from harboring domestic **extremist** groups, foreign ones have entered the areas and created camps there as well. However, the presence of these groups has often been a good lever for attaining political objectives in bordering Afghanistan and India, but there have been some recent operations on the part of the internal security forces (the Inter-Services Intelligence [ISI]) to repress these groups.

There is definitely a dynamic relationship between the ISI and foreign militant groups, especially the Taliban. Until 2001, the Pakistani state acknowledged the Taliban rule in Afghanistan and even supported it for diplomatic reasons. Even after American troops entered Afghanistan in the fall of 2001, Pakistan rarely joined its **Western** ally in thwarting the extremism in Afghanistan—although it announced that it broke ties with the Afghani state. It was then believed by many in the U.S. military intelligence that the ISI still had a close relationship with the Taliban army.

In 2007, *Tehreek-e-Taliban* Pakistan was formed as a conglomeration of Pakistani militants, al-Qaeda affiliates, and Taliban soldiers. The extremist group has conducted numerous attacks on the Pakistani state and has been accused of killing thousands of civilians within its borders. Another Pakistani extremist group is known as the Haqqani Network. Named after the militant Jalaluddin Haqqani, the organization works with the Taliban to fight against the Western forces within Afghanistan. The group targets military personnel as well as politicians and diplomats and has a range of alliances with various Islamic groups. Pakistan's desire to eliminate any Indian influence in Afghanistan has incited the ISI to allegedly support the Haqqani Network, which has repeatedly attacked Indian embassies and outposts.

Lashkar-e-Tayyiba and *Jaish e-Muhammad* have also been mainstays in the tribal regions of Pakistan and, like the Haqqani Network, have not been repressed by the ISI because of their anti-Indian policies. Pakistan's history of allowing these groups to flourish has led to the state coming under criticism for being the catalyst to operations such as the **Mumbai attacks of November 2008**. However, in the wake of this attack, the ISI did arrest several militant leaders and liquidated a few training camps. As far as the general population is concerned, most Pakistanis support the existence of these groups since many have also provided much-needed social welfare, medical, and educational programs. Still, because of international pressure (mostly on the part of the United States), Pakistan officially banned *Jaish e-Muhammad* in 2002. *Lashkar-e-Tayibba*, on the other hand, has moved its core to Afghanistan, especially in light of the Taliban's reemergence within the country.

Over the past few decades, aside from the Soviet-Afghan War (1979–1989) and Pakistani presidential policies of **Islamization**, the **Deoband** revivalist movement has had the most influence in the contemporary Islamic cultural climate. Although there are conservative elements like the Deoband school of **Islam** and Islamic **fundamentalism** within the country, the people as a whole are mainly moderate. In addition, the Pakistani population is constantly suffering from economic setbacks, foreign and domestic attacks, and a lowered standard of living. This turmoil has also made the Sufi school even more appreciated among its inhabitants and has dictated many of the country's ideological stances. The use of Islam as a means to unite the country and arouse a political consciousness has been integral to southern Asia's Muslim community since the later part of the 19th century.

Jamaat-e-Islami is the oldest Islamic fundamentalist party in Pakistan that represents these ideals. Established in 1941, the group sought to create an **Islamic state** throughout the country and remove all secular influence. The group was also adamantly against the Hindu religion and Western culture. The new Pakistani government began to repress the group, and in turn the group began to reinforce its platform of Islamization. Now, the popular consensus seems to be one that desires a secular democratic state that uses Islam as a means of creating nationalism and identity. *Jamaat-e-Islami* is still active on the political circuit in Pakistan but has performed only moderately well in elections over the past years. However, the group still influences popular opinion despite its poor electoral successes.

The Deoband movement, although it originated in India, has been part of Pakistani culture since its inception. When a split emerged within the movement by 1920, one group wanted to pursue an Indian nationalist platform (*Jamaat Ulema-e-Hind*), and the other sought the creation of an independent Pakistani state. The latter became known as *Jamaat Ulema-e-Islam* (JUI). Now a major **political party** within Pakistan, the group has also been affiliated with the Afghan Taliban. The JUI has worked with *Jamaat-e-Islami* especially on issues such as ousting Western troops from the surrounding regions—a topic that is very popular among the Pakistani people.

Also within the Pakistani general public, there is a lack of religious pluralism and, with that, a large degree of discrimination. In the past few years, the **Shiite** community in particular has been targeted by sectarian violence. The **Ahmadiyya Muslim community**, which has an approximate 4 million adherents in Pakistan, has been severely repressed throughout the country and has even been declared non-Muslim in 1974 and heretical. The situation for the small **Christian** minority is just as bad. The *madrasa* also plays a key role within the culture, serving as a center for Islamic education and, more controversially, for allegedly being financed by Islamic groups both foreign and domestic. It has also been speculated that these schools have been used to promote and spread bigoted attitudes, and some civilians have been accused of **blasphemy** and other "crimes" against Islam. Pakistan's religious shrines and locations have also come under attack because of the Islamic fundamentalist belief that the veneration of idols or saints is sacrilegious. In July 2010, a famous Sufi shrine in Lahore was attacked by Islamic extremists, resulting in the deaths of an estimated 40 and injuring over 200.

Suicide bombings and attacks have increased within Pakistan especially since 2007. This has also led to a growing distaste for militant Islamic groups within the country, and public support for such organizations as al-Qaeda and the Taliban has gone into a rapid decline. Although, as mentioned previously, the public does share in the groups' anti-Western sentiments, their militant approach and attacks on civilians have led to their lack of popular backing. However, reports have indicated that a vast majority of new, young recruits for various Islamic extremist groups have come from Pakistan from the outside.

The state's security forces have been forced to use aggressive tactics to repress these extremist activities, but many of the operations have also led to an increase in civilian casualties, making them much less popular among the ordinary people. Many have also criticized the state for being the catalyst of the extremist violence after having been tolerant of the radicals in the first place. A divide has been created since many people agree with the ideologies of the group but disagree with their tactics and means of enforcing their austere devotion to Islam.

Diplomatically, the Pakistani government has tried to facilitate the U.S. military efforts to fight al-Qaeda and the Taliban in neighboring Afghanistan by allowing the use of its airspace and providing logistical information. However, as mentioned, there still is a duality within Pakistan for accepting to help fight these extremists and then allegedly giving support to the Islamic groups as well. The government has even made peace overtures to these groups, but this has resulted only in weakening the state and increasing offensives in Afghanistan. This is due to the view that the peace deals are merely military surrenders on the part of Pakistan.

The fate of Pakistan's relationship with the Islamic insurgents will depend considerably on its political practices. Since **democracy** was established within the country on February 2008, a platform of **Islamization** has been embraced by political parties but not so much on the part of the military. However, this Islamization has had its lapses, too, since state leadership has tried to support the election of Islamic parties over secular ones, a move that has been viewed as supportive for all brands of Islam—both moderate and radical. This view has resulted in the Islamic political parties performing poorly in recent elections, as the public is wary of combining Islam with the state directly. Rather, it seems that Islam should remain within the culture and not dictate policy and practices. For example, during the 2008 elections, all the Islamic political parties combined only won 2 percent of the popular vote.

The main problem that needs to be addressed is that the Pakistani security forces often rely on the use of Islamic militants during operations. This joining of state security with religious-based combative groups has been one of the main reasons that Pakistan cannot extricate itself from the Islamic insurgency both internally and externally. This has also led to an increase in frustrations in Pakistan's American allies. However, to placate this tension with the United States, the state has captured and/or killed a number of extremist operatives and high commanders. Yet when **Osama bin Laden** was found out by American intelligence to be living in a safe house in Abbottabad and was subsequently killed by American forces on 2 May 2011, many questions arose as to why the Pakistani government and security forces were not aware of his presence there. Suspicions grew, especially because of the location's proximity to the capital of Islamabad and the state's previous support of the Taliban army (which notoriously had harbored bin Laden before). In addition, the U.S. administration had only two years earlier passed the Kerry-Lugar bill in September 2009. Referred to as the Enhanced Partnership with Pakistan Act, this authorized the American government to give Pakistan $7.5 billion in civilian aid in return for military assistance and intelligence.

To many, it is unclear as to why the Pakistani state has neglected to bring down some Islamic cadres but has demonstrated itself to be quite capable of doing so. Therefore, it becomes not a matter of ability but rather a matter of interest. As the state keeps playing both sides of the insurgency, its economy and central government are redoubtable challenges. The fear of an Islamic revolution has even come up in recent public polls, but the desire of the people to maintain their Islamized democracy still seems to overshadow it. *See also* AL-GHURABAA PAKISTAN; *JUND ALLAH* IN PAKISTAN; *PASBAN-E-ISLAMI*; *PASBAN KHATM-E-NABUWWAT*; *SIPAH-E-SAHABA PAKISTAN*; *TEHRIK-E-JAFARIA PAKISTAN*.

PALESTINE/PALESTINIAN AUTHORITY. The Islamic current in the Palestinian Authority, more commonly referred to simply as Palestine, is overwhelmingly focused on the destruction of the state of **Israel**. Islamic ideology, agenda, and tactics are all based on the concept that the state of Israel is one with the infidel and abhorrent to **Islam**. Many of the **Islamic groups** within Palestine also have roots in other countries, making them immensely international and interdoctrinal. These groups include **Hamas**, the **Islamic Jihad of Palestine**, *Jund Ansar Allah*, *Jaysh al-Islam*, **al-Fatah**, **Force**

17, and the **Muslim Brotherhood in Palestine**. Many of these groups have splintered from each other and have interrelated members.

With regard to legislative divisions in Palestine, the **Palestinian Liberation Organization** created the Palestinian National Authority after the 1993 Oslo Accords to serve as the interim **government** of the state. The accords mandated that the Palestinian Authority must replace the Israeli military that was established in the West Bank and Gaza Strip. The Palestinian Legislative Council now has over 130 parliamentary seats from the West Bank and Gaza alone, and since 2007 Hamas has controlled all the Palestinian groups in the Gaza Strip. This has made Hamas the most influential group in the legislature, along with the Islamic Jihad of Palestine, while *al-Fatah* has regularly lost influence.

A splinter group from the Muslim Brotherhood in Palestine, Hamas was created in 1987 with the sole purpose of replacing Israel with an **Islamic state** and reestablishing the **caliphate** based on *sharia* (Islamic law). Its primary tactic has been an aggressive application of the **jihad** since it is viewed by its members that only through militancy can Israel come under Islamic control. The group has thousands of supporters throughout Palestine and the Palestinian Territories of Gaza and the West Bank. This **Sunni** group has easily gained public support since it is widely believed that the territory that encompasses Israel truly belongs to **Islam**. Since Israel has been designated as the sovereign land of Judaism, a corrupt (*jahili*) religion in the eyes of many Muslims, the land is even more controversial. Israel's boundaries also house Jerusalem, a sacred site to Islam.

Hamas has played off this popular notion and has used Arab nationalism as one of its main avenues of support. The group has also provided social services to the Palestinian people and has used **Islamization** in the hope of more easily channeling the public into an austere Islamic state. Hamas has even fathered the **Izz ad-Din al-Qassam Brigade**, which has proven to be even more extreme in its vigilantism. The increased militancy surrounding Hamas, the rising popular support it has garnered, and its refusal to recognize Israel have resulted in many countries, especially the **United States**, refusing to send aid to Palestine. However, the group is still allegedly state sponsored by **Iran** and receives plenty from private donations throughout the Gulf states.

The Islamic Jihad of Palestine is another Muslim Brotherhood offshoot that was formed after being inspired by the **Iranian Islamic Revolution of 1979**. Similar in aggressiveness to Hamas, the Islamic Jihad of Palestine also completely rejects Israel. However, unlike its counterpart, the group is unusually secretive and illusive. Although it is an educated guess that a majority of this outfit is Palestinian, its exact size is unknown. The group has conducted numerous attacks against Israelis and the Israel security forces yet still continues to operate against it, primarily underground in secrecy. However, since 2008, the Israeli army has made great defensive strides and has arrested or killed numerous Islamic Jihad of Palestine members.

Jund Ansar Allah is a relatively new group (established in 2008) operating in Palestine with the same jihadist platform as the two previously mentioned groups. In fact, the group was formed out of former members of both Hamas and the Islamic Jihad of Palestine. The dissension took place because it was felt that these groups were not effective enough in toppling Israel and creating an Islamic state there. This group also seeks the establishment of the caliphate on a **pan-Islamic** level. The group has even gained a large following in the Gaza Strip. Hamas has been particularly critical of *Jund Ansar Allah* and, in August 2009, killed its leader, Abdel-Latif Moussa, and has tried to slander its name by linking it with the better-known *al-Fatah* organization along with **al-Qaeda**.

Jaljalat, *Jaysh Al-Ummah*, and *Hizb ut-Tahrir* are other Islamic groups active in Palestine. Although *Jaljalat* is a splinter group from the Izz ad-Din al-Qassam Brigades, it has also been known to have an alliance with *Jund Ansar Allah* and has joined the former in its criticisms of Hamas. *Jaysh al-Ummah* has been suspected of being an affiliate of al-Qaeda and also stands on the platform of fighting against Israel. However, the group is small and remains to function only in Gaza while opposing the activities of Hamas. *Hizb ut-Tahrir*'s presence in Palestine is very small but nevertheless has some following in the country with its pan-Islamic ideals. However, it must be noted that the group does not support the radical brand of militant Islam, nor does it refuse to recognize the legitimacy of Israel.

Al-Fatah has been dominating the Palestinian Authority for years and has a military wing known as **al-Aqsa Martyrs' Brigade**. The brigade is etymologically derived from the al-Aqsa mosque, which is known for its promotion of **suicide bombings**—illustrating the group's primary means of **violence**. *Al-Fatah* was led by the prominent Arab leader Yasir Arafat until his death in 2004. The group is seen as controversial because of its support of both sectarian and secular beliefs as well as its interest in both Islamic **extremism** and diplomatic solutions. The group often clashes with Hamas leading to even more palpable tensions since both are major players on the Palestinian stage. However, *Al-Fatah* has received international aid from both **Western** and Middle Eastern countries over the years.

Particularly in the past decade, the Palestinian Authority has been divided between those supporting and electing *Al-Fatah* members and Hamas members. Hamas's war against Israel in 2008 led many within the public to not support it for some time, although in 2006 it won the majority in the election. *Al-Fatah* is usually favored because of its platform of Islamization, but immense corruption within the group has led many to turn away from it. There have also been data collected from polls that brought to light the conflicting desires of people within the Palestinian Territories—some polls show a support of secularism, and others advocate for the implementation of *sharia*. With this in mind, it seems as if the Palestinian current is one that is ever changing and uncertain.

The situation in Gaza and the West Bank has also been a big part of the Palestinian diplomatic problems, recently almost as much as the Israeli situation. Gaza and the West Bank ceaselessly call for their right to self-government while being patrolled by both Palestinian and Israeli security forces. However, Palestine claims that the increased presence of radical Islamic **fundamentalists** within the West Bank is the reason for the heightened security. Gaza has seen an increase in Islamic **extremism** over the past years, too. In addition, since Palestinian militants have been basing their operations in and conducting their attacks against Israel in these two territories, Israel, in retribution, has continued to launch counterattacks on Gaza and the West Bank—putting even more of its people in harm's way.

Since Arafat's death, the Palestinian Authority and *Al-Fatah* have been led by Mahmoud Abbas. His moderate prescriptions have gained him support from many foreign bodies and countries but also led to opposition from many domestic groups. Arafat's hard-line ideologies made him a popular leader in Palestine for many years, but with this conversion to a more conciliating, secularist ruler, groups that were once in opposition to one another have joined forces and formed a united front against the Abbas government. With the January 2009 extension of Abbas's presidential term, Hamas was becoming even more vocal about condemning his government, calling it illegal and illegitimate and vowing to overthrow his administration. This internal opposition to the government has served only to weaken the Palestinian Authority in recent years. As of 2011, Hamas and *Al-Fatah* are still vying for complete control of the Palestinian Territories, and a solution to the separate state of Israel has yet to be reached. *See also* INTIFADA; JUDAISM.

PALESTINIAN ISLAMIC JIHAD. *See* ISLAMIC JIHAD OF PALESTINE.

PALESTINIAN LIBERATION MOVEMENT. *See AL-FATAH.*

PALESTINIAN LIBERATION ORGANIZATION (PLO). Formed on 2 June 1964 at the Arab League summit in Cairo, **Egypt**, the PLO is a political consortium of various groups that seek to raise the morale and clout of the Palestinian population. Paramilitary as well as diplomatic, the PLO was recognized by the United Nations in 1974. However, because of the anti-Zionist undertones that pervaded the organization for many years, it was deemed a threat to **Israel** until the signing of a peace agreement in 1993 whereby the Jewish state recognized the PLO as being the representative body of the Palestinian nation.

Originally, the organization focused its goals on the liberation of **Palestine** using all necessary means, including military intervention. However, over the decades, it defined itself more through diplomatic bargaining to sustain the state. At the time of its inception, the nation was still territorially defined as the British Mandate for Palestine, and in trying to erect a new geographic boundary and rectify the displacement of thousands of Palestinians with the creation of the Israeli state, the PLO and its affiliates were held responsible for multiple attacks in Egypt, **Jordan**, **Lebanon**, and **Syria**.

Structurally, the PLO has an executive committee that is comprised of 18 members who are elected by the Palestinian National Council, which also has a legislative body but is much smaller in size. One of the main reasons for the PLO gaining legitimacy from the United Nations and other entities is that its members represent a range of political, social, and religious ideologies. Originally considered representative of the Palestinian nation, the organization has tried to account for a majority of the sentiments felt among its people. Currently, it is led by Mahmoud Abbas, who replaced the famous Yasser Arafat after his death on 11 November 2004. Members of the PLO include the **Democratic Front for the Liberation of Palestine**, *al-Fatah*, **Democratic Islamic Arab Movement**, **Arab Liberation Front**, and **Hamas** (which won over two-thirds of the PLO seats during the 2006 elections).

Although the group focuses on the needs and desires of Palestinians as a whole, the main doctrine of the PLO has been pan-Arabism (as a way to unite the people) and to abolish the territorial boundaries that were set up after 1948. The main reason why the PLO was initially a very aggressive group was due mostly to the loss that the Arab states suffered during the Six-Day War (5–10 June 1967) at the hands of the Israeli army. This defeat enraged and radicalized the Palestinian populations (as well as much of the Arab world) and made way for the militant Arafat to rise to power as chairman of the organization on 4 February 1969. With him, many *fedayeen* joined the PLO and began to launch attacks on Israel that year.

Throughout the 1970s, the PLO was relatively small and merely an umbrella group of various organizations but had incredibly close ties with Lebanon. However, as the group tried to come to grips with its ideology and identity (by balancing between being a pan-Arab nationalistic group and a hard-line anti-Zionist organization), dissension occurred internally, and many splinter organizations formed from the PLO. These consisted mostly of members who thought that the doctrines of the PLO were too mild and not aggressive enough to be successful. It was during this time that militants such as **Abu Nidal** started to defect from the organization.

The failure of the 1979 Camp David Accords between Egypt and Israel, which promised to resolve the Palestinian situation, only enraged members throughout the Arab world and promoted dissatisfaction with Egypt for agreeing to a peace accord with Israel without securing the rights of their Arab brethren in Palestine. After witnessing the failure of diplomacy, many Arabs and displaced Palestinians were more than willing to allow aggressive tactics to flourish in the hopes that that could bring a resolution.

When Israel occupied Lebanon from 6 June 1982 to 17 May 1983, the PLO had to relocate its headquarters from Beirut to Tunis, **Tunisia**. Then, on 1 October 1985, the Israeli air force raided the headquarters in the Tunis neighborhoods, killing an estimated 60 people. Although the period of the mid-1980s was unquestionably marked a low point for the PLO, on 15 November 1988 the Palestinian Declaration of Independence was announced by Arafat. Although over 100 states recognized the declaration, which also called for Palestine to gain control over the lands of Gaza Strip and the West Bank, Palestine had yet to become a recognized state.

However, on 13 September 1993, when the historic Oslo Accords were signed between Arafat and Israeli Prime Minister Yitzhak Rabin, Palestine was given authority over the Gaza Strip and parts of the West Bank. This led to the creation of the Palestinian Authority (PA). Arafat was then elected president of the PA in January 1996. It must be stressed here that the PLO and the PA are not completely or officially linked bodies. The headquarters of the PLO then relocated from Tunis to Ramallah, West Bank. As part of the Oslo Accords, Arafat proclaimed the legitimacy of Israel and declared that a state of peace should exist between the two nations. However, Israel never expressed its acceptance of the rightfulness of Palestine in return. The signing of these accords seemed to provide only temporary fixes, as the PLO is still heavily at odds with the state of Israel. Both participated in the Second **Intifada** and conducted numerous attacks against each other during that time and since. *See also* BLACK SEPTEMBER ORGANIZATION; FATAH REVOLUTIONARY COUNCIL; FORCE 17; *HAWARI*; ISLAMIC JIHAD OF PALESTINE; ISLAMIC POLITICAL PARTIES; *AL-JIHAD AL-ISLAMI* IN THE WEST BANK AND GAZA STRIP.

PAN-AM FLIGHT 103 BOMBING. On 21 December 1988, a Boeing 747 commercial airliner departing from London en route to New York exploded while approximately 30,000 feet above the Scottish village of Lockerbie. All 259 passengers and crew members died, as did 11 within Lockerbie who were killed as a result of falling debris. An intensive forensic analysis and investigation ensued and concluded that the explosive was made from Semtex and was concealed within a Toshiba cassette player that was placed within a piece of luggage. It was also deduced that the timing mechanism was intended to go off while the plane was flying over the Atlantic, but since the flight had a 25-minute takeoff delay, it exploded over Scotland. If not for this delay, such analysis would not have been possible.

Investigators surmised that the Popular Front for the Liberation of Palestine–General Command made and planted the bomb since months before, on 26 October 1988, a similar bomb and timing device had been found in the possession of a member in West Germany. However, there was no conclusive evidence aside from the similarities between the two devices, resulting in mere speculation. Another hypothesis centered around the **Guardians of the Islamic Revolution** being at fault after a telephone call was placed allegedly by a member of the group who claimed responsibility. More evidence from the investigation also revealed that the luggage the bomb was packed in came from Malta, leading experts to surmise that the bomb was Libyan sponsored.

The Pan-Am bombing quickly grew into a diplomatic and economic crisis for **Libya**, and the country soon faced incredible effects in the aftermath of the investigation. As a result of the bomb being assumed as Libyan manufactured, the **United States** indicted two Libyan officials (Al-Amin Khalifa Fahimah and Abdel Basset al-Megrahi) on 14 November 1991 in connection with the explosion, but the **Muammar Qadhafi** regime refused to extradite them. This complicated relations between the Libyan government and the United States as the latter imposed an air traffic embargo, cut off military aid, and limited diplomacy to Libya in 1992. Furthermore, the UN Security Council imposed economic sanctions on Libya for not complying with the U.S. demands, a move that eventually cost the North African state more than $23.5 billion between 1993 and 1997. The effects were still felt over the next few years as oil prices fell, severe inflation occurred, and a shortage of basic goods overcame the nation. Finally, the Libyan **government** agreed to give the suspects up for trial at the International Court of Justice at The Hague, but the United States and Scotland disagreed since they felt that the two men should be tried in either America or Scotland since it was an American airliner and the act occurred over Scottish soil.

On 19 March 1999, an agreement was reached with the mediation of South African President Nelson Mandela that Fahimah and Al-Megrahi would be tried at The Hague under Scottish laws and using three Scottish judges. The trial began on 3 May 2000, and the men were charged with conspiracy, murder, and violations of the Air Security Act of 1982. On 31 January 2001, Fahimah was found not guilty, but Al-Megrahi was sentenced to 27 years at Glenrock Prison in Scotland and appealed his case to the Scottish Court of Criminal Appeals. Then, on 15 August 2003, Ahmed Awn, Libya's UN ambassador, submitted a letter to the UN Security Council claiming responsibility for the 1988 bombing. As a result, Libya paid $8 million to each victim's family, the United Nations lifted its economic sanctions, and the United States resumed diplomatic relations with the country. Finally, Al-Megrahi was released on 20 August 2009 for medical reasons and sent back to Libya, where he was treated as a hero, something that shocked the British population.

PAN-ISLAMISM. Ideologically, pan-Islamism is a concept that promotes the unification of the Muslim world under one political entity. This notion emerged in the 1880s during the Middle East's rebellion against **Western** colonial forces. As a propaganda tool, pan-Islamism reached its pinnacle before the turn of the 20th century. Instrumental in purveying the idea was Islamic thinker **Jamal al-Din al-Afghani**, who stated that a united Islamic entity would be the key to reviving world civilization and releasing it from its imperialistic constraints. Pan-Islamism is based on the proposition that all ideologies, governments, and societies should be merged into one popular and stable **government**. From this, al-Afghani argued, **liberation** and reformation would ensue.

Although the movement began to wane in popularity in the early 1900s, 'Abdullah al-Sharawardy created the Pan-Islamic Society while in London in 1903. He hoped to unite the ever-conflicting **Shiites** and **Sunnis** and continued to oppose the West using his publication *Pan Islamism* to spread his beliefs. However, when the Ottoman Empire fell after the Young Turk Revolution in 1908, the notions of pan-Islamism were suspended—marking an end for the first wave of the movement. Although minor resurgences occurred during the 1920s and 1930s, they had no significant impact.

Following World War II, there was, however, a notable revival of the pan-Islamist ideals. The new wave was centered in **Pakistan**, and there new feelings of economic, political, and social commonalities began to take hold. However, there was no great emphasis on ideological unity. Governmental goals seemed to be of more importance than religious reformation during this time. It is significant to note that pan-Islamism was never officially implemented and has now turned into a sort of utopian ideal. Some scholars have argued that the constant conflicts between the various schools and sects of **Islam** lie at the core of why such a concept can never truly exist.

PAN-MALAYSIAN ISLAMIC PARTY. Ideologically, this **Islamic political party** in Malaysia seeks to create an **Islamic state** within the country based on austere **interpretations** of the **divine texts**. A majority of the group's support comes from the northern regions of the state, which boast a more conservative Muslim population. The party has its origins in the March 1947 first Pan-Malayan Islamic conference, in which prominent Islamic figures gathered to form a progressive Malaysian-Muslim political movement. Members who were more in support of a clerically led **theocratic** government joined together and formed the Pan-Malayan Islamic Association (which was then renamed the Pan-Malaysian Islamic Party in 1955). However, during the 1970s, the group went under the name of *Parti Islam Se-Malaysia*.

The Pan-Malaysian Islamic Party coalesced with two other groups in 1999 to form the *Barisan Alternatif*—a party in opposition to the *Barisan Nasional*, the leading Malaysian political party since the 1957 independence from Great Britain. Mildly successful, the group gained control over Terengganu during its establishment. However, over a period of only five years, the group's support significantly waned. It lost control of Terengganu and most seats in the state assembly. In fact, by 2005, the Pan-Malaysian Islamic Party controlled only one seat in the legislature. Yet the party seemed to regain its prominence by the 2008 elections, winning 23 seats in the Malaysian Parliament.

Following the 8 March 2008 elections, the Pan-Malaysian Islamic Party joined with two other similar groups to form the *Pakatan Rakyat* (People's Alliance) coalition, which now controls 4 of the 13 federal Malayan states. Currently, the party is led by Abdul Hadi Awang and is spiritually advised by Nik Aziz Nik Mat. Still an opposition force to the *Barisan Nasional*, it has accused the dominant party of being the reason for the socioeconomic problems of the Malay Muslims. Ideologically, the group feels that these problems can be overcome if an **Islamic state** and *sharia* (Islamic law) are established throughout Malaysia since Islam can create a more morally upright citizen and therefore a just society.

PAN-SAHEL INITIATIVE (PSI). Launched by the **United States** in October 2002, the PSI was created to help countries in the Sahel region combat the increased activity of **al-Qaeda in the Islamic Maghreb**. This U.S. training program began with approximately 1,200 troops from **Mauritania**, **Mali**, Niger, and Chad. It is designed to help remove **Islamic groups** from the Sahel area, track Islamist activity, promote **peace**, and maintain ongoing security. In June 2005, the group expanded with the inclusion of other nations and was renamed the **Trans-Saharan Counter-Terrorism Initiative**. A major criticism of the multi-million-dollar security program has been its neglect of recognizing the underlying economic and political problems in the area as well as radicalizing groups purely because of their proximity to the Saharan region. The tactics used by the PSI focus more on special operations than on the large-scale heavy military occupation that is implemented in **Afghanistan** and **Iraq**.

PARTIE DE LA JUSTICE ET DU DÉVELOPPEMENT. *See HIZB AL-ADALA WA AL TANMIA*/JUSTICE AND DEVELOPMENT PARTY.

PARTY OF LIBERATION. *See HIZB U-TAHRIR.*

PARTY OF THE YEMENI ASSOCIATION FOR REFORM/*HIZB AL-TAJAMMU' AL-YEMENI LI AL-ISLAH.*** Founded by a prominent tribal chief, Sheikh 'Abd Allah al-Ahmar, the group gained its following through the **Muslim Brotherhood**. The group was quite successful in the political arena of Yemen, in the three years after its establishment in 1990, and al-Ahmar was elected as speaker of the parliament. After the 1993 elections, *Hizb Al-Tajammu' Al-Yemeni Li Al-Islah* became the second-strongest **Islamic political party** in the country. Still maintaining its ties to the Brotherhood, the deputy head of *Al-Islah*, Sheikh Yasin 'Abd Al-'Aziz, is also the supreme guide of the Brotherhood. In addition, a former supreme guide of the Muslim Brotherhood, 'Abd Al-Majid al-Zandani, is the head of the *Al-Islah* **shura** council. However, the party has come under some criticism from radical **fundamentalists** for its participation in **democratic** elections. Nevertheless, the group has made great strides in the educational, religious, and political fields of Yemen.

PASBAN-E-ISLAMI/PASBAN **VOICE AGAINST INJUSTICE.** *Pasban-e-Islami* is a **Pakistani** political group led by Altaf Shakoor. Now an independent group, it began as the student faction of *Jamaat-e-Islami*. Preferring to use verbal rather than violent means, the group protests against various cases of social injustices as perceived through the lens of **Islam**. *See also* ISLAMIC POLITICAL PARTIES.

***PASBAN KHATM E-NABUWWAT*/GUARDIANS OF THE SEAL OF THE PROPHET.** A **Pakistani** organization that ideologically believes that there will not be a future prophet and considers itself the "guardians" of the orthodoxy of the **Prophet Muhammad**. *Pasban Khatm e-Nabuwwat* has also taken up arms against the **Ahmadiyya Muslim Community** within the country. In fact, the group was able to get the Pakistani Parliament to declare the Ahmadiyyas infidels in 1974. Since then, reportedly hundreds of Ahmadiyyas have been murdered, mostly at the hands of *Pasban Khatm e-Nabuwwat* affiliates. This radical group has also been successful in influencing other Pakistanis to be aggressive toward members of the unorthodox Muslim community. *See also* HERESY; *JAHILI* SOCIETIES.

PAST/*AL-MADI*. One significant feature of **Islam** is its almost complete disregard of past applications of **government**, **theology**, **jurisprudence**, and so forth. Even earlier scholars had claimed that their doctrines were never intended to be for prolonged use and were created merely to deal with a current social climate at hand; that is, in Islamic thought, the past is something that should remain forgotten, and new **innovations** should take place since society and its needs change. However, that is not to say that former ideas were not **legitimate** since they did apply the teachings of **Allah**, the **Quran**, and the **Hadiths**. In addition, it should be stressed that the past way of the **Prophet Muhammad**, his companions, and the following generations of **caliphs** is the desired way of life for many Islamic **fundamentalists**. On the other hand, the fundamentalists argue that the past should be looked at by reexamining the way of life as exemplified by the Salafs (pious ancestors) but reformulated and transformed, along with textual interpretations, in the formation of an **Islamic society**. The past, therefore, should serve only as a model, not an entity deserving of literal emulation. Using this discourse, it is believed that Muslims can establish a **modern** civilization without turning their backs on its history. Therefore, the past should be a heavy inspiration and viewed as the ideal for modern society but cannot and should not be imitated exactly. *See also* MODERNITY; SALAFI.

PATANI UNITED LIBERATION ORGANIZATION (PULO). The PULO was established in 1998 and has become the largest militant Muslim organization in southern Malaysia. Its political wing is called the New PULO and has a more visible Islamic ideology.

PEACE/*AL-SALAM*. In radical Islamic doctrine, peace is based on the dominance of one group over another, and this would result in the establishment of **justice** and therefore peace. However, peace is a gradual process that must first take place in the individual, then the family, and finally the society. It must happen primarily in the individual because it is within man that a positive, spiritual peace can exist and the soul can be cleansed. When peace encompasses the family, justice becomes a foundation on which the rest of society can build. In his discourse *Peace in Islam* (*Al-Salami fi Al-Islam*), **Hasan al-Banna** uses Quranic explanations to emphasize how peace must grow in this way. He further states that differences in ideologies or politics must not be treated with contempt but rather can be used as a way to understand others' differences. With this notion, mercy becomes the avenue for peace. However, this understanding is conditioned by the guarantee that Islamic practices and dogmas must never be undermined or repressed. Peace relies on nonviolence, **justice**, and no entity getting in the way of **Islam**'s *da'wa* (call). To many of the fundamentalists, Islam is the only way to gain peace because it adheres to all these guidelines. *See also DAR AL-HARB*; VIOLENCE.

***PEMUDA*/YOUTH.** This organization of Muslim Youth in the south of Thailand was established as a charitable organization along with the *Pusaka* (Heritage) group. These two groups, *Pemuda* and *Pusaka*, were founded to create a new generation of Muslim separatists that would become responsible for the recovery of the Islamist insurgency in January 2004.

PENTAGON GROUP. A Philippine criminal organization, the Pentagon Group is active in the Muslim area of Mindanao and was formed by members of the **Moro Islamic Liberation Front**.

***PERSANTUAN ISLAM*/ORGANIZATION OF ISLAM.** Created in 1923 in Bandung, *Persantuan Islam* was a radical reform movement that was founded by Natsir Muhammad. Although small in size, it had an important influence on radical **Islam** in Indonesia.

PESHAWAR SEVEN. Officially formed in May 1985 when seven Afghani *mujahideen* groups aligned together to fight in the Soviet-Afghan War (1979–1989), the Peshawar Seven represented a united front that was comprised of both political Islamists and **fundamentalists**. Predominantly of **Sunni Muslim** groups, its members included the Khalis Faction, *Hizb-e-Islami*, *Jamaat-e-Islami*, the Islamic Union for the Liberation of Afghanistan, the **National Islamic Movement of Afghanistan**, the Afghanistan National Liberation Front, and the Revolutionary Islamic Movement.

Prior to its formal organization, this group was originally a loosely organized political union since May 1979. This formation was in reaction to the **Pakistani** government's restriction of foreign powers providing aid to the country. Coming mostly from **Saudi Arabia** and the **United States**, this decrease in accessible funds was imposed to hinder the advances of resistance groups within Pakistan. These seven groups were then provided with supplies, monies, and other resources by the Inter-Service Intelligence, which distributed them in Peshawar, Pakistan, hence the name.

Saudi Arabia certainly made sure that the assistance was still given to these *mujahideen* groups not only to present itself as being anticommunist (with the Soviet invasion of **Afghanistan** that took place shortly after) and pro-Muslim but also to combat **Iran**'s increasing popularity in the Muslim world. This was due to the formation of Iran's **Tehran Eight**, which assisted the **Shiite** Afghanis on similar pretenses. The United States under the Jimmy Carter administration also continued to send supplies via Pakistan to help the Afghan fighters resist the Soviet forces. During this period, the support provided by the Peshawar Seven proved to be the greatest and most dominant external backing for the Sunni *mujahideen* resistance fighters in Afghanistan.

PHILOSOPHY/*FALSAFA*. A negative association is frequently applied to philosophy, especially in the eyes of the radical **fundamentalists** (although moderate ones often agree on this point). As explained sufficiently by **Sayyid Qutb**, in the past when many Muslims were influenced by the Greek philosophers (notably Aristotle), they started to construct an **Islamic society** based on the **Western** notions of **reason** and logic that the Greek philosophical schools produced. They did this because they felt that it was this new discourse that was the most mature and universal way of thinking and thereby turned their backs on the fundamentals of **Islam**. In the fundamentalists' perception, this then led to disharmony and corruption because *tawhid* was replaced by the **pagan** theoretical political and ideological trend. So, with this **history** in mind, it is understandable why many Islamic fundamentalists reject the application of philosophy when discussing Islamic doctrine.

PLEDGE. *See* ALLEGIANCE.

PLURALISM/*TA 'ADDUDIYYA*. Although political pluralism (a multi-party **system**) is generally a moderate **fundamentalist** view, these Islamic leaders do believe that the lack of political pluralism is at the root of many of **Islam**'s societal problems. Therefore, it is also the cause of much of the contemporary violence in the Muslim world. Moderate fundamentalists wish to be included within the **government** sector along with other religious groups. They believe that this multicultural participation will lead to **justice** and **peace**, and thereby be the salvation of Islam. When adopting this system of government, it is important to apply **Islamization** in order to distance the Muslim government from that of the **West**. *See also* ISLAMIC POLITICAL PARTIES.

POPULAR ARAB AND ISLAMIC CONFERENCE. Also referred to as "the Congress" or "General Assembly," the Popular Arab and Islamic Conference (*Al-Mutamar Al-Arabi Al-Shabi Al-Islami*) took place from 25 to 28 April 1991 in Khartoum, **Sudan**. Orchestrated by **National Islamic Front** leader **Hassan al-Turabi**, the Congress was organized to unify various *mujahideen* and Islamic insurgent groups. After the **Iraqi** defeat in the Gulf War, there was a great need within the Islamic community to create a unified front and thereby continue with the goal of pan-Arabism and **pan-Islamism**. The Congress hoped to align the Islamists under a single nationalist cause by putting all conflicts aside to work toward a greater end. The main function of the conference, which was intended to be an annual event, was to serve as a forum for discussion among different **extremist** leaders and members of the Islamic cause.

Attendees of the Popular Arab and Islamic Conference allegedly included **Osama bin Laden**, Ilich Ramírez Sánchez (**Carlos the Jackal**), **Ayman al-Zawahiri**, and members of **Hamas**, *Hizbullah*, and the **Iranian Revolutionary Guard**. However, it was reported that some 300 Sudanese and 200 representatives from 45 other countries were also in attendance. Among the issues discussed at the General Assembly were the installation of an Islamist government in Sudan, making Khartoum a base for future meetings of this sort, setting up Afghan-Arab training camps in Khartoum, and obtaining financial and military support from the other Islamic countries represented to ensure the survival of the cause. The Popular Arab and Islamic Conference offered a great opportunity for increased cooperation, especially under the direction of al-Turabi, who had past experiences in the **Muslim Brotherhood in Sudan** and the National Islamic Front. But it has not been convened since.

PROPHET MUHAMMAD (570–632). Born in Mecca, **Saudi Arabia**, the Prophet Muhammad is considered to be the personification of moral and ethical righteousness in **Islam**. In Islamic **history**, **Allah** chose Muhammad as his final prophet and recited the **Quran** to him so that he could spread His doctrines throughout the world. Years later, his companions would compile and record Muhammad's words on Islam, creating the **Hadiths** (also known as the Traditions, or *Sunna*, of the Prophet).

The history of the Prophet Muhammad is commonly acknowledged as follows. Working as the average man would, Muhammad became discontent with his existence and in 610 left his banal life behind and went into the mountains to contemplate his life. While there, Allah spoke to Muhammad, revealing what would become the Quran. After this awakening, Muhammad returned to Mecca in 620 and began to spread the words of Allah. Although he gained his companions and followers, they were nevertheless confronted with hostilities and were driven to Medina. While in Medina, Muhammad attracted thousands of followers and returned to Mecca in 630, conquering the city. Shortly after, the Prophet fell ill and died, but by then almost the entirety of the Arabian Peninsula had converted to Islam, resulting in the first-ever pan-Arabian unification.

Muhammad is especially important to the **Sunni** school of Islam, for its adherents follow precisely the teachings and behavioral examples that are explicitly outlined in the Hadiths, hence their namesake. Sunni Muslims strictly apply the guidelines of these "Sayings of the Prophet" to their lives in everyday as well as spiritual practices. The long-standing point of contention between Sunni Islam and **Shia Islam** is actually centered on the Hadiths.

Where the *Sunna* of the Prophet is the guideline for Sunnis, Shiites take into greater consideration the teachings of his cousin, Ali ibn Abi Talib.

Muhammad is then incredibly important for the Islamic **fundamentalists**, especially as most of them are **Salafi**. This devotion goes further since not only do these fundamentalists believe that the Prophet is the sole example of how humans should act and worship here on earth, but they also wish for all people to live exactly in the image and likeness of Muhammad, his companions, and the immediate ancestors who followed (known as the Pious Ancestors, or *Salaf al-Salih*).

As one can see, the names of these different schools and sects of Islam are etymologically related to their devotion to the Prophet and his companions. Further, each and every Islamic movement or group uses quotes from the Hadiths that correspond and illuminate their specific ideologies. For example, **jihadi** groups will constantly quote from Muhammad's sayings about the holy struggle and therefore will view him as the model for defending Islam, whereas Sufists will use more peaceful sayings of the Prophet because that is how they choose to approach promoting Islam. Thus, by examining the name of a group, the name of its school in Islam, and the sayings from the Prophet that it utilizes, one can determine the ideologies and goals of these groups.

Q

QABALAN, JAMAL AL-DIN (1926–1995). Founder of the radical movement the Union of Islamic Associations and Groups of Turkey, Qabalan has also served as the deputy head of religious affairs in Turkey. A supporter of the *Milli Selamet Partisi* (National Salvation Party) branch *Munazzamat Al-Nazra Al-Wataniyya* (Organization of the National Perspective), he was given the moniker the "Black Voice" and even set up an Islamic "embassy" in Germany. In Anatolia, Turkey, during the late 1970s, when an **Islamic state** was declared there, he was named **caliph** and called for the abolition of secularism. He also accused all Turkish leaders of being **apostates**, including *Milli Selamet Partisi* leader **Necmettin Erbakan**, because of their devotion to a secular state.

AL-QADARIYYA/**THE LIBERTARIANS.** Ideologically similar and a derivative of the *al-Mu'tazila* school of **Islam**, *al-Qadariyya* takes its name from the doctrine that refers to predestination. Ideologically, it asserts that evil is a creation not of **Allah** but of man and that in creating man Allah also gave him free will—which is the provenance of all evil. This free will, in turn, gives power to man and the ability to fully act and be without Allah's **divine governance**. This stance led to its believers being ostracized within the Muslim community, and they were often labeled heretics for their position on free will. These views on the origins of evil and man's possession of free will is what makes *al-Qadariyya* one of the most unique and controversial schools of Islam. *See also* HERESY.

QADHAFI, MUAMMAR (1942–2011). Commonly referred to as Colonel Qadhafi, the former Libyan ruler Muammar Qadhafi took power over the country after a bloodless military coup d'état on 1 September 1969 led by the Revolutionary Command Council, resulting in his becoming one of the longest-ruling nonroyal leaders of the century. He attended the Libyan military academy in Benghazi from 1961 to 1966 but reached only the rank of lieutenant when he rose to power in 1969 despite his formal title of colonel. The Israeli defeat of the Arab armies in 1967 aroused feelings of Arab nationalism since it was felt that the monarchies that were leading many of the

Arabic states were not strong enough to protect the interests of the people. Using this banner of Arab nationalism, Qadhafi and his forces rather easily took control of **Libya** from King Idris, the first and only king of Libya, who ruled from 1951 to 1969. Afterward, the country was formally declared the Libyan Arab Republic.

After gaining power, Qadhafi redrafted the Libyan **constitution** and based the revised **legislation** on what he referred to as the Third International Theory. His political ideologies were outlined in detail in his 1975 publication *The Green Book.* Made mandatory reading in Libyan schools, his underlying theory combined Islamic socialism with Arab nationalism, which also underscored the prestige of military education and participation. In the early years of his regime, Libya's booming oil exports resulted in the country achieving some of the highest standards of living in Africa. This also allowed an upper-class and oil-rich entrepreneurial class (most of whom were patrons of the Qadhafi regime) to control the bulk of the wealth in the country, resulting in a large lower-class and impoverished populace.

In fact, only three months after gaining control of the country, a rebellion broke out but was quickly put down. Immediately thereafter, Colonel Qadhafi made all political dissent and insurrection illegal. He also created Revolutionary Committees to control and monitor any acts of resistance, often imprisoning or executing political nonconformists. Throughout his reign, several **assassination** attempts on his life were made. His close alliance with **Egypt** was a constant throughout his regime and a relationship that many in the population were weary of. Throughout the 1970s, power and control within the country were monopolized by Qadhafi's family and followers, and he even sought to remove **Western** oil companies and their interests from Libya. The laws and regulations that were imposed on social life were also incredibly strict and led to a constant stream of imprisonments and arrests and an overwhelming rise of a strict **Islamic society**.

Qadhafi continued to promote this Islamism, especially in the Maghreb, claiming that he wanted to unify the North African states under one **Islamic state** of the Sahel. Through this, he also supported the Islamization of Chad and **Sudan** by allowing their Islamic forces to set up bases within Libya. In 1972, he created the Islamic Legion in the hope of foisting this **pan-Islamic** nation on North Africa. During this time, he also tried to strengthen his ties with Egypt, especially with the Arab Socialist Union, but to no avail, especially while Anwar al-Sadat was in power (1971–1980). Outraged by Egypt's rebuking of a Libyan-Egyptian union and Egypt's participation in the Camp David Accords, a small war broke out between the two nations from 21 to 24 July 1977. During the late 1970s and the 1980s, Qadhafi's Islamic Legion was losing influence, and plans of union with other African states (notably Chad, **Morocco**, and **Tunisia**) repeatedly failed. Libya soon began to engage in conflicts with these nations, especially Chad in 1987 (known as the Toyota War).

Qadhafi's international reputation and foreign policy continued to attract negative attention throughout the 1970s, 1980s, and 1990s. The first serious blow was due to the **Pan-Am Flight 103 bombing** in 1988. Equally negative in certain ways was his expulsion of approximately 30,000 Palestinians living within Libya's borders in response to the 1995 Israeli peace negotiations with the **Palestinian Liberation Organization**. Questions of Libya's possession of weapons of mass destruction during this time also arose and peaked in 2003 when the **United States** began its policy of investigating such allegations. However, during the turn of the century, Qadhafi began to publicly stress his disappointment with his pan-Arab movement and how Arab nationalism had failed to materialize. He turned his diplomacy instead to the support of African nations, especially to aid **Omar al-Bashir** in Sudan, while sealing many African alliances. In fact, on 1 February 2009, Qadhafi was elected for a one-year term as president of the African Union. Beyond Africa, the Qadhafi regime also supported radical groups, such as the **Moro Islamic Liberation Front**.

With the **Arab Spring** revolutions taking place in neighboring Tunisia and Egypt, by February 2011, protests began in Libya as well. On 17 February 2011, massive social demonstrations and rebellions broke out within the country aimed directly at overthrowing the Qadhafi regime. Serious resistance came from the pro-Qadhafi forces, and the situation within the country quickly worsened and turned more violent. The anti-Qadhafi rebels then established a base in Benghazi and named a National Transitional Council (NTC). By March, the United Nations became directly involved in the protection of civilians against the warfare that was taking place. The following month, NATO forces also intervened, and Libya was declared to be in a state of civil war. The intense brutality that Qadhafi's forces used against the rebels also resulted in his being charged by the UN International Criminal Court.

In August 2011, after the Battle of Tripoli, Qadhafi fled to his hometown of Sirte, where the final stronghold of the pro-Qadhafi forces was located. The Qadhafi regime formally lost power on 16 September 2011 when the NTC obtained Libya's seat in the United Nations. However, while the rebellion expanded its position to wipe out any remains of the dictatorship, he was located in Sirte. The NTC announced that Qadhafi was captured while traveling in a convoy the previous day by a group of rebels just outside. After being beaten by the group, he was shot on 20 October 2011 and later buried at an unknown location in the desert.

AL-QAEDA. This global, multifaceted **Sunni** Islamic **fundamentalist** umbrella group is probably the most well-known **extremist** and **terrorist** organization in the world. Founded by the Saudi **Osama bin Laden** in August 1988, al-Qaeda's ideological platform hinges on the necessity of the **jihad** to establish a **pan-Islamic** state. Al-Qaeda has claimed responsibility for numerous attacks and the deaths of thousands over the past two decades. Its **World Trade Center and Pentagon attacks of September 11, 2001** even prompted the U.S. "War on Terror" campaign, which began in October 2001 and continued officially until President Barack Obama declared an "end" to his predecessor's "war on terror" on 23 January 2009. However, it was the **East African United States Embassy attacks** in 1998 that originally brought al-Qaeda to the attention of the media.

Ideologically, the group is totally against any **Western** presence or non-Muslim influences, seeks the establishment of a **caliphate** and the implementation of *sharia* (Islamic law), and even opposes schools of **Islam** that are not Sunni (leading to even more sectarian violence). In 1998, al-Qaeda was also known under the name "International Islamic Front for Jihad against the Crusaders and the Jews"—further illustrating its agenda. The term "al-Qaeda," interestingly enough, comes from the Arabic word meaning "base." This refers to fundamentals as a base and a militaristic type of base. Although the group dominates the contemporary jihadist movement and influences many other groups, it is by no means the only driving force behind contemporary Islamic fundamentalist extremism.

After Osama bin Laden's death on 2 May 2011, **Ayman al-Zawahiri** was made *amir* of the organization on 16 June 2011. The *shura* council of al-Qaeda consists of an estimated 20 to 30 people who transmit orders among the various al-Qaeda groups and still remains a unified but decentralized whole. Under the *shura* council, there is also a military committee that focuses its efforts on recruitment, training, arms acquisition, and tactical intelligence. A committee that concerns itself only with monetary funding of the group also exists. Through the *hawala* system, members of this committee ensure the financial solvency of al-Qaeda. There are also committees that deal with issuing *fatwas*, reviewing Islamic law decrees, and providing media outlets (in 2005, the *As-Sahab* production team was created in order to maintain all media communication facilities internally).

With regard to membership, al-Qaeda has several thousand adherents and has even aligned itself with other like-minded militant groups—in some cases absorbing them into the al-Qaeda organization and creating new branches (as is the case with **al-Qaeda in Iraq** and **al-Qaeda in the Islamic Maghreb**). It is also common practice for groups to **pledge** (*bay'a*) their alliance not only to al-Qaeda but also to its leaders when creating relationships. In doing this, it is perceived that all actions that the newly aligned group undertakes are therefore in the name of al-Qaeda as a whole. In addition, the group's leadership is highly decentralized and therefore efficient in both delegation and execution. Since al-Qaeda is present in multiple countries and continents, this type of structure is the key to its internal stability. The groups that directly fall under the banner of al-Qaeda include the **East Turkestan Islamic Movement**, the **Egyptian Islamic Jihad**, the Somali *Shebaab* Movement (*Harakat al-Shabaab*), the **Libyan Islamic Fighting Group**, **al-Qaeda in the Arabian Peninsula**, al-Qaeda in Iraq, and al-Qaeda in the Islamic Maghreb.

Tactically, the group implements primarily the use of **suicide bombings** and could be considered the group that has projected the issue of Islamic **martyrdom** into Western knowledge. Al-Qaeda has even issued *fatwas* to justify its **jihad**. It has been estimated that the militants active in the al-Qaeda system are so well trained, well organized, and numerous that they could easily carry out the missions of the father group without ever being given any direct orders. They could also sustain themselves quite well if ever communications were completely cut off from al-Qaeda leaders and its cadres. This military effectiveness is due partly to the fact that many members of the al-Qaeda forces are **Afghan Arabs** and former *mujahideen* and therefore are in possession of vast experience and tactical knowledge. Al-Qaeda has also taken advantage of domestic terrorist tactics as well as international ones. The domestic tactics are unique in that they target the people of their country and its leaders in the hope of toppling the regime and undermining the economy, which would then destroy the state and make way for the desired **Islamic state** to be established.

It can be argued that the ideology of al-Qaeda has its basis in the Islamic revivalist movement, which has been operating throughout the Muslim world for the past half century. **Sayyid Qutb** has also been noted as being the most influential radical Islamic thinker who has influenced the group. The organization has developed this austere notion of Islam into not only an ideology but also a way of life. Following Qutb's discourses, to al-Qaeda adherents, Islamic fundamentalism should dictate all facets of everyday life for the devoted Muslim—going beyond mere worship. The present leader of al-Qaeda, al-Zawahiri (who also was second in command to bin Laden), strongly supported Qutb's ideologies and studied them at length. Probably the most influential of Qutb's discourses was the idea that **apostates** could be prosecuted under *sharia*, which would therefore give **legitimacy** to al-Qaeda's jihad.

The formation and rise of al-Qaeda can be divided into four sections: development, consolidation, growth, and networking. The development period started with the Soviet-Afghan War (1979–1989). As the communist forces began to take control of **Afghanistan**, the United States became involved in order to thwart the advances of the Eastern bloc troops. As the Afghan Arabs launched their jihad against the Soviet Union, the United States began to provide them with tactical and military support, fueling their fight. Many of these *mujahideen* were also adherents of the extremist brand of Islam, so, in providing for the *mujahideen*, the United States was also promoting the Islamic radicals by proxy. During this time, Osama bin Laden was also rising in the Afghan Arab ranks and by the close of the insurgency was one of its leading fighters. Meanwhile, prominent Islamists also began to notice the vigor that the *mujahideen* displayed during the war, especially after finally expelling the Soviet troops in 1989. Many affluent Muslims (especially from **Saudi Arabia**) started donating money to the *mujahideen* cause and created camps for them within Afghanistan. However, this resulted in many of the Afghan Arabs being displaced, and various alliances were formed in an almost chaotic manner.

While these various groups of fighters were living austerely, there seemed to be a common belief that their Islamic program should not be restricted only to Afghanistan. Many wanted to continue their jihad in other areas. Of these many pockets of fighters, one was led by bin Laden. This group held its first meetings in August 1988. While still in Afghanistan, the group constructed its platform of Islamic fundamentalism and proclaimed its further promotion of the jihad. Soon, other similar groups joined bin Laden's plea that unity among the Islamists would lead to greater advances.

After leaving Afghanistan in 1990, bin Laden returned to his native Saudi Arabia and offered the kingdom the assistance of his militant force—an assistance that was needed because of the **Iraqi** invasion of Kuwait in August of that year that threatened Saudi Arabia. When **al-Saud** turned down the help of al-Qaeda forces in favor of American military aid, the group went to **Sudan** in 1992. Here, the pan-Islamic ideas began to spread, especially in light of Saudi Arabia seeking non-Muslim help for the protection of the lands that are integral to Islam (Mecca and Medina). Al-Qaeda was welcomed in Sudan by **Hassan al-Turabi**, and time that members spent there was interesting, especially since the country had just experienced a military coup d'état that resulted in the government being revamped on the basis of Islamic ideals. This made it even easier for al-Qaeda to spread and grow.

Meanwhile, the Egyptian Islamic Jihad (which was now an intrinsic segment of al-Qaeda) was becoming more aggressive in its attacks in **Egypt**, and bin Laden's verbal criticism against Saudi Arabia was increasing as well. These events eventually resulted in the al-Qaeda organization being exiled from Sudan in 1996 because of international pressure on the Sudanese government. The group then returned to Afghanistan and rejoined its *mujahideen* brothers who had remained in the country. This was the same year that the

Taliban army rose to power in Afghanistan. Ideologically and structurally similar to al-Qaeda, the group already had strong support from the Afghan Arabs, and al-Qaeda soon came to recognize its **legitimacy**. In September 1996, the Taliban captured the capital of Kabul and claimed the land as the "Islamic Amirate of Afghanistan." This atmosphere in Afghanistan made it possible for al-Qaeda to develop and propagate itself freely. The two groups began to rule the country with a shared militancy and were largely insulated from any opposing forces. Although the Taliban army was declared the official rulers of the land, they provided al-Qaeda with a cover of protection.

In Kashmir, al-Qaeda also attracted the interest of the ***Harakat-ul-Mujahideen*** organization, which declared its support of the former's jihad against the **West** in 1998. The group was attracted to al-Qaeda's rage against the West (and specifically the American forces) since the West's diplomatic relations with India supported the Indian acquisition of the Jammu and Kashmir regions. This support clearly caused separatist groups such as *Harakat-ul-Mujahideen* to favor any military front that would be conducive to the removal of Jammu and Kashmir from Indian control. Al-Qaeda's supposed relationship with **Pakistan**'s Inter-Services Intelligence also further supported this alignment. In 2001, there were also reports that *Harakat-ul-Mujahideen* was harboring bin Laden and other high-profile al-Qaeda leaders within the Pakistani-controlled portions of Kashmir. Pakistani-based Kashmiri groups such as ***Harakat-ul-Jihad al-Islami***, ***Jaish-e-Muhammad***, and ***Lashkar-e-Tayyiba*** have also been allegedly affiliated with al-Qaeda. These allegations are due to the relationship that many leaders within these groups have with al-Qaeda senior officers.

However, after the 11 September 2001 World Trade Center and Pentagon attacks when U.S. forces entered Afghanistan, the Taliban army (which refused to surrender bin Laden) was swiftly ousted, and al-Qaeda relocated to the Pakistani border. Yet, by this time, despite the American pressure, al-Qaeda had already effectively spread its pan-Islamic jihadist program through most of the Middle East, North Africa, and parts of Asia through its vast system of networking.

The American presence in the Middle East did result in some advantages for al-Qaeda, however. For example, when U.S. forces toppled the **Baathist** Iraqi regime in 2003, this allowed many Islamic groups (which were formerly repressed) to grow within the country. Al-Qaeda saw this as a beneficial event and in September 2004 established al-Qaeda in Iraq after aligning itself with **Abu Musab al-Zarqawi**'s ***Jamaat al-Tawhid wa al-Jihad***. Within Iraq, the **Shiite** community (which was arguably the most repressed group during the Baathist regime) began to increase its influence, and the Sunni al-Qaeda saw this union as a chance to undercut these efforts. A jihad against Iraqi Shiites was then declared, and many Shiite people and locations were attacked by *Tanzim Qaidat al-Jihad fi Bilad al-Rafidayn* (Organization of Jihad's Base in the Land of Two Rivers; al-Qaeda in Iraq's official title). This sectarian violence, marked mostly by suicide bombings, came to a peak by 2007.

By the middle of the decade, al-Qaeda also began to concentrate a majority of its training camps and bases along the Afghanistan-Pakistan border and gain influence in African nations like **Algeria**, **Mali**, and **Somalia**. On 11 September 2006, al-Qaeda in the Islamic Maghreb was officially announced and has been active in the Sahara Desert regions of the continent. Since its inception, the group has grown into a formidable force, and **violence** in North Africa has increased because of it. It became such an influential force in the African country that, by 2009, Somalia's *al-Shabaab* pledged allegiance to al-Qaeda. Because of bin Laden's animosity against the Saudi regime, an al-Qaeda network was placed there for quite some time and in January 2009 merged itself with its comrades in **Yemen** to form al-Qaeda in the Arabian Peninsula and based itself in Yemen.

Even in the United States, al-Qaeda has contingents. The most notorious leader was **Anwar al-Awlaki**. A spiritual motivator and Islamic recruiter, almost every notable al-Qaeda affiliate that has been on American soil has had a relationship with him. These include three of the 11 September 2001 hijackers, Fort Hood shooter **Nidal Malik Hasan**, and possibly **John Phillip Walker Lindh**. For the past decade, he was the primary American-born voice in promotion of the jihad against the Western forces. Al-Awlaki was successful in using propaganda methods, such as his online publication *Inspire*, which effectively combines Western communication techniques and Islamic ideological content.

With regard to communication of propaganda, since 2001, al-Qaeda has focused almost all its efforts on online media outlets. Since publication of periodicals or pamphlets and the like is too easily restricted in many of the countries in which the group located, the Internet has proven to be a viable and fluid tool for the organization to spread its ideologies. Over the years, its methods have increased in both sophistication and breadth. Its forums now encompass a variety of subjects and can be accessed in multiple languages in various countries. The publicity that the Internet has provided for the group has become an invaluable resource for its networking, financing, and recruitment as well. A variety of media is also used, such as videos, sound recordings, photographs, and testimonials. Many are impressively stylized and use common **master narratives** that are easily recognizable and relatable to the group's audience. In addition, by creating its own online platforms, al-Qaeda avoids the risk of other third-party distributors editing or removing significant portions of its content. However, many of these sites and online publications are highly monitored and often are swiftly removed by internal security agents in a large number of countries.

Although the al-Qaeda network has continued to spread its ideologies and remains the most formidable jihadist organization in the world, the group is by no means supported by a large number of Islamic fundamentalists. The group's brutality against fellow Muslims and its civilian domestic violence have been the main causes of opposition by many Islamic scholars and militants. Many moderate Islamists also do not fully support the jihadi doctrine against the West or are highly critical of it and therefore of al-Qaeda since it is al-Qaeda's primary ideology. Interestingly enough, one of the first supporters of al-Qaeda, Egyptian Islamic Jihad ideologue Sayyed Imam al-Sharif, even retracted his support for the group in his 2007 publication *Wathiqat Tarshid Al-'Amal Al-Jihadi fi Misr wa al-'Alam* (Rationalizing Jihad in Egypt and the World). The general public's support of al-Qaeda in many countries has also been slowly declining since 2008, according to reports. Yet the organization continues to prosper throughout Africa, the Middle East, and South Asia.

Although there is no doubt that the 2 May 2011 death of bin Laden had an impact on al-Qaeda's morale, the group proved resilient and has been persistent in its insistence that although the group owed a big debt to him and that he was an obvious asset, he was merely one man. Al-Qaeda continued by stating that the movement is greater than one person but that bin Laden will always be held up as one of the greatest **martyrs** because of his accomplishments. Throughout the 2011 events of the **Arab Spring**, al-Qaeda initially remained rather quiet despite many reports that certain demonstrations were instigated by the organization. As the year passed, al-Qaeda eventually announced more and more support for various rebellions, but it seems as if the group is letting the events fully take their course before influencing the newly rearranged states. *See also* AL-QAEDA IN THE ISLAMIC MAGHREB IN ALGERIA; AL-QAEDA IN MALI; AL-QAEDA IN MAURITANIA.

AL-QAEDA IN THE ARABIAN PENINSULA (AQAP). A branch of the **al-Qaeda** organization, AQAP is active mostly in **Saudi Arabia** and **Yemen**. Formerly led by **Osama bin Laden**, it shares in the same **jihadi**-Islamic **fundamentalist** ideologies as its umbrella group but focuses its operations on overthrowing the **al-Saud** kingdom. It was officially formed in January 2009 after al-Qaeda's Saudi and Yemenite branches coalesced. However, the Saudi governmental and security forces have been successful in containing AQAP advances in the country for some years. This has led many of its militants and affiliates to remain based in Yemen.

AQAP remains al-Qaeda's most dynamic and dangerous faction outside **Afghanistan** and **Pakistan**. It is even sometimes considered to be more active and hostile than its umbrella organization. AQAP has a rich history in Yemen, especially since that is the ancestral land of bin Laden, and his forces had been operational there for some time well before the actual organization of what is formally known as al-Qaeda. Countless attacks and insurgencies have been conducted in the name of AQAP, including the August 2009 attempted **assassination** of Saudi Prince Muhammad bin Nayef, the so-called Christmas Day Bombing in Detroit on 25 December 2009, the 3 September 2010 crash of a UPS Boeing 747 in Dubai, and the initiation in November 2010 of what the group referred to as "Operation Hemorrhage," which sought to launch a large number of small-scale attacks on American soil, among many others. AQAP has also called for **Somalia**'s *Harakat Al-Shabaab Al-Mujahideen* to assist the organization in its call for jihad and especially during its 8 February 2010 blockade of the Red Sea.

The group possesses an online media platform for generating propaganda and spreading its ideologies called *Sada al-Malahim*, or "Echo of the Battlefield," and *Inspire*, the English-language online magazine. The unstable sociopolitical and economic conditions in Yemen have made it a suitable location for AQAP, as its **violence** can easily be fostered there amid the widespread corruption that already exists. In addition, many of its members come from the tribes of Yemen and therefore can operate even more freely since many operate within the tribal alliance system. AQAP continues to have the most dominant presence in the region surrounding Sanaa, where very little Yemenite governmental control exists. Notable members of AQAP have included **Anwar al-Awlaki**, Qassim al-Raimi, Ibrahim Suleiman al-Rubaysh, Said Ali al-Shihri, and Naser al-Wuhaysh. *See also* ALLEGIANCE.

AL-QAEDA IN IRAQ (AQI). The **Iraqi** branch of the **jihadist** militant group **al-Qaeda**, AQI was founded in 2003. Originally led by **Abu Musab al-Zarqawi**, a Jordanian extremist, the group was known as *Jamaat al-Tawhid wa al-Jihad* (translated as "Group of Monotheism and Jihad") until September 2004, when its allegiance was **pledged** to the al-Qaeda organization. However, when **Osama bin Laden** accepted Zarqawi's allegiance in 2004, the official name of the group was announced as *Tanzim Qaidat Al-Jihad fi Bilad Al-Rafidayn*, or "Organization of Jihad's Base in the Land of the Two Rivers." The group is comprised of both foreign and native Iraqis, Islamists, and Kurds.

Zarqawi obtained his military experience in the Soviet-Afghan War (1979–1989) and originally formed *Jamaat al-Tawhid wa al-Jihad* in the hope of overthrowing the Jordanian monarchy. To achieve this goal, he started networking with other militant Islamic organizations, such as *Ansar al-Islam*, *Fatah al-Islam*, and *Salafia Al-Mujahidia*, and relocated to Iraq. It was as a result of this that he developed relations with other **extremists**, leading to the group's merger with the much more prominent al-Qaeda.

Soon, the main goals of the group shifted from overthrowing the Jordanian monarchy to expelling the U.S. forces from Iraq, reforming the Iraqi government to one based on *sharia* (Islamic law), and, above all, establishing an **Islamic state**. Tactically, the group makes use of **suicide bombings**, improvised explosive devices, and the ransoming of hostages more than the conventional guerilla tactics that were characteristic of earlier insurgent groups. The group is spiritually advised by the Palestinian Abu Anas al-Shami and uses verses from both the **Quran** and the **Hadiths** to support its actions. Numerous high-profile attacks on civilian, humanitarian, religious, and secular entities have been executed at the hands of AQI members since its inception. The group has also successfully carried out the **assassination** of several prominent politicians, including Iraqi Governing Council President Ezzedine Salim and Egypt's Iraqi envoy Ihab al-Sherif and numerous UN and embassy personnel. In January 2006, AQI announced the formation of the *Mujahideen Shura* Council (MSC), a group that brought together six **Sunni** Islamic insurgent organizations in the hope of unifying them under the same cause to achieve greater effects and recruit more Iraqi Sunni nationalists. However, the group's reputation for violent force and civilian aggression impeded its attempts to gain substantial support.

MSC was then reformed as the Islamic State of Iraq (ISI), headed by Abu Abdullah al-Rashid al-Baghdadi. The ISI, as the name indicates, plans to overthrow the Iraqi government and replace it with a pure Sunni Islamic state of **governance**. AQI and its umbrella organizations continue to attract masses of new members and recruits, leading analysts to conclude that the group's strength is in the tens of thousands. AQI's affiliates are also not limited to Iraqi nationals, but considerable foreign support has been obtained by the group as well; in fact, a majority of its top leaders are not Iraqi. There is a large network of extremist groups from Europe, the Middle East, North Africa, and central and southern Asia all in alliance with each other within the same al-Qaeda enterprise.

On 7 June 2006, AQI suffered the loss of its leaders al-Zarqawi, Sheik Abd-al-Rahman, and Hamid Juma Faris Jouri al-Saeedi (deputy leader and second in command of AQI) at the hands of American allied forces. The Egyptian militant **Abu Ayyub al-Masri** (a.k.a. Abu Hamza al-Muhajir) assumed power after al-Zarqawi's death. AQI has also not limited itself to domestic Iraqi attacks but has also carried out strikes in **Egypt** and **Jordan**. The year 2007 saw some dissension between Sunni tribes and AQI as tribal members wanted to distance themselves from the increasingly aggressive AQI because of its aim to retain sole control over the Sunni Islamic communities. Many of these conflicts took place in and around the capital city of Baghdad, and AQI suffered for a brief period from a loss of support and popularity. However, in 2009, the United States began to withdraw many of its forces from Iraq, allowing AQI fighters to step up their attacks in order to further destabilize the country. This increase of Iraqi attacks also parallels an increase in native Iraqi members within the group. On 18 April 2010, AQI's al-Masri and the ISI's al-Baghdadi were killed during a U.S.-Iraqi strike near Tikrit in northwestern Iraq. According to reports, as of early June 2010, nearly 80 percent of the group's 42 leaders had been killed or captured. Al-Masri was replaced by Abu Suleiman Al-Nasser li-Din Allah as leader of AQI, but on 25 February 2011, he was killed in Hit in the Anbar province of Iraq. *See also JAYSH AL-ISLAM.*

AL-QAEDA IN THE ISLAMIC MAGHREB (AQIM). The most violent and active **Islamic group**, AQIM is a new manifestation of **Algeria**'s **Salafi Group for Preaching and Combat**. On 11 September 2006, the group was officially recognized by **al-Qaeda** as its representative in North Africa. AQIM's field of activity has shifted from Algeria to the larger Sahel and Sahara desert regions in the past years. The group's motives have also become more opportunistic rather than ideologically inspired since its merger with al-Qaeda. Drug trafficking and the ransoming of hostages are the main ways in which the group obtains financing. These actions have led to its classification as a criminal organization with a facade of religious ideology. The group preaches a global **jihad** against **Western** society and has roots in the Algerian Civil War of 1991.

With the adoption of its name, the group has displaced its focus from overthrowing the **government** in Algeria to a global warfare with the **Unites States**, Europe, and **Israel**. AQIM's targets are mainly Americans and Europeans touring, working, or living in northern Africa. The group primarily implements political and cultural propaganda to gain its support. The group is led by the Algerian **Abdelmalek Droukdel** (a.k.a. Abu Mussab Abd al-Wadud), and the main commanders in the Sahel region are **Moktar Belmokhtar** and **Abdelhamid Abu Zeid**. However, an extensive knowledge of AQIM's organizational structure is lacking, but it is known that the group is divided into geographic zones, each constituting a combatant unit (*kata'ib*). The entire organization is presided over by a national leadership that consists of the *amir*, religious scholars, a consultative committee (*shura*), a political committee, a financial committee, and a media committee. It is also understood that AQIM has more than 1,000 members who are mostly former **Afghan Arabs**, *mujahideen*, and other veterans from the Soviet-Afghan War (1979–1989). *See also* BIN LADEN, OSAMA; AL-QAEDA IN IRAQ; AL-QAEDA IN THE ISLAMIC MAGHREB IN ALGERIA.

AL-QAEDA IN THE ISLAMIC MAGHREB (AQIM) IN ALGERIA. Before becoming **al-Qaeda in the Islamic Maghreb** in 2007, the **Salafist Group for Preaching and Combat** was a militant organization that followed the Salafist ideology, sought the implementation of *sharia* (Islamic law), and encouraged the **jihad** in **Algeria**. Algeria, they believe, abandoned **Islam** and brought oppression on the Muslim people. Although the group has been reformulated as AQIM, its members still follow the same basic principles. AQIM is concentrated mostly in the Kabylia and Sahel regions of Algeria. However, Algerian forces have been relatively successful in assaulting AQIM forces in the Kabylia, compelling its members to relocate, although about 500 fighters still remain in the Kabylia region, forming the majority, while another 300 to 500 are located in the Sahel region. AQIM's leader, **Abdelmalek Droukdel**, has stated that a large portion of its *mujahideen* are Algerian and that **Osama bin Laden**'s financial backing provided the majority of its support. The group follows al-Qaeda's practices in implementing propaganda, recruiting the younger generations, videotaping, and **suicide bombings**.

However, AQIM claims that it does not target civilians in Algeria; rather, it targets the *taghut* (non-Islamic state). The most significant acts of suicide bombing took place in Algiers in April, September, and December 2007, when government buildings, security barracks, and the Constitutional Council were targeted, killing dozens of people. Similar attacks took place again in March, June, August, and October 2009, again resulting in a large number of casualties. Aside from suicide bombers, AQIM also adopted al-Qaeda's method of vehicle-born improvised explosive devices, leading to numerous casualties since 2007. However, this internationalization within AQIM has created some friction within the Algerian Islamist movement as the domestic focus has shifted. Certain methods adopted by AQIM, such as suicide bombings, have not been well received among the Algerian supporters, who claim that those tactics are repulsive to Algerian society.

As in the other countries, AQIM forces in Algeria also finance themselves through drug trafficking, smuggling of weapons, and the ransoming of foreign hostages. In the summer of 2010, AQIM received 3.8 million euros as ransom for two Spanish hostages. Canada, Austria, and France have also paid substantial amounts of money for the release of their nationals. AQIM has resorted to kidnapping Algerian citizens as well. In 2009, more than 20 Algerians were kidnapped from the Kabylia region. These actions have consequently deterred foreign investors from Algeria, resulting in a weakening of the current regime. This has been seen as positive for the Islamists and encourages their vicious activities. Despite these events, Algerian security forces claim that they had suppressed hundreds of AQIM members in 2009 and 2010 as a result of special operations. Algeria has also joined the

U.S.-led **Trans-Saharan Counter-Terrorism Initiative** in attempts to combat the Islamists in the Sahel-Maghreb region.

AL-QAEDA IN MALI. Since 2007, there has been an alarming increase in the number of kidnappings, operations, and attacks that have been carried out by **al-Qaeda of the Islamic Maghreb** (AQIM) in the northern region of **Mali**. AQIM bring their captives to the desert region since operatives have a large knowledge of the geography. The kidnappings not only supply monetary gain to AQIM through the ransoming of hostages but also drive possible investors away from the country, continuing the cyclic impoverishment and suffering of the lower classes. These oppressed citizens are also the targeted population that al-Qaeda tries to gain support from. AQIM forces in Mali also use routes in the Sahel that run to northern Mali for smuggling and the transportation of fighters. To improve their actions in the country, AQIM has formed ideological relations with some of the northern communities in Mali (namely, the Tuaregs), making their activities relatively unnoticed and constantly growing.

Although the group has yet to begin large-scale offensives in Mali, the radical Islamist activity still remains a grave threat to the country and its people. In July 2010, AQIM attacked an Algerian security post on the Algerian-Malian border, killing 11. In the same month, French, **Mauritanian**, and Malian forces attacked an AQIM camp in Mali in order to rescue a French hostage, Michel Germaneau, who was taken in April 2010. The counter-Islamist forces killed seven members of AQIM there, and Germaneau, who was not present at the camp, was later executed.

AL-QAEDA IN MAURITANIA. Throughout 2009, **al-Qaeda in the Islamic Maghreb** (AQIM) seriously disrupted political developments in the country. Overall support among the Mauritanian population is unclear, although local endorsement is highly unlikely given the minimal number of native Mauritanians who have participated in pro-Islamist activities. These participants are primarily from the younger, urban generations who may be influenced by the media's images of the conflicts in **Iraq** and **Afghanistan** and between the **Israelis** and **Palestinians**, among other causes. **Mauritania**'s large expanse of desert has made the country desirable for the group's operations, and the internal struggles between the two dominant populations (the "black Moor" Haratins and the "white Moor" Beidanes) have left the country susceptible to **terrorist** activity.

AQIM has altered Mauritanian positions and attitudes toward Islamists because of the group's increased violence and **government** repression. In June 2009, an American aid worker was killed in the capital of Nouakchott, and then, in July 2009, **Mauritania**'s first **suicide bombing** was carried out near the French embassy, injuring three people. AQIM has claimed responsibility for both of these attacks. Despite these terrorist activities, local political parties have supported military attacks against AQIM targets, notably on 22 July 2010, when Mauritanian and Malian security forces with French technical assistants raided an AQIM camp in northern **Mali** with the intention of rescuing a French hostage, Michel Germaneau. The attack resulted in the killing of seven AQIM members, and Germaneau was later reported to have been executed. The government's counterterrorism measures have included intensified security measures and the arresting of suspected Islamist activists in its crackdowns against Islamist activity. *See also* AL-QAEDA; AL-QAEDA IN MALI.

QAHTANIYA AND JAZEERA BOMBINGS. On 14 August 2007, in the **Iraqi** cities of Qahtaniya and Jazeera, four vehicles laden with explosives were simultaneously detonated by *istishhadyun*. The attacks resulted in the deaths of an estimated 796 and injured at least 1,562 people, mostly of Kurdish descent. Although no group claimed responsibility for the **bombings**, it has been speculated that it was the work of **al-Qaeda in Iraq**. The worst mass-casualty event since the 2003 U.S. occupation of Iraq, the coordinators of the attacks seem to have been **Sunni** Muslim extremists since both areas contain a large population of Yazidis and Kurds—two groups constantly denounced by Sunni radicals. The bombings are also believed to have been a result of diplomatic moves that the Iraqi Prime Minister Nouri al-Maliki was making to unite the different political groups within the parliament.

AL-QARADAWI, YUSUF. A member of the **Muslim Brotherhood** and a scholar from Al-Azhar University, al-Qaradawi is one of the most prominent Islamic figures of the moderate **fundamentalist** movement. His writings have influenced many and continue to do so. His popularity peaked when he came to **Egypt** (he was at the time living in Qatar) at the bequest of President Anwar al-Sadat and spoke during ceremonies that were attended by thousands. While in Qatar, he was the dean of the Faculty of Law at Qatar University. After Egyptian President Hosni Mubarak resigned on 11 February 2011, al-Qaradawi returned to Egypt and became one of the most popular scholars thanks to his show on the Al-Jazeera channel.

AL-QASIMI, JAMAL AL-DIN (1866–1914). A leading modernist and scholar of **Islam**, Jamal al-Din al-Qasimi lived in Damascus, **Syria**, where he was also the imam at the al-Sham mosque. Al-Qasimi spent the majority of his life traveling to different areas in the Arab world, including Jerusalem and

Medina. The varying forms of Islamic ideologies that al-Qasimi encountered led him to base the corpus of his work on dispelling rivalries between the schools of thought in Islam. Based on Arab nationalism, he advocated for diversity through unity and stressed the rationality driving Islamic thought. His written works vary from commentaries on exegesis, jurisprudence, **history**, **interpretations**, law, literature, **science**, and **theology**. Over 2,000 individual writings can be found by al-Qasimi. Even today, he remains influential in the modern reforms of Arab innovation, thought, understanding, and unity. See also MODERNITY; *AL SHARI'A*.

QATADA, ABU (1960–). Palestinian-born Islamist militant and dominant figure in the **al-Qaeda** organization, Abu Qatada was expelled from Kuwait after its liberation from **Iraq** in February 1991 because of his pro-Iraqi sentiments. In 1993, he then traveled to Great Britain, claiming asylum from religious persecution. In August 2005, he was arrested for being affiliated with the **London bombings of 7 July 2005**. He has been imprisoned in Britain ever since despite countless efforts of the government to deport him to **Jordan**. He was even sentenced to life imprisonment prior to his arrest by the Jordanian government in 2000 for his participation in a plot to bomb a millennium celebration in the country.

Before his arrest, Qatada served on the *fatwa* committee of al-Qaeda, was the spiritual guide for the organization's followers in Europe, and possessed close ties with the **Armed Islamic Group** (AIG), the **Salafi Group for Preaching and Combat**, and the **Tunisian Combatant Group**—even acting as the spokesperson for the AIG for some time. He was also in contact with many of the *mujahideen* participating in the **Chechen terrorism** and with the assailants of the **World Trade Center and Pentagon attacks of September 11, 2001**.

Ideologically, Qatada is a strong supporter of the global **jihad** and believes that no truce can ever be made between Muslim and non-Muslim countries. His release has been demanded by many groups over the years, including *Jaysh Al-Islam* and **Supporters of *Sharia***. *See also* SALAFI JIHADISM.

QURAN. The revealed word of **Allah**, the Quran (*Al-Quran*) is the founding, central, and commanding text of **Islam** for both social and ideological issues and literally means "recitation." It is composed of 114 chapters called *sourat* (the first is the *Fatiha* Opening). Each *sourat* is composed of 6,219 *ayat*, or "verses." Written in Arabic, Muslims believe that the Quran was verbally revealed through the angel Gabriel (*Jibril*) from Allah (God) to the **Prophet Muhammad** between the years 610 and 632. Muslims also regard the Quran as the main miracle of Muhammad, hence the proof of his "Prophethood"

(*I'jaz*). For the **religion**, it provides the moral and cardinal rules for *sharia* (Islamic law) and is the guide for gaining truth and **morality**.

According to Quranic doctrine, Allah has created man (the believer) so as to be His custodian until humanity has reached maturity. Because of his role, man tries to persuade others toward Islam not for personal gain but in order to create salvation. In other words, man should also be the guide of Islam. The guide should also not restrict himself to territorial boundaries (for those are man-made), but instead the call (*da'wa*) to Islam should be global. The Quran is seen as the ultimate source, and the level of man's **knowledge** will directly affect his **interpretation** of Allah's words. Therefore, this holy text is the only **legitimate** and eternal place to find revelation in Islam. Without adherence to the Quran, it is understood that man will never find salvation.

QURANIC PRESERVATION SOCIETY/*JAM'IYYAT AL-HIFADH 'ALA AL-QUR'AN*. Founded in 1970 at the Al-Zaytuna mosque in **Tunisia**, the group eventually became highly influential to many Tunisian political movements that emerged in the 1980s and 1990s (notably *Ennahda* **in Tunisia** and the Tunisian Islamic Renaissance Movement). The Quranic Preservation Society was originally supported by the Tunisian **government** as it sought to counteract the leftist groups that were emerging at the universities. However, soon it became a powerful way of social Islamization used by *Ennahda* to gain a broader, popular audience and influence. The Quranic Preservation Society opened many *kutatid* (Quranic schools) where the **Quran** was taught to young children.

QUTB, MUHAMMAD (1919–). Like his famous brother, **Sayyid Qutb**, Muhammad Qutb was a member of the **Muslim Brotherhood in Egypt** and served as an inspiration to many Islamic **fundamentalists**. Now living in **Saudi Arabia** and teaching his ideology in Mecca, Qutb also helped his brother write the influential *Al-Atyaf Al-Arab'a* (The Four Phantoms). Muhammad Qutb also mentored **Ayman al-Zawahiri**, who would later become a dominant member of the **Egyptian Islamic Jihad** organization and counselor to **Osama bin Laden**.

QUTB, SAYYID (1906–1966). A leading theologian, thinker, and founding radical Islamist, Sayyid Qutb was one of the most influential and daring figures in the **Muslim Brotherhood** in **Egypt**. From an early period, the Islamist was active in his literary career as both writer and critic. The author of 24 works that deal specifically with his perception of the cultural and political role of **Islam**, Qutb's most declarative work is his 30-volume *Fi Zilal Al- Quran* (In the Shade of the Quran). He is also the author of *Hadha*

Al-Din, *Ma'alim fi Al-Tariq*, and *Al-Mustaqbal li Hadha Al-Din* (The Future of the Hadha Religion). Qutb has been criticized as being the leading influence behind the **modern** Islamists and **jihadists** because of his encouragement of the use of **violence** to purge Islam of **Western** influences. Conversely, supporters have deemed him a visionary and **martyr**. In his discourse, he hoped to rework the modern view of Islam and support Islam's ability to be a basis for a civil society within Egypt and throughout the Arab world.

Born in Musha, Egypt, on 9 October 1906, Qutb was most likely influenced at an early age by his father, who was also a political activist. From 1929 to 1933, Qutb attended the university in Cairo and then became, in 1939, an official at the Ministry of Education. After receiving a grant to study **Western** educational methods, Qutb attended the University of Northern Colorado (then Colorado State College of Education), Stanford University, and Wilson Teachers' College (now District of Columbia Teachers College) from 1948 until 1950. While there, he published his first major work of social and theological critique, *Al-'Adala Al-Ijtima'iyya fi-l-Islam* (Social Justice in Islam). It is believed that this is the time when Qutb developed his contempt for American culture and materialism. Consequently, he developed anti-Western, anti-Zionist sentiments and heightened his pride as a member of the Muslim civilization. On his return to Egypt, he joined the Egyptian Muslim Brotherhood after resigning from his post at the Ministry of Education. Rising quickly, Qutb became the editor in chief of the Brotherhood's weekly propaganda publication, *Al-Ikhwan Al- Muslimin*, and a member of its **Shura** Council.

After the attempted **assassination** of Egyptian President Gamal Abdel Nasser in 1954, many Muslim Brotherhood members were imprisoned, including Qutb. During his incarceration, he wrote works that encompassed his radical antisecular and pro-Islamist beliefs based solely on a strict adherence and **interpretation** of the **Quran** and therefore further enforced his political **activism**. It is also understood that during his time in prison, he was subjected to harsh treatment, provoking him to move to an **extremist** platform of dissolving the state of Egypt. In 1964, he was released from confinement but only eight months later was again interned on accusations of plotting a coup and being involved with the Brotherhood's secret military branch. His trial concluded with corporal punishment, and, on 29 August 1966, he was hanged, making him a heroic martyr in the eyes of many Islamists.

Qutb's desire for the implementation of *sharia* (Islamic law) in a total **Islamic state** has remained the basis for many jihadists and Islamists, as he believed that these political doctrines were the only way to attain a purely beneficial **Islamic society**. His writings dealt primarily with the need for **divine governance** and true obedience to the Quran, which helped bring about an intellectual development for Islamic fundamentalism, especially among Muslim Brotherhood members and extremists alike. Qutb's beliefs that only Islam is the path to moral **justice** and civility has resulted in his becoming one of the premier revolutionary Islamists. He continues to influence Islamic fundamentalist groups throughout the world to this day. *See also* AL-AWLAKI, ANWAR.

R

***RABITAT AL-ALAM AL-ISLAMI* (RAI)/MUSLIM WORLD LEAGUE.**
RAI was a group of **Saudi Arabian** nongovernmental organizations involved in supporting Islamist fighters.

RABITAT-UL-MUJAHIDEEN*/LEAGUE OF THE *MUJAHIDEEN*.** The *Rabitat-ul-Mujahideen* was an informal organization that was created to meet in conference. It was first established in 1999 by Abu Bakar Bashir and Riduan Isamuddin Hambali to unite various Islamist organizations fighting for Southeast Asia in favor of the regional strategy of the ***Jemaah Islamiyah.

RADICALISM/*TATARRUF*. The defining feature when distinguishing between moderate and radical Islamic **fundamentalists** is that the radical Islamists seek to implement their agenda in every facet of daily life. Radicals usually claim that social incoherence, the exploitation of the population, political aggressions, and illegitimacy are rampant throughout society and that it is only through the application and return to a pure form of **Islam** that civilization can be saved. They also view ***shura*** (consultation) as being the most desirable legislative practice because it supports the public, not the **government** or the individual. Ideologically, radicalism is characterized by a strict adherence to dogmatic traditions and views any deviation from those teachings as **apostasy**. Politically, there is no desire for **pluralism** since it may lead to friction or division within the Muslim community (***umma***). Rather, they want an **Islamic state** since it is constructed within the framework of **Allah**'s guidance. Therefore, radical Islam is completely exclusive, focuses on the rights of the community and not the individual, and sees the **religion** as practically and theoretically the best way to attain a civil **Islamic society**. *See also* EXTREMISM.

RADIO *DAKWAH ISLAMIYAH SURAKARTA*/RADIO PREACHING MUSLIM *SURAKARTA*. Founded by Indonesian Islamists Abdullah Sungkar and Abu Bakar Bashir in 1967, Radio *Dakwah Islamiyah Surakarta* was quickly banned by the Indonesian authorities in 1973.

RAFSANJANI, 'ALI AKBAR (1934–). An important figure in the opposition to the first president of the **Islamic Republic of Iran** (**Abul Hasan Bani Sadr**), Rafsanjani also helped organize the clerical opposition to the shah during the **Iranian Islamic Revolution of 1979**. A colleague of **Ayatollah Ruhollah al-Musawi Khomeini**, he was repeatedly jailed for his participation in the rebellion. Also a member of the Islamic Republican Party and a member of the Revolutionary Council's *Majlis-al-Shura*, he became a popular politician in Iran throughout the 1980s and 1990s. In fact, in 1989 and 1993, he was elected president of the Islamic Republic of Iran. His last major position was in 1997, when he became the president of the *Majlis Tashkhis Maslahat Al-Nizam* (Council for Characterizing the Regime's Interest). Since the 2008 Iranian protests, he has been marginalized by President Mahmoud Ahmadinejad and lost most of his influence within the Iranian establishment.

RAJAH SULEIMAN MOVEMENT (RSM). A Filipino Islamic extremist group close to the **Abu Sayyaf** organization, RSM consisted of approximately 50 converts from Balik **Islam** and was active primarily in the Manila region. Led by Ahmed Santos, the group was largely dismantled in August 2005.

REASON/'AGL. Reason plays an interesting role in the doctrine of **Islam** since it is thought that reason can impede man's **knowledge** of **Allah**'s divine message. Reason is therefore cautioned but not restricted since it can also be a viable tool for knowledge. It is important to note that although reason is carefully used within the **religion**, Islam is not against intellectual freedoms. Nor do Islamic **fundamentalists** want to limit man's search for truth; rather, they warn people from falling victim to fallacies or being trapped by a dependence on reason. Reason is supported, however, because it can also help the individual interpret the **Quran** as well. It is emphasized, though, that the heavenly realm of the Quran is unattainable for man, so reason can take him only so far. The fundamentalists also underline the importance of relying solely on the **divine texts** and not on reason when encountering personal, political, or social problems since the texts are the ultimate source of Islamic authority.

REFAH PARTISI/**WELFARE PARTY.** Established in 1983, *Refah Partisi* has become the most important **fundamentalist** party in Turkey. It was first led by 'Ali Turkmen, and in 1987 **Necmettin Erbakan** became its leader. Ideologically similar to the *Milli Nizam Partisi* (Party for National Order), the group also encourages educational freedom and economic equality for all in Turkey. *Refah* was highly successful electorally during the 1990s, winning 43 seats in parliament in its first election. The year 1996 also saw great strides when the group gained 158 of the 550 seats, making it the strongest **Islamic**

political party in the country. Consequently, Erbakan became prime minister of Turkey and formed *Al-Tariq Al-Qawim* (The Straight Path). However, Turkey's Constitutional Court disbanded the party in January 1998 following the February 1997 events when the Turkish army forced Erbakan and the group out of the political sector. Nevertheless, *Refah Partisi*'s experience in Turkey's government is considered one of the most distinguished and notable legislative attempts of any contemporary Islamic movement.

REFORM STAR PARTY/*PARTAI BINTANG REFORMASI.* This Indonesian **Islamic political party** was formed out of the United Development Party (UDP). When members of the UDP began a campaign to remove its leader Hamzah Haz from his post after recently being elected to the Indonesian vice presidency in 1998 (it was generally felt that both positions were too much for one man to handle), the Reform Star Party was formed. Its future members began to defect from their father organization, and in order to maintain a viable unity among all members (Haz supporters and opponents), the Reform Star Party was founded after Haz's resignation from the UDP on 8 January 2002. Still, the party continues to struggle with internal dissension, and many members have been removed (as was the case in April 2006) or left to create other organizations (such as the Great Indonesia Movement Party). This conflict within the group has resulted in poor electoral results. Although the Reform Star Party won 14 of 560 seats within the country's parliament (the People's Representative Council) in the 2004 elections, it lost all seats at the 9 April 2009 polls.

RELIGION/*AL-DIN.* To the Islamic **fundamentalists**, **Islam** as a religion goes beyond being a mere **philosophy** because it constitutes an entire **system** and **method** of living one's life in harmony. They believe that all aspects of life are either man-made or **God** given, and since religion is God given, it is superior to all other systems, which are man-made. Islam is explained as a system since it encompasses economics, education, ethics, daily life, metaphysics, politics, and **society** within the moral bracket of religion. This **morality** means that Islam attracts only what is beneficial to the world and repels the harmful. Although many Muslims long for and romanticize the Islam of the past, fundamentalists warn against trying to adopt new ideologies or theories in hopes of regaining that former Islam.

Moderate and radical fundamentalists alike agree that religion should always be a way of life based on dogmas and ideas that govern individual and societal behavior. With this understanding of how Islam is a substantial and practical system, it can then replace all theories and philosophies. **Sayyid Qutb**, for example, stated that all forms of decent **government**, intellect, and happiness stem from Islamic doctrines. With regard to illegitimate religions, they are deemed so if they cannot bring man closer to his *fitra* (**intuition**). The sign of true adherence to a religion, or true believers, is that which focuses on deepening their relationship with **Allah**, further developing their interpretations, increased activism (***harakiyya***), and the rejection of other ideologies that do not follow these stipulations. To the fundamentalists, Islam as a religion develops society as a whole: it revives awareness and **consciousness**, promotes morality, develops charity, removes the individual from the material, provides a goal for the soul, and creates unity.

While it is universally agreed by all Islamists that Islam is the superior religion and the one to be sought after by all (even violent) means, there is a distinction with regard to how they view other religions. **Judaism** and **Christianity**, for example, are expected to be treated with more consideration since they are also **monotheistic** and hierographic like Islam. All three also share the same geographic **history** and sacred areas, even though this has become a source of contention, especially with regard to Jerusalem and the Temple Mount.

This dispensation does not exist for other religions, such as Buddhism and Hinduism, with which Muslims are in closer contact because of their proximity to Asia. These religions, to the fundamentalists, are seen as even more idolatrous than the previously mentioned religions. However, given the mind-set of Muslims in general and Islamists in particular, there is no true respect whatsoever for those who do not believe in a god. Thus, their treatment of atheists and even agnostics is even more extreme. This point of view has definitely carried over to their perception of secular societies and governments, which are viewed as *jahili*.

Over the centuries, Islam has extended from **Morocco** all the way to China and India and therefore has been in contact with other major religions, such as Buddhism and Hinduism. In some cases, a subtle mix of the Islamic religion and these local religions has been made by the missionaries and was often accepted by the local people and spread easily. One of the basic points is that the believers of Buddhism, Hinduism, or Shintoism were considered to be not unbelievers but rather more believers of prophets unknown to the Muslims. This is because in the **Quran**, it is said that Allah sent thousands of prophets to all the people in the world, so Muslims should accept the followers of these prophets since they are not necessarily polytheists. Thus, when the Muslim conquerors and missionaries first discovered the Asian religions, they interpreted them as monotheistic religions, not idolaters.

For instance, Buddha has been assimilated in the Muslim point of view as a "prophet" since his followers do not believe in multiple gods. This tolerance regarding the local religions made Asian Islam more open to religious diversity, more tolerant to differences, and less focused on the Arabic cultural foundations. To some extent, Asian Islam can be considered a successful religious eclecticism. **Tunisia** (the largest Muslim country) is a good example of this openness and eclecticism.

As for the treatment of agnostics and particularly of atheists, it should be dealt with according to two distinctions. The first one is the "unthinkable," and the second is the "unthought." Indeed, in the mind-set of Muslims in general, it is unthinkable to not believe in any God—or, rather, any force of any type that manages the universe and the ordering of things on Earth. So atheism appears as an absurdity and is vigorously condemned. As for the agnostics, to Muslims, they belong to the "unthought" in Islamic mind-set because most of them do not understand why people who believe that there is "something" do not go farther and give it a name and believe in God. So agnostics are not as vigorously condemned as atheists because, from the Islamist point of view, there is still the hope that one day an agnostic will convert to the true religion of God.

This way of thinking raises problems for societies and governments that want to be secular since Islam is considered both religion and "regime" (*din wa dawla*); it makes it almost impossible to let people choose to believe or not. The major fear for Islamists is about the division of the ***umma*** (nation) because of these religious differences.

REVOLUTION/*AL-THAWRA*. With regard to revolution, Islamic **fundamentalists** believe that *tawhid* (oneness of **Allah**) is itself a revolution because it goes against all **systems** that claim any authoritative role. So, in linear thought, because *tawhid* is revolutionary and because it is the basis of **Islam**, Islam is revolutionary itself. More literally, a revolution is seen as the conscious desire to change current systems so that they adhere to the Islamic system. Although it is stipulated that a person does not have to convert to Islam, he or she should, however, never obstruct or undermine the progress and provisions of the **Islamic state**. On this point, radical fundamentalists think that there is no compromise, for if concessions took place, then aspects of Islam might be abolished in order to accommodate others, and therefore it would not be a complete system. A revolution must also be a complete upheaval and replacement of the old society because renovation will not suffice—the revolution must destroy the old way and build on its ruins. Furthermore, the individuals of that society should be liberated from their ancient way of life and be given a new one in accordance with Islamic principles and morality.

Contemporarily, the idea of the revolution has gone beyond dogmatic ideals and is now full of political connotations since it is believed that it is not just the people but the state itself that needs to be overhauled. To the fundamentalists, revolution is a duty that is not restricted to just rebelling against the enemies of Islam. Internal Islamic corruption, whether moral or political, must be dispelled as well. Hence, since revolution is so wide in breadth, *harakiyya* (activism) is needed, and **jihad** (struggle) and *da'wa* (call) have to be implemented in its development. To the radical fundamentalists, revolution is the only complete and proper way to install an Islamic state and **Islamic society**. To them, the Islamic state will replace all those that are devoted to and that yield to man-made laws, or *jahili* **societies**, which, according to the radicals, characterize all current societies in one way or another. Conversely, for moderate fundamentalists, revolution (*thawra*) has become synonymous with friction and division (*fitra*) within the Muslim nation (*umma*). Hence, revolution is dangerous since it threatens social peace and creates disunity and thereby should be condemned and avoided. That is why the scholar's council of **Saudi Arabia** prohibited all violent actions during the **Arab Spring** in 2011.

RIDA, MUHAMMAD RASHID (1865–1935). An Islamic reformer and promoter of the Islamic **modernist** movement, Rida worked alongside other Islamic revolutionary thinkers like **Jamal al-din al-Afghani** and **Muhammad 'Abdu**. He also created a magazine, *Al-Manar* (The Lighthouse), which he used to spread his thoughts on the positive effects of modernism, the need for a reinterpretation of the **Quran**, the benefits of **reason**, and his antisecular sentiments. He also stressed that **Islam** must return to the teachings of the ancestors, embrace **consensus**, and implement *shura* in order to abolish the tyranny that existed throughout the Islamic world. Rida believed that the Islamic nation (*umma*) became repressed because of elitists who ignored the needs of the people. He has been regaled as one of the first Muslim thinkers to employ **Islamization** and to demand the formation of an **Islamic state**. **Hasan al-Banna** and the **Muslim Brotherhood** repeatedly cited him as a direct source of inspiration.

RIDDA. See APOSTASY.

RIYAD AS-SALIHEEN **MARTYRS BRIGADE.** Meaning "The Gardens of the Righteous," the name was intentionally chosen to prove that all members of *Riyad as-Saliheen* Martyrs Brigade are willing to become **martyrs**. Organized in October 1999 by Shamel Basayev, the *Riyad as-Saliheen* Martyrs Brigade is an **extremist** militant group partaking in **Chechen terrorism**. Rather small in size, the group was originally known as *Riyad as Saliheen* Reconnaissance and Sabotage Battalion of Chechen Martyrs and then the Islamic Brigade of Shaheeds. The group was originally formed as a result of the Grozny missile attack on 21 October 1999. The incident resulted in the deaths of over 118 Chechens when Russian missiles struck the Chechen capital of Grozny during the Second Chechen War (1999–2000).

The group conducted a series of **suicide bombings**, including the 2002 **bombing** of the Chechen Republic headquarters in Grozny, which killed an estimated 80 people, and the 2003 Federal Security Service bombing in Znamenskoye, which killed 50, and also carried out multiple hostage kidnappings from 2002 to 2004 that led to the death of over 400 captives. *Riyad as-Saliheen* also has had a large number of **women** volunteer for suicide missions.

However, after September 2004, the group (allegedly because of pressure from the Chechen president, Sheikh Abdul Halim) rendered itself inactive with the hope that Basayev could enter the Chechen political sphere. Unsuccessful, *Riyad as-Saliheen* appeared again after the *amir* of the Caucasus emirate, Dooka Umarov, announced its revival in 2009.

The group continued with its original platform of bombings and in 2009 killed approximately 25 people in Ingushetia and took responsibility for the 17 August 2009 Sayano-Shushenskaya hydroexplosion, which killed about 75. Most recently, the group has been accused of bombing the Domodedovo International Airport on 24 January 2011, which killed over 30 and injured more than 100. Since 2011, the group has been led by Aslan Byutukayev.

RIYADH BOMBINGS. Riyadh, **Saudi Arabia**, has experienced three notable **bombings** that have been allegedly conducted by **al-Qaeda** and have targeted both U.S. and Saudi compounds. These occurred on 13 November 1995, 12 May 2003, and 8 November 2003.

On 13 November 1995, a Saudi National Guard U.S. Training Center known as the Office of the Program Manager/Saudi Arabian National Guard (OPM/SANG) was attacked using two separate bombs that were detonated almost simultaneously. The first bomb was located within a van that was parked just outside the OPM/SANG office and was made of 150 to 225 pounds of explosives, whereas the second bomb was located close by. The explosions resulted in the deaths of seven (four U.S. federal employees, two Indian government workers, and one U.S. serviceman) and injured 60. Notable in this attack was that it was the first bombing of a U.S. military compound in Saudi Arabia. Immediately after the incident, three different Islamic **fundamentalist** groups claimed credit for the attack, but it was not until 22 April 1996 that four Saudi nationals confessed to conducting the bombings. Claiming that they were trained in **Afghanistan**, the four men are suspected of being al-Qaeda affiliates. They were executed on 30 May 1996.

On 12 May 2003, three **suicide bombings** were conducted at the *Dorrat Al-Jadawel* housing compound and the *Al-Hamra* Oasis Village housing compound. The attackers of *Dorrat Al-Jadawel* exchanged fire with the Saudi security forces of the compound, resulting in the car being detonated outside its gates. The *Al-Hamra* Oasis Village insurgents were able to place the remaining two car bombs within the perimeter of the compound before detonating them. In the end, 47 were killed (including the 12 assailants), and 160 were injured. Days later, al-Qaeda claimed credit for the attack, and after a forensic investigation ensued, it was concluded that all 12 suicide bombers were Saudi nationals.

The 8 November 2003 attack took place at the Muhaya Complex and resulted in the deaths of 18 and injured approximately 188. In this bombing, a truck full of explosives was detonated by an *istishhad* and actually killed many Arabs who were working on contract from **Egypt** and **Lebanon**. Since many Muslims died as a result of this particular bombing, public support for al-Qaeda (which claimed responsibility) began to wane.

AL-RIYATI, BADR (1947–). One of the founding members of the **Islamic Action Front** Party (*Hizb JabhatAl-'Amal Al-Islami*), Al-Riyati's sociopolitical influence gained him a seat in the Jordanian Lower House of Parliament in 1993.

ROHINGYA SOLIDARITY ORGANIZATION (RSO). An Islamist militant group, the RSO was formed in 1980 by Rohingya refugees from Cox's Bazar, **Bangladesh**. The RSO was aided financially and militarily by *Rabitat al-Alam al-Islami*. The group has clearly stated its strategy of independence in religious terms.

RUSHDIE, SALMAN. Famous for his book *The Satanic Verses*, Rushdie is an Indian Muslim who grew up in Great Britain. Published in 1988, *The Satanic Verses* was received with an exceptional amount of criticism by the Muslim world. Considered blasphemous to the teachings of **Islam**, almost every Muslim country has banned the book, and thousands of copies were destroyed. The story revolves around a fictional character who is a revered religious figure in the Islamic world in the book. After its publication, Rushdie was accused of insulting the **divine texts**, making ill-based statements about *tawhid* (oneness with **Allah**), and criticizing the life of the **Prophet Muhammad** (including the relationship he had with his companions and wives). The outrage was so high that even **Ayatollah Ruhollah al-Musawi Khomeini** issued a *fatwa* against him in 1989. This *fatwa* then had an effect on **Iran**'s relationship with the West as the West defended Rushdie's freedom of expression and condemned those who chastised him. Years later, in 1998, Khomeini's *fatwa* and one-million-dollar reward for his death were lifted by the Iranian government. Most notable about the book's reception was the immense protests and demonstrations that occurred because if it. One such protest in Bombay got so out of hand that it resulted in the death of 12 people. *See also* BLASPHEMY.

S

SAADET PARTISI/FELICITY PARTY. Established on 20 July 2001, this Turkish **Islamic political party** was formed out of the Virtue Party—which also spawned the *Hizb al-Adala wa al-Tanmia*. The party was formed to protect the interests of the conservative Muslim population in Turkey. *Saadet Partisi* also concerns itself with other political issues and functions as a social organization as well. As a social force, the party has been successful in organizing rallies and demonstrations—specifically against the 2004 assault on Fallujah, **Iraq**, and the **Israeli** invasion of Gaza in 2008. Notable leaders of the party include Necmettin Erbakan (d. 2011), Numan Kurtulmus, and Recai Kutan.

The party has not been particularly successful electorally. In 2002, it failed to gain enough votes to be admitted into the Turkish Grand National Assembly; in 2004, it won only 4.1 percent of the votes; and at the 2011 polls, support dropped to 1.24 percent of the votes. It has been speculated that the party's lack of voter support is due to the incredible success of its counterpart, *Hizb al-Adala wa al-Tanmia*. Ideologically, *Saadet Partisi* has a nationalist vision that emphasizes the need for **Islam** in daily life and the cultural morality that faith can bring and warns against **Western** influences on the country. These sociopolitical ideas are derived largely from Erbakan's *Millî Görüş* (National Vision) Party.

SADA AL-MALAHIM/ECHO OF THE BATTLEFIELD. The online media platform of **al-Qaeda in the Arabian Peninsula**, *Sada Al-Malahim* first appeared in 2007. Using the Internet as a propaganda tool, *Sada Al-Malahim* first began by publishing audiovisual messages and footage. Thought to be the creation of **Anwar al-Awlaki**, *Sada al-Malahim* has taken on other avenues of publication, including the first English-language **jihadist** magazine, *Inspire*. Specifically affiliated with **al-Qaeda** in **Yemen**, *Sada al-Malahim* publishes a variety of works, including poetry, letters from family members of *mujahideen*, messages from Islamic leaders, and events pertaining to the jihad, among others.

AL-SADR, MUHAMMAD BAQIR (1935–1980). A distinguished **Shiite** Muslim **fundamentalist**, al-Sadr combined politics and scholarship in his establishment of the **Islamic Call in Iraq** (*Hizb Al-Da'wa Al-Islamiyya*), which sought to eradicate **Baathist** and communist influence within **Iraq**. However, the Iraqi **government** constantly kept an eye on his and the group's activities, especially in the wake of the **Iranian Islamic Revolution**, as the Iraqi regime feared a similar uprising. Because of this surveillance, many acts of aggression took place between the Shiite groups and the Iraqi regime, resulting in the execution of al-Sadr in 1980. Despite his death, al-Sadr's influence still remains and has even flourished. His views on **constitutional** rule and socioeconomic reforms are still discussed ideologically and philosophically by many Shiite fundamentalists. Today, one of the most prominent members of his family is Moqtad al-Sadr, who leads the *Al-Mahdi* **Army** and is also one of the most radical opponents of the U.S. presence in Iraq.

SADRIST TREND IN IRAQ. The Sadrist Trend was established in the 1990s by Muhammad Sadeq al-Sadr and focused its efforts on providing socioeconomic relief to the impoverished **Shiite** communities, particularly in Baghdad and southern **Iraq**. Ideologically, the group also wished to apply *sharia* (Islamic law) and create a theocratic system of **government**. The Sadrist Trend also wanted its **theocracy** to be headed by a supreme leading cleric rather than a council of clerics. After the **assassination** of Ayatollah Muhammad Sadeq as-Sadr (1943–1999), most of its members dispersed and went underground, but after the 2003 events, the organization reemerged. Now its platform is based on the removal of the U.S. forces from Iraq, and it has formed the *Jaish al-Mahdi* to be an aggressive opposition force to the **Western** occupation. However, many of the group's offensives were suppressed by American security forces, and the Sadrist Trend has reformulated itself by returning to its original platform of social and economic improvements. This reorganization has enabled the group to gain more influence during elections, but it still remains in total disagreement with the Western forces.

SAHRAOUI, NABIL (1969?–2004). Algerian Islamist militant and extremist, Nabil Sahraoui (also known as Ibrahim Mustafa) was briefly the leader of the **Salafist Group for Preaching and Combat** (GSPC) and was born in Batna, Algeria. In August 2003, Sahraoui became the head of the GSPC and looked forward to pledging his allegiance to **Osama bin Laden**'s **al-Qaeda** organization. Soon after, Sahraoui's death came after he was killed during a fight with Algerian security forces. He was then succeeded by Abu Musab Adb al-Wadoud as commander of the GSPC.

SALAFI. A Salafi is a person who follows the Islamic movements that are based on the patriarchal, or Salaf, period of ancient **Islam**. *Salaf* translates from Arabic to mean "predecessor" or "forefather." Historically, these pious predecessors are part of the first three Muslim generations: the *Sahabah* (Companions), the *Tabi'un* (Followers), and the *Tabi' Al-Tabi'in* (Those after the Followers). Salafis turn to these ancient Muslims as a model for Islamic **fundamentalism** and orthodoxy since the Salafis believe that these three generations established the purest forms of Islam and therefore are the ultimate in authority for the fundamentals of Islam, or *'Aqeedah*. Salafis believe themselves to be the direct followers of the **Prophet Muhammad**'s teachings, and the term is used mostly by **Sunni** Muslims as an explanation for their methods of worship, morality, piety, and conduct. With regard to the nondoctrinal aspects of the Salafi community, the followers are also strict in their emphasis on ritual in daily life.

The ideological doctrine of Salafism has contemporarily become increasingly popular and used by Islamists to attract supporters because of its associations with Muslim purity and authenticity. The younger generations, which are the target audience of Islamic fundamentalists, are drawn to Salafism because it can appropriate a new sense of identity and universality. Contemporarily, the term *Salafi* has been replaced by *Wahhabi*, which etymologically is issued from the doctrine of Sheikh **Muhammad Ibn Abd al-Wahhab**. This interjection of the two words is often used by the **Western** media to give derogatory meaning to the Islamists extremists. More generally, a Salafi conforms to a belief in staunch **monotheism** and a rejection of speculative theology (the use of rhetoric and debate to develop an understanding of Islam), turns to the **Quran** and **Hadiths** only for guidance, abstains from any innovations in the religion, desires the implementation of *sharia* (Islamic law), and strives for an idealized and pure **Islamic society**. Salafi extremists believe that the only way to attain such purity is to purge the Muslim world of any and all non-Muslim forces and influences. These extremists have led to a contemporary association of Salafism to Islamists, making the belief tainted in many eyes. *See also* EGYPTIAN SALAFI; MOROCCAN SALAFIST JIHADISM; SALAFI GROUP FOR PREACHING AND COMBAT; SALAFI JIHADISM; *SALAFIA JIHADIA*.

SALAFI GROUP FOR PREACHING AND COMBAT (SGPC). Active since 1996, the SGPC seeks to establish an **Islamic state** within **Algeria** and destroy all that is considered "**Western** occupation." An outgrowth of the **Armed Islamic Group** (AIG), the SGPC is reportedly led by radical **Abdelmalek Droukdel** and was founded by former AIG commander **Hassan Hattab** in 1998. In 2003, Hattab was overthrown by what is known as SGPC's

"Council of Chiefs" because he refused to send fighters to **Iraq** in order to help the Iraqi insurgency groups. These insurgency groups are considered by SGPC fighters as "brothers" who need to be helped against the American occupying troops. **Nabil Sahraoui**, also known as Ibrahim Mustafa, replaced him as the leader of the group. However, Sahrawi was killed one year later by Algerian military forces and then replaced by Abdelmalek Droukdel.

Droukdel adopted the strategy of the global **jihad** and made efforts to merge the SGPC with **al-Qaeda** to become its African branch. In order to complete this relationship, he was introduced to **Osama bin Laden** by the al-Qaeda in Iraq leader, the Jordanian **Abu Musab al-Zarqawi**, who was killed in a U.S. air strike on 6 June 2006. On 11 September 2006, Abdelmalek Droukdel pledged allegiance to bin Laden, and the SGPC became **al-Qaeda in the Islamic Maghreb** (AQIM) on 11 January 2007. Financed by the smuggling of goods and the ransoming of Western hostages, AQIM has numerous camps and bases throughout North Africa and is the primary link to al-Qaeda regional operatives.

SALAFI JIHADISM/*AL-SALAFYYA AL-JIHADIYYA*. The term *Salafi Jihadism* refers to the school of strict Muslims who support the violent action against **Western** countries. Salafi Jihadism is a combination of an absolute veneration of the Islamic **divine texts** and a complete commitment to the Holy War (**jihad**). An extreme form of **Sunni** Islamism, followers of this ideology reject all things non-Muslim, Western, and **democratic**. The preeminence of the jihad against infidels, the rejection of all **innovations** toward Islam, and the intense emphasis on one's unity with **Allah** are central characteristics of modern Salafi Jihadism. Members of the movement are active all over the Muslim world and have launched numerous attacks on the Western democracies since the end of the Cold War in 1991. Notable members include **Abu Qatada, Abu Ayyub al-Masri**, Mustafa Setmariam Nasar, and **Osama bin Laden**, among many others. The leaders hope to install an Islamic rule based on *sharia* (Islamic law) comparable to the **Taliban** regime found in **Afghanistan** between 1996 and 2001. Believing themselves to be the only true interpreters of the **Quran**, these extremists seek the domination of fundamental Islam over the entire world. *See also* INTERPRETATION.

SALAFIA JIHADIA. Arabic for "**Salafi** Combat," *Salafia Jihadia* is an extremist Islamic combatant group operating in **Morocco**. Founded at the beginning of the 1990s in the hope of imposing an Islamic **caliphate** on the country, little is known about this rather small group (approximately 400 members). Their spiritual guidance comes from Muhammad Fizazi, while other notable leaders include Omar Hadouchi in Tétouan and Zacaria Miloudi and Ahmed Raffiki, both in Casablanca. The **Islamic group** prefers adopting aggressive tactics of **suicide bombing** and uses the ideology of **martyrdom** to attract members. However, the group has been severely depleted by arrests, particularly after the May 2003 Casablanca Metro bombings, which resulted in the arrest of Fizazi and many other members of the group. Structurally, the group is divided into many small clusters, each of which contains its own leading *amirs*. Some of them joined **al-Qaeda in the Islamic Maghreb** after 2006 and organized a series of 10 suicide bombings in Casablanca on 10–14 April 2007. *See also* FIZAZI, MUHAMMAD; MOROCCAN ISLAMIC COMBATANT GROUP.

SALAFISM. *See* SALAFI.

AL-SALAFYYA. A movement that calls for the improvement and renewal of **Islam**, it must be stressed that *Al-Salafyya* is not an established organization or a strict doctrine; instead, it is a program of ideals that has gained advocates throughout the Islamic world. Muslim scholars and thinkers who contributed to the notions of *Al-Salafyya* included 'Abd Al-Razzaq Al-Bitar, Jamal Al-Din Al-Qasimi, and Tahir Bin Al-Tazairy, all of whom kept their beliefs secret until the end of World War I. After that, the movement went public and subsequently spread to **Egypt** (it was notably influential on the **Muslim Brotherhood**), **Saudi Arabia**, and **Syria**. Doctrinally, the group is based on the teachings of *Al-Salaf Al-Salih*, "the righteous ancestors." Those who adhere to *Al-Salafyya* believe that Islam must return to the period of these ancestors in order for modern-day Islam to regain its former role of intellectual and social superiority because that was when Islam prospered.

AL-SALAFYYA AL-JIHADIYYA. *See* SALAFI JIHADISM.

AL-SANUSIYYA. A movement established by Muhammad Ibn 'Ali Al-Sanusi, it calls for a reevaluation and renovation of the Islamic doctrines and intellect. Al-Sanusi's ideologies were based on **reason**'s role in the modernization of **Islam**. He also stated, in many of his writings, that traditional interpretations are no longer effective in Islam. Al-Sanusi was also known for his opposition to **Western** forces in North Africa, but he was accused of **heresy** for his insistence on using **reason** in Islamic theology. *See also* MODERNITY.

***SAREKAT ISLAM*/ISLAMIC LEAGUE.** The first Indonesian independence movement, *Sarekat Islam* was founded in the early 20th century. Based on Islamist ideology, the organization went through various leaderships because of power struggles and eventually collapsed in 1962.

AL-SAUD/HOUSE OF SAUD. The ruling family of the Kingdom of **Saudi Arabia**, it is currently led by King Abdullah bin Abdul-Aziz Al Saud since his appointment on 1 August 2005. All the members of the ruling family are descendants of Muhammad bin Saud (founder of the First Saudi State who died in 1765) and support the **Salafi** school of **Islam** throughout their kingdom. Interestingly enough, power is passed on between brothers, not from father to son (although this was not always the case), and the entire extended family is comprised of over 7,000 members.

There have been three phases of Al-Saud: the First Saudi State (1773–1818), the Second Saudi State (1835–1891), and the current nation of Saudi Arabia (1932 to present). The First Saudi State was imposed by the alliance between tribal leader Muhammad bin Saud and Islamic cleric **Muhammad Ibn Abd al-Wahhab**, a relationship that marked the beginning of the state and continued until its collapse at the hands of the Ottoman Empire. The Second Saudi State was characterized by little territorial expansion and continuous internal conflicts within the royal family, causing its downfall. The current state of Saudi Arabia has proven to be the most influential and powerful of all. The kingdom has also become one of the most prominent and significant states in the Middle East.

Al-Saud's financial eminence can be traced back to the 1930s, when, in 1932, Ibn Saud united his kingdom in the Arabian Peninsula and created the current territorial boundaries, which consist of the majority of the peninsula. The kingdom's large territory encompassed what was discovered in 1937 to be a vast oil reserve. This huge acquisition of land with its lucrative resource is what made Saudi Arabia the economic power that it is today. In addition, the boundaries of the nation include the two holiest sites in Islam, Mecca and Medina, making Saudi Arabia hugely important to the Islamic community as well. The country then entered the world stage and engaged in diplomatic relations with the **West** after creating a strategic political alliance with the **United States** in 1945.

Politically, the king and therefore head of the House of Saud is a monarch and head of state, hence possessing absolute legislative power. The appointment to lucrative positions within the **government** is done by the king, and many of the Al-Saud family members hold important military and political positions. Although the monarchy wields ultimate authoritarian power, it is supported by the Saudi community. This support from the population has been particularly instrumental in the maintenance of the kingdom. A large part of the population's support stems from the monetary prosperity. The state's wealth makes it easy for the kingdom to give social benefits to its people, thereby improving the socioeconomic climate and buttressing a favorable status quo. However, there have been incidents over the years by opposition groups that were against the totalitarian regime. After the first Gulf War (1991), the House of Saud has been subject to the attacks of **Al- Qaeda** led by **Osama bin Laden**, who was against its relationship with the West and especially its strategic alliance with the United States.

SAUDI ARABIA. The first kingdom of Saudi Arabia was established in 1773 after a merger between tribal chief Muhammad Ibn Saud and **Islamic** thinker **Muhammad Ibn Abd Al-Wahhab** resulted in the creation of the first amirate within the country. From 1818 to 1835, the monarchy took refuge with the Arab Bedouin tribes in the desert until its return. The second kingdom was then established in 1835 and lasted until 1891, when the family went into exile in Kuwait. The third kingdom was then created in 1932 and has been ruling the country to the present day.

Since then, the Wahhabi school has been the dominant sect of Saudi Arabia. The introduction of the modern Islamic **fundamentalist** movement in the country began in the 1960s, when **Muslim Brotherhood** members came to Saudi Arabia seeking political and ideological refuge and subsequently became so integrated in Saudi society that many members began to hold lucrative posts in the educational and legislative system. However, the brand of Islam that was promoted by the Brotherhood contrasted with the Wahhabism teachings, bringing the first religious challenge to the kingdom since its inception. The creation of new Brotherhood-funded *madrasas* in Saudi Arabia also brought further contestation to the nation.

The year 1979 was also a significant one for Saudi Islamic change, as many joined the fight against the Soviet occupation of **Afghanistan** that year and the **Islamic Revolution in Iran** (a longtime rival of the Saudi state) began to influence a number of the small **Shiite** communities living in the eastern part of the country. After returning from the war, many *mujahideen* brought back with them the new **interpretations** of **Islam** that they were exposed to. This, along with the tensions rising within the Shiite community, encouraged the Saudi regime to reenact its long-dormant program of forcibly repressing any opposition to its ideological prescriptions. Successful in combating the competing forms of Islam, the political Wahhabism that the government exuded began to dictate Saudi foreign and domestic policy. It is within this context that contemporary Islamic opposition movements started to form.

The problem that many Islamic groups have with the Saudi brand of Islam is that it contradicts itself. Internally, the state promotes and encourages its people to adhere to a conservative Islamic interpretation based on Wahhabism, whereas its foreign policy has reformulated itself into secularism. This conflict created a breeding ground for various trends, moderate and radical alike, that still impact the state to this day. One such trend has been labeled "rejectionist," and its followers refuse to participate in any political activity within the state and focus primarily on religious discourse. Completely orthodox in practice, these adherents reject all attempts at Islamic **jurisprudence** and rely only on the **divine texts** to dictate their lives. The most well known group of this trend is *Al-Jama'a Al-Salafyya Al-Muhtasiba*, which was formed in the 1970s. Another trend, the *Sahwa* (meaning "awakened") movement, is practically a combination of **Salafism** and Wahhabism. Influenced by the Muslim Brotherhood teachings, members of the *Sahwa* movement encourage political **activism** (*harakiyya*) and came into the spotlight during the early 1990s as the Saudi regime combined forces with the United States to fight against Saddam Hussein's **Iraqi** invasion of the Arabian Peninsula.

Another Islamic trend within Saudi Arabia is the **Shiite** school of Islam. Shiites have been marginalized within Saudi culture since its inception, and they are still labeled as heretics by a majority of the population. However, with the onslaught of the **Arab Spring** protests in 2011, Saudi Shiites have been the dominant voice for reform within the country, probably because of their history of repression. They have called for social reforms and the end of segregation and have pushed for a constitutional monarchy. However, many of their efforts have been thwarted by Saudi security forces, and their small numbers are proving to be ineffective.

The final trend within the country is the influence of the **al-Qaeda** network throughout Saudi society. When the Saudi government petitioned the **United States** for military help in combating Saddam Hussein's regime after the latter invaded Kuwait in 1990, the *mujahideen* of al-Qaeda were greatly offended especially since they offered their tactical service to King Fahd. After this, the monarchy was deemed by al-Qaeda a betrayer of the Muslim nation (*umma*) and a promoter of the infidel **Western** forces, resulting in attracting a large number of Saudi nationals to join the **jihadist** organization. From 1999 to 2001, al-Qaeda trained a number of Saudi militants in its Afghani training camps, and it has been regularly speculated that the organization has received plenty of funding from Saudi nationals and groups.

However, when Afghanistan's **Taliban army** fell in 2001, the Saudis who were training there returned to the kingdom, bringing with them their **violence** and brutality. From 2003 to 2006, al-Qaeda forces in Saudi Arabia **assassinated** numerous diplomats, targeted security forces, killed both foreigners and civilians alike, and injured approximately 1,000. After a serious crackdown on these actions by Saudi officials, the al-Qaeda presence regrouped in **Yemen** and in January 2009 formed (along with its Yemenite brethren) **al-Qaeda in the Arabian Peninsula** (AQAP). Although AQAP cells are still very active in Saudi Arabia, security forces have arrested hundreds of affiliates since 2010.

Even though, as these trends illustrate, there have been numerous instances of Saudi Islamic insurgencies, the majority of the population has yet to react to these trends and seriously oppose the monarchy. This is perhaps due to the country's conservative history, the wealth and economic expansion it enjoys, and the traditional Wahhabist doctrine of adhering to the *amir*. In fact, any major support for an extremist or jihadist agenda has been extraordinarily lacking throughout the country, and the House of Saud has a long history of successfully defending itself against any opposition to its rule. Yet Saudi Arabia still has come under a good deal of scrutiny for allegedly financing many extremist Islamic groups. These criticisms have been directed at both private and public entities for the past 30 years. But little can be done since Muslims see charitable contributions as one of the Pillars of Islam, and a majority of the population thinks that it is an Islamic duty to provide support for defenders of Islam and *mujahideen* factions. It has also been noted that Saudi Arabia has deep interests in protecting its economic and political resources abroad, and this may also be a reason for its support of groups—in order to further its own foreign objectives.

In order to counter this radicalization trend, the government has implemented a two-pronged program designed to "rehabilitate" radical extremists. Through this Tranquility (*Al-Sakina*) program, Islamic clerics engage in theological discussions with former members of radical groups to rework their views of Islam and society. However, the program is open only to those who have not committed an act of terror on Saudi soil. With successful completion of the program, these people are given viable jobs and government stipends for education and housing, although there have been critical reports that the program has only a 20 percent success rate. With the onset of the Arab Spring in 2011, it seems as if the government has been encouraging and buying the population's peace by providing thousands of government jobs and hundreds of thousands of new homes and increasing the minimum wage and subsidy packages. *See also* AL-SAUD; *AL-WAHHABIYYA*.

SCIENCE/'ILM. The role of science in **Islam** is a special matter because of its origins in **Western civilization**. To the **Islamic fundamentalists**, since modern science is predominantly a product of the West, it is inherently distrusted and is feared to bring about *kufr* (unbelief). However, they also agree

that Islam has historically contributed to the development of science. Therefore, the topic of science is one that represents both potential progress and
downfall. Moderate fundamentalists support the first claim that science can
bring about the necessary revival of Islam. A compromise is therefore created
between both radicals and moderates—one that states that civil, economic,
and political rebirth can occur by using science as long as it is founded on
the spirit of Islam.

**SEPTEMBER 11, 2001, WORLD TRADE CENTER AND PENTAGON
ATTACKS.** *See* WORLD TRADE CENTER AND PENTAGON AT-
TACKS OF SEPTEMBER 11, 2001.

SEVEN PARTY *MUJAHIDEEN*. *See* PESHAWAR SEVEN.

AL-SHABAAB. *See HARAKAT AL-SHABAAB AL-MUJAHIDEEN.*

***SHABIBA ISLAMIYA* (ISLAMIC YOUTH)/MOROCCAN ISLAMIC
YOUTH MOVEMENT.** The first known **Moroccan Islamist jihadist**
group, *Sahbiba Islamiya* (Islamic Youth) was organized in 1969 by Ab-
delkrim Moutiiy and is often referred to as the Moroccan Islamic Youth
Movement. The group was structured to have an ideological branch that
performed such functions as preaching its Islamic dogmas and a militant
branch for use in armed actions that was headed by Abdelaziz Nouamani.
The group's members were comprised mainly of teachers and students who
shared the same aims of spreading orthodox Islamic education and opposing
nationalist political parties (especially the Socialist Union of Popular Forces/
Union Socialiste des Forces Populaires).

The early 1980s saw a splintering within the group, and in 1981 Moutiiy
created a new armed organization called Combat Faction. Nouamani soon
followed suit in 1984 and founded the *Harakat Al-Mujahedeen Al-Maghribia*
(Moroccan Mujahideen Movement), but by 1985 both of these groups were
internally dissolved. Former *Shabiba Islamiya* member Abdelilah Ziyad also
went on to create the Islamic Combat Movement in 1993. Other splinter
groups include Abdelilah Benkirane's more moderate *Al Jama'a Al-Islamiya*
(currently *Hizb Al-Adala wa Al-Tanmia* or **Justice and Development Party**),
but most members left Morocco for **Afghanistan** or **Iraq** after 2003. *See also*
MOROCCAN ISLAMIC COMBATANT GROUP.

SHAHID. Although in Arabic this simply means "witness," *shahid* (plural,
shihada) is an Islamic doctrinal term that almost always refers to a martyr.
The word is reserved solely for the glorification of Muslim martyrs and has

connotations of scrupulousness and distinction. According to the **Quran**, a *shahid* is promised a place in paradise for being killed in the name of **Allah** and therefore is deemed to be among the most faithful. A *shahid* is thought to have struggled to achieve both internal and external betterment and therefore is regarded with sincerest praise and honor. According to Muslim ideologies, a *shahid* can be granted *istishhad* (or martyrdom) through a variety of ways, not only through participating in the **jihad**. The *shahid* goes to Paradise (heaven) and can intercede for 72 people to enter heaven. The status of a *shahid* is very prestigious and brings respect to the family since one of its members is a *shahid*. In **Sunni** Islam, a *shahid* must be killed by a non-Muslim, whereas in **Shiite** Islam, a *shahid* can be killed by other Muslims.

AL-SHAHRISTANI, HIBAT AL-DIN (1883–1967). Al-Shahristani became a notable figure in **Islamic** philosophical and political platforms after World War I, when he struggled against the British invasion of **Iraq**. Associated with many different ideological schools, he also became head of the Appeals Court in Iraq, although prior to this appointment he was imprisoned for a short period over his activities against the British. Al-Shahristani spent a good deal of his life teaching Islamic doctrine and also became a member of the Iraqi Parliament, a position he held until his death.

*AL-SHARI'A/SHARIA/*ISLAMIC LAW. Arabic for "path," *sharia* is the sacred law of **Islam**. *Sharia* is composed of two basic parts: thorough dedication to the teachings set forth in the **Quran** and striving to live one's life as exemplified by the Prophet Muhammad. Although there is a general **consensus** among Muslims that *sharia* is the law of **Allah**, individual sects of Muslims interpret and practice *sharia* differently. Furthermore, *sharia* can implement and **Islamize** non-Islamic doctrines and ideas if they are beneficial and necessary to the society and do not oppose the Quran. The Islamists' intent to implement *sharia* is political in nature and has posed countless threats to secular **governments**. Sometimes referred to as neo-Sharism, this school of thought targets the young, urban poor and completely opposes the **Western** culture and way of life. Extremists, however, use *sharia* to justify their acts of violence against westerners and Western sympathizers.

For the extremists, *sharia* should govern all aspects of a Muslim life, and one of the primary goals of the Islamic **fundamentalists** is to reintroduce *sharia* into every aspect of society. This means that *sharia* would be applicable not only to the religious and ideological but to the political and prosaic issues as well (the way to wear clothes, to clean oneself, to speak, and so on). It moves society away from the alienating laws of man and establishes a moral system based on the divine. To the advocates of Islamic law, it represents an ethical, dogmatic, and communal index of Allah's will. The more radical fundamentalists desire to return **Islamic society** to the most basic of Muslim laws and virtue and have used violence toward those who interfere with their efforts. They also have permanently linked *sharia* with morality and have stated that nonadherence to it is characteristic of a non**legitimate** establishment. This imposition of Allah's law on different cultures has been one of the primary causes of violence, controversy, and dissonance throughout the Middle East and North Africa during the past few decades. *See also* APOSTASY; CALIPHATE; CONSTITUTION; DEMOCRACY; *ENNAHDA*; HUMAN RIGHTS; *IJMA'*; ISLAMIC ACTION FRONT; ISLAMIC GROUPS; ISLAMIC SALVATION FRONT; ISLAMIC STATE; *JAHILI* SOCIETIES; JIHAD; JURISPRUDENCE; KHOMEINISM; MODERNISM; MUSLIM BROTHERHOOD; PAGANISM; RADICALISM; REVOLUTION; *SHURA*; THEOCRACY; AL-TURABI, HASSAN; ZANDANI, SHEIKH 'ABD AL-MAJID.

SHARI'ATI, ALI (1933–1977). Although not strictly an Islamic **fundamentalist**, Shari'ati's thoughts on **Islamic society** continue to influence many Muslims throughout the world. He began his political **activism** (*harakiyya*) with his father and was subsequently imprisoned for one year for his participation in pro–National Front rallies. After his incarceration, he obtained a doctorate at the Sorbonne and moved to Mashhad, **Iran**, where he taught humanities at the Mashhad University. While there, he joined *Husayniyah-yi Irshad*, a group that promoted educational and intellectual reforms, and delivered many lectures that were well attended. Although he gained popularity with the intellectual community, he did not become very prominent with the political and religious groups. The government of Iran carefully watched many of his actions and jailed him for two years in 1973 for preaching his radical views. Many extremists disagreed with his ideas that **modernism** should be applied to **Islam** and that the **religion** should be viewed as a **philosophy**.

   He spent a majority of his remaining years confined under house arrest but nevertheless continued his studies and promoted his thoughts. Shari'ati supported **revolution** and saw it as a way to fulfill **Allah**'s message. Furthermore, he believed that liberation would ensure **justice** and give the Islamic society the freedom it needs to gain **consciousness**. Notably, he also **Islamized** philosophies such as Marxism when examining the issue of social justice within the Muslim world.

SHEKAU, ABUBAKAR. A radical **Islamic fundamentalist**, Abubakar Shekau has been in command of the Nigerian militant group *Boko Haram* since the death of its founder **Muhammad Yusuf** on 30 July 2009. Days after Yusuf's death, Shekau proclaimed that he was his successor since he served as Yusuf's number two in command. However, on 26 July 2009, during the sectarian violence that ravished the state of Borno, killing over 700, it was thought that Shekau was killed. It was not until a video was released months later of Shekau that it was verified that he was in fact alive and now in command of *Boko Haram*. Influential and ferocious, Shekau has been wanted by the Nigerian government for years, and since 2009, it is suspected that he is hiding in the desert between Chad and **Sudan**.

SHIA ISLAM. The second-largest sect of Islam (the first being **Sunni Islam**), Shia Islam is based on the teachings of the **holy texts** and is short for the phrase "*Shi'at Ali*," meaning "Followers of Ali." Shiite and Sunni Muslims believe in similar doctrines and discourses surrounding the **religion**, but they do vary in their interpretations of the **Quran** and the **Hadiths**. In addition, Shiites constitute only about 15 percent of the Islamic population—the rest being Sunni Muslim. For Shiites, the interpretations given by the family of the Prophet Muhammad are preferred, whereas Sunni Muslims follow those set out by Muhammad himself and his companions. In addition, adherents believe that the family of Muhammad was imbued with extraordinary spiritual power and political authority. Therefore, Shiites reject the **legitimacy** of the first four **caliphs** and rather look to the Twelve Imams. Imam Ali, Muhammad's cousin, is thought to be the first of the Twelve Imams. The Twelve Imams, in Shiite Islam, were the rightful leaders of Islam since their legitimacy came from **Allah**. This constitutes the school's etymology as "Followers of Ali." Those within Shia Islam who strictly adhere to the divinity of the Twelve Imams and the return of the 12th are called Twelvers. Twelvers constitute 85 percent of the Shiite community. Perhaps the most famous Twelver in contemporary Islamic history is **Ayatollah Khomeini**. **Muhammad Baqir al-Sadr** is another contemporary Shiite notable.

In addition to the Twelver branch of Shia Islam, there are also the Ismaili and Zaidi branches, which constitute 10 percent and 3.5 percent of this Shiite population, respectively. Within the Muslim world, **Iran** possesses the largest Shiite population with 90 percent of the people adhering to the Twelver school. **Bahrain**, **Iraq**, and **Lebanon** also have a Shiite majority within the country. However there is a significant amount of followers in **Afghanistan**, Kuwait, Qatar, **Pakistan**, **Saudi Arabia**, **Syria**, Turkey, and **Yemen**. Historically, the Shiite ideologies began to form in the eighth century, and by the ninth century the whole Shiite communities and theocracies were formed.

A main component of Shiite ideology is based on eschatology and states that the Mahdi (redeemer) is currently on Earth but is "hidden" and will come forth at the end of time. Because of the secretive nature of the Shiite Mahdi, he is often referred to as "the hidden imam." Another doctrinal belief for Shia Islam is that the legitimacy of Ali was given to him by the Prophet Muhammad himself speaking for Allah. This is verified to them in the Hadith of the Pond of Khumm—named after the place (Ghadir Khumm, near al-Juhfah, Saudi Arabia) where the Prophet bestowed this power to Ali. On the Islamic calendar, this event occurred on 10 March 632 AD. Therefore, like Sunni Muslims, adherents feel that true legitimacy can be appointed only by the divine.

A difference between the Sunnis and Shiites lies within this narrative and the preceding event: the election of Abu Bakr as the first caliph. According to Sunni tradition, after the Prophet's death, the leaders of Medina appointed Bakr as their new leader, whereas, as previously mentioned, the Shiites claim that it was Ali who was deemed the true and rightful ruler of Islam. This question of legitimacy of Ali and the first caliph is a large point of contention between these two schools of thought. If one questions the legitimacy of the first generation of caliphs (here, it would be the first three since Ali was appointed the fourth caliph in 656 AD), then one questions a major doctrine of Sunni Islam. Also significant is that the capital of Ali's caliphate was Kufah in present-day Iraq, and his body is supposedly buried at the Imam Ali mosque in Najaf, Iraq. The symbol of Shia Islam is the sword of Ali, which is called the Zulfiqar and was presented to him by the angel Gabriel during a battle in which the Prophet was also fighting.

The theology behind the *imam* (plural, *imamis*) is also a large factor of the Shia faith. For believers, an *imam* is anyone who is legitimately the authoritative, political, and spiritual guide of Islam on Earth—interpreters rather than rulers. This legitimacy is provided only for the descendants of Ali and his wife Fatimah az-Zahra (the Prophet's daughter). Because of their lineage, *imamis* are also considered the successors of the Prophet. Not sharing in these views of the divine decree and true power given to the *imamis*, Sunni Muslims have long persecuted them, therefore making these *imamis* martyrs in the eyes of Shiites.

These slight differences of belief within the Shiite community have manifested themselves in the sect only following the Hadiths written by the Ahl al-Bayt (the family of Muhammad and their descendants) and excluding those written by the companions. In addition, in both Twelver and Ismaili Shia Islam, **reason** (*'aql*) was at the center of the Prophet. Thus, it is this that gave them and the future *imamis* **divine knowledge** (*hakimiyya*). Hence, although *imamis* are not divine, they have such a direct closeness with Allah that they are inherently guided by Him. The belief in such a divine guide, or Imamate, is fundamental to Twelvers and Ismailis. Further, adherents reassert this belief by stating that Allah would not desert humanity without such a guide and that these people are infallible. This infallibility, however, comes from their pure devotion to Allah and Islam. As in Sunni Islam, Shiites also believe in *tawhid* (oneness of Allah) and the Prophethood of Muhammad. In addition, *tawhid*, Prophethood, and Imamate are the three cornerstones of Shia Islam.

Therefore, with this knowledge, it is evident that Shia Islam has its developmental roots in being a political party (one that favored and supported the rule of Ali as true caliph) and then evolved into a religious one. One could also say that Shiites have a long history of repression and conflict with Sunni Muslims (those who believe in the validity of the first three caliphates). In fact, many cite that the decisive break between Sunni and Shiite Muslims was when Ali's son, Hussein ibn Ali, was killed by the troops of the Umayyad Caliph Yazid I. Called the Day of Ashura, Hussein's martyrdom is celebrated each year in the Shiite tradition.

Historically, as previously mentioned, the Shiite community has been constantly suppressed and discriminated against. Notably and contemporarily, examples include the official decree of the **House of Saud** to chastise Shiites and the **Arab Socialist Baath Party**, which severely persecuted Shiite adherents. Other groups that have encouraged the suppression of Shiites are the **Deoband Islamic Movement**, the **al-Qaeda** organization, and **the Taliban army**. On the contrary, some Shiite groups include *Amal*, **Islamic Call in Iraq**, *Hizbullah* **in Lebanon**, **Islamic Jihad in the Hijaz**, *Jaish al-Mahdi*, **Sadrist Trend in Iraq**, and *Tehrik-e-Jafaria* **Pakistan**. These groups are hostile to any Sunni government or supporter to Sunnis. *See also* GUARDIANS OF THE ISLAMIC REVOLUTION; IRANIAN ISLAMIC REVOLUTION OF 1979; *MAJLIS-AL-SHURA*; TEHRAN EIGHT; THEOCRACY.

SHIITE. *See* SHIA ISLAM.

SHURA/**CONSULTATION.** *Shura* is understood as the way in which the community becomes the source of executive power in economic, personal, political, and social, or everyday, matters. *Shura* ensures that there is communal, not authoritarian, rule. It is based on **Quranic** doctrine and therefore also maintains **Allah**'s will and **divine governance**. Islamic **fundamentalists** use the Quranic verses to support their claim of the legitimacy of *shura* and have made it the basis of their political ideologies. Most fundamentalists also state that any nonadherence to *shura* implies *kufr* (unbelief) and can lead to a *jahili* society. Moderate fundamentalists have even introduced **modernism** into their interpretation of *shura*, stating that a contemporary *shura* must take into account the current sociopolitical climate and adjust accordingly—as long as those adjustments do not go against the basic fundamentals of *shura* as stipulated by the Quran.

Shura has also been explained as an **Islamization** of **democracy** since it directly involves the people in legislation; however, *shura* is based primarily on Allah's guidance. Another difference between *shura* and democracy is the former's roots in a **divine text**, whereas the latter is based on **reason**. To Islamic fundamentalism, *shura* is the way in which an Islamic society will prosper and remain faithful to *tawhid* (oneness of Allah). Consultation must be understood as the primary fundamentalist way in which **Islam** can combine the ideological with the sociopolitical.

SIPAH-E-SAHABA PAKISTAN (SSP). With origins in the Indian **Deobandi** military organization, the SSP Pakistan was established in 1985 in Jhang, **Pakistan**, and was briefly a legal Pakistani **political party** until August 2001, when it was banned by President Pervez Musharraf. Founded by Zia-ur-Rehman Farooqi, Haq Nawaz Jhangvi, Eesar-ul-Haq Qasmi, and **Azam Tariq**, the group intended to reduce the **Shia** population's influence in Pakistan and was originally known as *Anjuman-e-Sipah-e-Sahaba* (The Army of the Friends of *Sahaba*; *Sahaba* refers to the companions of the Prophet Muhammad). Although Jhangvi was declared leader of the group, after his **assassination** in 1990 Tariq assumed power until his death in 2003. The group has actively supported making Pakistan a Deobandi republic and was briefly operating under the name of *Millat-e-Islamia* Pakistan but currently is known as *Ahle Sunna Wal Jamaa* (People of the Tradition and the Congregation). In 1996, many members of the SSP left the group, claiming that it was not aggressive enough, and in turn formed ***Lashkar-e-Jhangvi*** and have aligned themselves with ***Jaish-e-Mohammed*** as of October 2000. *See also* BASRA, RIAZ.

SOCIAL JUSTICE/*ADALA ISTIMA'IYYA*. Justice in **Islam** is an ethical concept and is an essential part of the Islamic **system** of government (a system that completely involves society in legislative matters). Therefore, social justice is based on a balanced and unified relationship between individuals or institutions and the understanding that they have a reciprocal responsibility to each other. For example, the right to private ownership is a form of social justice since it also has legal limits placed on it so that exploitation or extortion cannot take place between individuals. *See also* ECONOMIC THEORY; ISLAMIC SOCIETY.

SOLIDARITY/*TAKAFUL*. As understood by **Islam**, mutual responsibility is a total system of taking care of the people by providing them with educational, health, and other social services. This goes beyond traditional interpretations of what charity is and is rather a public duty to one another. In other words, mutual responsibility is a communal responsibility that should involve the state only when it cannot fulfill its responsibilities. The lack of intervention by the state emphasizes the importance that **Islamic society** has in being greater than the **government**.

SOMALIA. This fragile and at times unstable African country has seen a great deal of **Islamic** activity over the years. A vast majority of the population adheres to the **Wahhabi** and **Sunni** schools of Islam, and Somalia has often been the locale for many militant training camps. The instability of the **government** and its widely unguarded coast's proximity to the Arabian Peninsula has helped make this country particularly desirable for many radical **Islamic groups** from **Afghanistan**, **Kashmir**, **Pakistan**, and others.

Since Somalia gained its independence from the Italian colonial power in 1960, many different Islamic movements have existed. The most dominant at the time, however, were the **Sufists** (adherents of the mystical side of Islam), although the **Ahmadiyya Muslim Community** also had a strong presence. *Sharia* (Islamic law) was also not an immediately popular idea since many of the country's inhabitants were pastoral and therefore subscribed to their own legislative customs that are specific to their tribes. However, by 1953, Islamic scholars from **Egypt** established the Mogadishu Institute of Islamic Studies, which was based on the Al-Azhar University in Cairo. This creation allowed for a considerable presence of the **Muslim Brotherhood** within Somalia even before ridding itself of its colonial masters. In fact, it could be argued that the influence of **activism**, organization, and sociopolitical change that the Brotherhood emphasized was highly instrumental in Somalia's independence.

The Egyptians continued to build Islamic schools throughout the country and thereby continued to promote their program of Islamic politics and **jurisprudence**. By the 1970s, the government (weary of the Brotherhood's influence on the population) repressed the organization, forcing it underground. This led to the formation of *Al-Islah Al-Islami* in 1978 and *Al-Itihad Al-Islami* in the early 1980s. Both these groups often merged with regard to membership and ideologies in the hope of creating an **Islamic state** within Somalia and the rest of the Middle East.

A strong Islamic movement did not occur until the 1980s and was then further supported after the 1991 collapse of the state. The resulting civil war, along with an external multinational intervention and internal Somali political reconstruction attempts, helped promote the current militant Islamic forces. Without these very specific events, which are new to the country, it is doubtful (according to experts) that the strong Islamic political movement would ever have grown past marginalization.

Groups such as **Harakat Al-Shabaab Al-Mujahideen** and *Hizb ul-Islam* have since dominated a majority of southern Somalia. *Harakat Al-Shabaab Al-Mujahideen* has even controlled large parts of the capital of Mogadishu and has set up a strict Islamic command there and has conducted a number of violent campaigns over the years. Although *Harakat Al-Shabaab Al-Mujahideen* has focused its goals on a more global scale, the two groups have worked together in the hope of implementing *sharia* and expelling **Western** forces from its territory. However, they have conflicted with each other, most notably in June 2010, when *Hizb ul-Islam* lost some territory to the other group.

Other lesser-known Islamic organizations also exist throughout Somalia, such as the *Mu'askar Ras Kamboni* (Ras Kamboni Brigades) and *Ahl Al-Sunna Al-Jama'a* (Followers of the Traditions of Muhammad). The former was aligned with *Hizb ul-Islam* for a period of time until 2010, when it decided to rather associate itself with *Harakat Al-Shabaab Al-Mujahideen*. The group is located primarily along the Kenyan border and has recently taken up arms with the **al-Qaeda** forces. Conversely, *Ahl Al-Sunna Al-Jama'a* was formed to counteract the growing brutality of *Harakat Al-Shabaab Al-Mujahideen*. More localized and focused on internal matters of **Islam** within the state, *Ahl Al-Sunna Al-Jama'a* trained within the boundaries of Ethiopia, is ideologically based on Sufism, and is present in southern and central Somalia.

The current **government** within the country is known as the Transitional Federal Government (TFG) of Somali. It is also the 15th interim government there since 1991. Considered a moderate Islamic state, its president is the former head of the **Islamic Courts Union**, Sheikh Sharif Sheikh Ahmed. Since his appointment, *Al-Islah Al-Islami* (Islamic Reform) has been recharged and is largely Sufi in nature. It is also suspected that these Islamic **fundamentalist** programs that the state is encouraging are receiving financial support from **Saudi Arabia** and other Persian Gulf countries. Lately, Islam is being increasingly seen as a viable alternative to the old tribal traditions and the recent violence that has permeated the countryside, making an Islamic state attractive to many Somalis.

Socially, many Islamic groups have established schools, and other civic structures have provided welfare aid and security particularly in the urban areas—increasing their popularity especially among the poorer classes. Therefore, the installation of *sharia* and an Islamic state is more welcome in the larger cities. Many also feel that the unity that **pan-Islamism** supports can help rebuild the segmented country. However, the increasingly weak TFG remains undecided on whether to promote a strict Islamic state or to completely hold back from it so as not to give more power to the Islamic **extremists**. Whatever happens, Islamism in Somalia is a complex and yet relatively new issue for the African state.

STRUGGLE. *See* JIHAD.

STUDENTS ISLAMIC MOVEMENT OF INDIA (SIMI). Formed in April 1977 in the northern Indian territory of Uttar Pradesh, SIMI seeks to liberate India from all **Western** influences and replace the country's **government** with an **Islamic state**. This organization has participated in many violent attacks, resulting in the group being monitored by many government organizations, and it has been officially banned in India (in 2001, 2003, and 2006). Some experts even believe that SIMI is now an affiliate of the **al-Qaeda** organization and is currently operating under the name of Indian *Mujahideen* (a.k.a. Al-*Arbi* and *Al-Hindi*).

Originally, the group began as the student faction of *Jamaat-e-Islami Hind* and was inspired by the **Iranian Islamic Revolution**. SIMI believes that only through the **jihad** can social change in India take place, but because of this radical ideology, the relationship between SIMI and *Jamaat-e-Islami Hind* began to deteriorate by the early 1980s. The group participated in protests against the **Palestinian Liberation Organization**, especially Yasir Arafat's signing of the U.S.-orchestrated Oslo Accords. The group's founding president, Muhammad Ahmadullah Siddiqi, pursued the SIMI extremist platform and adopted the slogan "**Allah** is our Lord, the **Quran** is our **constitution**, Muhammad is our leader, Jihad is our way and *Shahada* is our desire," a modified version of the **Muslim Brotherhood**'s, in order to further illustrate the group's campaign.

The violence of the group only seemed to increase, especially in the light of the Hindu-Muslim conflicts that were taking place in India during the 1980s and 1990s. The secularist and **democratic** constitution of India is also felt to be completely contrary to the essence of **Islam**, and this is why the group wants to establish a **pan-Islamic government** (**caliphate**) and unify the Islamic nation (*umma*) within the country. SIMI has released several publications in various languages in the hope of spreading its ideologies and attracting members. Although there are reports that the group's support network is in the thousands, it has only hundreds of registered members. This is most likely due to the age limit (30 years old) placed on membership. After being banned by the Indian government in 2001, the current SIMI president, Misbahul Islam, stated that the group was against any form of armed struggle, probably with the aim of gaining more positive support throughout the population.

However, the group has been known to organize a number of protests, has been accused of various **bombings**, and has often clashed with the Indian security forces. In the wake of the 11 July 2006 Mumbai train bombings, over 300 alleged accomplices were arrested, a majority reportedly SIMI members. The 2008 Ahmedabad, Delhi, and Jaipur bombings are also thought to be the work of SIMI militants. Most affiliates of the Indian government also believe that the group has been responsible mostly for the major insurgencies and explosions throughout India in the past decade.

SUDAN. An estimated 70 percent of the population of Sudan are practicing Muslims and are living primarily in the northern part of the country. This demographic proximity to **Egypt** has helped filter Islamic ideologies into Sudan, such as those of the Egyptian **Muslim Brotherhood**. As the first country to adopt the group's principles, Sudan has been a key player in the contemporary Islamic **fundamentalist** movement since the 1950s. This movement was promoted by the influential **Hassan Al-Turabi** and his **Islamization** platform. However, throughout the years, Sudan has proven to be willing to project a more radical brand of **Islam** and at the same time be open to a more moderate form of fundamentalism.

Historically, Islamic politicization and rebelliousness has been part of Sudan since the 1881 Islamic rebellion, when a **jihad** was launched against the British colonial powers there. Defeating the **Western** forces in 1885, Muhammad Ahmad Ibn Abdullah's *Mahdiyya* **government** ruled the country until 1989, when it fell once again to the British. Yet, decades later, the Islamic Charter Front (also referred to as the **Muslim Brotherhood in Sudan** and later renamed the **National Islamic Front**) was established in 1964 in the hope of returning to a pure **Islamic state** based on *sharia* (Islamic law). The work of this group under the leadership of Al-Turabi helped make Sudan one of the most formidable staging grounds for Islamic politics throughout the Arab states. A legislative turnover happened again on 30 June 1989, when Al-Turabi's group aligned itself with **'Umar Hasan Ahmad Al-Bashir**'s forces and overthrew the **democratic** government of Sadiq Al-Mahdi and formed what is known as the First Islamic Republic of Sudan. However, between 1999 and 2004, Al-Turabi's and Al-Bashir's relationship seriously deteriorated because of Al-Turabi's support of the radical trend in Islam throughout the 1990s and his support of two coup attempts between 1999 and 2004.

During the early 1990s, Sudan's national unity was strained by two major events: the welcoming of **Osama bin Laden** into the country in 1991 and the Darfur conflict in 1993. The presence of bin Laden and his **al-Qaeda** followers in the country was largely to help Al-Turabi set up his long-sought-after Islamic state that Al-Bashir was proving not to be establishing, but they also brought with them radical jihadists. Over the five years that bin Laden was in Sudan, over 20 training camps were established (used by Sudan's Popular Defense Forces), and even some viable financial ventures were created. However, even after bin Laden and his forces left the country in 1996, Sudan still maintained a relationship with his organization for years to come. The huge humanitarian catastrophe that was the Darfur conflict was essentially an Arab apartheid in which non-Sudanese Arabs were repressed and brutally attacked by militant Sudanese Arab nationalists. The result was the deaths of over 300,000 mainly southern Sudanese in just a six- to seven-year period.

With the onset of the foreign al-Qaeda within Sudan and the nationals committing atrocities, radical Islamic groups blossomed throughout the 1990s in the country. Militant organizations, such as *Ansar Al-Sunna* and **Takfir wAl-Hijra**, began to rise and indiscriminately attack civilians, foreigners, and security forces. The Islamic movement within Sudan began to shift from revising its diplomatic links to domestic militant **activism**. The camps that al-Qaeda and other groups set up would continue to be used by various jihadist groups as well. In fact, this use of the country as a safe haven for Islamic movements dates back to the August 1989 Muslim Brotherhood Conference in London, where members agreed that Sudan should play this role for the displaced organizations.

Demographically, this importing and supporting of Islamic extremists only worsened the already strained relationship of the dominant Muslims in the north and the populations in the south. The southern Sudanese feared any establishment of Islamic law, especially after the atrocities that they had been subjected to during the Darfur conflict. The 80 percent Muslim population of the north, to the contrary, wanted to see its implementation. However, despite Al-Turabi's support of the Islamic movements, Al-Bashir's legislation has proven to be conducive to the counterterrorism measure implemented by many of the Western governments (especially the **United States**) since the **World Trade Center and Pentagon attacks of September 11, 2001**.

Moreover, this growing resentment of the al-Bashir regime led to further uprisings within southern Sudan, and the region was allowed to secede from the nation. Known as the Republic of South Sudan, it gained independence on 9 July 2011 and even became a member of the United Nations shortly thereafter on 14 July. Despite this heavily desired separation (over 98 percent of all Sudanese voted in favor of secession), conflict still exists. Known as the Kordofan conflict, it revolved around Sudan's desire to benefit from the oil-rich province of Abyei (which territorially lies in the Kordofan area), which borders both the north and the south. Beginning in May 2011, the short yet intense conflict has resulted in the displacement of tens of thousands, although a cease-fire was declared in August of that year.

Administratively, the Sudanese government has agreed to prevent the spread of violent Islamism and to work within the international conventions to suppress radical regimes. However, in 2010, al-Bashir was indicted for crimes against humanity by the International Criminal Court (ICC) stemming from the Darfur conflict, but this has not kept him from ruling the state and even more so from continuing to have diplomatic relations with other Muslim countries—which he has repeatedly visited without being turned over to the ICC. In short, for the past century, Sudan has been a country of contrasts marked by a northern desire to Islamize the nation and religious oppression that has turned most of the population away from any type of religious dominance. The country initially allowed extremists to enter and train and then, conversely, has worked with other nations to help suppress such violence. Nevertheless, Sudan's history is one of exporting as well as importing Islamic militantism.

SUFISM. Commonly referred to as the mystic side of **Islam**, Sufism is a type of existentialism. Adherents (sufis) believe that through proper devotion, one can enter within the presence of **Allah** and purify the soul. Most practice asceticism (not pursuing earthly pleasures in order to gain spiritual ones), meditation, pilgrimage to burial places of notable figures in Islam, and verbally repeating phrases from the **holy texts** (called *dhikr*). Historically, it is believed that this branch of Islam began in the seventh or eighth century as a reaction to the indulgences practiced by the Umayyad caliphate. Over time, it has attracted both **Sunni** and **Shia** Muslims alike as well as other branches of Islam and various other religions. Contemporarily, **Hassan al-Banna** and **Taqiyuddin al-Nabhani** have been noted for studying Sufism from an early age. In addition, **Abul Alaa al-Maududi** came from a prominent Sufi family.

Practicing an obscure and mysterious brand of Islam, Sufis are usually excluded from the sphere of Islam by many **fundamentalists**. Perhaps the main difference between Sufism and other forms of Islam is that for the Sufis, it is possible to attain closeness to Allah while here on Earth. Most Muslims, on the contrary, believe that this intimate relationship will happen only while in paradise or after the apocalypse. For Sufis, one reaches this state by returning their minds (and then eventually souls) back to their original state of pure **intuition**, or *fitra*. This idea to return back to a primordial state is the reason why many abstain from indulging in the self, whether that is through material or psychological means. In addition, to become closer, practitioners participate or perform actions only if they are for the will of Allah and would increase the value of the individual's soul.

Traditionally, the practitioner (*murid*) of Sufism begins by aligning himself with a teacher (*sheikh*) who will then show him the proper way to purify his mind and soul. This master must have then been approved by another master to give his teachings legitimacy. However, this guidance should not be given from mouth to ear but rather from heart to heart. Since this process is intense and requires the believer to adopt a new way of living, the student usually lives with the master for many years. Personally intimate and arguably an internalization of Islam, Sufis argue that they are the adherents who are closest to the Prophet and Allah. However, Sufis receive little opposition or harassment from the other schools of Islam, perhaps because of their austere nature and devotion to the **holy texts**. This devotion to the **Quran** and the **Hadiths** is why many Islamic scholars have concluded that Sufism adheres to *sharia* (Islamic law) and therefore is **legitimate**, although this is questioned by others.

Some also give credit to the Sufis for spreading the faith into Africa and Asia. Currently, the school is most prominent in **Afghanistan**, **Morocco**, **Pakistan**, Senegal, and **Somalia**. However, since 2009, the government of the **Islamic Republic of Iran** has been considering banning Sufism within its borders. Among the major schools of Sufism are *al-Naqshabandiyya*, *al-Qadariyya*, and *al-Tijaniyya*. Although for the most part Sufism is tolerated throughout much of the Muslim world, that does not make it exempt from militant Islamic fundamentalist persecution because fundamentalists regard it as the source of Muslim's underdevelopment and diffusing fatalism within **Islamic societies**. Opponents to the order include the **Association of Muslim Scholars**, **Egyptian** *Salaf*, *Harakat al-Shabaab al-Mujahideen*, 'Abd al-Hamid ibn Badis**, and *al-Wahhabiyya*. *See also* HERESY.

SUICIDE BOMBING. The most common ways suicide bombings are executed is by a bomber driving a vehicle riddled with explosives into the target or by wearing explosives on his or her person and then detonating the bombs. The idea of this tactic is to kill both victim(s) and bomber(s). In contemporary culture, suicide bombing is often equated to radical Islamic **fundamentalists**, but it has been implemented by other types of sociopolitical extremists throughout the world (most of which are not religiously based). The association with the fundamentalists and suicide bombings can be traced to the **Israeli** occupation of Lebanon (6 June 1982–17 May 1983). This event encouraged radical violence in the Islamic world as **Islamic groups** such as *al-Fatah*, **Hamas**, *Hizbullah*, and the **Islamic Jihad of Palestine** surfaced as the first groups to implement these types of attacks.

Over time, it has been understood that most of these perpetrators are attacking in order to preserve that sanctity of **Islam** and its people from those whom they feel are threats. By performing this act of martyrdom (*istishhad*), these men and women are referred to in Islam as *istishhadyun*. The *istishhadyun* are frequently austerely pious Muslims who believe that through sacrificing themselves for Islam, their sins as well as those of their family members will be absolved. For the martyrs, death has already been embraced and antici-pated well before the actual act takes place. In addition, the bomber expects to be instantly welcomed into paradise as a hero of Islam. Although these attacks are supposed to just target military forces, many civilians have also been victims of domestic **terrorism** as well. From a preventive standpoint, the martyrs provide a particular challenge to security forces because of their welcoming their own death. For counterterrorist agencies, the most effective methods of thwarting these plans is to identify the demographic and specific type of person or persons who would most likely be attracted to *istishhad* and when and where these attacks would take place (almost always they are symbolic). These types of predictive strategies have thus far proven to be the most successful.

There has also been a recent trend of **women** participating in suicide bomb-ings. These women are chosen on a voluntary basis most of the time. It is also often the case that when a woman loses her husband in a suicide bombing, she is more apt to do the same. Another reason for a woman's volunteerism is that it is her way of retribution for a man of the family—father, brother, husband, and so on. Finally, women who are deemed remarkably pious or are known for their piety are sometimes approached with the idea of participating in a suicide mission in order to become an example and edification for the people. However, there is reason to believe that not all the women accept this honor voluntarily but rather come under considerable social or familial pressures.

Suicide bombings have been used by both **Sunni** and **Shiite** extremist groups, such as ***Mujahideen-e-Khalq*** and **al-Qaeda**. Perhaps the most fa-mous suicide mission was the **World Trade Center and Pentagon attacks of September 11, 2001**. Suicide bombings have mixed reactions. There is no doubt that it has impressed and also frightened non-Muslims, who regard it as a form of barbarity more than an honorable act and therefore tend to regard the martyrs as anything but symbols of honor and those who use them as cruel and deviant. Yet even within the Muslim community, there is far from una-nimity since, among other things, along with infidels and persons who might be regarded as the enemy, any number of quite ordinary, innocent bystanders, most of them Muslim, also are killed, and life becomes increasingly harsh for all. For this reason, most Islamic groups do not always use such practices, and even some moderate Muslim leaders have spoken out against them. *See also* IZZ AD-DIN AL-QASSAM BRIGADES; *JAMAAT AL-TAWHID WAL-JIHAD*; *AL-JIHAD AL-ISLAMI* IN THE WEST BANK AND GAZA STRIP; RIYADH BOMBINGS; *SALAFIA JIHADIA*.

SUNNA (TRADITION) OF THE PROPHET. *See* HADITHS.

SUNNI ISLAMISM. The largest branch of **Islam**, Sunnism, is considered the most orthodox variation of the religion and accounts for 80 percent of the total Muslim population. The term stems from the Arabic word *sunna*, which refers to the **Hadiths** and traditions of the **Prophet Muhammad**. Despite the faith's desire to unify through the teachings of Muhammad, there are slight variations in Sunni Islamic schools of thought throughout the Muslim world, and these varying schools do fragment the overall Sunni population.

These differences have turned into the foundation of political discordance and social instability for many Islamists. There are four main schools: Malikism (mainly in North Africa), Hanafism (**Central Asia**, **Afghanistan**, **Pakistan**, and so on), Shafiism (**Egypt**, **Sudan**, Indonesia, and so on), and Hanbalism (**Saudi Arabia** and Arabian Peninsula). The Malakite school of Islamic thought is the most followed one, but since the 1990s, it has been challenged by the salafi Hanbalite's school wing.

Some groups that are ideologically adherents of Sunni Islamism are *Ansar al-Islam*, *Boko Harum*, **Brigades of the Revolution of the Twenty**, *Fatah al-Islam*, **Iraqi Islamic Party**, **Islamic Jihad of Palestine**, **Islamic Liberation Party**, *Jamaat Ansar al-Sunna*, *Al-Menbar*, the **Muslim Brotherhood** (and all its branches), and *Sipah-e-Sahaba*.

Although not every Sunni-based Islamic group is hostile toward the **Shiite** populations, some are. These include the former governing **Baathist Party of Iraq** (which is interesting considering the majority of Shiites within the country; in fact, Iraq has historically repressed Shiite Muslims), *Jund Allah in Iran*, *Lashkar-e-Jhangvi*, the **al-Qaeda** organization, and the **Taliban army**. In addition, many countries within the Middle East, North Africa, and Asia are dominated by Sunni Muslims. Examples of these countries are **Bangladesh**, **Jordan**, **Mali**, **Somalia**, and **Yemen**. *See also* DEOBAND ISLAMIC MOVEMENT; IBN TAYMIYYA, TAQIY AL-DIN AHMAD; LATIF MOUSSA, ABDEL; SALAFI JIHADISM.

SUPPORTERS OF ISLAM. *See ANSAR AL-ISLAM.*

SUPPORTERS OF THE *SHARIA*/SUPPORTERS OF ISLAMIC LAW. A Tunisian Islamist group that formed as a result of the January 2011 **Arab Spring** revolution in the country, Supporters of the *Sharia* was established in April 2011 by its spiritual leader, Sheikh Abu Iyad al-Tunisi. The group has approximately 500 to 1,000 members and was inspired by the Tunisian Salafi preacher Al-Khatib al-Idrissi, who was imprisoned for years under the Zine al-Abidine Ben Ali regime (1987–2011).

Supporters of the *Sharia* are active mostly in Tunis and Bab al-Khadra, where most of the population is from the poorer working classes. Since April

2011, the group has been spreading its platform in the streets and through the Internet, calling for the establishment of *sharia* (Islamic law) and a **caliphate in Tunisia**. Its online media platform, the Kairouan Media Company, takes its name from the first Islamic city in North Africa, which was founded by Muslim armies in 670 AD. Through this medium, the group is calling for a new Tunisian **government** that will release the Tunisian fighters who were imprisoned for going to **Iraq** from 2005 to 2007 and joining **al-Qaeda in Iraq** (which, at that time, was under **Abu Mussab Al Zarqawi**'s command). Radical in its nature, this group has links to multiple international **jihadi** organizations that dictate many of its goals. For example, the group has also called for the freeing of **Egyptian** Islamist leader **Sheikh Omar Abdul Rahman**, who has been imprisoned in the U.S. penitentiary system after being connected to the bombing of World Trade Center in 1993. The group also demands the release of the European former spiritual leader of al-Qaeda, **Abu Qatada**, who is in jail in Great Britain. In addition, Supporters of the *Sharia* considers all the dead leaders of al-Qaeda as *shahid* and praised **Osama bin Laden** after his death on 2 May 2011.

SYRIA. The trend in Syria for the past 50 years has been to use the struggle against Islamic **extremism** to further advance the regime's internal and external sociopolitical goals. However, there have been some slight changes in these methods as circumstances have evolved. Since the Syrian **government** can be labeled a militant republic, it can more easily create its own state-financed radical organizations as well as provide foreign support. The Syrian regime has even supported different groups with varying ideologies, such as the **Shiite** *Hizbullah* **in Lebanon**, the **Sunni-Salafi** *Fatah Al-Islam* **in Lebanon**, and the Sunni **Hamas** in **Palestine**. The Syrian government has also worked with the **Islamic Republic of Iran** to support these groups and even supported the entry of **jihadists** into **Iraq** after Saddam Hussein's fall in 2003. Despite this large range of support, the country has repeatedly repressed the **Muslim Brotherhood in Syria**.

The Arab secularism that characterizes the current legislation has been in effect since the Iraqi **Baath Party** seized control of Syria in 1963. This eventually led to the decline of the Muslim Brotherhood within the country as the **government** controlled all religious and educational activities with a policy of repressing all who opposed its regulations. Since the Muslim Brotherhood's doctrine is based on Islamic educational reforms, its movement was swiftly dissolved. However, when Hafiz Al-Asad came to power in November 1970, there were some attempts to try to soften the anti-Islamic regulations that the Baathists had imposed. Yet these attempts to improve relations were quickly reversed in 1976, when a group of Islamic militants (many former Muslim Brotherhood members) tried to revolt against the state and topple the regime. Drawing significant support from the urban middle classes, the revolt lasted until February 1982, when the Asad government finally put an end to it by defeating a large faction of rebels in Hama. During this insurgency, tens of thousands were reportedly killed or imprisoned, and many were forced into exile. To this day, thousands are still officially considered missing or imprisoned.

However, by the 1990s, the Syrian government again tried to improve its relations with Islamic factions both internally and externally. Believing that a greater acceptance of the **religion** would help dispel any religious-based protests, the regime claimed to officially sponsor **Islam**, although its policies are still of a secular nature, not an Islamic one. The state even released many of the prisoners from the 1976–1982 revolt in the hope of mending relations even further. Yet the Brotherhood was still not allowed to reenter the Syrian socioreligious realm, and even when al-Asad's son, Bashar, became president on 10 June 2000, he continued the government's stance on Islam within the country and the repression of Brotherhood members. Interestingly enough, in March 2006, the former vice president of Syria, Abd al-Halim Khaddam, collaborated with the Muslim Brotherhood in Syria leader, Sadr al-Din Bayanuni, and thereby formed the National Salvation Front. Combining both secular and Islamic interests, the group was short lived, however, since it split in 2009 after the Brotherhood faction left over differences in **methods**.

Nevertheless, radical **Islamic groups**, such as *Jund al-Sham* (Army of the Levant) and *Ghurabaa al-Sham* (Strangers of the Levant), do exist within the country. The Islamic militant organization *Jund al-Sham* carried out a series of attacks between 2005 and 2006 but has recently been inactive. With regard to *Ghurabaa Al-Sham*, the group has denounced the teachings of the Muslim Brotherhood and seeks cooperation with the Syrian government in the hope of achieving a national Islamic unity. Because of this wish for collaboration with the regime, it has been speculated that the group may have been created by the state or is at least state sponsored. Another group, the **Islamic Liberation Party**, is more political in nature and has called for the establishment of a **caliphate** within Syria, but frequent arrests by security forces have resulted in a small support base for the group within the country.

More recently, Sunni Islamism has gained popularity specifically in the larger populated urban areas, but the populace has not been able to provide effective financial or membership support. This lack of backing and the government's strict stance on repressing any Islamic group has made it almost impossible for these groups to flourish within Syria. It is also interesting to note that the Shiite Muslim population, although still marginal, has increased significantly throughout the country. Another growing trend within Syria is the move toward a more conservative practice of daily routine. Traditional dress for men and **women** as well as the separation of the sexes in public has become more prevalent in recent years.

With regard to foreign affairs, the Syrian government's long-standing relationship with Lebanon's *Hizbullah* movement can be traced all the way back to *Hizbullah*'s inception in 1982. In addition, Syria has been friendly to the **Iranian Revolutionary Guards** by allowing them to train in parts of eastern Lebanon that Syria occupied. An "Agreement of Fraternity and Cooperation," signed in May 1991, gave Syria control over the Lebanese political sector, an action that allowed the Asad regime to acquire even more influence and use *Hizbullah* as a viable tool against **Israel**. The Syrian government has been helpful in providing a number of militants and arms to the group and may have forced the Israelis to withdraw from southern Lebanon in 2000. It has also been speculated that from 2000 to 2006, Syria gave an approximate 80 percent of the arms used by *Hizbullah* in the Israeli-*Hizbullah* War of 2006. The importation of weapons has only increased in both quantity and quality over recent years, and this trafficking of arms has been one of the most valuable resources for militant extremists.

Even in the wake of the 14 February 2005 **assassination** of Lebanese Premier Rafiq Hariri, when Syria was pressured to remove its troops from Lebanon, the **government** still had its hand in Lebanese affairs through its sponsorship of the Shiite *Hizbullah* and Salafi fundamentalist group *Fatah al-Islam*. Damascus is also the headquarters of the **Islamic Jihad of Palestine**, which repeatedly enjoyed support from the Syrian regime. Also within Palestine, Syria has been a major sponsor of **Hamas** by giving the group tactical training, financial funding, and arms. Through this relationship, Syria has been allowed to have significant political influence within the country. It may also be noted that it gave support to many of the jihadists who were entering Iraq after the fall of Saddam Hussein's government in 2003 in the hope that the extremists would oust the U.S. occupation forces. It was also reported that Syria has allowed Iraqi **al-Qaeda** members to use Syrian territories for safe houses and has provided them with weapons since 2003.

Syria has not been immune to the protests of the 2011 **Arab Spring** either. Constant and continued detention of its citizens for minor crimes has heightened the tensions, especially when security forces tried to disperse the crowds by force. The Asad regime's harsh reaction to the protests has only encouraged more civil disobedience. As is the case in the other Arab states experiencing the Arab Spring, the establishment of an **Islamic state** is not the overall goal of these riots, but the religion has played a role. Specifically in Syria, the precursor of many of the demonstrations has been the Friday sermons at the local mosques. However, the government's continued repression of the protests has made it difficult for the activists to make any real headway. Yet these uprisings have also put some strain on Syrian-Hamas relations, as the latter has refused to publicly denounce the protests. The Syrian regime could risk losing its influence on events within Palestine if Hamas decides not to support the government in the treatment of its own population.

The tensions between the people of Syria and the al-Asad regime have only increased throughout 2011, bringing the country to the brink of civil war. The Free Syria Army of the rebellion, which includes many Islamic militants, has been clashing with the state security forces at a heightened rate since November 2011. The Syrian army has been accused of violently repressing and killing hundreds of protestors and rebels. Because of this, many have argued that the Syria rebellion is akin to the brutality seen in **Libya**, especially in the way **Muammar Qadhafi** tried to thwart the protestors. As for February 2012, there have been large death tolls on both the pro-Asad and the anti-Asad sides.

SYSTEM/*NIZAM*. Significant to **Islam** is that it goes beyond doctrinal adherence and **interpretation** but also is a complete social way of life and **government**. The system of Islam can be applied to all aspects of daily and religious life, as it uses **fundamentals** and **methods** to create this framework. In order for the system to be effective and still retain its foundation in Islam, the **Quran** and the **Hadiths** are used to guide the community in their application of *shura* (consultation) and *ijma'* (consensus). To the fundamentalists, Islam is the ultimate dogma since it is the only system that possesses universality. Furthermore, the wholeness of the system can make possible the preservation of the **Islamic society** and nation (*umma*).

T

TABLIGHI JAMAAT/SOCIETY FOR SPREADING FAITH. *Tablighi Jamaat* is an Islamic organization that seeks to instill a pure profession of **Islam** throughout the Muslim nation (*umma*). **Muhammad Ilyas** established this ideological movement in 1926 in Mewat, North India, as part of the **Deoband Islamic movement**. The main headquarters, *Nizamuddin Markaz*, of the group is in Delhi, India. The group was formed primarily to counter the Hindu revivalist movements in the country, which were thought to be detrimental to India's Muslim population. The group quickly gained momentum and had thousands of followers attending its meetings in nearly two decades (its 1941 annual conference, called *ijtema*, had 25,000 attendees). Over the century, *Tablighi Jamaat* has spread throughout Africa, Asia, Europe, and North America but remains absent from the political sector, focusing primarily on ideological reform. Doctrinally rudimentary, the group adheres purely to the **divine texts** of **Islam** and does not defer from the strictest of Muslim practices. Although the group remains nonmilitant and denies any association with **jihadist** groups, it has been cited as influential to many **extremist** groups.

The group's slogan (Oh Muslims! Become Muslims!) dictates how Ilyas and his followers desired to unite the Muslim community and not lose their identity by espousing the teachings of the **Prophet Muhammad** in every aspect of their lives. The group believes that through *da'wa*, education, and personal reforms, Islam can attain stability and social prominence. The group's funding is provided solely through member donations, and it has systematically eschewed the media, never having released any official statements. Structurally, the group is led by an *amir* who is appointed for a lifelong term and consults with the *shura* council of that sector. The reason for this division of power and consultative organization is to ensure that all the needs of the large organization are met. The *amir* also helps guide members on issues such as dogma, as his faith is considered to be of the utmost quality.

This notwithstanding, the group has come under some criticism from other **Islamic groups** because of its apolitical, nonaggressive policies. In response, members defend their neutral stance by pointing out that if they had aligned themselves with a political platform or taken up arms, they would never have gained such substantial membership through so many countries. Today, *Tablighi Jamaat* is one of the largest Muslim movements in the world, spanning dozens of countries, although the majority of its followers are in South Asia, thereby attracting millions of followers; however, no official membership list has ever been released.

TAFSIR. See INTERPRETATION.

TAGHUT. Translated as "false leader," *taghut* also refers to believing in any other being or object (i.e., icons, animals, money, and so on) than **Allah**. Essentially idolatry, *taghut* is considered to be a completely impure psychological condition. Through *taghut*, one denounces **Islam**'s monotheistic teachings and therefore denounces the **religion** itself, a dogmatic crime punishable by the gravest of consequences. Many Islamic **fundamentalists** have used accusations of *taghut* to justify their insurgencies against Arab and Islamic regimes. *See also* BLASPHEMY; HERESY; *TAKFIR*.

TAHIR, 'ISAM MUHAMMAD. *See* AL-MAQDISI, ABU MUHAMMAD.

TAKFIR. According to Islamic dogma, *takfir* (or *takfeer*) refers to the practice of declaring someone or some group a nonbeliever or nonbelievers of **Islam** and thereby as **apostate**(s) or infidels. The accuser is referred to as a *mukaffir*. Under *sharia* (Islamic law), the sentence for this apostate is traditionally execution. Because of the severe consequences of such an accusation, traditional Islam requires stringent evidence to support these claims and usually requires an Islamic court to pass the judgment (*fatwa*) on the group or individual in question. What constitutes *takfir* differs among the various sects and schools of Islam. For example, in **Sunni** Islam, the denial of fundamental Islamic practices constitutes *takfir*, whereas the Kharijites of early Islam believed that any Muslim who sinned was a *kafir*. *Takfir* has been used by the Islamist **extremists** to legitimize their warfare against different groups, which they deem to be *kafirs*. Since most Islamists follow the Sunni school of Islam and seek to implement *sharia*, it is only natural that they would use *takfir* to condemn their targets. Notably at the present, the **Algerian Armed Islamic Group** uses *takfir* in defense of its attacks on Muslim civilians. *See also* HERESY; *TAGHUT*.

AL-TAKFIR WA AL-HIJRA/**APOSTASY AND IMMIGRATION.** Founded by Shukri Mustapha in 1969 as a splinter group from the **Muslim Brotherhood** in **Egypt**, the group is known for its militant **extremism**. What is extreme in the group's ideology is its belief that an **Islamic society** cannot be attained through any type of peaceful discourse or cooperation. It feels that only through violent aggression can an **Islamic state** or **caliphate** be established. In addition, it views any person outside of the group as an infidel (*kafir*), un-Islamic, and worthy of a **jihad** against them.

Mustapha segmented his group's path into two phases: *Al-istid'af* (weakening, to make weak) and *al-tamkin* (enabling). In the first stage of *al-istid'af*, the group leaves Egypt and retreats into the desert region in order to rebuild itself. Then, in *al-tamkin*, the group becomes strong and returns to the *jahili* society in order to overthrow it and rule. This program was enacted by Mustapha on his release from prison in 1971. Many feel that the group's extremist view was inspired by **Sayyid Qutb** since many of the members were exposed to his writings while incarcerated. Interestingly enough, the group also rejects any form of **consultation** or **governance**—it simply relies on the jihad.

TALIBAN ARMY. Arabic for "students," the Taliban army was established in September 1994 and eventually ruled the majority of **Afghanistan** from 1996 to 2001. The founding members were followers of Mullah Muhammad Omar, who wanted to create a more substantial organization after seeing how the *mujahideen* were beginning to fragment. Quickly progressing, on 27 September 1996, the Taliban conquered Kabul and by 1999 was in control of most of Afghanistan. Ideologically, members of the organization are radical Islamic **fundamentalists** who adhere to the **Salafi** school of **Sunni Islam**. Puritanical and similar to **Wahhabism**, members do not believe in Islam's adoption of any **modern** or **Western interpretations** (**democracy**, elections, and so on) and are particularly prejudiced against the **Shiite** school of thought. They have become staples in the contemporary militant extremist brand of Islamic fundamentalism since the group has carried out numerous attacks and has granted asylum (most famously to **Osama bin Laden**) and provided military training to plenty of other radical fundamentalist groups, notably **al-Qaeda**. The group is also known for its steadfast refusal to have extradited Osama bin Laden and its promotion of the Islamic **Kashmiri separatist** movement.

When the U.S. military forces entered Afghanistan on 7 October 2001 in the wake of the **World Trade Center and Pentagon attacks of September 11, 2001**, the Taliban army lost much of the area it controlled to the Northern Alliance. Notably, after weeks of persistent air strikes, Kabul fell to American forces on 13 November 2001, and the Taliban organization began to flee to the mountainous regions of the country and to the tribal areas of Waziristan. Prior to the 2001 occupation, the Taliban army reportedly had a membership numbering from 30,000 to 40,000, but afterward it is speculated that the group lost an approximate 10,000 during the fight against the Northern Alliance.

Known for its brutal tactics of militant **extremism**, an estimated 1,500 civilians and security personnel alike were killed by the merging Taliban and al-Qaeda forces during 2002 alone. Over the next two years, as the Taliban began to lose control in Afghanistan, it seemed as if the new Afghani **government** was making notable strides toward maintaining stability within the country. However, in 2005, the Taliban army and its al-Qaeda comrades began launching more attacks on Afghani as well as NATO security forces. Using improvised explosive devices, rockets, **suicide bombings**, and various other types of insurrectional tactics, from 2005 to 2006, the militants caused over 5,000 deaths—many civilian.

Membership of the organization during this time seemed to renew itself, as there were an estimated 40,000 militants within the Taliban's ranks. Many Pakistani nationals began to join the Taliban army, and public support began to increase for opportunistic reasons since the Taliban allowed nefarious activities to go on, whereas the Afghani government did not. By the latter part of 2007, the Taliban successfully regained control of and support in more than half of Afghanistan. The political climate within the country (and **Pakistan**) also helped maintain the group's dominance. A poll conducted in 2006 revealed that 54 percent of the Afghani population was open to a coalition government between the Taliban forces and the Afghani Senate. With this information and the hopes of limiting the rampant **violence**, Afghanistan's President Hamid Karzai offered to enter into negotiations with the Taliban army, but the latter has repeatedly refused to do so until all foreign occupants leave the country.

TAMANRASSET, ALGERIA. The capital of Tamanrasset province in southern **Algeria**, Tamanrasset is the primary city of the Algerian Tuareg tribe. This oasis city was originally sustained as a military base to guard the trans-Saharan trade routes during the French colonial occupation and was then called Fort Laperrine. Presently, Tamanrasset is the headquarters of the Joint Military Staff Committee focusing on combating **al-Qaeda in the Islamic Maghreb**. The countries of Algeria, **Mali**, **Mauritania**, and Niger are members of this committee and hope to put down the increasing Islamist trafficking and kidnapping activities in the pan-Sahel region. This poses a great problem demographically since many Islamists have created familial alliances with a number of Tuareg tribes and therefore have gained significant support among the dominant population in Tamanrasset.

TANZEEM-E-ISLAMI. Based in Lahore, **Pakistan**, *Tanzeem-e-Islami* is an **Islamic political party** that was founded in 1975 by Israr Ahmed. Ideologically, the group seeks the implementation of an Islamic **caliphate** not only in Pakistan but also worldwide. Currently, Ahmed's son, Hafiz Akif Sayyed, leads the group and has followers in some European countries where Pakistani immigrants are numerous.

Ideologically, the group is similar to *Hizb-u-Tahrir* and looks strictly to the **divine texts** in order to lead a morally just, Islamic life that is focused on the submission to **Allah**. Members also support the necessity of the **jihad** and the recitation of the **Quranic** passages. The group has emphasized the scholarship behind the Arabic language, stating that it can directly lead toward **knowledge** (*ma'rifa*). According to its adherents, it is the duty of the **nation** (*umma*) to spread the doctrines of **Islam** to the world. Although *Tanzeem-e-Islami* supports the holy struggle (**jihad**), Israr Ahmed emphasizes the need for passive resistance and perseverance in order to gain a substantial foothold and momentum within society.

TAQLID. See TRADITIONALISM.

TARIQ, AZAM (1962–2003). Born in Bahawalpur, **Pakistan**, in March 1962, Azam Tariq was one of the founders of *Sipah-e-Sahaba* **Pakistan** (SSP), a **Deobandi** movement. Leader of the SSP from 1990 until his death in 2003, Tariq was also the head of *Lashkar-e-Jhangvi* (a SSP splinter group from 2000 to 2003). Tariq became head of the SSP following the death of fellow founder Haq Nawaz Jhangvi. Tariq shared, along with the other founding members like Jhangvi, the belief that the **Shia** population should be repressed, as the **Sunni** school of **Islam** is the purest form of the **religion**. In August 2001, the SSP was officially banned by Pakistani President Pervez Musharraf, and Tariq was imprisoned. In response, many followers of Tariq carried out a number of Shia-targeted killings. Released from custody in November 2002, Tariq was also elected to the National Assembly of Pakistan three times, once while still imprisoned and all times in areas predominantly Sunni. Tariq was killed during an attack on 4 October 2003 along with fellow SSP founder Zia-ur-Rehman Farooqi near Islamabad, Pakistan. Although Shia sectarians were blamed for the deaths, they remain unsolved.

TAWHID. Tawhid (oneness of **Allah**) is understood by the **fundamentalists** to be beyond human comprehension and **reason** because His existence supersedes the limits of time and space, whereas man's existence is limited to those boundaries. Therefore, the only way man can interact with Allah is through the **divine texts** of **Islam**. It is because of this doctrine that the fundamentalists believe that Muslims should adhere only to the texts and then act in accordance with them. It is also through this ideology that the fundamentalists reject **philosophy** or any other **method** of reasoning or **theology,** especially **Sufism** (the mystic side of Islam that claims to be able to arrive at an understanding of Allah). Allah is seen as the supreme authority of all **legislation**, and therefore a true belief in Him would implement *sharia* (Islamic law), which would establish a new **Islamic society**. To arrive at this new society, the fundamentalists believe that a revolution must take place, and that is where their justification of **jihad** lies.

As the most basic component of Islam, *tawhid* is the dogma that promotes man's life in the likeness and conformity of Allah and accepting his divine laws and **divine governance**. More simply, *tawhid* is the belief that Allah is the ultimate authority on and divine architect of all material and spiritual things. It demands that man follow Allah's path in all matters from the sacred to the administrative and even in daily life. When the individual accepts Allah's word as omnificent and supreme, Islam is then transformed from doctrine to **system**, eliminating the cardinal laws of man and transforming the individual's **consciousness**. This elimination of man's earthly laws has made *tawhid* the basis of many of the fundamentalist ideologies. This, in turn, gains momentum for the fundamentalists since many Islamic communities are unhappy with the current political climate in their country and yearn for a change in the administration to a more Islamic way of **government**.

Tawhid reinforces the Islamic system since it unites all aspects of economics, ethics, politics, and theology. Since *tawhid* is a political doctrine, it also provides for the evaluation of political behavior and the production of political guidelines. Seeking guidance from Allah is also the reason why many fundamentalists reject employing **philosophy** or implementing a non-Islamic political structure to shape society. To the radical fundamentalists, any system that is not based on *tawhid* is illegitimate and not beneficial to society since it is seen (by the radicals) as the only true way of life. **Sayyid Qutb** made the declaration, "No god but God," which comprehensively and simply illustrates the fundamental discourse on *tawhid*.

TAWHID AL-JIHAD. *See JAMAAT AL-TAWHID WAL-JIHAD.*

TAWHID AND JIHAD IN SYRIA/MONOTHEISM AND JIHAD IN SYRIA. An offshoot of **Abu Musab al-Zarqawi**'s *Jamaat al-Tawhid wal-Jihad*, *Tawhid* and **Jihad** in **Syria** formed specifically because its brother organization had a large number of Syrian nationalists within its ranks (in fact, many splinter groups use the name "*Tawhid* and Jihad" to express their goals and ideologies). When *Jamaat al-Tawhid wa al-Jihad* became part of the **al-Qaeda** organization in September 2004, many of its Syrian members returned to Syria in the hope of replacing the country's secular **government** with an **Islamic state** based on *sharia* (Islamic law). *Tawhid* and Jihad in Syria also has sprouted a more militant faction called *Jund Al-Sham*.

The group first became public in November 2006, when its leader, Abu Jandal al-Dimashqi, attacked Syrian security forces on the Syrian-Lebanese border and detonated a bomb that was attached to him. The group has been radical in its claims that all Arab states are *jahili* **societies** since they are not based on *sharia* and therefore must be removed and reestablished under Islamic **jurisprudence**. Today, the group has some militants in **Lebanon** but has not claimed responsibility for any of the attacks there.

TAYA, COLONEL MAOUYA OULD SID AHMED (1941–). Colonel Maouya Ould Sid Ahmed Taya exercised control over **Mauritania** from 1984 until 3 August 2005 after the deposition of Colonel Muhammad Khouna Ould Haidallah. On his assuming control, Colonel Taya continued Haidallah's policies, such as a pro-Algerian stance and imposing various restrictions sanctioned by **Islam**, including the ban on alcohol consumption. However, in order to protect his rule, Taya did not allow Islamist-oriented political and social movements to gain enough power in politics or society. Despite his efforts to suppress the Islamist political presence, poverty, unemployment, a frustrated urban population, low standards of living, and lack of ideological direction led to an increase in Islamist activity in Mauritania. Although a supporter of Islam, Taya's regime claimed an opposition to Islamism. In 1991, Taya officially banned any formation of religious-based parties in order to strengthen the country's ties with the **United States**. However, this was seen as a way to curry favor with the **West** and reduce criticism of Mauritania's abysmal **human rights** record. This idea is further enhanced by Taya's close cooperation with **Iraq** and his pursuance of a strongly Arab nationalist line in the late 1980s. In 2005, Taya's regime was overthrown as a result of a bloodless political coup led by Colonel Ely Ould Mohammed Vall. *See also* AZIZ, GENERAL MUHAMMAD OULD ABDEL.

TEHRAN EIGHT. Composed of eight *mujahideen* groups that aligned together to protect the **Shiite Muslim** interests in **Afghanistan**, the Tehran Eight is also known as *hashtgana*. Similar to the **Peshawar Seven**, this coalition served to fight against the Soviet forces during the Soviet-Afghan War (1979–1989). However, in 1987, the group was forced to unite with the Islamic Coalition Council of Afghanistan, which gave rise to the **Islamic Unity Party** in 1989.

***TEHRIK-E-JAFARIA PAKISTAN* (TJP)/MOVEMENT OF THE PAKISTANI SHIITES.** A **Shiite**-based **Islamic political party** in **Pakistan**, TJP was formed in 1979 under the name *Tehrik-e-Nafaz-e-Fiqah-e-Jafaria*. The group was created specifically in reaction the 2 December 1978 Pakistani laws that were introduced that directly affected the Shiite community—especially those employed in Pakistani civil service positions and the armed forces. Since its inception, TJP has been led by Sajid Ali Naqvi. However, founding member Arif Hussein was **assassinated** in 1988. The group has been banned by the Pakistani **government** twice, yet it continued to advocate for the rights of the Shiite community. Uncharacteristic of many similar groups, TJP has also worked together with **Sunni** Muslims and does not advocate a purely Shiite **Islamic state**. These progressive positions allowed it to join the **United Council of Action**. However, with the election of Benazir Bhutto as the Pakistani prime minister on 19 October 1993, the Shiite population did not feel as threatened, and therefore the need for such groups as the TJP fell into decline. This climate did not last long, as 2005 saw increased oppression of the Shiite by groups such a *Jaish-e-Muhammad*.

TEHRIK-E-JIHAD. A Kashmiri *mujahideen* group, *Tehrik-e-Jihad* was formed in March 1997 as a result of a merger between *Ansar al-Islam* and a splinter group of *Al-Barq* (The Thunder). Led by Farooq Qureshi and serving as the militant front for the Muslim Conference in Kashmir, the organization seeks the liberation of Kashmir from Indian control and the absorption of that territory into **Pakistan**. Reportedly, the group is comprised of a number of Kashmiri nationals as well as **Afghans** and Pakistanis (many of whom were former members of the Pakistani army). Militarily successful on various levels, its most notable victory came on 22 May 1999, when *Tehrik-e-Jihad* announced that it had captured a sizable area of the Kargil district in Jammu and Kashmir. *See also* KASHMIRI SEPARATISM.

TEHRIK-E-KHATME NABUWWAT/TEHRIK-E-TAHAFUZ-E-KHATM-E-NABUWAT. *Tehrik-e-Khatme Nabuwwat* (Last Prophethood Movement) is a Pakistani religious movement that is ideologically focused on the finality of the **Prophet Muhammad**, namely, that Muhammad was the last Prophet of **Islam**, as illustrated in many verses in the **Quran**. With origins in the 1947 formation of **Pakistan**, the movement began to take shape and was officially called *Kul Jamati Majlis-e-Aml Tahafuz-e-Khatm-e-Nabuwat*. The theological thrust of this group can be traced back to the first foreign minister of Pakistan, Chaudhry Zafarullah Khan. During his time in office, he began to lend support to the **Ahmadiyya Muslim community**. The problem with his patronage of the group is that it believes that Mirza Ghulam Ahmad (1835–1908) was the final prophet of Islam, not Muhammad. So, in retaliation for this deemed **apostasy**, the *Tehrik-e-Tahafuz-e-Khatm-e-Nabuwat* movement was formed. This was the first group that formed despite any individual differences in order to protect the legacy and finality of Muhammad. It set out to remove Khan from his legislative post, remove any Ahmadis from their positions in the **government**, and declare them as non-Muslim infidels.

The group began taking shape in 1949 under the name *Majlis-e-Khatm-e-Nabuwat*, and by 1954 its protests had earned it illegality, and it renamed itself *Majlis-e-Tahafuz-e-Khatm-e-Nabuwwat*. The year 1973 saw success for the movement, as the Ahmadis were declared non-Muslim by the Jammu and Kashmir president and the *Rabta-e-Alam-e-Islami* Conference in **Saudi Arabia**. The next year, in December 1974, Pakistan's government unanimously voted on its second amendment, which declared the group non-Muslim. Throughout the 1980s, the organization dealt with enforcing the sanctions and continuing to oppress the Ahmadi people. Another group that arose for the same purpose as the *Tehrik-e-Khatme Nabuwwat* is the ***Pasban Khatme Nabuwat***. *See also* HERESY.

TEHRIK-UL-MUJAHIDEEN* (TuM)/MUJAHIDEEN MOVEMENT.** Established in June 1990 by the head of the Jammu and Kashmir *Jamaat-e-Ahle Hadith*, Yunus Khan, TuM hopes to have the territories of Jammu and Kashmir secede from India and merge within **Pakistan**. Using the tactic of **pan-Islamism**, TuM has also received protection and support from many small **Sunni** Muslim communities throughout the area. Currently, Jamal ur-Rehman is the *amir* of the group and receives further assistance from **Fazul ur-Rehman**, the leader of ***Jamaat Ulema-e-Islam and a member of the Pakistani National Assembly. However, the group suffered some major setbacks during the 1990s, when its main leaders (Khan in 1991 and commander Abu Waseem Salafi in 1999, among others) were killed by security forces.

The organization has a military-type structure with the *amir* at the top, followed by a deputy chief, an operations chief, a military adviser, an intelligence chief, and then district commanders, divisional commanders, and finally regiment commanders at the field level. TuM is composed primarily of Jammu, Kashmir, and Pakistan nationals and operates almost exclusively in the Kashmir Valley. **Bangladesh**, the Persian Gulf states, and Pakistan have all provided financial assistance to the group over the years, especially **Saudi Arabia**'s Haramain Islamic Foundation. Most of the funds received by TuM have been transmitted using *hawala* transactions. The group is also a member of the **United Jihad Council** and has a close relationship with the Jammu and Kashmir Liberation Front and ***Lashkar-e-Tayyiba***. *See also* KASHMIRI SEPARATISM; *MUJAHIDEEN*.

TERRORISM. It is of the utmost importance to stress that there is no consensus on the definition of terrorism, and for that reason the use of the term in this dictionary has been severely limited for didactic reasons. What is commonly called "Islamic terrorism" has no foundation in the **Quran** and the **Hadiths** and is rather the result of ideological choices and certain biases in **interpretation** of the Islamic teachings (*irhaab*). However, a case can be made that terrorists are aggressive **extremists** who attack both civilians and nonmilitants as often as security and military targets. Different groups' tactics can also help in defining which type of target they wish to attack. For example, antiaircraft artillery would be used more for antimilitary aggressions, whereas car bombs would result in more civilian casualties. These examples, of course, are not always consistent but are general. Another defining characteristic of terrorists is that the insurgencies are almost always politically motivated and that, in using their tactics, they hope to instill a sense of fear so that the observers of their aggressions will respond in some way that would benefit their cause.

There are, however, two types of terrorism: domestic and international. Domestic terrorism is understood to be limited only to a certain area and is conducted by an internal force that often seeks official recognition. Motives for domestic terrorism are usually to harm the economy and to hurt those representatives of the **government** who are seen as impeding the terrorists' goals. International terrorism is not defined by one specific territory or country and is usually focused on creating turmoil throughout a particular government or governments in the hope of influencing their **legislation**, and it is sometimes state sponsored. Furthermore, domestic terrorists are often part of a separatist movement that seeks to be recognized as an independent, legitimate nation-state. Conversely, international terrorists usually try to injure a particular state for ideological or political reasons.

Radical Islamic **fundamentalist** groups have often transcended territorial boundaries in attempts to further promote their Islamic agenda of creating a **pan-Islamic state** throughout the Muslim nations. In addition, their international barbarism has been justified through their **jihad** to protect **Islam** from its perceived enemies (Europe, **Israel**, and the **United States**). Other defining characteristics of international terrorism include the use of psychological warfare, which is described as targeting civilians rather than security targets in the hopes of creating a state of public anxiety. In doing this, there is also a communications outlet created that can induce the public spectators to hear and possibly understand their political and ideological goals (common for the jihadist groups that justify their military actions as being secondary to their religious aims). This can also result in pressuring governments to consent to their demands. These tactics are often used to serve a greater sociopolitical end that is larger in breadth than the actual **violence** itself. When this characteristic is applied, it is often seen as a form of low-intensity conflict that is often promoted by other governments. This type of conflict combines tactical insurgency with diplomatic pressure and is incredibly cost effective for the sponsoring state. It forces the attacked government to spend more money on protecting its people and deters tourism, which is a valuable industry for many of these states.

A great deal of incongruity comes with terrorist attacks, making it hard to define and difficult for the defending state to repress. For example, if these attacks are viewed as mere criminal infractions, then it should be repressed by using simple police force, which is a minimal type of resistance. If the government views the attacks as military aggressions, then maximum and high-cost force should be used. Third, if seen as a political matter, then diplomatic resolutions would be in order in the form of negotiations. One of the main reasons why terrorism has become an effective **method** for many extremists is because of the diffuseness that it creates. *See also* RADICALISM.

THEOCRACY. Islam's governmental policies are ones based on *sharia* (Islamic law) and the **divine governance** of **Allah** (*hakimiyya*) and thus are theocratic in nature. However, *sharia* merely guides society based on the essence of Islam and the **consensus** of the community. Theocracy, by definition, usually also calls for the establishment of a group of religious clerics who would oversee the adherence to the **religion** within the administration—this quality is found only in the **Shiite** school of Islam. In **Sunni** Islam, clerics are seen merely as Islamic scholars who do not possess any authority with regard to legislation. Therefore, a Shiite Islamic society could be more appropriately defined as a theocracy as opposed to a Sunni one.

Ayatollah Ruhollah al-Masawi Khomeini made his argument for the necessity of the clerical body in Islamic law in his book *Islamic Government*, in which he states that **Islamic government** should be based on **jurisprudence** and that the jurists (the council of clerics) should play a key role in the development of an **Islamic society**. Some deny this discourse, stating that no specific group, no matter how well versed in the **divine texts**, should ever hold an authoritative position since Allah is the ultimate authority and possesses divine governance. Most **fundamentalists** will therefore agree that Islam is not a theocracy since an individual or group cannot have a position of ideological rule. This opposition over a clerical authority versus consensus and **consultation** is one of the main differences and sources of disagreement between the Shiite and Sunni schools of Islam. *See also* GOVERNMENT; ISLAMIC REPUBLIC OF IRAN; ISLAMIC STATE.

THEOLOGY. Many Islamic **fundamentalists** deny any **legitimacy** to theology since they believe that no individual can ever completely understand the divine no matter how well versed he or she is in the **divine texts**. Some also agree that since Islamic **interpretations** have historically and contemporarily been in a constant state of evolution, there cannot be a universal theology with regard to Islam. However, moderate fundamentalists have encouraged the idea of opening intellectual circles so that traditional interpretations can continue to evolve to create an **Islamic state** that takes into account **modernity**. There is also a **consensus** between the varying degrees of fundamentalism in that the individual's positive, Islamic interpretation of the texts is what is most important when discussing theology.

AL-TIJANIYYA. Established in North Africa as far back as 1801, *al-Tijaniyya* is a Turkish **Sufi** movement. The group was led by Turkish businessman Kamal Billo Oghlo and was ideologically focused on the destruction of **paganism**. In 1925, when members of *al-Tijaniyya* attempted a failed revolt in Minaman, Turkey, many of its leaders and affiliates were executed. Although the group's power waned a great deal because of the 1925 event, a minor resurgence occurred after World War II. Numerous followers of the *al-Tijaniyya* Sufi movement still exist in many Muslim countries, especially those states that were under the rule of the Ottoman **caliphate** until 1924.

TOURÉ, GENERAL AMADOU TOUMANI (1948–). Born in Mopti, **Mali**, General Amadou Toumani Touré was the leader of the coup d'état that led to the deposition of General **Moussa Traoré** in March 1991. Afterward, Touré assumed control of the country and became the leader of the Transitional Committee for the Welfare of the People until elections took place in April 1992. These elections were the first multiparty elections in the country, and Alpha Oumar Konaré then became the first president under the new legislature. Touré was instrumental in the formation of the **Constitution** of Mali and eventually gained the nickname "The Solider of Democracy." In 2002, Touré ran in the Malian presidential elections after his retirement from the army in 2001. Winning 64.35 percent of the votes, Touré was sworn in on 8 June 2002. On 8 June 2007, Touré was again sworn in as president of Mali after running for reelection and obtaining an overwhelming 71.20 percent of the votes.

TRADITIONALISM/*TAQLID*/IMITATION. Although looking to the past is usually regarded unfavorably by the Islamic **fundamentalists** because they feel that **history** has proven to not adhere to the Islamic ideal, most fundamentalists do support turning to the generation of the **Prophet Muhammad** and the first four **caliphs** (some validate only the first three caliphs). The imitation of these generations is endorsed because, to the fundamentalists, they were marked by Islamic purity. Traditionally viewed dogmas have, over time, resulted in false **interpretations** or have lost their true meaning over the course of time—another reason for which imitation of past Islamic **theologies** is frowned on. When employing traditionalism, doctrines also run the risk of being boiled down to a **philosophy** that can be reinterpreted or modified using more **reason** and so forth. Some fundamentalists have also alleged that past periods in Islam have submitted to political authoritarianism, resulting in neglect of the **Quran**, an event that should not be repeated. Traditionalism has also led to the exclusion of Islam from both religious and political authorities.

TRANS-SAHARAN COUNTER-TERRORISM INITIATIVE (TSCTI). Constructed by the **United States**, the TSCTI seeks to dispel **terrorism** in trans-Saharan Africa through military and civil organizations. The TSCTI began in June 2005 with its initial operation, Exercise Flintlock. Eleven African countries (**Algeria**, Burkina Faso, Chad, **Libya**, **Mali**, **Mauritania**, **Morocco**, **Niger**, Nigeria, Senegal, and **Tunisia**) have joined in membership to provide training and political assistance to prevent the growth of or to eliminate Islamist occupation in the desolate desert areas of these countries. A successor of the **Pan-Sahel Initiative**, the TSCTI has been criticized as stimulating antagonism between the African countries. The United States African Command, or AFRICOM, has overseen TSCTI operations since 1 October 2008.

TRAORÉ, GENERAL MOUSSA (1936–). Born in Kayes, **Mali**, General Moussa Traoré led the country for 23 years under a military dictatorship from 19 November 1968 to 26 March 1991. Traoré came to power as a lieutenant after leading the ousting of President Modibo Keïta in 1968. Traoré's rule is stained by a police state in the country, hostile monitoring of Malian citizens, and single-party politics. The early 1990s brought political opposition to Traoré's regime and peaked during a demonstration on 22 March 1991, when Malian troops assaulted participants during a pro**democracy** gathering in the capital city of Bamako. The orders to open fire apparently came directly from Traoré, and the **violence** killed an estimated 300 protestors. Four days later, on 26 March, Traoré's reign ended as a result of a military coup organized by Malian General **Amadou Toumani Touré**. Traoré was condemned to death twice, once in 1993 for the crimes committed during the March 1991 protests and again in 1999 with his wife, Mariam Traoré, for economic crimes of embezzlement. However, their sentences were reduced to life imprisonment, and in 2002 the couple was officially pardoned. Traoré has since retired from politics.

TUNISIA. In Tunisia, most political and radical opposition groups were swiftly suppressed because of its postcolonial regime, which has regularly and successfully thwarted Islamist attempts to disrupt its social order. Tunisians also take pride in their moderate views on **Islam**, making it difficult for a domestic or foreign Islamic **fundamentalist** group to take root. In fact, most **extremists** have imported their ideologies into the country from elsewhere. It has also been deemed illegal by the **government** to participate in Islamist activities. However, despite the government's fairly successful attempts to marginalize the Islamists, Tunisia's overly secular policies and socioeconomic problems have paved the way for the emergence of new **Islamic political parties** that desire a return to orthodox Islam.

The history of the contemporary Islamic fundamentalist movement in Tunisia is marked by the 1970 inception of the **Quaranic Preservation Society**. Apolitical in its foundation, the group was permitted by the government and focused on the education and encouragement of piety in the Muslim community. Under the first Tunisian president, Habib Bourguiba, who was in office from 25 July 1957 to 7 November 1987, the group was admitted by the Ministry of Religious Affairs since it did not seek the implementation of an **Islamic state**. However, by the end of the decade, social instability had led to a splintering of the group. Most of these fragments were radicals, such as **Rashed al-Ghannushi**, who went on to establish the **Islamic Tendency Movement**. Renamed *Ennahda* (Renaissance Party) and calling for an overthrow of Bourguiba's one-party regime, the group is the most influential and dominant Islamist party in Tunisia. Although it was banned by the government, it has been estimated that over 90 percent of Tunisian Islamists support *Ennahda*. Other, smaller Islamic extremist groups do exist within the country, but *Ennahda* is one of the few that is based within the territory of the country and is comprised primarily of nationals.

Another group that has taken hold is *Tabligh wa Da'wa* (Transmission and Preaching). **Pakistani** in origin, the group nevertheless retained significant influence among Tunisian reformers. The **Islamic Liberation Party** also gained a foothold but is relatively small in size and more radical in its aims to forcibly replace the government with a **caliphate**. More recently, the **Tunisian Combatant Group**, formed in 2000, has allegedly established connections with **al-Qaeda** and has participated in violent attacks with the goal of creating an orthodox Islamic regime. Although **al-Qaeda in the Islamic Maghreb** (AQIM) apparently does not have a significant military or organizational base in Tunisia, it still has carried out some tourist kidnappings in the south as well as attacks near the capital Tunis on 24 December 2006 and 3 January 2007. This obliged the Tunisian army to intervene to get rid of the affiliated group of AQIM.

In Tunisia, the university has become a place of heightened political **activism**, a forum in which confrontation, debate, rhetoric, and discussion among varying tendencies in Tunisian sociopolitical ideologies can occur. The highly historical, structured, and increasingly fractured politics within the country has created a place for early theories of political Islam to be fostered. Not only have these administrative ideologies been growing, but they have been organized and discussed in such a way that the country can now take on a new political discourse because of its educated and informed classes of university students and graduates.

The increasingly deplorable socioeconomic situation in Tunisia has been the main cause of growing Islamist support and sympathies throughout the country. However, it has been noted that the citizenry has witnessed the incredible strife that their neighbors in **Algeria** faced because of the rise of **Islamic groups**, leading to a more convincing restraint on Islamists in Tunisia. Adhering to the trends in membership, the younger university-enrolled populations in particular have been susceptible to this proliferation of Islamic political ideologies and, along with the poorer males in general, have been the biggest supporters of the Islamists. All Islamic groups have gained influence since the **Arab Spring** revolutions of 2011.

The most prominent and popular Islamic group in Tunisia is the ***Ennahda*** Party. The main impediment to Islamist groups in Tunisia is the country's strong secular tradition. Since its independence from France in 1956, the Tunisian government has been rooted in a secular Arab nationalist ideology that conflicts greatly with the strictly traditional Muslim beliefs of the Islamist groups. This foundational party, the Neo-Destour Party and then *Rassemblement Constitutionel Démocratique*, was renamed the Party of Ben Ali in 1987. Instrumental in Tunisia gaining independence from France, it has been not only a party marked by violence but also the only ruling party in the country since independence.

During the early 1990s, the government of Tunisia sought to eliminate Islamists from public life and put hundreds of people on trial on allegations obtained through torture and sentenced party leaders to imprisonment or exile. Supporters of these Islamist groups hid their sympathies and financial backing to avoid arrest, and members had to keep an extremely low profile. However, this all changed in 2011 as Tunisia became the place that ignited the Arab revolutions.

On 14 January 2011, the political regime of President Zine al-Abidine Ben Ali collapsed, and the ruler was forced into exile. Because of these events, many previously marginalized and harassed opposition figures are expected to establish themselves as mainstream politicians in Tunisia. If **democracy** prevails, as seems to be the case presently, it could directly benefit these

Islamist groups since they appeal primarily to the lower classes. Yet the idea that anarchy could be caused by the Tunisian Islamic groups alarms the population, especially the middle classes and the army, while any outbreak of violence or fighting could result in a new dictatorship.

However, on 23 October 2011, an election for the Constituent Assembly was held in the country. Comprised of 217 members, it marked the first free election held in Tunisia since its independence in 1956. In addition, it was the first election held in the countries that participated in the Arab Spring. The assembly's First Party was won by *Ennahda*, led by Hamadi Jebali, and obtained 90 of the 217 seats. Possibly the most notable aspect of these elections was that there was a total of 11,686 candidates running on 1,517 lists. This participation more than illustrates the national pride and success of the Tunisian rebellion. *See also* TUNISIAN ISLAMIC FRONT.

TUNISIAN COMBATANT GROUP (TCG)/*GROUPE COMBATTANT TUNISIEN*. The TCG also operates and is also known as the Tunisian Islamic Fighting Group. The TCG's goals reportedly include establishing an Islamic **government** in **Tunisia** and targeting Tunisian and **Western** interests. Founded in 2000 by Tarek Maaroufi and Saifallah Ben Hassine, the group has come to be associated with **al-Qaeda** and other North African Islamic **extremists** in Europe who have been implicated in anti-U.S. terrorist plots there during 2001. In December 2010, Belgian authorities arrested Maaroufi and charged him with providing stolen passports and fraudulent visas for those involved in the **assassination** of Ahmed Shah Massood, which took place just before the **World Trade Center and Pentagon attacks of September 11, 2001**. Tunisians associated with the TCG are part of the support network of the international **Salafi** movement. TCG members are engaged in the trafficking of false documents and recruitment for Afghan training camps. Some TCG associates are suspected of planning an attack against **United States**, **Algerian**, and Tunisian diplomatic interests. Members reportedly maintain ties to the Algerian **Salafi Group for Preaching and Combat**.

TUNISIAN ISLAMIC FRONT/*FRONT ISLAMIQUE TUNISIEN* (FIT). A **Tunisian** militant **Islamic group**, the FIT has been allegedly working in conjunction with the **Algerian Armed Islamic Group** (AIG) by sending its members to train in the AIG camps. When a change in Tunisia and a greater increase in **democratic** political ideology were rebuffed by the **government** of Ben Ali, **Abdullah Bin Omar** set up FIT at the end of the 1980s. The group has claimed responsibility for a number of attacks and deaths, especially along the Tunisia-Algeria border. The **extremist** FIT warns all foreigners to leave Tunisia and has become the armed wing of the *Ennahda*

in Tunisia political group. Members of FIT include Riyad Bil Mohammed Tahir Nasseri and Abdullah Al-Hajji Ben Amor. FIT also has a range of contacts with other extremist and Islamic movements.

AL-TURABI, HASSAN 'ABD ALLAH (1932?–). Hassan 'Abd Allah al-Turabi, commonly referred to simply as Hassan al-Turabi, is a political Islamist leader who was born in Kassala, **Sudan**, and was a member of the Islamic Charter Front, a splinter organization of the **Muslim Brotherhood in Sudan**. During his membership in the Islamic Charter Front, the **Islamic political party** appointed al-Turabi as secretary-general in 1964. While in this position, al-Turabi worked with the Ansar and Khatmiyyah factions of the Sudanese Islamic Movement to draft a new Islamic **constitution** for the country (he had also once helped **Pakistan** and the United Arab Emirates draft their constitutions). Also a leader of the **National Islamic Front**, al-Turabi came to the forefront of the Sudanese Socialist Union and was made minister of justice in 1979 and also held posts as minister of foreign affairs and deputy prime minister.

In June 1989, the Salvation Revolution (*Thawrat al-Inqadh*), led by General **'Umar al-Bashir**, overthrew the democratic regime in Sudan. Al-Turabi, being the ideological leader of the group, rose to significant power along with his National Islamic Front and introduced a period of heavy repression throughout the country. Al-Turabi also had a close working alliance with **Osama bin Laden** and encouraged the **jihadist** to relocate his operations to Sudan from 1992 to 1996. In 1991, al-Turabi convened the **Popular Arab and Islamic Conference**, which brought many **Islamic groups** together for an annual meeting. This meeting, also referred to as the "Congress," consisted of members of the **Palestinian Liberation Organization**, **Hamas**, **Egyptian Islamic Jihad**, Algerian Islamic Jihad, and *Hizbullah* **in Lebanon**.

Although al-Turabi is an ideological figure especially in the northern part of the Sudan, the National Islamic Front saw a decline in its influence during the 1990s, when the Sudanese public opted for a more pragmatic leadership. This change in political direction was a direct result of the unanimous votes by the United Nations to place economic sanctions on the Sudanese for their assistance in the attempted **assassination** of President Hosni Mubarak of **Egypt** in 1995. Because of these actions and the increasingly harsh violence enacted by the National Islamic Front, al-Turabi's power became synonymous with **human rights** violations and primitive **theologies**. Regardless of his party's decline in popularity in Sudan, al-Turabi was elected speaker of the parliament in March 1996. But in March 2004, on orders from his former associate, President **'Umar Hasan Ahmed al-Bashir**, he was imprisoned in Khartoum at the Kobar prison until 28 June 2005. Despite his incarceration, al-Turabi is still seen as a leading theoretician and ideologist for North Africa and the Middle East, especially in terms of his willingness to adopt Western discourses and to use Islamization as a means to modernize Islamic society.

TYRANNY/*TAGHUT*. **Islam** does not tolerate or give **legitimacy** to tyrannical rule since such **governance** is based on the laws of man, not **Allah**. **Fundamentalists** also blame tyranny for the marginalization of many Muslims and the oppression of **Islam** since totalitarianism has forced specific political and religious platforms on the governed populations, creating a society of restricted freedoms. In Islam, *sharia* (Islamic law) is the preferred form of **legislation** since it is based on Allah's will as **interpreted** through the **Quran** and places the community at the forefront of administrative decisions. Fundamentalists insist that the only form of commitment should be to Allah, not to any other institution.

U

UKHUWWA/BROTHERHOOD. This concept, in the eyes of Muslims, refers to the belief that all Muslims are "brothers" with each other. **Women**, then, are also considered to be their "sisters" and are engaged in a sort of sisterhood as there is a brotherhood. This idea of brotherhood not only is the cornerstone of many Islamic social groups and **Islamic political parties** (most notably the **Muslim Brotherhood**) but also is shared among even the most inactive members of **Islam**. Brotherhood, conceived as being related to fraternity and solidarity, is translated in the Muslim perception as being the reason for charity and aid. Charity, being one of the Pillars of Islam, also then corresponds directly to family and the *umma* (**nation**). Therefore, for the Muslim, brotherhood is a type of solid bond that strengthens the universal Muslim world and perpetuates a moral and social prosperity.

AL-UMAR MUJAHIDEEN (AuM)/THE *MUJAHIDEEN* OF UMAR. AuM was formed by Mushtaq Ahmad Zargar in December 1989. The group's name comes from the Srinagar cleric Maulvi Umar Farooq, who backed the inception of AuM as a group seeking to oust India from Jammu and Kashmir. Since it is a Jammu and Kashmir separatist group, a majority of the group's members came from Srinagar, the capital of the Indian state of Jammu and Kashmir. Primarily active in Srinagar, the group's main center of operations lies in Muzaffarabad, **Pakistan**. Accused of perpetrating over 40 murders, Zargar was arrested in Srinagar on 15 May 1992 (released on 3 December 1999) and was replaced by Manzoor Ahmad Ganai as commander of the organization. Other high-ranking leaders of AuM include Latif-ul-Haq and Jamshed Khan.

AuM also possesses a military outfit called the al-Umar Commando Force, and the entire entity is divided into the supreme command and the field formations. The group has approximately 700 militants in its force. AuM made use of the ransoming of hostages, attacks on political officials, and civilian offensives in its attempts to gain control of Kashmir and incorporate it into the Pakistani Islamic structure. *Jaish-e-Muhammad* has worked with *al-Umar Mujahideen* on a number of these attacks. A member of the **United Jihad Council**, the group supposedly received financial support from Pakistan's Inter-Service Intelligence. *See also* KASHMIRI SEPARATISM.

UMMA. *See* NATION.

UNBELIEF. *See KUFR.*

UNITED COUNCIL OF ACTION/*MUTTAHIDA MAJLIS-E-AMAL* (MMA). Established in 2001 by a number of **Islamic groups** from **Pakistan**, MMA serves as a coalition for these organizations with hopes of altering the Pakistani application of *sharia* (Islamic law) throughout the country. These groups include *Jamaat Ahl al-Hadith*, *Jamaat-e-Islami*, **Jammu and Kashmir** *Jamaat-e-Islami*, *Jamaat-e-Islami-e-Pakistan*, *Jamaat-ul-Ulema-e-Islam Fazal*, *Jamaat-ul-Ulema-e-Pakistan*, *Jamaat-ul-Ulema-Islami Sami*, and *Tehrik-e-Jafaria* **Pakistan**. Since its formation, MMA stands as an opposition force to the Pakistani Parliament and has become the foremost **Islamic political party** since. The major grievance of MMA is that despite the country's **constitution** declaring *sharia* as the law of the land, it is not applied to foreign policy. Pakistan's relationship with the **United States** makes this especially difficult, considering that most hard-line Islamists (which the coalition is comprised of) want the complete elimination of all **Western** presence within the Muslim world.

MMA achieved electoral successes, notably in 2002, but accusations of the results being manipulated by Pakistani President General Pervez Musharraf and the Inter-Services Intelligence have led to some criticism of the coalition's legitimacy. Nevertheless, the opposition group was the ruling political party in Balochistan province and North-West Frontier province until 2008. Among the groups that form MMA, the *Jamaat-ul-Ulema-e-Islami Fazal* (JuI-F) is the largest and most influential. Coincidently, in 2005 the *Jamaat-ul-Ulema-e-Islami Sami* left the organization because of differences with JuI-F and *Jamaat-e-Islami* leaders. *See also* UR-REHMAN, FAZAL.

UNITED DEVELOPMENT PARTY (UDP). An **Islamic political party** in Indonesia led by Suryadharma Ali, the UDP was formed out of a merger of four ideologically similar parties during the 1971 legislative elections. The groups coalesced after the **government** declared that too many parties were running on the ballot, so in order to keep a political presence, the UDP was created on 5 January 1973. Politically, the party began to oppose the increasingly authoritarian regime of President Suharto (in office 12 March 1967–21 May 1998), so the government began to publicly associate the group with the Jihad Commando in order to derail any social support the party might gain. This propagandistic tactic proved to be successful, and the UDP lost the 1977 legislative elections to the pro-Suharto Golkar Party.

Throughout Suharto's rule as Indonesian president, the UDP continued to be one of the leading opposition parties in the country. Constantly criticizing, protesting, and accusing the presidency of fraudulent acts, the party was oppressed by the government for its use of Islamic symbols and ideologies. Although this repression did not necessarily weaken its strength, the withdrawal of one of its leading members in 1984, Abdurrahman Wahid, did. However, shortly after, the group was strengthened briefly when in 1988 its chairman, Jaelani Naro, was nominated as a vice-presidential candidate—an act that Suharto condemned, citing the oppositional nature of Naro's allegiance and forcing him to resign from his candidacy.

Undermined by the events leading up to the 1988 elections, the UDP was quiet until the fall of Suharto in 1998 and the Indonesia New Order began. With the New Order in power, the UDP returned as the second-largest party in the country, resumed its Islamic associations, and ran in the 1999 legislative elections. During these elections, the group aligned itself with other Islamic political parties and formed the Central Axis coalition. This saw the return of Wahid to the group as he was nominated as Indonesian president during the elections. The Central Axis also nominated UDP Chairman Hamzah Haz for the vice presidency. However, after Wahid won the election and became the fourth president of Indonesia on 20 October 1999, many of his former supporters began to withdraw their patronage after allegations that Wahid wanted to reestablish diplomatic relations with **Israel**—an action that many of the Islamic parties had a problem with.

As the years passed, the UDP began to lose more and more public support and by the 2004 elections only won 8.1 percent of the votes (making it only the third-largest political party in Indonesia). After realizing its decrease in public support, the party refrained from aligning with other Islamic political groups and in so doing was rewarded with lucrative positions within the government. Chairman Ali was made minister of cooperatives and state and medium-size enterprises within the president's cabinet, and the party (although receiving only 5.3 percent of the votes in the 2009 elections) was given 37 seats in the People's Representative Council (the Indonesian Parliament).

UNITED JIHAD COUNCIL (UJC). Also referred to as the *Muttahida* Jihad Council, the UJC is an amalgamation of **Islamic** militant groups. Established in 1994, the UJC is currently led by Syed Salahuddin, who is also the head of the largest **jihadi** group in Jammu and Kashmir, *Hizb-ul-Mujahideen*. Created to unify the different militant groups in order to more efficiently achieve their goal of removing Kashmir from India's control, the UJC is also a sort of forum for various information and resources to be exchanged between the groups. The UJC benefits from Kashmiri and **Pakistani** financial support.

Allegedly, both sources also provide arms, ammunition, recruits, and tactical information. By 1999 the UJC had roughly 15 groups as members, but currently only 5 of them remain effective: *Al-Badr*, *Harakat-ul-Mujahideen*, *Hizb ul-Mujahideen*, *Lashkar-e-Tayyiba*, and *Tehrik-e-Jihad*. *See also* KASHMIRI SEPARATISM.

UNITED MALAYS NATIONAL ORGANIZATION (UMNO). Malaysia's largest **Islamic political party**, the UMNO is ideologically centered on establishing an **Islamic state** throughout the country. Using Malay nationalism, members claim that through doctrinal similarity the national culture of Malaysia can be preserved and ethnic diversity can be diminished. The group's origins are rooted in the return of the British forces to the state following World War II. After this, the Malayan Union was formed on 11 May 1946 as a nationalist party in favor of the Malayan identity. Although not originally a political party, the newly formed UMNO tried to work with the British, especially with the onslaught of communist forces that were threatening the country. However, by 1949, UMNO became more politically active after the Malayan Union re-formed itself into the Federation of Malaya.

The party was strict in its pronationalist platform and was unwelcoming to non-Malay people, resulting in many members defecting from the group. However, UMNO gained massive public support and along with the **Pan-Malaysian Islamic Party** began to dominate the political scene of the 1950s. The group was also particularly instrumental in achieving the Malaysian independence from Great Britain on 31 August 1957. The new **constitution** that was drafted then declared **Islam** as the official creed of Malaysia. During the first elections of the new Malayan federation in 1959, UMNO won the majority of the seats in parliament (74 of 104). With the power of UMNO at hand, the organization began to spread throughout the surrounding areas of Malaysia (specifically in Singapore), and support therefore increased. Still in alliance with the Pan-Malaysian Islamic Party, UMNO continued with its platform of strengthening Islam's influence over the nation during the 1960s.

However, as the country began slipping into economic decline and political corruption, many university students (mostly from the Islamic Youth Movement of Malaysia) and professors began to protest against the National Front and were arrested. Many of these protestors were also members of UMNO and the Pan-Malaysian Islamic Party. Public demonstrations and assemblies that could undermine the **government** were banned in 1975. Still, the pro-Malay/pro-Islam UMNO tried to work with the Malaysian government (since it continued to gain majorities in elections) to achieve a positive relationship. In fact, UMNO's president, Mahathir Muhammad, was Malaysia's prime minister for 12 years.

Throughout the 1980s, more and more UMNO-related branches began to emerge, so much so that on 4 February 1988 a ruling was made that declared UMNO illegal since it was the umbrella group to many unregistered (and thereby illegal) political parties. In light of this judgment, UMNO was turned into UMNO Malaysia but was quickly disbanded after not being allowed to register legally. This led to the formation of UMNO (New) and then the UMNO (Baru)—the formation of both was spearheaded by Mahathir Muhammad.

However, in 2003 Muhammad retired and Abdullah Ahmad Badawi became the new president of UMNO (Baru) and consequently prime minister of Malaysia. Badawi continued with the group's platform of nationalism and the promotion of Islam, although the tide was changing in favor of a more moderate rather than conservative approach. For example, non-Malay and non-Muslim people may now join the party. Yet **extremist** factions do exist within the organization, such as the UMNO Youth. To counteract allegations of racial tensions and segregation against non-Malay nationals, UMNO adopted the ideologies of Malaysia (created on 16 September 2008), standing for ethnic harmony and unity. *See also ANGKATAN BELIA ISLAM MALAYSIA*; PAN-MALAYSIAN ISLAMIC PARTY.

UNITED STATES OF AMERICA. The foundations of the U.S. relationship with the Arabic world were laid in February 1945, when President Franklin Delano Roosevelt (1933–1945) met with Saudi king and founder Ibn Saud (1932–1953) on the USS *Quincy*. That year, **Saudi Arabia** entered a strategic alliance with the United States that implied mainly that the United States will give protection and support to Saudi Arabia as long as the Saudi kingdom provides oil to the U.S. economy and companies. This alliance was unique at the time and passed the baton from Great Britain, which was the dominant power in the region before World War II. For the United States, this alliance with Saudi Arabia in the 1950s enabled it to counter the Soviet communist influence that was rising in the region. Thus, it was very important for the United States to secure these oil resources in the Middle East and to deter the Soviet Union from gaining power there. This was especially important because **Egypt**'s leader at that time, Gamal Abdel Nasser (1952–1970), decided after the "Triple Aggression," which was Great Britain, France, and **Israel** attacking Egypt, in 1956 to join the Soviet bloc and apply socialism in Egypt. Saudi Arabia was the only regional power that could balance the impact of Egypt's decision.

This Saudi-U.S. alliance was then reinforced during the end of the decade by the Eisenhower doctrine on 5 January 1957, stating that the United States would give support to any country in the world aiming to resist the communists.

During the 1967 Israeli-Arab War (5–10 June), the United States militarily and politically supported **Israel** against its Arab foes. This was the first
time that the United States, as a world superpower, appeared as an enemy to
the Arab interests and more of a strategic ally to Israel. After this war, the
Islamist forces almost everywhere in the Islamic world began to question the
alliance made between the United States and Saudi Arabia. In addition, the
Islamists began to see the American forces as servants of the holy wars of
Islam.

This image was then reinforced during the 1973 Israeli-Arab War (6–25
October), when the United States gave even more support to Israel, which
was critically endangered. As evidence of Saudi Arabian independence from
the United States and to express its anger with the United States supporting
Israel, Saudi Arabia along with other countries decided to raise the price of
oil dramatically. This was the cause of the U.S. economic crisis of 1973. But
both Saudi Arabia and the United States had to remain allies since the communist threat was still there. It was especially important since almost all the
other Persian Gulf countries had became independent from Great Britain:
Kuwait (in 1961), Qatar (in 1971), **Bahrain** (in 1971), and Oman (in 1962).
The United States then had to secure all the oil in these surrounding countries
as well by making alliances with these new, independent Gulf monarchies.

Each one chose to align itself with Washington, which was especially important since **Yemen**, Saudi's neighbor and fellow Gulf country, had chosen
to become an ally of the Eastern bloc. During the 1960s, a minor competition
arose between Saudi Arabia and Yemen that was heightened when Yemen
established a communist government in Sanaa. Therefore, the United States
(which was in full support of the other Gulf countries) entered into a proxy
war with the Soviet Union that was still being supported by Egypt.

American relations with the Gulf countries had to be reinforced again after
the **Iranian Islamic Revolution of 1979**. From the beginning, Iran's leader
Ayatollah Ruhollah al-Musawi Khomeini asserted his will to counter the
U.S. presence in the Middle East, especially since the United States was a
longtime supporter of the shah of Iran. Therefore, the United States appeared
as an enemy of the new **Islamic Republic of Iran**. Part of Khomeini's agenda
was also to spread and expand the ideals of Iran's Islamic revolution to the
other countries in the surrounding region. It was his declared objective to
control all the oil resources in the Middle East as well. This, then, was the
beginning of a new alliance between the United States and **Iraq**'s Saddam
Hussein. During the early 1980s, Hussein was an Arab nationalist leader who
presented himself as the next Nasser and clearly had support of the secular
West, especially the United States, France, and Great Britain. Hussein was
also well equipped and encouraged to counter Khomeini's will to expand the

Islamic revolution in the region. This was the second proxy war in the region that the United States was involved in. This conflict, both verbal and military, between Iran and Iraq lasted from 1980 to 1988. During all these years, the Iraqi armed forces were supported by the West and the Iranian army by the Soviet Union. The war ended in a draw, concluding without any definitive winner. However, it enabled the West to block the expansion of Iran's Islamic revolutionary agenda in the Middle East.

At the same time, the Soviets entered **Afghanistan** in 1979, occupied the country, and established a communist government there. This led to the Soviet-Afghan War (1979–1989) and was a new opportunity for the United States and Saudi Arabia to tighten their relationship. During the 1980s, while Iraq was still fighting Iran, Saudi Arabia was encouraged by the United States to send Islamist fighters to Afghanistan to fight against the Soviets and aid the **Afghan Arabs**. Saudi Arabia swiftly agreed to this support, and one of its nationals, **Osama bin Laden**, a millionaire whose family was very close to the Saudi monarchy, was appointed by the Saudi military to lead what was known as the "Arab Bureau," or *maktab al-khadamat*. He was given the mission of training and managing all the Arab volunteers coming from all over the Arab world to fight against the Soviets in Afghanistan. Like the Afghan fighters, these Arab *mujahideen* were supported militarily and tactically by the Central Intelligence Agency (CIA) and the other Arab countries' intelligence services. The Afghan experience enabled the United States to connect with many of the other Arabic governments and intelligence services that were not in the Gulf region, especially **Jordan**.

Ties between Egypt and the United States were tightened when the U.S. government mediated the peace treaty between Israel and Egypt during the 1979 Camp David Accords. By doing this, the United States succeeded in making a new major ally with Egypt. This new alliance was especially important to Egypt because the other Arabic countries rejected the peace agreement with Israel and expelled Egypt from the Arab League until 1990. Thus, by the end of the 1980s, the Soviet Union had lost two proxy wars in the Middle East, and communism was thereby contained. But most of the countries that took part in these conflicts, especially Iraq, were livid with the outcome. Many had lost a lot of money, people, and economic stability, leaving these countries in bankruptcy. As a result, they wanted to increase the oil price on the global market. The desire of Iraq to get more money from the oil trade was countered by the allies of the United States in the region—the Gulf countries and especially Iraq's neighbor Kuwait.

A major event and error on the part of Hussein's Iraq was the decision to invade Kuwait on 2 August 1990. Hussein thought that there would not be any repercussions or reactions from the United States or the Gulf countries since Iraq had fought for them against the communists just years before. Therefore, he thought that they would quietly accept the annexation of Kuwait. But this alliance between the United States and Saudi Arabia worked so well at that time that half a billion American soldiers were sent to the Gulf, and an international coalition was set up to free Kuwait from the Iraqi forces. Although this conflict lasted only a few months (2 August 1990–28 February 1991), it gave the evidence to the entire world that, after the collapse of the Soviet Union in 1991, the United States was the only superpower able to police the world.

After the Kuwait conflict (known as the Persian Gulf War), the United States was beginning to be viewed as an enemy to the Muslims and Arabs. This was due to the fact that the U.S. Army and troops of other Western countries had been hosted in the sacred land of Islam: Saudi Arabia. Prior to this perspective, the United States was not really seen as a threat to the Muslim or Arab people. Since then, many Muslims, especially those Islamist fighters who were in Afghanistan fighting against the Soviets (Afghan Arabs and *mujahideen*), perceived this presence of the United States in the region as an invasion and occupation of the holy lands of Islam. After having been an ally to the Arab world for decades, the United States quickly became the main enemy of the Afghan Arabs. The ideology of these militants was to overthrow the existent Arab regimes and replace them with **Islamic states** because they considered these countries as infidels since they made alliances with infidel countries.

The militant strategy of these groups, which was made explicit in 1998 by bin Laden, was that of global **jihad** as a response to the American global imperialism. After witnessing the failed experience of the Algerian Afghans (i.e., the Algerians who fought in Afghanistan during the Soviet-Afghan War and went back to their country at the end of 1989) who, from 1992 to 1997, used all forms of **violence** and civil war without being able to actually establish an Islamic state in Algeria, bin Laden opted for the "indirect strategy" of jihad. He believed that the Arab regimes could not be overthrown as long as they are economically and militarily supported by the West and especially by the United States. This was the turning point of **terrorism** in the Islamic world, and since then the United States and the other major Western countries (France, Great Britain, Spain, and Germany) have been priority targets of jihadi terrorism.

The major actions that signified this shift occurred during the 1990s with the **East African American embassies attacks** in 1998 in Nairobi and Dar al Saleem and then the **suicide bombing** of the USS *Cole* in the Gulf of Aden in 2000. Many of the jihadist leaders during the 1990s and especially then second in command of **al-Qaeda**, the Egyptian **Ayman al-Zawahiri** (the current leader of al-Qaeda), were also arguing that the United States would not "understand" the Islamist claims as long as the country was not targeted and attacked on its own homeland. This led to the planning and execution of the first attack on the World Trade Center in 1993. This was a warning from the jihadists, but their greater motive was still there.

The **World Trade Center and Pentagon attacks of September 11, 2001**, became the apex of their strategy and made the United States reconsider its strategy with the Islamic world. Even if the Muslims as a whole were conceived, in the common perception, as the new enemies of the United States, the United States was happy to rely on its traditional allies in the Middle East, especially Saudi Arabia, which made many efforts to eradicate the Islamist threat against the United States. But the period from 2001 to 2008 was also an extraordinary period for the United States to create or tighten relations with all the other Arab and Islamic countries. Despite the invasion of Iraq in March 2003, the "global war on terror" led by the George W. Bush administration from 2001 to 2008 was an extraordinary opportunity to form these relationships with new countries, such as Algeria and **Libya**. These two countries engaged in the ultimate contest against Islamist and jihadist groups within their own countries and abroad and therefore had much experience.

The Libyan case is particularly interesting with this "new global order" being established because of the global war on terror. Until then, Libyan leader **Muammar Qadhafi** had been widely regarded as a rogue leader and was placed under embargo for years only to resurface as an ally in the global war on terror. On the other hand, almost all the moderate and even some radical Arab and Islamic leaders came to be perceived as traitors by a section of their population and, most of all, by all Islamist and jihadi groups. This perception is due to these governments entering in the struggle against other Muslims and siding with an "infidel" country—the United States.

By the end of the 2000s, the situation in the Islamic world was explosive, and the United States was literally hated by a large part of Muslims all over the world. Despite the efforts of the newly elected Democratic President Barack Obama (2009–) to pacify the relationships with the Muslim world with his discourse in Cairo on 4 June 2009, the fact that the United States was still giving unconditional support to Israel would not change the negative perception of the United States in the Middle East. As the United States was also seen as a supporter of dictatorships, the 2011 **Arab Spring** was a new turning point in the relationship between the United States and the Arabic world. It also occurred at the same time that al-Qaeda leader Osama bin Laden was killed (2 May 2011). The U.S. administration also clearly expressed its support to the popular uprising in all these countries, showing that its alliance was to democracy and no longer dictatorships. By doing so, the United States is preparing itself for a long-term alliance with the newly elected governments in the Arab world even though most of these governments are dominated by **Islamic political parties**. At the same time, the Obama administration has also decided to withdraw a major portion of U.S. troops from the occupied lands of Islam, a major point of contention for years.

The fact that, at the same time in 2011, Iran was developing its nuclear program and explicitly threatening Israel and the other Gulf countries makes all these countries, aside from Israel, objective allies against America's new "enemy": the **Islamic Republic of Iran**.

UNITED TAJIK OPPOSITION (UTO). Led by **Sayid Abdullod Nuri**, the UTO was formed by members of the **Islamic Renaissance Party of Tajikistan**. During 1993 and 1998, the Tajik government banned the Islamic Renaissance Party, forcing many to go into exile in **Afghanistan**. It was at this time that the UTO was established. A militant **Islamic group**, the UTO fought in the Tajik Civil War (1992–1997) and focused particularly on ousting Tajik President Emomali Rahmonov, who was sworn into office on 20 November 1992. Peace accords, through mediation of the United Nations, were signed between the Tajik government and the UTO on 27 June 1997, ending the war. On 25 December 1998, Nuri announced that he would close all foreign UTO bases and called on fighters to return to the country, yet insurgencies continued to crop up for some time thereafter. Although many of the associates of the UTO are no longer in operation, some have aligned themselves with the **Islamic Movement of Uzbekistan**, and some were even granted positions within the Tajik security force.

UNIVERSALISM. A large part of the discourses for both moderate and radical Islamic **fundamentalists** is their insistence that **Islam** is a **system** that has a universality that can expel the **paganism** (and therefore, to them, the corruption) of the world as well as bring man closer to his intuition (*fitra*). This universality would first be embodied by complete submission to **Allah**'s **divine governance**, according to the fundamentalists. However, a submission of this magnitude does not mean that all personal freedoms and liberties would be excluded. Since Islam rests on the dynamic relationship between individuals, as long as different groups still adhere to *sharia* (Islamic law) and do not undermine the **religion**, tolerance is absolutely desired.

Islamic scholars have also argued for Islam's universalism in stating that the religion creates a **balance** between the moral, the physical, and the spiritual aspects of life. Islamic universalists also feel that territorial, dogmatic, political, and racial boundaries should be broken down in order for society to exist peacefully. In order to gain this universality, Islam employs *da'wa* (call), ideas of **justice**, brotherhood (***ukhuwwa***), and the teachings of the **divine texts**. To many, Islam is a comprehensive, complete system of political and social regulations that can bring about revolutionary changes. The religion is argued to have the ability to replace the earthly pleasures of carnal life and **materialism** by an existence based on truth, morality, and dignity. *See also* WORLD ORDER.

UR-REHMAN, FAZAL (1953–). Commander of *Jamaat-ul-Islami Fazal* (JuI-F), Fazal-ur-Rehman was born in Dera Ismail Khan, **Pakistan**, on 19 June 1953. Rehman entered the political scene in the 1988 elections and gained considerable support, especially because of his family's notable history in Pakistani politics, particularly in his native region, where his father (Mufti Mahmood) was provincial chief minister. Although his party's politics are those of antisecular, pro-Islamic *sharia* (Islamic law)-implemented legislation, the Muslim League has criticized some of his actions. This included, notably, his support of Benazir Bhutto's reelection as prime minister of Pakistan (victorious in her campaign, her second term lasted from 19 October 1993 to 5 November 1996). Many of his supporters claimed that it was merely a publicity stunt to deflect *Jamaat-ul-Islami Fazal*'s reputation of **human rights** violations and antifeminist regulations. In addition to being JuI-F's leader, the Islamic politician also sits on the opposition benches in the National Assembly of Pakistan, the Parliamentary Committee on Foreign Affairs, and the Senate of the Islamic Republic of Pakistan. *See also HARAKAT-UL-JIHAD AL-ISLAMI*; *JAMAAT ULEMA-E-ISLAM*; UNITED COUNCIL OF ACTION.

AL-'UTAYBI, JUHAYMAN BIN SAYF (?–1979). Juhayman bin Sayf al-'Utaybi's emergence as a militant Islamic **fundamentalist** in **Saudi Arabia** is seen as the beginning of the rise of contemporary **Islamic groups**. He is most remembered as leading a group of radicals in hopes of taking over the Great Mosque in Mecca in 1979. However, when Saudi troops intervened, al-'Utaybi was killed in the wake of the skirmish, and the mission was deemed unsuccessful. Yet the efforts and demonstration of the radical resolve during that incident are still remembered, as it took place in a very symbolic Muslim location.

V

VANGUARD/*TALI'A*. An Islamic vanguard is simply a group of committed adherents who are self-sacrificing and hope that through the **jihad**, an **Islamic state** and thereby an **Islamic society** can successfully be brought into existence. Many radical **fundamentalists** believe that the vanguard is essential to the promotion of **activism** and is specific to **Islam**. **Sayyid Qutb** extensively discussed the importance of the vanguard's exclusive and uncompromising attitude in his book *Ma'alim fi Al-Tariq*.

VIOLENCE. Many **Islamic groups** and **fundamentalist** organizations have resorted to the use of violence since they believe that compromise, moderation, and restraint have historically been proven ineffective when trying to establish an **Islamic state** and expel **tyrannical** rule. Economic inequality, exploitation, repression, and oppressive political policies that undermine the power of the populace imposed by such rulers have all also led radical fundamentalists to resort to violence, as they feel that no **peace** can be achieved without it. Differences in doctrinal and political ideologies between the diverse fundamentalist groups have also led to competition, resulting in a rancorous cycle of inner turmoil and violence between the groups themselves.

Nevertheless, the groups still show a great deal of unity when fighting outside persecution. Political violence has become especially popular in trying to oust political regimes and leaders. Groups such as **Hamas**, *Hizbullah* **in Lebanon**, *Jama'at al-Muslimin*, and *al-Jihad al-Islami* have all been described as Islamic fundamentalist organizations that have employed violence on numerous occasions in hopes of reaching their goals. However, it must be noted that if one removes the violent actions and radicalism from these Islamic groups, their ideologies and adherence to Islam is very similar to most of the Muslim community's.

Some fundamentalist groups eschew violence entirely, such as *Ennahda*, *Hizb-u-Tahrir*, **Movement for the Society of Peace**, the **Muslim Brotherhood**, and *Tablighi Jamaat*. On the contrary, other groups use violence because it is seen that political means are not enough. These groups include **al-Qaeda**, the **Taliban army**, *Boko Haram*, *Harakat al-Shabaab al-Mujahideen*, and the **Egyptian Islamic Jihad**, among others. *See also* EXTREMISM; RADICALISM.

AL-WAHHAB, MUHAMMAD IBN ABD (1703–1792). Born into the Banu Tamim tribe in Uyaynah, central **Saudi Arabia**, Muhammad Ibn Abd al-Wahhab was an influential Islamic scholar from which the *Wahhabism* movement derived. Al-Wahhab also came from a long line of *Hanbali* scholars, *Hanbali* being one of the four schools of **Sunni** Islam that emphasizes a strict adherence to the **divine texts** and *sharia* (Islamic law). While studying among Muslim scholars in Basra, **Iraq**, it is believed that al-Wahhab developed his reformist ideologies. On his return to Uyaynah, al-Wahhab began to influence his local kinsmen, including the area's ruler, Uthman ibn Mu'ammar. After a more prominent leader who controlled the nearby oasis towns of Al-Hasa (present-day Bahrain) and Qatif (located on the Persian Gulf coast of Saudi Arabia) called for al-Wahhab's execution, al-Wahhab left Uyayna. After this, he relocated to nearby Dir'iyya in 1740.

Here, he became closely acquainted with **al-Saud**, which would eventually take over the kingdom of Saudi Arabia in 1932, and al-Wahhab's Islamic teachings were spread in the area. This relationship between al-Wahhab and the Saud kingdom has been the source of funding and support for **Salafi** activity in Saudi Arabia. The acquisition of Mecca and Medina by Saudi Arabia, which came under Saud control in 1924, has also influenced the Salafi movement throughout the Muslim world.

Al-Wahhab wished to purify **Islam** through a return to the most basic **fundamentals** of the **religion**, especially the teachings of the Salaf. Many Sunni Muslims will agree that al-Wahhab sought to purify the religion through a revival of **monotheism** and a deep devotion to the sacred texts of Islam (the **Quran** and the **Hadiths**), and this has led him to be perceived as the most significant contemporary Muslim. Al-Wahhab's prominence as the first figure in the modern Islamic era is emphasized in his great work *Kitab at-Tawheed* (The Book of Unicity). Genealogically, the current Saudi Arabian minister of justice, Muhammad bin Abdul Kareem al-Eissa, and the country's grand *mufti*, Abd al-'Aziz al-Ashaikh, are descendants of al-Wahhab. *See also AL-WAHHABIYYA.*

WAHHABISM. *See AL-WAHHABIYYA.*

AL-WAHHABIYYA. A movement founded by **Muhammad Ibn 'Abd al-Wahhab**, *al-Wahhabiyya* (Wahhabism) promotes the use of *da'wa* to create a complete and everlasting **Islamic society**. Originally, the movement was used during the political revolt against the Ottoman **caliphate**, which was promoted by **al-Saud** in the hope of establishing an **Islamic state**. Ideologically, **reason** is believed to be able to play a fickle role in society and should be approached with caution as well as **traditionalism** (*taqlid*). Furthermore, *al-Wahhabiyya* supports the return to the **fundamentals** of **Islam** as well as adherence to the **holy texts** (**Quran** and the **Hadiths**). Also referred to as the **modern Salafi interpretation** of Islam, this movement is strictly in adherence with *tawhid* and supports the necessity of the **jihad** in order to abolish political oppression and Sufi tendencies. Many modern Islamic fundamentalist figures and groups have also adopted the basic principles of *al-Wahhabiyya* in forming their own ideologies, such as **Muhammad 'Abdu**, **Jamal al-Din al-Afghani**, **Muhammad Iqbal**, *al-Mahdiyya*, and *al-Sanusiyya*.

WALIY AL-FAQIH/**THE JURIST'S GUARDIAN.** In the Iranian **system**, *Waliy al-Faqih* is the supreme authority in the *Murshid al-Thawra* (Revolution's Guide) and the first guide of all authorities in the **Islamic Republic of Iran** in the absence of the *Mahdi*. The individual holding this post is also the supervisor of the military in Iran (the regular security forces as well as the **Iranian Revolutionary Guards**) and therefore has the power to declare war. His other duties include the appointment of the highest clerics in the constitutional council, the approving of presidential elections, the calling for votes, and the supervision of all electoral processes. A Twelvers' structure, the guardian is elected by members of the Council of Experts through anonymous ballots and can be removed by that council if he loses his abilities to lead. The first *Waliy al-Faqih* was **Ayatollah Ruhollah al-Musawi Khomeini**, who was succeeded by Ayotollah Ali Khamanei, the present *Waliy al-Faqih*.

WALKER LINDH, JOHN PHILLIP (1981–). The U.S. citizen John Phillip Walker Lindh was captured in the Battle of Qala-i-Jangi during the 2001 American invasion of **Afghanistan**. Currently serving a 20-year jail sentence for his membership in the **Taliban**, Lindh trained in al-Farouq camp in Afghanistan and with the Pakistani *Harakat Al-Mujahideen*. Aliases include Sulayman al-Faris and Abu Sulayman al-Irlandi. Although born in Washington, D.C., Lindh was raised in San Anselmo, California, and developed an interest in Islamic cultural studies during his adolescence. In 1997, he converted to **Islam** and the following year traveled to **Yemen**, where he studied Quranic Arabic. By May 2001, he was enlisted in the Taliban army in Afghanistan. On 25 November 2001, Lindh was seized by the Afghan

Northern Alliance and brought to a makeshift military garrison called *Qala-i-Jangi*, where he was interrogated. Soon after, a turbulent Taliban-provoked skirmish occurred at the prison, resulting in the death of hundreds. Lindh was one of 80 survivors and was recaptured a week later on 2 December 2001. In December, he was recognized as a U.S. citizen and was transferred to numerous places, including Camp Rhino (the first U.S. land base set up in Afghanistan during Operation Enduring Freedom), the USS *Peleliu*, and then finally the USS *Bataan*.

While aboard the two U.S. Navy vessels, Lindh signed confessions that revealed his memberships in **al-Qaeda** and the Taliban, and he was extradited back to the United States to face charges. On 13 February 2002, Lindh pled not guilty to 10 criminal charges against him, including conspiracy to murder U.S. nationals and supplying services to al-Qaeda and the Taliban. Due to fears that the confession would be thrown out by the court because of the disputed means by which it was attained, Lindh was offered a plea bargain that included a 20-year jail sentence, conviction of carrying armed weapons, participation in the Taliban, and a gag order. Lindh also had to drop any assertions that he was mistreated while in military custody. On 15 July 2002, he accepted the offer and was sentenced on 4 October 2002 to 20 years without parole. Lindh is currently imprisoned in Terre Haute, Indiana.

WAR/*AL-HARB*. *See DAR AL-HARB.*

AL-WEFAQ NATIONAL ISLAMIC SOCIETY/ISLAMIC NATIONAL ACCORD ASSOCIATION. The largest and most dominant **Islamic political party** in **Bahrain**, al-Wefaq (Bloc of Believers) is a **Shiite** group that is led by Sheikh Ali Salman. Claiming to have thousands of supporting members, the group also has ties with the Islamic Scholars Council. This relationship helped win al-Wefaq 17 of the 18 seats its members ran for in the 2006 Bahraini parliamentary elections (62 percent of the population voted for the party). By the 2010 elections, the group secured all 18 desired seats of the 40 within the parliament. However, on 27 February 2011, the 18 members protested against the **government**'s **violence** toward the Bahraini reformist protestors in the **Arab Spring** by submitting resignation letters.

The group's formation has its origins in the succession of King Hamad bin Isa al-Khalifa to the Bahraini throne on 14 February 2002. After he began his rule and initiated reform processes within the kingdom under his National Charter, the group began to support the **legislation** but then boycotted the 2002 elections when that year's **constitution** stated that a chamber of the parliament (which would be solely elected by the king) would share power with the popularly elected chamber. However, members still ran in the municipal elections of that year and slowly reemerged as a viable entity in the political sector.

Members of al-Wefaq are also heads of the Manama and the Muharraq City Councils (two of the largest cities within the kingdom) and have worked with the **Salafi** *al-Asalah* **Islamic society** on a variety of issues. With regard to religious legislation, al-Wefaq has been adamant in supporting **theocratic** rule, stating that secular authorities cannot pass Islamic-oriented laws since that power should be reserved for the spiritual leaders who are well versed in Islamic doctrine. The group has also been progressive in bringing many sociopolitical issues to the fore in Bahraini society, including electoral scandals and fraudulent activities among parliamentary members.

WEST, THE. Islamic **fundamentalists** associate the West with the Western imperialist colonialism, which dominated the lands of **Islam** for over two centuries, leading to the rejection of any doctrine, ideology, or **philosophy** associated with the West by many Muslims. The global inferiority that the Islamic world felt after the period of Western oppression still lingers to some extent today, as many feel skeptical of the benefits that Islam claims to be able to bring. On the contrary, many fundamentalists are skeptical of the West and believe that it has not provided anything beneficial to the Muslim world. Fundamentalists also agree that the West has often promoted the rule of repressive political regimes and has not assisted the majority of the population that suffers from illness and poverty. Furthermore, many claim that the Western powers will not completely abandon the Islamic world because of the large market the raw materials within their lands provide for.

Since many blame Western colonization for the current problems within the Islamic world, it is not encouraged to be a role model for imitation, according to the radical fundamentalists, and Islam should completely separate itself from the West. The moderate fundamentalists, however, feel that an open dialogue with the Western powers could be beneficial to **Islamic society**. More specifically, they encourage the adoption of Western **sciences** and technologies. **Islamization** has therefore been used in transforming Western ideologies and disciplines into discourses that are compatible to the Islamic community.

To the Islamic fundamentalists, Western civilization is the continuation of the ancient Greek and Roman civilizations that are the foundations of Western society. For many fundamentalists, there is a belief that Greco-Roman ideologies were focused only on the material aspects of life and that this led to a dependence on the carnal pleasures and lack of spirituality that has lasted in Western culture up to today. The Roman emphasis on power and authoritarian organization served only to enhance the materialistic tendencies. To the fundamentalists, Roman society collapsed because of its lack of morals. Furthermore, Greco-Roman **philosophies** were based on the power of the human intellect and the ability to apply **reason**, whereas Islam is founded on a divine discourse. This difference is what leads many fundamentalists to believe that their ideology is pure and, if practiced properly, will not collapse. Although some moderate fundamentalists believe that Islam should borrow some ideas from the West (Islamization), the radicals feel that Western civilization lacks any and all characteristics befitting a decent society.

For Islamic fundamentalists, many of the problems that the Muslim society has had to endure over the past two centuries have been directly related to the Western imperialist colonization. For them, the colonial period was the reason why the fracturing of the **Islamic states** and the depletion of natural resources has occurred. According to the fundamentalists, the West's interest in the Islamic lands led to an unnatural development in these lands, and their society is now too influenced by Western ideologies, political doctrines, and economic structures. Many Islamic fundamentalist movements have developed out of a reaction to the colonialist period and have tried to reform the education system in order to revive the Islamic way of life that was suppressed by the colonialists. *See also* UNITED STATES OF AMERICA.

WOMEN. The women's liberation movement in **Islam** has taken shape in many Islamic **fundamentalist** feminine groups and among influential figures. This includes notably the **Muslim Brotherhood** Sisters of **Egypt** and Nadine Yassine, leader of the feminine branch of *Al-Adl Wal Ihsane*. The movement, like many throughout the world, is focused on the role of women and their identity in Islam. Advocates desire full equality in both public and private life. These two spheres of the female space and the way in which women act in both illustrate a specific nuance in the Islamic feminist movement. Underlying questions have also risen concerning the patriarchal elucidations of the faith and how it can be reinterpreted to include the female population as well.

The lack of women's rights in Islam is deeply rooted, as in most **monotheistic**, male-dominated religions in both the East and the **West**. Still, although most of these faiths have seen progressive reformulations of the role of women, Islam still remains austere for the most part. This is partly explained by historical and psychological reasons. Historically, when Islam appeared in the seventh century as the last monotheistic religion, it was perceived as the most progressive one compared to **Christianity** and **Judaism**. However, over the centuries, as the **Quranic** text has been declared sacrosanct, there has been almost no adaptation of its content with regard to women. This fossilized perception has been strengthened also by the fact that almost the entire Islamic world has been under Western domination since the beginning of the 19th century. Given the fact that Western powers always promoted a defensive agenda with regard to women, the Muslim countries and leaders under Western domination reacted by maintaining what they considered to be their identity with regard to this topic. Yet this did not mean that changes in rights were not wanted and welcomed. Today, the differences in rights between Muslim and Western women are the consequence more of traditional and conservative societies among the former than of Quranic or Islamic dogmas and principles. Nevertheless, some of these differences have legal consequences and appear as contrary to UN **Human Rights legislation**. However, the main differences deal with family. For example, if *sharia* (Islamic law) is applied, polygamy and reputation are authorized, a Muslim woman must marry a Muslim man, and a sister will inherit half her brother's property.

Nonetheless, there have been some significant strides made in legislation over the past decades. Most notable has been the granting of financial, economic, property, and inheritance rights to the women of a family. Women have also been playing an increasingly noteworthy role in Islamic academia. The importance of a proper education for women has even been appropriated into patriarchal society in that an intelligent mother can then raise an intelligent son. Advocates have also noted that Muhammad's first wife was allegedly an effective businesswoman and that his second was a renowned intellectual. Even during the first **caliphates**, women continued to play effective roles in society, although their legal rights waned under *sharia*. Interestingly enough, 1899 saw the publication of Qasim Amin's *Tahrir al-Mar'a* (Women's Liberation), which reevaluated the wearing of the veil and polygyny. The work is still cited and influential to this day for many feminists.

Currently, the more pressing questions in the Islamic women's movement are concerned with their equality in mosque participation, unsegregated prayer, and political involvement. The countries that have seen some sizable form of Islamic feminist activism include **Egypt**, Indonesia, **Libya**, **Pakistan**, **Saudi Arabia**, Senegal, **Sudan**, and **Tunisia**. Wearing of the veil has become probably the most palpable symbol for Islamic feminism. In some countries, such as **Afghanistan**, it is absolutely necessary, whereas in nations like Tunisia, it was outlawed in public areas for decades. Within the feminist realm, some players advocate for its use as a personal sign of heritage and devotion, whereas other Muslim women see it as a sign of repression and subjugation. Within the mosque, there has been a desire to remove the gender-dividing partition, but this change has occurred mostly in Western mosques. Even within the house, there still exists the practice of having women and men pray in different spaces.

Supporting feminist groups has also proven to be a way for fundamentalists to influence a greater share of the population from a sociopolitical standpoint as well as to showcase their ideologies even further. For example, the **Muslim Brotherhood** in Egypt has stressed the platform that both genders should be equal in order to create a more positive society while retaining the individual values of each group. The Brotherhood especially concentrated on the need to formally and thoroughly educate women in society by setting up educational, health, and social programs that were constructed solely for this purpose. In addition, the Muslim Brotherhood Sisters of Egypt was formed in 1932 as a subgroup of **Hasan al-Banna**'s organization. Since then, they have become one of the most notable and visible Islamic feminist groups in the Muslim world. Many of its members are also daughters, wives, and sisters of male Muslim Brotherhood members. Notable events not only for the Muslim Brotherhood Sisters of Egypt but also for Muslim women worldwide were the 2000 nomination of Jihan al-Halafawi and the 2005 nomination of Makarem al-Deeri in the Egyptian parliamentary elections. *See also DUKHTARAAN-E-MILLAT*; *LASHKAR-E-JABBAR*.

WORLD ORDER. To Islamic **fundamentalist** ideologies, any sense of world order can come only from an adherence to **Islam** since it represents the equality, righteousness, and scruples that an ideal **civilization** needs. In an **Islamic society**, according to moderates, the government would also guarantee the rights of non-Muslims and not force other religions to assimilate into Islam in order to provide liberty and progress. However, to the radicals, an Islamic world order would mean that all people would eventually have to adopt Islam so that the **Islamic state** can stay secure. *See also* UNIVERSALISM.

WORLD TRADE CENTER AND PENTAGON ATTACKS OF SEPTEMBER 11, 2001. At 8:46 a.m. on 11 September 2001, American Airlines Flight 11 crashed into the north tower of the World Trade Center in New York City. In addition, at 9:02 a.m., United Airlines Flight 175 struck the south tower of the World Trade Center complex. Both flights were en route from Boston, Massachusetts, to Los Angeles, California. Later, at 9:40 a.m., American Airlines Flight 77 from Dulles, Virginia, to Los Angeles crashed into the east side of the U.S. Pentagon building in Arlington County, Virginia. Finally, at 10:07 a.m., United Airlines Flight 93 from Newark, New Jersey, to San Francisco, California, crashed in a field in Stonycreek Township, Pennsylvania. These commercial airliners had been hijacked by three groups of five hijackers and one group of four (aboard United Airlines Flight 93). By 9:48 a.m., the Federal Aviation Administration grounded all aircraft without exception—a decision that lasted for several days.

Calamity ensued, particularly in New York City, after the initial crashes, when, at 9:59 a.m., the south tower collapsed and shortly after, at 10:28 a.m., the north tower. The immense destruction that the collapse of these two huge landmarks wrought resulted in the deaths of not only the occupants of the building who did not evacuate in time but also the emergency responders and civilians on the ground. The force from the collapse also resulted in serious damage to four other buildings in the World Trade Center complex. In Virginia, the eastern side of the Pentagon almost completely collapsed and was engulfed in flames, whereas United Airlines Flight 93 apparently crashed after a struggle between the hijackers and the passengers.

In total, 2,993 people were killed—2,603 at the World Trade Center, 125 at the Pentagon, and 40 in Pennsylvania. All 19 of the hijackers perished, and all crew members and passengers of each flight died. In addition, 342 firefighters, 23 New York City policemen, 37 Port Authority police, and 10 emergency medical personnel were killed. To this day, approximately 24 people remain listed as officially missing at the World Trade Center. Deemed as one integrated operation, the attacks on 11 September 2001 remain the worst mass-casualty foreign act of **violence** that any country has endured.

As a result, on 14 September 2001, U.S. President George W. Bush declared that a state of war existed between the **United States** and any state or organization that supported the attacks. After the president's address, the U.S. Congress passed Joint Resolution 23, which allowed for the use of military force against any and all suspected perpetrators of the 11 September hijackings. Days later, on 17 September, evidence concluded that **Osama bin Laden**'s militant Islamic **fundamentalist** group, **al-Qaeda**, was responsible for and the coordinator of the attacks. The U.S. government ordered the Afghani **Taliban army**, longtime protectors of bin Laden, to extradite him to American authorities but to no avail. In retaliation, Operation Enduring Freedom commenced on 7 October 2001—a U.S. military operation focused on combating the Taliban and al-Qaeda forces within **Afghanistan**. Still an ongoing, active mission, Operation Enduring Freedom in Afghanistan has resulted in the death or capture of over 30,000 belligerents and the loss of over 1,500 American troops.

In terms of American domestic legislative repercussions, the Bush administration passed the 2001 Patriot Act on 25 October. Passed in the hope of preventing similar acts from occurring and to maintain security within the country, the act is often perceived as restricting civil liberties and was not welcomed by much of the American population. Some of the criticisms were that it allowed for immigrants to be detained without warrant, granted the right for security agencies to have access to jury information, permitted legal monitoring of electronic communications, and gave the Federal Bureau of Investigation access to all citizens' documents. In the wake of the hijackings, the Office of Homeland Security was created to deal specifically with air traffic and domestic security measures. Furthermore, the 9/11 Commission (officially known as the National Commission on Terrorist Attacks) was formed on 27 November 2003 to investigate the September incidents and make procedural recommendations on how to avoid a comparable act from occurring again. The main criticism of this group was that it was partisan and that most of the information gained was applied in such a way as to benefit the party in power. Its final report was published on 22 July 2004 and resulted in the formation of the National Counterterrorism Council.

YASIN, AHMAD (1936–2004). The former spiritual leader of **Hamas** in **Palestine**, Yasin was a blind man and cleric (sheikh) who was also once a member of the **Muslim Brotherhood in Gaza Strip**. He was extremely vocal and dedicated to protecting the rights of Muslims in Gaza, especially during the Israeli occupation of the 1970s, and was sentenced to a 12-year prison term in 1984. However, he was released 11 months later in a prisoner exchange between **Israel** and *al-Jabha al-Sha'biyya: al-Qiyada al-'Amma* (a Palestinian militant group). During the 1987 Palestinian uprising, Yasin helped form Hamas and was arrested again by Israeli forces in 1989. He served six years (1991–1997) of his life sentence for murder and inciting violence as a result of negotiations after a failed Israeli assassination attempt on **Khalid Mashaal**. Sheikh Yasin was killed in 2004 by a targeting missile detonated by the Israeli Secret Services.

YASSINE, SHEIKH ABDESSLAM (1928–). Born in Marrakesh, **Morocco**, Sheikh Abdesslam Yassine, known as "The Blind Sheikh," is the leader of *al-Adl Wal Ihsane* (Justice and Charity Movement). A member of the Ministry of Education in Morocco, Yassine is a **Sufist** and created *al-Adl Wal Ihsane* because he wished to focus more on ideological and social matters of **Islam** rather than entering into the political realm. He was jailed after writing a letter that spoke out against King Hassan II (1961–1999) but was released by his successor, King Muhammad VI (1999 to present). He is known for his publication, *L'Islam ou le deluge* (Islam or the Flood). His daughter Nadina Yassine is now the spokesperson for *al-Adl Wal Ihsane*.

YEMEN. The republic of Yemen has a Muslim population that is mainly **Sunni** in the central and southern parts of the country and **Shia** in the north. Yemen in particular has a long history of allowing many extremist Islamic **fundamentalist** groups to operate within its borders. This is especially true for the southern part of the country, which hosted **Palestinian** militants specifically before the unification of the north and the south in 1990. After the civil war (1990–1994), radical groups continued to occupy the southern lands, but these groups were focused more on expelling the monarchy of

Saudi Arabia. In northern Yemen, however, a group called the Al-Houthi Rebellion has dominated the area and posed serious security threats to the then-ruling **government** of President Ali Abdallah Saleh.

This Shia group seeks to replace the Saleh regime with an **Islamic state** and has been conducting attacks throughout the country since 2003. Led by Abdul Malik al-Houthi (younger brother of founder Sheikh Hussein Badreddin al-Houthi), the Al-Houthi Rebellion is trying to suppress the **Wahhabi** Muslims within Yemen and claims that the country's economic decline and political corruption is a direct result of the government's association with the **Western** powers, specifically the **United States**. Although numerous attempts at cease-fire agreements and peace accords between the Al-Houthi rebels and the Yemeni security forces have occurred, tensions are still present. In fact, in 2009, Saudi Arabian forces had to intervene after fighting in the north hit a peak. February 2009 saw the signing of the latest cease-fire between the insurgent group and the Saleh regime, but the 2011 civil protests and anti**government** demonstrations of the **Arab Spring** have strained the already fragile agreement.

The **al-Qaeda** organization also has a long history of operating within Yemen's borders. In fact, a large percentage of al-Qaeda militants are Yemeni nationals and former *mujahideen* from the Soviet-Afghan War (1979–1989). This war also had a major effect on the presence of militant **Islamic groups** within the country. During the 1990s, al-Qaeda established a number of training camps throughout Yemen, and many Yemenites also trained with al-Qaeda in **Afghanistan** camps. However, after the stiff U.S. counterterrorism efforts in the wake of the **World Trade Center and Pentagon attacks of September 11, 2001**, Saleh's government began to tighten its security measures on the militant groups—an effort that started to wane by early 2006. It has been speculated that this laxity in ousting the Islamic radicals within the country is due to the government's reorganization of security forces to tackle other, more pressing matters posed by the al-Houthi Rebellion. This has resulted in an even greater presence of al-Qaeda troops within many areas of southern Yemen.

This fragile country now serves as home to **al-Qaeda in the Arabian Peninsula** (AQAP). Formed out of the merger between Saudi and Yemenite al-Qaeda forces, AQAP has become one of the most active branches of the al-Qaeda organization. The group has also been successful in establishing alliances with the eastern Yemenite tribes, resulting in the creation of a broad internal protective force. This protection that AQAP has gained has resulted in even more operations that are conducive to the organization's global **jihad** agenda. With the onset of the 2011 public demonstrations during the Arab Spring, the Saleh government faced ruin and, with that, collapse, at which point AQAP activity within Yemen might rise significantly.

This country has an overwhelming stretch of underdeveloped, secluded regions that suffer from an incredible lack of education and a huge amount of economic poverty. These areas are more likely to become susceptible to the jihadists as their socioeconomic situation makes the civic programs that the Islamic groups promise that much more desirable. On a larger scale, the prevailing economic downturn of the country, social inequality, the array of segmented tribes, the weak central government, and internal civil conflicts have also helped make Yemen a desirable location for extremist groups, both domestic and foreign. All the country's negative factors contribute to a mood in the population of being subjugated by militant organizations. Furthermore, in Yemen, a massive illegal arms market exists, making the acquisition of weapons that much easier for militant groups and tribesmen, further endangering state and global security.

Moreover, as many other countries, Al Iman University in the capital city of Sanaa has been repeatedly accused of merely being a front for raising Islamic radicals. However, locals contest that the institution is simply a *madrasa* for Islamic learning. This opinion that the university is an ideological training ground is promoted by the fact that the financier and spiritual guide to **Osama bin Laden**, Adbel Majid Al-Zindani, is the head of Al Iman. Provocative **Western** Islamists, such as **John Walker Lindh**, are also among its alumni. Al-Zindani also established the *al-Islah* Islamic movement in 1990. Now an **Islamic political party**, the group is also known as the Yemenite **Muslim Brotherhood**. The political **activism** that this group promotes is one that calls for a stricter adherence to *sharia* (Islamic law) within the **constitution**. In 1993, the party won key positions within the government, resulting in a great deal of tension, and Saleh eventually agreed to govern along with *al-Islah*. Many members of this Islamic fundamentalist organization now hold lucrative posts in the education, justice, and trade departments of the state.

Currently, the entry and promotion of Islamic groups within Yemen's borders continue. Increasingly, the security forces have shifted their focus from the jihadist groups directly and have placed more efforts on containing the popular protests of 2011. Since the national guards have been accused of using violence against the demonstrators, dissatisfaction and animosity toward the government have grown. Members of the government have begun to stray, and al-Zindani, along with his *al-Islah* Party, is hoping to replace the central government with an Islamic one. As these protests escalate, it is clear that *al-Islah* (and therefore Islamic fundamentalists) and the other opposition parties (such as the Yemeni Socialist Party) will play a key role in the shaping of reforms within the country. These demonstrations, which follow the ones that toppled the Zine Al-Abidine Ben Ali regime in **Tunisia** and the Hosni Mubarak regime in **Egypt**, have many speculating that the Yemenite government will suffer the same fate. Given the presence of al-Qaeda within the country and the political prominence of fundamentalists within the legislature, if the secular government does fall, it is most likely that an **Islamic state** will prevail throughout Yemen. *See also* ISLAMIC JIHAD IN YEMEN; PARTY OF THE YEMENI ASSOCIATION FOR REFORM; YEMENI ASSOCIATION FOR REFORM.

YEMENI ASSOCIATION FOR REFORM/*AL-TAJAMMU' AL-YE-MENI LI AL-ISLAH.* Formed as a result of a union between many tribal leaders in northern **Yemen**, the group became one of the most powerful **Islamic political parties** in the Yemen elections during the early 1990s and was led until 2007 by the leader of the Hashid tribal confederation, Sheikh al-Ahmar 'Abd Allah. The party focused its platform on **constitutional** reform and the application of Islamic ideologies. During the time of its formation, it was also concerned with combating the radical leftist factions that were rising in Yemen. Eventually, even the **Muslim Brotherhood** aligned itself with the Yemeni Association for Reform and became active in Yemenite sociopolitical affairs. The Brotherhood faction of the group, led by **'Abd al-Majid al-Zandani**, also sought to reform the educational system within the country. Many members of this organization eventually became indoctrinated into the Islamic Renaissance Movement (***Ennahda***). *See also* PARTY OF THE YEMENI ASSOCIATION FOR REFORM.

YO'IDOSH, TOHIR (1967–2009). Tohir Yo'Idosh was known for the December 1991 establishment of the **Islamic Movement of Uzbekistan** (IMU) with fellow Islamist Juma Namangani (1969–2001). A native of the Fergana Valley in Uzbekistan, Yo'Idosh also helped organize the Justice Movement in 1991 in the wake of the formation of the Central Asian republics brought about by the Soviet Union's collapse and worked with the Turkistan Islamic Party. By 1995, Yo'Idosh had established a reputation throughout Uzbekistan as a noteworthy Islamic militant who resorted to brutal tactics that aimed to rid Central Asia of all **Western** occupying forces. Yo'Idosh sought to overthrow the government of Uzbekistan's president, Islam Karimov, in office since 24 March 1990, and replace it with an Islamic **caliphate** state based on *sharia* (Islamic law). In 2000, as a result of a number of **assassination** attempts on Karimov during 1999, Yo'Idosh was sentenced to death in absentia by the Uzbekistan courts.

Yo'Idosh and Namangani effectively and equally led the IMU until the latter's death in November 2001. No replacement was appointed, and instead Yo'Idosh headed the party alone, along with the newly formed (in 2002) Islamic Jihad Union, with no equal until his own death in 2009. A U.S. Air Force–led strike that took place on 27 August 2009 in South Waziristan in northwestern **Pakistan** resulted in the death of the militant Islamist, but the IMU did not officially confirm his death until almost a year later on 16 August 2010. Announced on the group's website, *Furqun*, Yo'Idosh was referred to as Shaheed Muhammad Tahir, an honorable name designated for Islamic **martyrs**. Although *Furqun* did not specify how or when Yo'Idosh died, it is speculated that he expired within days after the air strike from wounds that he sustained (around 27 August 2009). The Islamist's former lieutenant Abu Usman Adil was named his successor on 17 August 2010. Yo'Idosh also served on **al-Qaeda**'s distinguished council *Majlis-al-Shura* and fought alongside the **Taliban** against the American forces in **Afghanistan**.

YUSUF, AHMAD RAMZI (1968–). Infamously known for his involvement with the 1993 World Trade Center bombings, Ahmad Ramzi Yusuf was also implicated in a plot to destroy 12 American commercial airliners (he claims in retaliation for the American support of **Israel**). He was sentenced to life imprisonment for his actions in January 1998. Born 'Abd al-Basit Bulushi in Kuwait, Yusuf is also known to have been involved with the **Islamic Salvation Front** and the **Armed Islamic Group**.

YUSUF, MUHAMMAD (1970–2009). Born in Girgiri in northeastern Nigeria, Muhammad Yusuf was the leader of the militant Nigerian **Islamic group** *Boko Haram* until his death on 30 July 2009. Radical in his ideologies, Yusuf studied theology in **Saudi Arabia** before founding the *Boko Haram* movement in 2002. Completely against all forms of westernization and **modernism**, his advocacy for the strict application of *sharia* (Islamic law) also inspired the **Taliban army** in **Afghanistan**.

Almost immediately following his group's establishment, it became increasingly hostile toward the Nigerian government, and Yusuf was arrested many times on various charges. As Yusuf declared a **jihad** in Nigeria, when the state decided to suppress and outlaw *Boko Haram*, the insurgencies only escalated. On 30 July 2009, he was captured by the Nigerian security forces in Maiduguri in northern Nigeria. After an interrogation, he was promptly executed.

Z

ZANDANI, SHEIKH 'ABD AL-MAJID. A provocative and model figure for the Yemeni Islamic **fundamentalists**, Zandani became a member of **Yemen**'s Presidential Council in 1993. During his time in that position, he was able to have *sharia* (Islamic law) recognized by the administration as the primary inspiration of **legislation**, securing a viable position for the Islamic fundamentalist movement within the **government**. Also once a member of the **Muslim Brotherhood**, he was active in the revolution and civil war of Yemen and became closely affiliated with *Hizb al-Tajammu' al-Yemeni li al-Islah* (**Party of the Yemeni Association for Reform**) leader 'Abd Allah al-Ahmar. Most recently, Zandani is the head of the group's *shura* council.

AL-ZARQAWI, ABU MUSAB (1966–2006). Born Ahmad Fadeel al-Nazal al-Khalayleh in Zarqa, **Jordan**, on 30 October 1966, Abu Musab al-Zarqawi has been implicated in numerous attacks, kidnappings, and **assassinations** throughout **Iraq**. One of the most significant figures in the contemporary Islamic **fundamentalist jihadi** circuit, he served as a *mujahideen* in the Soviet-Afghan War (1979–1989). It is there that al-Zarqawi began his relationship with **al-Qaeda** leader **Osama bin Laden**. In 1999, the militant organized *Jund al-Sham* (Army of the Levant) with the financial help of bin Laden. However, this organization (which was reportedly small) was dismantled sometime just prior to the 2001 U.S. Operation Enduring Freedom. After a failed attempt to bomb a Radisson Hotel in Amman, **Jordan**, al-Zarqawi fled to **Afghanistan** and then returned to Iraq following the fall of the **Taliban army** in 2001. While there, he joined *Ansar al-Islam* in 2002 and was accused of taking part in the assassination of U.S. diplomat Laurence Foley on 28 October of the same year.

Al-Zarqawi continued with his attacks and planned a series of **bombings** in 2003 at the UN headquarters in Iraq. He went on to become the founding member and exclusive leader of *Al-Tawhid wal-Jihad*. In 2004, he merged his group with the al-Qaeda organization—resulting in the formation of **al-Qaeda in Iraq** (AQI), known as *Tanzim al-Qa'ida fî bilâd al-Râfiday* (Organization of al-Qaeda in the Land of the Two Rivers). Regularly carrying out attacks against the American military presence in Afghanistan and Iraq, al-Zarqawi also supported the repression of the **Shiite** Muslim community. He was implicated in the attacks on the Shiite shrines in Iraq in March 2004 and the Najaf and Karbala car bombings in December 2004. Some intelligence reports claim that in total al-Zarqawi had a hand in over 1,000 deaths by 2004 alone.

Over the decade and after countless attacks (which he either executed or planned), al-Zarqawi was second only to bin Laden in being the most wanted man in the Middle East. He was also implicated in the 2006 Al-Askari Mosque attack, which was an attempt to ignite violence between the Shiite and **Sunni** communities in Iraq. He turned out to have indispensable tribal connections, tactical prowess, military acuteness, and a great ability to gain immense amounts of intelligence, thereby making him one of the towering figures in the Islamic **jihadist** program of the 21st century.

Finally, after years of being hunted by multiple countries for his atrocities, al-Zarqawi was killed by a U.S. Air Force strike on 7 June 2006 in his safe house in Baqubah, Iraq—six others died during the bombing as well. Following his death, **Egyptian Islamic Jihad** leader **Abu Ayyub al-Masri** was named the new leader of AQI on 15 June 2006.

AL-ZAWAHIRI, AYMAN (1951–). Ayman Muhammad Rabaie Al-Zawahiri was born on 19 June 1951 into a prominent family in Maadi, **Egypt**. At the early age of 14, Al-Zawahiri joined the **Muslim Brotherhood** (*Ikhwan*) in Egypt and was devoted to implementing an Islamist vision throughout the Egyptian **government**. Al-Zawahiri was also briefly imprisoned along with many other suspected conspirators following the 1981 **assassination** of Egyptian President Anwar al-Sadat and subsequently served a three-year sentence for weapons dealing. After his imprisonment, he fled to **Saudi Arabia** and then **Pakistan**, where he began to reorganize the **Egyptian Islamic Jihad** (EIJ) and reformed the organization by adopting the tactics of *takfir*, the killing of Muslim blasphemers.

In 1991, al-Zawahiri became the leader of EIJ after the group split from the original leader, Abud al-Zummar. Second in command and leader of **al-Qaeda**, al-Zawahiri successfully conflated the EIJ with al-Qaeda in 1998 and has since been an incredible force in the Islamist movement. As the commander of the EIJ, al-Zawahiri has recruited not only civilians but military officers and personnel as well in order to be more efficient and militaristic in the group's practices. Since al-Qaeda's inception, al-Zawahiri has served on the group's *shura* (consultation) council and he worked closely with **Osama bin Laden** on many Islamist activities and terrorist attacks.

In 1999, al-Zawahiri, along with his brother Muhammad al-Zawahiri, were sentenced to death in absentia by an Egyptian military tribunal. Since 2003, numerous attempts have been made to locate and kill al-Zawahiri, but all have proven to be unsuccessful. On 30 April 2009, the U.S. Department of Homeland Security announced that al-Zawahiri was the operational and strategic commander of al-Qaeda and that **Osama bin Laden** was merely the ideological figurehead of the organization. After bin Laden's death in May 2011, al-Zawahiri was announced the following July as the new leading figure of the al-Qaeda organization. *See also* BLASPHEMY.

ABU ZEID, ABDELHAMID (1966–). Born in Touggourt, **Algeria**, Abdelhamid Abu Zeid joined the **Islamic Salvation Front** in 1990 at the age of 24 and has become one of the most prominent and brutal leaders of **al-Qaeda in the Islamic Maghreb** (AQIM). The first formal acknowledgment of Abu Zeid came when he appeared as the assistant chief to **Saifi Ammari** (Abderrazak Al-Para) during the kidnapping of 32 European tourists in southern Algeria in 2003. When, in September 2006, **Abdelmalek Droukdel**, the leader of the **Salafist Group for Preaching and Combat**, pledged allegiance to **Osama bin Laden**, Abu Zeid followed Droukdel and formed what would be known as AQIM. Using great mobility and knowledge of the Sahara Desert region, Abu Zeid moves hostages, soldiers, and arms throughout northern Africa with great ease. Abu Zeid also commands a northern **Mali**–based *katiba* (a small company or section of armed men who specialize in moving quickly and secretly over great distances), Tariq Ibn Ziyad. Through his tactics, Abu Zeid has opened up northern Mali, northern **Niger**, and southern **Tunisia** to Islamist activities and **violence**.

AL-ZINDANI, ABDUL MAJEED (1942–). A Yemeni national and leader of the **Muslim Brotherhood** within his country, Abdul Majeed al-Zindani also founded Iman University in Sanaa, the capital. Among his many positions within the Islamic **fundamentalist** movement, he is also a prominent member of *Ansar al-Islam* and *al-Islah*. Al-Zindani is known for his relationship with **al-Qaeda**'s former leader **Osama bin Laden**, serving mostly as his spiritual adviser. However, there is also evidence that suggests that he facilitated the recruitment of new members as well as the raising of funds for the organization. Al-Zindani also seemed to have a similar relationship with **Anwar al-Awlaki** and possibly **John Walker Lindh** through Iman University. An advocate for **jihad** and the absolute implementation of *sharia* (Islamic law) throughout the Muslim world, al-Zindani has made numerous *fatwas* calling for a holy struggle against the American troops that are stationed throughout the Islamic states.

ZITOUNI, DJAMAL (1964–1996). The fifth *amir* of the **Armed Islamic Group** (AIG), Djamal Zitouni was a former member of the **Algerian Islamic Salvation Front**. On 26 September 1994, Zitouni replaced Ahmed

Abu Abdullah as the AIG's leader in **Algeria**. During his regime, the AIG grew increasingly violent, especially toward France and its nationals. Zitouni claimed responsibility for a number of attacks on civilians, including the 3 August 1994 attack on the Max Marchand French school in Ain Allah that left five French nationals dead. More infamously, Zitouni is suspected of having kidnapped and killed seven Trappist monks from a monastery in Tibhirine on 21 May 1996. Zitouni also attacked other Islamic militant groups, including the **Islamic Salvation Army**. His brutality and malevolence, especially toward Algerian civilians and other Islamists, could be what contributed to his death, as he was allegedly killed by a rival Islamic faction.

ZOUABRI, ANTAR (1970–2002). Also known as Abou Talha Antar, Antar Zouabri was born on 10 May 1970. He succeeded **Djamal Zitouni** as *amir* of the **Armed Islamic Group** (AIG) in **Algeria** after Zitouni's death in July 1996 and became one of the group's longest-serving *amirs*, with his rule lasting until his death on 8 February 2002. During Zouabri's leadership, the AIG gained a reputation of increased **violence** and mindless brutality, especially toward Algerian civilians, resulting in the group's exclusion from Algerian society. The AIG under Zouabri's command pushed Islamic doctrine to an extreme to justify the massacre and slaughter of hundreds of lives. Zouabri remained *amir* of the AIG until he was killed by Algerian security forces in his hometown of Boufarik, Algeria.

Glossary

Abu: Father (of)
Adala: Justice
Adl: Equity
'Aql: Reason
Ahl: Family (of)
Al: From
Alami: Global
Amir/Emir: Commander
Ansar: Supporters
Arabiya: Arabian
Asala: Authenticity
Aswad: Black
Baath: Resurrection
Bid'a: Heresy; innovation
Caliphate: Kingdom
Dar: Abode
Da'wa: Call
Dimucratiyya: Democracy
Din: Religion
Ennahda: Renaissance
Falsafa: Philosophy
Faqih: Jurist
Fatwa: Legal opinion
Fedayeen: Resistors
Fi: In
Fiah: Section
Filastin: Palestine
Fiqh: Jurisprudence
Fitra: Intuition
Furqan: Proof
Gama'a: Group
Hadatha: Modernity
Hakimiyya: Divine governance

Haq: Truth
Harakat: Movements
Harakiyya: Activism
Harb: War
Hashashin: Assassin
Hawari: Disciples
Hifadh: Protection
Hijra: Emigration
Hind: India
Hiwar: Dialogue
Hizb: Party
Hudud: Deterrents
Hukuma: Government
Huquq: Rights
Hurriyat: Liberties
Hurriyya: Freedom
Ihsan(e): Beneficence
Ijma': Consensus
Ikhwan: Brethren
'Ilm: Science
Insan: Human
Islah: Reform
Islami: Islamic
Islamiyya: Muslim
Istishhad: Martyrdom
Istishhadyun: Martyrdom seekers
Itihad: Union
Ittijah: Tendency
Jabha: Front
Jabhat: Fronts
Jafaria: Chiite
Jahili: Pagan
Jahiliyya: Paganism

Jaish: Army
Jamaat: Groups
Jamal: Beauty
Jam'iyyat: Associations
Jazira: Island
Jebheye: Front
Jemaah: Community
Jihad: Struggle, holy war
Kaff: Bring to a halt
Kafir: Infidel
Katibat: Brigade
Khairiyya: Beneficence
Khalq: People
Khatm: Closing
Khilafat: Caliphate, kingdom
Kirdas: Company
Kufr: Unbelief
Kurdiyya: Kurdish
Lashkar: Army
Li: Of, in order to
Madi: Past
Madrasa: School
Majlis: Assembly
Malahim: Battles
Manhaj: Method
Mantiqi: Region
Ma'rifa: Knowledge
Marji': Guide
Menbar: Pulpit
Millat: Tenet
Milli: Adherent
Mosharekate: Participation
Moulathamoun: Turbaned
Mujahideen: Holy fighters
Mujtama': Society
Munazzama: Organization
Muqatila: Combating, fighting
Muqawama: Resistance
Murtadd: Apostate
Musawat: Equality
Muslimin: Muslims

Muttahida: Unified, united
Nubuwwa: Prophethood
Nizam: System
Partisi: Party
Ridda: Apostasy
Sada: Echo
Sahaba: Companions
Salafiyya: Revivalist
Salam: Peace
Sariyah: Group
Shabaab: Youth
Shabiba: Young people
Shahid: Martyr
Shar'iyya: Legitimacy
Sheikh: Leader, scholar
Shura: Consultation
Subb: Blasphemy
Sulh: Truce
Ta'addudiyya: Pluralism
Tablighi: Missionary
Tafsir: Interpretation
Taghut: Tyranny
Tahrir: Liberation
Tajammu': Assembly
Tajdeef: Blasphemy
Takaful: Solidarity
Takfir: Accusing of apostasy
Talai': Vanguard
Tanmia: Development
Tanzeem: Organization
Taqlid: Traditionalism, imitation
Tarikh: History
Tashri': Legislation
Tatarruf: Extremism, radicalism
Tawazun: Balance
Tawhid: Monotheism
Tehrik: Movement
Thawriyya: Revolutionary
Tijaniyya: Sufi
Toifah: Group
Ukhuwwa: Brotherhood

'Ulama, Ulema: Scholars
Umma: Nation
Usuliya: Fundamentalism
Wa: And

Wahdat: Union
Wakalah: District
Waliy: Governor
Wefaq: Harmony

Bibliography

CONTENTS

INTRODUCTION

The amount of scholarly research performed and publications produced about Islamic fundamentalism is as vast and diverse as the subject itself. This bibliography includes an array of materials that covers geographical differences and similarities, general histories on Islam, socioeconomic theories, reflections on warfare, and comparative studies as well as many other topics. Different movements, groups, organizations, and leading figures that have helped shape the current Islamic fundamentalist trend are also cited within this bibliography. However, many of these works cover more than just one aspect. In these cases, the works have been put in the category that seems most appropriate. Therefore, it would be advantageous of the reader to peruse the entire bibliography to gain the most comprehensive knowledge on the works available on this topic. A reader who refers to these works will certainly be richly rewarded, as they provide useful information on many topics that are all too often not acknowledged.

Along with being fairly broad and large, a second strength of this bibliography is its use of both theoretical and practical works. Most of the recent scholarship focuses on the practical, historical aspects of the fundamentalist trends in Islam, but here, the not-as-often-studied theoretical side is as thoroughly covered. Just as one cannot separate the culture from the context, neither can one separate this movement from its global context. Many recent scholars have avoided this notion of an everlasting Islamic fundamentalism, but even if the movement disappears, the history will not.

Various publications have appeared in numerous languages: English, French, German, as well as Arabic, Iranian, and many others. In this bibliography, the bulk of the works are in English, although significant contributions in other languages are also included. The emphasis on English is a clear choice given the primary audience of this historical dictionary, but titles in other languages have made a significant contribution to this field and should certainly not be overlooked. It should also be noted that publications listed within cover not only books but also papers and articles taken from scholarly journals.

The bibliography has been subdivided first by geographical regions (including Europe, North America, and Russia but also obviously the Middle East, Africa, and other related regions). The further sections deal with the theoretical perspectives and approaches used in the studies. Another important subsection of titles involves the Islamic movements and its leaders who have played a prominent role, although these are limited to the more prominent ones on which scholars and others have written extensively about. Finally, there is an assortment of reference works, basic sources, and other historical dictionaries. Obviously, this bibliography does not encompass every work written on these subjects, but it does contain a representative array of scholarly and also nonscholarly resources that provides a broader outlook.

While there are numerous works cited for the various regions, some of the more useful ones are *Islam without Fear: Egypt and the New Islamists* by Raymond William Baker, *Islamic Fundamentalism in Egyptian Politics* by Barry M. Rubin, *Faith in Moderation: Islamist Parties in Jordan and Yemen* by Jillian Schwedler, *Hizbu'llah: Politics and Religion* by Amal Saad-Ghorayeb, *Islamic Fundamentalism in the West Bank and Gaza: Muslim Brotherhood and Islamic Jihad* by Ziyad Abu-'Amr, *The Islamist Challenge in Algeria: A Political History* by Michael Willis, *Islam and the Political Discourse of Modernity* by Armando Salvatore, *The Imamte Tradition of Oman* by John C. Wilkinson, *Religion and State in the Kingdom of Saudi Arabia* by Ayman al-Yassini, *Violence in Nigeria: The Crisis of Religious Politics and Secular Ideologies* by Toyin Falola, *The Course of Islam in Africa* by Mervyn Hiskett, *The First Islamist Republic: Development and Disintegration of Islamism in the Sudan* by Abdullah Gallab, *Afghanistan: A Military History from Alexander the Great to the War against the Taliban* by Stephen Tanner, *Muslim Shrines in India* by Christian W. Troll, *Islam in Indonesia: Modernism, Radicalism and the Middle East* by Giora Eliraz, *Sacred Space and Holy War: The Politics, Culture and History of Shi'ite Islam* by Juan Cole, *Piety and Politics: The Shifting Contours of Islamism in Contemporary Malaysia* by Joseph Chinyong Liow, *Political Islam in Southeast Asia: Moderates, Radicals and Terrorists* by Angel Rabasa, *Islamic Fundamentalism in Pakistan, Egypt, and Iran* by Mahmood Suhail, *Newer Islamic Movements in Western Europe* by Lars Pedersen, *Islam in America* by Jane Smith, and *Islam in Post-Soviet Russia* by Hilary Pilkington and Galina M. Yemelianova.

For the political and theoretical works, those of particular interest include *Moderate and Radical Islamic Fundamentalism: The Quest for Modernity, Legitimacy and the Islamic State* by Ahmad S. Moussalli, *Radical Islam: Medieval Theology and Modern Politics* by Emmanuel Sivan, *Political Islam: Religion and Politics in the Arab World* by Nazih N. Ayubi, *The Political Language of Islam* by Bernard Lewis, and *Tolerance and Coercion in Islam: Interfaith Relations in the Muslim Tradition* by Yohanan Friedman.

The most delicate area in some ways is the works on movements and leaders since that is where more bias tends to emerge. This bias can lean in either direction, presenting these groups and figures as either more or less harmful than in actuality. Thus, one should be careful in choosing among these titles. Some of the more recommendable ones are *Egypt's Islamic Militants* by Saad Eddin Ibrahim, *The Society of the Muslim Brothers in Egypt* by Brynjar Lia, *Five Tracks of Hasan al-Banna'* by Charles Wendell, *The Jihadi Salafist Movement in Jordan after Zarqawi: Identity, Leadership Crisis and Obscured Vision* by Mohammad Rumman and Hassan Abu Hanieh, *Religion and Regime Legitimacy: The al-Saud, Wahhabism, and Saudi Arabian Politics* by M. Openshaw, *Terrorism and Public Opinion: A Five Country Comparison* by Christopher Hewitt, *Leaders and Their Followers in a Dangerous World* by Jerrold Post, and *Political Parties and Terrorist Groups* by Leonard Weinberg.

The reference works are usually much more balanced but do offer a variety of information. The works that are particularly useful are *Political Terrorism: A New Guide to Actors, Authors, Concepts, Data Bases, Theories, and Literature* by Alex P. Schmid, *The Idea of Women in Fundamentalist Islam* by Lamia Rustum Shehadeh, *Pride, Faith, and Fear: Islam in the Sub-Saharan Africa* by Charlotte A. Quinn and Frederick Quinn, *Islam in Revolution: Fundamentalism in the Arab World* by R. Hrair Dekmujian, and *Historical Dictionary of Islamic Fundamentalist Movements in the Arab World, Iran, and Turkey* by Ahmad S. Moussalli.

THE MACHREK

Egypt

Abaza, Mona. *Debates on Islam and Knowledge in Malaysia and Egypt: Shifting Worlds.* London: Routledge, 2002.

Abdalla, Ahmed. "Egypt's Islamists and the State: From Complicity to Confrontation." *Middle East Report* 23 (1993): 29–31.

Abdo, Geneive. *No God but God: Egypt and the Triumph of Islam.* New York: Oxford University Press, 2002.

Adams, Charles C. *Islam and Modernism in Egypt.* New York: Russell and Russell, 1968.

Baker, Raymond William. *Sadat and After: Struggles for Egypt's Political Soul.* London: I. B. Tauris, 1990.

———. *Islam without Fear: Egypt and the New Islamists.* Cambridge, MA: Harvard University Press, 2003.

Gaffney, Patrick D. *The Prophet's Pulpit: Islamic Preaching in Contemporary Egypt.* Berkeley: University of California Press, 1994.

Goldschmidt, Arthur, Jr., and Robert Johnston. *Historical Dictionary of Egypt*. Lanham, MD: Scarecrow Press, 2003.

Jansen, Johannes J. G. *The Neglected Duty: The Creed of Sadat's Assassins and Islamic Resurgence in the Middle East*. New York: Macmillan, 1996.

Kepel, Gilles. *Muslim Extremism in Egypt: The Prophet and Pharaoh*. Berkeley: University of California Press, 2003.

Kerr, Malcolm. *Islamic Reform: The Political and Legal Theories of Muhammad 'Abduh and Rashīd Ridā*. Berkeley: University of California Press, 1966.

Kupferschmidt, Uri M. "Reformist and Militant Islam in Urban and Rural Egypt." *Middle Eastern Studies* 23 (1987): 403–20.

Murphy, Carlyle. *Passion for Islam: Shaping the Modern Middle East: The Egyptian Experience*. New York: Scribner, 2002.

Rubin, Barry M. *Islamic Fundamentalism in Egyptian Politics*. New York: Palgrave Macmillan, 2002.

Shukr, Abdelghaffar. *Al-Ahzâb as-Siyâsiyya wa Azmat at-Ta'addudiyya fî Misr* (Political Parties and Pluralism Crisis in Egypt). Cairo: Al-Ward, 2010.

Sullivan, Denis J., and Sana Abed-Kotob. *Islam in Contemporary Egypt: Civil Society vs. the State*. Boulder, CO: Lynne Rienner, 1999.

Waterbury, John. *Exposed to Innumerable Delusions: Public Enterprise and State Power in Egypt, India, Mexico, and Turkey*. Cambridge: Cambridge University Press, 1993.

Wickham, Carrie Rosefsky. *Mobilizing Islam: Religion, Activism, and Political Change in Egypt*. New York: Columbia University Press, 2002.

Iraq

Baram, Amatzia. *Culture, History and Ideology in the Formation of Ba'thist Iraq, 1968–89*. New York: St. Martin's Press, 1991.

———. "From Radicalism to Radical Pragmatism: The Shi'ite Fundamentalist Opposition Movements in Iraq." In *Islamic Fundamentalisms and the Gulf Crisis*, edited by James Piscatori, 28–50. Chicago: American Academy of Arts and Sciences, 1991.

Chapman, Steve. "The Sobering Reality of the Iraq War." *Chicago Tribune*, 2 June 2005.

David, Eric. "State-Building in Iraq during the Iran-Iraq War and the Gulf Crisis." In *The Internationalization of Communal Strife*, edited by Manus Midlarsky, 69–91. London: Routledge, 1993.

———. *Memories of State: Politics, History, and Collective Identity in Modern Iraq*. Berkeley: University of California, 2005.

Dodge, Toby. *Inventing Iraq: The Failure of Nation Building and a History Denied*. New York: Columbia University Press, 2003.

Everest, Larry. *Oil, Power and Empire: Iraq and the U.S. Global Agenda*. Monroe, ME: Common Courage Press, 2003.

Farouk-Sluglett, Marion, and Peter Sluglett. *Iraq since 1958: From Revolution to Dictatorship*. London: I. B. Tauris, 1990.

Ghabreeb, Edmund A. *Historical Dictionary of Iraq*. Lanham, MD: Scarecrow Press, 2004.

Grummond, Stephen. *The Iran-Iraq War: Islam Embattled*. Westport, CT: Praeger, 1982.

Gunter, Michael M. *The Kurdish Predicament in Iraq: A Political Analysis*. London: Palgrave Macmillan, 1999.

Hashim, Ahmed. "Military Power and State Formation in Modern Iraq." *Middle East Policy* 10 (2003): 29–47.

Hiro, Dilip. *The Longest War: The Iran-Iraq Military Conflict*. London: Routledge, 1991.

Hoffman, Bruce. *Insurgency and Counterinsurgency in Iraq*. Pittsburgh, PA: RAND, 2004.

Jabbar, Faleh. "The State, Society, Clan, Party, and Army in Iraq: A Totalitarian State in the Twilight of Totalitarianism." In *From Storm to Thunder: Unfinished Showdown between Iraq and US*, 1–27. Tokyo: Institute of Developing Economies, 1998.

Khadduri, Majid. *Socialist Iraq: A Study in Iraqi Politics since 1968*. Washington, DC: Middle East Institute, 1978.

Lukitz, Laura. *Iraq: The Search for National Identity*. London: Frank Cass, 1995.

Marr, Phebe. *The Modern History of Iraq*. Boulder, CO: Westview Press, 2004.

Nasr, Vali. *The Shia Revival: How Conflicts within Islam Will Shape the Future*. New York: Norton, 2006.

Rosen, Nir. "Iraq: Enemies and Neighbors." *Asian Times*, 24 February 2004.

Simon, Reeva, and Eleanor Tejirian, eds. *The Creation of Iraq, 1914–1921*. New York: Columbia University Press, 2004.

Sluglett, Peter. *Britain in Iraq, 1914–1932*. Reading: Ithaca Press, 1976.

Sluglett, Peter, and Marion Farouk-Sluglett. *Iraq since 1958: From Revolution to Dictatorship*. London: Kegan Paul, 1987.

Tripp, Charles. *A History of Iraq*. Cambridge, MA: Cambridge University Press, 2000.

Jordan

Adams, Linda. "Political Liberalization in Jordan: An Analysis of the State's Relationship with the Muslim Brotherhood." *Journal of Church and State* 38 (1996): 507.

Bank, André, and Oliver Schlumberger. "Jordan: Between Regime Survival and Economic Reform." In *Arab Elites: Negotiating the Politics of Change*, edited by Volker Perthes. Boulder, CO: Lynne Rienner, 2004.

Braizat, F. "Opinion Poll: Democracy in Jordan 2008." Center for Strategic Studies at the University of Jordan. http://www.css-jordan.org (accessed 7 September 2011).

Brand, Laurie A. *Jordan's Inter-Arab Relations: The Political Economy of Alliance Making*. New York: Columbia University Press, 1994.

———. "The Effects of the Peace Process on Political Liberalization in Jordan." *Journal of Palestine Studies* 28 (1999): 52.

Central Intelligence Agency. "The World Factbook: Jordan." Central Intelligence Agency. http://www.cia.gov/library/publications/the-world-factbook/geos/jo.html (accessed 7 September 2011).

Fischbach, Michael R. *State, Society and Land in Jordan.* Leiden: E. J. Brill, 2000.

Hammerstein, Ralf P. *Deliberalization in Jordan: The Roles of Islamists and U.S.-EU Assistance in Stalled Democratization.* Munich: University of the German Federal Armed Forces, 1999.

Hanieh, Hassan Abu. *Women and Politics: From the Perspective of Islamic Movements in Jordan.* Edited by Friedrich Ebert Stiftung. Amman: Economic Printing Press, 2008.

Lucas, Russell. "Deliberalization in Jordan." *Journal of Democracy* 14 (2003): 137.

———. *Institutions and the Politics of Survival in Jordan: Domestic Responses to External Challenges, 1988–2001.* Albany: State University of New York Press, 2005.

Robinson, Glenn E. "Can Islamists Be Democrats? The Case of Jordan." *Middle East Journal* 51 (1997): 373.

———. "Defensive Democratization in Jordan." *International Journal of Middle East Studies* 30 (1998): 387.

Ryan, Curtis. "Islamist Political Activism in Jordan: Moderation, Militancy, and Democracy." http://www.meriajournal.com/en/asp/journal/2008/june/ryan/index.asp (accessed 7 September 2011).

Wiktorowicz, Quintan. *The Management of Islamic Activism: Salafis, the Muslim Brotherhood and State Power in Jordan.* Albany: State University of New York Press, 2001.

Lebanon

Abraham, Antoine J. *The Lebanon War.* Westport, CT: Greenwood, 1996.

Barakat, Halim. "Social and Political Integration in Lebanon: A Case of Social Mosaic." *Middle East Journal* 27 (1973): 301–18.

Binder, Leonard, ed. *Politics in Lebanon.* New York: Wiley, 1966.

Ellis, Kail C., ed. *Lebanon's Second Republic: Prospects for the Twenty-First Century.* Gainesville: University Press of Florida, 2002.

Gordan, David C. *Lebanon: The Fragmented Nation.* London: Hoover Institution Press, 1980.

Gunderson, G. "Faces of Lebanon Sects, Wars, and Global Extensions." *Digest of Middle East Studies* 6 (1997): 78–83.

Hamzeh, A. Nizar. "The Future of Islamic Movements in Lebanon." In *Islamic Fundamentalism: Myths and Realities*, edited by Ahmad S. Moussalli, 249–74. Reading: Ithaca Press, 1998.

Harik, Iliya F. "Political Elite of Lebanon." *Political Elites in the Middle East* (1975): 201–20.

Harik, Judith Palmer. *Hezbollah: The Changing Face of Terrorism.* London: I. B. Tauris, 2004.

Harris, William W. *Faces of Lebanon: Sects, Wars, and Global Extensions.* Princeton, NJ: Markus Wiener, 1997.

Jaber, Hala. *Hezbollah: Born with a Vengeance.* New York: Columbia University Press, 1997.

Khalaf, Samir. *Civil and Uncivil Violence: The Internationalization of Communal Conflict in Lebanon.* New York: Columbia University Press, 2002.

Qazzi, Fayiz. *Min Hassan Nasrallah ilâ Michel Aoun: Qirâ'a Siyâsiyya li Hizb Allah* (From Nasrallah to Aoun: A Political Analysis of Hizbullah). Beirut: Riyâdh ar-Riyyis, 2009.

Ranstrop, M. *Hizballah in Lebanon: The Politics of the Western Hostage Crisis.* London: Macmillan, 1996.

Rubin, Barry M. *Lebanon: Liberation, Conflict, and Crisis.* London: Palgrave Macmillan, 2009.

Saad-Ghorayeb, Amal. *Hizbu'llah: Politics and Religion.* London: Pluto Press, 2002.

Salibi, Kamal S. *A House of Many Mansions: The History of Lebanon Reconsidered.* London: I. B. Tauris, 2003.

Winslow, Charles. *Lebanon: War and Politics in a Fragmented Society.* London: Routledge, 1996.

Palestine

Abu-'Amr, Ziyad. *Islamic Fundamentalism in the West Bank and Gaza: Muslim Brotherhood and Islamic Jihad.* Bloomington: Indiana University Press, 1994.

Ahmad, Hisham H. *Hamas: From Religious Salvation to Political Transformation.* Jerusalem: Palestine Academic Society for the Study of International Affairs, 1994.

Anti-Defamation League of B'nai B'rith. *ADL Special Background Report: Hamas, Islamic Jihad, and the Muslim Brotherhood: Islamic Extremists and the Terrorist Threat to America.* New York: Anti-Defamation League of B'nai B'rith, 1993.

El-Awaisi, Abd al-Fattah Muhammad. *The Muslim Brothers and the Palestine Question, 1928–1947.* London: I. B. Tauris, 1998.

Elad, Shlomo, and Ariel Merari. *The International Dimension of Palestinian Terrorism.* Tel Aviv: Tel Aviv University Press, 1986.

Hadawi, Sami. *Bitter Harvest: A Modern History of Palestine.* Northampton, MA: Interlink, 1998.

———. *Palestinian Rights and Losses in 1948: A Comprehensive Study.* London: Saqi Books, 1998.

Hatina, Meir. *Islam and Salvation in Palestine: The Islamic Jihad Movement.* Syracuse, NY: Syracuse University Press, 2001.

Kushner, David, ed. *Palestine in the Late Ottoman Period: Political, Social, and Economic Transformation.* Leiden: E. J. Brill, 1986.

Laqueur, Walter. *Voices of Terror: Manifestos, Writing, and Manuals of Al Qaeda, Hamas, and Other Terrorists from around the World and throughout the Ages.* Naperville, IL: Sourcebooks, 2004.

Lybarger, Loren D. *Identity and Religion in Palestine: The Struggle between Islamism and Secularism in the Occupied Territories.* Princeton, NJ: Princeton University Press, 1964.

Mattar, Philip. *Encyclopedia of the Palestinians.* New York: Facts on File, 2005.

Milton-Edwards, Beverley. *Islamic Politics in Palestine*. London: I. B. Taurus, 1999.

Nassar, Jamal, and Roger Hickocks, eds. *Palestine Intifada at the Crossroads*. New York: Praeger, 1989.

Nawfal, Ahmad Said, ed. *Munazzmat at-Tahrîr al-Filistiniyya: Taqyîm at-tajruba wa I'âdat al-Binâ'* (Palestinian Liberation Organization: Experience Assessment and Reconstruction). Beirut: Markaz az-Zaytun, 2007.

Smith, Charles. *Palestine and the Arab-Israel Conflict*. New York: St. Martin's Press, 2001.

Uwaysi, Abd al-Fattah Muhammad. *The Muslim Brothers and the Palestine Question, 1928–1947*. London: I. B. Tauris, 1998.

Zureik, Elia. "Palestinian Refugees and Peace." *Journal of Palestine Studies* 25 (1994): 6.

Syria

Abd-Allah, Umar F. *The Islamic Struggle in Syria*. Berkeley, CA: Mizan Press, 1983.

Commins, David Dean. *Historical Dictionary of Syria*. Lanham, MD: Scarecrow Press, 2004.

Daftary, Farhad. *The Isma'ilis: Their History and Doctrines*. Cambridge: Cambridge University Press, 1992.

Federal Research Division. *Syria: A Country Study*. Whitefish, MT: Kessinger, 2004.

Human Rights Watch. *Far from Justice: Syria's Supreme State Security Court*. New York: Human Rights Watch, 2009.

Kulick, Amir, and Yoram Schweitzer. "Syria and the Global Jihad: A Dangerous Double Game." *Strategic Assessment* 11 (2009): 67.

Leverett, Flynt Lawrence. *Inheriting Syria: Bashar's Trial by Fire*. Washington, DC: Brookings Institution, 2005.

Rabil, Robert G. "The Syrian Muslim Brotherhood." In *The Muslim Brotherhood: The Organization and Policies of a Global Movement*, edited by Barry Rubin. New York: Palgrave Macmillan, 2010.

Rabu, Annka. "Nation-State Building in Syria: Ba'th and Islam—Conflict or Accommodation?" In *Islam: State and Society*, edited by Klaus Ferdinand and Mehdi Mozaffari, 117–26. London: Curzon Press, 1988.

Roberts, David. *The Ba'th and the Creation of the Modern Syria*. New York: St. Martin's Press, 1987.

Wikas, Seth. "Battling the Lion of Damascus: Syria's Domestic Opposition and the Asad Regime." *Policy Focus* 69 (2007): 24.

THE MAGHREB

Algeria

Adamson, Kay. *Algeria: A Study in Competing Ideologies*. New York: Continuum, 1998.

Bedjaoui, Youcef, Abbas Aroua, and Meziane Ait-Larbi, eds. *An Inquiry into the Algerian Massacres*. Geneva: Hoggar, 1999.

Ciment, James. *Algeria: The Fundamentalist Challenge*. New York: Facts on File, 1997.

Entelis, John P., and Phillip C. Naylor, eds. *State and Society in Algeria*. Boulder, CO: Westview Press, 1992.

Fuller, Graham E. *Algeria: The Next Fundamentalist State?* Santa Monica, CA: RAND, 1996.

Hunter, Shireen. *The Algerian Crisis: Origins, Evolution and Lessons for the Maghreb and Europe*. Brussels: Centre for European Policy Studies, 1996.

Laremont, Ricardo Rene. *Islam and the Politics of Resistance in Algeria, 1783–1992*. Trenton, NJ: Africa World Press, 1999.

Malley, Robert. *The Call from Algeria: Third Worldism, Revolution, and the Turn to Islam*. Berkeley: University of California Press, 1996.

Martinez, Luis. *The Algerian Civil War, 1990–1998*. New York: Columbia University Press, 2000.

Naylor, Phillip. *Historical Dictionary of Algeria*. Lanham, MD: Scarecrow Press, 2006.

Roberts, Hugh. *The Battlefield: Algeria, 1988–2002—Studies in a Broken Polity*. London: Verso, 2003.

Volpi, Frederic. *Islam and Democracy: The Failure of Dialogue in Algeria, 1988–2001*. London: Pluto Press, 2003.

Willis, Michael. *The Islamist Challenge in Algeria: A Political History*. New York: New York University Press, 1999.

Libya

Allen, J. A. *Libya since Independence: Economic and Political Development*. London: Croom Helm, 1982.

Bearman, Jonathan. *Qadhafi's Libya*. London: Zed Books, 1986.

Boucek, Christopher. "Libyan State-Sponsored Terrorism: A Historical Perspective." *Jamestown Foundation Terrorism Monitor* 3 (2005).

Deeb, Marius K. "Libya: Internal Developments and Regional Politics." In *The Middle East: Annual Issues and Events* 4. Boston: G. K. Hall, 1985.

Deeb, Marius K., and Mary Jane Deeb. *Libya since the Revolution: Aspects of Social and Political Development*. New York: Praeger, 1982.

Obeidi, Amal. *Political Culture in Libya*. Surrey: Curzon Press, 2001.

Pargete, Allison. "Political Islam in Libya." *Jamestown Foundation Terrorism Monitor* 3 (2005).

Royce, Ed. *U.S.-Libya Relations: A New Era? Hearing before the Committee on International Relations, U.S. House of Representatives*. Darby, PA: Diane, 1999.

Simons, Geoff. *Libya: The Struggle for Survival*. New York: St. Martin's Press, 1993.

St. John, Ronald Bruce. *Libya and the United States: Two Centuries of Strife*. Philadelphia: University of Pennsylvania Press, 2002.

———. *Historical Dictionary of Libya*. Lanham, MD: Scarecrow Press, 2006.

Mauritania

Bennoune, Mahfoud. "The Political Economy of Mauritania: Imperialism and Class Struggle." *Review of African Political Economy* 12 (1978): 31–52.

Curtin, Phillip D. "Jihad in West Africa: Early Phases and Inter-Relations in Mauritania and Senegal." *Journal of African History* 12 (1971): 11–24.

Diallo, Garba. *Mauritania, the Other Apartheid*. Uppsala: Nordiska Afrikainstitutet, 1993.

Eagleton, William, Jr. "The Islamic Republic of Mauritania." *Middle East Journal* 19 (1965): 45–53.

Gerteiny, Alfred G. *Mauritania*. New York: Praeger, 1967.

Human Rights Watch/Africa. *Mauritania's Campaign of Terror: State-Sponsored Repression of Black Africans*. New York: Human Rights Watch, 1994.

Jourde, Cédric. "The President Is Coming to Visit! Dramas and the Hijack of Democratization in the Islamic Republic of Mauritania." *Comparative Politics* 37 (2005): 421–40.

Norris, H. T. "Muslim Sanhaja Scholars of Mauritania." In *Studies in West African Islamic History: The Cultivators of Islam*, edited by John Ralph Willis. New York: Routledge, 1979.

Ould-Mey, Mohameden. *Global Restructuring and Peripheral States: The Carrot and the Stick in Mauritania*. London: Littlefield Adams, 1996.

Pazzanita, Anthony G. "Political Transition in Mauritania: Problems and Prospects." *Middle East Journal* 53 (1999): 44–58.

———. *Historical Dictionary of Mauritania*. Lanham, MD: Scarecrow Press, 2008.

Stewart, Charles Cameron, and E. K. Stuart. *Islam and Social Order in Mauritania: A Case Study from the Nineteenth Century*. Gloucestershire: Clarendon, 1973.

Morocco

Ahmida, Ali Abdullatif, ed. *Beyond Colonialism and Nationalism in the Maghreb: History, Culture and Politics.* New York: Palgrave, 2000.

Ashford, Douglas E. "Politics and Violence in Morocco." *Middle East Journal* 13 (1959): 11–25.

———. *Political Change in Morocco*. Princeton, NJ: Princeton University Press, 1961.

———. *Knowledge and Power in Morocco: The Education of a Twentieth Century Notable*. Princeton, NJ: Princeton University Press, 1985.

Bennison, Amira K. *Jihad and Its Interpretation in Pre-Colonial Morocco: State-Society Relations during the French Conquest of Algeria.* New York: Routledge Curzon, 2002.

Benomar, Jamal. "The Monarchy, the Islamist Movement and Religious Discourse in Morocco." *Third World Quarterly* 10 (1988): 539–55.

Brace, R. M. *Morocco, Algeria, Tunisia*. Englewood Cliffs, NJ: Prentice Hall, 1964.

Buskens, Léon. "Recent Debates on Family Law Reform in Morocco: Islamic Law as Politics in an Emerging Public Sphere." *Islamic Law and Society* 10 (2003): 70–131.

Entelis, John Pierre. *Comparative Politics of North Africa: Algeria, Morocco, and Tunisia*. Syracuse, NY: Syracuse University Press, 1980.

———. "Kingdom of Morocco." In *The Government and Politics of the Middle East and North Africa*, edited by David E. Long and Bernard Reich. Boulder, CO: Westview Press, 1980.

———. *Culture and Counterculture in Moroccan Politics*. Lanham, MD: University Press of America, 1996.

Hart, David M. *Tribe and Society in Rural Morocco*. London: Frank Cass, 2000.

Hirchi, Mohammed. "Political Islam in Morocco: The Case of the Party of Justice and Development (PJD)." http://concernedafricascholars.org/bulletin/77/hirchi.

Ismail, Salma Mahmud. *As-Sirâ' al-Ithni wal Madhhabî fîl Maghrib al-Aqsa* (Ethnic and Doctrinal Struggle in Morocco). Cairo: Ru'a lil Nash, 2010.

Moore, Clement Henry. *Politics in North Africa: Algeria, Morocco, and Tunisia*. Boston: Little, Brown, 1970.

Munjib, Al-Muti. *Muwâjahât Bayna al-Islamiyyîn wal 'Ilmâniyyîn bil Maghrib* (Confrontations between Islamists and Laicists in Morocco). Rabat: Wijhat Nazar, 2009.

Munson, Henry, Jr. "The Social Base of Islamic Militancy in Morocco." *Middle East Journal* 40 (1986): 267–84.

———. *Religion and Power in Morocco*. New Haven, CT: Yale University Press, 1993.

Park, Thomas K., and Aomar Baim. *Historical Dictionary of Morocco*. Lanham, MD: Scarecrow Press, 2000.

Seddon, David. "Morocco and the Western Sahara." *Review of African Political Economy* 38 (1987): 24–47.

Spaulding, Jay, et al. *The Enigmatic Saint: Ahmad Ibn Idris and the Idrisi Tradition*. Evanston, IL: Northwestern University Press, 1994.

Tunisia

Allani, Alaya. "The Islamists in Tunisia between Confrontation and Participation, 1980–2008." *Journal of North African Studies* 14 (2009): 258–66.

Anderson, Lisa. "Tunisia and Libya: Responses to the Islamic Impulse." In *The Iranian Revolution: Its Global Impact*, edited by John L. Esposito, 157–75. Miami: Florida International University Press, 1990.

Borowiec, Andrew. *Modern Tunisia: A Democratic Apprenticeship*. Westport, CT: Praeger, 1998.

Boulby, Marion. "The Islamic Challenge: Tunisia since Independence." *Third World Quarterly* 10 (1988): 590–614.

Charrad, Mounira M. *States and Women's Rights: The Making of Postcolonial Tunisia, Algeria, Morocco*. Berkeley: University of California Press, 2001.

Dunn, Collins. "The *Al-Nahda* Movement in Tunisia: From Renaissance to Revolution." In *Islamism and Secularism in North Africa*, edited by J. Ruedy. Basingstoke: Macmillan, 1994.

Al-Ghannushi, Rashid. *Harakat al-Itijah al-Islami fi Tunis*. Kuwait: Dar al-Qalam, 1989.

Hamidi, Muhammad al-Hashimi. *The Politicization of Islam: A Case Study of Tunisia.* Boulder, CO: Westview Press, 1998.

Hermassi, Abdelbaki. "The Rise and Fall of the Islamist Movement in Tunisia." In *The Islamist Dilemma: The Political Role of Islamist Movements in the Contemporary Arab World*, edited by Laura Guazzone, 105–27. Reading: Ithaca Press, 1995.

Labyadh, Salem. *Al-Huwiyya, al-ʿUrûba, at-Tawnasa* (Identity, Arabity and Tunisianity). Beirut: Markaz Dirâsât al-Wihda, 2009.

Moore, Clement Henry. *Tunisia since Independence.* Berkeley: University of California Press, 1972.

——. "Tunisia and Bourguibisme: Twenty Years of Crisis." *Third World Quarterly* 10 (1988): 176–90.

Murphy, Emma. *Economic and Political Change in Tunisia: From Bourguiba to Ben Ali.* London: Palgrave Macmillan, 1999.

Perkins, Kenneth J. *Tunisia: Crossroads of the Islamic European Worlds.* Westview, CT: Westview Press, 1986.

——. *Historical Dictionary of Tunisia.* Lanham, MD: Scarecrow Press, 1997.

——. *A History of Modern Tunisia.* Cambridge: Cambridge University Press, 2004.

Rowland, Jacky. "Tunisia: 'More Repressive Than Ever.'" *Africa Report* 37 (1992): 50–51.

Ruedy, John, ed. *Islamism and Secularism in North Africa.* New York: St. Martin's Press, 1994.

Sadiki, Larbi. "Bin Ali's Tunisia: Democracy by Non-Democratic Means." *British Journal of Middle Eastern Studies* 29 (2002): 57–78.

Salvatore, Armando. *Islam and the Political Discourse of Modernity.* London: Ithaca Press, 1997.

Waltz, Susan. "The Islamist Appeal in Tunisia." *Middle East Journal* 40 (1986): 651–70.

Zartman, I. William, ed. *Tunisia: The Political Economy of Reform.* Boulder, CO: Lynne Rienner, 1991.

GULF STATES

Bahrain

Belgrave, James H. D. *Welcome to Bahrain.* Manama: Augustan Press, 1975.

Dekmejian, R. Hrair. *Islam in Revolution.* Syracuse, NY: Syracuse University Press, 1982.

Gause, F. G. *Oil Monarchies: Domestic and Security Challenges in the Arab Gulf States.* New York: Council on Foreign Relations Press, 1994.

Al-Khalifa, Abdullah bin Khalid, and Michael Rice, eds. *Bahrain through the Ages: The History.* New York: Kegan Paul, 1993.

Khury, Fuad. *Tribe and State in Bahrain: The Transformation of Social and Political Authority in an Arab State.* Chicago: University of Chicago Press, 1980.

Lawson, Fred. *Bahrain: The Modernization of Autocracy*. Boulder, CO: Westview Press, 1989.

Naqeeb, Khaloun. *Society and State in the Gulf and Arab Peninsula: A Different Perspective*. London: Routledge, 1990.

Nugent, Jeffery B., and Theodore Thomas. *Bahrain and the Gulf: Past Perspectives and Alternative Futures*. New York: St. Martin's Press, 1985.

Pasha, A. K. "Demography, Political Reforms and Opposition in GCC States." In *The Political Economy of West Asia: Demography, Democracy and Economic Reforms*, edited by G. Pant. Delhi: Mank, 1994.

Peterson, J. E. *The Arab Gulf States: Steps toward Political Participation*. New York: Praeger, 1988.

Piscatori, James, ed. *Islamic Fundamentalisms and the Gulf Crisis*. Chicago: American Academy of Arts and Sciences, 1991.

Zahlan, Rosemarie. *The Making of the Modern Gulf States*. London: Unwin Hyman, 1989.

Kuwait

Abu-Hakima, Ahmed M. *The Modern History of Kuwait. Kuwait: 1750–1965*. London: Luzac, 1983.

Crystal, Jill. *Oil and Politics in the Gulf: Rulers and Merchants in Kuwait and Qatar*. Cambridge: Cambridge University Press, 1995.

Ghabra, Shafeeq. "Kuwait and the Dynamics of Socio-Economic Change." *Middle East Journal* 51 (1997): 358–72.

Halliday, Fred. "Letter from Kuwait." *Middle East Report* 215 (2002): 43–45.

Hassan, Hamdi A. *The Iraqi Invasion of Kuwait: Religion, Identity, and Otherness in the Analysis of War and Conflict*. London: Pluto Press, 1999.

Ismael, Jacqueline S. *Kuwait: Dependency and Class in a Rentier State*. Gainesville: University Press of Florida, 1993.

Kazan, Fayad E. "Kuwait." In *Mass Media in the Middle East: A Comprehensive Handbook*, edited by Yahya R. Kamalipour and Hamid Mowlana. Westport, CT: Greenwood Press, 1994.

King, John. *The Invasion of Kuwait: Days that Shook the World Series*. Oxford: Raintree, 2004.

Levins, John. *Days of Fear: The Inside Story of the Iraqi Invasion and Occupation of Kuwait*. Dubai: Motivate, 1997.

Rashoud, Claudia Farkas. *Kuwait: Before and After the Storm*. Kuwait City: The Kuwait Bookshop, 1992.

Tetreault, Mary Ann. *Stories of Democracy: Politics and Society in Contemporary Kuwait*. New York: Columbia University Press, 2000.

Oman

Allen, Calvin H. *Oman, the Modernization of the Sultanate*. Boulder, CO: Westview Press, 1987.

———. *Oman under Qaboos: From Coup to Constitution, 1970–1996*. London: Frank Cass, 2000.

Allfree, P. S. *Warlords of Oman*. Kent, 2008.

Hill, Ann, and Daryl Hill. *The Sultanate of Oman: A Heritage*. London: Longman, 1986.

Al-Kahlili, Majid. *Oman's Foreign Policy: Foundation and Practice*. New York: Praeger, 2009.

Kechichian, Joseph A. *Oman and the World: The Emergence of an Independent Foreign Policy*. Santa Monica, CA: RAND, 1995.

Owtram, Francis. *A Modern History of Oman: Formation of the State since 1920*. London: I. B. Tauris, 2003.

Peterson, John E. *Oman in the Twentieth Century: Political Foundations of an Emerging State*. London: Croom Helm, 1978.

———. *Oman's Insurgencies: The Sultanate's Struggle for Supremacy*. London: Saqi Books, 2008.

Pridham, Brian R., ed. *Oman: Economic, Social and Strategic Developments*. London: Croom Helm, 1986.

Rabi, Uzi. *The Emergence of States in a Tribal Society: Oman under Sa'id bin Taymur, 1932–1970*. Sussex: Sussex Academic Press, 2011.

Riphenburg, Carol. *Oman: Political Development in a Changing World*. New York: Praeger, 1998.

Risso, Patricia. *Oman and Muscat: An Early Modern History*. New York: St. Martin's Press, 1986.

Wilkinson, John C. *The Imamate Tradition of Oman*. Cambridge: Cambridge University Press, 1987.

Yousef, Mohamed bin Musa Al-. *Oil and the Transformation of Oman: The Socio-Economic Impact*. London: Stacey, 1996.

Qatar

Crystal, Jill. *Oil and Politics in the Gulf: Rulers and Merchants in Kuwait and Qatar*. Cambridge: Cambridge University Press, 1990.

Fakhr, M. El-Islam. "Intergenerational Conflict and the young Qatari Neurotic." *Ethos* 4 (1976): 45–56.

Ferdinand, Klaus. *Bedouins of Qatar*. New York: Thames and Hudson, 1993.

Global Investment Center. *Qatar: Foreign Policy and Government Guide*. Washington, DC: International Business Publications, 2011.

Hamzeh, A. Nizar. "Qatar: The Duality of the Legal System," *Middle Eastern Studies* 30 (1994): 79–90.

El-Mallakh, Ragael. *Qatar: Energy and Development*. London: Croom Helm, 1985.

Rahman, Habibur. *The Emergence of Qatar*. New York: Routledge, 2006.

Rathmell, Andrew. "Political Reform in the Gulf: The Case of Qatar." *Middle Eastern Studies* 36 (2000): 47–62.

U.S. Library of Congress. *Qatar Federal Research Study: Comprehensive Information, History, and Analysis—Politics, Economy, and Military*. Washington, DC: Progressive Management, 2011.

Zahlan, Rosemarie Said. *The Creation of Qatar*. London: Croom Helm, 1979.

Saudi Arabia

Abir, Mordechai. *Saudi Arabia: Government, Society, and the Gulf Crisis.* New York: Routledge, 1993.

Bill, James A. "Resurgent Islam in the Persian Gulf." *Foreign Affairs* 63 (1984): 108–27.

Buchan, James. "Secular and Religious Opposition in Saudi Arabia." In *State, Society and Economy in Saudi Arabia*, edited by Tim Niblock. London: Croom Helm, 1982.

Dekmejian, R. Hrair. "The Rise of Political Islamism in Saudi Arabia." *Middle East Journal* 48 (1994): 627–43.

Fandy, Mamoun. *Saudi Arabia and the Politics of Dissent.* New York: Palgrave Macmillan, 2001.

Al-Farsy, Fouad. *Saudi Arabia: A Country Study in Development.* London: Kegan Paul, 1986.

Goldberg, Jacob. "The Shi'i Minority in Saudi Arabia." In *Shi'ism and Social Protest*, edited by Juan R. I. Cole and Nikki R. Keddie, 230–46. New Haven, CT: Yale University Press, 1986.

Habib, John. *Ibn Saud's Warriors of Islam: The Ikhwan of Najd and Their Role in the Creation of the Saudi Kingdom, 1910–1930.* Leiden: E. J. Brill, 1978.

Helms, Christine Moss. *The Cohesion of Saudi Arabia: Evolution of Political Identity.* London: Croom Helm, 1981.

Holden, David, and Richard Johns. *The House of Saud: The Rise and Rule of the Most Powerful Dynasty in the Arab World.* New York: Holt, Rinehart and Winston, 1981.

Howarth, David. *The Desert King: Ibn Saud and His Arabia.* New York: McGraw-Hill, 1964.

Jacquard, Roland. *In the Name of Osama Bin Laden: Global Terrorism and the Bin Laden Brotherhood.* Durham, NC: Duke University Press, 2002.

Nehme, Michel G. "The Islamic-Capitalist State of Saudi Arabia: The Surfacing of Fundamentalism." In *Islamic Fundamentalism: Myths and Realities*, edited by Ahmad S. Moussalli, 275–302. Reading: Ithaca Press, 1998.

Niblock, Tim, ed. *State, Society, and Economy in Saudi Arabia.* New York: St. Martin's Press, 1982.

Openshaw, M. "Religion and Regime Legitimacy: The Al-Saud, Wahhabism, and Saudi Arabian Politics." *Journal of Arabic, Islamic and Middle Eastern Studies* 1 (1994): 76–89.

Peterson, J. E. *Historical Dictionary of Saudi Arabia.* Lanham, MD: Scarecrow Press, 2003.

Al-Rasheed, Madawi. "Saudi Arabia's Islamic Opposition." *Current History* 95 (1996): 16–22.

Yamani, Mai. "Saudi Arabia and Central Asia: The Islamic Connection." In *From the Gulf to Central Asia: Players in the New Great Game*, edited by Anoushiravan Ehteshami. Exeter: University of Exeter Press, 1994.

Al-Yassini, Ayman. *Religion and State in the Kingdom of Saudi Arabia.* Boulder, CO: Westview Press, 1985.

United Arab Emirates

Abdullah, Muhammad Morsy. *The United Arab Emirates: A Modern History*. London: Croom Helm, 1978.

Ballantyne, W. M. "The New Civil Code of the United Arab Emirates: A Further Reassertion of the Shari'a." *Arab Law Quarterly* 1 (1986): 245–64.

Feulner, Gary R., and Amjad Ali Khan. "Dispute Resolution in the United Arab Emirates." *Arab Law Quarterly* 1 (1986): 312–18.

Heard-Bey, Frauke. "The United Arab Emirates: Statehood and Nation-Building in a Traditional Society." *Middle East Journal* 59 (2005): 357-375.

Khoury, Enver. *The United Arab Emirates: Its Political System and Politics*. Hyattsville, MD: Institute of Middle Eastern and North African Affairs, 1980.

McCoy, Lisa. *United Arab Emirates*. Philadelphia: Mason Crest, 2004.

Romano, Amy. *A Historical Atlas of the United Arab Emirates*. New York: Rosen Publishing Group, 2004.

Rugh, William A. "The Foreign Policy of the United Arab Emirates." *Middle East Journal* 50 (1996): 57–70.

Soffan, Lina U. *The Women of the United Arab Emirates*. London: Croom Helm, 1980.

Taryam, A. O. *The Establishment of the United Arab Emirates*. London: Croom Helm, 1986.

Yemen

Bidwell, Robin. *The Two Yemens*. Boulder, CO: Westview, 1983.

Bonnefoy, Laurent. "Varieties of Islamism in Yemen: The Logic of Integration under Pressure." *Middle East Review of International Affairs* 13 (2009): 26–36.

Burrowes, Robert D. *Historical Dictionary of Yemen*. Lanham, MD: Scarecrow Press, 2010.

Carapico, Sheila. "Elections and Mass Politics in Yemen." *Middle East Report* 23 (1993): 2–6.

Cigar, Norman. "Islam and the State in South Yemen: The Uneasy Coexistence." *Middle Eastern Studies* 26 (1990): 185–203.

Donaldson, William J. *Sharecropping in the Yemen: A Study in Islamic Theory, Custom and Pragmatism.* Leiden: E. J. Brill, 2000.

Dresch, Paul. *A History of Modern Yemen.* Cambridge: Cambridge University Press, 2000.

———. *Economic Growth in the Republic of Yemen: Sources, Constraints, and Potentials*. Washington, DC: World Bank, 2002.

Dresch, Paul, and Bernard Haykel. "Stereotypes and Political Styles: Islamists and Tribesfolk in Yemen." *International Journal of Middle East Studies* 27 (1995): 405–31.

Latta, Rafiq. *Yemen: Unification and Modernization.* London: Gulf Centre for Strategic Studies, 1994.

Mackintosh-Smith, Tim. *Yemen: The Unknown Arabia*. New York: Woodstock, 2001.

Pridham, Brian, ed. *Contemporary Yemen: Politics and Historical Background*. London: Croom Helm, 1984.

Schmidt, Dana Adams. *Yemen: The Unknown War*. London: Bodley Head, 1968.

Schwedler, Jillian. *Faith in Moderation: Islamist Parties in Jordan and Yemen.* Cambridge: Cambridge University Press, 2007.

Stookey, Robert W. *Yemen: The Politics of Yemen Arab Republic*. Boulder, CO: Westview Press, 1978.

AFRICAN STATES

Mali

Bratton, Michael, Massa Coulibaly, and Fabiana Machado. "Popular Views of the Legitimacy of the State in Mali." *Canadian Journal of African Studies* 36 (2002): 197–238.

Conrad, David C. "Islam in the Oral Traditions of Mali: Bilali and Surakata." *Journal of African History* 26 (1985): 33–49.

Cutter, Charles H. "Mali: A Bibliographical Introduction." *African Studies Bulletin* 9 (1966): 74–87.

Economist Intelligence Unit. "The Political Scene." In *EIU Country Report: Mali.* London: Economist Intelligence Unit, 2002.

Imperato, Pascal James, and Gavin H. Imperato. *Historical Dictionary of Mali*. Lanham, MD: Scarecrow Press, 2008.

Pringle, Robert. "Mali's Unlikely Democracy." *Wilson Quarterly* 30 (2006): 31–39.

Schulz, Dorothea E. "'Charisma and Brotherhood' Revisited: Mass-Mediated Forms of Spirituality in Urban Mali." *Journal of Religion in Africa* 33 (2003): 146–71.

———. "Political Factions, Ideological Fictions: The Controversy over Family Law Reform in Democratic Mali." *Islamic Law and Society* 10 (2003): 132–64.

Soares, Benjamin F. "Muslim Proselytization as Purification: Religious Pluralism and Conflict in Contemporary Mali." In *Proselytization and Communal Self-Determination in Africa*, edited by Abdalladh A. An-Na'im. Maryknoll, NY: Orbis, 1999.

———. "Islam and Public Piety in Mali." In *Public Islam and the Common Good*, edited by Armando Salvatore and Dale F. Eickelman. Leiden: E. J. Brill, 2004.

———. *Islam and the Prayer Economy: History and Authority in a Malian Town*. Ann Arbor: University of Michigan Press, 2005.

———. "Islam in Mali in the Neoliberal Era." *African Affairs* 105 (2006): 77–95.

Nigeria

Aborisade, Oladimeji, and Robert J. Mundt. *Politics in Nigeria*. London: Longman, 2002.

Achebe, Chinua. *The Trouble with Nigeria*. Enugu: Fourth Dimension, 1982.

Agbese, Pita. "The Impending Demise of Nigeria's Third Republic." *Africa Today* 37 (1990): 23–44.

Ajaeqbu, H. I. *Urban and Rural Development in Nigeria*. London: Heinemann, 1976.

Akeredolu-Ale, E. O. *The Underdevelopment of Indigenous Entrepreneurship in Nigeria*. Ibadan: Ibadan University Press, 1975.

Albert, I. O. *Inter-Ethnic Relations in a Nigeria City: The Historical Perspective of the Hausa-Igbo Conflict in Kano, 1953–1991*. Ibadan: Institut Français de Recherche en Afrique, 1993.

Clarke, Peter Bernard, and Ian Linden. *Islam in Modern Nigeria: A Study of a Muslim Community in a Post-Independence State, 1960–1983*. San Francisco: Grünewald, 1984.

Doi, Abdur Rahman I. *Islamic in Nigeria*. Zaria: Gaskiya Corporation, 1984.

Falola, Toyin. *Violence in Nigeria: The Crisis of Religious Politics and Secular Ideologies*. Rochester, NY: University of Rochester Press, 1998.

Falola, Toyin, and Ann Genora. *Historical Dictionary of Nigeria*. Lanham, MD: Scarecrow, Press, 2009.

Ihonvbere, Julius Omozuanvbo. *Nigeria: The Politics of Adjustment and Democracy*. New Brunswick, NJ: Transaction, 1994.

Jarmon, Charles. *Nigeria: Reorganization and Development since the Mid-Twentieth Century*. Leiden: E. J. Brill, 1988.

Onimode, Bade. *Imperialism and Under-Development in Nigeria: The Dialectics of Mass Poverty*. Charlottesville: University of Virginia Press, 1983.

Paden, John N. *Faith and Politics in Nigeria: Nigeria as a Pivotal State in the Muslim World*. Washington, DC: United States Institute of Peace Press, 2008.

Uwazie, Ernest E., Isaac O. Albert, and Godfrey N. Uzoigwe, eds. *Inter-Ethnic and Religious Conflict Resolution in Nigeria*. Lanham, MD: Lexington Books, 1999.

Wright, Stephen. *Nigeria: Struggle for Stability and Status*. Boulder, CO: Westview Press, 1998.

Somalia

Barnes, Cedric, and Harun Hassan. "The Rise and Fall of Mogadishu's Islamic Courts." *Journal of East African Studies* 1 (2007): 160.

Fitzgerald, Nina J. *Somalia: Issues, History, and Bibliography*. Hauppauge, NY: Nova, 2002.

Fukui, K., and J. Markakis. *Ethnicity and Conflict in the Horn of Africa*. London: Currey, 1994.

Gudurn, C., ed. *The Horn of Africa*. London: UCL Press, 1994.

Hiskett, Mervyn. *The Course of Islam in Africa*. Edinburgh: Edinburgh University Press, 1994.

Latin, David D., and Said S. Samatar. *Somalia: Nation in Search of a State*. Boulder, CO: Westview Press, 1987.

Levtzion, Nehemia, and Randall L. Pouwels, eds. *The History of Islam in Africa*. Athens: Ohio University Center for International Studies, 2000.

Lewis, Ioan M. *A Modern History of Somalia: Nation and State in the Horn of Africa*. London: Longman, 1980.

———. *Understanding Somalia: Guide to Culture, History and Social Institutions.* Kent: HAAN, 1993.

———. *A Modern History of the Somali.* Oxford: James Currey, 2002.

———. *Understanding Somalia and Somaliland: Culture, History, Society.* New York: Columbia University Press, 2008.

Marchal, Roland. "A Tentative Assessment of the Somali Harakat al-Shabaab." *Journal of Eastern African Studies* 3 (2009): 389.

Menkhaus, Kenneth J. "Risks and Opportunities in Somalia." *Survival* 49 (2007): 5–20.

Mukhtar, Mohamed Haji. *Historical Dictionary of Somalia.* Lanham, MD: Scarecrow Press, 2002.

Pham, J. Peter. "Peripheral Vision: A Model Solution for Somalia." *RUSI Journal* 154 (2009): 84–90.

Shay, Shaul. *Somalia between Jihad and Restoration.* New Brunswick, NJ: Transaction, 2007.

Sudan

El-Affendi, Abdelwahab. *Turabi's Revolution: Islam and Power in Sudan.* London: Grey Seal, 1991.

Bechtold, Peter. *Politics in Sudan: Parliamentary and Military Rule in an Emerging African Nation.* New York: Praeger, 1976.

Burr, Millard. *Revolutionary Sudan: Hasan al-Turabi and the Islamist State, 1989–2000.* Leiden: E. J. Brill, 2003.

Collins, Robert O. *A History of Modern Sudan.* Cambridge: Cambridge University Press, 2008.

Deng, F. M., and P. Gifford. *The Search for Peace and Unity in Sudan.* Washington, DC: Wilson Center Press, 1987.

Gallab, Abdullah A. *The First Islamist Republic; Development and Disintegration of Islamism in the Sudan.* London: Ashgate, 2008.

Hamdi, Mohamed Elhachmi. *The Making of an Islamic Political Leader: Conversations with Hasan al-Turabi.* Boulder, CO: Westview Press, 1999.

Holt, P. M., and M. W. Daly. *A History of the Sudan: From the Coming of Islam to the Present Day.* London: Longman, 1988.

Johnson, Douglas Hamilton. *The Root Causes of Sudan's Civil Wars.* London: International African Institute, 2003.

Jok, Madut. *Sudan: Race, Religion and Violence.* London: OneWorld, 2007.

Khalid, Mansour. *War and Peace in the Sudan: A Tale of Two Countries.* London: Kegan Paul, 2003.

Kobayashi, M. *The Islamist Movement in Sudan: The Impact of Dr. Hassan al-Turabi's Personality on the Movement.* Doctoral dissertation, University of Durham, OCLC # 48469721.

Lesch, Ann Mosely. *The Sudan: Contested National Identities.* Bloomington: Indiana University Press, 1999.

Lobban, Richard A., Jr., Robert S. Kramer, and Carolyn Fluehr Lobban. *Historical Dictionary of Sudan*. Lanham, MD: Scarecrow Press, 2002.

Petterson, Donald. *Inside Sudan. Political Islam, Conflict and Catastrophe*. Boulder, CO: Westview, 1999.

Prunier, Gérard. *Identity Crisis and the Weak State: The Making of the Sudanese Civil War*. London: Writenet, 1996.

Sidahmed, Abdel Salam. *Politics and Islam in Contemporary Sudan*. New York: St. Martin's Press, 1996.

Tvedt, Terje. *Southern Sudan: An Annotated Bibliography*. London: I. B. Tauris, 2004.

ASIAN STATES

Afghanistan

Adamer, Ludwig A. *Historical Dictionary of Afghanistan*. Lanham, MD: Scarecrow Press, 2004.

Blank, Jonah. *Mullahs on the Mainframe: Islam and Modernity among the Daudi Bohras*. Chicago: University of Chicago Press, 2002.

Clements, Frank. *Conflict in Afghanistan: A Historical Encyclopedia*. Santa Barbara, CA: ABC-CLIO, 2003.

Dupree, Louis. *Afghanistan*. Princeton, NJ: Princeton University Press, 1973.

Fuller, Graham E. *Islamic Fundamentalism in Afghanistan: Its Character and Prospects*. Santa Monica, CA: RAND, 2008.

Gohari, M. J. *The Taliban: Ascent to Power*. Oxford: Oxford University Press, 2001.

Goodson, Larry P. *Afghanistan's Endless War: State Failure, Regional Politics, and the Rise of the Taliban*. Seattle: University of Washington Press, 2001.

Griffin, Michael. *Reaping the Whirlwind: Afghanistan, Al Qa'ida and the Holy War*. London: Pluto Press, 2003.

Kaplan, Robert. *Soldiers of God: With Islamic Warriors in Afghanistan and Pakistan*. New York: Vintage Books, 1990.

Magnus, Ralph H., and Eden Naby. *Afghanistan: Mullah, Marx, and Mujahid*. Boulder, CO: Westview Press, 2002.

Malley, William. *Fundamentalism Reborn? Afghanistan and the Taliban*. New York: New York University Press, 1998.

———. *The Afghanistan Wars*. New York: Palgrave Macmillan, 2002.

Rashid, Ahmed. *Taliban: Militant Islam, Oil and Fundamentalism in Central Asia*. New Haven, CT: Yale University Press, 2001.

———. *Taliban: The Story of the Afghan Warlords*. London: Pan Books, 2001.

———. *Jihad: The Rise of Militant Islam in Central Asia*. New Haven, CT: Yale University Press, 2002.

Roy, Olivier. "The New Political Elites of Afghanistan." In *The Politics of Social Transformation in Afghanistan, Iran, and Pakistan*, edited by Myron Weiner and Ali Banuazizi. Syracuse, NY: Syracuse University Press, 1994.

Shahrani, Nazif M., and Robert L. Canfield. *Revolution and Rebellions in Afghanistan: Anthropological Perspectives.* Berkeley, CA: Berkeley Institute of International Studies, 1984.

Tanner, Stephen. *Afghanistan: A Military History from Alexander the Great to the War against the Taliban.* Cambridge, MA: Da Capo Press, 2009.

Williams, Brian Glyn. *Afghanistan: The Longest War.* Philadelphia: University of Pennsylvania Press, 2011.

India

Ajithkumar, M. P. *India-Pakistan Relations: The Story of a Fractured Fraternity.* New Delhi: Kalpaz, 2006.

Buehler, Arthur F. *Sufi Heirs of the Prophet: The Indian Naqshbandiyya and the Rise of the Mediating Sufi Shaykh.* Columbia: University of South Carolina Press, 1998.

Dixit, Jyotindra Nath. *India-Pakistan in War and Peace.* Oxford: Routledge, 2002.

Eaton, Richard M., ed. *India's Islamic Traditions, 711–1750.* Oxford: Oxford University Press, 2003.

Ganguly, Šumit. *The Crisis in Kashmir: Portents of War, Hopes of Peace.* New York: Cambridge University Press, 1997.

Hasan, Mushirul. *Islam in the Subcontinent: Muslims in a Plural Society.* New Delhi: Munshiram Manoharlal, 2000.

Mansingh, Sarjit. *Historical Dictionary of India.* Lanham, MD: Scarecrow Press, 2000.

Minault, Gail. *The Khilafat Movement: Religious Symbolism and Political Mobilization in India.* Oxford: Oxford University Press, 1999.

Ozdalga, Elisabeth, ed. *Naqshbandis in Western and Central Asia: Change and Continuity.* Richmond, VA: Curzon, 1999.

Qureshi, M. Naeem. *Pan-Islam in British Indian Politics: A Study of the Khilafat Movement, 1918–1924.* Leiden: E. J. Brill, 1999.

Schimmel, Annemarie. "Islam in India and Pakistan." *Iconography of Religions* 9 (1982): 34.

Sharif, Ja'Far, Gerhard Andreas Herklots, and William Crooke. *Islam in India: Or the Qānūn-i-Islām: The Customs of the Musalmāns of India.* New Delhi: Atlantic, 1999.

Swami, Praveen. *India, Pakistan and the Secret Jihad: The Covert War in Kashmir, 1947–2004.* New Delhi: Routledge, 2007.

Thomas, Raju G. C. *Indian Security Policy.* Princeton, NJ: Princeton University Press, 1986.

———. *Democracy, Security and Development in India.* New York: St. Martin's Press, 1996.

Troll, Christian W., ed. *Islam in India: Studies and Commentaries.* Uttar Pradesh: Vikas Publishing House, 1985.

———. *Muslim Shrines in India.* Oxford: Oxford University Press, 2003.

Indonesia

Abaza, Mona. "Some Research Notes on Living Condition and Perspectives among Indonesian Students in Cairo." *Journal of Southeast Asia Studies* 22 (1991): 347–60.

Abdullah, Taufik. "The Sociocultural Scene in Indonesia." In *Trends in Indonesia: Proceeding and Background Paper*, edited by Leo Suryadinata and Sharon Siddique, 65–85. Singapore: Singapore University Press, 1981.

Abu Rabi', Ibrahim. "Christian-Muslim Relations in Indonesia: The Challenge of the Twenty-First Century." *Studia Islamika* 5 (1998): 1–23.

Baswedan, Anies Rasyid. "Political Islam in Indonesia: Present and Future Trajectory." *Asian Survey* 44 (2004): 675–77.

Cribb, Robert, and Audrey Kahin. *Historical Dictionary of Indonesia*. Lanham, MD: Scarecrow Press, 2004.

Eliraz, Giora. *Islam in Indonesia: Modernism, Radicalism and the Middle East Dimension*. Brighton: Sussex Academic Press, 2004.

Federspiel, Howard M. *The Usage of Traditions of the Prophet in Contemporary Indonesia.* Tempe: Arizona State University Program for Southeast Asian Studies, 1993.

———. *A Dictionary of Indonesian Islam.* Athens: Ohio University Press, 1995.

———. *Islam and Ideology in the Emerging Indonesian State: The Persatuan Islam (Persis), 1923–1957.* Leiden: E. J. Brill, 2001.

Hefner, Robert W. *Civil Islam: Muslims and Democratization in Indonesia.* Princeton, NJ: Princeton University Press, 2000.

Hitchcock, Michael. *Islam and Identity in Eastern Indonesia.* Hull, NY: Hull University Press, 1996.

Holt, Claire, ed. *Culture and Politics in Indonesia.* Ithaca, NY: Cornell University Press, 1972.

Laffan, Michael Francis. *Islamic Nationhood and Colonial Indonesia: The Umma below the Winds.* New York: Routledge Curzon, 2002.

Latif, Yudi. "The Rupture of Young Muslim Intelligentsia in the Modernization of Indonesia." *Studia Islamika* 12 (2005): 373–420.

Riddell, Peter G. *Islam and the Malay-Indonesian World: Transmission and Responses.* Honolulu: University of Hawaii Press, 2001.

Robinson, Kathryn. *Gender, Islam and Democracy in Indonesia (ASAA Women in Asia Series).* London: Routledge, 2008.

Woodward, Mark R., ed. *Toward a New Paradigm: Recent Developments in Indonesian Islamic Thought.* Tempe: Arizona State University Program for Southeast Asian Studies, 1996.

Iran

Abrahamian, Ervand. *Iran between Two Revolutions.* Princeton, NY: Princeton University Press, 1982.

———. *The Iranian Mojahedin.* New Haven, CT: Yale University Press, 1989.

———. *Khomeinism: Essays on the Islamic Republic.* Berkeley: University of California Press, 1993.

Cole, Juan R. I. *Sacred Space and Holy War: The Politics, Culture and History of Shi'ite Islam.* London: I. B. Tauris, 2002.

Cole, Juan R. I., and Nikki R. Keddie, eds. *Shiism and Social Protest.* New Haven, CT: Yale University Press, 1986.

Dabashi, Hamid. *Theology of Discontent: The Ideological Foundations of the Islamic Revolution in Iran.* New York: New York University Press, 1993.

Ehteshami, Anoushiravan. *After Khomeini: The Iranian Second Republic.* New York: Routledge, 1995.

Esposito, John L., ed. *The Iranian Revolution: Its Global Impact.* Oxford: Oxford University Press, 2001.

Farsoun, Samih K. *Iran: Political Culture in the Islamic Republic.* London: Routledge, 1992.

Ghamari-Tabrizi, Behrooz. *Islam and Dissent in Post-Revolutionary Iran: The Religious Politics of Abdolkarim Soroush.* London: I. B. Tauris, 2001.

Haseeb, Khair El-Din, ed. *Arab-Iranian Relations.* New York: St. Martin's Press, 1998.

Hashim, Ahmed S. *The Crisis of the Iranian State.* Oxford: Oxford University Press, 1995.

Hooglund, Eric, ed. *Twenty Years of Islamic Revolution: Political and Social Transition in Iran since 1979.* Syracuse, NY: Syracuse University Press, 2002.

Keddie, Nikki, ed. *Roots of Revolution: An Interpretive History of Modern Iran.* New Haven, CT: Yale University Press, 1981.

———. *Religion and Politics in Iran.* New Haven, CT: Yale University Press, 1983.

Lorentz, John H. *Historical Dictionary of Iran.* Lanham, MD: Scarecrow Press, 2007.

Momen, Moojan. *An Introduction to Shia Islam.* New Haven, CT: Yale University Press, 1985.

Mottahedeh, Roy P. *The Mantle of the Prophet: Religion and Politics in Iran.* New York: Simon and Schuster, 1985.

Nabavi, Negin. *Intellectuals and the State in Iran: Politics, Discourse and the Dilemma of Authenticity.* Gainesville: University Press of Florida, 2003.

Sanasarian, Eliz. *Religious Minorities in Iran.* Cambridge: Cambridge University Press, 2000.

Stewart, Devin J. *Islamic Legal Orthodoxy: Twelver Shiite Responses to the Sunni Legal System.* Salt Lake City: University of Utah Press, 1998.

Van den Bos, Matthijs. *Mystic Regimes: Sufism and the State in Iran, from the Late Qajar Era to the Islamic Republic.* Leiden: E. J. Brill, 2002.

Wright, Robin. *In the Name of God: The Khomeini Regime.* New York: Simon and Schuster, 1989.

Malaysia

Abdul Rahman, Tunku. *Contemporary Issues on Malaysian Religions.* Selangor: Pelanduk, 1984.

Ackerman, Susan E., and Raymond Lee. *Heaven in Transition: Non-Muslim Religious Innovation and Ethnic Identity in Malaysia.* Honolulu: University of Hawaii Press, 1988.

Gin, Ooi Keat. *Historical Dictionary of Malaysia.* Lanham, MD: Scarecrow Press, 2009.

Hefner, Robert W., and Patricia Horvatich, eds. *Islam in an Era of Nation-States: Politics and Religious Renewal in Muslim Southeast Asia.* Honolulu: University of Hawaii Press, 1997.

Hooker, Virginia Matheson, and Norani Othman. *Malaysia: Islam, Society and Politics.* Pasir Panjang: Institute of Southeast Asia Studies, 2003.

Ibrahim, Ahmad. "Islamic Law in Malaysia." *Journal of Malaysian and Comparative Law* (1981).

———. "The Position of Islam in the Constitution of Malaysia." In *Readings on Islam in Southeast Asia*, edited by Ahmad Ibrahim, Sharon Siddique, and Yasmin Hussain. Pasir Panjang: Institute of Southeast Studies, 1985.

Liow, Joseph Chinyong. *Piety and Politics: The Shifting Contours of Islamism in Contemporary Malaysia.* New York: Oxford University Press, 2008.

McAmis, Robert Day. *Malay Muslims: The History and Challenge of Resurgent Islam in Southeast Asia.* Grand Rapids, MI: William B. Eerdmans, 2002.

Meddeb, Abdelwahab. *The Malady of Islam.* New York: Basic Books, 2003.

Metzger, Laurent. *Stratégie islamique en Malaisie (1975–1995).* Paris: L'Harmattan, 1996.

Millard, Mike. *Jihad in Paradise: Islam and Politics in Southeast Asia.* Armonk, NY: M. E. Sharpe, 2004.

Mutalib, Hussin. *Islam in Malaysia: From Revivalism to Islamic State?* Kent Ridge: Singapore University Press, 1993.

Rabasa, Angel M. *Political Islam in Southeast Asia: Moderates, Radicals and Terrorists.* New York: Oxford University Press, 2003.

Schottman, Sven Alexander. "Muslim Democrats: The Changing Face of Political Islam in Malaysia." In *Islam and the Question of Reform: Critical Voices from Muslim Communities*, edited by Kylie Baxter and Rebecca Barlow. Victoria: Melbourne University Publishing, 2008.

Pakistan

Ahmed, Akbar S. *Jinnah, Pakistan and Islamic Identity: The Search for Saladin.* London: Routledge, 1997.

Ahmed, Ishtiaq. *The Concept of an Islamic State in Pakistan.* Lahore: Vanguard, 1991.

Barki, Shahid Jared. *Historical Dictionary of Pakistan.* Lanham, MD: Scarecrow Press, 2006.

Cohen, Stephen Philip. *The Idea of Pakistan.* Washington, DC: Brookings Institution, 2004.

Decasa, George C. *The Qur'anic Concept of Umma and Its Function in Philippine Muslim Society.* Rome: Gregorian University Press, 1999.

Hiro, Dilip. *Between Marx and Muhammad: The Changing Face of Central Asia.* London: HarperCollins, 1995.

Mullick, Fatima, and Mehrunnisa Yusuf. *Pakistan: Identity, Ideology, and Beyond.* London: Quilliam, 2009.

Nasr, Seyyed Vali Reza. *The Vanguard of the Islamic Revolution: The Jamaat-I-Islami of Pakistan.* Berkeley: University of California Press, 1994.

Pirzada, Sayyid A. S. *The Politics of the Jamiat Ulema-I-Islam Pakistan, 1971–1977.* Karachi: Oxford University Press, 2000.

Suhail, Mahmood. *Islamic Fundamentalism in Pakistan, Egypt and Iran.* Lahore: Vanguard, 1995.

White, Joshua T. *Pakistan's Islamist Frontier: Islamic Politics and U.S. Policy in Pakistan's North-West Frontier Province.* Arlington, VA: Center on Faith and International Affairs, 2008.

Philippines

Abuza, Z. Balik. *Terrorism: The Return of the Abu Sayyaf.* Carlisle, PA: Strategic Studies Institute, 2005.

Banlaoi, Rommel C. "'Radical Muslim Terrorism' in the Philippines." In *A Handbook of Terrorism and Insurgency in Southeast Asia*, edited by Andrew Tian Huat Tan. Cheltenham: Edward Elgar, 2007.

Guillermo, Artemco. *Historical Dictionary of the Philippines.* Lanham, MD: Scarecrow Press, 2005.

Haqqani, Husain. "The Ideologies of South Asian Jihadi Groups." *Current Trends in Islamist Ideology* 1 (2005): 12–21.

Majul, Cesar Adib. *Muslims in the Philippines.* Quezon City: University of the Philippines Press, 1999.

Robinson, Francis. *Islam in South Asia.* Cambridge: Cambridge University Press, 2003.

Turkey

Ahmad, Feroz. *Turkey: The Quest for Identity.* Oxford: OneWorld, 2003.

Davison, Andrew. *Secularism and Revivalism in Turkey: A Hermeneutic Reconsideration.* New Haven, CT: Yale University Press, 1998.

Gunter, Michael M. *The Kurds and the Future of Turkey.* London: Palgrave Macmillan, 1997.

Heper, Metin, and Nur Bilge Criss. *Historical Dictionary of Turkey.* Lanham, MD: Scarecrow, 2009.

Houston, Christopher. *Islam, Kurds and the Turkish Nation State.* Oxford: Berg, 2001.

Kayal, Hasan. *Arabs and Young Turks: Ottomanism, Arabism, and Islamism in the Ottoman Empire, 1908–1918.* Berkeley: University of California Press, 1997.

Kuran, Timur. *Islam and Mammon: The Economic Predicaments of Islamism.* Princeton, NJ: Princeton University Press, 2004.

Mardin, Serif. *Religion, Society and Modernity in Turkey.* Syracuse, NY: Syracuse University Press, 2002.

Noyon, Jennifer. *Islam, Politics, and Pluralism: Turkey, Jordan, Tunisia, and Algeria.* Washington, DC: Brookings Institution Press, 2002.

White, Jenny B. *Islamist Mobilization in Turkey: A Study in Vernacular Politics.* Seattle: University of Washington Press, 2003.

Yavuz, M. Hakan. *Islamic Political Identity in Turkey.* Oxford: Oxford University Press, 2003.

EUROPE

Allievi, Stefano, et al., eds. *Muslim Networks and Transnational Communities in and across Europe.* Leiden: E. J. Brill, 2003.

Cardini, Franco. *Europe and Islam.* Malden, MA: Blackwell, 2001.

Laidi, Ali, and Ahmed Salal. *Le Jihad en Europe: Les filières du terrorisme islamiste.* Paris: Seuil, 2002.

Maréchal, Brigette, et al., eds. *Muslims in the Enlarged Europe.* Leiden: E. J. Brill, 2003.

Mazower, Mark. *The Balkans: A Short History.* New York: Modern Library, 2002.

Mohammad Shahid Raza. *Islam in Britain.* Leicester: Volcano Press, 1991.

Moussalli, Ahmad S. "Discourses on Human Rights and Pluralistic Democracy." In *Islam in a Changing World: Europe and the Middle East*, edited by A. Herichow and J. B. Simonson. Surrey: Curzon Press, 1997.

Norris, Harry T. *Islam in the Balkans: Religion and Society between Europe and the Arab World.* Columbia: University of South Carolina Press, 1994.

Pedersen, Lars. *Newer Islamic Movements in Western Europe.* Aldershot: Ashgate, 1999.

Poole, Elizabeth. *Reporting Islam: Media Representations of British Muslims.* London: I. B. Tauris, 2002.

Ramadan, Tariq. *Musulmans d'Occident face à l'avenir.* Paris: Sindbad, 2003.

———. *Western Muslims and the Future of Islam.* Oxford: Oxford University Press, 2003.

Rath, Jan, ed. *Western Europe and Its Islam.* Leiden: E. J. Brill, 2001.

Rodinson, Maxime. *Europe and the Mystique of Islam.* London: I. B. Tauris, 2002.

Al-Sayyad, Nezar, and Manuel Castells, eds. *Muslim Europe or Euro-Islam: Politics, Culture, and Citizenship in the Age of Globalization.* Lanham, MD: Lexington Books, 2002.

Shatzmiller, Maya, ed. *Islam and Bosnia: Conflict Resolution and Foreign Policy in Multi-Ethnic States.* Montreal: McGill-Queen's University Press, 2002.

Vertovec, Steven, and Ceri Peach, eds. *Islam in Europe: The Politics of Religion and Community.* London: Palgrave Macmillan, 1997.

NORTH AMERICA

Avella, Valerie N. Y. "The Domestic War on Terrorism: Fighting the Roots of Jihadist Extremism in the United States." *Defense Intelligence Journal* 15 (2006): 13–24.

Curtis, Edward E., IV. *Islam in Black America: Identity, Liberation, and Difference in African-American Islamic Thought.* Albany: State University of New York Press, 2002.

Feldman, Noah. *After Jihad: America and the Struggle for Islamic Democracy.* New York: Farrar, Straus and Giroux, 2003.

Haddad, Yvonne Yazbeck, ed. *The Muslims of America.* New York: Oxford University Press, 1993.

Khan, M. A. Muqtedar. *American Muslims: Bridging Faith and Freedom.* Beltsville, MD: Amana, 2002.

Lawrence, Bruce B. *New Faiths, Old Fears: Muslims and Other Asian Immigrants in American Religious Life.* New York: Columbia University Press, 2002.

Lebor, Adam. *A Heart Turned East: Among the Muslims of Europe and America.* New York: St. Martin's Press, 2001.

Mamdani, Mahmood. *Good Muslim, Bad Muslim: America, the Cold War, and the Roots of Terror.* New York: Pantheon, 2004.

Nyang, Sulayman S. *Islam in the United States of America.* Chicago: ABC, 1999.

Simon, Jeffery D. *The Terrorist Trap: America's Experience with Terrorism.* Bloomington: Indiana University Press, 1994.

Smith, Jane I. *Islam in America.* New York: Columbia University Press, 1999.

Smith, Jane I., and Yvonne Y. Haddad, eds. *Muslim Communities in North America.* Albany: State University of New York Press, 1994.

Telhami, Shibley. *The Stakes: America and the Middle East.* Boulder, CO: Westview Press, 2002.

RUSSIA

Abu Khalil, As'ad. "Ideology and Practice of Hizballah in Lebanon: Islamization of Leninist Organizational Principles." *Middle Eastern Studies* 27 (1991): 390–403.

Akiner, S. *Islamic Peoples of the Soviet Union.* London: Kegan Paul, 1983.

Bennigsen, A. A., and C. Lemercier-Quelquejay. *Islam in the Soviet Union.* London: Pall Mall Press, 1967.

Broxup-Bennigsen, M., ed. *The North Caucasus Barrier: The Russian Advance towards the Muslim World.* London: Hurst, 1992.

Bukharaev, Ravil. *Islam in Russia: The Four Seasons.* New York: St. Martin's Press, 2000.

Dudoignon, Stéphane A., and Komatso Hisao, eds. *Islam in Politics in Russia and Central Asia.* London: Kegan Paul, 2002.

Eickelman, Dale F. *Russia's Muslim Frontiers. New Directions in Cross-cultural Analysis.* Bloomington: Indiana University Press, 1993.

Fowkes, B., ed. *Russia and Chechnya: The Permanent Crisis.* London: Macmillan, 1998.

Gammer, M. *Muslim Resistance to the Tsar: Shamil and the Conquest of Chechnya and Daghestan.* London: Frank Cass, 1994.

Pilkington, Hilary, and Galina M. Yemelianova, eds. *Islam in Post-Soviet Russia.* New York: Routledge-Curzon, 2002.

Russell, John. *Chechnya-Russia's "War on Terror."* London: Taylor and Francis, 2007.

Yemelianova, Galina M. *Russia and Islam: A Historical Survey.* New York: Palgrave, 2002.

ISLAMIST MOVEMENTS AND LEADERS

Movements

Abdelmajid, Wahid. *Al-Ikhwân al-Muslimûn Bayna at-Târîkh wal Mustaqbal* (Muslim Brotherhood between History and Future). Cairo: Wakâlat Al-Ahrâm, 2010.

Al-Ali, Najde. *Secularism, Gender, and the State in the Middle East: The Egyptian Women's Movement.* Cambridge: Cambridge University Press, 2000.

Arrabiu, Turki Ali. *Al-Harakât al-Islâmiyya min Manzûr al-Khitâb al-'Arabî al-Mu'assir* (The Islamic Movements in the Contemporary Arabic Discourse). Casablanca: Al-Markaz ath-Thaqâfî al-'Arabî, 2006.

Al-Awadi, Hisham. *As-Sirâ' alâ ash-Shar'iyya: Al-Ikhwân al-Muslimûn wa Mubârak* (The Struggle for Legitimacy between the Muslim Brotherhood and Mubarak: 1982–2007). Beirut: Markaz Dirâsât al-Wihda, 2009.

Batatu, Hanna. *The Old Social Classes and the Revolutionary Movement of Iraq.* Princeton, NJ: Princeton University Press, 1979.

Boulby, Marion, and John Obert Voll. "The Muslim Brotherhood and the Kings of Jordan, 1945–1993." *South Florida-Rochester-Saint Louis Studies on Religion and the Social Order* 18 (1999).

Guidère, Mathieu, and Nicole Morgan. *Le Manuel de recrutement d'Al-Qaïda.* Paris: Le Seuil, 2007.

Ibrahim, Saad Eddin. "Anatomy of Egypt's Militant Islamic Groups: Methodological Note and Preliminary Findings." *International Journal of Middle East Studies* 12 (1980): 423–53.

———. "Egypt's Islamic Militants." *MERIP Reports* (1982): 5–14.

———. "An Islamic Alternative in Egypt: The Muslim Brotherhood and Sadat." *Arab Studies Quarterly* 4 (1982): 75–93.

Kepel, Gilles. *Jihad, expansion et déclin de l'Islamisme.* Paris: Gallimard, 2000.

Khayyun, Rashid, and Muhammadand Assaf. *Lâhût as-Siyâsa: al-Ahzâb wal Harakât ad-Dîniyya fil Iraq* (Politics Religion: Religious Parties and Movements in Iraq). Baghdad: Dirasât Iraqiyya, 2009.

Lia, Brynjar. *The Society of the Muslim Brothers in Egypt: The Rise of an Islamic Mass Movement, 1928–1942.* Reading: Ithaca Press, 1998.

Al-Mahbub, Abdulsalem. *Al-Harakât al-Islâmiyya as-Sûdâniyya* (Sudanese Islamic Movements). Cairo: Dar Mudârik, 2010.

Al-Mashhadâni, Saadun. *Al-Islâm as-Siyâsî: Min al-Khawârij ilâ al-Mintaqa al-Khadrâ'* (Political Islam: From the Kharijis Movement to the Green Zone). Amman: Dar Ward, 2009.

Misbar Center. *Al-Ikhwân al-Muslimûn wal Salafiyyûn fîl Khaleej* (Muslim Brotherhood and Salafists in the Gulf). Dubai: Misbar Center, 2010.

Mitchell, Richard P. *The Society of the Muslim Brothers.* Oxford: Oxford University Press, 1969.

Muhafaza, Ali. *Harakât al-Islâh wa at-Tajdîd fîl Watan al-'Arabî* (Reform and Renovation Movements in the Arab World). Beirut: Al-Mu'assa al-'Arabiyya, 2011.

Rizk, Yunan Labid. *Al-Ahzâb al-Misriyya 'abra Mi'at 'Amm* (Egyptian Parties through One Century). Cairo: Al-Hay'a al-Misriyya, 2006.

Rougier, Bernard, dir. *Qu'est ce que le salafisme?* Paris: PUF, 2008.

Rumman, Mohammad, and Hassan Abu Hanieh. *The Jihadi Salafist Movement in Jordan after Zarqawi: Identity, Leadership Crisis and Obscured Vision.* Edited by Friedrich Ebert Stiftung. Amman: Economic Printing Press, 2009.

Ternissien, Xavier. *Les frères musulmans.* Paris: Fayard, 2005.

Triaud, Jean-Louis. *La légende noire de la Sanûsiyya: Une confrérie musulmane saharienne sous le regard français.* Paris: HSM, 1995.

Warghi, Jalal. *Al-Haraka al-Islâmiyya at-Turkiyya: Ma'âlim at-Tajriba wa Hudûd al-Minwâl fîl 'Âlam al-'Arabi* (The Islamic Movement in Turkey: The Experience and Its Limits for the Arab World). Beirut: Ad-Dar al-'Arabiyya, 2011.

Leaders

Gardet, Louis. *Les hommes de l'islam: Approche des mentalités.* Paris: Complexe, 1999.

Al-Habbab, Mustafa. *Al-Islâmiyyûn fîl 'Âmm 1431H* (Who Are the Islamists in the Year 2010). Beirut: Markaz Sina'at al-Fikr, 2011.

Kane, Ousmane, and Jean-Louise Triaud, dir. *Islam et islamismes contemporains au sud du Sahara.* Paris: Karthala, 1998.

Kepel, Gilles, and Jean-Pierre Milelli. *Al-Qaïda dans le texte, Ecrits d'Oussama ben Laden, Abdallah Azzam, Ayman al-Zawahiri et Abou Moussab al-Zarqawi.* Paris: PUF, 2005.

Merad, Ali. *Ibn Badis Commentateur du Coran.* Paris: Paul Geuthner, 1971.

Nafii, Bashir Mussa. *Al-Islâmiyyûn* (Islamists). Doha: Al Jazeera Studies Center, 2010.

Ramadan, Tariq. *Aux sources du renouveau musulman: D'al-Afghani à Hassan al-Banna, un siècle de réformisme islamique.* Paris: Bayard/Centurion, 1998.

Roy, Olivier. *Généalogie de l'islamisme.* Paris: Hachette, 1995.

Sayah, Jamil. *Philosophie politique de l'islam: L'idée de l'Etat d'Ibn Khaldoun à Aujourd'hui.* Paris: L'Atelier de l'Archer, 2000.

Shepard, William. *Sayyid Qutb and Islamic Activism.* Leiden: E. J. Brill, 1996.

Wendell, Charles, trans. *Five Tracts of Hasan al-Banna, 1906–1949.* Berkeley: University of California Press, 1978.

GENERAL REFERENCE WORKS

Bibliographies and Dictionaries

Anderson, Sean, and Stephen Sloan. *Historical Dictionary of Terrorism.* Lanham, MD: Scarecrow Press, 2009.

Choueiri, Youssef M. *Islamic Fundamentalism.* Boston: Twayne, 1990.

Combs, Cindy C., and Martin W. Slann. *Encyclopaedia of Terrorism* (Facts on File Library of World History). New York: Facts on File, 2002.

Crenshaw, Martha, and John Pimlott, eds. *Encyclopaedia of World Terrorism.* Armonk, NY: M. E. Sharpe, 1997.

East, R., and T. Joseph. *Political Parties of Africa and the Middle East: A Reference Guide.* Harlow: Longman, 1993.

Esposito, John L. *The Oxford Encyclopaedia of the Modern Islamic World.* New York: Oxford University Press, 1991.

Haddad, Yvonne Y., and John L. Esposito. *The Islamic Revival since 1988: A Critical Survey and Bibliography.* Westport, CT: Greenwood Press, 1998.

Korbani, A. G. *The Political Dictionary of Modern Middle East.* Lanham, MD: University Press of America, 1995.

Lakos, Amos. *Terrorism, 1980–1990: A Bibliography.* Boulder, CO: Westview Press, 1991.

Lentz, Harris M., III. *Assassinations and Executions: An Encyclopaedia of Political Violence, 1865–1986.* Jefferson, NC: McFarland, 1988.

Micklous, Edward F. *The Literature of Terrorism: A Selectively Annotated Bibliography.* Westport, CT: Greenwood Press, 1980.

Momen, Moojan. *An Introduction to Shi'i Islam.* New Haven, CT: Yale University Press, 1985.

Moussalli, Ahmad S. *Historical Dictionary of Islamic Fundamentalist Movements in the Arab World, Iran and Turkey.* Lanham, MD: Scarecrow Press, 1999.

Mullins, Wayman C. *A Sourcebook on Domestic and International Terrorism: An Analysis of Issues, Organizations, Tactics, and Responses.* Springfield, IL: Charles C. Thomas, 1997.

Nielson, Niels C. *Fundamentalism, Mythos, and World Religions.* Albany: State University of New York Press, 1993.

Prunckun, Henry W. *Shadow of Death: An Analytic Bibliography on Political Violence, Terrorism, and Low-Intensity Conflict.* Lanham, MD: Scarecrow Press, 1995.

Schmid, Alex P., and Albert J. Jongman. *Political Terrorism: A New Guide to Actors, Authors, Concepts, Data Bases, Theories, and Literature.* Edison, NJ: Transaction, 2008.

Sfeir, Antoine. *Dictionnaire mondial de l'islamisme.* Paris: Plon, 2002.

———. *Dictionnaire géopolitique de l'islamisme*. Paris: Bayard, 2009.

Sourdel, Dominique and Janine. *Dictionnaire historique de l'Islam*. Paris: PUF, 1996.

Tachau, Frank, ed. *Political Parties of the Middle East and North Africa*. Westport, CT: Greenwood Press, 1994.

Directories and Yearbooks

Abraham, Antoine J., and George Haddad. *The Warriors of God and Jihad and the Fundamentalists of Islam*. Bristol, IN: Wyndham Hall Press, 1990.

Annual Editions. *Violence and Terrorism*. Boston: McGraw-Hill Higher Education, 2011.

Appleby, R. Scott. *Spokesmen for the Despised*: *Fundamentalist Leaders of the Middle East*. Chicago: University of Chicago Press, 1996.

Hunter, Thomas B. *The A to Z of International Terrorist and Counterterrorist Organizations*. Lanham, MD: Scarecrow Press, 2000.

Khuri, Fuad. *Imams and Emirs: State, Religion and Sects in Islam*. London: Saqi Books, 1990.

Chronologies and Databases

Alexander, Yohad, ed. *Terrorism: An International Resource File, 1988*. Ann Arbor, MI: University Microforms, 1989.

Gordan, Avishag. "The Spread of Terrorism Publications: A Database Analysis." *Terrorism and Political Violence* 10 (1998): 190–93.

Hewitt, Christopher. *Political Violence and Terrorism in Modern America: A Chronology*. Westport, CT: Praeger, 2005.

ICT-Herzliya. *International Institute for Counter-Terrorism* (ICT) research publications, chronologies, and databases. http://www.ict.org.il (accessed 11 September 2011).

Mickolus, Edward F., and Susan L. Simmons. *Terrorism, 1996–2001: A Chronology*. Westport, CT: Greenwood Press, 2002.

———. *Terrorism, 2002–2004: A Chronology*. Westport, CT: Greenwood Press, 2005.

National Consortium for the Study of Terrorism and Responses to Terrorism (START). *Global Terrorism Database* (GTD). http://www.start.umd.edu/data/gtd (accessed 11 September 2011).

Rummel, Rudolph J. *Statistics of Democide: Genocide and Mass Murder since 1900*. Charlottesville: Center for National Security Law; School of Law, University of Virginia, 1997.

South Asia Terrorism Portal. *Weekly Assessment and Briefings*. http://www.satp.org (accessed 11 September 2011).

TWEED Project. *Terrorism in Western Europe: Events Data* (TWEED). http://www.uib.no/People/sspje/tweed.htm (accessed 11 September 2011).

U.S. National Counterterrorism Center. *Worldwide Incidents Tracking System*. http://wits.nctc.gov/Main.do (accessed 11 September 2011).

PHILOSOPHICAL AND THEORETICAL BOOKS

Abed Al-Jabri, Mohammed. *Arab-Islamic Philosophy: A Contemporary Critique.* Austin: University of Texas Press, 1999.

Abou Zaid, Nasr. *Critique du discours religieux.* Paris: Actes Sud, 1999.

Abu-Nimer, Mohammad. *Nonviolence and Peace Building in Islam.* Gainesville: University Press of Florida, 2003.

Abu-Rabi', Ibrahim M. *Intellectual Origins of Islamic Resurgence in the Modern Arab World.* Albany: State University of New York Press, 1996.

Ajami, Fouad. *The Arab Predicament: Arab Political Thought and Practice since 1967.* Cambridge: Cambridge University Press, 1992.

Arojomand, Said Amir. *The Shadow of God and the Hidden Imam.* Chicago: University of Chicago Press, 1988.

Al-Ashmawy, Muhammad Saïd. *L'islamisme contre l'islam.* Paris: La Découverte, 1991.

Benzine, Richard. *Les nouveaux penseurs de l'Islam.* Paris: Albin Michel, 2004.

Berque, Jacques. *Quel Islam?* Paris: Sindbad-Actes Sud, 2003.

Bonnaud, Christian. *Le Soufisme (al-tasawwuf) et la spiritualité islamique.* Paris: Maisonneuve and Larose, 2002.

Boullata, Issa J. *Trends and Issues in Contemporary Arab Thought.* Albany: State University of New York Press, 1990.

Choueiri, Youssef M. "Theoretical Paradigms of Islamic Movements." *Political Studies* 41 (1993): 108–16.

Corbin Henry. *History of Islamic Philosophy.* New York: Columbia University Press, 2002.

Dozon, Jean-Pierre. *Les nouveaux conquérants de la foi.* Paris: Karthala, 2003.

Eickelman, Dale F., and James Piscatori. *Muslim Politics.* Princeton, NJ: Princeton University Press, 1996.

Esposito, John L., and John O. Voll. *Islam and Democracy.* New York: Oxford University Press, 1997.

Ferjani, Mohammed Chérif. *Islamisme, laïcité et droits de l'Homme.* Paris: L'Harmattan, 1991.

Ferro, Marc. *Le choc de l'Islam.* Paris: Odile Jacob, 2003.

Gardet, Louis. *L'islam, religion et communauté.* Paris: Desclée de Brouwer, 1970.

Geoffroy, Eric. *Initiation au soufisme.* Paris: Fayard, 2003.

Haddad, Yvonne, et al. *The Contemporary Islamic Revival: A Critical Survey and Bibliography.* Westport, CT: Greenwood Press, 1991.

Hardacre, Helen. "The Impact of Fundamentalisms on Women, the Family, and Interpersonal Relations." In *Fundamentalism and Society: Reclaiming the Sciences, the Family and Education,* edited by Martin E. Marty and R. Scott Appleby. Chicago: University of Chicago Press, 1993.

Hiro, Dilip. *Neighbors, Not Friends: Iraq and Iran after the Gulf Wars.* New York: Routledge, 2001.

Jochen Hippler, and Andrea Lueg. *The Next Threat—Western Perceptions of Islam.* London: Pluto Press, 1995.

Karawan, Ibrahim A. *The Islamist Impasse.* Oxford: Oxford University Press, 1998.

Keddie, Nikki R. *An Islamic Response to Imperialism: Political and Religious Writings of Sayyid Jamāl ad-Dīn "al-Afghānī."* Berkeley: University of California Press, 1983.

Kedourie, Elie. *In the Anglo-Arab Labyrinth: The Mac-Mahon/Hussein Correspondence and Its Interpretations, 1914–1921.* Cambridge: Cambridge University Press, 1976.

Kepel, Gilles. *Fitna. Guerre au cœur de l'islam.* Paris: Gallimard, 2004.

Khalsa, Jeffery. *Forecasting Terrorism: Indicators and Proven Analytical Techniques.* Lanham, MD: Scarecrow Press, 2004.

Laqueur, Walter. "The Origins of Guerrilla Doctrine." *Journal of Contemporary History* 10 (1975): 341–82.

Lawrence, Bruce B. *Defenders of God: The Fundamentalist Revolt against the Modern Age.* Columbia: University of South Carolina Press, 1995.

———. *Shattering the Myth: Islam beyond Violence.* Princeton, NJ: Princeton University Press, 1998.

Lory, Pierre. *Alchimie et mystique en terre d'Islam.* Paris: Verdier, 1989.

Martin, C. Augustus. *Understanding Terrorism: Challenges, Perspectives, and Issues.* Thousand Oaks, CA: Sage, 2006.

Merkl, Peter H., and Leonard Weinberg, eds. *The Revival of Right-Wing Extremism in the Nineties.* Portland, OR: Frank Cass, 1997.

Miller, David. "The Use and Abuse of Political Violence." *Political Studies* 32 (1984): 401–19.

Moaddel, Mansoor, and Kamran Talattof. *Contemporary Debates in Islam: An Anthology of Modernist and Fundamentalist Thought.* New York: St. Martin's Press, 2000.

———, eds. *Modernist and Fundamentalist Debates in Islam: A Reader.* New York: Palgrave Macmillan, 2002.

Mottahedeh, Roy. "The Islamic Movement: The Case for Democratic Inclusion." *Contention* 4 (1995): 107–27.

———. "The Clash of Civilizations: An Islamist's Critique." *Harvard Middle Eastern and Islamic Review* 2 (1996): 1–26.

Nasr, Seyyed Vali Reza. *Mawdudi and the Making of Islamic Revivalism.* New York: Oxford University Press, 1996.

———. *The Islamic Leviathan: Islam and the Making of State Power.* Oxford: Oxford University Press, 2001.

Newman, Graeme R., and Michael J. Lynch. "From Feuding to Terrorism: The Ideology of Vengeance." *Contemporary Crises* 11 (1987): 223–42.

O'Sullivan, Noel, ed. *Terrorism, Ideology and Revolution.* Brighton: Wheatsheaf Books, 1986.

Poland, James M. *Understanding Terrorism: Groups, Strategies, and Responses.* Englewood Cliffs, NJ: Prentice Hall, 2004.

Quotb, S., and W. E. Shepard. *Sayyid Qutb and Islamic Activism: A Translation and Critical Analysis of Social Justice in Islam.* Leiden: E. J. Brill, 1996.

Qureshi, Emran, and Michael Sells, eds. *The New Crusades: Constructing the Muslim Enemy.* New York: Columbia University Press, 2003.

Rahnema, Ali. *An Islamic Utopian: A Political Biography of Ali Shari'ati.* London: I. B. Tauris, 1998.

Roberson, B. A. *Shaping the Current Islamic Reformation.* London: Frank Cass, 2003.

Roy, Olivier. *The Failure of Political Islam.* Cambridge, MA: Harvard University Press, 1994.

Shehadeh, Lamia Rustum. *The Idea of Women in Fundamentalist Islam.* Gainesville: University Press of Florida, 2007.

Snowden, Lynne L., and Bradley C. Whitsel, eds. *Terrorism: Research, Readings, and Realities.* Upper Saddle River, NJ: Prentice Hall, 2005.

Sonn, Tamara. *Interpreting Islam: Bandali Jawzi's Islamic Intellectual History.* Oxford: Oxford University Press, 1996.

Sterling, Claire. *The Terror Network: The Secret War of International Terrorism.* New York: Holt, Rinehart and Winston, 1981.

Stern, Jessica. *Terror in the Name of God: Why Religious Militants Kill.* New York: HarperCollins, 2003.

Voll, John. "The Revivalist Heritage." In *The Contemporary Islamic Revival: A Critical Survey and Bibliography.* Westport, CT: Greenwood Press, 1991.

Weinberg, Leonard. *Global Terrorism: A Beginner's Guide.* Oxford: OneWorld, 2008.

Willis, Henry H., Andrew R. Morral, Terrence K. Kelly, and Jamison J. Medby. *Estimating Terrorism Risk.* Santa Monica, CA: RAND, 2005.

CASE STUDIES

Abuljobain, Ahmad. *Radical Islamic Terrorism or Political Islam?* Annadale, VA: Association for Studies and Research, 1993.

Adams, James. *The Financing of Terror.* London: New English Library, 1986.

Ahmed, Akbar S. *Postmodernism and Islam: Predicament and Promise.* New York: Routledge, 1992.

Ahrari, M. E., and J. H. Noyes, eds. *The Persian Gulf after the Cold War.* Westport, CT: Praeger, 1993.

Alexander, Yonan, and Seymour M. Finger, eds. *Terrorism: Interdisciplinary Perspectives.* New York: John Jay Press, 1977.

Alexander, Yonan, and Robert A. Kilmarx, eds. *Political Terrorism and Business: The Threat and Response.* New York: Praeger, 1979.

Attaii, Hashem Abderrazak. *At-Tayyâr al-Islâmî fil Khaleej al-'Arabî: Dirâsa Târîkhiyya* (The Islamic Trend in the Arab Gulf: A Historical Study). Beirut: Muassat al-Intishar al-'Arabî, 2010.

Al-Azm, Sadik. "Islamic Fundamentalism Reconsidered: A Critical Outline of Problems, Ideas and Approaches." *South Asia Bulletin* 13, nos. 1–2, pt. 1 (1993): 93–131; 14, no. 1, pt. 2 (1994): 73–98.

Babès, Leïla. *L'Islam positif: La religion des jeunes musulmans de France.* Paris: De l'Atelier/Ouvrières, 1997.

Barnett, Roger W., and Stephen J. Cimbala. *Asymmetric Warfare: Today's Challenge to U.S. Military Power.* Washington, DC: Brassey's, 2003.

Ben Achour, Yadh. *La deuxième Fâtiha: L'islam et la pensée des droits de l'homme.* Paris: PUF, 2011.

Benkheira, Mohamed Hocine. *L'amour de la loi: Essai sur la normativité dans l'Islam.* Paris: PUF, 1997.

———. *Islam et interdits alimentaires, Juguler l'animalité.* Paris: PUF, 2000.

Bell, J. Bowyer. *The Dynamics of the Armed Struggle.* London: Frank Cass, 1998.

Binder, Leonard. *Islamic Liberalism: A Critique of Development Ideologies.* Chicago: University of Chicago Press, 1988.

Bunker, Robert J., ed. *Networks, Terrorism and Global Insurgency.* London: Routledge, 2006.

Burgat, François. *L'Islamisme au Maghreb.* Paris: Editions Payot, 1995.

———. *L'Islamisme en face.* Paris: La Découverte, 2002.

———. *L'Islamisme à l'heure d'Al-Qaida.* Paris: La Découverte, 2005.

Coulon, Christian. *Les musulmans et le pouvoir en Afrique: Religion et contre-culture.* Paris: Karthala, 1988.

Dassetto, Felice. *La construction de l'Islam Européen: Approche socio-anthropologique.* Paris: L'Harmattan, 1996.

Djalili, Mohammad-Reza. *Iran: L'illusion réformiste.* Paris: Presses de Sciences Po, 2001.

Dovert, Stéphane, and Rémy Madinier, dir. *Les musulmans d'Asie du Sud-Est face au vertige de la radicalisation.* Paris: IRASEC-Les Indes savantes, 2003.

Dozon, Jean-Pierre. *La cause des prophètes: Politique et religion en Afrique contemporaine, suivi de La leçon des Prophètes.* Paris: Le Seuil, 1995.

Feillard, Andrée, and Rémy Madinier. *Islam et armée dans l'Indonésie contemporaine, les pionniers de la tradition.* Paris: L'Harmattan, 1995.

———. *L'Islam en Asie, du Caucase à la Chine.* Paris: La documentation française, 2001.

———. *La fin de l'innocence? L'islam indonésien face à la tentation radicale de 1967 à nos jours.* Paris: IRASEC-les Indes savantes, 2006.

Fourchard, Laurent, dir. *Entreprises religieuses transnationales en Afrique de l'ouest.* Paris: IFRA/Karthala, 2005.

Guidère, Mathieu. *Les "Martyrs" d'Al-Qaïda.* Paris: Temps, 2005.

———. *Al-Qaïda à la conquête du Maghreb: Le terrorisme aux portes de l'Europe.* Paris: Le Rocher, 2007.

———. *Les Nouveaux terroristes.* Paris: Autrement, 2011.

Juergensmeyer, Mark. *Terror in the Mind of God: The Global Rise of Religious Violence.* Berkeley: University of California Press, 2001.

Kaplan, Lawrence, ed. *Fundamentalism in Comparative Perspective.* Amherst: University of Massachusetts Press, 1992.

Khosrokhavar, Farhad. *Les Nouveaux Martyrs d'Allah.* Paris: Flammarion, 2002.

Labari, Brahim. "*Islam, islamisme et le 11 septembre. Le grand imbroglio.*" *Esprit critique* 5, no. 2 (2003).

Lancaster, C. "Democratization in Sub-Saharan Africa." *Survival* 35 (1993): 38–50.

Lawson, Fred. *Oppositional Movements and U.S. Policy toward the Arab Gulf States.* New York: Council on Foreign Relations, 1992.

Moore, Clement Henry. "Political Parties." In *Polity and Society in Contemporary North Africa*, edited by I. William Zartman and William Mark Habeeb, 42–67. Boulder, CO: Westview Press, 1993.

Piscatori, James, ed. *Islamic Fundamentalisms and the Gulf Crisis.* Chicago: American Academy of Arts and Sciences, 1991.

Quinn, Charlotte A., and Frederick Quinn. *Pride, Faith, and Fear: Islam in Sub-Saharan Africa.* Oxford: Oxford University Press, 2003.

Robinson, David, and Jean-Louis Triaud. *La Tijâniyya en Afrique subsaharienne: Une confrérie musulmane à la conquête de l'Afrique.* Paris: Karthala, 2000.

Ruedy, John, ed. *Islamism and Secularism in North Africa.* New York: St. Martin's Press, 1994.

Sfeir, Antoine, dir. *"L'islamisme à l'assaut de l'Asie du Sud-Est."* Les Cahiers de l'Orient 78 (2005).

Shahin, Emad. *Political Ascent: Contemporary Islamic Movements in North Africa.* Boulder, CO: Westview Press, 1997.

Turki, Abdelmajid. *Théologiens et juristes de l'Espagne musulmane.* Paris: Maisonneuve, 1982.

Vinatier, Laurent. *L'Islamisme en Asie centrale: Géopolitique et implantation des réseaux religieux radicaux dans les républiques d'Asie centrale.* Paris: Armand Colin/VUEF, 2002.

Zubaida, Sami. *Islam, the People and the State: Essays on Political Ideas and Movements in the Middle East.* London: I. B. Tauris, 1993.

SOCIOLOGICAL AND PSYCHOLOGICAL STUDIES

Abou El Fadl, Khaled, et al. *The Place of Tolerance in Islam.* Boston: Beacon Press, 2002.

Abu Rabi', Ibrahim. *Intellectual Origins of Islamic Resurgence in the Modern Arab World.* Albany: State University of New York Press, 1996.

Ahmed, Akbar S. *Postmodernism and Islam: Predicament and Promise.* New York: Routledge, 1992.

———. *Islam under Siege: Living Dangerously in a Post-Honour World.* London: Polity Press, 2003.

Anawati, Georges, and Maurice Borremans. *Tendances et courants de l'islam arabe contemporain.* Munich: Kaiser and Grünewald, 1982.

Arkoun, Mohammed. *Essais sur la pensée islamique.* Paris: Maisonneuve, 1973.

———. *Vers une critique de la raison islamique.* Paris: Maisonneuve Larose, 1984.

———. *L'islam, morale et politique.* Paris: Desclée de Brouwer, 1987.

Ayoob, Mohammad. *The Politics of Islamic Reassertion.* New York: St. Martin's Press, 1981.

Ayubi, Nazih. *Political Islam: Religion and Politics in the Arab World.* New York: Routledge, 1991.

———. *Over-Stating the Arab State: Politics and Society in the Middle East*. London: I. B. Tauris, 1995.

Al-Azmeh, Aziz. *Islam and Modernity*. London: Verso, 1997.

Bloom, Mia. *Dying to Kill: The Allure of Suicide Terror*. New York: Columbia University Press, 2005.

Bunt, Gary. *Virtually Islamic: Computer-Mediated Communication and Cyber-Islamic Environments*. Cardiff: University of Wales Press, 2000.

Butterworth, Charles, ed. "Political Islam." *Annals of the American Academy of Political and Social Sciences* 524 (1992).

Crenshaw, Martha. "The Logic of Terrorism: Terrorist Behavior as a Product of Strategic Choice." In *Origins of Terrorism: Psychologies, Ideologies, Theologies, States of Mind*, edited by Walter Reich, 7–24. Cambridge: Cambridge University Press, 1990.

Durrani, K. S. *Impact of Islamic Fundamentalism*. Bangalore: ISPCK, 1993.

Eickelman, Dale F. "Changing Interpretations of Islamic Movements." In *Islam and the Political Economy of Meaning*, edited by William R. Roff, 13–30. London: Croom Helm, 1987.

Etienne, Bruno. *L'Islamisme radical*. Paris: Hachette, 1987.

———. *Islam, les questions qui fâchent*. Paris: Bayard, 2003.

———. *L'islamisme comme idéologie et comme force politique*, *Cités* 14. Paris: PUF, 2003.

Ferjani, Mohamed, and Dominique Cusenier. *Les voies de l'islam*. Paris: Cerf, 1997.

Finianos, Ghassan. *Islamistes, apologistes et libres penseurs*. Bordeaux: Presses Universitaires de Bordeaux, 2002.

Fluehr-Lobban, Carolyn. *Islamic Societies in Practice*. Gainesville: University Press of Florida, 2004.

Fuller, Graham, and Iran Lesser. *A Sense of Siege: The Geopolitics of Islam and the West*. Boulder, CO: Westview Press, 1995.

Haddad, Yvonne Yazbeck, Byron Haynes, and Ellison Finfly, eds. *The Islamic Impact*. Syracuse, NY: Syracuse University Press, 1984.

Haddad, Yvonne Yazbeck, and Jane I. Smith, eds. *Muslim Minorities in the West: Visible and Invisible*. Lanham, MD: AltaMira Press, 2002.

Haeri, Shaykh Fadhlalla. *Living Islam East and West*. Longmead: Element Books, 1989.

Hewitt, Christopher. "Terrorism and Public Opinion: A Five Country Comparison." *Terrorism and Political Violence* 2 (1990): 145–70.

Hunter, Shireen T., ed. *Islam, Europe's Second Religion: The New Social, Cultural and Political Landscape*. Westport, CT: Praeger, 2002.

Huntington, Samuel P. *The Clash of Civilizations and the Remaking of World Order*. New York: Simon and Schuster, 1996.

Karim, Karim. *Islamic Peril: Media and Global Violence*. New York: Black Rose Books, 2000.

Karpat, Kemal, ed. *Political and Social Thought in the Contemporary Middle East*. New York: Praeger, 1982.

Khouri-Dagher, Nadia. *L'islam moderne: Des musulmans contre l'intégrisme*. Paris: Hugo and Cie, 2008.

Laroui, Fouad. *De l'islamisme: Une réfutation personnelle du totalitarisme religieux*. Paris: Robert Laffont, 2008.

Lawrence, Bruce. *Defenders of God: The Fundamentalist Revolt against the Modern Age*. San Francisco: Harper and Row, 1989.

Munson, Henry. *Islam and Revolution in the Middle East*. New Haven, CT: Yale University Press, 1988.

Post, Jerrold, ed. *Leaders and Their Followers in a Dangerous World*. Ithaca, NY: Cornell University Press, 2004.

Rejwan, Nissim, ed. *The Many Faces of Islam: Perspectives on a Resurgent Civilization*. Gainesville: University Press of Florida, 2000.

Richards, Alan, and John Waterbury. *A Political Economy of the Middle East*. Boulder, CO: Westview Press, 1990.

Sahliyeh, Emile, ed. *Religious Resurgence and Politics in the Contemporary World*. Albany: State University of New York Press, 1990.

Sayid, Bobby Z. *A Fundamental Fear: Eurocentrism and the Emergence of Islamism*. London: Zed Books, 1997.

Shahin, Emad Eldin. "Secularism and Nationalism: The Political Discourse of 'Abd al-Salam Yassin." In *Islam and Secularism in North Africa*, edited by J. Ruedy. Basingstoke: Macmillan, 1994.

Simons, Thomas W., Jr. *Islam in a Globalizing World*. Stanford, CA: Stanford University Press, 2003.

Turner, Bryan S., and Akbar Ahmed, eds. *Islam: Critical Concepts in Sociology*. New York: Routledge, 2003.

Viorst, Milton. *In the Shadow of the Prophet: The Struggle for the Soul of Islam*. New York: Anchor Books, 1998.

Waardenburg, Jacques. *Muslims and Others: Relations in Context*. Berlin: Walter de Gruyter, 2003.

Weinberg, Leonard, ed. *Political Parties and Terrorist Groups*. London: Frank Cass, 1992.

Zaman, Muhammad Qasim. *The Ulama in Contemporary Islam: Custodians of Change*. Princeton, NJ: Princeton University Press, 2002.

Ziadeh, Nicol A. *Sanusiyah: A Study of a Revivalist Movement in Islam*. Leiden: E. J. Brill, 1958.

ANTHROPOLOGICAL AND HISTORICAL STUDIES

Ajami, Fouad. *Dream Palace of the Arabs: A Generation's Odyssey*. New York: Vintage, 1999.

Armstrong, Karen. *Islam: A Short History*. New York: Random House, 2002.

Al-Azmeh, Aziz. *Arabic Thought and Islamic Societies*. London, I. B. Tauris, 1986.

Bamyeh, Mohammed. *The Social Origins of Islam*. Minneapolis: University of Minnesota Press, 1999.

Bloom, Jonathan, and Sheila Blair. *Islam: A Thousand Years of Faith and Power.* New York, TV Books, 2000.

Brockelman, Carl. *A History of the Islamic Peoples.* London: Routledge and Kegan Paul, 1964.

Butterworth, Charles E., and I. William Zartman, eds. *Between the State and Islam.* Cambridge: Cambridge University Press, 2001.

Cragg, Kenneth, and R. Marston Speight, ed. *Islam from Within: Anthology of a Religion.* Belmont, CA: Wadsworth, 1980.

Davidson, Lawrence. *Islamic Fundamentalism.* Westport, CT: Greenwood Press, 1998.

Davis, Joyce M. *Between Jihad and Salaam: Profiles in Islam.* New York: Palgrave Macmillan, 1997.

Dekmejian, R. Hrair. *Islam in Revolution: Fundamentalism in the Arab World.* Syracuse, NY: Syracuse University Press, 1995.

Dessouki, Ali E. Hillal, ed. *Islamic Resurgence in the Arab World.* New York: Praeger, 1982.

Dilip, Hiro. *Islamic Fundamentalism.* London: Paladin Grafton Books, 1989.

Esposito, John L., ed. *The Oxford History of Islam.* New York: Oxford University Press, 2001.

Esposito, John L., and John O. Voll. *Makers of Contemporary Islam.* New York: Oxford University Press, 2001.

Fuller, Graham E. *Islamic Fundamentalism in the Northern Tier Countries: An Integrative View.* Santa Monica, CA: RAND, 1991.

Graham, Mark. *How Islam Created the Modern World.* Beltsville, MD: Amana, 2006.

Herichow, A., and J. B. Simonson, eds. *Islam in a Changing World: Europe and the Middle East.* Richmond: Curzon Press, 1997.

Hourani, Albert. *History of the Arab Peoples.* Cambridge, MA: Harvard University Press, 1990.

Humphreys, R. Stephen. *Islamic History: A Framework for Inquiry.* Princeton, NJ: Princeton University Press, 1991.

Juan, Cole. *Sacred Space and Holy War: The Politics, Culture, and History of Shi-ite Islam.* New York: I. B. Tauris, 2002.

Landau, Jacob M. *The Politics of Pan-Islam: Ideology and Organization.* Oxford: Clarendon Press, 1992.

Lawrence, Bruce B. *Religious Fundamentalism.* Durham, NC: Duke University Press, 1993.

———. *Shattering the Myth: Islam beyond Violence.* Princeton, NJ: Princeton University Press, 1998.

Lewis, Bernard. *Islam in History: Ideas, People, and Events in the Middle East.* Chicago: Open Court, 1993.

———. *Islam and the West.* New York: Oxford University Press, 1994.

———. *The Muslim Discovery of Europe.* London: Norton, 2001.

Lindholm, Charles. *The Islamic Middle East: Tradition and Change.* Malden, MA: Blackwell, 2002.

Maudoodi, Syed Abul 'Ala. *Towards Understanding Islam*. Lahore: Islamic Publications, 1967.

Mohaddessin, Mohammad. *Islamic Fundamentalism: The New Global Threat*. Washington, DC: Seven Locks Press, 1993.

Moussalli, Ahmad S., ed. *Islamic Fundamentalism: Myths and Realities*. Reading: Ithaca Press, 1998.

———. *Moderate and Radical Islamic Fundamentalism: The Quest for Modernity, Legitimacy and the Islamic State*. Gainesville: University Press of Florida, 1999.

Nasr, Seyyed Hossein. *Ideals and Realities of Islam*. London: Unwin Hyman, 1988.

Pasha, Nihad Ibrahim. *At-Tanmiya al-Mustâdâma fîl Mujtama' al-Islâmî* (Sustainment Development in the Islamic Society). Beirut: Dar an-Nahâr, 2009.

Peters, Rudolph. *Jihad in Classical and Modern Islam*. Princeton, NJ: Princeton University Press, 1995.

Peterson, J. E. *The Arab Gulf States: Steps toward Political Participation*. New York: Praeger, 1988.

Piscatori, James, ed. *Islamic Fundamentalisms and the Gulf Crisis*. Chicago: American Academy of Arts and Sciences, 1991.

Rahnema, Ali, ed. *Pioneers of Islamic Revival*. London: Zed Books, 1994.

Saikal, Amin. *Islam and the West: Conflict or Cooperation?* New York: Palgrave Macmillan, 2003.

Sidahmed, Abdel Salam, and Anoushiravan Ehteshami, eds. *Islamic Fundamentalism*. Boulder, CO: Westview Press, 1996.

Sivan, Emmanuel. *Radical Islam: Medieval Theology and Modern Politics*. New Haven, CT: Yale University Press, 1990.

Tamimi, Azzam, and John L. Esposito, eds. *Islam and Secularism in the Middle East*. New York: New York University Press, 2000.

Umer Chapra, M. *Islam and the Economic Challenge*. Riyadh: International Islamic Publishing House, 1992.

Voll, John. *Islam: Continuity and Change in the Modern World*. Syracuse, NY: Syracuse University Press, 1994.

LEGISLATION AND POLITICS

Abootalebi, Ali Reza. *Islam and Democracy: State-Society Relations in Developing Countries, 1980–1994 (Comparative Studies of Democratization)*. New York: Garland, 2000.

Abou El Fadl, Khaled, et al. *Islam and the Challenge of Democracy*. Princeton, NJ: Princeton University Press, 2004.

Abu-Rabi', Ibrahim M. *Intellectual Origins of Islamic Resurgence in the Modern Arab World*. Albany: State University of New York Press, 1996.

Abu Rumman, Muhammad. *Al-Islah as-Siyâsi fîl Firk al-Islâmî* (Political Reform in the Islamic Thought). Beirut: Shabaka 'Arabiyya, 2010.

Abu Taha, Anwar, ed. *Ma'zaq ad-Dawla Bayna al-Islâmiyyîn wal Libirâliyyîn* (The State Dilemma between Islamists and Liberals). Cairo: Maktabat Madbulî, 2011.

El-Affendi, Abdelwahhab. *Who Needs an Islamic State?* London: Grey Seal, 1991.

Akbarzadeh, Shahram, and Abdullah Saeed, eds. *Islam and Political Legitimacy.* London: Routledge Curzon, 2003.

Aldeeb, Abu-Sahlieh. "Les mouvements islamistes et les droits de l'Homme." *Revue trimestrielle des droits de l'Homme* 34: 251–290.

Ansari, Ali M. *Iran, Islam, and Democracy: The Politics of Managing Change.* London: Royal Institute of International Affairs, 2003.

Arat, Yesim. *Rethinking Islam and Liberal Democracy.* Albany: State University of New York Press, 2005.

Ayubi, Nazih N. *Political Islam: Religion and Politics in the Arab World.* London: Routledge, 1991.

Babès, Leïla, and Tarek Obrou. *Loi d'Allah, loi des hommes: Liberté, égalité et femmes en Islam.* Paris: Albin Michel, 2002.

El-Bahnassawi, Salem. *Women between Islam and World Legislation.* Kuwait: Dar al-Oalam, 1985.

Barber, Benjamin. *Jihad vs. McWorld: Terrorism's Challenge to Democracy.* New York: Ballantine Books, 1995.

Beinin, Joel, and Joe Stork, eds. *Political Islam: Essays from Middle East Report.* Berkeley: University of California Press, 1997.

Bilqaziz, Abdellilah. *An-Nubuyya wal Siyâsa* (Prophethood and Policy). Beirut: Markaz Dirâsât al-Wihda, 2011.

Bin Sayeed, Khalid. *Western Dominance and Political Islam.* Albany: State University of New York Press, 1995.

Binder, Leonard, ed. *Ethnic Conflict and International Politics in the Middle East.* Gainesville: University Press of Florida, 1999.

Black, Antony. *The History of Islamic Political Thought: From the Prophet to the Present.* Edinburgh: Edinburgh University Press, 2001.

Dumper, Michael. *The Politics of Sacred Space: The Old City of Jerusalem in the Middle East Conflict.* Boulder, CO: Lynne Rienner, 2002.

Eickelman, Dale F., and James Piscatori. *Muslim Politics.* Princeton, NJ: Princeton University Press, 1996.

Esposito, John L. *Islam and Democracy.* New York: Oxford University Press, 1998.

Fuller, Graham. *The Future of Political Islam.* New York: Palgrave Macmillan, 2003.

Gerges, Fawaz A. *America and Political Islam: Clash of Cultures or Clash of Interests?* Cambridge: Cambridge University Press, 1999.

Ghalioun, Burhan. *Islam et politique: La modernité trahie.* Paris: La découverte, 1997.

Gomez-Perez, Muriel, dir. *L'islam politique au sud du Sahara: Identités, discours et enjeux.* Paris: Karthala, 2005.

Guazzone, Laura, ed. *The Islamist Dilemma: The Political Role of Islamist Movements in the Contemporary Arab World.* Reading: Ithaca Press, 1995.

Haddad, Y. Y. *Islamists and the Challenge of Pluralism.* Washington, DC: Georgetown University Press, 1995.

Hafez, Kai, et al., eds. *The Islamic World and the West: An Introduction to Political Cultures and International Relations.* Leiden: E. J. Brill, 2000.

Hamzawi, Amru. *Khiyârât al-'Arab wa Mustaqbaluhum: Ad-Dîmuqratiyya wal Islam as-Siyâsî wal Muqâwama* (The Future and Options of the Arabs: Democracy, Political Islam and Resistance). Beirut: Dar an-Nahâr, 2010.

———. *Bayna ad-Dîn wal Siyâsa: al-Islâmiyyûn fîl Barlamânât al-Arabiyya* (Between Religion and Politics: Islamists in the Arabic Parliaments). Beirut: Shabaka Arabiyya, 2011.

Haynes, Jeff. *Religion in Third World Politics*. Boulder, CO: Lynne Rienner, 1994.

Hibbard, Scott W., and David Little. *Islamic Activism and U.S. Foreign Policy*. Washington, DC: United States Institute of Peace Press, 1997.

Hroub, Khaled. *Hamas: Political Thought and Practice*. Washington, DC: Institute for Palestine Studies, 2000.

Al-Ishsha, Faraj. *Nihâyat al-Usûliyya wa Mustaqbal al-Islâm as-Siyâsî* (The End of Islamic Fundamentalim and the Future of Political Islam). Beirut: Riyâdh ar-Riyyis, 2009.

Jones-Pauly, Chris. *Women under Islam: Gender Justice and the Politics of Islamic Law*. London: I. B. Tauris. 2007.

Kedourie, Elie. *Politics in the Middle East*. Oxford: Oxford University Press, 1992.

———. *Democracy and Arab Political Culture*. London: Frank Cass, 1994.

Kurzman, C. *Liberal Islam: A Source Book*. New York: Oxford University Press, 1998.

Lambton, Ann K. S. *State and Government in Medieval Islam: An Introduction to the Study of Islamic Political Theory: The Jurists*. Oxford: Oxford University Press, 1981.

Lamchichi, Abderrahim. *Islam, islamisme et modernité*. Paris: L'Harmattan, 1994.

———. *Géopolitique de l'islamisme*. Paris: L'Harmattan, 2001.

———. *L'Islamisme politique*. Paris: L'Harmattan, 2001.

Laoust, Henri. *Pluralismes dans l'Islam*. Paris: Geuthner, 1983.

Laroui, Abdallah. *Islamisme, modernisme, libéralisme: Esquisses critiques*. Casablanca: Centre culturel arabe, 1997.

Lewis, Bernard. *The Political Language of Islam*. Chicago: University of Chicago Press, 1991.

Mansour, Camille. *L'autorité dans la pensée musulmane: Le concept d'ijma' et la problématique de l'autorité*. Paris: J. Vrin, 1975.

Mernissi, Fatima. *Islam and Democracy: Fear of the Modern World*. London: Virago, 1994.

Mirish, Mussa. *Ad-Dînî wa as-Siyâsî fî al-Yahûdiyya wal Islâm* (Politics and Religion in Judaism and Islam). Algiers: Muassat Iqra, 2009.

Musa, Saleem. *The Muslims and the New World Order*. London: Institute for Strategic and Development Studies, 1993.

Owen, Roger. *State, Power, and Politics in the Making of the Modern Middle East*. London: Routledge, 2004.

Piscatori James P., ed. *Islam in the Political Process*. Cambridge: Cambridge University Press, 1983.

Roy, Olivier. *L'échec de l'islam politique*. Paris: Seuil, 1992.

———. *The Failure of Political Islam*. Cambridge, MA: Harvard University Press, 1994.

Samih, Muhammad Ismail. *Idiulûjiâ al-Islâm as-Siyâsy wa sh-Shuyu'iyya* (Political Islam Ideology and Communism). Beirut: Dar Saqi, 2010.

Sayeed, Khalid Bin. *Western Dominance and Political Islam*. Karachi: Oxford University Press, 1995.

Shaarawi, Hilmi. *Al-Fikr as-Siyâsî wal Ijitimâ'î fî Ifrîqiyâ* (Political and Social Thought in Africa). Cairo: Markaz Al-Buhuth, 2010.

Shadid, Anthony. *Legacy of the Prophet: Despots, Democrats, and the New Politics of Islam*. Boulder, CO: Westview, 2002.

Sheikh, Naveed S. *The New Politics of Islam: Pan-Islamic Foreign Policy in a World of States*. New York: Routledge, 2003.

Sisk, Timothy. *Islam and Democracy: Religion, Politics and Power in the Middle East*. Washington, DC: Institute for Peace and Press, 1992.

Sonn, Tamara. *Between Qur'an and Crown: The Challenge of Political Legitimacy in the Arab World*. Boulder, CO: Westview Press, 1990.

Souaiaia, Ahmed E. *Contesting Justice: Women, Islam, Law, and Society*. Albany: State University of New York Press, 2008.

Al-Sulami, Mishal. *The West and Islam: Western Liberal Democracy versus the System of Shura*. London: Routledge, 2004.

Tibi, Bassam. *The Challenge of Fundamentalism: Political Islam and the New World Disorder*. Berkeley: University of California Press, 2002.

———. *Islam between Culture and Politics*. New York: Palgrave Macmillan, 2002.

COMBATIVE DISCOURSES

Abou El Fadl, Khaled. *And God Knows the Soldiers: The Authoritative and Authoritarian in Islamic Discourses*. Lanham, MD: University Press of America, 2001.

Akbar, M. J. *The Shade of Swords: Jihad and the Conflict between Islam and Christianity*. New York: Routledge, 2003.

Ali, Tariq. *The Clash of Fundamentalisms: Crusades, Jihads and Modernity*. New York: Verso, 2002.

Amghar, Samir. "Les mouvements islamistes, des armes aux urnes." *Revue Maghreb-Machrek* 194 (2008).

Appleby, R. Scott, ed. *Spokesmen for the Despised: Fundamentalist Leaders of the Middle East*. Chicago: University of Chicago Press, 1997.

Al-Ashmawy, Muhammad Said, and Carolyn Fluehr-Lobban, ed. *Against Islamic Extremism: The Writings of Muhammad Said Al-Ashmawy*. Gainesville: University Press of Florida, 2003.

Atkinson, Rick. *Crusade: The Untold Story of the Persian Gulf War*. New York: Houghton Mifflin, 1994.

Baud, Jacques. *Encyclopédie des terrorismes et violences politiques*. Paris: Panazol, 2003.

Bergen, Peter. *Holy War, Inc: Inside the Secret World of Osama bin Laden*. New York: Free Press, 2001.

Challiand, Gérard. *Histoire du terrorisme, de l'antiquité à Al Qaïda*. Paris: Bayard, 2006.

Charfi, Mohamed. *Islam et liberté: Le malentendu historique*. Paris: Albin Michel, 1998.

Charnay, Jean-Paul. *L'Islam et la guerre: De la guerre juste à la révolution sainte*. Paris: Fayard, 1986.

Cooley, John. *La Charia et l'Occident*. Paris: L'Heurne, 2001.

———. *Unholy Wars: Afghanistan, America and International Terrorism*. London: Pluto Press, 2002.

Darwish, Adel, and Gregory Alexander. *Unholy Babylon: The Secret History of Saddam's War*. London: Diane, 1991.

Davis, Joyce M. *Martyrs: Innocence, Vengeance and Despair in the Middle East*. New York: Palgrave Macmillan, 2003.

Esposito, John L. *The Islamic Threat: Myth or Reality?* New York: Oxford University Press, 1999.

———. *Unholy War: Terror in the Name of Islam*. New York: Oxford University Press, 2002.

Filali-Ansari, Abdou. *L'islam et les fondements du pouvoir de Ali Abderraziq*. Paris: La Découverte, 1994.

———. *L'islam est-il hostile à la laïcité?* Paris: Actes Sud, 2002.

Firestone, Reuven. *Jihad: The Origin of Holy War in Islam*. Oxford: Oxford University Press, 2002.

Hafez, Mohammed M. *Why Muslims Rebel: Repression and Resistance in the Islamic World*. Boulder, CO: Lynne Rienner, 2003.

Hiro, Dilip. *Holy Wars: The Rise of Islamic Fundamentalism*. New York: Routledge, 1989.

———. *War without End: The Rise of Islamist Terrorism and the Global Response*. New York: Routledge, 2002.

Hoveyda, Fereydoun. *The Broken Crescent: The "Threat" of Militant Islamic Fundamentalism*. Westport, CT: Praeger, 1998.

Hubbard, Mark. *Warriors of the Prophet: The Struggle for Islam*. Boulder, CO: Westview Press, 1998.

Ibrahim, Hasanin Tawfiq. *Zâhirat al-'Unf as-Siyâsî fî an-Nuzum al-'Arabiyya* (Political Violence in the Arab Regimes). Beirut: Markaz Dirâsât al-Wihda, 2011.

Kepel, Gilles. *Jihad: The Trail of Political Islam*. Cambridge, MA: Harvard University Press, 2002.

Lewis, Bernard. "The Roots of Muslim Rage." *Atlantic Monthly* 226 (1990).

———. *The Crisis of Islam: Holy War and Unholy Terror*. New York: Modern Library, 2003.

Maalouf, Amin, and Jon Rothschild. *The Crusades through Arab Eyes*. Berlin: Schocken Books, 1989.

Marret, Jean-Luc. *Les fabriques du Djihad*. Paris: PUF, 2005.

Martinez-Gros, Gabriel, and Lucette Valensi. *L'Islam en dissidence, genèse d'un affrontement*. Paris: Seuil, 2004.

Miller, Judith. *God Has Ninety-Nine Names: Reporting from a Militant Middle East*. New York: Touchstone, 1997.

Pelletiere, Stephen C. *Mass Action and Islamic Fundamentalism: The Revolt of the Brooms*. Carlisle Barracks, PA: Strategic Studies Institute, U.S. Army War College, 1992.

Peters, Rudolph. *Islam and Colonialism: The Doctrine of Jihad in Modern History*. Berlin: Mouton de Gruyter, 1984.

———. *The Jihad in Classical and Modern Times: A Reader*. Princeton, NJ: Markus Wiener, 1996.

Rashid, Ahmed. *Taliban: Militant Islam, Oil and Fundamentalism in Central Asia*. New Haven, CT: Yale University Press, 2001.

———. *Jihad: The Rise of Militant Islam in Central Asia*. New Haven, CT: Yale University Press, 2002.

Roy, Olivier. *Le croissant et le chaos*. Paris: Hachette, 2007.

Rubin, Barry, and Judith Colp Rubin. *Anti-American Terrorism and the Middle East: Understanding the Violence*. New York: Oxford University Press, 2002.

Ruthven, Malise. *A Fury for God: The Islamist Attack on America*. London: Granta Books, 2002.

Telhami, Shibley. *The Stakes: America and the Middle East*. Boulder, CO: Westview Press, 2002.

Wright, Robin B. *Sacred Rage: The Wrath of Militant Islam*. New York: Simon and Schuster, 1985.

———. *Sacred Rage: The Crusade of Modern Islam*. New York: Simon and Schuster, 2001.

Al-Zawahiri, Ayman. *L'absolution des oulémas et des moudjahidines de toute accusation d'impuissance et de faiblesse*. Paris: Milelli, 2008.

Zunes, Stephen. *Tinderbox: U.S. Middle East Policy and the Roots of Terrorism*. Monroe, ME: Common Courage Press, 2002.

IDENTITY AND RELIGION IN ISLAM

Abdelfattah, Sayfeddin. *Al-Awlama wal Islâm: Ru'yatân lil 'Âlam* (Globalization and Islam: Two Views of the World). Damascus: Dar al-Fikr, 2009.

Afkhami, M. *Faith and Freedom: Women's Human Rights in the Muslim World*. Syracuse, NY: Syracuse University Press, 1995.

Ahmed, Leila. *Women and Gender in Islam: Historical Roots of a Modern Debate*. New Haven, CT: Yale University Press, 1993.

Amuli, Sayyid Haydar. *Inner Secrets of the Path*. Longmead: Element Books, 1989.

Arjomand, Said Amir, ed. *From Nationalism to Revolutionary Islam*. Albany: State University of New York Press, 1984.

Asad, Talal. *Genealogies of Religion: Discipline and Reasons of Power in Christianity and Islam.* Baltimore: Johns Hopkins University Press, 1993.

———. *Formations of the Secular: Christianity, Islam, Modernity.* Stanford, CA: Stanford University Press, 2003.

Ask, Karin, and Marit Tjomsland, eds. *Women and Islamization: Contemporary Dimensions of Discourse on Gender Relations.* Oxford: Berg Publishers, 1998.

Azumah, John. *The Legacy of Arab-Islam in Africa: A Quest for Inter-religious Dialogue.* Oxford: OneWorld, 2001.

Barazangi, N. H., et al. *Islamic Identity and the Struggle for Justice.* Gainesville: University Press of Florida, 1996.

Barlas, Asma. *Believing Women in Islam: Unreading Patriarchal Interpretations of the Qur'an.* Austin: University of Texas Press, 2002.

Bencheikh, Khaled. *La Laïcité au regard du Coran.* Paris: Presses de la Renaissance, 2005.

Bill, James A., and John Alden Williams. *Roman Catholics and Shi'i Muslims: Prayer, Passion, and Politics.* Raleigh: University of North Carolina Press, 2008.

Bowen, John R. *Islam, Law and Equality in Indonesia: An Anthropology of Public Reasoning.* Cambridge: Cambridge University Press, 2003.

———. *Why the French Don't Like Headscarves: Islam, the State, and Public Space.* Princeton, NJ: Princeton University Press, 2006.

Brown, L. Carl. *Religion and State: The Muslim Approach to Politics.* New York: Columbia University Press, 2000.

Bullock, Katherine: *Rethinking Muslim Women and the Veil: Challenging Historical and Modern Stereotypes.* Herndon, VA: International Institute of Islamic Thought. 2007.

Burgat, François, and William Dowell. *The Islamic Movement in North Africa.* Austin: Center for Middle Eastern Studies, University of Texas, 1997.

Burlas, Asma. *Believing Women in Islam: Unreading Patriarchal Interpretations of the Quran.* New Delhi: Munshiram Manoharlal Publishers, 2005.

Al-Bushri, Tariq. *Nahwa Tayyâr Asâsi lil Umma* (Toward an Essential Trend of the Umma). Doha: Al Jazeera Studies Center, 2008.

Carré, Olivier. *Mystique et politique, Lecture révolutionnaire du Coran par Sayyed Qutb, Frère musulman radical.* Paris: Cerf, 1984.

———. *L'Islam laïque ou le retour à la Grande Tradition.* Paris: Armand Colin, 1993.

Choueiri, Y. M. *Islamic Fundamentalism.* London: Pinter, 1990.

Cole, Juan. "Modernity and the Millennium: The Genesis of the Baha'i Faith in the Nineteenth-Century Middle East." *Studies in the Babi and Baha'i Religions 9.* New York: Columbia University Press, 1998.

Donnan, Hastings, ed. *Interpreting Islam.* London: Sage, 2002.

Eickelman, Dale F., and Jon W. Anderson, eds. *New Media in the Muslim World: The Emerging Public Sphere.* Bloomington: Indiana University Press, 2003.

Esack, Farid. *Qur'an, Liberation, and Pluralism.* Oxford: OneWorld, 1997.

Esposito, John L., and François Burgat, eds. *Modernizing Islam: Religion in the Public Sphere in Europe and the Middle East.* New Brunswick, NJ: Rutgers University Press, 2003.

Friedmann, Yohanan. *Tolerance and Coercion in Islam: Interfaith Relations in the Muslim Tradition.* Cambridge: Cambridge University Press, 2003.

Gatje, Helmut. *The Quran and Its Exegesis: Selected Texts with Classical and Modern Muslim Interpretations.* Rockport, ME: OneWorld, 1996.

Gerami, Shahin. *Women and Fundamentalism, Islam and Christianity.* New York: Garland, 1996.

Al-Ghidhami, Abdallah. *Al-Qabîla wal Qabâ'iliyya aw Hawiyyât mâ-ba'd al-Hadâtha* (Tribes and Tribalim or Postmodern Identities). Casablanca: Al-Markaz ath-Thaqâfî al-'Arabi, 2009.

Haddad, Yvonne Yazbeck, ed. *Muslims in the West: From Sojourners to Citizens.* New York: Oxford University Press, 2002.

Halliday, Fred. *Islam and the Myth of Confrontation: Religion and Politics in the Middle East.* London: I. B. Tauris, 1996.

———. *Nation and Religion in the Middle East.* London: Saqi Books, 2000.

Hassan, Riaz. *Faithlines: Muslim Concepts of Islam and Society.* Oxford: Oxford University Press, 2002.

Hikmat, Anwar. *Women and the Koran: The Status of Women in Islam.* New York: Prometheus Books, 1997.

ISCWA. *Târikh al-Harakât an-Nisâ'iyya fil 'Âlam al-'Arabî* (History of the Women Movements in the Arab World). Beirut: ISCWA, 2006.

Jansen, Johannes J. G. *The Dual Nature of Islamic Fundamentalism.* Ithaca, NY: Cornell University Press, 1997.

Karpat, Kemal H. *The Politicization of Islam: Reconstructing Identity, State, Faith and Community in the Late Ottoman State.* Oxford: Oxford University Press, 2002.

Kazemzadeh, Masoud. *Islamic Fundamentalism Feminism.* Lanham, MD: University Press of America, 2002.

Khuri, Fuad I. *Imams and Emirs: State, Religion and Sects in Islam.* London: Saqi Books, 1990.

Khurshid, Ahmad. *Islamic Resurgence.* Tampa, FL: World and Islam Studies Enterprise, 1994.

Kramer, Martin, ed. *The Islamism Debate.* Syracuse, NY: Syracuse University Press, 1997.

Laoust, Henri. *Comment définir le sunnisme et le chiisme.* Paris: Geuthner, 1985.

Laroui, Abdallah. *Islam et modernité.* Paris: La Découverte, 1987.

———. *Islam et histoire: Essai d'épistémologie.* Paris: Flammarion, 2001.

Lewis, Bernard. *The Shaping of the Modern Middle East.* New York: Oxford University Press, 1994.

———. *What Went Wrong? Western Impact and Middle Eastern Response.* New York: Oxford University Press, 2001.

Mansi, Bishara. *Al-Urûba wal Usûliyya ad-Dîniyya* (Arabism and Islamic Fundamentalism). Beirut: Riyadh ar-Rayyis, 2007.

Medded, Abdelwahab. *La maladie de l'Islam.* Paris: Seuil, 2002.

Mernissi, Fatima. *Le harem politique: Le Prophète et les femmes.* Paris: Albin Michel, 1987.

Moghissi, Haideh. *Feminism and Islamic Fundamentalism: The Limits of Postmodern Analysis.* London: Zed Books, 1999.

Munson, Henry. *Islam and Revolution in the Middle East.* New Haven, CT: Yale University Press, 1988.

Nielsen, Niels C., Jr. *Fundamentalism, Mythos, and World Religions.* Albany: State University of New York Press, 1993.

Noorani, A. G. *Islam and Jihad: Prejudice versus Reality.* London: Zed Books, 2003.

Rahman, Fazlur. *Revival and Reform in Islam: A Study of Islamic Fundamentalism.* Oxford: OneWorld, 1999.

Ramadan, Tariq. *L'Islam en questions.* Paris: Actes Sud, 2002.

Rougier, Bernard. *Le Jihad au quotidien.* Paris: PUF, 2004.

Roy, Olivier. *L'islam mondialisé.* Paris: Seuil, 2002.

Said, Edward W. *Covering Islam: How the Media and the Experts Determine How We See the Rest of the World.* New York: Vintage Books, 1997.

Scott, Joan Wallach. *The Politics of the Veil.* Princeton, NJ: Princeton University Press, 2007.

Shahâta, Marwân. *Tahawwulât al-Khitâb as-Salafî: Al-Harakât al-Jihâdiyya* (Changes in Salafi Discourse: Jihadi Movements). Beirut: Shabaka 'Arabiyya, 2010.

Sharify-Funk, Meena. *Encountering the Transnational: Women, Islam and the Politics of Interpretation.* Aldershot: Ashgate, 2008.

Sorman, Guy. *Les enfants de Rifaa, musulmans et modernes.* Paris: Fayard, 2003.

Talbi, Mohamed. *Plaidoyer pour un islam moderne.* Paris: Desclée de Brouwer, 1998.

———. *Un penseur libre en Islam.* Paris: Albin Michel, 2002.

Urvoy, Dominique. *Les penseurs libres dans l'Islam classique.* Paris: Albin Michel, 1996.

Watt, William Montgomery. *Islamic Fundamentalism and Modernity.* New York: Routledge, 1988.

Zakarya, Fouad. *Laïcité et islamisme: Les Arabes à l'heure du choix.* Paris: La Découverte, 1991.

SELECTED U.S. GOVERNMENT DOCUMENTS

Erickson, Richard J. *Legitimate Use of Military Force against State-Sponsored International Terrorism.* Maxwell Air Force Base, AL: Air University Press; Washington, DC: U.S. GPO, 1989. D 301.26/6: T 27/3.

National Commission on Terrorist Attacks upon the United States. *The 9/11 Commission Report: Final Report of the National Commission on Terrorist Attacks upon the United States.* Washington, DC: U.S. GPO, 2004. Y 3.2: T 27/2/FINAL. ISBN 0160723043.

U.S. Congress. House Committee on Government Reform, Subcommittee on National Security, Emerging Threats, and International Relations. *Overseas Security: Hardening Soft Targets: Hearing before the Subcommittee on National Security, Emerging Threats and International Relations.* 108th Cong., 2nd sess., 22 September 2004. Washington, DC: U.S. GPO, 2005. Y 4.G 74/7: T 27/27.

U.S. Congress. House Committee on International Relations. *Palestinian Anti-Terrorism Act of 2006: Report Together with Additional Views (to Accompany H.R. 4681)*: *Report of the Committee on International Relations.* 109th Cong., 2nd sess. Washington, DC: U.S. GPO, 2006. Y 1.1/8: 109-462/PT-f: hr46281.109. http://purl.access.gpo.gov/GPO/LPS70128 (accessed 11 September 2011).

U.S. Congress. House Committee on International Relations, Subcommittee on Africa. *Terrorism in Algeria: Its Effect on the Country's Political Scenario, on Regional Stability, and on Global Security: Hearing before the Subcommittee on Africa of the Committee on International Relations.* 104th Cong., 1st sess., 11 October 1995. Washington, DC: U.S. GPO, 1996. Y4.IN 8/16: AL 3.

U.S. Congress. House Permanent Select Committee on Intelligence. *Resolution of Inquiry Concerning Terrorist Bombings in Beirut, Lebanon.* 99th Cong., 1st sess. Washington, DC: U.S. GPO, 1985. Y 1.1/8: 99-171.

U.S. Congress. House Staff Report of the Permanent Select Committee on Intelligence, Subcommittee on Intelligence Policy of 23 August 2006: *Recognizing Iran as a Strategic Threat: An Intelligence Challenge for the United States.* http://intelligence.house.gov/Media/PDFS/IranReport082206v2.pdf (accessed 11 September 2011).

U.S. Congress. Senate Committee on Armed Services. *State-Sponsored Terrorism: Hearing before the Committee on Armed Services.* 99th Cong., 2nd sess., 28 January 1986. Washington, DC: U.S. GPO, 1986. Y 4.Ar 5/3: S.HRG.99-795.

U.S. Congress. Senate Committee on Banking, Housing, and Urban Affairs, Subcommittee on International Trade and Finance. *Hawala and Underground Terrorist Financing Mechanisms: Hearing before the Subcommittee on International Trade and Finance.* 107th Cong., 1st sess., 18 December 2001. Washington, DC: U.S. GPO, 2002. Y 4.B 22/3: S.HRG.107-660.

U.S. Congress. Senate Committee on Foreign Relations. *Iran: Security Threats and U.S. Policy: Hearing before the Committee on Foreign Relations.* 108th Cong., 1st sess., 28 October 2003. Washington, DC: U.S. GPO, 2004. Y 4.F 76/2: S.HRG.108-353.

U.S. Congress. Senate Committee on Foreign Relations. *Iran: An Update: Hearing before the Committee on Foreign Relations.* 110th Cong., 2nd sess., 22 April 2008. Washington, DC: U.S. GPO, 2008. Y 4 SCI 2: 110-189.

U.S. Congress. Senate Committee on the Judiciary. *Able Danger and Intelligence Information Sharing: Hearing before the Committee on the Judiciary.* 109th Cong., 1st sess., 21 September 2005. Washington, DC: U.S. GPO, 2006. Y 4.J 89/2: S.HRG.109-311.

U.S. Congress. *Uniting and Strengthening America by Providing Appropriate Tools Required to Intercept and Obstruct Terrorism Act of 2001* (USA PATRIOT ACT). Washington, DC: U.S. GPO, 2001. AE 2.110:107-156.

U.S. Department of Defense. *Terrorist Group Profiles.* Washington, DC: U.S. GPO, 1988. D 1.2: T 27. Last printing 1989, with U.S. Department of State presenting profiles of terrorist groups in its annual *Patterns and Global Terrorism* (1985–2003) and its subsequent *Country Reports on Terrorism* (2004 to present), which are published annually each May.

U.S. Department of State. *Country Reports on Terrorism*. Washington, DC: U.S. GPO. Published 2004–2007. Can be accessed through http://www.state.gov/s/ct/rls/crt/index.htm (accessed 11 September 2011).

SELECTED INTERNET RESOURCES

Air University, Maxwell Air Force Base. "Terrorist and Insurgent Organizations." http://www.au.af.mil/au/aul/bibs/tergps/tg98tc.htm (accessed 11 September 2011).

American Foreign Policy Council's World Almanac of Islamism. http://almanac.afpc .org (accessed 15 February 2011).

Blackwater, USA: Lessons Learned: Infantry Squad Tactics in Military Operations in Urban Terrain during Operation Phantom Fury in Fallujah, Iraq. http://www .blackwaterusa.com/btw2005/articles/041805aar.html (accessed 11 September 2011).

Center for Strategic and International Studies. Terrorism and Transnational Threats Page. http://www.csis.org/researchfocus/TNT (accessed 11 September 2011).

Emergency Response Research Institute (ERRI). Counterterrorism Archive: A Summary of Worldwide Terrorism Events, Groups, and Terrorist Strategies and Tactics. http://www.emergency.com/cntrterr.htm (accessed 11 September 2011).

International Association for Counter-Terrorism and Security Professionals (IASCSP). http://www.iacsp.com (accessed 11 September 2011).

Naval Postgraduate School, Dudley Knox Library. Terrorist Group Profiles and U.S. State Department. http://www.nps.edu/Library/Research/SubjectGuides/Special Topics/TerroristProfile/TerroristGroupProfiles (accessed 11 September 2011).

RAND Corporation. Terrorism and Homeland Security. http://www.rand.org/pubs/online.terrorism/1 (accessed 11 September 2011).

U.S. Department of Justice, Federal Bureau of Investigation (FBI) Homepage and Terrorism Publications and Reports. http://www.fbi.gov and http://www.fbi.gov/publications.htm (accessed 11 September 2011).

U.S. Department of State. *Patterns of Global Terrorism* reports (1976–2003) and succeeding *Country Reports on Terrorism* (2004 to present). http://www.terrorisminfo .mipt.org/Patterns-of-Global-Terrorism.asp (accessed 11 September 2011).

U.S. Department of State, Foreign Terrorist Organizations, Office of Counterterrorism. http://www.state.gov/s/ct/rls/fs/08/103392.htm (accessed 2 June 2011).

University of St. Andrews. Centre for the Study of Terrorism and Political Violence (CSTPV). http://www.st-andrews.ac.uk/~wwwir/research/cstpv/resources/resources.php (accessed 11 September 2011).

About the Author

Mathieu Guidère (BA, MA, and PhD, Sorbonne University, Paris) is a full professor of Islamic and Middle Eastern studies at the University of Toulouse II, France, and senior fellow at the Center for Advanced Defense Studies, Washington, D.C. Dr. Guidère has been the director of the Radicalization Watch Project since 2006 and was the chair of the Strategic Information Analysis Laboratory at the French military academy of Saint-Cyr from 2004 to 2007. He also was chief editor of *Les Langues Modernes*, an academic journal of the French Association of Language Professors, from 2001 to 2003. Dr. Guidère received a Fulbright grant in 2006 to study radical groups and was professor of multilingual monitoring at the University of Geneva, Switzerland, from 2007 to 2011. He regularly publishes research on Islamic movements in the Middle East and on radical groups in the Arab world. He has published more than 20 books in French, including *Le Printemps islamiste* (2012), *Le Choc des révolutions arabes* (2011), *Les Nouveaux terroristes* (2010), and *Irak in Translation* (2008). Dr. Guidère is frequently consulted by the press and various media outlets to explain the risks and new trends of groups and parties within the Islamic world. Familiar with the Arab societies, Dr. Guidère has lived in many different countries throughout the Middle East and is fluent in almost all of the Arab dialects. This dictionary was compiled with the participation of Amanda Gawlowicz, MA.